CRYSTAL LAKE MEMORIES

CRYSTAL LAKE MEMORIES

THE COMPLETE HISTORY OF

PETER M. BRACKE

FOREWORD BY SEAN S. CUNNINGHAM

TITAN BOOKS
IN ASSOCIATION WITH SPARKPLUG PRESS

Editorial
Editor—Daniel P. Farrands
Crystal Lake Entertainment consultant—Geoff Garrett

Design
Cover Design & Title Treatment—Mark Matsuno for Matsuno Design Group
Art Direction and Layout—Peter M. Bracke
Design Consultant—Joel Vendette for Vendetta Designs
Stills Restoration—John McCloy for Matsuno Design Group

The publisher would like to thank all at Crystal Lake Entertainment, New Line Cinema and Paramount Pictures
for their invaluable support and involvement in the production of this book,
in particular Sean Cunningham, Lourdes Arocho, David Imhoff, Larry McCallister and Martin Blythe.

The publisher would also like to give special thanks to seven individuals without whom this book would not have been
possible: Sean Cunningham, Daniel Farrands, Geoff Garrett, Garrett Hicks, Adrienne King and Larry Zerner.

Additional thanks for the use of still images: John Carl Buechler, Bill Butler, Jason Paul Collum, Juliette Cummins,
Noel Cunningham, Sean Cunningham, Darcy DeMoss, Dennis Dermody, Daniel Farrands, Richard Feury, John Furey,
CJ Graham, Rob Hedden, Tiffany Helm, Jim Isaac, Adrienne King, Paul Kratka, Lar Park Lincoln, Frank Mancuso, Sr.,
George Mansour, Tom & Nancy McLoughlin, Laurel Moore, Carey More, Erik Lee Nash, Greg Nicotero, Kerry Noonan,
Tracie Savage, Tom Savini, Jeannine Taylor, Bill Terezakis, Dick Wieand and Larry Zerner.

Library of Congress Control Number: 2005924310

A CIP catalogue record for this title is available from the British Library.
ISBN: 1-84576-343-2
ISBN-13: 9781845763435

Published by Titan Books, a division of
Titan Publishing Group Ltd
144 Southwark St
London, SE1 0UP

In association with Sparkplug Press, Los Angeles. www.sparkplugpress.com

First Titan edition October 2006
8 10 9 7

Did you enjoy this book? We love to hear from our readers. Please e-mail us at: **readerfeedback@titanemail.com**
or write to Reader Feedback at the above address. To subscribe to our regular newsletter for up-to-the-minute news,
great offers and competitions, email: **titan-news@titanemail.com**

Printed and bound in China

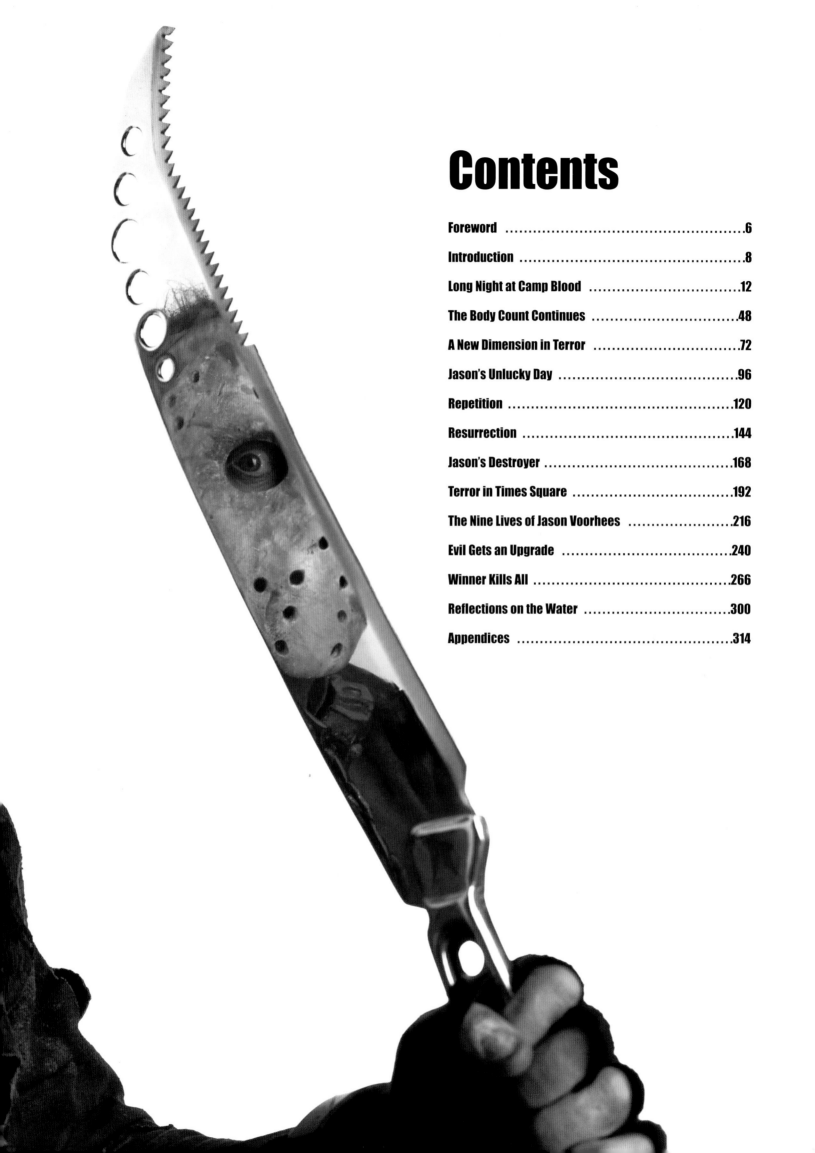

Contents

Foreword by Sean S. Cunningham

As this book goes to press, it's hard to believe that it has been over twenty-five years since I made the original *Friday the 13th*. It's even harder to imagine that a book has been written to define and memorialize the original film and the subsequent installments. Over the past few years, I have gotten to know Peter Bracke, the author, as he has carefully and painstakingly assembled his research. At this point, I'm sure that Peter's the world's most informed expert on the subject. Now, I think it's hilarious that when I have a question about events concerning any one of the movies, I always call Peter to ask him what really happened. Peter knows.

Back in the summer of 1979, things were tight. I had just finished *Manny's Orphans*, the second of two independently financed family films but it had yet to be distributed. I was worried about how I was going keep everything going until some money came in. I was married, with two beautiful children, and was working out of a home office in Westport, Connecticut where I had produced *Last House on the Left* with my friend Wes Craven. I needed to come up with a new idea that I could sell.

So why not make a scary movie? I had not revisited the horror genre since *Last House on the Left* but I had this movie title banging around in the back of my head that I thought would be terrific: *Friday the 13th*. I had no idea what the movie would be, but with that title I thought, at least, I'd be off to a good start.

That's when I went to Steve Miner, my friend, producer, editor and collaborator with a half-baked idea about taking out an ad in *Variety* announcing the production of a movie called *Friday the 13th*. We both knew it was crazy since we didn't have a script, no production funds and we weren't sure we could even get the rights to use the title. I said to Steve, "First, let's see if we can use the title and we'll work the rest out from there. If the ad runs and nobody sues us, I say we have the rights."

I scraped together just enough money to run a full-page ad in the July 4th weekend edition of *Variety* announcing the production of: "Friday the 13th—The Most Terrifying Film Ever Made!" I ran the ad expecting to receive letters from lawyers telling me that I couldn't make the movie because I didn't have the rights, blah, blah, blah. But to my amazement, nobody objected! And here's

the thing we didn't anticipate. People loved the ad and wanted to see the movie. I got distribution queries from all over the world, plus I got several offers from people willing to loan me money or to invest in the movie.

Virtually overnight we were in pre-production.

The next weeks were a frantic obsessive scramble as we tried to figure out how to actually make "The Most Terrifying Film Ever Made." We decided on a budget of $500,000—more money than I had ever raised before—and then tried to put together a script. Instrumental in all this was my friend Victor Miller, a writer who had collaborated with me on the two earlier kids movies. We'd meet every morning to discuss the story, and then Victor would go off to sketch out scenes while Steve and I wrestled with the logistics of casting and production. And every day we'd ask ourselves the same questions: what's really scary, and how can we shoot it on our budget?

Sometime during pre-production we interviewed Tom Savini, who had driven up from Pittsburg with his pet Chinchilla and a car full of clothes and makeup tools. Tom had been trained by Dick Smith, the master makeup effects wizard, and had worked with George Romero on *Dawn of the Dead*. We all hit it off perfectly and Tom didn't go home until we finished the movie. Some of my fondest memories from that time were of Victor, Steve, Tom and I trying to plan storyboards for stuff that had never been done before. Surely someone on the outside might have found it bizarre to see us trying to figure out the best way to chop off somebody's head or the most effective way to drive an arrow through a camper's throat. But we were energized with laughter and adrenaline and the naughty hope of putting on a kind of crazy magic show. We kept pushing forward, one foot in front of the next, until we found ourselves at a Boy Scout Camp in Blairstown, New Jersey, getting ready to shoot the movie at a place we renamed Crystal Lake.

Making movies is difficult under the best conditions. But when you have no money, it's even harder. Looking back I realize how lucky I was to have been put together with such a dedicated, caring, passionate group of people. Steve Miner, Victor Miller,

Tom Savini. Barry Abrams, my cinematographer and our tireless crew of commando filmmakers. In post Bill Freda, my skillful editor and my musical mentor and maestro, Harry Manfredini, the genius who created the signature musical sounds of *Friday the 13th*. And I was particularly lucky to have Barry Moss and Julie Hughes as my casting agents. They worked diligently to assemble such a terrific cast of unselfish actors willing to do anything to make the movie better. I was grateful then and I'm even more grateful now.

So it is with continued shock and amazement that I sit here twenty-five years later, in the middle of developing a sequel to *Freddy vs. Jason* and a television series set in Crystal Lake. Who would've thought it? Certainly not us back in 1979. Although it wasn't planned, the film completely changed the course of my life. It opened doors in Hollywood and offered me opportunities that I never even conceived of back in my little office in Westport. Jason Voorhees has been good to me.

I want to thank you, Peter, for creating this book which has allowed me to look back at one of the craziest and most wonderful times of my life.

It's been one hell of a ride so far!

Sean S. Cunningham directs *Friday the 13th*.

Introduction

It was an idyllic scene. Rays of early morning sunshine pierced the trees as ripples gently caressed the cool waters of Crystal Lake. A young girl lay in a canoe, her fingertips gingerly testing the glassy surface. All around, the sounds of nature were peaceful, almost a lullaby. Then, suddenly, a figure burst through the once-calm water. Some creature, some *thing*, moss-covered and horribly disfigured, pulled the screaming girl down into the depths below. The legend of Jason Voorhees had claimed his first victim.

It was a moment that inspired a nation to let out a collective scream. A scream so loud and bloodcurdling that it continues to send aftershocks twenty-five years later.

It was the final scene of a film called *Friday the 13th*—and the start of a phenomenon that has become as inexplicable to its critics as it is beloved by its fans. Who could have anticipated that the story of a group of carefree camp counselors being stalked by an unseen assailant, only to be dispatched one by one in a series of ever more gruesome kills, would inspire ten sequels, a television series and a lucrative line of tie-in merchandise? And who would have known that it would catapult its star villain, Jason Voorhees—a hockey mask wearing, machete-wielding manic with a deformed face and one serious mother fixation—into an icon of terror recognized around the world?

Amazingly, for a concept as seemingly straightforward as that of *Friday the 13th*, the series—like the seemingly indestructible Jason Voorhees—has continued to rejuvenate itself for twenty-five years. Diehard fans typically point to the first installment of any long-running horror film series as being the best, but in fact the eleven installments (and counting) of *Friday the 13th*, collectively, form as admirably diverse and ambitious a franchise as any in motion picture history. While not all of the cinematic permutations of Jason have met with unanimous approval by the series' dedicated fan base, *Friday the 13th* nevertheless continues to prove that it cannot be stopped. Having survived no less than two "final" chapters, a telekinetic teen, the gimmick of 3-D, a shipwrecked voyage to Manhattan, a journey into outer space and even a Jason imposter, it is hard to deny the character's universal and enduring appeal. The series has also had not just one but two parent studios: Paramount Pictures, who "adopted" eight installments of the franchise during the 1980s, as well as *Friday the 13th: The Series*, a popular television show that ran for three seasons in first-run syndication; and

New Line Cinema, who acquired the rights to the franchise in 1992 and continue to release its own successful new sequels. In 2003, Jason even did battle with his greatest challenger: Freddy Krueger of the *A Nightmare on Elm Street* series. Not only did Jason survive the resulting bloodbath, *Freddy vs. Jason* managed to inject new life into two of Hollywood's most enduring faces of evil. The battle between the terror titans became one of the biggest hits of the year as well as the most commercially successful sequel that either series had ever spawned on its own. Although few would have predicted it at the time—including its own creators—the specter of Jason Voorhees still seems to be unstoppable twenty-five years after he made his first big-screen appearance.

The seed for this remarkable, if somewhat redoubtable, success was planted on May 9, 1980, when the original *Friday the 13th* made its debut on over 1,100 screens across the United States. Though the basic formula of *Friday the 13th* was not entirely new—its blueprint had, in fact, already been established by *Halloween* two years prior (and arguably *Psycho* eighteen years before that)—the presentation was unique, as was the film's attitude, modern dress and innate understanding of the collective fears of its audience. After all, horror films involving teenagers—ones usually preoccupied with sexual exploration—under threat from murderous forces, whether human, monstrous or other-worldly, had already been a staple of the genre for decades. And certainly many a great mystery-thriller, particularly Agatha Christie's *Ten Little Indians*, had fine-tuned the plot device of introducing a group of unwitting victims only to pick them off, one after another, until the identity of the evildoer was revealed in the last reel. But what proved so effective about *Friday the 13th* was that this unassuming, low-budget exploitation picture could so cannily and craftily reformulate the classic conventions of yesteryear and turn them on their head into something that was contemporary, resonant and unapologetically shocking.

At the time of its release, *Friday the 13th*'s cinematic language was hip and cutting-edge. Bathed in dark shadows and filled with roving point-of-view shots—usually from the perspective of the killer—the audience was kept perpetually off-balance. The film's attenuated shock moments, gingerly but relentlessly modulated, were then sprung without mercy. Like a giant exclamation point at the end of a carefully worded sentence, the film's incredibly visceral and graphic murder sequences, executed with state-of-the-art makeup effects, literally left audiences gasping, "How did they do that!?" *Friday the 13th* pushed the boundaries of what was permissible to be seen in mainstream cinema, and did it with mood, suspense and unforgettable imagery. Driving it all was an unsettling, almost atonal musical score, complete with a classic aural motif for its unseen killer—the stuttered words, "Ki, ki, ki, Ma, ma, ma" have undeniably become as synonymous with Jason as John Williams' unforgettable three-note score has with the man-eating shark in *Jaws*.

Friday the 13th also presented a group of young characters purposely stereotypical, even archetypal. So relatable were these carefree counselors of Camp Crystal Lake to young audiences that the boundary between spectator and participant all but disappeared. The horrors of *Friday the 13th* became not something just to watch but to experience. More akin to a rollercoaster ride than a motion picture, even the film's harshest critics could not deny that the "*Friday the 13th* formula" had connected with young audiences on an almost primal level. Even more unsettling to some observers was that the point of identification for the audience—the character with whom their allegiance was strongest—varied throughout the film, a narrative device that became even more pronounced in all of the subsequent sequels. In one moment, audiences could have empathy for the hapless human victims as they were stalked one by one, while in the next they could "cheer on" Jason as he dispatched his prey in ever more elaborate and shocking ways. Yet, by film's end, their sympathies were once again aligned with the (usually) female protagonist, as she (or he) defeated Jason, if only temporarily. Film as spectator sport was and continues to be one of *Friday the 13th*'s signature attributes.

Friday the 13th was more than just a well-executed, if thriftily-made thrill ride: it was ground zero for a new mythology of fear. Almost immediately upon its release, *Friday the 13th* became the new campfire tale for the largest generation in American history—the children of the baby boomers. For them, its shocks were new, its visuals arresting, and its chair jumper of an ending totally unanticipated. Just as urban legends are passed from ear to ear, house to house, town to town—and transformed from local superstition into revered folklore in the process—so, too, would *Friday the 13th*'s tale of the young Jason Voorhees and his revenge-seeking mother be whispered in hushed tones in schoolyards across America. And as Jason became more powerful, more indestructible and more iconic with each sequel—eventually donning his now trademark hockey mask in 1982's *Friday the 13th Part 3 in 3-D*—he has legitimately become as potent and vital a symbol of fear to our modern culture as Dracula, Frankenstein and the Wolf Man were to the early twentieth century.

The people who create low-budget, independent genre movies often don't produce a film because they imagine it will break fresh ground or set grand new aesthetic standards or expand the horizons for the next generation of moviemakers. *Friday the 13th* was not created because its filmmakers wanted to inject something bold and alive into the cinematic bloodstream. And certainly none of them had any notion of creating a franchise that would spawn eleven films over a period of three decades and take in nearly half a billion dollars at the box office. *Friday the 13th* was conceived purely by chance and out of desperation by an ambitious independent producer and director named Sean S. Cunningham who wanted to create a potboiler just profitable enough so that its success might allow him to make another movie. Cunningham—having reached the milestone age of forty and left nearly insolvent after a decade of paying his dues—had only one true hit on his resumé, the notorious 1972 exploitation cult classic *Last House on the Left*. Fresh off the commercial failure of his two previous films, a couple of sports-themed, family-friendly entertainments, he pulled out the one great title he had once stored away in his mental Rolodex—*Friday the 13th*. Reluctant at first to return to his horror roots, Cunningham nevertheless crafted his new suspense shocker out of a little money, a lot of spit and polish, and a game cast and crew out to make something special—and, they hoped, successful.

When Sean Cunningham sold the domestic distribution rights for *Friday the 13th* to Paramount Pictures, the studio was at a crucial juncture in its history. Looking to augment their product pipeline of in-house productions, the studio turned to its then-Vice President of Distribution & Marketing, Frank Mancuso, Sr., to find independently-produced motion pictures that they could acquire quickly and cheaply, then widely distribute and market for maximum profit. When Mancuso took a chance on Cunningham's seemingly unremarkable horror film, he immediately sensed its commercial potential. Then Mancuso and Paramount thought big. They gifted *Friday the 13th* with a launch on over a thousand screens across the United States—an unheard-of number for a "negative pick-up" at that time—and the kind of saturated multimedia marketing campaign previously afforded only to high-gloss, first-class studio pictures. The result was historic for an exploitation movie: *Friday the 13th* was not only a smash success, it helped to create a whole new paradigm in the way motion pictures are made, marketed and exhibited.

In the twenty-five years since the release of *Friday the 13th*, the execution of its pattern for success has become a template copied by the entire motion picture industry. By the beginning of the 1990s, negative pickups would become *de riguer*, and by the new millennium most of the major studios had created their own in-house specialty divisions to produce and distribute the kind of niche genre entertainment previously disregarded as strict exploitation fare. Companies like Dimension Films, a subsidiary of The Walt Disney Company, and, most notably, New Line Cinema, owned by Time-Warner, continue to see profits from such popular horror franchises as *A Nightmare on Elm Street*, *Halloween* and *Hellraiser* serve as a major source of annual revenue on their parent companies' financial ledgers. Concurrent with major studio production of genre films in the 1980's came a sea-change in how they exhibited them. Today, the type of no-holds-barred horror fare that once might have played only in drive-ins and seedy grind-houses is now being shown in multiplexes across America. And advertising campaigns that were once considered taboo are now accepted across all forms of mainstream media, from network television to major magazines to the Internet. Thanks in part to the success of *Friday the 13th*, the distinction between the "A" and "B" film has been, if not entirely erased, then at least blurred.

The evolution of *Friday the 13th* has not been without its aches and pains, however. The scorn that was heaped upon the franchise, particularly in its early years, was of the type usually reserved only for the most reviled of exploitation films, or pornography. The creative murder sequences for which the *Friday the 13th* films have become infamous were considered not just offensive to many but downright obscene. Almost immediately upon the release of the original *Friday the 13th* the barrage of criticism began: countless attacks by high-brow commentators, irate op-ed pieces in local newspapers, complaints from concerned parents on syndicated talk shows, and even the official condemnation of the Catholic League of Decency were among the firestorm of charges being leveled at the film and its makers. *Friday the 13th* became not just a lightning rod for controversy, but the most visible representation of a so-called "cynical new wave of horror filmmaking" that reveled in sadistic violence, misogyny and nihilism. Further inciting the backlash was the immediate and overwhelming wave of imitators that followed in the wake of the success of *Friday the 13th*. Knock-offs that were, arguably, even more crass, derivative and prurient than the film that had already been derided as the most base form of cinematic exploitation imaginable. *Friday the 13th*, along with *Halloween* and *The Texas Chainsaw Massacre*, were among the first in the cycle of American "slasher films," a whole new subgenre of motion pictures united by their most basic elements—sex-crazed teens, a virtuous heroine, a masked killer with a knife and graphic bloodletting. That *Friday the 13th* and its seemingly endless parade of sequels would remain the most financially successful of the slasher craze—released unapologetically by a major studio, no less—only emboldened the Moral Majority in their cause.

But perhaps the greatest nemesis of the *Friday the 13th* series was, ironically, the least publicly vocal. The Motion Picture Association of America's ratings board had always maintained a vise-like grip on the series' graphic content, but as the sequels wore on, the constraints began to feel like a strait-jacket being placed on the creative backs of the filmmakers. The battle eventually took on political dimensions, with the producers and directors often loudly complaining that the board—or the "censors," as some foes labeled them—held an unfair bias towards the franchise. While such theories could never be proven, it was an assumption that had all but become accepted as fact by the genre press and the series' most ardent fans. Nevertheless, it remains an undisputed fact that most of the films in the series required extensive trimming of their violent imagery in order to earn an R classification from the

board. Whether or not the imposed cuts harmed or dimished the intended impact of the films, the issue continues to be hotly contested by fans and the filmmakers today.

By the mid-1990s, the MPAA's stance against the kind of graphic imagery seen in films like *Friday the 13th* clearly began to soften. Whether American culture had, in the intervening years, grown more accepting of graphic depictions of violence in motion pictures, video games and the broadcast media—or if we simply were becoming densensitized to it—the stigma that had marginalized the *Friday the 13th* franchise had seemed to dissipate to a large degree. Ironically, by the end of the 1980s, the key elements of the "slasher film" that had once sparked such public outrage were suddenly (if not subversively) being adopted by more mainstream movies. From the high-gloss thrills of *Fatal Attraction* to any of the big-budget action extravaganzas starring Bruce Willis or Arnold Schwarzenegger, many of the most derided elements of the *Friday* films—over-the-top violent deaths, the seemingly unstoppable killer and that now-expected "One Last Final Scare"—seemed to have migrated over to the more "socially acceptable" Hollywood blockbuster. Today, even the most repudiated aspect of the *Friday the 13th* series—its gore quotient—can now be seen in greater clinical detail (and for free, no less) on such television shows as the top-rated *CSI* and *ER*.

Occasionally, those opposed to *Friday the 13th* won some of their battles. By the end of 1990, *Friday the 13th: The Series*, a weekly syndicated television drama that ranked second only to *Star Trek: The Next Generation* in weekly ratings, would be cancelled after its third season amid protests from the Religious Right. So synonymous had the title *Friday the 13th* become with sex, nudity and gratitious violence that the television series, which otherwise had no connection to the motion picture franchise, suffered its untimely demise sheerly as a result of guilt by association. Although neither Paramount Pictures nor New Line Cinema has ever publicly commented on the critical and moral backlash, the repercussions have been felt mostly by the actors and the filmmakers, some of whom have come under harsh personal attack from both outside and within the industry just for having their name associated with something as prurient and offensive as *Friday the 13th*.

Now, as *Friday the 13th* celebrates its silver anniversary, the horror series that refuses to die has, at last, come full circle. Reinvigorated by the success of 2003's *Freddy vs. Jason*, *Friday the 13th* has gone from a surprise mainstream success to a cult phenomenon, survived a nearly decade-long hibernation, and then re-emerged as an enormously viable commercial franchise whose appeal now spans multiple generations. The series has achieved the simultaneous feat of being both a source of nostalgia for older audiences who grew up on the original films, as well as relevant for a new generation of moviegoers. While perhaps not quite as all-American as "Mom and Apple Pie," *Friday the 13th* has nonetheless hacked, slashed and stabbed its way into the annals of pop culture, with Jason Voorhees' iconic hockey-masked visage recognized around the world as a symbol of movie mayhem. For many, *Friday the 13th* is one of the signposts of the adolescent experience. To initiate a younger sibling or friend into the mythology of *Friday the 13th* is like telling your favorite scary story around a campfire. And for those who have never before experienced a Jason film, the event is akin to a rite of passage. *Friday the 13th* has become a phenomenon far larger than the sum of its bloody parts. It is currently the longest-running film series in cinema today, second only to James Bond. Its profits have exceeded those of any other horror franchise around the world. And its durability has defied even the most vocal of its detractors. *Friday the 13th* may truly be eternal.

This book tells the complete story of *Friday the 13th* for the first time in the words of the people who created it. Whether the success of the franchise left them elated or disgruntled, amused or bewildered, they talk about their experiences with passion and candor, in a wide array of views about the series, its making, its controversies and its legacy. Their recollections are also proof positive that even in the world of *Friday the 13th*, there may never be one pure, objective reality, only several subjective perspectives of the same event. With the compiling of this book, I have aspired to do justice to the people and their stories, to celebrate their accomplishments and respect the cultural impact of what they have created.

What you are holding in your hands is also the culmination of my own twenty-five year journey, one that began when I sat in a darkened movie theater back in 1980 and watched, with rapt fascination, as *Friday the 13th* unspooled in front of my ten-year-old eyes. But unlike the science fiction and fantasy-adventure films that proved so popular and resonant to the youth of my generation, I was not so much transported to a different universe by *Friday the 13th* as I was inspired to reckon with the sometimes harsh realities of my own very real world—to confront my adolescent fears and mortality, stimulate my sexual curiosities, find a sense of belonging within my peer group through our shared love of the genre and ultimately to realize my own ambition to work in the entertainment industry. If, inevitably, the question of why I would write such a book as this must be asked, specifically by those unfamiliar or outright offended by the series, I can only answer with another question: where would I be without *Friday the 13th*?

Never could I have anticipated that it would have taken me three years to complete *Crystal Lake Memories*. But in that time, I have had the great fortune to meet more than two hundred people who lent their considerable talents to the *Friday the 13th* franchise over its twenty-five-year lifespan. Never, in my opinion, has there been such an unfair schism between the reputation of a film series and the caliber of talent, passion, integrity and intelligence of the people who created it. And I certainly cannot forget the many, many enthusiastic and devoted fans that I have met over the course of this journey—not only the next generation of teenagers who have discovered their passion for the *Friday* films in today's world of special edition DVDs, but also their parents who, not so long ago, made up the young audience for whom these films were so unabashedly intended. It has been good to hear others talk so passionately about the impact these films have had on their lives. I also cannot forget the many new friends I have made among the series' alumni, especially the team at Crystal Lake Entertainment and, of course, Sean Cunningham, who has not only graciously contributed a new Foreword for this book, but whose support and belief made this project possible. To all of you, I do not know what my life would have become had I not had this experience and this privilege.

So huddle around the campfire, whisper "Ki-ki-ki, Ma-ma-ma," and turn the page to discover the secrets of the mythical place called Crystal Lake. Inside you'll find stories of fear and fortitude, told with much humor and reverence, as well as tales of courage, of conquering seemingly insurmountable obstacles, and ultimately of good defeating evil. Because *Crystal Lake Memories* is a book about survivors—both real-life and fictional—who have come to learn that, while there is darkness in the world, we can, with great resourcefulness and a little luck, survive the night. I hope that once you have finished reading this book you will realize that the world would be a much darker place indeed without *Friday the 13th*.

Peter M. Bracke
Los Angeles, July, 2005

1.

Long Night at Camp Blood

Near the end of 1969, Sean S. Cunningham, then twenty-nine years old, sat down with his wife, Susan, at their home in Westport, Connecticut. Almost four years married, and with a second child on the way, Sean outlined to his wife his strategy for making it in the film business. Despite having already achieved a prodigal level of success as a Broadway theatre director and stage manager, Cunningham was eager to make the transition to the cinematic arts. "I didn't know enough to be intimidated," he would admit thirty-five years later. "Since then, I've been stupid enough and lucky enough to have achieved great success in my career." Stupid and lucky—Cunningham gives the words equal weight. Throughout his career, he has defied the odds and achieved commercial success on his own terms. Brash, pragmatic and resolutely independent, Cunningham retains to this day the tireless work ethic instilled in him as the son of first-generation Irish immigrants. He is also a devout family man and fiercely loyal to the people he chooses to work with—a dichotomy that, in the early days of his career, left him torn between maintaining financial security and realizing his own artistic ambitions.

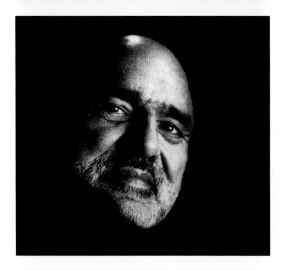

Top: Sean Cunningham (left) and Steve Miner, circa 1986. After Cunningham hired the young Miner as a production assistant on 1972's *Last House on the Left*, they formed a close friendship that continues to this day. Miner went on to direct the first two *Friday the 13th* sequels, as well as the hit 1986 horror-comedy *House*, which Cunningham produced.

Middle: Frank Mancuso, Sr., in a 1982 publicity pose. He began his career as a booking agent for Paramount Pictures in 1962, and by 1983, was named the studio's Chairman and CEO. He would acquire *Friday the 13th* for the studio in 1980.

Bottom: Hallmark Releasing's George Mansour. In 1971, Mansour acquired Sean Cunningham's second directorial effort, *Together*, for the company. The founders of Hallmark eventually went on to fund *Last House on the Left*, which Cunningham produced, as well as *Friday the 13th*.

Sean Cunningham's beginnings were inauspicious at best. He struggled to make a name for himself in New York's "anti-establishment" film scene of the early 1970s, scraping by on a diet of industrial shorts and commercials—and the occasional soft-core porn. Yet Cunningham's drive and determination remained unflappable. He was once heard to boast, even before he produced his first motion picture, "All you need in order to be a film producer is a telephone and some stationery!"

Although Sean Cunningham would toil in the trenches of low-budget, unremarkable exploitation pictures for the ten years before the unprecedented success of *Friday the 13th*, his youthful bravado proved magnetic. And many of those drawn into his rag-tag filmmaking family would come to play a crucial part in the birth of the *Friday* franchise—a group whose backgrounds were as disparate as their talents were unique, and often united by little more than raw ambition. There was Wes Craven, an ex-Humanities professor-turned-aspiring filmmaker; Steve Miner, a former ski-bum on the verge of his first Hollywood break; Harry Manfredini, a New York-based composer and part-time session musician; Bill Freda, editor-for-hire; and Victor Miller, the Yale-educated screenwriter torn between prestige and schlock. But those most influential to Cunningham's destiny would be three men of great mystery, owners of the Boston-based regional chain Esquire Theatres who were about to make an unexpected transition from shady back-door dealmakers to major studio-supported financiers.

All were anxious to make their mark on motion picture history. And they would.

SEAN CUNNINGHAM, Producer & Director: My first film was called *The Art of Marriage*. At the time, we had what were called "white coaters." They allowed you to get away with showing hardcore XXX-rated movies as long as they were under the guise of freedom of speech. You billed it as an "educational" or "medical" movie. At the beginning, someone would come out in a white coat and say, "We're now going to show you marriage practices in Denmark and these are the ways you can improve your marital bliss." And then for the next 80 minutes you saw people fucking like crazy. At the end, the same guy with the white coat would come out again and say, "Now that you have experienced these practices, you can go home with your mate and practice these things at home." We didn't have anybody actually fucking onscreen, just two people without clothes on lying on top of each other.

I just can't tell you how simple things are when you don't know anything. I had never even touched a camera before. I had no idea whatsoever what I was getting into. *The Art of Marriage* cost something like $3,500 that I had scraped together. I think we had three crew members, and I don't even know why we had to have that many. We just were afraid of getting arrested. That was how I embarked upon my filmmaking career. This was 1970, approximately.

GEORGE MANSOUR, Distributor, Esquire Theatres: Back in the late '60s, I was working for Warner Bros. as a "short-booker"—in other words, I wasn't trusted with major films. There were big books and you had a number of prints and you wrote in where the prints were going and the name of the movie house. And I knew all of them. So I would fill in for this drunk guy all the time and call up and try to get dates and make sure that the prints went out to the proper movie houses.

Esquire Theatres was one of Warner's accounts. They owned and operated about one hundred screens, mostly on the East Coast. Esquire were not the best payers—they were a little shady and shaky—but they also had a lot of good movie houses. I got a rapport going between myself and the owners—Phil Scuderi, Steve Minasian and Robert Barsamian. One thing led to another, they had an opening and offered me a job. So I went from a trainee booker for Warner, who was selling to movie houses, to working a distribution company who was booking movies from them.

RON KURZ, Screenwriter, *Part 2*: I had known of Phil Scuderi and Esquire since my days in the early 1970s as a theater manager in Baltimore. I became aware of Phil because of some of his distribution tricks. He was like William Castle—taking out insurance policies against dying of fright or having kids handing out logo-imprinted toilet paper on downtown street corners. Phil, who has since died, was quite a force in the schlock movie business—just picture a cross between Roger Corman and Michael Corleone: a trained lawyer, crude and suave at the same time, and full of street smarts. And when he got into movie production, he could rip off the latest box office hit and have something on screen in a matter of months. I should know—I wrote a few of them.

SEAN CUNNINGHAM: I was in completely uncharted waters. It was one of those scenes right out of an old B-movie. As dreadful as *The Art of Marriage* was, I had to find a theater that would make some sort of deal with me to play it. So I literally figured out who owned the local movie theaters in my area and just looked them up in the phone book. One guy I got on the phone was Bingo Brant, part of the Brant family, and I went over to his offices and showed him the picture, and he says he wants to play it. He kept the first $3,500 or something, and then after that, we'd get a piece of the box office.

The Art of Marriage was first released at the Brant Theater on 42nd Street in Manhattan. And it played for twenty-seven weeks! We probably got over $100,000. So I had what most people in the film business never had, a hit movie. But *The Art of Marriage* was crummy, so I thought if we could make a real version of it, we could play it in suburban theaters. That was how my next film, *Together*, evolved.

I ended up renting office space in New York with the profits from *Marriage*. And I raised another $50,000 from my family, friends and people I knew. Everybody was in for $1,000 or $1,500. It was kind of a lark, a silly crapshoot for them, like, "Crazy Sean doesn't know what he's doing, but he seems to think that this might work." It was a nifty time. It was the 1970s and this was alternative filmmaking. My belief was that you didn't need those big Hollywood trucks and shit like that. All you needed was a 16mm camera, throw it on your shoulder and shoot.

WES CRAVEN, Filmmaker: The late 1960s was not a successful time for me. I think at that point in my life I was still trying to please my parents, unconsciously trying to be the good boy that went off to school and then became a teacher. This was an acceptable profession and very respectable. But about four or five years into teaching I just realized I was profoundly bored and out of place. It just wasn't me, and so I made one of those big leaps. I said, "I'm gonna take a shot at doing something that I would really enjoy." So I quit and went to New York to work in filmmaking.

It was a very intense year and a half of doing everything, from sweeping floors upwards. Before I met Sean Cunningham, I was working around the clock, just going from one job to another, from managing post-production to synching up dailies for various documentaries. It was very intense. My marriage collapsed. I lived on virtually nothing. But it was a real watershed in my life—within a few weeks of meeting Sean, I had this job synching up dailies on this little feature he was directing, *Together*. It had already been shot, and Sean hired me to synchronize the dailies from a three or four-day reshoot of additional material. After that, they asked me to come aboard as assistant editor. Sean and I got that film ready for mix under horrendous conditions of no money and no sleep for practically two weeks. We stayed up all hours just working through the night and we bonded. We really became war buddies at the end of that process.

GEORGE MANSOUR: Hallmark Releasing was one of the names for Esquire's many distribution arms. Sean was shopping around a print of this movie, *Together*, and he had heard about Hallmark and came up to our offices. He didn't even have $90 to fly up from New York City. I looked at the film and said, "It's pretty crude and stupid, but I think that people would pay to see this." It has a very pretty girl, Marilyn Chambers, and it had this one incredible sequence with this tremendously good-looking black man. Very handsome. Fantastic

Background: Some of Sean S. Cunningham's varied directorial efforts include (clockwise from top) 1971's soft-core "sexutainment" *Together*, starring Marilyn Chambers; the light-hearted family soccer comedy *Manny's Orphans* (1978); and the disastrous X-rated sex comedy *The Case of the Smiling Stiffs* (1974).

body. And Marilyn Chambers took a yellow flower and she runs it along his flaccid penis, and as she runs it along, the penis becomes erect. I said, "You know, Phil. There's a big group of people out there who have never seen a big black dick before. We can exploit this." So Hallmark bought *Together* for $10,000 flat.

SEAN CUNNINGHAM: Phil saw what I saw. If you marketed this right, it could play in suburban theatres. We'd take out big ads in local papers that read, "What can your children teach you about S-E-X? Find out Tuesday—Special Screening at 10:00 am. Free!" Who's going to come at ten o'clock in the morning? Housewives. And the buzz was off the charts. We just did phenomenal business. People were literally lining up around the block to see it. Nobody had seen anything like this. It was 1971— before *Deep Throat*. "Porn chic" happened later. That's when censorship came, and everything changed at that point.

Of course, it felt great. It was glorious. But *Together* wasn't an aesthetic success. After that, Hallmark said, "Well, what do you want to do?" And Wes and I said, "Something else. If you guys will write us a check, let's figure out another movie."

The film Wes Craven and Sean Cunningham created, Last House on the Left, *remains one of the most notorious horror-exploitation films of the 1970s. Based loosely on Ingmar Bergman's* The Virgin Spring, *Craven's tale of a pair of innocent teenage girls, kidnapped, raped and murdered by a band of thugs was unflinching in its depiction of violence, with a* cinema verité, *news-reel like realism that was violent, unapologetic and, to some, obscene. Aided by an aggressive marketing campaign by Hallmark, including the famous tagline "To Avoid Fainting, Keep Repeating, 'It's Only a Movie…'" the film was a big hit on the exploitation and drive-in circuit, and has since become a cult classic. But its success proved to be something of an albatross for Craven and Cunningham, who seemingly overnight were crowned cinema's new reigning* enfant terribles, *a sobriquet they would be unable to shake for years to come. It would be the last film Cunningham and Craven would make together. But* Last House *would also introduce Cunningham to an aspiring young filmmaker named Steve Miner, a relationship that would become integral to the creation of* Friday the 13th.

WES CRAVEN: Sean had been offered $90,000 as the whole budget for a scary movie as a result of *Together*. He asked me if I wanted to write it and direct it and cut it. I said sure, even though I never thought of writing a scary movie before. So I said, "Okay, what's a horror film?" Films about violence at that time had become tremendously stylized. I was watching Peckinpah's films— violence becoming legitimized as balletic and almost beautiful. The critics were all swooning about how it could be handled so artistically. At the same time, Vietnam was going on, there was much there that was brutal and protracted and awful and ugly. So I set out to start a film that seemed to be a typical B-movie. Then, at the moment it gets violent, I wanted to make it very real, not swerving away, fading to black or dissolving or seeing a shadow do it, but just looking right at people at the moment they did it. That was very subversive and very threatening to people.

STEVE MINER, Associate Producer: I always say in interviews, "Yeah, I loved horror movies as a kid" and stuff, but no, I never really did. I'm not one of the children of Forry Ackerman. But my mom was a film librarian, and she would always bring home movies for us to watch. I'd see a lot of 16mm films and that's when I really started to fall in love with cinema and decided that I should try to make them.

In the early 1970s, I was a ski bum in Colorado, and I had decided that I wanted to get into the film business. I grew up in

Above: One of the many shocking images from *The Last House on the Left*.

Distributed theatrically in 1972 by Hallmark Releasing, this notorious cult classic was directed by Wes Craven and produced by Sean Cunningham. The film was initially tested under different titles, including *Sex Crime of the Century* and *Krug & Company*. It was not until the film was renamed and coupled with an inventive ad campaign that recommended to terrified patrons, "To avoid fainting, keep repeating, 'It's only a movie...'" (**below**) that it became one of the most successful exploitation films of the early 1970s.

Such publicity gimmicks would prove influential to *Friday the 13th* when, almost a decade later, Hallmark helped create ad concepts for the film. "The original marketing for *Friday the 13th* was Hallmark's," says the company's former publicist George Mansour. "And it could easily have been the idea of any of the guys in the office, because it was very loose and crazy. We didn't have an ad agency or anything like that. It wasn't until Paramount really came in on the third *Friday* that they were involved in the marketing."

Westport, and I knew that there were a number of industrial and educational filmmakers there. So I moved back home to Connecticut in hopes of finding some work. I heard that somebody in town was shooting a movie, and it turned out to be Sean Cunningham, who was producing *Last House on the Left* with Wes Craven. I didn't know Sean at the time, but I had grown up with his younger brothers. So I asked Sean to give me a job, and he did, at something like fifteen dollars a week. I was a gofer, but I ended up doing a little bit of everything. I held the boom mike, I carried lights, I took script notes, anything that was needed. I remember a lot of twenty-four hour days, trying to finish up and get out of a given location. And we didn't have script boards, so we would be going through the script, crossing out pages, wondering, "Did we shoot this part yet?"

SEAN CUNNINGHAM: *Last House* became a kind of double-edged sword. Since it was very cheap and exploitative, and successful at its own level, all people thought of me was with the notion that, "If you want to get puke in a bucket—and get it cheap—boy, I've got just the guy for you!" I'm certainly glad to have made it, because it made a whole bunch of other things possible. But at the time, there was no thought of, "Is this something that I'm even going to be talking about twenty-five years from now?"

WES CRAVEN: At this point in my life, *Last House* is so far back in my past that it's more of an oddity than a sore point. I see it, in a way, as a protest film. There was an initial stage in horror cinema, during which *Last House* was made, where gore stood for everything that was hidden in society. Guts stood for issues that were being repressed, so the sight of a body being eviscerated was exhilarating to an audience, because they felt, "Thank God, it's finally out in the open and slopping around on the floor." But that gets very old very fast.

I don't think *Last House* was really the progenitor of what Sean did in *Friday the 13th*... the violence in that film was bizarre, but it wasn't real; it was goofy. I was more interested in psychological underpinnings and irony, and I think Sean discovered after *Last House* that he was much more interested in being entertaining rather than assaultive. *Last House* didn't allow you to have fun at all.

SEAN CUNNINGHAM: In terms of film politics and possibilities, *Last House* is important. But it is very, very hard to watch. It's not a fun movie at any level. And boy, did I not want to make *Last House on the Left Part II* or *III*. Wes and I were also striking off in slightly different directions. I was trying to do documentary films and commercials. Steve Miner had been working for me, and he was trying to cut some NHL film. We were all just learning.

I also did not want to deal any longer with Phil and the folks in Boston. They were and continue to be very difficult people to deal with. In a perfect world, you wouldn't have to deal with people who cause you problems. So after *Last House*, Wes and I just decided to stay away from them. We were friendly, and I didn't want to quite close the door, but I didn't particularly want to work with them again.

Eventually, I wound up going to Spain to do a tax shelter movie called *Blind Planet*. I was somehow the American who had brought in the financing and they wanted to make their own movie, and they didn't want my input. And in Spain they have siesta, so I was getting drunk twice a day. Plus, I didn't have too many responsibilities, so I could get drunk as much as I wanted to. And I had two alcoholic parents, so I knew a lot about booze. I thought I had decided that I wasn't going to become a drunk like my parents. And I didn't. I became a drunk unlike my parents.

When I came home, my wife had had it. I went to AA on Mondays to get her off my back—meeting after meeting. And as it turned out, I was one of those fortunate guys—I discovered sobriety. That's when my life really changed dramatically. Sobriety brings with it very different perspectives. I no longer had interest in the "naughty factor." I just wasn't going to do that anymore. That was a big turning point.

So after coming back from Spain and still wanting to do something else, one day, out of the blue, I got a call from Phil Scuderi to come out to Boston. I said, "What the hell?" So he sits me down in his office, this is around Labor Day, 1976, and he has this thick Boston accent: "Have you ever seen that *Bad News Bears* movie?" So a writer named Victor Miller and I put together this silly little rip-off movie called *Here Come the Tigers* with only three weeks of prep and script.

VICTOR MILLER, Screenwriter: I was very impressed with Sean. He had an incredible mind and seemed to know a lot. And, of course, he had done *Last House on the Left*, which was a lot more than I had done. It's funny, because Sean was anything but scary. He was goofy and sort of carefree at that point. I also always liked his metaphor that a good movie was putting together a good rollercoaster for people. We both wanted to make a living at it, we definitely thought about movies as entertainment, not as teaching tools for the universe.

SEAN CUNNINGHAM: I think *Here Come the Tigers* cost like $250,000, if that. It could be much lower. It was guerrilla filmmaking. It was all kids from the local little leagues; it was like being on a three-week field trip with a bunch of sixth-graders. It was good and bad, frustrating and exciting. I loved it.

VICTOR MILLER: Those where the days when everybody said, "What America needs is a good G-rated movie." I guess *Here Come the Tigers* made its money back, but they lied about America wanting G-rated films. But that did not stop us from making another G-rated film, *Manny's Orphans*—or *Kick*, depending on which version you saw. Steve Miner had come up with the idea for it and I wrote the screenplay and we did it, another low budget film, and shot it around Bridgeport, Connecticut.

SEAN CUNNINGHAM: We had this notion of a bunch of orphans in a halfway house, they put together a soccer team and the underdog wins. So we raised the money to do what became known as *Manny's Orphans*. It was a lot of fun to make, and again I loved working with the kids. I really thought it was going to be a breakthrough film for me. Then we went out to try and sell it and the reaction was lukewarm. United Artists said, "Let's take this and use it as a pilot for a TV series," and they optioned the movie. That was the good news. The bad news was all they did was option it, they didn't buy it.

I was trying to figure out what the heck we could do to keep the lights on, to support my wife and my kids. I loved this notion of doing a warm, fuzzy children's series, but that wasn't gonna pay the bills. I decided I had to make some kind of a movie. I didn't want to go back to horror, but we were broke. And the most important thing you can do in a film career is make money. Because if you make money, people will let you make more films and take chances and nobody will blame you.

Sean Cunningham would find the inspiration he needed with the release in 1978 of a low-budget, independently financed and distributed horror film entitled Halloween. *The story of an escaped mental patient named Michael Myers who returns to his hometown to stalk and murder a trio of babysitters, along with the film's stylish direction by John Carpenter and easy-to-replicate elements—a simple but effective structure, limited locations, a masked killer and a fresh-faced cast of relative unknowns—served as the blueprint for a new sub-genre of the horror film that would soon become known as the "slasher movie."*

Although excited by the commercial possibilities of following in the success of Halloween, *Cunningham's return to horror was still a reluctant one. Even if the film that would become known as* Friday the 13th *was more calculated rip-off than genuine inspiration, the roots of the film's conception, development and financing would, ultimately, begin with the relationships Cunningham had forged eight years prior—and the three men with whom he had sworn he would never do business again.*

VICTOR MILLER: Around early 1979, I was living in Stratford. Sean and I were going to each other's houses probably two, three or four days a week just working on things. We were coming up with projects that we thought would be great for Clint Eastwood and other stuff that, of course, never got made. Then one day he called me up and said, "*Halloween* is making a lot of money at the box office. Why don't we rip it off?"

STEVE MINER: I loved the original *Halloween*. It was a breakthrough for American cinema really. It pioneered several concepts, of the independent film having mainstream success, and of a certain type of horror film as a genre. And it was really well done, a really terrific film. It relied on classic suspense and situations, and not gore. With *Friday the 13th*, we tried to copy the success of *Halloween*, clearly. We did it to break into the movies. At the time, we were working out of a garage in Connecticut. And we didn't even have a script.

SEAN CUNNINGHAM: Victor and I sat down at the kitchen table and started kicking around ideas. We'll take a remote location and put a lot of young people in jeopardy. Then we went down the list: are they in jeopardy from a real force or

"Those were the greatest times I ever had making movies."

Sean Cunningham on *Here Come the Tigers* and *Manny's Orphans*

Below: The trade ad that launched *Friday the 13th*. Appearing in the July 4, 1979 issue of *International Variety*, the ad, while placed by Sean Cunningham primarily to generate investment capital, also served a second, more covert purpose. "I talked with Steve Miner about it," remembers Cunningham, "and the two of us thought that while we liked the title 'Friday the 13th,' we didn't know if we could legally use it or not. So that is in part why we took out that big ad, because then if somebody was gonna sue us, they'd let us know. And as it turned out, we had no problems with the title at all."

However, George Mansour, who worked for Phil Scuderi, one of the co-owners of Georgetown Productions, the company that would eventually fund *Friday the 13th*, disputes that claim. "Actually, there was a problem with the title," says Mansour. "There was a movie before ours called *Friday the 13th: The Orphan*. Moderately unsuccessful. But someone still threatened to sue. I don't know whether Phil paid them off, but it was finally resolved. So, another *Friday the 13th* did exist."

FROM THE PRODUCER OF *LAST HOUSE ON THE LEFT* COMES
THE MOST TERRIFYING FILM EVER MADE!

FRIDAY THE 13TH

PRODUCED AND DIRECTED BY SEAN S CUNNINGHAM

CURRENTLY IN PRODUCTION AVAILABLE IN NOVEMBER 1979

CONTACT

> ## "With our budget, I had to be very selective about what I put on camera. There's nothing we shot that isn't up there on the screen." Sean Cunningham

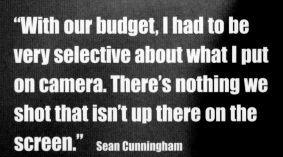

The sequence in *Friday the 13th* that transformed the most from script to screen was the film's opening prologue, a flashback to the murder of two amorous counselors at Camp Crystal Lake in 1958. "Originally, we planned to shoot that scene in quite a different way," reveals director Sean Cunningham. "It was written to occur by the lake on the campgrounds, there was to be a chase through a boat house and by the water, and a few other things."

Eventually, the sequence had to be streamlined, largely due to production constraints. "The first night we tried to film the scene, it snowed," laughs associate producer Steve Miner. "Then when we did it the second time, the generator died. So we were forced to choose the barn, as it eventually appeared in the movie, out of necessity, because that was the one location we could think of that had its own power source. And I liked what we ended up with, but the original sequence would have been very exciting."

Top: This still was taken by unit photographer Richard Feury, leading many fans to believe that a more graphic murder was shot for the prologue's doomed heroine, Claudette (Debra S. Hayes). Special makeup effects artist Tom Savini clarifies: "The first two kids in the movie, we *should* have killed them gloriously. But we didn't. Because when nothing happens to them, you're thinking, 'Okay, well I can deal with that, it's not that scary, they're not gonna shock me too bad.' And then from there on out, with every increasingly gruesome murder, the audience just went, 'Oh my god!'"

an imaginative one? Who's going to survive, if anyone? Locations were kicked around, too. How about an apartment building, or a funhouse or an amusement park or an island off the coast of Spain?

VICTOR MILLER: Everything happened really fast. This was the middle of 1979. My first week's work was coming up with about fifty different venues. Anywhere that kids would be. Like high schools, play rooms, forests, whatever. I would go over and pitch my ideas to Sean and we would say, "Nah, nah, nah." Then I remembered that going away to summer camp was just too scary for me. I was a wuss. My older brother went to camp and I did not like the stories he came back with. The whole idea of living in these big rooms with people with double bunk beds sounded pretty awful. So I finally went over to Sean's and said, "I think I got it—it's a summer camp before it opens." And we both said, "Yippie!"

Then I went off to my little office, typing my life away. And after I started writing I came up with the highly unfavorable title of "Long Night at Camp Blood." That was its working title until about the third or fourth draft, when Sean said, "I've got the name of the movie."

SEAN CUNNINGHAM: While I was working on *Manny's Orphans*, I was trying to figure out a campaign for that movie, and distributors were telling me, "The title's no good. 'Manny' is too ethnic. 'Orphans' sounds too sad. We should have another title." So I started making these long lists of titles and one that just came into my head was "Friday the 13th." I didn't know what it would be about, but the title intrigued me. And out of frustration I said, "Christ, if I had a picture called *Friday the 13th*, I could sell that! But what am I supposed to do with this?" I kept toying around with it. What would it be? It just kinda stuck in the back of my mind.

So I took out this ad in Variety over the Fourth of July weekend of 1979. A full-page ad that said, "Friday the 13th" in great big block letters, crashing through a mirror. And underneath it read, "The Most Terrifying Film Ever Made! Available December 1979." I started getting all of these telexes from different foreign distributors all around the world, who said they'd love to see this picture.

I had gone away from the investors in Boston, but after I placed the ad they called and said they would like a piece of it. I was trying to syndicate it for $500,000, and they came in with an initial offer of $125,000. It was a good start. They came back to me after we had an early draft of the script and they had said that they changed their mind—they wanted to invest the entire $500,000. They really wanted to control it all. We tried to negotiate the deal in a certain way that I thought I could live with, but they wouldn't cave on a few points that I considered to be crucial, like who gets the money and when, and cash flow.

Finally, one night I was having a phone conversation with Phil Scuderi. I said, "No. I just can't do it." And I hung up on him. It wasn't the wrong thing to do—it was the right thing to do. And I think it would still be the right thing to do if it were only me involved. On the one hand, they're putting up all the money, so we get to make the movie. But on the other hand, it was just going to be like signing up for a root canal. It was a way to go forward, but it was another way to go backwards.

That was a very troubled night. I spent the night tossing and turning, and I got up early in the morning and went jogging. I remember this so clearly. Sometimes when you run you wind up being free-associative. All this stuff bubbled up. I thought, "It's not the deal you want, but it's not the movie you want, either. You're just trying to put it together and all these people are counting on you. Fuck, what's the big deal? So you didn't get what you wanted." Sometimes we do the right things for the wrong reasons.

So I come back to the house, it's 6:45 a.m. and the kids had just gotten up. I called Phil at home and said, "I thought about our conversation last night, and I changed my mind. I'm willing to do it on the terms you suggest." And he said, "I'm glad you called because I was just leaving the house." He was about to go take the money and invest it in a shopping center.

That's how we got to make *Friday the 13th*. It really came down to, if I had called him twenty minutes later it never would have happened.

Dated August 21, 1979, Victor Miller's third draft of "Long Night at Camp Blood" deviated unusually little from the final shooting script of Friday the 13th. *It was with this draft in hand that Sean Cunningham would begin pre-production for the film: scouting locations, assembling a crew and beginning casting sessions in a non-descript warehouse in New York City.*

The hodgepodge of characters that pepper Miller's script are undeniably generic, albeit dependable, archetypes: roughly a half dozen thinly-sketched, would-be victims familiar to any American teenager—the good girl, the practical joker, the jock, the slut, the potential boyfriend. And in the film's heroine, Alice, Miller would build upon the foundation laid by Carpenter's prototypical babysitter Laurie Strode in Halloween, *while also granting his creation a resourcefulness and intelligence transparently lacking in scream queens past.*

Few answering the open casting calls could have expected anything more than just another low-budget horror film in the wake of Halloween's *success, but for one group of fresh-faced young actors,* Friday the 13th *would be a very lucky day indeed.*

VICTOR MILLER: I was sitting in the waiting room at Columbia Pictures after *Friday the 13th* had come out and was such a success, and I heard one of the guys describing the movie as "the Pepsi Generation being horribly killed."

SEAN CUNNINGHAM: I remember thinking what was so scary about *Jaws* was looking up at the legs of all these innocent children and lovers and parents. It wasn't that they did anything wrong, or right. So when I was doing *Friday the 13th*, I wanted to create this world of young lovely kids, and that somebody is going to bite their legs off without any rhyme or reason. And therein lies the fear.

When we decided to cast the film, we'd never used a casting agency before. I was very fortunate to run into Barry Moss in New York. He worked with Julie Hughes at TNI Casting, and they were primarily theatrical agents. And for whatever reason, Barry really responded to it. Julie wasn't quite so sure. But they just broke their necks to get me the best actors they could find, and were absolutely instrumental in getting us the credible cast that we wound up with.

BARRY MOSS, Casting Director: We had done *Hero at Large* and *The Champ* before *Friday the 13th*. We didn't think it was a comedown, not at all. This was before the stigma of horror movies. There was *Halloween*, which was a big hit, and then this was the next one. Then a few years after that it became sort of like a grade-B thing to do. At the time, it was not. It wasn't grade-A, but in New York actors loved to do movies because there are so few opportunities. And I loved the script. I remember reading it one night on my little terrace, "Oh, no, not Jack! Don't kill Jack!"

KEVIN BACON, "Jack": Ever since I was a little kid, I always had an overdeveloped fantasy life and plugged myself into those fantasies whenever I could. By the time I was nine, I wanted to be a painter. When I was thirteen years old, I wanted to be a conga drum player. Then, when I reached fifteen or sixteen, it came to me that I was going to be an actor. I had a really strong sense that I was going to make a living even though I was going to be an artist. That was a big driving force, because I wanted to be free from any financial connection to my parents as soon as I possibly could. I didn't want to owe anybody anything. I still think of myself as a workhorse. The summer I turned eighteen, I remember coming up out of the New York subway with my little suitcase at Seventy-Second Street and Broadway, thinking it was the center of the universe.

My first movie was *Animal House*. I was attending Circle in the Square at the time, and the casting director called up the school and said, "We're looking for preppy freshman, wet behind the ears." It didn't register as anything real. The guy said, "How's scale?" and I said, "Scale is fine." I had no idea what scale meant. I ended up with a couple of scenes in that movie in which I get whacked on the backside with a paddle, and I get flattened into the cement at the end. And after five weeks on the set in Oregon, I figured I was a movie star and didn't have to go back to school. Six months later there I was, back in New York, waiting tables.

I heard about *Friday the 13th* because I traveled in some of the same acting circles as Mark Nelson, and I knew Jeannine Taylor as well. I think the casting directors just thought we worked well together as a threesome.

SEAN CUNNINGHAM: At that point he wasn't Kevin Bacon the movie star as we know him now, he was just a kid from New York trying to figure out how to make it happen. And he had a chance to be in a movie, to have a bunch of lines and show what he could do. I thought he was really smart. And I guess he still is great looking, but he was a *great* looking kid. It was kind of a no-brainer to hire him.

JEANNINE TAYLOR, "Marcie": I had the bug pretty early. I began to take voice lessons at the age of fourteen and then sang in school assemblies and at church and community events. Then I got some parts in school plays, and began to yearn to be a serious actress. Right after college I immediately moved to New York. I couldn't wait. I had the great good fortune to work with really fabulous, renowned artists very early. I was incredibly lucky. I was living many American girls' dreams.

But as far as acting in major motion pictures—frankly, I didn't think I was pretty enough. I didn't ever think of myself in that way. It was kind of a fluke, really. Barry Moss and Julie Hughes were a big

"She was just all bubbly and light and fun," says Sean Cunningham of Robbi Morgan, who plays *Friday the 13th*'s doomed Annie. "Robbi's scene was basically the prologue," continues Cunningham, "so she didn't work that much, but boy, she was a real treat." For the actress, being cast in the film was an unexpected but pleasant surprise. "I went in to audition for Barry Moss and Julie Hughes for something else," remembers Morgan. "They said, 'You know, Robbi, you're not really right for this, but there's a movie called *Friday the 13th* and they need an adorable camp counselor.' I was seventeen or eighteen years old. And when Sean called me to tell me I had gotten the part, he just said, 'I just want to make sure you're joining us!' And I said, 'Absolutely!' It was only a day or two of work, but I was just thrilled."

part of my auditioning for *Friday the 13th* because they were very well regarded—as they both still are. I was very confident that any part that came through that office would be a good opportunity. I didn't even really think of this movie as a horror film. To me, this was a small independent film about carefree teenagers who are having a rip-roaring time at a summer camp where they happen to be working as counselors. Then they just happen to get killed.

MARK NELSON, "Ned": *Friday the 13th* was my first movie. I had done an off-Broadway play at the Joseph Papp Public Theatre right after college, and some other small theater jobs. I had also done a few plays with Jeannine Taylor.

I got sides from the script, a comedy scene among the counselors. Then I got called back and my agent told me that they wanted me to come to the second audition in a bathing suit. That was when I was clued in that something was unusual about this movie. It certainly was not a straight dramatic role, and it was only after they offered me the part that they gave me the full script to read and I realized how much blood was in it. I did wonder how it would turn out, but I knew that Kevin Bacon was going to be in it and I liked Sean from the auditions. And I was anxious to start an acting career.

ADRIENNE KING, "Alice": I did my first commercial when I was six months old. I didn't have a lot to say about it. My mother had my sister and my brother and I in commercials. Then I quit school. I'd commute to New York, take my lessons, do commercial stuff, a few soaps, off-off-off Broadway, just the thing every young actor in New York does when they want to be a serious actor: you do it 100 percent of the time, whatever you can.

At that point, in 1979, I had spent a few weeks as a dancing extra on *Saturday Night Fever*. I'm one of like two blondes in the dance scene. They used us for everything—the continuity is so off that I had different hairstyles and dresses during the same song! But it was great—I felt like things were clicking and happening. At the same point I was auditioning for *Friday the 13th*, I was auditioning for *Grease* on Broadway. It was a very exciting time.

BARRY MOSS: There was an open casting call for Alice, a promotional thing to get people excited about the project. Adrienne was a friend of somebody who worked in our office, who had told us about this girl she thought was marvelous. So we brought her in as a favor to this woman, and after she read, Sean said, "You sneaky guys! You saved the best one for last!"

SEAN CUNNINGHAM: They brought in every young actress in New York. I liked Adrienne King when I met her. Vulnerable, girl next door. She didn't seem like an actress, she seemed like a kid, which was true for most of the actors in the movie. I wanted a sense of real people who could act and behave naturally, and Adrienne gave me that sense. I liked what she brought to the table. It's one of those things where she just had *something*.

ADRIENNE KING: The audition process took an entire summer. The first time I auditioned was in one of those rehearsal houses and there were hundreds of people in the hallway. Hundreds. And it wasn't even a scene, it was just "Hello, here's my picture. I'm young and nubile and I can scream really well." And I think that's what locked it for me, I really do. Because my scream was bloodcurdling. My mother was in the room at the time and she jumped up and thought I had been hurt. It's true—my scream has done me well.

It wasn't until late August, almost Labor Day, when I got a letter and that made it official. It was magical, just magical. I didn't sleep that whole summer.

Production on Friday the 13th *began on September 4, 1979. Budgeted at approximately $600,000, the film was shot on location in rural Blairstown and Hope, New Jersey, over a period of seven weeks. If the adventurous team of filmmakers was frequently aghast at the marginal accommodations afforded by the movie's modest budget, the early days of the production would see a cast and crew brimming with an enthusiasm and optimism that assuaged any complaints. It was, by all accounts, a true filmmaking summer camp—albeit one with a body count.*

SEAN CUNNINGHAM: I had discovered that a Friday the 13th fell in June 1980, and hoped to be able to get it into national release by then. All of this was, of course, speculative. We set about trying to lay the foundation over the month of July and August, casting and finding locations. I used my former art director Virginia Field and sent her out to find camps to get the thing rolling. We went in completely below the radar out at a Boy Scout camp, waiting for the Boy Scouts to go back to school before we could camp out there for four weeks while we shot the movie. And we were only able to come in after we made a contribution to the Boy Scouts of America. We set up shop in these little rustic cabins, with the production offices next to bunk beds.

MARK NELSON: Jeannine, Kevin and the rest of the cast and I were all on the same bus out of Port Authority in New York. I remember the first day; people just introduced themselves to each other on the bus as we got closer. And the motel was on the highway, and so they would pick us up and bring us to the location. It really was like summer camp.

JEANNINE TAYLOR: Some people might think it surprising that the set of *Friday the 13th* was so sunny and devoid of neuroses. But it was in absolute contrast to the movie's eerie, ghoulish subject matter. There was a jokey, breezy, carefree atmosphere on the set. We didn't really have to act that—that was real. The location was part of it. It was a real summer camp in a beautiful, bucolic setting. We ate a lot of our meals together in the dining hall. We were even given the option of staying in the cabins, but I didn't care to be that much of a method actress. So the cast fell into a kind of laugh-a-minute relationship with one another and I think it added to the movie.

ADRIENNE KING: It was Camp No-Be-Bos-Co, or as we all called it, "Not-a-Very-Good-Boy-Scout-Camp." It was the scary atmosphere of being out there in the middle of nowhere and it was an independent feature. It was one of those things where there immediately was a great bonding energy because there was no money. When there's nothing you just have to hang in there. For all of us, it was everyone's first big possibility. Everybody was so psyched and hopeful. That was the feeling on the entire set. I think that's why the first one is so special. Everybody just dug in his or her heels and said, "You know, something's happening here." And Sean was right there with us.

SEAN CUNNINGHAM: The wonderful part about making a movie at that point in everyone's career is that we were so thrilled just to be seeing an image. We'd look at the dailies and it had color and sound. It's a wonderful place to be, because a big part of our industry is about becoming jaded and spoiled. This was young film-making by young people.

BILL FREDA, Editor: I had cut *Here Come the Tigers* for Sean. When I took that job, I had heard of *Last House on the Left*, but I wasn't interested in background—it gave me a chance to cut dialogue and that was about it. Then Sean called and he said he was doing *Friday the 13th* and that he was going to make me famous. I said, "I don't want to be famous, I just want to be rich." I never forgot that. That goes to show you the kind of attitude we're talking about here. Anyway, it was nothing more than another movie. I don't even think we talked about it being a horror movie.

The dailies weren't very impressive, to be honest. It was like home movies. Everyone was young and overacting. It wasn't anything to get negative about. They were actors, they were doing a good job, but they were young.

VICTOR MILLER: I thought they did a fabulous job. The kids were interesting and real. If it had been cast in Los Angeles, I think the look would have been quite different. Clearly these are New York actors. The women were not pneumatically endowed, which was a fantasy of mine, so I missed that. But I thought it made it much more real.

SEAN CUNNINGHAM: When you are casting low budget films, what you ask the actors to do is be consistent with who they are personally. That makes it easier and credible to the piece. Sometimes it is a double-edged sword, because it can work great or it can turn out to be a real embarrassment. But if you're fortunate enough, you wind up with a situation where you just turn the cameras on and your actors behave how they would behave in real life. No matter how scripted it was, it would appear natural.

JEANNINE TAYLOR: Sean was very easygoing and he knew exactly what he wanted, and he conveyed that mostly non-verbally. If he didn't like something, he wouldn't say,

"I can't remember why we called him 'Ralph the Rat Man,' but Walt played him very well. I loved the way he looked. He was so strange!"

Sean Cunningham on the late Walt Gorney

"The scene where Annie (**above**) comes into the tiny diner and announces she's going to Crystal Lake, and the people just stare?" says director Sean Cunningham. "That was just trying to set mood. So the audience would think, 'Oh, there's something out of the ordinary going on here!'"

The sequence also introduced the character of Crazy Ralph (**top**), played by the late Walt Gorney. Though a favorite of many *Friday the 13th* fans, the film's director is not as convinced. "One character I did have reservations about was Crazy Ralph, and I still do," admits Cunningham. His function, in the classical tradition, was to be the foreshadower. It was also predicated on the fact that I needed, for at least a while, somebody who might be the murderer. I can't tell you if I really accomplished my intention."

So effective was Gorney in the role that many in the cast believed him to be a local town crazy. In truth, he was an accomplished stage and television actor. "I remember going to see Walt in a play called *Trelawny of the Wells* when I was in college," recalls Mark Nelson. "He played the butler in that. It was a huge cast with Meryl Streep and John Lithgow. And Walt was terrific! It is still one of my favorite plays I have ever seen."

"No" or "Don't," or any of the negative words that make actors—especially young, inexperienced actors—freeze and feel upset with themselves. He was very good that way. The silent message was: "Okay, kid, if I don't say anything, you're doing all right and if you're messing up I'll gently redirect you."

I remember when Kevin Bacon and I made the entrance into the cabin to do the sex scene, I was extremely nervous because I was going to do this very private, naughty thing. I was a modest person—I still am, really. So I did it very clumsily. I was just really bad on that first take. And I knew it—I was inwardly cringing. With that, just to show you what kind of person Sean was, he said "Cut," took me by the hand, privately walked me away from the rest of the crew and said very slowly and quietly in my ear: "Now, we can all do better than that." He was very gentle and compassionate about it—like talking to a skittish horse or something—it calmed me down immediately. I did a little better on the next take.

ADRIENNE KING: I think the reason that *Friday the 13th* has endured is because we were the kids next door. I think a lot of the teens that saw the movie could identify with the characters: "That could have been me out there, stuck in the middle of nowhere." I felt that innocence when I was shooting it. I don't know if that's because we didn't have any money, or because everyone was pitching in to make it the best they could. But we made something special.

KEVIN BACON: When I first started out, I had the idea that there were two sides to acting—"out of work" and "star." That was a misconception that was blown apart when I realized that there was this whole middle range of actors who were making a living in the theatre, playing a wide variety of roles, tuning and tightening and mastering their craft. So I took whatever acting work I could get at that time. I worked as an extra, and tried unsuccessfully to land commercials. I did soap operas. That being said, I think I was still really careful not to make work decisions based on money. *Friday the 13th*, honestly... it was material that, for whatever reason, I didn't necessarily feel connected to. But I tried to take the size of the budget and the size of the part and the size of the paycheck out of the equation. And then a huge variety of things open up to you. Because there is something about a truly collaborative effort that really feels right. Movies are an isolated medium. You're taught or learn to look out for number one—yourself. Rarely do you encounter something that's really my concept of what an ensemble is.

As production on Friday the 13th *continued through long days and even longer nights, relations became increasingly strained between Sean Cunningham, Victor Miller and Steve Miner on one side, and Phil Scuderi, Steve Minasian and Robert Barsamian, the film's Boston-based financial backers, on the other. The situation would grow even more contentious when Scuderi brought in screenwriter*

Ron Kurz to incorporate additional "comic relief" into Miller's shooting script. The creative and financial tensions that had started to simmer during production of Last House on the Left *some eight years earlier were about to reach a boiling point.*

VICTOR MILLER: The only scene in *Friday the 13th* that I did not write was the motorcycle cop. I was told that it was the brainstorm of the man who came up with the cash, Phil Scuderi. And when I heard about it I was just appalled, because the entire point was to create an environment in which there was no way these kids could get any help from the outside. Officer Dorf worked so far against that.

With the adult characters, I was not trying to save the kids from buffoons, you know? I like to think that outside their world there were very effective adults who could have helped them, but they were unable to get them or even knew what was going on. That scene with the cop is the only one that I am aware of that has nothing to do with me whatsoever.

RON KURZ: After writing a couple movies for Phil, I heard he was approached by a somewhat down-and-out Sean Cunningham. Sean basically had a great title in *Friday the 13th*, but what Phil viewed as a rather tepid script by Victor Miller. Before Phil would put up any money he wanted script changes. He brought me in to do the revisions—Phil wanted some humor added, my forte, and he knew the script needed something. He didn't know what at the time, but something.

I have no apologies for any humor I put into the script. Despite Victor's or Sean's sense that it was detrimental, I'm afraid I disagree. If done right, humor and horror can work extremely well together—complimenting one another—often lulling the audience to a point where the horror, when it strikes, is more effective.

SEAN CUNNINGHAM: Ron Kurz? I don't know that I ever met the guy. I think that potentially Scuderi gave him money to write, but he never wrote for me.

RICHARD FEURY, Unit Photographer: I remember Sean and Steve got everyone together one day not far into the shoot and said they were having money problems, asking would the crew consider, in lieu of salary, having a fraction of a point in the film? Yet we all said "No." Because we all thought this movie was going to go absolutely nowhere. But to be fair to Sean and Steve, they had to deal with this throughout the picture. And I had worked on some really skanky

Adrienne King won the lead role of Alice in *Friday the 13th* over hundreds of other girls—and to the surprise of no one more than King herself. "The funny thing was, I heard that they were looking for a star name," smiles King. "I even heard Sally Field was being considered at one point. Thankfully, she didn't do it!"

"My haircut was, uh, *lovely.* But I was just so excited to be starring in my first movie that they could have turned it purple for all I cared!" Adrienne King

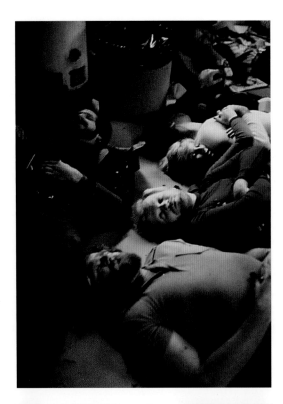

Top: Often working long hours and throughout the night, the crew of *Friday the 13th* manage to steal a catnap between setups.

Above: Director of photography Barry Abrams grabs a few winks during a break in filming. Abrams would also work with Sean Cunningham on such films as *Here Come the Tigers* (1976) and *A Stranger is Watching* (1982).

Opposite page: Actors Jeannine Taylor (left) and Mark Nelson (right) rehearse a scene as Kevin Bacon (far left) looks on. This still was taken on the very first day of principal photography on *Friday the 13th*—September 4, 1979.

low-budget things in New York, where we'd all run to the banks to cash our checks and there would be no funds. And it was never like that on this. I would mail the check home, and after the first one or two cleared I stopped worrying about it. Of course, after the movie came out and was a big hit, I'd run into people who worked on it and we'd say, "Oh, shit, maybe we should have taken the points!"

SEAN CUNNINGHAM: Georgetown Productions was just another name for Hallmark. It was just another corporate entity. They had to change things every once in a while. It sounds so low-rent, but it wasn't like they'd write a check and the money would be in the bank. They would say they would write a check and then they wouldn't, and then it wouldn't arrive, and then you can't make payrolls and you're trying to pay the laboratories and stuff like that. They were theater owners, and cash would come in on the weekends, and they would have a limited number of places where they could spend the money. It was the squeaky wheel thing—there was a lot of that going on. Every week it was always a battle. You had to fight so hard just to pay the bills, which is a fight that was completely separate from how hard it is to make any movie, even when you have the money.

What poor Steve Miner had to go through—I couldn't have done it without him. And Steve didn't even want to do this picture at all. I had to beg him to do it. He said that he would work as the Line Producer and the Unit Production Manager and make all that stuff happen. He had to keep dealing with these people day after day until we finally got to the end of it.

GEORGE MANSOUR: Sean Cunningham got a better deal on *Together* than he would ever have gotten from anybody else. And he would never have had the opportunity to make *Last House on the Left* and *Friday the 13th* if Hallmark hadn't bought *Together*. Sure, we paid him very little money, and we made a lot of money on those films. But no one else would have invested that kind of publicity and prints and attention. If Sean had made *Friday the 13th* for Sony Pictures now, he would have been fucked. The majors would have written off everything and he would have had nothing. He got a substantial amount of money out of *Friday the 13th*. And after that Sean never made a decent movie, or one that could make any money.

However, I will say this about Phil and Steve and Bob—I won't characterize them as more than shady, without mentioning any other kind of word. They would lie about things they didn't need to lie about, and they sort of liked to portray themselves as worse than they were. There was a certain frisson for them about being outlaws. But they were nice people underneath it all. All movie companies are tough. Just try dealing with Harvey Weinstein. At least Phil and Steve and Robert, after everything was said and done, they were okay. Maybe they'd fuck Universal, but if you were a little guy, they'd be less inclined to fuck you. They'd only fuck you half the way.

SEAN CUNNINGHAM: I don't resent all the money that Scuderi and Minasian made. Nobody else had that kind of faith in me and wrote those kinds of checks. They took an enormous risk. And as a result, they made an enormous amount of money. Okay, fair enough. The problems that they caused me are problems that some people would love to have.

But it was always a push-pull relationship. It was always an incredible ordeal to extract the money to make the movies. They'd tell me, "I'll give you $25,000 on Friday." And they wouldn't give me the money. It was never, ever easy. But to give them full credit, they were people who, when I said I was going to go do something, they'd believe me and I'd go do it. Phil trusted me—I think Phil trusted me. But I can't complain. If it hadn't been for them, I would have never made *Friday the 13th*.

ADRIENNE KING: Everyone else was complaining about the money situation. But Sean was very organized and kept everyone calm. No matter what was going on, the actors didn't know about it. I'm sure they were having money problems left and right, but Sean would just say, "It's going to be a big hit!" For us, we knew going in that everyone was on minimum, so that was just the deal. I was just thrilled to be there.

Not that money was never a factor. At the beginning of the shoot, the wardrobe person had bought me a pair of boots and they were too small. So being that we were on this tight budget, she started walking around in my boots with three pairs of socks on, trying to get my boot to fit my foot. So I put them on and I did my first scene with my tight boots, and afterwards I said to Sean, "I have to do a lot of running in this film and I really need boots that fit." He goes, "Jeez, okay, when you go back to New York this weekend go find a pair of boots. Just make sure they're on sale."

Minimalist, thrifty and occasionally crude, Friday the 13th *both suffered and benefited from the limitations of its small budget. Cunningham and his crew had to be inventive with the resources at their disposal—limited equipment, the moodiness of the location, and creative production design. But the result was a dark, sparse, neo-verité nightmare influenced as heavily by the documentary makers with whom Cunningham had rubbed shoulders during his early years as by the more stylized films of the era that critics accused him of shamelessly swiping from.*

SEAN CUNNINGHAM: I wasn't creatively invested in *Friday the 13th*. I didn't have "artistic" inklings. The style was, "What does it take to tell the story?" And we created technical problems that you wouldn't believe. We were out in this totally remote location in New Jersey. Then, in the script, the storm comes in. And on top of that, the lights have to go out. So I have to shoot this film with no source light whatsoever, not even moonlight. There I am, out in the middle of nowhere, trying to maneuver everyone. Consequently, it takes forever to go from here to there. Anything you want to do is three to four hours of setup time.

There have been criticisms of the way *Friday the 13th* looks. But my poor DP, Barry Abrams, he begged me for more light. I didn't have the money. I was like, "Barry, you're killing me! Why do we need all those lights!?" *Friday the 13th* was almost the definition of minimalist filmmaking at the time. How low can we light it to qualify as a movie that somebody would pay us money to see? And reality is perhaps the most effective method to present horror. "This could happen to me" is what truly scares the wits out of an audience. I think another reason why the film is seductive in its own way is that the amateurishness gives it a verité kind of reality, which a slick movie doesn't create. You feel like you're witnessing a real event, which I suppose is an accomplishment.

ADRIENNE KING: It was like *The Blair Witch Project* twenty years beforehand. That's what we felt like in the dark, in the woods. It wasn't a handheld camera, but it was close.

PETER STEIN, Camera Operator: We shot *Friday the 13th* with a very small crew. A gaffer and an assistant cameraman, that was about the size of it. And you've got to figure out where to place the lights so they're not going to be in the shot, but they're going to do the job. And do it all without front-lighting the action, because that is not horror film lighting. You want to edge-light and backlight, and just have a little bit of fill to give it that dramatic, scary look. And for the effects, you want to light them even darker, to not feature them too much. The lighter it is, the more the audience's attention goes to it. So if you keep it dark and in the shadows, it works better. I think it was those considerations that really contributed to the look of *Friday the 13th*.

SEAN CUNNINGHAM: There's a technique that has since become a cliché, which is the stalker POV. I used it in *Friday the 13th*, and John Carpenter certainly used it before I did. It's the notion that there is an unexplained, unexpected person in the story. And that by switching to that point of view you can create a certain kind of anxiety. Because the camera is in the wrong place and it's telling you, non-verbally, that there's somebody else possibly present. And that we, the audience, have information that the characters don't have. So whereas the character might just wander into the equipment shack thinking everything is fine, we're saying, "No, there's somebody out there, don't ya' see?" That is one of the many devices that we used to try to increase the tension, and it's certainly the main visual dynamic of *Friday the 13th*.

JEANNINE TAYLOR: As an actress, it was interesting to do those switches. When Marcie recounts her dream, I think her fear does come across. That was one part of my performance that I thought was pretty okay. The sound of the storm triggers this happy-go-lucky girl's only real terror. The film changes tone at that point and goes into a darker place. That's an aspect that I can say was interesting to try and do.

The actual shower scene—my death scene—I'm just goofing around. My character is in love, she's in this great place and has all

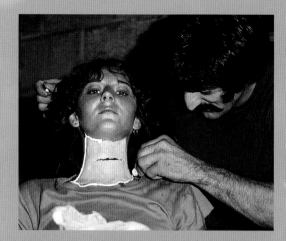

Above: "I was strongly aware of that setup for *Psycho*—that the first girl you are introduced to dies," explains director Sean Cunningham of *Friday the 13th*'s initial scenes, which subvert traditional narrative convention by introducing the audience to who they presume will be the film's the main protagonist, the soon-to-be-doomed Annie. "I purposely set up Annie as the lead, and she isn't the lead at all. That's why I think the audience is so surprised when she becomes the first victim, because they didn't expect her to die." Screenwriter Victor Miller concurs: "*Psycho* totally spun horror movies around, in that you could kill off a major contract player. I certainly knew I had to establish in *Friday the 13th* how helpless these characters would be. So that after Annie is killed, the audience would say, 'Whatever this movie is about, the people who made it are not taking prisoners!"

Shooting the effect of Annie getting her throat slit was one of the many examples of the wizardry of makeup effects artist Tom Savini. "It really is a magic trick," says Savini. "What do I need to do to make the audience believe what they're seeing is really happening? With Robbi Morgan's death, all you saw was a knife come up into the frame, then the blade go across her throat. So we cast Robbi's neck and built a rubber appliance with a slit in it already, so when she tilted her head back, you'd see the wound open. It is a primitive effect today, but still in use. In fact, after *Friday the 13th*, I think there was a cut throat gag in every movie that was offered to me."

Filming the scene proved a memorable one for Morgan. "It was really fun," she remembers. "It was just Tom, his assistant Taso Stavrakis and I being goofy and fun and silly. The actual shooting was uneventful—we got it all in one take. And in between shots, we'd be walking on our hands along the dirt road all the time. We were totally pals."

"Robbi, Tom and I hung out a lot," agrees Stavrakis. "We even had shirts made up for each of us. Robbi's read 'Mini Maniac,' Tom's read 'Major Maniac,' and mine read 'Minor Maniac.' We were three maniacs, and we had a great time."

these neat new friends. She's just read this clumsy little graffiti that the kids left on the bathroom stall and it's put her in a silly, child-like mood. So the reality is wholesome and safe. The safety is broken the second she hears a noise. But then it's back to a childish game as she looks into each shower stall and there's nothing there. The only things that aren't safe and child-like in that scene are the first noise that might be something bad, and the last split-second, seeing what's going to happen.

SEAN CUNNINGHAM: I discovered Bruno Bettelheim and his book *Uses of Enchantment* when, back in the mid-1970s, I had tried to develop an update of *Hansel & Gretel*. He says one of the values of these grim, ugly fairy tales is that younger people have unnamed fears. Fears of abandonment, fears of death, fears involving sexual repression. We don't quite know what they are, but it's scary stuff.

We the parents read them and get spooked, but the kids love it, because at a young age we don't have words or names to go around these things, we just know they are out there lurking. What fairy tales can do, and by extension certain kinds of horror movies can do, is take the fear, dress it up in a costume, look at it in the safety of a story, and then put it away. As a result of listening to the story a number of times, each time the fear becomes more and more manageable and less and less scary. It was armed with that notion that I went into *Friday the 13th*.

I also believe that, as teenagers, we think of ourselves as invulnerable. Bad things happen to other people, but not to us. And everybody has that story of somebody in high school who got on a motorcycle and hit a tree and died. And the school is in shock. "How could this possibly happen?" It's simple—you get onto a motorcycle, you run into a tree, you die. And these events call into sharp focus the fact that we are vulnerable, yet we put it out of our minds. This is where we wanted to go with *Friday the 13th*, to deal with untimely, unwarranted death. That there is a hostile world out there that wants to destroy you and eat you up. I still think that's at the core of the most successful horror films.

VICTOR MILLER: From a very early age, my mother and father called me a worry wart, because I was always creating these dire scenarios. If I had an infected finger, well clearly I was going to die by the morning. And surely the idea that my mind instantly leaps to a negative outcome made it possible for *Friday the 13th* to happen.

Each of the killings in the film did not need to be particularly gory but they had to be inventive. They certainly had to be something very personal and a kind of a hand-to-hand thing. It was one of Sean's pieces of wisdom that we always worked under, which was that guns are terribly impersonal weapons for movies. Unless I can wrap my hands around your throat, it is really not killing you, because murder is a very personal thing and you have to take full responsibility for it.

SEAN CUNNINGHAM: We also had a really tough bullet to bite—that there is no discount for the patron at the box office to see a low-budget movie. On any particular night, people are either going to see your film or someone else's. They are all first-run movies. Even at that time, the whole idea of a second feature, the B-movie that plays drive-ins and exploitation houses, almost didn't exist anymore as a viable alternative to conventional distribution. That was the reality. So when Victor and I were playing with this we were very aware that what we needed to do was create something that had an element of circus to it.

I had, in fact, no notion of the tradition of the European body count movies or the gross-out, Grand Guignol kind of thing. I wasn't a fan, and I only found out about a lot of these films after the fact. I never saw movies like *Twitch of the Death Nerve* or any of those other movies—the first time I ever heard the name Mario Bava was when I went to a film festival in 1986 or '87. I knew that Hammer made some movies, but the idea of Spanish or Italian or Japanese horror films, I didn't know anything about it. I was not even aware of horror films in the United States.

With the relentless shocks of Halloween *still fresh in the minds of young movie-goers, Sean Cunningham realized that he needed to do more than simply replicate the modern scare techniques and camera trickery employed by the likes of John Carpenter and Alfred Hitchcock before him. What could his film bring to the marketplace that was fresh and commercial? Could the inspiration for Cunningham's aborted attempt to film* Hansel & Gretel—*the disturbing, often graphic imagery of the Grimm's fairy tales—be updated for the sophisticated, sensation-starved youth audiences of 1980? And how could the creative and graphic murder sequences suggested in Victor Miller's script be realized practically and logistically on a limited budget?*

With the arrival of a 26-year-old makeup effects artist named Tom Savini, Cunningham would have his answer.

TOM SAVINI, Special Makeup Effects: The whole reason I got into effects was seeing *Man of a Thousand Faces*, the story of Lon Chaney. He was a silent screen actor, a make-up artist and a stunt man—all the things I wanted to be when I grew up. Lon was my first inspiration, and of course Jack Pierce, the guy who created *Frankenstein* and the *Wolf Man*. Then after that Dick Smith, who is still the greatest living make-up artist today. And of course Rick Baker, Rob Bottin—those guys are in a class all by themselves. They're my idols, my inspiration, who I strive to be like.

My first memory of Sean Cunningham is a whirling dervish. I remember I went to his house in Connecticut and we talked about the film, effect by effect. Sometimes the script was pretty descriptive as to what it wanted, sometimes it wasn't. But that was the fun—inventing how to do this stuff. Then, I could give Sean a budget and how many people I needed, and how long it would take to prepare.

VICTOR MILLER: I remember it was a hot summer afternoon in 1979 and this guy came up in his car with Pennsylvania plates, and it was Tom Savini. We sat around Sean's patio and I was stunned. This guy was saying things like, "Okay, on page 43 you've got an ax in the face. Now, do you want a fake ax on a real face, or do you want a fake face with a real ax in it?" I looked at Sean and said, "My God, I just write this shit, what's this?"

SEAN CUNNINGHAM: Whereas Victor and I had this sense of a story, I think it was when Savini came on board with this notion of what we could or could not do that the film really started to take on a visual character of its own.

Once production began, Tom arrived at the camp with his truck, his assistant Taso, a chinchilla and a bunch of makeup. And he didn't leave until we wrapped. He became part of our extended filmmaking family. I remember Steve Miner and Tom and I trying to block stuff

out—trying to figure out where a prosthetic would go and how we would make the switch via cuts. It was Special Effects 101.

TASO STAVRAKIS, Effects Assistant: Tom Savini and I were best friends in college. We both grew up in Pittsburgh. I was an actor, and Tom was teaching acting and makeup classes. I went on to do *Dawn of the Dead* with him. It was low-budget and they didn't have any stunt guys, so we said, "Hey, we can do that, too!" And we just kept finding these low-budget pictures like *Friday the 13th*—it was great. It was just a big game.

TOM SAVINI: It was just me and my best friend, Taso. We decided not to live in the hotel. We were just out there every night in the middle of the woods, in this little camp by the lake, where somebody's supposedly running around killing people. And here we were creating the victims. We had everything at our disposal, and free reign of the kitchen—we even baked prosthetic appliances in the pizza oven at this Boy Scout camp. And in those days I had a Betamax, and we only had two movies, *Barbarella* and *Marathon Man*. We watched one of them every night for two months—I can quote you every line from those movies. So, when I think of *Friday the 13th*, I think of living at the camp, watching the same two movies over and over again and hanging around at night. It was a blast.

Below: "When I wrote *Friday the 13th*, I had no background in horror movies whatsoever," says screenwriter Victor Miller. "I was a wuss. But Sean Cunningham made me go dutifully to see *Halloween*. I loved it. I think that John Carpenter and Debra Hill did such a wonderful job. And one of the things I noticed is that the first act of *Halloween* is filled with the more innocent scares. So I wrote a scene early on in *Friday the 13th* that called for a snake to be killed. I wanted to show that these kids could fight back, if necessary, and use violence."

Filming the scene—which called for the actual killing of the snake, live on the set—was far more gruesome than what Miller had written. "It was an important moment in the film," says Sean Cunningham. "It was tone setting. But it was very upsetting that we actually chopped up that snake with a machete." Cunningham was not alone. "I was shocked," shudders Adrienne King. "And thank God PETA wasn't around when we shot that. I remember that the owner of the snake was just standing off to the side, tears running down his cheeks!"

"It was a movie about kids having a blast at a summer camp, and we really were a bunch of young, carefree actors having a blast. A little bit of *cinema verité* there." Jeannine Taylor

NOEL CUNNINGHAM, Producer, *Jason X*: I always knew what my dad did. It's the same as being the son of a train conductor, it's just dad's job. Especially doing low-budget films—back then it didn't have as much allure as it does now. So going to the set was very much like just going to see dad at work. On weekends, I'd go out to the set. I even played one of the kids in the opening prologue. Just for a brief little stint in the cabin, the flashback scene where the killer's P.O.V. walks around. I'm the kid in the second bunk on the left.

Most of the crew just dropped themselves into this camp. They lived there and ate there and slept there. I was around the shop all the time. I became pretty good friends with Tom Savini and Taso, or rather, they put up with me because I was the director's son. They were great. I was like twelve years old and these guys were stuntmen and special effects guys. They'd be fencing and sword-fighting all over the camp. One night, everyone was eating lunch in the cafeteria and then out of the darkness— because it was a night shoot—this big gorilla comes running into the mess hall screaming and flipping up tables. Then Savini jumps up on the table and draws a blank gun. He's rigged the gorilla suit with squibs and he starts blasting. Everyone was screaming and yelling. No one had any idea what was going on. They did stuff like that all the time.

TASO STAVRAKIS: Tom's specialty was that he didn't want to cut away from the horror moments. He wanted to watch it and see it, like a cartoon, which is something that no one else had done. It was thinking in reverse. And Tom and I both come from a theatre background, so we kept saying, "How can we do this stuff live? How can we do it here in front of a live audience?" And that helps the movie a lot.

TOM SAVINI: I was a combat photographer in Vietnam. My job was to photograph the damage done to people, so I kind of had a safety looking through the camera, seeing the live gore, because to me it became special effects. So when I create the fake stuff, it doesn't give me the same feeling that I got when I saw the real stuff. And there's a big difference.

I hate when I'm watching a war movie or something and somebody's dying and as soon as he dies, he assumes this very pleasant look, because he doesn't want to look bad. That's not the way it happens. Sometimes people die with one eye open and one eye half-closed; sometimes people die with smiles on their face as their jaw is always slack. That's the way it goes. So when I make fake heads and cadavers, I incorporate the feeling I got seeing the real stuff in Vietnam. I think that's where my reputation comes from. Because the average person doesn't see this stuff. When they do see it in that kind of a motif, it registers somewhere in some subliminal way, that inherited primitive thing. They've been given a taste of what death is really like.

SEAN CUNNINGHAM: The murder sequence with Kevin Bacon and the arrow is, I suppose, the signature creative death of *Friday the 13th*. And the best example of something that could not have been done or even remotely considered without Savini being there, telling us how to do it. Now everybody knows how to do it, but at the time we had no idea how we were gonna pull it off.

TOM SAVINI: The mindset was, "What do I need to see?" I need to see a guy, looking like he's lying down on a bed. We cast Kevin and did a fake body. He's actually under the bed with his head coming up through and the fake body was lying in the bed. We put the same shirt on the fake body, and we had him wear a chain that we also put on the fake body. As long as the real head is in there, you kind of accept the fake neck, and I always try to do that—keep the real person in it as much as possible. So cutting from the real Kevin with the shirt and the necklace to the fake body with the shirt and the necklace, you believed that was Kevin. And whatever I did to the neck is not going hurt the actor because his body's not there. So we just drove the arrow in and pumped blood out of it. And it looked great.

SEAN CUNNINGHAM: I think the reason that gag worked so well is because of that misdirection. Your whole focus was somewhere else. Two people, in what you think is a loving, sexually-charged environment. But what the people in bed don't know is that there is a dead body above them, and we don't know what's going to happen. All our focus is up. She leaves, and we're saying, "Oh my goodness, he is going to discover that the body is above!" The last thing we expect is that something is going to happen from below.

Sean Cunningham wanted a surprise for Friday the 13th's *third act revelation of its heretofore unseen villain, Mrs. Voorhees. It was highly unlikely that the production could land an A-list actress such as a Meryl Streep or Shirley MacLaine, let alone afford her on such a low budget film. In his search for the soon-to-be-crowned "Queen of the Slashers," casting director Barry Moss would look to the past, finding an unlikely match in Betsy Palmer, a veteran of wholesome 1960's network television. Palmer's arrival on set during its final ten days of shooting added a touch of class to the film. Fully in command of her Method stage training, Palmer would invigorate the production with her witty, worldly style, battle to the death with its plucky leading lady and provide the film with its most memorably gruesome* piece de resistance.

VICTOR MILLER: I learned from *Halloween* that you had to start with some evil that had happened before the movie ever began, so there is kind of that Gothic sense, a historical evil lurking around that had never quite been avenged. The idea for Mrs. Voorhees came to me about the first or second week that I was working, because we had the summer camp and I needed that prior evil. Once I had that her kid had drowned, it all sort of came together fairly quickly. Because clearly what had been done to her had to justify an awful lot of bad activity, so I figured this would certainly do it.

We were also using the Donald Pleasence formula, which means that you have a maximum of five shooting days with

"Many people have criticized some of the early scenes in *Friday the 13th*, that they are too slow and chit-chatty," says director Sean Cunningham. "Take the scene where Ned fakes his own drowning. By itself this scene doesn't play, but in the context of the film and our expectation of what is in store for these characters, it means something different. All of this is eventually what will make the last act of the film work—if you play the hour that precedes it, you carry that emotional investment in what happens to these characters."

whoever your name player is. But I think we made a more interesting choice by saying that our Donald Pleasence is actually going to be the killer, rather than just the failed psychiatrist. That made it much more fun, and it saved us an incredible amount of money.

SEAN CUNNINGHAM: Betsy Palmer had worked in television on the morning talk shows. And she was squeaky clean, like a completely scrubbed up Katie Couric. As a person, and certainly as a personality, Betsy was perceived to be somebody that would never get her hands dirty, who would never do anything wrong. So that was one of the reasons that I thought it was kind of fun to cast her as the main villain. I was hoping to fool a few people, and I think we did fool a few people, initially. Although that kind of reverse casting is, I think, a little self-conscious.

BARRY MOSS: Originally, Sean wanted Estelle Parsons, who had won an Oscar for *Bonnie & Clyde*. But Estelle was smart enough to want several points in the film. So I thought, "How great would it be if, when we look out the window at who we think is the killer, and here comes the wonderful, sweet Betsy Palmer." To have it totally be someone you would never, ever suspect.

BETSY PALMER, "Mrs. Voorhees": At the time I was on Broadway doing *Same Time Next Year* and living in Connecticut. One night I was driving home from the theatre and my dear old Mercedes broke down. So, I said to the universe, "I need a new car." This was on a Tuesday or something, and then my agent called on Friday. He said, "How would you like to do a movie?" And I said "Great! I haven't done a movie since the 1960s." And he said, "Well, it's ten days' work and they'll give you $1,000 a day." And I had already picked out the car I wanted, and it was a little VW Sirocco, and it was going to be about $9,999.50. Really, it was that close. So

I thought, great, I have myself a car. Then he said, "Now, I have to tell you... it's a horror film." I asked my agent to send me the script anyway. I read it and thought, "What a piece of shit." Just dumb, dumb, dumb. I just could not envision this thing.

Then I thought about the car again. And that nobody is going to see this, ever. It's going to come, it's going to go, I will have my little Sirocco, and everything will be fine. So I called him back and I said, "Great, I'll do it."

BILL FREDA: Betsy was beautiful and when she came in I was surprised, because she had aged. I remember her as a kid and she was really good-looking. She always created this society act. She was from the upper-crust of New York City, and all the stuff she did on TV reflected that. It was weird. It's like having Rosie O'Donnell be in your horror movie. She was a little out of place for me. But I think she really wanted to do it, although I don't know if she knew what she was getting into.

BETSY PALMER: My first day on the set, I drove up in my Mercedes that was still clunking along. I just made my way out, and I see the sign "Crystal Lake," and I say, "Wow! That's a good omen!" Because I had spent my summers as a kid growing up on Crystal Lake in Warsaw, Indiana. So I arrive and the first person they shoo me off to is Tommy Savini because he's got to make the mock-up of my head. And the first thing he says is, "Do you have claustrophobia?" Then he mixed up some goop and put it on my face, with straws in my nose so I was able to breathe. And Tom had this cute little chinchilla—we would all be putting raisins in our mouths, and the chinchilla's eating raisins from our puckered lips.

RICHARD FEURY: Betsy was great. I kept thinking, "What is she doing in a horror film?" But she was just like me. She needed to work

and the price was right. But to her everlasting credit, she could have come in there, not wanting to do it, and have been a real bitch. A lot of people who come up and are successful in Hollywood would be hard to deal with. But I think she came from a different era. She was a woman from the 50s, she had Broadway training and the morals and the backbone to say, "I signed on to do this. I'm going to do the best I can and be the best person I can be." How many actors—leading ladies—sit every night with the crew? There are actors who will just go to their dressing room for lunch and it has to be brought to them by a production assistant. Then there are actors who will stand in line with everybody else. That was Betsy.

MARK NELSON: The first time I met Betsy Palmer, I had just gotten there the night before. I was a fan because I had grown up watching her on *I've Got a Secret*. So I go to Tom Savini's cabin to get my makeup and he says, "Hey Mark, I want to introduce you to Betsy Palmer!" I looked over in the corner and she is leaning against a worktable with a down jacket draped over her shoulders, her hands both on the table. Or what I thought were her hands. So I walked over and said, "Oh Betsy, I'm so glad to meet you!" And her real right hand came out from inside the middle of her shirt to shake hands with me and I screamed. She was wearing prosthetic hands that Tom had set her up with to fool me. After that, I was too suspicious to fall for any of their tricks again.

VICTOR MILLER: In the years since the writing of the movie, I have had a very helpful psychiatrist explain Mrs. Voorhees to me. He said, "My God, don't you know what you've done?" And I said, "I'm totally clueless." He pointed out to me that I had created a mother, in some ways very much like my mother, but a better version of her because she was killing people because they had not taken good care of her son. In some ways she was the best mother of all—she loved her son so much that she would continue committing these horrible acts for eternity just to make up for her loss.

Not to say, of course, that any of this was on a conscious level as I was writing it. But it was perfect for me that the two counselors were making love when they should have been watching that poor little boy Jason. And it is a theme that I would repeat throughout the movie, so that we knew right from the get-go that this whole thing has a lot to do with psychosexual craziness.

The cast of *Friday the 13th* has fond memories of working with future star Kevin Bacon. "I remember Kevin as being very much an all-around nice guy," recollects co-star Jeannine Taylor (**top**, with Bacon). "I knew he'd be a star. He had that kind of focus. He was very serious without really seeming to be—in some ways mature beyond his years."

"I was very impressed with Kevin," says actor Ron Millkie, who plays the dim-witted Officer Dorf. Although Millkie only shares a single scene with Bacon (**opposite page**), he praises the young actor's naturalness. "Kevin was improvising with me; I didn't expect him to do that," says Millkie. "He came over to my motorcycle and I didn't know what to say, but I indicated for him to get away. Kevin made that whole scene spontaneous and fresh."

Millkie was cast in the role of Officer Dorf after spotting an ad for an open call in *Variety*. "I had known director Sean Cunningham back in the days when he was doing industrial films, so I called him up and he said, "Come to think of it, there might be a part for you. I was going to play Dorf myself. Why don't you come on up?" Millkie found the comedic character enjoyable to play. "Officer Dorf is a jerk, a dork. I know cops like that. Very filled with themselves, big men."

Although Millkie worked only a single day on the film, his memorable motorcycle riding proved hilarious both onscreen and off. "I can't even ride a motorcycle," admits Millkie. "Sean said, 'Just hold on!' And I did—then I tumbled, and the motorcycle fell on top of me. Everyone was laughing. So they had to hire a real state trooper as my 'stunt double.' I only made the motion of starting the damn thing, and they cut to him riding off. Pretty embarrassing!"

BETSY PALMER: I'm a very sincere actress. I was taught "The Method." So I did this whole autobiography of Mrs. Voorhees. She was a gal my age, and she had grown up in the forties like I did. And in the script she had a class ring. Back in school you went steady, and in those days girls did not go to bed with anybody. So I said "OK, what happened to her was she's in love with this guy, and they did make love, and she became pregnant. And after a while she said to him 'I'm pregnant,' and he said, 'Well, don't brush it off on me. Bye, bye.'" He tosses her off, she tries to hide it from her family, and pretty soon six months or so she's showing. Her father has a cat fit and throws her out of the house. So here's this poor thing, wandering around pregnant. She hasn't even finished high school; she has no way of earning a living. I figure she probably went to the Salvation Army. They always took in a lot of the girls, the unmarried girls, and let them have their babies in the home. And then she has the kid, and now he's a mongoloid! When it rains on her parade it pours. The bluebirds are dropping doo-doos all over her. So she makes the best of life and her little boy. She gets this job to cook at summer camp. And she thinks, "Wonderful, my little boy can be with other kids, and he can swim, and he can have this wonderful camp thing, and we'll be there together." And of course you know what happens, the kids go off and make love and her boy drowns.

I was in some city once, doing a radio show and the kids were calling in to talk to "Mrs. Voorhees." And I asked one of the girls, "Why do you kids love this woman so much?" And she said, "Because we know why you did it." That is the reason why I think the character has stayed alive as long as she has. I didn't think I was a bad lady. I thought I just got the short-shrift in life. If her little boy hadn't drowned she never would have killed all those counselors. I just tried to save those other children every summer when they tried to reopen the camp. Doesn't the movie talk about how I had set fires and poisoned the water, and it eventually closes the camp down? Doesn't it make sense?

SEAN CUNNINGHAM: You're always a little worried about stage actors for a lot of reasons. The biggest is that they are in complete control of their performance. You can give direction, but when the curtain goes up, the actor does whatever he or she wants to. In a film, it's the absolute opposite. And when that lack of control is realized by the actor, panic often sets in. So in film, what

"I went out to the set once to see what was going on, and there's Jeannine Taylor's head on a stick. I never went back to the set again." Barry Moss

has to happen is that he or she has to trust you as a director. And Betsy decided to trust me on the decisions she made. Consequently, when we were rehearsing her stuff, it started off very big. A lot of time was spent toning her down, and keeping her madness limited to subtler eye and head movements. But Betsy always had something cooking inside that I liked.

BARRY MOSS: I hope I don't get shot over this, but I would have directed it a little differently. I think Sean tried to make Betsy look a little like Estelle. When he put her in this windbreaker and this short haircut so she could look as tough as possible, it was just the opposite of what I had in mind when I recommended her for the part. I just thought it was such a cool idea to have it be someone you would never suspect.

ADRIENNE KING: This is what I really want to know: do audiences feel cheated that she only shows up in the last part of the film?

BETSY PALMER: When my character makes her entrance at the end of the movie, I said to Sean, "You know, you're not fighting fair, fella. You're not even giving anybody a loose clue that I'm on the scene. They should at least have a glimpse of this woman somewhere earlier in the film. You should at least put me in that little diner Steve Christy visits, or at a stoplight in my Jeep. Whatever, just a flash somewhere." And he said, "The hell with it. Just let 'em guess."

VICTOR MILLER: Sean would say things that I always thought were really campy and right on. Like that it is a good idea to keep your villains masked, because if you start seeing your villain brush his or her teeth it becomes very ordinary. So I guess we went to the furthest extreme possible. It is a cheat, obviously, because you never even know that there is a neighbor of any sort. But it seems to have worked.

SEAN CUNNINGHAM: We had high ambitions for the climactic fight between Alice and Mrs. Voorhees. We couldn't afford have stunt people, so I thought we'd do the "easier" dialogue stuff first. We had Betsy come out and shoot her long revelation scene in the cabin, which took a long time to do. Once that was done, we started staging a ballet of the fight. And that was the beginning of the longest two days of the film. We just could not get the action staged correctly. We spent the next two nights doing stuff I thought we'd get done in two hours. It was hard, but Betsy and Adrienne were both good sports and never complained once.

ADRIENNE KING: We jokingly called it the "Ballet du Machete." We rehearsed and rehearsed and rehearsed. And then when we shot it, it was like gangbusters. We had all this adrenaline. And Sean wanted to make sure that nobody got hurt, which I was thankful for, because we were really on a beach and it was a real machete and there really was somebody smacking my head into the sand.

BETSY PALMER: Before we went down to the beach. I said to Adrienne, "Let's rehearse our scene." She says, "Great!" This lovely young thing. So I haul off and I hit her. Because when you're onstage in the theater, you do. You cup your hand, and you get it along the jawbone so you don't break somebody's face. So I just gave her a potchky right on her cheek. And she fell to the ground, "Sean! Sean! She hit me!" Sean came over and I said, "Well, we were rehearsing this thing and I just hit her." He said, "No, Betsy, you don't hit people in movies. You miss them, and then we put a sound effect in later!"

ADRIENNE KING: Betsy and I did have a couple of very intense days and nights in the cabin. We had a few great fight scenes together. And she loves to tell that story where she slaps me and she says I broke into tears. Well, she did slap me really hard and I went flying through the air. She beat me up, man. It got to fisticuffs. I walked away from that scene with bruises. No stunt double. When she grabbed me, she really grabbed me. It's not like she tried to hurt me. But she's a stage actress, and you can only train so much.

But she was a real trooper to be cast in this film. She was bigger than life and funny off the set. On the set she was really into it, and she scared me. Betsy's very theatrical and very intense, but very sweet. But she was a hoot, and I can't imagine anyone else that could have done a better job.

Background: Perhaps the most famous murder sequence in *Friday the 13th* is the impaling of Kevin Bacon from below with an arrow. "That was the biggest scene for us to do," recalls effects assistant Taso Stavrakis. "There were four or five of us underneath that bed. And Kevin, of course—sitting in a harness with his head and neck sticking out of the mattress, and a fake body glued to his chest. And then Richard Feury, the unit photographer, was brought in to be Mrs. Voorhees' hand that reaches up and grabs Kevin by the forehead."

"The arrow was attached to an ice bag that was glued to the plastic support of the neck," continues Tom Savini. "It was a sealed compartment that we pumped blood into, so the action of me pushing the arrow through Kevin's neck was also pushing against the ice bag and forcing the blood to come out And right off-camera, Sean Cunningham was screaming, 'More blood!' Only there was none."

The effect almost went completely awry until Stavrakis saved the day. "So there we are, all cramped under the bed," he laughs. "And my knees were getting wet because the tube came off by mistake and I was pumping blood all over us. So I grabbed the tube and started blowing with all my might. And that's why, in the finished film, what you see coming out of Kevin's neck are two or three spurts of arterial spray. It was terrific.

"Then, after we got the shot, I spit out all the blood and ran down to the lake and jumped in, still hacking, trying to get that shit out of my mouth!"

Opposite page: "The special effects were fascinating to me," says Jeannine Taylor of filming the death scene of her character Marcie. "After my scream and the slow slide down the shower stall, I got to be almost an audience member. I remember that I really had a lot of fun watching the special effects being created. The ax was hot-glued to my face. It didn't burn me—I was quite relieved at that. And I saw all the fake but very real looking blood, which was pumped through tubing. But oddly enough, I had no sense of how gory the end product would be. I didn't even think about it—the process was just so interesting!"

The scene also earned high praise from co-star Betsy Palmer: "I remember when the audience saw it—when Jeannine looked over her shoulder at the shower curtain—they gasped. 'Did that move!?' That to me was one of the scariest moments in the whole film because it lets you use your imagination. That's what's really wonderful about a lot of *Friday the 13th*."

TOM SAVINI: The fight between Adrienne King and Betsy Palmer is almost like the Road Runner and the Coyote, you know? If, at last, the Road Runner was going to get his comeuppance, you want him to die gloriously because of all the torment he's been giving the poor Coyote. So here's Betsy Palmer wiping out all these people. Well she has to die in a glorious way, so the idea was to cut her head off.

VICTOR MILLER: Decapitation has always been one of those things that I have found particularly disquieting ever since the French Revolution was explained to me. I thought that was just one of worst things that could possibly happen to someone.

SEAN CUNNINGHAM: It hadn't been done before, and all we could keep thinking was, "How in the world can we chop somebody's head off and make it look as if it actually happened?" We had to be sure that we knew when we were gonna cut because it only works for maybe a second or two. I knew that if I had those seconds covered then I could sell the moment. You think you see a lot more than you actually do.

ADRIENNE KING: Tom Savini's head was actually under the sweater and they put Betsy Palmer's head on top of his neck. It didn't feel fake because I was cutting somebody's head off. I worked very hard on the moment after I deliver the fatal blow. Sean talked me through that whole scene. He said to me, "Just put yourself in the moment. What would your reaction be if you really did this?" I was supposed to be like, "I can't believe I'm doing this, but thank God I did. I'm alive." Those mixed emotions. I think I look perplexed. And I'm happy with that look, because it works.

Filming that shot was the culmination of everything we'd done. I wouldn't trade it for the world, because how many times in your life do you get to do something like that? It's hysterical. If there is going to be a memory of what I did in this lifetime, it is that I'm the person who decapitated Betsy Palmer with a machete.

For six weeks, the production of Friday the 13th *had gone through highs and lows, surviving a lack of cash flow, constant practical jokes by Tom and Taso, and weeks of intense all-night shoots that left cast and crew wrung out. But there was one final, crucial element left to complete. One that, in retrospect, would ultimately spawn a franchise.*

Almost an afterthought, the emergence of a little boy named Jason from the watery depths of Crystal Lake would prove to be more than a last-minute, tagged-on "chair jumper." It would be the birth, albeit a seemingly inauspicious one, of a cinematic icon.

VICTOR MILLER: I went to school with a girl named Van Voorhees. I was always struck by the sound of the name because

it was just creepy-sounding. My son Ian was born in 1968 and my other son Josh was born in 1972. I mixed the two together and that's how I came up with the name Jason Voorhees.

Originally, my script ended with Alice killing Mrs. Voorhees. Then Sean called me up and said we need a chair jumper after the climax. So I wrote the sequence where Alice is in the little canoe, she sets off, the sun rises, we think she's safe and Jason comes out of the water. Then she wakes up in the hospital bed. Which was as close as I could steal from *Carrie* without being arrested.

TOM SAVINI: At that point there still wasn't an ending to the film—Betsy Palmer's killed and that's it. But I had just seen *Carrie*, and it's ending was terrific. You think the movie is over: Amy Irving is walking to Carrie's grave and the music is playing as if the credits are going to roll any second, then suddenly this hand pops out of the grave—that scared the piss out of everybody. So great, let's do the same thing. But how are we going to do that here when everyone's dead? So I said, "It might be psychologically disturbing if Jason suddenly pops out of the water and grabs her." Because Jason is already registered in your head. You've kind of dismissed him, he's gone, and that's why Betsy Palmer ia killing everybody. Then just have Alice wake up out of a dream. Which worked, because if it's a dream, you can show anything and get away with it no matter how preposterous it is.

RON KURZ: Everyone will, of course, have their own version of events, but here's mine. In Victor Miller's script Jason was merely a normal kid who had drowned one year, followed by two camp counselors being killed the next year. Everything centered on the unseen Mrs. Voorhees and her revenge when the camp is about to reopen. In rewriting, I came up with the idea of making Jason "different"—a mongoloid—and having him appear out of the lake in the shocker scene at the end, still in the form in which he drowned. A scene that, I've been told more than once, made the movie.

TOM SAVINI: I can't say, in all honestly, that I completely remember. He wasn't deformed in the screenplay. Maybe it was my idea that instead of a boy, why not a deformed kid? There's a little more pathos in that. If he's mentally challenged then obviously he can't take care of himself. And that is why he died, because he wasn't being taken care of. And it seems to me that would provide the motivation for the mother to wipe everybody out.

When I designed the look of Jason, I just kept thinking of this guy that I saw in my neighborhood when I was a kid. His name was Bill Bailey—a derelict and a drunk. And he was misshapen. He had one ear that was lower than the other one, and one eye was kind of lower, like Quasimodo. Originally we were thinking Jason was gonna have hair, but it just didn't look quite right. So we just

Opposite page, left: "The 'Strip Monopoly' scene came out of nowhere," chuckles Adrienne King. "We just totally laughed about it. And it became the unwritten rule of the movie—because my clothes don't come off, I got to live!"

Opposite page, right: Adrienne King (left) and Harry Crosby clown around between takes.

This page: "I think much of the success of the suspense and murder sequences in *Friday the 13th* was because Sean didn't want anyone to go over the top," says Adrienne King of her director, Sean Cunningham. "When I wake up from my nightmare and I go off looking for Bill in the woods, I knew that Harry Crosby was on the back of the door but I didn't know what he was doing there or how he was going to look. Sean purposely did not let me see him beforehand. So when I close the door to the generator shed that was a real, serious scream, from the gut—because Sean was able to keep it pure."

left him bald as if he was like a hydrocephalic, mongoloid pinhead or something. I also gave him more of a dome head for the final make-up. And we just went with that—we didn't do any tests or mockups at all. It was low-budget filmmaking. And that's been the look of Jason ever since.

BETSY PALMER: Taso said, "Why don't you look at these Polaroids that we've been taking of the special effects that we've been doing?" And I come upon this one little photograph. I didn't have my glasses on because I usually wear contact lenses, but I said, "Wait a minute! Who's this?" Taso said, "That's your son." I say, "Why does he look so strange?" And he says, "Well, that's your son Jason. We figured that he just looked too normal, so we made him a mongoloid." And I said, "What!? That wasn't in the script!"

VICTOR MILLER: Betsy is absolutely correct. Again, time plays tricks on me, but I think it would be fair to say that I may have intimated that Jason was not a normal kid, that maybe he was slow. But I think it was when Tom and Sean got together that they cooked up this grotesque mask for the character, which was fine, because Tom's ideas are very seductive. If you think about it, the only time Jason actually appears in the movie, when you actually see his face, it is a fantasy, so he could be anything you wanted him to be. But certainly when I let go of the screenplay, Jason was just a slow kid who probably needed more help than your average camper.

RON KURZ: I remember being out to dinner in Boston with Phil and his secretary and I told him of my idea to change the Jason character. He then got up without a word and left the table, going into the lobby where we saw him pacing around. His secretary looked at me and said, "Wow, you got him good with that one." After that, the ending lake scene became Phil's obsession. From what I understood, he was all over Sean to do it right, Phil all but directing it himself by some accounts I've heard. But let me make one thing crystal clear—the idea of making Jason "different" was mine, the scene of him leaping out of the lake at the end was mine. The ending was mine. I conceived it, I wrote it. Phil, having the power over Sean, carried it through onto film.

Yet despite my contribution to the original film I've never gotten any formal credit, although I'm told some sequels state "based upon characters created by Victor Miller and Ron Kurz." It's not something I'm particularly proud of, nor something I have ever trumpeted, but Jason, as we know him, is my creation.

SEAN CUNNINGHAM: There was no particular reason that Jason looked the way he did. It was just something that Tom Savini and Steve Miner and I came up with. Make him look weird and just, you know, not normal. Whether it was Victor Miller or Phil Scuderi's

"When Brenda flies through the window, I was so freaked out! I didn't know when the moment was going to come, and it was done entirely in one two-minute take. It was a totally real situation."

Adrienne King

original idea, I really don't remember. Anyway, what scenes would you like credit for? You can have it. Who gives a shit? It was really Victor Miller, Steve Miner, Tom Savini and me. We were the four people who, for all intents and purposes, were sitting around the table every day trying to figure out how to make the movie.

ARI LEHMAN, "Jason Voorhees": When I walked into the casting room they handed me sides for a different character, Jack. I was about thirteen years old. I remember they said the character goes off to make out with another counselor, and I was like, "Wow, this is great! I really want to be in this movie!" But then Sean walked in and said, "No, no, no! We want Ari to play *this* role." I ended up not even having to say a word for the part. Sean just took one look at me and said, "You're the right size, you've got it!"

ADRIENNE KING: The first time we shot the scene, it wasn't winter yet and the water was still warm. But I don't think they had more than one camera shooting and they didn't get what they needed. Then the second time was about three weeks later, and the water was colder. And they had two cameras going. It still didn't work. And the last time we did it, it was three weeks after the end of the shoot. This is November in upstate New Jersey. You'll notice the leaves have changed color and are actually starting to fall off the trees. And this time they had three cameras, and one was in slo-mo. Finally, Sean finally got everything he needed.

It was tough. I remember that morning, before we started, there was a little snow falling and—I'll never forget this—over the radio a weatherman says, "…And it's twenty-eight degrees." Everybody stopped. "Twenty-eight degrees! Are you sure the lake isn't frozen?" It was a good-sized lake, but still!

ARI LEHMAN: By the third time we shot the ending, we just had this energy. We were like, "Yeah, we're going to knock it out of the park with this one!"

Every time we had to shoot the scene, I would have to reach down into the lake and rub mud all over myself and all I had on was a jockstrap. In the shot, it looks like Adrienne is out there in the middle of the lake in thirty feet of water. Barry Abrams framed it in such a way where all you can see is the water. We had to wait for it to calm so I could come up and out and the illusion of great force would created. And there could be no bubbles on the surface. So I would have to go under and count to ten. And there was buoyancy to the prosthetics. It was like holding a beach ball underwater. So that is why I came up with the momentum I did.

SEAN CUNNINGHAM: I was never sure the ending was going to work and I didn't quite know how to do it. Phil thought that the disgusting creature from the lake was going to be great. But his emphasis was on how much seaweed you could put on this monster that comes from the lake floor. My belief was that if you were going to make the gag work, it wasn't about the seaweed or whatever, but getting the surprise right.

We accomplished it in three ways. It had to be idyllically staged, with Adrienne in the canoe. Second, there is a shot where you see the police coming to the rescue, just to create that sense of safety. And third, Harry Manfredini figured out a piece of music that just mellowed you out, so when the kid comes up out of the bottom of the lake, he comes up at a point musically where it's so unexpected. Then all hell breaks loose.

HARRY MANFREDINI, Composer: If you listen closely at the beginning of the movie when the girl who's on her way to the camp, Annie, goes into the local convenience store, there's a country and western song playing on the radio. Originally, when the film was being edited, they had a Dolly Parton song in there called "Fly Away Little Bluebird." Well, we couldn't afford Dolly Parton, obviously, so I sat down and wrote this song called "Sail Away Tiny Sparrow." A typical country song, about a girl who got married when she was in high school and her husband's an asshole. We also used it in the diner scene later on in the film, too. And then again at the end. That gentle music before Jason comes out of the water, that's her theme song. It literally becomes the catalyst that starts this music up.

ADRIENNE KING: After we wrapped, two weeks later we did the final scene up in Connecticut in some kind of little hospital set. Sean said, "Let's wrap it up somehow." That was the last scene we shot, and the last time I saw anybody before the screening.

SEAN CUNNINGHAM: I insisted that we couldn't end the film on that scene with Jason coming out of the water. Everybody thinks the movie ended there. But there's an epilogue, and without it, the movie doesn't make any sense. And in writing the

The sequence where Alice finds the body of Brenda (Laurie Bartram) proved terrifying to audiences but at times humorous for Adrienne King. "Alice is not the smartest person in the world, is she?" laughs the actress. "When I run into the cabin, protecting myself from God knows who, I'm supposed to throw a rope over the beam to brace the door, and then start throwing all this stuff against it. Until I realized afterwards that the door opened *out*. Still, I was told to intentionally do it that way. What sense does this make? Hello! But my fans love to delight in the fact that after piling all this furniture up against the door, I then have to leap over all this stuff and run back out. I guess when you're scared, you are not really thinking ahead."

Below: Who is that strange woman crashing through the window? "That is actually me in a costume and a wig," says Tom Savini. "We didn't have any stunt people, so I suggested to Sean that I should go through the window with ropes around me, and it'll be Laurie. Then we cut to the real actress after I ended up on the floor. So that was my big stunt."

The reality of the situation also inspired one unlucky improvisation for Adrienne King: "You'll notice that I'm so into that scene that I didn't realize I caught my slicker on the oven door. I sort of did myself in there, because at that point it was established that I would be running the rest of the shoot without the slicker on—in the rain! And we weren't gonna do that scene over because Sean got what he wanted. Although I actually didn't want to do it over, either, because it felt so real. So I ended up freezing the whole rest of the shoot."

epilogue I went through the hammers of hell. As it turns out it was like four sentences, but that was four out of four hundred that we tried. How do you explain Alice's dream? I think those two scenes back to back, in terms of the overall presentation of the film, were the most important.

RONN CARROLL, "Sgt. Tierney": Sean Cunningham called and asked if I would come in and read for this policeman. I had no idea what kind of movie it was, except that they said it was "sort of a horror film." So for one week, I went out there and did all the scenes. I never saw an entire script. I only saw sides of my scenes. And my scenes were like, "There's trouble down at camp! Where are we going?"

When we shot the final scene, when I say, "Ma'am, we didn't find any boy," to me, even at the time, that meant here comes number two. I'm thinking, "Mmm-hmm!" I asked Sean how to play it, and he said, "Draw yourself over to the camera here." And you know that when a director moves his camera in close, it's an obvious setup. I almost said the line with tongue in cheek. Because I had a feeling that they didn't want it to end here. I would laugh about it with my friends after the film came out: "I knew there was going to be a sequel!"

In early 1980, the directive given by Paramount Pictures to Frank Mancuso, Sr., the company's then forty-six year-old Executive Vice-President of Distribution & Marketing, was as clear as it was direct: augment the studio's slate of in-house motion picture productions by acquiring low-cost, independently-produced product. While the concept of the "negative pickup" was not an entirely new one in late 1970s Hollywood, the zeal with which Mancuso was to go about his task would instigate a major change in motion picture distribution and exhibition, blurring the previously steadfast division between the "A" and "B" picture and the marketing of low-budget acquisitions. But even Mancuso did not know what lay just around the corner.

Following a series of screenings in February 1980, a bidding war broke out over the rights to Friday the 13th *between representatives of four major motion picture studios—Paramount, Warner Bros., MGM and United Artists. The film eventually would be picked up by Paramount for domestic distribution, with Warner taking international markets. After ten years in the trenches of low-budget film-making, and his fortieth birthday just past by the turn of 1980, fate was about to smile upon Sean Cunningham. Back in 1971, unable to afford a ninety dollar airline ticket, he once schlepped by bus the film cans containing his first full-length theatrical feature,* Together, *to the offices of Hallmark Releasing. Now, he would never have to worry about the price of a plane ticket ever again.*

SEAN CUNNINGHAM: When you finish a film, all you have to do is call distribution companies. Literally, you can cold call them. That doesn't mean they'll buy it, but they're delighted to look at it. That's as true today as it was in 1980. And with *Friday the 13th*, my investors were guys that had a background in exhibition. They knew distributors because they'd worked with them every day of the week—they'd call up their friends, and their friends told their friends. The selling of *Friday the 13th* happened very, very quickly, really within a matter of two weeks.

FRANK MANCUSO, SR., VP of Distribution & Marketing, Paramount Pictures: I was raised in Buffalo, New York. I was mesmerized by film from the time I was small. When I was a teenager, I started working as an usher in a movie theater. Then I progressed through the action side of the business. I managed a theater, then got into booking movies into different demo areas throughout Upstate New York, Ohio and Pennsylvania. I would match the population with the movies that were available. I was hired by Paramount in 1959 to do distribution, and stayed with them until 1991.

Phil Scuderi was a customer and I met him many times. Paramount used to have these events where we would show a reel of our upcoming product. We would fly out to the West Coast, then you'd fly out to the East Coast and do the same thing. And I don't even know if it was Phil or Sean who contacted me first about *Friday the 13th*. I just remember seeing it at a screening with our distribution guys.

BETSY PALMER: I first saw it at a screening at the Paramount Theater. The other kids from the film were there, everybody brought their families and we were all eager to see it. And I remember that Sean was a good 45 minutes late because he was putting in that "Ch-ch-ch, ha-ha-ha" sound in. That was a brilliant move.

HARRY MANFREDINI: I was looking for a sound, a signature for a killer who does not appear in the movie until reel eight or something. That's a long time, so it was essential to establish something that brought the villain into the movie from the beginning without ever showing him—or her. You didn't see the shark in *Jaws*, but when you heard that motif, it was the shark! It's the same thing with old Jason, or in this case, actually, Mrs. Voorhees. The audience has to be aware of what's going on, and the music was the thing that said, "Uh-oh, the killer's there."

SEAN CUNNINGHAM: Harry is an equipment junkie, and he had something called an echo reverb machine. I don't know what Harry was saying, but it is like guttural sounds, hard sounds. The two words that he used were "kill" and "mother." "Ki, ki, ki. Ma, ma, ma." That is were it started. If he had tried "dog" and "peach" it wouldn't have had the same flair. But I still don't know exactly why it works. The peculiarity of this kind of stuff is that you don't know until you put it up with the movie and see how it actually plays in context. And I think there was something about the repetition of it.

I was very fortunate. Harry really knew timing. His score is very mathematical. From here to here, there's a certain amount of time. And if you break that down into a rhythm pattern, like a metronome, then there are a certain amount of beats. He didn't write music that just worked. It was measured so it happens in time. That's what scoring is all about.

HARRY MANFREDINI: I wrote the score in a couple of weeks, maybe three. The recording took much longer, because there was so little room, and so few players—oddly enough, thirteen—and it was recorded in a friend's basement studio in New Jersey. The original budget was five or six thousand dollars, and I could only do the strings for two sessions, and then the brass later. All the rest of the instruments were played one at a time by me. So I would have to go through the whole score numerous times to add each part.

When I do a film, I always try to create a world where that score lives. And that's what I tried to do with *Friday the 13th*. I learned about being limited and being really concise and using the material in many different ways. And sometimes you write your best when you don't know what you're doing. You just let it happen—when you're more in control of it, it doesn't come through. In *Friday the 13th* there are two chords in the whole picture. They are just colors that relate to various parts of the story. It's very intense in the sense that it all comes out of itself. Every single note can be explained from these two chords. I was also was not a big fan or user of electronic instruments at the time. I wanted to stay orchestral. So things that you might think were synthesized were just me making sounds. I spent a lot of time scraping and hammering on the piano of the poor studio owner, and playing screeching sounds on an Irish tin whistle.

ADRIENNE KING: I asked Sean if I could bring my mother to the screening and he said, "Sure." So we were sitting up front and all the guys are sitting in the back. And my mother's all nervous because she thinks I'll probably take my shirt off in the Monopoly scene or something like that. Anyway, at the end, she's easing into her seat and she thinks the movie was over. Then Jason comes out of the water, and I'm telling you—she bolted six feet out of her chair. She screamed so loud that she could have aced my audition better than I did. If Sean didn't have a deal with the folks in the back at that point, then trust me, she sealed it. I think that's the day Sean sold the film.

FRANK MANCUSO, SR.: Obviously, the ending was a highlight. I said, "Oh, boy! The audience is going to leave the theater talking about this movie for days because of that ending!" Because it is a truly visceral moment. Half the people in the distribution group jumped out of their seats.

I left that screening saying, "If we could get this for the right price, it will have a market. I know exactly who will want to see this, and I know who doesn't want to see this. And we have many slots coming up in the year where we could use a movie like this."

Background: A classically-trained stage actress, Betsy Palmer is devilish perfection as Mrs. Voorhees. She also lent a rather unique vocal talent to the film. "A few weeks after we wrapped," Palmer remembers, "Sean called me up one night and said, 'Betsy, we need you back to do some insert shots. You're going to be Jason's voice.' So we went over to a university in Bridgeport, Connecticut, because there was a big campus with a lawn. But it was already wintertime, so when they were shooting the close-ups of my mouth, my breath was coming out like steam. I said, "Get me some ice cubes." So there I stood, with ice cubes in my mouth, talking up in a high voice, to my dead son, Jason."

Above: The decapitation of Mrs. Voorhees was conceived and executed by Tom Savini and his crew down to the tiniest detail. "Tom and I went to New York to get the fake eyes for Mrs. Voorhees' head," recalls effects assistant Taso Stavrakis. "There was this old, dark, dingy shop in the Empire State Building where you could go and buy them. You walk in and they just say, 'Go over there and help yourself.' And there's a little drawer that you pull out, filled with eyes of every different shape and size, all staring back at you..."

Opposite page: "When Betsy Palmer's head goes off her body, her hands actually come up into the frame, as if looking for the head?" says Tom Savini. "That's just our way of making fake stuff look real. But if you notice, her knuckles are full of black hair because that's Taso's hands. He was actually slumped over with Betsy's fake head stuck to the body with toothpicks. So that the machete, when it hit, would just break the toothpicks and the head would spin off. Another glorious death!"

"Tom just amazed us with his imagination. The decapitation appeared on the screen in the most powerful and visceral way possible!" Steve Miner

SEAN CUNNINGHAM: We started to screen it for distributors and it had just incredible success. Mostly because of the sucker punch in the last reel. They loved it. Then all of a sudden we're setting up another screening and they bring in all the secretaries and their other friends and they would sit in the back and wait and wait for the ending, to watch their friends get scared. Then they'd jump up and they'd laugh and they'd high-five each other. It was exactly that kind of fun that created this little bidding war between United Artists, Warner Bros. and Paramount.

You have to understand the world of distribution at that point did not exist the way it does now. The notion that an independent film would ever be released nationally had never occurred. When I went out to do *Friday the 13th*, I wasn't going out to try to jump into or resurrect a previously established pattern. It was a pattern that didn't exist. I wasn't even conscious that it would become one. What I looked to do was make a movie for the $500,000 we were able to raise. And hopefully get our investors their money back. And maybe United Artists would pick up the option and we could go on and do something else, make enough money to keep the lights on and keep the people around me working.

GEORGE MANSOUR: To be honest, we all just thought it was going to be another rip-off movie. I didn't think it was very good. I wasn't keen on it. I liked *Last House on the Left* better. I never thought it would do as well as it ultimately did. But this was quite a coup for Esquire and Hallmark, to have this association with a major company like Paramount.

VICTOR MILLER: Sean and I had done two movies before and they were nice and respectful and nothing happened, so I was used to nothing happening. Then I got a call from Sean saying Paramount had picked up *Friday the 13th* and was going to release it in a thousand movie theaters, which was an unheard of number. I just went, "Holy shit!"

One charge that plagued Friday the 13th *was that it was a cynical gorefest, reveling in the kind of lurid, sadistic violence that tested not only the standards of the Motion Picture Association of America's ratings board, but all manner or good taste, propriety and social responsibility. Yet after only two submissions, the MPAA requested a mere nine seconds of deletions from the film's graphic murder sequences before granting it an R classification.*

In the years since the film's domestic release, the unexpurgated international version of Friday the 13th, *which Warner Bros. issued overseas, remained a highly sought-after collectible on the American market. But even today, with the international version widely available on DVD, rumors persist of even bloodier and more violent versions of the film, a claim its filmmakers continue to deny.*

VICTOR MILLER: I think the funny thing about *Friday the 13th*, and I will go to my grave saying this, is that it is not grossly violent. What I think was so great about the editing and the special effects is that everything had a buildup, and then you finally you saw this one shot of this thing and nobody lingered on it. We got in and we got out real fast. It was more of the thought of having an ax in your face that lingers with you, rather than seeing real sheep's blood dripping down or whatever.

SEAN CUNNINGHAM: It's like the relationship between pornography and erotic storytelling. That, when all is said and the specifics are presented, it's not what you think. It's off-putting. It doesn't take you to the right fantasy places. We needed to have long attenuated moments that would end in a moment of surprise in them. We were trying to see how long we could maintain suspense. That was the goal, rather than extreme gore. We had to push the envelope, not rip it open.

BILL FREDA: I think the build-up is more of what Sean was trying to create rather than focus on the actual murder. That moment of impact is all that matters. And then let them imagine what happened. When you start showing it three or four times it loses its effect.

SEAN CUNNINGHAM: There has been a lot of talk about additional scenes and all this extra gore stuff that was shot and not released. The truth is that we had so little money. We used every scene, every possible shot we had. We didn't have the luxury of shooting an extra twenty minutes and deciding what worked the best, and then taking those twenty or thirty minutes out of the movie. We did an we could do and used every resource to come up with a ninety-minute movie. And I had to be very selective with what I was going to put on the camera—there is nothing that I didn't plan to use at some point.

BILL FREDA: There were no bloody, gory scenes left on the cutting room floor, I feel quite certain of that. I'm being completely honest—after that screening at Paramount, the final domestic version didn't change much from the original cut. Plus, it was a low-budget film and you're only going to have so much footage—there wasn't the kind of coverage you have with a big-budget production. Yes, I do recall a few seconds being excised. It was hardly a big deal. And remember, Sean had been making very low-budget movies, so he was more than willing to make cuts to allow a major distributor like Paramount to pick up the movie.

Frank Mancuso, Sr. was taking a gamble on Friday the 13th. *He eschewed the regional platform distribution pattern usually afforded to prestige pictures of the era, yet did not discard the film directly into the dumpster of the drive-in and exploitation circuit. Instead, he gifted his low-budget acquisition with an unprecedented—at least for a low-budget negative pickup—mass media marketing campaign that highlighted the film's key selling point: its succession of creative murder sequences. Mancuso also shrewdly refused to screen the picture in advance for critics.*

Mancuso's conceit, combined with a release date set strategically placed well ahead of the summer's expected blockbusters, would pay off. Handsomely. Friday the 13th *opened on 1,127 screens on May 9, 1980 and topped the box office with a three-day opening gross of $5.8 million. But even more remarkable to observers was the film's staying power. Unusual for a horror film, whose receipts traditionally decline after its opening weekend,* Friday the 13th *remained second only behind* The Empire Strikes Back *as the top money-earner of the summer, and would go on to best such higher-profile major studio rivals as Stanley Kubrick's* The Shining *and Brian DePalma's* Dressed to Kill. *By the end of its run,* Friday the 13th *would pull in an impressive $39.7 million, inspiring over 14 million ticket holders to sleep with the lights on.*

If the popularity of Friday the 13th *baffled the industry and mystified critics, it would shock no one more than its cast and crew, who were expecting little from the film on which they labored so enthusiastically. For its creator, investors and studio, it was a financial windfall that would change their lives—and the face of the horror genre—forever.*

SEAN CUNNINGHAM: I didn't know what was going to happen. I just hoped that if the film were to do more than $6 or $7 million then I would see some real money. But back then, how many pictures saw that kind of return? Very few. Independent films? Almost none. So we were really fortunate there wasn't anything else going on at that time approaching the format of the film. And the success of *Friday the 13th* could never have been accomplished without Paramount and Warner Bros. They had the money and the resources to sell it, to put it into theaters and present it in such a way that it reached a mass audience.

FRANK MANCUSO, SR.: What we started doing with a picture like *Friday the 13th* was target marketing, because I never believed we would have a demographic spillover for the film beyond, say, someone in their early twenties. That was it. The early 1980s was the beginning of when Hollywood started to realize that the teenage market was the driving force at the box office. The attraction of acquiring *Friday the 13th* for a studio like Paramount was that it served a natural, frequent movie-going demographic. It was the right subject matter and the right title.

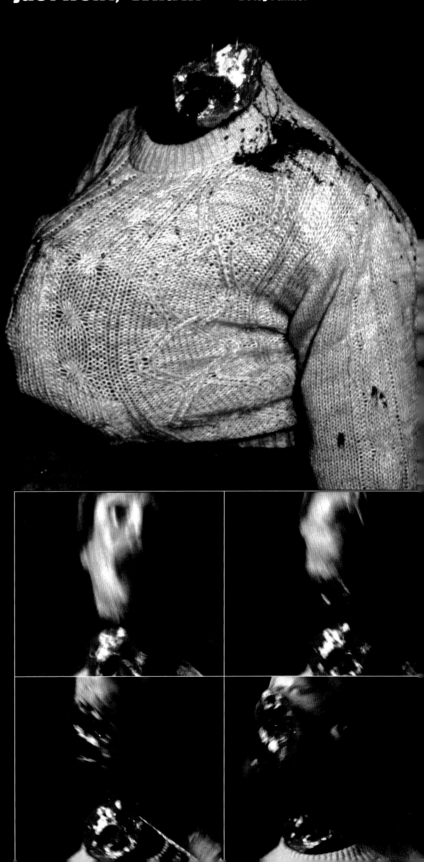

"One of the crew came to me and said, 'Hey, Betsy, we're going to cut your head off. Don't you wanna come down and see?' I just went, '*What!?*'" Betsy Palmer

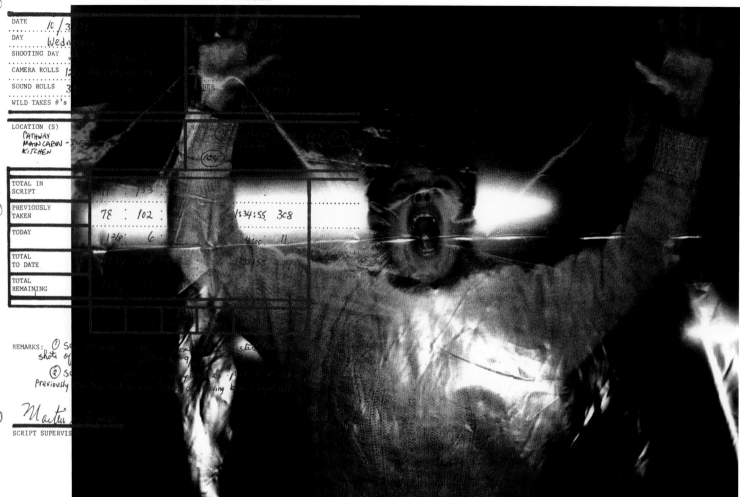

TITLE: FRIDAY 13
PROD. NO.:
PROD./DIR.: SEAN S. CUNNINGHAM

Everything we did was targeted, as opposed to something like *Jaws*. That was a mass audience picture, so their coverage in print, television and radio was much more general in purpose and intent. What we needed to discover was much more specific. What do teenagers listen to? What do they watch? Where do they go? What do they read? So in many ways our campaign for *Friday the 13th* was less expensive but much more effective.

GEORGE MANSOUR: It's like what Miramax does today. They're totally publicity-driven. They make much better movies, obviously, and they have much better taste and much higher budgets, but when it comes down to it, the people who run Miramax run it on the basis of publicity and advertising. In a lot of ways, they're a high-class rip-off of the old Phil Scuderi school of film distribution. There are definite parallels there.

SEAN CUNNINGHAM: Frank Mancuso decided to take a chance on this low budget film with no stars and release it nationally. That had never been done before. He could have fallen on his face, but he believed in the film and he took enormous chances. And as it turns out, he was absolutely correct. We happened to be at the right time at the right place, and we were very, very lucky. The success of *Friday the 13th* was completely unanticipated by everybody, except maybe Mancuso. But we sure didn't expect it.

ADRIENNE KING: We did have a proper premiere, just a very small opening at the Loews on Broadway. But it was a huge theater, and packed. And before the showing was over there was a line around the corner for the next showing. I mean, it didn't stop. I was amazed at how successful it became the very first night.

I know it opened up at number one for the weekend. It was a love fest for *Friday the 13th*. The fans just adored it and they kept on coming back. I remember opening *Backstage* and it showed *Friday the 13th* above *Kramer vs. Kramer* on the charts. After that it was overwhelming. I was living in a little studio apartment in New York on 56th Street between 2nd and 3rd. I would get stopped all the time on the subway. It was just the most amazing thing that could have happened to me. And it has been the highlight of my career, since it was the only time it has happened so far.

RON KURZ: Everyone with their name on it was becoming rich overnight. Sean, down in Westport, traded his station wagon for a new Mercedes. I was at lunch with Phil after the first weekend grosses were in and I've never seen a happier man in my life.

MARK NELSON: I saw it on opening night. I went to the Plaza on 44th Street in New York City, which is probably a 1,500 seat theater, and it was packed. I remember Barry Moss was coming up the escalator as we were going down, and he said, "There was a heart attack at the first show where it hit." It was huge.

KEVIN BACON: Whatever steps forward I have taken, I was always able to take a few back and sabotage it. I've been through so many ups and downs. But I feel pretty good from a career standpoint. I was never the fresh new face, and I'm happy about that. *Friday the 13th*—I think that success gave me the confidence I needed at that time, after the lull following *Animal House*. And it was a great conversation piece. For a while I was known as "the guy that got it with an arrow through the neck, making love to a girl in a camp bunk."

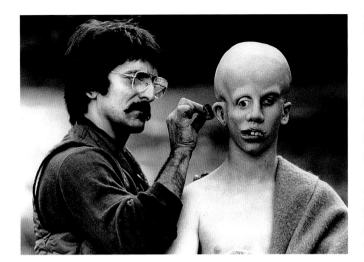

TOM SAVINI: I've done a lot of stage work where the reward is right there—the applause, the laughter, the screaming. But a movie, you don't get your reward until like a year later when the movie comes out. So I always go to the theater, and I hardly watch the movie. I pick somebody in the audience and watch the evolution of their heart attack. It was just like watching fireworks. And *Friday the 13th* was a great one to watch, I mean, my god—when Kevin Bacon's death scene came up, the reaction—the audience screamed at the top of their lungs. I remember staying in the lobby waiting to watch the people leave. *Friday the 13th* was a very rewarding film.

VICTOR MILLER: I saw it with a real audience in Milford, Connecticut, and it was absolutely terrifying. But the most interesting moment was the end. Half the audience got up and headed toward the exit. So when Jason came out of the water, the half that were still seated were trying to see over the people who were leaving. Everyone screamed. It was absolutely the most wonderfully chilling sound I have ever heard in my life. And everybody who was headed for the exit whipped around and I saw nothing but white faces, all pissed off that they had been had by this wonderful chair jumper.

HARRY MANFREDINI: One of my favorite things to do with Sean Cunningham was to sit in the front row of the theater, and we'd slide down in our chairs, turn around, face the audience and watch them react. People would fly out of their seats, and Sean would scream, "I got 'em! I got 'em all!"

SEAN CUNNINGHAM: The dynamics of that ending scene have been copied any number of times and consequently, any time you even come near it, everybody says, "Oh, yeah, I know what you guys are up to. You can't fool me with that stuff

Opposite page: The most famous promotional photograph taken from *Friday the 13th* was actually a fluke. "We were eating in the dining hall at this Boy Scout camp," remembers unit photographer Richard Feury. "It was basically open-air, so it got very cold, and they set up sheets of plastic with space heaters inside. I said to Betsy Palmer, 'Why don't you just lean into that plastic and scream?' She did, and the photo wound up in *Time Magazine*. And it's really funny, because it's not from any scene in the movie at all."

This page: Tom Savini puts the finishing touches on his famous creation (left, top), while Steve Miner (left, bottom) poses with actor Ari Lehman and Sean Cunningham.

Although audiences were suitably terrified by Savini's handiwork, the character's appearance did attract some unwanted attention. "There was some controversy after the movie came out in *Fangoria* magazine about the use of the term 'mongoloid,'" recalls Miner. "That word was used to describe Jason to the press, but not to belittle or make fun of handicapped people—only to describe someone who might be horribly deformed and at the same time might be mentally incapable of taking care of himself. Tom Savini might have just latched onto the word mongoloid and made him look that way. But I'm not going to pass the buck."

anymore." But it was so much fun at first. I think that was probably the biggest scare I've ever seen in a movie theater. The only one that got me in a similar way is when Ridley Scott had the alien come out of John Hurt's stomach in *Alien*. Ours was great, but that was spectacular!

BETSY PALMER: When I first went to see *Friday the 13th* in a theater, I went in Connecticut where I lived and I brought my daughter. And it was Mother's Day, so I said, "Well, let's go see this damn thing." And there's nobody in this movie house except for six young boys. No audience. Well, the film finishes, nobody screams, nobody yells, nobody's frightened, nobody laughed. And I said to Melissa, "I told you it was going to be a turkey. It's a bomb. Nobody's ever going to see this movie."

Then after it began to become such a big hit, we went over to the Paramount on Hollywood Boulevard and it's just filled with kids. They were crazy for it! They had found it by then. And there were three black girls sitting in front of me. A friend that was with me leans over and whispers, "You've got to! You've got to tap them on

the shoulder!" So the lights came up, we were all getting ready to leave, and as the girl stands up I just poke her on the shoulder, and she turns around and says, "Oh my God! It's her! It's her!" And they all started screaming and running out of the theater.

That is my last memory of seeing the film. I've never seen it since.

The critics hated Friday the 13th. *It was not merely reviewed, it was eviscerated. But while poor notices were nothing new for low-budget exploitation films, what came as a surprise was the virulent and personal nature of the attacks.*

The most vocal of the film's detractors was the late Gene Siskel, then still a local critic for the Chicago Tribune *who, in his May 8th, 1980 review, took the unprecedented step of not only revealing the identity of the film's killer to potential moviegoers, but also calling Sean Cunningham "one of the most despicable creatures ever to infest the movie business." Siskel's review went on to urge those just as outraged as he was by* Friday the 13th *to write letters to both Paramount Pictures and Betsy Palmer to express their contempt and disgust for them and their film. Perhaps as further incentive to get his*

Friday the 13th's famous "chair jumper" took three arduous filming attempts to perfect. It also saw a last-minute casting change in the role of young Jason. "He was originally meant to be played by my eleven year-old son, Noel," says Sean Cunningham. "He thought it would be fun, but when his mother found out, she was having no part of it. Forget about missing school, there was damn near ice on the lake, and he would have had to get in and stay under the water. So we wound up hiring Ari Lehman, who had been in *Manny's Orphans*." Much to the disappointment of the younger Cunningham. "I went through a lot of therapy after that," jokes Noel. "I think about it now, and man, I could have been Jason! I would have gotten on the cover of *Fangoria*. Chick magnet! Can you imagine all the tail I could get with that story?"

Linda Gross lamented in the Los Angeles Times *that "Cunningham has evidently no respect for a good murder mystery...the villain is as much a surprise as a sunburn after a July 4th beach party."*

The few critics who did bestow any virtues to Friday the 13th did so begrudgingly. Janet Maslin admitted that "...Cunningham's brand of horror is reasonably suspenseful, though none too new," while Rob Edelman in Films in Review *at least acknowledged that "Friday the 13th is almost unbearably scary," and was made for an audience "who like to be terrified out of their wits as they munch popcorn and convince themselves that they are only watching a movie."*

But critical brickbats did little to quell audience interest. By the time the Catholic League of Decency officially added Friday the 13th *to its list of condemned motion pictures on June 12, 1980, such publicity only guaranteed its status as the sleeper hit of the year. The film that had been proclaimed the most dangerous of the summer by moral watchdogs was now the one every kid in America wanted to see.*

TONY TIMPONE, Editor, *Fangoria Magazine*: It's funny, when *Friday the 13th* first came out in 1980, I was seventeen years old and it was the same summer as *The Shining*. All my friends were arguing about which horror movie we should see that weekend, and I was kind of taking the highbrow approach and saying Stanley Kubrick. The other group was like, "No, let's go see *Friday the 13th*." Somehow, I thought it was going to be a sleazy slasher film. So I dragged some of the group to see *The Shining*, and the others went to see *Friday the 13th*. We came out of *The Shining* bored stiff, but the people who went to see *Friday the 13th* couldn't stop talking about it. And that's all they talked about in the schoolyard the next day—they got off on all of the horrible murders and the cast getting knocked off one by one. But the box office was the true test. *Friday the 13th* was the big hit, not *The Shining*. I think the public ruled on that one.

STEVE MINER: The enjoyment with this kind of film is audience participation. The audience didn't even mind the dumb stuff, because they could talk back to it. They really stayed with the story. What does happen with a lot of these movies is that they have terrific ad campaigns but then don't deliver. I don't think that that was the case with *Friday the 13th*, because business continued strong for weeks and weeks. Practically all of the advertising money was spent during its first week of release, which means that its continued success was based on good word of mouth. I think a film like *Friday the 13th* is just pure entertainment, like a roller-coaster ride is pure entertainment.

SEAN CUNNINGHAM: It wasn't like I was creatively invested in *Friday the 13th* and then misunderstood. My personal delights lie with stories that are well told. *Friday the 13th* is just not a story. It seems like a story, but it's not. It doesn't have that integrity and elevation that good stories have. I was just trying to create a fun horror film, and people called me names because of it. Horror films don't get good reviews. Horror films, like several other genres but more than any of them, speak to your subconscious. And they are meant to be manipulative—if they aren't, they don't work. And people who write critical evaluations of movies characteristically resist anything that is not cerebral. They want the information to come in through the brain—more often than not, verbally—and they want to be able to filter it, and only then maybe it feels good. But if it comes through the eyes and goes to the guts and then bubbles up to the brain, then it's dangerous.

I knew that then, so I didn't need vindication. I was amused. When critics said the film was manipulative, it was a pejorative word, and one I considered a huge compliment.

*readers on his anti-*Friday the 13th *bandwagon, Siskel even went so far as to publish Ms. Palmer's home address. Siskel, along with his co-critic Roger Ebert, then devoted the entire October 23, 1980 episode of the pair's weekly, nationally syndicated television program* Sneak Previews *to what they called the "gruesome and despicable" new genre of the "splatter" film. During the show's twenty-four minutes, a disgusted and disgruntled Ebert accused* Friday the 13th *and its ilk of "expressing a hatred of women," and decried the phenomenon of "audiences cheering the killers on." The pair concluded the program with an outright call for censorship, with a smug Siskel remarking, "After all, bullfights were outlawed, too!"*

Joining in the fray were the vast majority of national critics, among them The Hollywood Reporter's *Ron Pennington, who lambasted the film as "a sick and sickening low-budget feature that's blatant exploitation of the lowest order." Archer Winsten complained in* The New York Times *that while "the performers are a good-looking set of youngsters, the dialogue and continuity are barely up to the level of competence." And echoing those who felt cheated by the out-of-the-blue third-act reveal of the film's killer,*

ADRIENNE KING: They called us "young and nubile." Do you think anyone my age read those things? It wasn't like I had this thing about being a serious actress, even though I did end up trying to train to be one after *Friday the 13th*. I had been doing this stuff since I was a kid. I'd put in my time and I just felt like this was probably the best thing that could happen to me, fame-wise. I can't control what happens outside of that. I learned that. And it didn't matter anyway. The thing was *huge*.

BETSY PALMER: There was that one critic, Ebert or Siskel, whatever his name was. I don't even know which one did it. He wrote in his review, "You write Betsy and tell her how awful it is that she should let us down this way, after being our girl next door all these years." It's so funny how they cannot delineate. They can't put it out of their heads that you're not really who you are when you're playing these roles. Anyway, it was too late. The die was cast. It was out. What was I going to do?

VICTOR MILLER: I had to be reminded of that Siskel review because I had totally forgotten it. That was just unconscionable, the idea of printing somebody's address. Although at that point, I was just thinking, "Boy, the more publicity they give, the better off we can be!" So that did not hurt. As a graduated Yaley, I was already used to people talking about how trashy I was. I was never fooling myself about what *Friday the 13th* was. It is a good show and we were building a roller coaster—the best damn roller coaster that we could. We just seemed to be the most visible at that moment and we caught all of the flack.

STEVE MINER: To be honest, my feeling was that if you have to show it, it's not strong enough. The audience can usually imagine something much worse than you can show them if you lead them in the right direction. But critics don't understand this kind of movie. I think, at the time, you had to show some realistic violence in order to make the setup frightening. You can't scare people nowadays without showing some kind of gore. You don't necessarily have to dwell on violence, however, to satisfy an audience. Still, I'm sure there will be people, especially critics, who still think we went overboard. But we couldn't worry about what the critics were going to say. If we made a movie to please the critics, we probably wouldn't have been doing justice to our audience.

Part of the backlash was also that less people were doing it. It was at the beginning of independent horror films like *Halloween* and *Friday the 13th*. They were much cheaper to make, much easier to get going. And there weren't that many film schools back then like there are now, filled with kids who are very smart and sophisticated. So critics called them cynical for watching *Friday the 13th*, and us cynical for making it.

TOM SAVINI: *Friday the 13th* was the beginning of the splatter craze. But it was not that we were getting pleasure out of creating gore or the monster attacking somebody. We were getting pleasure out of fooling and scaring people. When I see something gory and I say, "Wow! That's beautiful!" it's because it was a magic trick that worked. That is dangerous sometimes, because I will look at the stuff exactly like what it is. It's a rubber head with glass eyes on remote control mechanisms. And the blood is Karo syrup. And then when I'm in the movie theater, I realize that I'm springing this on objective, unaware people. And sometimes their reaction really surprises me. But that's why they're there, right? They pay their money to get scared, the same reason they go to an amusement park to get strapped into a machine that catapults them into the air and turns them upside down and makes them fly in loops.

BILL FREDA: I remember one comment Sean made during the editing that I think really paid off. It was a chase scene, and I was moving it along. He said, "Slow it down." That was a big influence. Because it's that pacing that, as an editor, you don't want so much. But Sean saw the overview of it. And that's a big compliment for him on that movie. Today, people would be like, "Let's get on with it." But at that time it worked. The audience waited for the next murder to happen, and to see how it happened.

I do think kids have a great sense of humor, this tongue-in-cheek sense of humor, and that's what *Friday the 13th* had. It wasn't serious. And kids loved the creative way the murders were executed. It was almost stupid. Today, people say, "How could you do a movie like that? It's so dumb." But *Friday the 13th* came in just before the realistic era arrived. It was still part of that almost '50s-era sensibility, where nobody really died and nobody really got hurt. That is why it was shocking.

JEANNINE TAYLOR: *Friday the 13th* had an artfully-designed plot and striking special effects and memorable music that added suspense. Was it a valid endeavor? I think it was. I really was shocked at the degree of hostility and the criticism and how emotional it all was. People got very exercised about vilifying everyone connected with the project. I don't think I—or anybody—deserved to be held personally responsible for the degradation of our culture. I did not think this merited that kind of scorn. I still don't.

But now when I think about the initial reaction to the film I realize that one must ask the question: who was being murdered in this way? The epitome of fresh-faced, all-American middle-class youth. We were the next step along the road of those squeaky clean kids in sitcoms. That's what enraged the press and some of the public so extremely. It was the first time that had ever been seen in exactly that way, except for *Halloween*. And Tom Savini is such an artist and so good at making these effects that it created this horrified reaction because it did look quite real. It was extremely disturbing.

No one of the older generation took it as fun. People Gene Siskel's age and older didn't think it was fun at all. There were still arbiters of taste who were the children of people whose sensibilities were formed during the end of the Victorian era. It's not really all that surprising that there was this kind of stigmatization of anything violent or sexual. Things have moved way beyond that now—and I don't know if that's good or bad; it just is.

> **"I wasn't offended by the violence. I had already gone through Vietnam and protested. I felt that was much worse—people having to die for a stupid war. I just thought this was not to be taken seriously."** Ron Millkie

SEAN CUNNINGHAM: I don't know when I started to hear it, probably in the mid-1980s and early '90s, but I began to get asked these questions about themes that were being superimposed upon *Friday the 13th* and other slasher films. That thing of, "Oh, the slut's gonna die for sure. And the good person, the blond virgin, she will survive." And honest to God, I thought they were nutty. Clearly, there have been a great number of

films made that do create that sort of morality, but that certainly wasn't what I intended in *Friday the 13th*. It wasn't meant to be a morality tale. I never bought into the notion of sex equals death. I grew up as an Irish Catholic, and like in most Irish Catholic families there comes a time after your First Communion where you say, "Oh, shit, I don't want to do this." Religion was not part of my life at all as an adult. So in my movies, you don't find any sense of preachiness or born-again stuff. In fact, I think that diminishes the form at some level. It was supposed to be, "Bad stuff happens. Let's take a look at it and it will be a little less scary." The fear comes from bad things happening to good people for no apparent reason. And reconciling yourself to the fact that bad things are out there. We think that we protect ourselves by being nice to our mothers, being polite, by being good people, going to church. And doing all the good things. But gnawing in the back of our minds someplace is the notion that they may not protect us. It's as cold as that. And that fear is the base root archetype for the genre.

Friday the 13th wasn't meant to be misogynistic. It certainly wasn't trying to demean women. We killed democratically. Yes, the primary audience is teenage boys and they are interested in what naked girls look like. And it is kind of fun at that level. But we didn't exploit nudity, particularly. Because there is always gonna be some version of a girlie calendar. But there are also calendars that exploit motorcycles or exploit gay men. It's just a part of our culture. I think if you make too big a deal out of it, you do yourself a disservice. I think when you try to over-analyze this stuff, you can get yourself into a big mess.

VICTOR MILLER: It is all about sex and violence. That was a lesson I learned from *Halloween*—if you make love without the benefit of marriage, you get killed. And anyway, what else would a bunch of kids be doing while opening up a camp? Painting canoes?

But it was not necessarily important that the heroine be a virgin, historically, just that you not fool around. Certainly at this camp. And I bent that rule around, because it was more interesting to me, and because I was forty years old writing this. Remember that line Alice says to Steve Christy, "You did last night?" That

used to be a more important exchange about the nature of their physical relationship, but it just got whittled down, both by budget and the time constraints of shooting. The reason it was even there is because I really wanted Alice to be more of an outsider. That is probably the only thing that I was conscious of doing with her, that the kids kind of fit in better with each other, but she had a history that was not all cool.

But if there is any scene in the film that is the most controversial, I think it is when the Jack and Marcie characters are having sex, and the camera pans up to Ned's dead body right at the point of orgasm. It all sort of works together. And it was all plotted out, that it just got creepier and creepier, that it really would make sex very creepy.

SEAN CUNNINGHAM: The movie has no emotional impact on me at all. It's all plumbing. The characters were thin at best. The person who calls *Friday the 13th* a film is pretentious. This is the movie business we're involved in. And there is a difference.

I don't think popular moviemaking create values in culture whatsoever. They project the values that are already a part of a culture. What we're doing as filmmakers is sitting around the campfire, telling these little fables, these little stories, that reflect what we think is important, what is valued, in our culture. We're just using different tools than we could before, and we're able to reach more people. And if you reach out with stuff that is bogus, that doesn't really relate to life, doesn't have any resonance, it will just get rejected. It might be popular for ten minutes. That's why, in general, people don't like to be surprised in movies. They want to have their feelings and prejudices affirmed.

My feeling about all the attention that *Friday the 13th* has gotten is that it's unwarranted. *Friday the 13th* is interesting maybe as a social document, in historical terms of what can happen in the movie business at a particular point of time, for whatever reasons. But it's a very simple, low-rent kind of movie. Certainly, if it was made today, it wouldn't merit a second look. I was very, very fortunate to have had a chance to make it and benefit from its success. But, on its own, it doesn't qualify as anything meaningful in the grand scheme of things. It's hardly a cure for cancer, is it?

2. By the end of 1980, *Friday the 13th* not only ranked as the top-grossing horror film of the year, it represented the new face of the genre itself: culturally resonant, with a modern sensibility and cutting-edge special effects. In the wake of *Halloween*, *Friday the 13th* tapped into the collective fears of its audience in a way few Hollywood films ever had—and it had done it outside of the

The Body Count Continues

establishment and without following any of the traditional rules. By benefit of the mass marketing campaign afforded it by Paramount Pictures, *Friday the 13th* bridged the gap between the wholly independent, regionally-distributed B-movie and the truly respectable, major studio A-picture. *Friday the 13th* was at the forefront of a coming sea change in exploitation moviemaking; the public was looking outside the mainstream for something that scared them, and now the mini and major studios were only too eager to sate their audience's taste for horror by looking outside established patterns of acquisition and exhibition. Following the success of *Halloween* and *Friday the 13th*, what had quickly been dubbed the "slasher film" was just as quickly becoming a staple of the industry, with the mandate to make them faster, cheaper and gorier than the last.

Opposite, top: "We were all so different, from different backgrounds and different types of work," remembers actor Russell Todd of the cast of *Part 2*. "It is the socialization of it that I still remember most, to be young and working, and that we all became a family during that time. And, eventually, that you have to move on. It was so sad when that project ended."

Opposite, center: Director Steve Miner pals around with actress Amy Steel.

Amy Steel (**below**) won the lead role of Ginny Field much to the delight of casting director Meg Simon: "We thought Amy Steel was terrific. She had everything we were looking for. Great spirit, great personality, she had talent, and she was gorgeous!"

The success of *Friday the 13th* had surprised no one more than its creator. It was not a film born out of creative passion but manufactured as a means to an end. For Sean Cunningham, the hope was to make enough of a profit to afford to make another movie. Now, he was being offered that chance—only it was a remake of the same movie he had already made once before. But more troubling for Cunningham was that a key creative question remained: what do you do when almost the entire cast of your original film—and its villain—are dead? But with Paramount Pictures eager to acquire a follow-up and financiers Phil Scuderi and his partners in Boston only too happy to oblige, *Friday the 13th* was about to take its first evolutionary step toward coining a now oft-used Hollywood phrase—a film franchise. And they would do it with or without Cunningham.

SEAN CUNNINGHAM, Executive Producer: I'd like to go on record to say that when we made *Friday the 13th*, we had no clue there would ever be a sequel. That was never part of our plan. You made a sequel to *Jaws*, maybe, but you didn't make sequels to horror films. We only started talking about doing a sequel within days of the initial success. And that came directly from Paramount, who wanted to book more. It was, "People are comin' to this, and you killed eight people. Maybe next year, you should kill twelve people?"

FRANK MANCUSO, SR., VP Distribution, Paramount Pictures: The first film was such an immediate success that we looked to establish it on a long-term basis almost immediately. We sought to buy the worldwide rights because it was a no-brainer—when you make an acquisition like *Friday the 13th* at that kind of price, the profit margin is built-in. And those profits will allow the studio to gamble a little bigger on something else, whether it be another acquisition or our own productions, because we know we already have profits on the way. And it became such a natural thing to open another one the next year, on a Friday the 13th. We wanted it to be an event, where teenagers would flock to the theaters on that Friday night to see the latest episode. That was the concept almost from the beginning.

SEAN CUNNINGHAM: We kicked around a lot of ideas of what a *Part 2* should be, or could be. I thought we should exploit the title, use *Friday the 13th* as a tentpole name for a series of scary movies not necessarily related to each other. But Phil Scuderi felt it was really important to bring back this Jason character. I thought that was just the worst idea I had ever heard. Of course, I have been proven completely wrong. But at the time Jason wasn't a villain, he was just a figment of somebody's imagination. Having Jason come up out of the lake was a device. It was justifiable, but it wasn't meant to be the beginning of a story. He was just a gag. The notion that Jason came back—how are you going to sell it?

Finally, as I considered whether or not to be involved, I just didn't get it. *Friday the 13th* was reality based. When you added Jason as a machete wielding character, you're shifting to a mythological base. Since then I have come to understand it, but in the beginning I just didn't get it at all.

STEVE MINER, Producer & Director: I thought it made sense that a *Part 2* would be about Jason. His mother was dead, and the ending of the first film just left itself open to it. I thought people were anxious to find out what happened. Who was that kid that came out of the lake? Was he a dream? Was he real? The ending of the first one didn't mean that Alice saw the real Jason. I approached it that Jason survived his drowning—we just had to give him a chance to grow a little so he could be menacing. I also thought a *Part 2* should follow the same structure of *Friday the 13th*, namely a bunch of teens in a camp situation who are being killed off, one by one. I really thought the first film was very good, and we should move ahead in the same way.

VICTOR MILLER, Screenwriter: I remember buying *Variety* every week when *Friday the 13th* was in the top ten and I just could not believe it. I was hot for about thirty seconds. Immediately, I went out and took all kinds of meetings. When *Part 2* came around, I thought there was no way they could have paid my new salary level. Which I think is one of the things about sequels—you always try to get a new writer because that way you can pay them minimum. And I would go with Sean that an anthology *Friday the 13th* would have been much more interesting. But who am I to argue with the fact that it has since had a life of its own? And Sean and Phil were the owners of this thing. I was not an owner. I wanted to go on a different kind of rollercoaster with *Part 2*. So I didn't do it.

STEVE MINER: I thought that I would just produce a *Part 2*. Then when Sean didn't want to do it, it just became clear that I was probably the best person to do the job. Working with Sean and Wes Craven, I'd learned the nuts and bolts of filmmaking on a grass-roots level. I'd done every job on a film that you could imagine. I had also directed a lot of industrial films and second unit stuff. And I thought I understood what the first picture's audience and fans of the genre would want. It was a natural transition for me. I felt like I was ready to direct. I wasn't scared, just excited.

SEAN CUNNINGHAM: Ultimately, I felt I had other films to make. I had done the two children's movies and this horror film. I didn't want to keep making the same movie over again. I thought it would be fine if other people wanted to do it and I could help. Steve Miner and I had been friends for ten years by the time we did the first *Friday the 13th*. He was an enormous help, a rock, and I really grew to count on him. Then when the first film was as successful as it was, Steve got the opportunity to direct the second one.

I was able to support him and help him get a directing career launched. I added very little to the second film, and certainly the third. Most of it came from Steve. I didn't interfere at all with his work. I just acted as a mentor, giving advice. I remained close to the next two only because of Steve, and then after that I was just off on the side, being a cheerleader. And I'm very grateful I had the opportunity to do it. I'm proud.

DENNIS MURPHY, Co-Producer: Sean had no interest in a *Part 2*. If you look at *Here Come the Tigers*, that's the stuff Sean loved. Then he got into all this other weird stuff. I also think Sean likes to do the family thing. His wife was on the first two pictures, and his son, so was Steve Miner. I think he really believed that when you do something that's not for you—that's important for somebody else—you wind up getting it back. He trusted Steve

and was happy for him. And I don't know how close Steve and Sean are now, but I'd feel bad if they weren't friends. That would be a shame, because they were so close.

FRANK MANCUSO, SR.: The people in Boston were our customers. We sold our pictures to them to play in their theaters. That's as much as I knew about them. We had a very simple arrangement. They would make the movie and we would negotiate how much we wanted to pay for it. And when the deal was done we'd distribute the film. Very clear lines. That's what we all wanted. And they were very respectful. We never got ourselves involved in the production, and they never got themselves involved in the distribution. They never interfered. They got their proceeds and that was it. But ultimately the payoffs and the profits were all handled by Paramount.

SEAN CUNNINGHAM: Because Phil Scuderi, Steve Minasian and Bob Barsamian put up the rights, they controlled the copyright in their investment entity. However, it was subject to a whole bunch of obligations to me. We had made *Friday the 13th* and it was very difficult. Over the course of the movie, there were some unconscionable stunts that a couple of people associated with them tried to pull. As it turned out, Steve Miner and I—particularly me—had anticipated the shit they were going to try to do and got in front of them and stopped it. Consequently, all my contracts never looked at Georgetown for money. Georgetown couldn't make the deals with Paramount and Warner Bros. without me cosigning, and agreeing that I was to be paid directly from Warner Bros. and Paramount. Absent that, I wouldn't sign. And if I wouldn't sign, Georgetown couldn't do it.

When *Part 2* happened, I signed off because the last thing I wanted to do was keep working with these people, subject only to token royalties. Georgetown was free to continue to do whatever the hell they wanted to do.

Much to the delight of fans, Adrienne King returned for a cameo death scene in the pre-title sequence of *Part 2*. "Alice was a very special character," confirms Steve Miner. "She was the hero in the first film, and indestructible in a way. So it was important that she be killed off dramatically, because *Part 2* was Jason's film—avenging the death of his mother is what motivates him."

The entire sequence was the last to be filmed during principal photography, and shot over the course of two days on the outskirts of Kent, Connecticut (**bottom**). "It was just me, a black cat and a head in the refrigerator," laughs Adrienne King. "I don't remember reading a script. Steve Miner simply told me what the story was going to be about. And that was fine with me, because while I was not contractually obligated to come back for *Part 2*, when the success of the first film happened, it was a dream come true. So why would I ever think twice about coming back? I felt like I owed it to them. Honestly, where would I be otherwise?"

Filming the prologue remains a memorable one for Miner. "I thought we really had fun doing the opening scene," the director enthuses. "I just loved the way it developed—I would tell Adrienne to walk a certain way and move at a certain pace. It was scary because you know that something's going to happen, but it keeps getting dragged out...and *then* the killer pounces!" But King's memories (**opposite page**) are not quite as fond. "My outfit was so horrible, wasn't it?" winces King. "The wardrobe lady must have hated me! I was so happy to get out of that and into the robe. A couple of people even asked me after the movie came out if I was pregnant!" Her death scene was also hampered by technical problems. "The ice pick was supposed to go straight into my temple and retract," she explains, "but the first time we shot it, it didn't work. And it hurt!"

Background: As would become commonplace throughout the sequels, the character of Jason Voorhees was often played by different performers for select "insert shots" of the killer. But the pre-title sequence of *Part 2* merits special distinction, because for the only time in the series' history, Jason was played by...a woman! The legs of Jason actually belong to the film's costume designer, Ellen Lutter.

"I couldn't believe it when Steve Miner called me and asked me to come in for *Part 2*," says Betsy Palmer of her cameo appearance (**opposite page, background**). "I thought to myself, 'Who's Jason?' Isn't he supposed to be dead? How is this happening?' But I liked Steve and thought I'd help him out." Palmer appears as a mental projection of Jason's during the film's climax, as well as a disembodied head found by Adrienne King in the prologue. "All I remember," Palmer recalls, "is sitting in a booth and being asked to read six or seven lines with the camera on me. I think I also had to come in so they could do another mockup of my head—I guess I end up in a refrigerator or something. And I've still never even seen the movie."

Friday the 13th was a tough act to follow. While its artistic merits remain debatable—no love would ever be lost between it and its critics—any film that achieves such a level of success still brings with it considerable expectations for a sequel. This weighed heavily on no one more than Steve Miner. With his mentor Sean Cunningham offering little more than encouragement, the success or failure of Part 2 would rest completely on the shoulders of the neophyte director. Undaunted, Miner chose the path often taken by sequel-makers—create a follow-up that's familiar yet different, one with a little more style, a little more gloss and, in the case of a horror film, a lot more scares.

To recapture the appeal of the original film, and likely surround himself with familiar and reassuring support, Miner assembled a team that included many of the same crew members who had worked on Friday the 13th, *with most receiving promotions. By the end of September 1980, just a few months since the release of the original film, Miner and company had already set up camp in Kent, Connecticut and its surrounding community, with their eight-week shoot commencing production in early October. Along with a new group of fresh-faced, eager young actors, the team set out to do the only thing they could: to try and top* Friday the 13th.

STEVE MINER: I don't begrudge the fact that people give Sean credit for *Friday the 13th*—he deserves a lot, for both the first film and for *Part 2*. But it was awfully difficult. I had always done things the hard way. I didn't go to film school. I didn't have the benefit of learning the craft out in Hollywood. I'm from the East and no one knew me. And here I was making a sequel to a type of horror movie no one in the industry at large particularly liked, even if they admired the amount of money they made. I was sure I was going to be typed that way, as the guy who makes sequels. But I could look out my window and see ten people who'd give their right leg to have the opportunities I've had. It was my obligation to make the most of it. This was my break. I would be judged on this film, and I really wanted to do better than *Part 1*.

DENNIS MURPHY: Steve was officially the producer of the movie. When I was offered the job, I didn't expect to be a producer, although at the end of the day I had a Co-Producer credit. It was a control thing. Steve wanted to do it his way, not only because there was a void and he stepped in, but because he was very dedicated and really wanted to make something good. This was his shot.

RICHARD FEURY, Second Assistant Director: *Friday the 13th* was really marginal in the context of the New York film community. There was porn, there was soft-core porn, and then

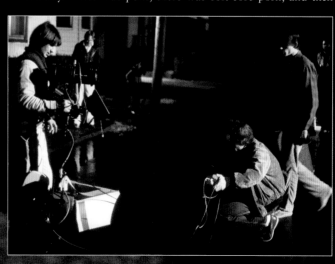

there was horror. The better projects were all Director's Guild, and at that point I wasn't in the DGA, and neither was Steve. So when the sequel came around a year after the first, and Steve called me up and asked me to again do the stills, I turned to him and said, "Well, I'm a first AD." I ended up as Second Assistant Director.

The feeling when we began *Part 2* was that we all knew what was going to be a hit, so there was no longer the same element of surprise. But we also wanted it to be a better film, and it was. We wanted it to be more polished, more professional. We all really went into it with the attitude that we didn't have to make an Academy Award-winning film, but because of the success of the first one, we had to top it.

PETER STEIN, Director of Photography: I actually shot a scene in the first *Friday the 13th* where Alice wakes up in the hospital and says, "The boy, is he dead, too?" I don't remember what the deal was, but Barry Abrams wasn't available so I shot it, and it worked out pretty well. I hadn't seen Steve Miner since the first film, but he thought of me and *Part 2* was to be my first big movie. I am still not a real horror film fan, but I thought career-wise it would be a very good move, knowing it would be a Paramount film. And we all thought this was going to be a bigger, better movie, and that we would all be in it together, gaining experience and shooting a feature.

RON KURZ, Screenwriter: After Phil Scuderi got a green light from Frank Mancuso, I was given the screenplay assignment. And with Paramount involved, I thought "screw this," I'm going legit. I eventually came clean with the Writers Guild about my errant ways, which was one of the smarter things I've ever done in my life. Honesty pays. I'm still getting quarterly residuals on *Part 2*. Although, despite my contributions, it was too late to do anything through the Guild about *Part 1*. Victor Miller got it all.

Anyway, Steve Miner was great. As I remember it, he had little if anything to do with the writing of the script, but after it was finished I did go down to Westport and spend some time with him in pre-production, making a few changes he wanted. Steve wasn't afraid to involve me. He was always positive and gracious, with a wonderful sense of humor. He was intent upon doing the best he could. Phil was taking a chance with him and had him under strict orders to follow the script word for word. And he did. I've never seen a finished film that so closely matched the script.

STEVE MINER: Saying there were some mistakes in the first script was not the way I approached it. I came to the project thinking that there were some very good things about the original film, mainly the structure. I felt that the overall framework worked. We tried, however, to improve upon some of the character and dialogue flaws. We attempted to make the characters a little more realistic. We did avoid "Strip Monopoly."

BARRY MOSS, Casting Director, *Part 1*: I got a call from Steve Miner, begging me and Julie to do *Friday the 13th Part 2*. I don't know what we were thinking, but we said no. We had done the first one, and thought that was enough. We got a little arrogant. We were young and stupid. But I loved Steve, and he was very angry at us. I've always regretted that. Looking back on it, I realize we were bailing out on him. He wanted us for the support because he knew who we were. And of course, after that, we were never asked back. So we recommended Meg Simon to do it.

MEG SIMON, Casting Director: I was from the theatre world. I studied set design, and I was a manager and then a Broadway producer. I probably cast over fifty Broadway shows. Then I formed a partnership with Fran Kumin, who had come out of Yale. We were these young women who had a couple of Broadway shows running and were working with a lot of hip young theatre directors. And we had just started our business in 1980, so it was really cool to get a movie.

We used an old Broadway audition studio called Broadway Arts on 7th Avenue between 56th and 57th. We had the cheapest room available, and probably spent a month on the casting. It was pretty straightforward—attractive young people who looked good in blood. I think at that point any young actor in New York was eager for work. No one thought this was going to make anybody's career, nor did anybody think it would hurt.

AMY STEEL, "Ginny Field": I was living in Florida, and a friend of mine wanted me to come to this modeling agency with her, and they took me on, then up to New York. I was about nineteen or twenty years old. It was all fast and fun. I did a lot of commercials, then I got the audition for *Part 2*. It was big. It was out there. I was doing this job in the Poconos and they said, "You're up for a role in *Friday the 13th*." And I was like, "Come on!"

I had to show up at the audition and pretend I was walking through the woods, screaming. And it was total typecasting—the outdoorsy, strong girl with blonde hair. And when I got it, it was great. It's nice to be wanted in any capacity, and *Friday the 13th* was cool. I just said, "It's sequel time!"

JOHN FUREY, "Paul Holt": I'll tell you something strange, and this is an absolutely true story. I was born on a Friday the 13th, and the first time I read for *Part 2* was on a Friday the 13th. So I consider Friday the 13th a very lucky day. My audition was kind of a fluke. Steve Miner said, "Pick a couple of scenes you want to read." I read the campfire scene. I thought he sort of

This page: Another group of naive counselors return to Crystal Lake (counterclockwise from top): Bill Randolph as Jeff; Marta Kober as Sandra; Kirsten Baker as Terri, with director Steve Miner; and Lauren-Marie Taylor as Vickie.

Part 2's all-night shoots and isolated location made for plenty of spooky times for the cast, particularly lead actress Amy Steel. "I remember Tom McBride had his face all made up for his death scene," Steel recollects. "He had all these wires on his head, and he couldn't eat dinner—he had to eat out of a straw. And others would have slashes in their heads. Seeing your friends hung upside down with gaping wounds...it got creepy. I was always sort of living in this zone of fear."

Opposite page: Adrienne King and Betsy Palmer were not the only Friday the 13th alumni to return for Part 2. Walt Gorney also reprised his role as Crazy Ralph. Unfortunately for Ralph (insert), his return would be short-lived.

liked me, but you never know. Then my agent said Steve wanted to meet with me again, and that was it.

I did have reservations. I had never seen a horror movie before. I didn't see Friday the 13th. So Steve actually took me to go see The Texas Chainsaw Massacre. It was insane. He kind of talked me into doing it.

LAUREN-MARIE TAYLOR, "Vickie": I started acting by doing Burger King commercials. That's all I had done. And I was only graduating high school when the audition came up—I don't even remember it. It was just another reading. My feeling was, "If I get it, great. If I don't, I'll go do another Burger King commercial." Then after I got the part, because I was about to turn eighteen, my mother had to sign a waiver to even let me go. At first I was a little wigged-out about being at a camp. Because growing up in the South Bronx, you don't go to camp; you go to Fire Island, you know? So I had to psych myself up. But it was an adventure for me, and I welcomed it.

RUSSELL TODD, "Scott": My first real acting gig came from reading Backstage, and there was an ad for this movie called He Knows You're Alone, which was Tom Hanks' first movie. In the opening of the movie, I'm making out with a girl in a car and you hear this tapping outside, and then I get killed. She screams and then you realize that it's a movie within a movie. Eventually I got an agent and he set me up on Part 2.

I had seen the first Friday the 13th. It is what it is. There was no pretense or anything. And even though it was a horror film, to me, that wasn't a negative. To be part of something that was popular was exciting. I don't know if people felt the same when they were doing Part V, VI or VII. Being part of something that was really recognizable, whether people thought it was a quality film or not, at least meant it would last and be remembered.

STU CHARNO, "Ted": Frankly, I was surprised that they were making a sequel. In those days sequels weren't quite as rampant as they are today. Of course, if something makes money they'll try to do it again. But I was happy to get the work. And as a beginning actor, you usually have very little idea of preparing for a role. It is just your natural personality coming out. I immediately knew which role they wanted me to play. The character Ted was the practical joker. Steve Miner actually just said, "Stu, you got any good jokes?" And I think all of the jokes I told in the film were ones that I came up with at the time. Steve was great that way. He knew when to direct and when to just let the actors go.

BILL RANDOLPH, "Jeff": I was doing stage in New York when I got the film. Seeing the first movie and then reading our script, it was obvious I was Kevin Bacon's carbon copy. You couldn't be more formulaic if you tried. But Kevin and I, being struggling actors in New York at the time, we were friends and had mutual girlfriends. And the last thing I wanted to do was be him. So I went up there with an idea of Jeff being more of a street kid from Jersey, and the only reason he was up there was because of his girlfriend and to get laid. And with this huge truck that he has, his only other interest is cars. It was also the first time he'd ever put on a pair of shorts, first time he's ever had tennis shoes. So I went into the audition with

"Walt Gorney was a great man, a very serious actor, and very fun to have around on *Part 1*. I just knew we had to get him back for *Part 2*." Steve Miner

an almost Blues Brothers kind of hat, and shades, and black socks, and smoking cigars all the time.

A lot of that stuff Steve Miner wouldn't let me keep in the film, but Steve was fun to work as far as being able to bounce ideas off him. Although, in terms of my performance, I would have liked to have fought more for some of the colors I wanted. So what I really appreciate now was that I had so much fun doing it, and I was so kind of unpretentious about it. I was much more relaxed, and I think that showed on screen. For all of us. Because as your career goes on, the more seriously you take the whole thing.

LAUREN-MARIE TAYLOR: Right before we took off for filming, they had a screening of *Friday the 13th* for those of us who hadn't seen it. And we all looked at each other after we saw it and thought, "Where did these people go?" Because at that time nobody had quite made it. Kevin Bacon hadn't made it; he was still doing a lot of stage work. So the big joke was, "Well, you never saw any of those people again, so maybe they really did kill them off!"

As the early weeks of filming progressed, the on-set presence of a baby-faced, incongruously well-dressed production assistant went largely unnoticed. While no one paid much attention to the ambitious young man, one of the most important figures in the future of the Friday the 13th *franchise was about to make his introduction.*

RICHARD FEURY: We had three production assistants and one of them was Frank Mancuso, Jr. Now, normally, a PA comes dressed very sloppily to work. Then I meet Frank and he has this very nice late-model Corvette and expensive shoes and slacks. And I had him getting refills on coffee. By the third night, he said, "I really can't be going off and getting coffee and stuff." My initial reaction was, "What are you talking about? You're a PA! Don't give me this shit!" And he goes, "Well, I'm really here to keep an eye on things for my father." So I ask, "Who's your father?" And he replies, "Frank Mancuso. He's a Vice-President at Paramount Pictures."

I just walked away, put on my walkie-talkie and yelled to Dennis Murphy, "Dennis! Do you know who Frank Mancuso is?" And Dennis acted as though he didn't. In retrospect, Dennis is a smart man and I am fairly sure he was just putting on a good act for me. He had to have known who Frank Mancuso was.

DENNIS MURPHY: I knew, but no one else did. I called Frank, Jr. right before we were to go up and said, "Frank, if you really want to be part of the company, do yourself a big favor and don't drive your nice Corvette up there." Sure enough, he came up with his Corvette. And I realized that he had no intention of disguising who he was. And that's okay. It's a choice he made and I think it was a right choice, actually, all things considered.

FRANK MANCUSO, JR., Associate Producer: I grew up in Buffalo, and then in Toronto. My dad was involved in film sales, but not too much in the making of movies. His influence on me was that, probably more than most people, I started to think realistically about a life in the industry earlier than I otherwise would have. In him, I saw somebody enjoying what he did, and that meant something.

In my middle-to-late teens, I worked at Paramount in different places and different departments—the acquisition of grosses, that kind of thing. And I learned a lot about marketing and distribution through my dad. But it became clear to me early on that this was less interesting to me, and what I was more interested in was coming up with ideas and making movies that I wanted to see. I had worked on several movies over summers where you're the gopher and did whatever needed to be done. And I liked the process. I liked the creative engagement. I loved watching people push themselves. Plus, I had no interest in acting nor did i want to direct. So what that really told me was that I wanted to produce. It became very clear to me.

The guys who financed the *Friday the 13th* movies were exhibitors out of Boston, so they had a relationship with Paramount. Because of my dad, they knew I was getting out of school and that I had worked on productions. So they said, "If he wants to work on this production, there's a space for him." I was probably close to twenty or twenty-one years old.

RICHARD FEURY: We had a different PA come in to replace Frank, and then Frank never left the set. The word was out by the next day that he was now an associate producer. But he was smart. He never lorded that over me or any of the other PAs. Everybody was ready to not respect him for not coming in and being upfront. But clearly he knew what to do in his situation. He didn't even have to put on any airs. I think his father had trained him well.

FRANK MANCUSO, SR.: Frank, Jr. getting into the movie business—that was never my choice. It was his choice. And when I was sure that that's what he really wanted to do, I did whatever I could to help him. And it's important that you define help. Help is nothing more than getting him the opportunity. Once he got in the door then it was totally up to him.

Nepotism? Nonsense. Frank, he earned everything—he paid his dues. The first job he ever had was on *Urban Cowboy* when he was still in college. He was directing traffic in a parking lot in Houston, Texas. That's literally what he was doing—making sure that nobody drove their cars through the set when they were shooting. And after a while, he got promoted to John Travolta's assistant along the way. Then, when *Friday the 13th Part 2* came around, I knew the boys from Georgetown and we put him on as a gofer. And that's exactly what he was, out there in the woods along with everyone else.

If I taught Frank anything, it's that it was invaluable that I was able to have all these different jobs along the way, starting the way I did in distribution and marketing, then international operations, and eventually production. Because ultimately, when you do come into a position of authority, if you have been there and done it yourself, you will understand when someone really knows or does not know what they're doing. And the only thing that is going to allow you to make those judgments is all that incredible, valuable experience.

AMY STEEL: Frank Mancuso, Jr. was incredible. He was a baby, but he was always very serious. All of us would be partying and he would be working. He could read the day-to-day budget boards like no one else. He was a really brilliant producer. He came out as "dad's kid" and when he left he had earned a lot of respect.

JOHN FUREY: I am sure everyone has their opinion of Frank, Jr., but here is mine. He was very young and he was learning, and probably very much unlike he probably is now. He just kept his mouth shut a lot. He wasn't in any way dictatorial. And he wasn't around that much—he sort of came and went a lot. A nice, young, innocent guy.

FRANK MANCUSO, JR.: I didn't have a title and I was making $175 a week. I don't think anybody paid any attention to who I was or why I was there. I was just another guy working on the movie. That was the grace. I didn't start off as the boss. It's unwise to do that. No matter how much you know, to go out there and presume that because you have a certain title you're the most informed.

I simply got the opportunity to do the gig based on certain fortuitous moves I made and I ended up with a good working relationship with the director and I had a keen understanding of the whole issue of fiscal responsibility. I had made certain fortunate moves in scheduling that they had benefited from. And because they seemed to like me, they just kept giving me more responsibility, and as I received more responsibility, I took advantage of it and continued to push it.

RON KURZ: There was an incident where we were viewing the completed footage at a local theater and Steve was concerned about some technical aspect. Frank got on the payphone in the lobby, said the word "Mancuso," and within minutes had the top technical man at Paramount on the line. He was just a kid although one with the right last name.

CLIFF CUDNEY, Stunt Coordinator: The scuttlebutt was that they were putting the dailies together and doing quick edits and Frank, Jr. was trying to help to get more money. One of the reasons we shot the movie more or less in order was so we could put a couple of scenes together at a time and the better the dailies would look. Then if it appeared promising enough, they could get some extra distribution money.

DENNIS MURPHY: Lisa Barsamian was our production manager and the liaison to the backers in Boston. And then when Frank eventually assumed more responsibility, he became kind of the watchdog for the money with Lisa. She still got a credit as a producer, while Frank received Associate Producer, which was well deserved. He was a very earnest young man. Somebody who wanted to learn the business. He clearly had a great potential future.

PETER STEIN: On *Part 2* we had a bigger budget and a bigger crew. Enough to do it right, I think. And halfway through the movie, there was a big discussion to bring in more elements including rain, which is always very expensive. And then the Steadicam came onboard. I think many of the shots were conceived for it originally by Steve and Marty Kitrosser, the script supervisor, who was very instrumental in helping plan shots with him. And then Steve became totally taken with it. Then all of a sudden, they decided to use it for a lot more scenes, which was great. I could focus more on the lighting, we could get more movement, and real coverage within the house, which wasn't even a set. It was all on location. I think all those factors really influenced the effectiveness of *Part 2*. I think that is why many people say it is, at least, a better-looking film than *Friday the 13th*.

RICHARD FEURY: Right from the beginning we all felt a lot more secure than we had on the first film, now knowing that there was a deal upfront with Paramount. At least it was "Great

"My last day on set was to shoot my death scene. The day before, I called my mother, and she said, 'Russell, don't you think that's a little odd? Are you sure this is legitimate?' She thought it was a snuff film. I said, 'Mom, this is Paramount. They're not going to kill me!'" Russell Todd

I'm going to get paid." Although nobody from the studio ever came up—it was just clear that they were involved once Frank, Jr. revealed who he was. And after his arrival, I think we all thought it was much more of a "real" picture after that. All of a sudden, we had six weeks of rain and six weeks of Steadicam. We knew were all going to be working a lot harder and we were going to be a lot wetter and a lot colder. But the Steadicam made the movie interesting. It was a new toy at that time, and to have the camera moving like that made it scarier. Steve Miner really pushed for it. It was a good idea, but there was a lot of discussion going on, "Can we afford this?" I think Frank was part of that decision, to spend the money. To this day, I believe that his presence truly elevated the movie.

No one could fully know it at the time, but in the character of Jason Voorhees, Friday the 13th *introduced one of the most enduring villains in motion picture history. Few had regarded his appearance in the original film as the key to its success—the audience would cite the film's creative death sequences and attendant grisly effects as its main appeal. For the sequel, crafting a believable explanation for the character of Jason would prove a challenge for screenwriter Ron Kurz. Working closely with an uncredited Phil Scuderi, the pair fashioned a script that faithfully replicated not just the original's overall structure, tone, pace and plot, but its characters, murder scenarios and suspense sequences—even to the extent that some claim* Part 2 *is more remake than sequel.*

Sean Cunningham and Victor Miller were not the only ones nonplussed by the promotion of Jason to the sequel's star antagonist. Special makeup effects impresario Tom Savini would turn down the follow-up to the film that, along with Dawn of the Dead, *made him a household name to horror fans around the world. Savini's departure also meant that* Part 2 *was now without its biggest "star," leaving Steve Miner to scramble to find a replacement who could not only equal the shocking illusions Savini and his collaborators had orchestrated in the original film, but successfully evolve Jason into a terrifying, murderous presence.*

The casting of Jason was also fraught with difficulties. Requiring its performer to wear a burlap sack, utter guttural sounds in place of dialogue and endure countless hours in the makeup chair, the role would prove so physically demanding that it ultimately required two actors to bring the character to life. Even if the Jason Voorhees of Friday the 13th Part 2 *was in his formative years—and without the hockey mask that would later become his indelible trademark—he was still a creation that would ultimately provide the foundation for the iconic monster to come.*

Filming *Part 2*'s famed murder sequences often proved emotionally trying for cast and crew. "The subject matter was difficult for me," admits director of photography Peter Stein. "I couldn't believe that throat cutting scene—it was amazingly gory! But every film has its own aesthetic and artistic rewards, so in that way it was a wonderful experience. I tried to make it look as scary as possible. We had to get the glint off the machete just right, and get the actor to move his head precisely to get the effect. I think for horror fans, it was fabulous."

The effect was especially tricky for makeup effects designer Carl Fullerton. "The character gets his throat cut in extreme closeup," says Fullerton. "The normal way to do that would be with a pre-slit appliance that the actor rips open by jerking his head back as the knife passes. But here the actor was hanging upside-down. So we shot it with the knife already on his neck, pulled the blade across, then pumped the blood. It's an editing trick Hitchcock used; you swear you see the incision, but you don't."

The death of Mark (Tom McBride) is "probably the best in *Part 2*, and my favorite," says director Steve Miner. "I had a special styrofoam mask built to cover Tom's face and catch the machete, which we constructed out of balsa wood. Then, with a quick reverse cut, it seems like the murder actually happens onscreen. Part of the thrill of the *Friday* films is that the audience knows that the guy or gal is going to get it, but the tension builds up as they're trying to guess when and from where it's going to come. So the build to the machete killing is nice because it really throws the audience off. I still think it's really cleverly conceived and executed."

RON KURZ: I couldn't really keep Jason as a child. You must understand, back then we had no idea Jason would continue to the extent he has, even becoming part of our popular culture. And Sean's idea of an annual series of anthology-like films was never discussed with me. I merely wanted to make Jason work in the script at hand. So I tried, with Paul's campfire speech and, later, Ginny's barroom ruminations, to flesh him out into an understandable character. And having him obsessed to the point of keeping an altar with his mother's severed head, obsessed with avenging her death and continuing her mission, offered the motivation needed.

TOM SAVINI, Special Makeup Effects, *Part 1*: Jason doesn't exist, OK? Jason died in the first movie. For Jason to be around today means what? He survived by living off of crawfish on the side of the lake? For thirty-five years? Nobody saw this kid walking around and growing up? It asks you to accept a lot. That was part of my concern about *Part 2* when they offered it to me. I got the script and here's Jason running around. I said, "What do you mean, Jason's running around?" So I turned down *Part 2* and did *The Burning* instead, which had sort of a *Friday the 13th* premise anyway.

STEVE MINER: It was a disappointment not to use Tom Savini again because he has such tremendous creative energy and is a joy to work with. And after *Friday the 13th* he even had certain box office appeal. So I turned to Stan Winston. He said that he wanted to do it but that he also had a bunch of conflicts. He told me to call Dick Smith, who then highly recommended Carl Fullerton. And when Carl brought a severed head that he had made for *Wolfen* to our first production meeting—it was so amazingly lifelike and extraordinary—I knew that he'd be up to the job.

CARL FULLERTON, Special Makeup Effects: I had applied for an apprenticeship at NBC-TV in New York for the simple reason that Dick Smith used to be the head of the department there. At the time, Dick was at the forefront of makeup. I finally had the opportunity to meet him when he would come in from time to time. Several years went by, and he got a very large project called *Altered States* and needed some people to work for him, basically to do grunt work.

Dick recommended me for *Part 2*. He had described *Friday the 13th* to me as the lowest form of sex and gore picture. I suppose that the whole appeal of it is to prurient interest and an audience's appetite for violence. I thought it was extremely comical. Perhaps that's because I'm in the makeup end of the business. Tom Savini did some fine work in it, but the dialogue and situations were extremely laughable. I was amazed that it was such a success.

I had to interview for Steve Miner. I drove up to Connecticut, and the only examples of my stuff that I had were some photographs and a decapitated head. I was exhilarated to have the opportunity to work, to have a job. It breaks down to that. And it was a wonderful opportunity to experiment.

STEVE MINER: On *Friday the 13th*, Tom Savini had taken over the editing studio in my house in Connecticut to build all of his stuff. I was with him all of the time, so I got a pretty good working knowledge of how all the various tricks work. With my background as an editor, I was able to easily visualize the effects sequences. In fact, I storyboarded very carefully how the effects scenes would work and how one shot would cover another. That enabled me to tell Carl to build only exactly what we needed. It was very enjoyable, like putting all the pieces together of a giant puzzle.

CARL FULLERTON: The kicker was that I started on the film in late July, and they gave me six weeks to do the whole thing. And that includes shooting. It was a race to beat the clock. We were making a pittance. I had very dedicated people, all very young men who were willing to work ungodly hours and come back the next day and do it again. It was very much a hurry-up-let's-get-it-done project. I had some preliminary conversations with Steve Miner in his office, figuring out how we would do the various effects. He kept telling me that it was imperative that they be good enough to shoot tight close-ups on, including Jason's makeup, which they couldn't do on the first film, despite Tom's marvelous work. So I designed them all that way. I went through the script and broke it down. And often it would just say, "so-and-so gets a hammer through their head."

"He was like Superman to me. I always dreamt of marrying him!"
Lauren-Marie Taylor on Tom McBride

Below: Actor Tom McBride passed away on September 24, 1995 due to AIDS-related complications. He was forty-two years old. The openly gay actor is remembered by his fellow cast as a man of true beauty, grace and humility. "I used to squeeze his muscles all the time, and mess with his hair," smiles co-stars Lauren-Marie Taylor, "because it was so amazing to me that a guy looked like that!" Fellow co-star Bill Randolph agrees: "Tom had a great physique. He was probably the best-looking guy there. And everybody knew he was gay, but nobody really talked about it on the set. It wasn't a problem because Tom never made it an issue."

"Tom wasn't in your face about his sexuality," says Taylor. "He wasn't like, 'Deal with me.' He was very natural. It is a testimony to Tom's genuineness, and his ability to share that trueness with everybody, and also his ability as an actor, that there was such a mutual respect amongst all of us, for each other."

The actor's haunting last days are unflinchingly depicted in Jay Corcoran's acclaimed documentary *Life and Death on the A-List*. McBride's passing remains all the more tragic as many of his creative aspirations went unfulfilled. "I ran into Tom a few times in the city," remembers Randolph, "and I know that before his death he was very angry, just at dying at such a young age. It always seemed like he had something he was working on—at one point, he was considering himself a photographer. It seemed like he really had expected a lot more, that it all would have led to greater success."

"After the film," continues Taylor, "I used to see Tom at commercial calls, and I actually went on a couple of auditions with him where we were supposed to play husband and wife. And it was hysterical because, after all those years, we still had an instant rapport. You know, looking back at the making of *Part 2*, I sometimes think that maybe Tom even felt sorry for me because I was such a dork! There was such a purity about our relationship, even in this little horror movie—we put a lot of ourselves into our characters. He always wanted to be true to being an actor. It wasn't like, 'Oh, here's Tom sitting in a wheelchair, playing make-believe.' It was almost intimidating to somebody like me, being only seventeen years-old. I learned so much from Tom. I will always miss him."

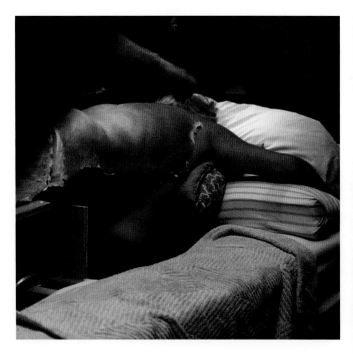

Above: *Part 2*'s famed "shish-ke-bob" murder of Jeff (Bill Randolph) and Sandra (Marta Kober) required the film's most complicated effect. "We wound up using a false-bottomed bed," explains makeup effects designer Carl Fullerton. "Marta laid underneath with her neck and head coming up through a hole we carved out, then Bill laid on top with his neck, head and arms exposed. The mid-portion of his back was a dummy. And in would go the spear." But all did not go according to plan. "We were all lit and ready to shoot," chuckles director of photography Peter Stein, "but the spear had to be put through this little hole in the fake back that was only a three-inch circle. So Carl takes the spear and he jams it down and...he missed! It took about six hours to clean it up before we could try again. That was a very tense moment for a low-budget shoot."

The experience was also quite an ordeal for the actors. "It was painful!" cringes Bill Randolph. "It took so many hours to shoot and I couldn't get out of position. No bathroom breaks, no food, no nothing. But it was a lot of fun to watch all the technical stuff. The funny thing is, doing a horror movie, it all becomes so antiseptic, it doesn't scare you at all."

Little of this ambitious effect can be seen in the finished film. *Part 2* would require extensive cuts to earn an R rating from the MPAA, and this photograph (**right**) is one of the few that remains of the uncut sequence.

RON KURZ: Credit where credit is due—although his name is nowhere on it, *Part 2* was a true collaboration between Phil Scuderi and myself. We worked extremely close together on it, meeting in his office, or at lunch or dinner three or four times a week. Phil was a creative force in his own right, often coming up with wild scenes, usually acted out in fancy Boston restaurants to the mortification of his secretary-cum-mistress, who would usually accompany us. All the dialogue, the character development, the pacing and shaping that any screenplay requires was mine, but Phil would come up with the most outrageous sequences, and from where they came I haven't a clue.

A film has been mentioned as an inspiration for *Part 2* called *Twitch of the Death Nerve*. I'd never seen it nor heard of it. Perhaps Phil had. He was not above lifting anything from anywhere. In *Part 2*, the scene of Ginny urinating under the bed is his, as is the "shish-ke-bob" scene where Sandra and Jeff get speared to the bed, as well as the Mark character being disabled and in a wheelchair and meeting his end tumbling down the stairs. In those cases I merely had to finesse them into my screenplay, usually with some character development and thought-out dialogue to make them work. Phil loved how I could make his ideas shine on paper. A writer, he was not. Then portions of the completed script were sent out to Frank Mancuso, Sr. from time to time. I never received any complaints.

TASO STAVRAKIS, Effects Assistant, *Part 1*: After *Friday the 13th* became this big thing, Steve Miner called me and said, "We're going to do a sequel. Do you want to play Jason?" And I said, "I don't think so." I remember silence over the line. Steve was like, "Are you serious?" But I hated the idea of sequels, and I was an actor. I also didn't want to do effects for the rest of my life. And Tom wasn't going to do it, either.

So I'm an idiot. That was one of the biggest mistakes of my life. Because I wish I had worked on *Part 2*, if only to have worked with Steve. I like Steve a lot. And since that day, I haven't spoken with the guy. Ever. If I could, I would say, "I'm sorry, I'm sorry. I wrecked my career. And I'm sorry I made it harder on you."

WARRINGTON GILLETTE, "Jason Voorhees": Like a lot of young artists, I had come to New York seeking fame and fortune. I was going to school at the time at the Lee Strasberg Institute and trying to get into the Actor's Studio. My agent submitted me

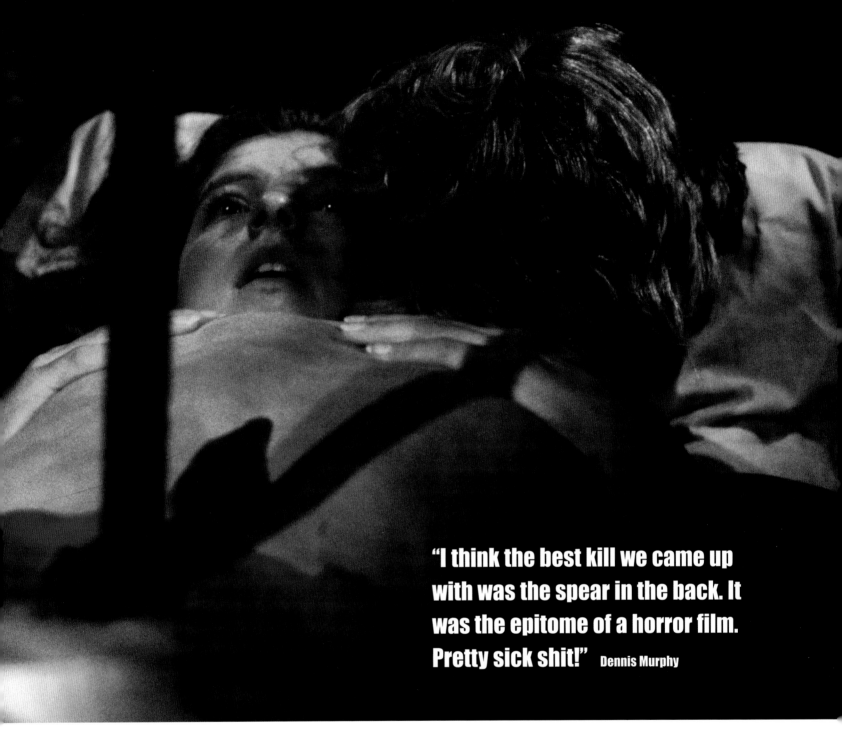

"I think the best kill we came up with was the spear in the back. It was the epitome of a horror film. Pretty sick shit!" Dennis Murphy

for the role John Furey ended up playing. I don't know what happened in the audition, but I didn't get the part, although they liked me and said, "We know you've been to the Hollywood Stuntman's School and that you can handle all the stunts. Would you like to be Jason?" And the idea of running around killing people and offering them to my mother's head seemed amusing. So I said, "I'd be happy to do anything you want."

CARL FULLERTON: Initially, Steve Miner told me that I should stick somewhat with Tom's concept of Jason at the end of *Friday the 13th*. Well, you can't stick with a concept "somewhat"—you either go with it or you don't. So I did a thumbnail sketch of what I thought Jason should look like and showed it to Steve, and I'm sure with all the other things on his mind he said, "Yeah, that looks great."

I say this reluctantly because I don't know how I would do it differently. It would have been fun to have designed a detailed character makeup for Jason, including body appliances, but hell, with six weeks to do it all in, including all the blood effects, there just wasn't time. As it was, I had exactly one day to design and sculpt Jason's head—that was it! Then one day

for research, sculpting, everything, the whole concept. That is unreasonably fast. I think it was a very crude approach. And certainly, the actor spent too many hours in the chair.

WARRINGTON GILLETTE: Carl was instructed by Steve Miner to make Jason look as bad as he could. So they went to a dentist to make Jason have the worst dental problems you've ever seen in your life. And the dentist made these horrendous sets of dentures with built-up gums that went in my mouth. It really distorted my face. Then they had rubber forms glued all over my head and closed one eye off, which is very painful for twelve hours at a time. Extremely uncomfortable. You get a little dizzy and lose your depth perception. And I had to do all these stunts not really knowing where I was. I had the fake eye, the teeth and all this mongoloid hair. It had a little bit of the *Elephant Man* look to the structures of the skull.

And add to that, you are living your day in reverse. You have breakfast at 6:00 p.m., lunch at midnight, dinner at sunrise. If I was in the makeup chair, I was there for six or seven hours. I might start at noon and then they'd be ready to film at seven, and that crap would be on me the entire day. So they can't feed you. All you could do was drink through a straw. And you look horrendous.

Normally, I'm not that hostile and violent. I'm more of an easy-going guy. However, I will tell you that the makeup made me very angry. It definitely put me in a state of mind that I was plenty pissed. They went overboard. The process was more shocking and painful than I had anticipated. But I dealt with it.

CLIFF CUDNEY: The whole situation with Warrington came to a head during the climactic scene when Jason is supposed to crash through the window at Amy Steel. Steve Miner wanted to film him in slow motion going up through the window, like he was heading for the ceiling, then almost freeze in mid-air. So I had to design a special rig that was like a pendulum. Warrington was on the end of it and it swung him up through the window, and when it got to the right height, we just held it there. And he was strapped in a harness under the clothing, and it came out his back so you couldn't see it. But when we tried putting him on the rig, he couldn't handle it. The first time we did it, he didn't even get halfway through the window.

WARRINGTON GILLETTE: They built a platform outside of the house and it was long enough so that I knew I had three steps to take before the stunt. Just one, two, three, then jump and bust the whole window out. And I did this about ten times. It didn't work the first time. The boards of the window pane didn't break—I just slammed into them and bounced right back. They scored them but they didn't cut them. Then they made some adjustments and we just kept doing it.

I was getting myself to cry underneath all that stuff, so you had eyes tearing and snot coming out of your nose. There was clotted blood and loose blood. It was quite a spectacle. No question, I was angry. There was no method acting requirement there at all. I wanted to kill somebody. I'm drooling and snot is coming out of my nose. I was hurting. I was in pain. The Jason face was horrific. There's no other way to explain it—somebody's in your way, you're angry, and you want to take them out.

AMY STEEL: That was so horrible. I remember one day Steve Miner said, "We have to drive into town." So we go on this drive, just talking, and it's beautiful. Then he said, "I have some news I need to tell you. We have to do *that* scene again." And I just thought, I can't believe it! Can I do this scene again?

Steve had to talk me through that. I'm sitting there going, "Muffin! Come here, Muffin!" Then they'd hook up the high-speed camera, which goes "Rrrrrrr!" And I know someone is behind me, waiting to go, "Bam!" I had to act all calm and the dog is coming up. And this guy's about to bash through behind me. The fake glass and the balsa wood and Jason behind me, swinging on one of those rig things—that was truly the worst part of making the whole movie.

PETER STEIN: It was really awful. We shot it in regular motion and in slow motion, with two cameras from two different angles. And poor Warrington. They had him on this swing contraption, and he was supposed to go through this sugar glass window, but his head went right into the top of the window frame. Oh, god, it was a really rough few days of shooting. Just really intense and unpleasant.

STEVE MINER: Jason's makeup was terribly uncomfortable. And the first time we filmed that sequence, it just didn't work. There was a lot to coordinate. I just didn't figure it out properly.

CARL FULLERTON: I think it didn't work because of the velocity. If the cowboy walks in and draws a gun, it's not as exciting as if the cowboy rides in full force, flies off the horse and shoots the guy from mid-air.

RICHARD FEURY: It was a half-day's work just to get this one shot—very little page count for a low-budget motion picture. And it just didn't look impressive. You could clearly see, without even looking at the film, that it didn't work. Even the camera operators were worried about it. And then they got the film back and it definitely didn't work—there was this big piece of window frame that stayed perfectly in line between the lens and Jason's face on the main camera, all the way through the shot. So there were a lot of meetings about it, and the whole thing had to be reshot.

BILL RANDOLPH: Warrington was a strange character. It was interesting because he was a good-looking guy. I don't know if he had a lot of money but he sure had the nicest clothes out of everybody else out there. He was kind of a fish out of water. He wasn't really an actor, and he wasn't really a crew guy. The rumor that was going around the set was, essentially, that he claimed to be a stuntman and I don't think he was. He and the stunt coordinator got into it: "What stunts have you actually done? Who has paid you to do stunts? What's the real deal here?" And instead of just saying, "Look, I'm here on a wing and a prayer, can you use me anyway?" kind of deal, Warrington wouldn't really come clean. And I think it became a situation of either he left, or the stunt coordinator fired him. It just ballooned.

JOHN FUREY: I remember Warrington was kind of a WASP-y rich kid or something. He quit after two weeks. I don't think he wanted to do the physical stuff and I don't know if he was any good at it, either. Steve Miner just said he sucked.

WARRINGTON GILLETTE: For someone twenty-one or twenty-two years old to be working in a motion picture, I thought, "Aw, man this is my break into Hollywood. This is great! I got a part! I'll be a big star." Then I get a bag on my head. Then I have to jump through a window to kill Amy Steel with a machete through my shoulder and blood squirting all over the place. It was a shock. When you're trying to break into the business and you get a part that requires you to have a bag over your head, stomping around and killing people, it's just not that exciting.

AMY STEEL: I had a personal connection with Warrington—I knew his family in Florida and we were from the same town and had friends in common. I knew he wasn't very happy because of all the prosthetics, and he realized that he was basically a stuntman wearing a mask. I think he wanted or expected it to be a little bit more of a thespian role. So he quit,

Above: Makeup effects designer Carl Fullerton originally envisioned a more protracted death for the character of Vickie (Lauren-Marie Taylor). "I saw this scene as a progression," Fullerton says. "Jason has her trapped and is teasing her, waving his knife around before he kills her. What we see in the finished film is that he cuts into her thigh through her pants. But this was to be followed by a cut on her bare arm, a direct hit, but we just did not have enough time to shoot it. We had to get so much in the can each day, constantly battling for the light, and Steve Miner chose to sacrifice it."

"People still say to me that, because my death is so prolonged, and that she sees it coming, it's just incredibly creepy and sad."
Lauren-Marie Taylor

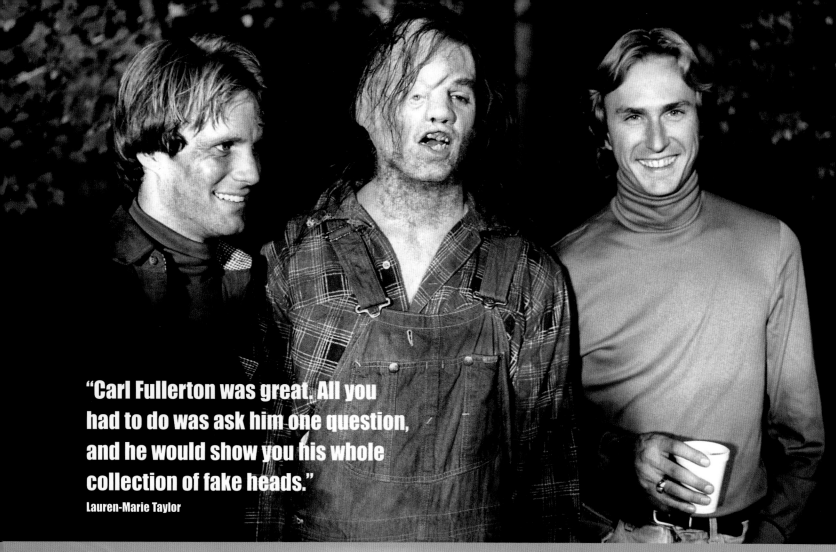

or they fired him. I don't know exactly what the term would be. I think we should all be thankful Jason ended up being played by a real stunt guy.

STEVE DASKAWICZ, "Jason Stunt Double": I had been acting since 1977. My very first movie I did was a film called *Wolfen*, then I got a part as a cop in *Nighthawks*." That is where I met Cliff Cudney. Then Cliff had gotten this show called "Jason." He called me and said, "Can you get up to Connecticut? The guy we hired to do the lead role didn't work out." I have to tell you, I was excited. A starring part in a film! This was the biggest thing in my life. I was ecstatic. I had to borrow twenty dollars from my brother-in-law for gas just to get up to the set because I had no money.

Then Cliff greets me and takes me in to see Steve Miner and the producer, Dennis Murphy. They looked me up and down and said, "He looks pretty good—take him over to wardrobe and see if he fits." So we get over there and he hands me the shoes, and they were too small. But they say, "You have to wear the shoes because we already shot some scenes of the character walking through the woods." Then they say, "Okay, he looks great. Get the bag." I said to Cliff, "What's the bag?" Cliff says, "Oh, I forgot to tell you. You're going to have a bag over your head." I'm like, "You're fucking kidding me! I'm going to have a bag over my head? I thought I had the lead role in a film! Now nobody's going to see me?" Then Cliff says, "Well, at the end, they take your bag off and you have this hideous face." So they put the bag on and I ask, "You want to give me a script?" And they say, "You don't really need a script. There's a lot of grunts and groans and you're chasing people and killing them." This is unbelievable. I have the lead role in a film and I don't have any lines and nobody's going to see my face. Then for the final insult, Steve Miner said, "There's one more thing. Warrington's agent won't release us from the Jason

credit, so we'll have to give you billing as Jason's stunt double." So I go from lead role to no role.

Needless to say, I was disappointed. But I said, "What the hell?"

DENNIS MURPHY: The bag was not a favorite of mine. Or anybody's. I believe the costume designer was the one who came up with it. Nobody else had a better idea how to do it. It came out of not having a great idea.

STEVE MINER: We had finished shooting right before *The Elephant Man* came out, and the whole thing with the bag was just an unfortunate coincidence. The mask wasn't meant as a joke. I never wanted people to laugh at Jason.

PETER STEIN: Just lighting the bag was very difficult. The thing was to keep it edgy. Because white's horrible—white and black are the hardest things to light. I just didn't want to front light Jason. It was a real challenge to make it scary, not silly.

STEVE DASKAWICZ: That fucking bag! We had a lot of problems with it. The bag would go around my head, there was a little rope on the bottom and it only had one eye hole. And I couldn't even see out of that because the bag would flop. So Cliff devised a way of putting double-faced tape over my eyebrow and double-face tape under my eye so I could see where I was going. I had no peripheral vision and I got burned on my face from taking the double-faced tape on and off. It was a nightmare.

With a new Jason on board, Friday the 13th Part 2 *would complete its first two weeks of production with relatively few problems. But the most rigorous tests were yet to come, with five more weeks of all night shoots, constant rain, and complex effects sequences that stretched the film's already low budget to the breaking point. But it would be a bonding experience for the film-makers, who would form a closely-knit community enlivened by juvenile hijinks, occasional youthful indiscretions and early-morning cocktails of alcohol and marijuana. With the average age of any individual cast or crew member just north of twenty, the experience was often more akin to survival training than a movie shoot—albeit one with a body count. By the end of production, war wounds would include frequent trips to the hospital, a minor revolt, fainting spells, and one missing finger.*

CARL FULLERTON: When you're a kid, summer camps are great. For an adult, they're awful. It was battlefield conditions. It is amazing that there is still a nice sense of fun in the picture, because everyone went through hell during the shooting. It was very physically demanding on both sides of the camera.

LAUREN-MARIE TAYLOR: The word that comes to mind is "ensemble." Doing a movie is an experience where you have to accept everybody for who they are, and just respect everybody for who they are—like going off to college for the first time, and being thrown in with a roommate you don't like. It doesn't matter. And it really hit home for me that, even if you wish you were elsewhere, or you're jealous of somebody, or you like somebody and it's obvious they don't like you back, making a movie is a living experience and you have to support each other.

I wanted to have big boobs like Marta Kober. I wanted to be smart like Amy Steel and be able to ride a horse. I wanted Tom McBride to move in with me and be my best friend forever. I wanted to jump John Furey. And I had the biggest crush on Bill Randolph. I just found him so hot and mysterious. And Russell Todd, he was beautiful. You're talking about a well-groomed man for 1980. I used to envy his nails.

AMY STEEL: You develop a family on the set. It's such a tight-knit thing. Everyone treated me so great. I was taken care of, and I liked everybody and we liked each other. And I didn't have to compete with a whole bunch of insecure actors. It kind of goes along with being an actor, that insecure, competitive thing. Everybody's just trying to keep their head above water.

Initially, all the cast members were segregated—girls in one cabin, boys in another. But we were all kids. There are always romances. Just like any set. It was cool to spend that much time with people. You couldn't really go into a town and go party anywhere. It all happened there, at the camp. I remember there were great roads around where I'd take a walk or run, or go fishing. How could it not be fun? It was only weeks, but it seemed like months.

DENNIS MURPHY: I look back and say, "How did I get these people to come up and do a movie like this in the middle of the woods?" Then I remember looking out over the lake one night and seeing people cavorting on the other side of the camp. It was indicative of the whole experience, this group of children out in the woods by ourselves, doing crazy things.

BILL RANDOLPH: There was always a lot of attention paid to jiggling and nudity. When I filmed the pre-murder sex scene with Marta, I was on this bed naked for like ten hours. It was the least sexy day I've ever had. Because there are all these guys hanging out, and of course they all can't wait until Marta gets in there. So I remember joking, "Hey, what about a pickle shot?" Although to be honest, I don't know whether I was just saying that to be socially correct, or to impress Marta. To make her more comfortable, in terms of, "Well, if she's going to have to hang out her tits, why isn't there equal exposure?"

But what a shame to have to worry about that. It's so high school, it's unbelievable. I can remember a couple of nights before they were going to shoot that scene with Lauren-Marie Taylor running around in her underwear, Steve Miner said something about what she was eating at dinner—"Don't forget, you're going to be running around in your underwear!" And then for the next two days she was eating nothing but celery.

LAUREN-MARIE TAYLOR: That underwear scene was uncomfortable because I was never comfortable with my body. I was very soft back then. I was representing seventeen year-old girls in 1980. And I never felt as though I was hot or anything like that. Ever. And they were like, "Oh, it will just be so quick." I know it's quick. It's not like you see the whole shebang or anything like that, but still. In retrospect, my mother should have signed something. But back then it was very different. Things were just more relaxed.

So when I did that underwear scene, I turned it into a joke—I started shaking my butt to annoy Steve Miner and the crew. If it was me today, I would take my underwear or whatever I was wearing in the scene, and just pull it into the crack of my butt and shake it, because that's the way I am now. And it's funny, because I think a lot of that movie helped me get over my body phobias.

Left: Makeup effects designer Carl Fullerton shows off his newest creation. Hired to reinterpret Tom Savini's original design concept of Jason Voorhees, Fullerton aged the character considerably but maintained a consistency in appearance to ensure continuity with the original film. "I basically took that bald-headed figure and distorted his face much more," explains Fullerton. "Not diseased or waterlogged so much as a congenital defect. He has a drooping eye and a massive fleshy portion that distorts one side of his face out."

Opposite page: Warrington Gillette (top, center), in full Jason makeup, poses with actor John Furey (left) and director Steve Miner.

The makeup application process (bottom background) ultimately proved quite arduous for stuntman Warrington Gillette. "It took about seven-and-a-half-hours to put the damned thing on him," opines Fullerton. "Ultimately, about one-fourth of Warrington's face is normal. The rest of his head is encased in very complicated latex appliances, with dentures and a false eye and bald cap that is functional in holding down his hair, and also gave me a base to glue on the other pieces. It was a very primitive technique."

Staging the climactic duel between Jason Voorhees and heroine Ginny Field was far more complex than it appeared onscreen. "We did do one terrific effect in that scene with a dummy Jason," says makeup effects designer Carl Fullerton. "There's a nice tight closeup as the machete goes into the dummy's shoulder, and its head moves with the impact. The dummy head was sawed through the neck and put on a pivot which came out the bottom and was turned as the machete hit. Then, there's a reverse cut, in which a prop machete was contoured and fitted into the body of the real stuntman playing Jason, and blood is pumped. I must say, all of these reverse angles were marvelously cut together in the completed sequence."

The experience of filming the scene, however, was not so pleasant for Jason stunt double Steve Daskawicz. "When Carl put on the device with the machete, they had to solder it in, and he burned me on my chest. I'm like, 'You're hurting me! I've been beaten up the whole shoot, and now you're going to burn me, too!?'"

Top: Director Steve Miner puts Steve Daskawicz, as Jason, through his paces. Some of the character's most memorable onscreen moments often came out of on-set improvisations. "When we were doing the scene where Amy Steel is attempting to fool Jason into thinking she is his mother, Steve Miner gave me about the only bit of directing in the entire film," says Daskawicz. "He said, 'You have to recognize that Amy is your mother. It's going to be hard because you've got the bag on your head, but just do your best.' So we did a rehearsal, and that's when, as I'm looking up at Amy, I tilted my head a little bit, like some sort of demented recognition. I'm very proud of that little moment—I thought it gave a little shading to the character that wasn't originally in the script."

That's when I started running. My butt looks better now than it did back then, let me tell you. I'm like Linda Hamilton in *Terminator* now.

JOHN FUREY: There were so many fun scenes. In Kent, there wasn't much to do. So sometimes we'd go to a hick bar, like the one we shot at. It was actually very funny doing that bar scene. I don't know where those people came from—they obviously had never been anywhere near a movie. We laughed so hard at the girl who played the cocktail waitress, because she was so bad. And in a way, it really helped the scene, because we thought she was hilarious. And we were teasing Amy so much. That's why we were laughing all the time. I think we got a little drunk, too. And she kept saying that there was a "man boy beast" or something out there, and we just thought that was hysterical. Every time she said it, we could barely keep a straight face. Steve Miner actually started to get pissed because we were fucking up takes.

LAUREN-MARIE TAYLOR: There was a lot of behind the scenes scaring. I fainted at one point. Stu, Tom and a couple of the other guys came to the window of my cabin and started scratching at the screens with one of those old man masks. I turned around, saw that, screamed bloody murder, and just fell flat on my face on the floor. I thought I was going to get killed.

RUSSELL TODD: The only scary part was going home at night from the actual lake location to the cabins. There was a long road with bushes on both sides, and the crew would be in the bushes going, "Kill, kill, kill!"

AMY STEEL: I think horror is the genre where you get people right off the bus. You don't have to pay them a lot of money. They're all excited, young and fresh-faced, ready to go with energy to burn. I don't remember anybody really complaining, but it was exhausting, no question about it. We were in these cabins without heat and there were no amenities. And there were no cell phones back then, only this phone booth where everyone made phone calls.

What I learned the most from *Part 2* is that a human being is not a nocturnal animal. Human beings are supposed to work during the day and sleep at night. To reverse that left me wasted afterward. We would work all night and then we would be fighting the sun. Dinner break would be a like 2:00 a.m. It was eggs, bacon, biscuits, and Jack Daniels.

BILL RANDOLPH: Being the wild, ridiculous kids that we were at the time, it was like, "Who can come up with the craziest drink for breakfast?" It became a competition between the crew and the cast to see who could come up with the drink that would knock your socks off.

CLIFF CUDNEY: It would be morning, and you're supposed to go to sleep and get a good period of rest, just so you can get up later that night and go to work again. But you're fired up—the dawn is breaking, you're getting your second wind and you've just had a meal—which is supper, but it's breakfast, actually—and now you're supposed to lay there and go to sleep? So everyone would have a couple drinks and mellow out and crash. I don't think we used drugs to keep going, it was more to come down.

LAUREN-MARIE TAYLOR: It was what it was back then; everybody did it. But not smoking ended up being the biggest issue I had during the movie, when my character was supposed to smoke a joint. I asked Steve Miner, "Does Vickie have to do this? Does she have to be high? Twelve years of Catholic school—I don't do that!" Now normally, Steve was really relaxed. He was always a calming presence in the midst of this insane movie. Maybe inside he was going, "We're way over budget!" but you didn't feel any stress from him whatsoever. So I never felt as though I was doing a horrible job. But when I tried to make believe I was smoking, that was the only time Steve got irritated with me, because he was like, "Haven't you ever smoked before!?" I was like, "No!" And I can't tell you how many takes it took him just to teach me how to hold the thing.

PETER STEIN: It all was fun for awhile, but eventually there was a crew revolt. They put us up in these cabins that didn't have heat, and it was October in Connecticut. So everybody got together and said, "This is not acceptable anymore. We want heat!" And they finally put us up in hotels.

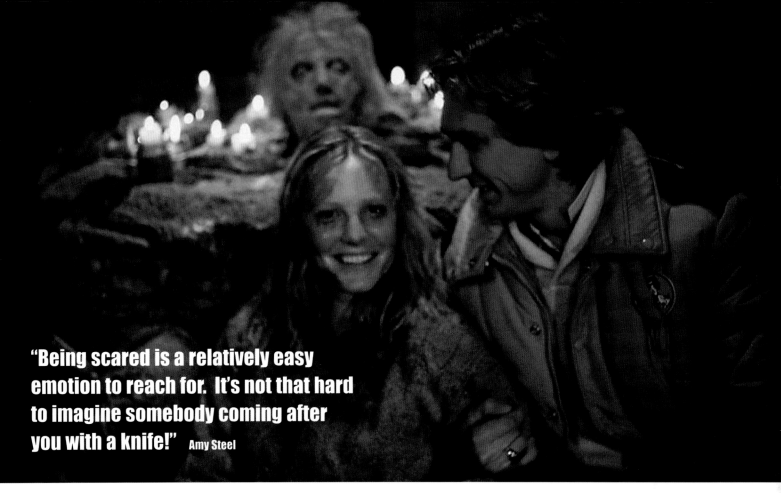

"Being scared is a relatively easy emotion to reach for. It's not that hard to imagine somebody coming after you with a knife!" Amy Steel

STEVE DASKAWICZ: One day Cliff and I went into town to get a toaster oven and a hot plate, because we had decided to turn our cabin into a house. We even sealed off the whole cabin with plastic to shield ourselves from the cold. So we go into town to this K-Mart or whatever it was, and I say to Cliff, as a joke, "You buy the stuff and I'll get the toaster oven. And I bet you I could walk right out of here with it and not get caught." So as I'm walking out, and one of the girls who worked there comes out—a very attractive girl—and she says, "You neglected to do one thing—pay for that." So I say to her, "I tell you what. I'm the guy playing Jason in *Friday the 13th Part 2* up at the camp. If you come up there tonight, I'll let you watch. And then I'll let you get laid. What do you think?" She did. She let me steal the toaster oven. Then she came up that night and I had sex with her.

CLIFF CUDNEY: You know, despite the conditions and the challenges and the craziness, *Part 2* is probably one of the most fun movies I've ever worked on because we had creative license. They had no idea how to do these things or what they wanted to do. As long as we make it gory and make it exciting and make it scary. I remember many of those days on *Part 2*, asking, "Hey Steve, instead of seeing Jason's face, how about if just his hand comes through the window?" And then we would just do it. The script was loose and it's like an improv show. And once everybody gets into it, you feed off each other and the ideas just flow. If you can come up with a surprise that scares the audience in a new and different way, it makes a world of difference.

DENNIS MURPHY: Looking back, to be honest, I thought most of the scares in *Part 2* were not executed very well. They were kind of flat. I thought the most exciting part of the film was the last third or so, when Jason is chasing Ginny. And during that chase, there's a scene where Ginny's in the kitchen of the cabin, holding tight on a doorknob, because she thinks Jason is on the other side. And she's reaching over to the window, thinking that is her escape route. And then, *bam!*, Jason smashes through the glass. Creatively, that and the chair jumper are the best scares in the movie. Those were great.

STEVE MINER: Suspense and scary moments are created by nothing happening so much. But you've got to be careful having nothing happen for too long. It'll get boring. You also can't have the same thing happen too often. You have to have chase sequences and humor and scares and suspense. *Part 2* is a quick movie. I just tried to mix it all together and keep the film moving. To get the rhythms of it going, knowing where to

Above: The filmmaker's original vision for *Part 2*'s final shot were considerably more animated. "Stan Winston had originally cast Betsy Palmer's head, the one that is seen at the film's beginning," says makeup effects designer Carl Fullerton. "But because Georgetown Productions wouldn't fly Betsy out to the East Coast, I had to totally re-sculpt her likeness from a photograph and create a new fake head for the climax. Steve Miner also wanted some movement in the film's final shot—he wanted Mrs. Voorhees' head to smile and for her eyes to open. So we hired an actress, Connie Hogan, and built the head so she could fit into it. Connie was then positioned in a false bottom altar, which created all kinds of unnecessary problems, considering the way the picture was cut. We had to cheat Mrs. Voorhees' neckline, which, in my opinion, makes the shot look a little awkward—if we had just used Stan's dummy head from the beginning, the last shot would be much better. Although I'm glad that, ultimately, they chose not to use that footage of the head opening its eyes and smiling, because quite frankly, it looked humorous rather than scary."

keep the frame open, and knowing how to create expectation in the audience that something is going to happen. Then sustain those moments, that tension, for as long as possible.

I never try to figure out what I think people are going to find scary. I just do what I think is scary. I'll sit there on the set and watch the scene unfold and try to watch it like I'm in the audience.

AMY STEEL: It was a television schedule. There was just so much to get done. It was so emotionally draining. I acted my ass off. And although I have always been physical, there were a whole bunch of times where I remember saying, "I don't want to do this." It was challenging.

But I felt really cool doing all my own stunts. For one sequence, where I'm supposed to fall out of the cabin window and run to the car, they said, "Just jump through this window and fall down and walk away." And I did it. The adrenaline started and just I broke open the screen on the window. Then the stunt guy comes up to me and says, "You know, you could be getting stunt adjustments for this," especially considering I was getting like $5 for six weeks.

CLIFF CUDNEY: The shot where she came out the window, hell, it was a big drop. And, boy, did she do a lot of running and clawing and being in the mud. And it was freezing. Amy did a lot of her stunts, as did most of the actors. We didn't have stunt doubles. But there was no time when she was in any danger of being seriously injured. There was never anything that was harrowing, other than wrestling with a stuntman. But I think she did great.

DENNIS MURPHY: Let it be known that Amy Steel was no prima donna. She definitely fought for her point of view and her character, but she didn't exhibit any of that kind of behavior at all. She was terrific.

CLIFF CUDNEY: Steve Daskawicz had it the worst. There is a scene where Jason has trapped Amy in a room, and he's supposed to break through a door with a pitchfork. So we took two thin sheets of wood and glued them together with grains going the opposite way. Well, unknowingly, the effects guys built the first door with crossed grain, so when Steve ran up there and hit that door with the pitchfork, all the pitchfork did was vibrate. It was like hitting a telephone pole with a baseball bat. It almost broke his wrist.

STEVE DASKAWICZ: When we were doing the scene where Jason is chasing Ginny at night through the woods, the camera was mounted on the back of a station wagon. Amy was running and I'm supposed to fly out of the woods to try and grab her. So they built this platform that was elevated—three feet up—and they dug the ground out where she'd run in front of where I landed, and put a mattress under there to soften my fall. I also had a pickax in one hand. So, I'm supposed to literally fly out of the woods and land on the ground with a real pickax! Amy was so scared that she was running incredibly fast, too fast, so by the time I leaped I wasn't even close to her and it didn't look right. They kept telling her to slow down, and we did take after take. Finally, the last time I jumped I landed with the pickax under me and it broke my ribs. I had to go to the hospital alot on that movie.

CLIFF CUDNEY: The climactic scene in Jason's shack—that was the only time Amy did anything with a real machete. It was an all-night shoot and it was very late, and we're filming the shot where Amy swings the machete down at Jason, and he blocks it with a pickax. Well, we had blocked this whole thing, and I had taken the machete and rounded off the blade so there were no

sharp angles on it. But then, at the last minute, Steve Miner decided to change the choreography. Amy got confused halfway through filming the real scene and swung the machete the wrong way. It caught Steve Daskawicz in the hand, and the machete came down right between two of his fingers.

STEVE DASKAWICZ: Cliff didn't want to use Amy for the machete scene in the first place; he wanted to use a stunt girl. Because Amy was scared to death of me. She never even talked to me for the three weeks I was on the set. She just wanted to play that Method actor thing up like you wouldn't believe. I kept saying, "This is fake. Calm down. It's only a movie!" But she wouldn't look at me during lunch or anything like that. Maybe I'm just an intimidating guy.

AMY STEEL: The timing was off, and I cut Steve's finger basically clear off. We had to stop filming, and he had to go to the emergency room. I felt so bad. I was really mad at Steve Miner. I yelled at him, "Oh, my God, why didn't we use a rubber machete?" But Steve was just like, "No, don't worry, he's a stuntman. It's just another scar. It's okay." And he was right! Eventually he came back, put the bag back on and just kept going. It was just another battle wound for him.

STEVE DASKAWICZ: You have to picture this: Amy takes the machete and she slices me. I'm lying on the floor and they yell, "Cut!" Cliff comes over, leans down and says, "Man, buddy, that was great!" Then they realize she cut me, and there's panic. You have to picture this: it's the middle of the night, we're in this makeshift shack, and the entire crew is running around, trying to find my finger, thinking it has been sliced off.

Then Cliff says, "I've got a great idea. Let's go to the hospital, but with the machete in your shoulder. It'll be hilarious!" And I was already a frequent flyer at the hospital anyway; we'd get accolades every time we arrived—"The actors are here!" They'd run around and pamper us. So we walk in through this big automatic door, and a nurse says, "Don't tell me you're back!" Then they see the machete in my shoulder. There are nine nurses standing there with their mouths hanging open. And I'm covered in blood and the whole thing. Then two or three interns and doctors ran out. They looked at Cliff, turned around and went back out. Everybody left. Then four or five of them came back in with cameras and started taking pictures.

CLIFF CUDNEY: Well, we finally got Steve's wound all taken care of—it was nothing too serious, just a couple of stitches. Anyway, while we were driving back, everyone at the set had decided to wrap for lunch, which was at like 1:00 a.m., and they had made arrangements to feed the crew in this restaurant downtown. We knew it was a bad night and everyone was in bad spirits. So Steve and I put on pink tutus and just went right into this restaurant. And everyone broke into hysterical laughter. That broke the down period and made everybody feel a lot better. That was some night.

Friday the 13th Part 2 was released on April 30th, 1981, on 1,350 screens across the United States. It was an instant financial success, with an initial three-day gross of $6.4 million that eclipsed the opening of the original film. However, its subsequent fall-off was noticeably sharper, and by the end of its run, Part 2 would earn $21.7 million, taking in a still-impressive 7.8 million admissions. Certainly, given its modest production budget of $1.25 million, Part 2 was a moneymaker. Yet the sequel's inability to scale the box office heights of its predecessor left some industry pundits searching for a reason for the *depression in ticket sales. Reviews were, predictably, atrocious. But then* Friday the 13th *never needed the endorsement of critics to bolster its box office appeal. More detrimental was the proliferation of slasher movies that had followed in the wake of* Halloween. *Had the primary appeal of the original film—its ultra-graphic murder sequences—already become passé? Was the character of Jason not as interesting a villain as Mrs. Voorhees? Or had the censors at the Motion Picture Association of America finally succeeded in draining the sequel of the one thing that mattered most at the box office: blood?*

Forced to submit his film nearly ten times to the ratings board, Steve Miner would excise fifty-four seconds of carnage from Part 2, *leaving many fans to complain that it not only lacked the visceral effectiveness of the original film, but that it failed to deliver on its very* raison de entré. *It would be only the first of many battles between the producers of the franchise and the MPAA. Two decades later, the ratings board remains the only foe Jason has yet to defeat.*

SEAN CUNNINGHAM: When we finished *Friday the 13th*, we took a very strong piece of work to the MPAA. And they asked us to make a couple of cuts, but basically they let the film go through, pretty much in the form that we expected. And because of the film's impact, there were a lot of imitators who kept pushing the envelope. And then when they submitted their films to the MPAA they would say, "You let *Friday the 13th* get by, and now you're tellin' us we can't do this?" Our film became held up as an example.

STEVE MINER: After *Friday the 13th*, the ratings board really cracked down, and it had a chilling effect. It wasn't an option to release the film in a form like *Dawn of the Dead* or *Last House on the Left*. This was a film that had to play in over a thousand movie theaters. We also had to watch our negative pickup deal with Paramount because they sure weren't going to release a film that was unrated. And it would have been too expensive to go back and do tons of reshoots.

I still feel *Part 2* worked really well, but some of the cuts did rob the film of its impact. The MPAA forced us to excise much of the great work that Carl and his team did. I was also concerned by the criticism of the first film, that it was just a bunch of mindless gore. I wanted the characters in *Part 2* to be a little more realistic, and that may have taken away from some of the scares.

CARL FULLERTON: I first learned of the cuts to the film when Steve called me on the phone one day in an almost apologetic tone. My first reaction was that I was disappointed and angry, but I also felt bad for Steve. I do remember being warned by him about the ratings board before the film came out, and he was genuinely apologetic. I knew that his hands were tied. I appreciated the phone call, and I thought that was a very kind thing for him to do.

I'm absolutely certain that, at the time, it was upsetting, simply from a selfish point of view. The result of our efforts was taken away from us. The only saving grace is that I was presented with creative challenges and productions problems, and I did solve them. At worst, it was a learning experience. You can't buy that kind of education. However, now, in the broad scope of things, it makes absolutely no difference to my life. Right now I'm having trouble even remembering what got cut.

GREG NICTOERO, Effects Supervisor, *Jason Goes to Hell*: At the time, I was just about to start my first film, *Day of the Dead*, with George Romero and Tom Savini. I had to drive to New York to rent molds from Carl Fullerton. Later, at his house, Carl said, "Hey, do you guys want to see some of the stuff from *Friday the 13th Part 2?*"

It was the unedited version of the scene where the couple is lying in bed and they get speared. The original effect as it is is now not even in the movie: you see the spear go in the guy's back, then you see her react, then you see more struggling, then the spear comes back out. And it was one of the most shocking things I had ever seen. To this day. Because the girl is lying there, the guy is on top of her, and as Jason comes in, the girl sees him—what was disturbing was the look on her face, and her struggling to get the guy off of her to save her own life before the spear goes in.

I remember watching that and being really horrified because I realized that it wasn't the effect that disturbed me the most, but the woman's reaction to her impending death. I think that's where a lot of people sort of get confused: it's not the gore that really is offensive, as much as it is the circumstance in which we see it.

Part 2's ending remains a source of confusion for many fans. After Jason crashes through the window at Ginny (**background**), the screen fades to white, and Ginny is rescued. But what has happened to Paul? Screenwriter Ron Kurz explains: "Jason's coming through the window was written as reality. My intent was this: Paul is, in fact, killed by Jason. Ginny survives. She asks, when found, "Paul! Paul! Where's Paul?" Then we cut to Jason's shack, and a close-up on Mrs. Voorhees' head. It's bathed in faint light, staring at the camera. Slowly, distinctly, a diabolical smile forms at the corners of its mouth. In other words, in answer to Ginny's question, the smile tells us that Jason has killed Paul. That is how I wrote it and that's how Steve Miner filmed it. Granted, as it appeared on screen, shot and edited as it was, I can see cause for some confusion. So whether it came across as such for the audience is up for debate."

Rumors continue to persist that the ending was actually altered due to friction between actor John Furey and director Steve Miner. "That's not true. That's bullshit!" replies Furey. "We got into discussions and might have raised our voices once or twice, but I was friendlier with Steve than anyone else on that movie. And we've remained friends ever since." Steve Miner concurs: "John was a total professional and he did everything that was asked of him. If the ending was vague, that was the film's fault, not his."

Above: "I first came to be involved with the *Friday the 13th* series when Paramount called me in to work on *Part 2*," remembers title designer Dan Curry, who also created the opening credit sequences for *The Final Chapter, A New Beginning* and *Jason Lives.* "Traditionally, the *Friday* titles were white letters over black, and the intent was that, working in tandem with the music, they would pop on the screen in different places and unsettle the audience. For the first sequel, Frank Mancuso, Jr. had the idea that we would see this block of wood that said 'Friday the 13th,' then it would explode, and inside it would say 'Part 2.'"

Although the actual filming of the effect was a success, it did result in one comical mishap. "We had some wax copies made of the block of wood, and a pyrotechnic expert, Pete Gerard, wired that up for us," explains Curry. "Then we mounted it on a motion control rig. We did one 'hero shot' of the actual wood block that looked great, and once it was in its final position, we replaced that and shot the same thing over with the wax one. Then we rigged a charge and blew it up. Finally, we did a third pass with 'Part 2' in virtual space, in the same position where it would have been inside the original block.

"The funny thing was, we had invited a bunch of executives over to watch the effect. And right before the charge was about to go off, I saw Pete dive behind a stack of plywood. So I ducked, too, and then the explosion shot molten wax pellets all over the place that embedded themselves into the suits of the executives. Which they were far from happy about!"

Opposite: The domestic theatrical one-sheet poster for *Friday the 13th Part 2.*

SEAN CUNNINGHAM: I think the MPAA may have thought that it had thrown a softball with *Friday the 13th* and then lived to regret it. The truth is that the MPAA is, as far as censorship goes, a political committee. And it's meant to evolve, to ride along with public opinion.

I know many will disagree with me on this, but in the MPAA we have one of the greatest political gifts to artists in the world. I think it's wonderful we live in a culture where you can do anything in a movie. Nobody tells you that you can't do something, except the marketplace. Anybody who goes out and makes a film that is just bathed in blood is trying to make an exploitation film. The only thing he or she can complain about is that they went so close to the edge they fell off. You don't have to be a rocket scientist to know what you're allowed to do. I think that the people complaining about it are the ones who are getting caught.

DENNIS MURPHY: I thought *Part 2* was fun. I thought we did a good job. And there is no reveling in the violence. But I forgot how sanitized these films were. I don't remember thinking of it that way when I saw it at the time, however.

WARRINGTON GILLETTE: They had a premiere party in New York, at a theater on 86th street. I brought my family, and we took Andy Warhol and some friends. It was a letdown because I had built it up to be something more than it was going to be. Everybody was saying, "Where are you?" I thought I had this really great part, and there I was on the big screen, saying absolutely nothing, just killing a bunch of kids.

LAUREN-MARIE TAYLOR: I went to a regular movie theater to see it and freaked out: "Oh, no! I showed my private parts! Look at my butt!" That's all I could think.

JOHN FUREY: I went to see it at the premiere screening and it was unbelievable, because I think sixty or seventy percent of the crowd was black, and they all were rooting for Jason. They got a kick out of Jason killing white people. They liked the mayhem. It's amazing.

CARL FULLERTON: At the time, 42nd Street was like a carnival in the worst sense. And it was loaded with movie houses. I recall going to see *Part 2* there and it was a very hot summer day. People were jammed in the theatre—perhaps, if no other reason, than to keep cool. And the people that were watching this film were participants. They would call out to the screen and scream out loud. People were walking over the seats to get to different seats. It was one of the best movie-going experiences I have ever had in my entire life.

CLIFF CUDNEY: It was like *The Blair Witch Project.* When I saw it, I thought, "What the hell is this?" It looked like somebody's home movie. It always astounds me that the film is still popular because I don't think there's much to it, and the acting is not that great. But some of the cinematography was good, and I was pleased with the way the stunts came out.

AMY STEEL: Technically, I think it is almost archaic compared to what they make now. But I thought Steve brought class to it, and he seemed to have a good grip on what the genre was, what the public wanted to see and what Paramount wanted from it. I think he got all of that, and raised the bar.

HARRY MANFREDINI, Composer: I was happy to do *Part 2.* Work was not that plentiful, and I was now a part of a dynasty—I like to think an important part. But I have to say I was not aware of the "iconicity" of the score at the time. I still find it hard to believe. The direction from Steve Miner was simply, "Do it again." The second one is a little more complicated. I got better. It was clearer what I had to do. On the first one, I was flying by the seat of my pants. I had never written music like that. This time, I knew what worked and I knew how to make it work. I think that is true of the second film as a whole.

Danny Elfman says there's a difference between puke and shit. Puke is where you take something, you eat it and then you throw it up. Shit is something that you eat, you digest and then turn it into something of your own. So I've gotten both sides of this. There are a lot of people who say to me of my score, "It's so derivative." I don't want to argue with them. But if you've never heard Bernard Herrmann, how are you going to do a horror picture? Not even so much what the music sounds like, but just the way the music approaches the picture. He understood the attitude of the music.

This is the way it's supposed to be done. If you want to go a different way, you can, but it won't work. Same with a sequel.

RON KURZ: My personal opinion is that Steve is a much better director than Sean. He's proven that with the films he's done since the two *Friday*s. On balance, I think *Part 2* is a better film than *Friday the 13th*. Brighter, smarter, better acted, better directed. Of course, the original did have the scene of Jason coming out of the water at the end...

STEVE MINER: What we did was set out to try and top *Friday the 13th*, and in many respects we did. And I feel that it showed people that I could direct. Ultimately, the film did very well, because you have to consider that it was released less than a year after the original. And if you combine both films into one, you've got a blockbuster level of success. Everyone was happy.

While the Friday the 13th *camp was celebrating, Sean Cunningham was finding that his attempts to distance himself from the film that had made him famous were being met largely with indifference. In the initial months following the success of* Friday the 13th, *Cunningham was heavily courted by the Hollywood establishment, and the doors that had remained shut to him for over a decade had suddenly opened. But success can be as limiting as it is liberating, especially in Hollywood, where the obligation to repeat the past often outweighs all other artistic considerations. The film Cunningham eventually chose as his follow-up to* Friday the 13th, *the adult thriller* A Stranger is Watching, *based on the best-selling novel by Mary Higgins Clark, was released by United Artists in 1982—and quietly flopped. Cunningham's subsequent efforts likewise found little favor with the moviegoing public: only* Spring Break, *a teen sex comedy he directed for Columbia Pictures, gave him a minor hit when it was released in August 1983. And Cunningham, still based on the East Coast, also saw his once tightly-knit filmmaking family begin to unravel. Following the release of* Part 2, *Steve Miner, like Wes Craven before him, would make the move to Los Angeles to pursue mainstream success, while Cunningham's once-thriving partnership with Victor Miller deteriorated into acrimony and, eventually, a lawsuit.*

SEAN CUNNINGHAM: Knowing now what I didn't know then, sure, it would have been much better business sense doing the sequels myself. But with *Friday the 13th*, they were making the same movie over and over again. Why would I want to do that? So much of that was my own naïveté. Suddenly, I had a successful film, and my attitude toward Hollywood was: "I know you guys have all these great scripts and great actors—what have you got for me?" I had no idea that they didn't have a file cabinet full of great material waiting for me, that all they wanted me to do was make them more money by doing the same thing over and over again.

I spent the better part of a year after *Friday the 13th* trying to find something else to do that was soft and warm and lovely. And I couldn't find it. Out of self-defense, I wound up doing what was supposed to be an upscale thriller in the form of *A Stranger is Watching*. But all that did was reinforce to the world that all I could do is horror movies.

VICTOR MILLER: *A Stranger Is Watching* was supposed to be the biggie, but the movie did not do very well at all. Then with *Spring Break*, lightning was supposed to strike twice. Sean called and told me to go see *Porky's* in just the same way he told me to go see *Halloween*. So I wrote two or three drafts. Then I got a phone call one morning. "Victor, I'm not going to go ahead with you on *Spring Break*." Either my screenplay, in his opinion, sucked, or the money people had some other writer they wanted to use. Or maybe it was just creative differences. But whichever it was, I was stunned. Not so much at my being fired, but to be fired over the phone by a guy who I had been working with for five years. I just could not believe that this was happening.

Sean did send me a letter at one point, but it did not really deal with what had happened and I never talked to him again. I don't think he treated me all that kindly.

SEAN CUNNINGHAM: When I got to do *A Stranger is Watching*, I had the opportunity to use some really high-level studio people. They were available to me, yet I didn't want to use them. I was afraid of them—I thought they might fuck me over because they're not really working for me, they're working for "the man." I don't know if my films, whether it was *A Stranger is Watching* or *Spring Break*, would have been any better, but I could have learned a lot more if I had surrounded myself with different people. If I made mistakes after *Friday the 13th*, that maybe was the biggest.

With *Spring Break*, I was at the point where I wasn't learning anymore from these people. What happens is, after you have success, you try and make commitments to the people who make commitments to you. You try to be loyal. When everybody starts off working for nothing and you're chasing this dream, and all of a sudden your ship comes in, it would seem wrong to just leave these people behind. But, of course, that's what everybody does.

VICTOR MILLER: I ended up suing Sean over *Friday the 13th*. My union was trying to get what was owed me, so I had to. And this was not for residuals, but the sequels, the cable showings and everything else. So I sued Sean, and Sean had to sue Georgetown. Getting money out of Phil Scuderi was always troublesome. I'm not a lawyer. Whatever my guild did, it did it the right way and I eventually got my money in 1988; it was a long time coming.

I would still probably hold Sean up for a point or two. I did bring up that subject to him way back when, and he said, "I can't afford you, I haven't got any points." That seems to be an ongoing problem that I hear about Sean. But anything I signed, I signed. I am not saying anybody pulled the wool over my eyes. But the stories I hated to hear later on were, "Well, George Lucas gave a point to the costume woman on *Star Wars*." And here I am, the screenwriter, and I don't have any points at all on *Friday the 13th*. So then I had to work, whereas Sean did not need to after that.

But I think Sean is going to be very surprised by this interview because I have nothing but good things to say about him. I mourn the loss of our friendship. I think we were the best for each other, and maybe history is bearing that out, I don't know. He gave me strength where I was weakest and I did the same for him. There was a wonderful shorthand that we had—we could use words or phrases that nobody else in the room understood. It was a symbiotic relationship that I never had before and have never had again.

3.

A New Dimension in Terror

Bolstered by the success of its first sequel, *Friday the 13th* had managed to survive its sophomore slump. Even if the filmmakers' decision to resurrect Jason Voorhees from the depths of Crystal Lake was a contrivance that critics—and even the most stalwart horror fans—found hard to swallow, the profits generated by *Part 2* were more than enough to convince Paramount Pictures that a third picture was a no-risk investment. The silhouetted image of a masked figure, brandishing a knife, with the words "Friday the 13th" splashed across a movie poster were a guarantee to sell tickets and bring in at least a strong opening weekend at the box office. But any new entry in the series had to compete not only with past success but rapidly fading interest in the slasher film itself. Aside from 1981's *Halloween II*, no other offering in the genre had generated the ticket sales of *Friday the 13th*. And no slasher film villain, including Jason Voorhees, had yet become truly iconic. There was also a vacancy in the leadership role of piloting the creative direction of future *Friday*s. After the departure of Sean Cunningham from the series, the opportunity was ripe for a changing of the guard as *Part 3* began pre-production at the end of 1981. The only question was: who would step up to the plate and apply for the job?

DENNIS MURPHY, Co-Producer, *Part 2*: At the end of filming *Part 2*, Frank Jr. came to me and said, "I have two job possibilities after this show. One of them is that I could be Robert Evans' assistant on his next movie. Or, I can produce my first film. Could you give me some advice?" I said, "Produce your first film." I had no idea it was going to be *Friday the 13th Part 3*.

FRANK MANCUSO, JR., Producer: The creative impetus of the early movies, certainly the second one, was Phil Scuderi. He was the most vocal about having input. The one guy I really don't have any experience with is Sean Cunningham. I might have met him, but I'm sure I wouldn't recognize him if I stepped on his foot. The person I originally started talking to the most was Bob Barsamian. He also had a daughter, Lisa, who was involved with the production. Then Bob would talk to Phil, and as Bob started carrying back to Phil more of the things I said and did, I started to get more involved with Phil. I'd say that certainly from the end of the second movie through the third movie, I dealt primarily with Phil.

Phil couldn't really pay me on *Part 2* because of the budget of the movie—nobody got paid much. But they gave me some points as a thank you for my participation. It ended up working out great. Subsequent to that on *Part 3*, Phil said, "It's yours—go do with it what you want." It started moving away from Phil and he started giving me larger parameters to operate in. I also happened to be in a unique situation, because as I continued to make these films my father continued to move up the ladder at Paramount. And I would say that each side's familiarity with me made them comfortable with the fact that it was okay that Paramount wasn't really involved. They knew I wouldn't act in a way that hurt them. I would never participate in something that would con them or steal money from them. The nature of who I was helped everyone get over the hump because otherwise, at that time, with negative pick-ups, there were so many scams where people were ripping off studios left and right.

GEORGE MANSOUR, Distributor, Esquire Theaters: It wasn't until after the second film that Paramount showed a vested interest in the *Friday the 13th* series, and wanted to back the movies directly. I think the last one any of the guys from Boston got any producing credit on was *Part 3*. After that, Paramount just sent them a check. "Here's some money for the title and we'll make the movie. Now go away!" But Phil Scuderi and Bob Barsamian were close with Frank Mancuso, Sr., and there were deals made for other pictures aside from *Friday the 13th* as well. There was a very incestuous thing going on. Frank Mancuso, Sr. was an executive at a big company, and while this was not shady, it wasn't exactly super-legitimate. It wasn't the kind of thing that Gulf & Western, who owned Paramount, wanted to be associated with, necessarily. But the studio made tons of money off of the first two. And I think Mancuso also profited personally from it.

FRANK MANCUSO, SR., VP Distribution, Paramount Pictures: *Friday the 13th* was not generally a product that a studio like Paramount would be interested in producing. That's number one. The creative executives just wouldn't have been attracted to that material. And second, the studio wouldn't know how to produce it anyway. They would spend way too much money. Independent film-makers like Georgetown Productions, who are in the business of selling their films, they are very cost conscious. Because they're putting up the risk money and hoping that someone will acquire their product, and their return on their investment is dependent upon that. And for the studio making the acquisition, that's exactly where you wanted it. Because then you usually got a break on the price you were paying for it.

One of the questions that continues to be asked is whether Paramount produced these movies. I would never have allowed Paramount to do that. That is simply a false assumption, one probably more due to the fact that my son produced so many of them. But it is not true. It would have cost us twice as much to make the films had they been studio productions, just the overhead alone. *Friday the 13th* movies were and should be like rebel films, where you take a camera and you go into the woods and you just shoot. And if your camera breaks down, you have to shut down for a couple of hours and get a new camera, whereas if you were a studio production you'd have five cameras already standing by as backup. It was simply a whole different culture.

One charge that has plagued the Friday the 13th *series since its inception is that they are not movies at all, but rather a series of creatively staged murder sequences caught on film—cynical exploitations successful only because of a grotesque gimmick. But* Friday the 13th *had been conceived from the start to excite the senses of its audience as much as involve them with its story and characters. And one good gimmick always deserves another. Enter 3-D.*

The concepts of three-dimensional photography had been around since the turn of the 20th century, but the widespread exhibition of full-length, theatrical 3-D motion pictures would not gain commercial acceptance until the early 1950s. But like most of the fads Hollywood had concocted during the decade to seduce Americans away from their television sets, the 3-D craze was short-lived, and by the end of the '50s the process was all but extinct. Fewer than a dozen full-length 3-D features were produced over the next two decades, all of them flops.

Then, like a phoenix from the ashes, 3-D returned in June 1981, with the success of a low-budget quickie from Spain called Comin' At Ya! *An unexceptional comedy western enlivened only by the novelty of its three-dimensional effects, the film still managed to gross over $12 million (back when tickets still cost three bucks a pop) and became one of the surprise hits of the season. Within a few weeks, independents and major studios alike announced over two dozen 3-D motion pictures. 3-D was back, and drawing in audiences of all ages, from nostalgia-starved adults longing to recapture the cinematic thrills of their youth, to a new generation running out to see what their parents' fuss was all about. The makers of* Friday the 13th *had finally found the fresh hook they needed for* Part 3.

STEVE MINER, Director: With the *Friday the 13th* films, we had always made a conscious decision to make the same movie over again, only each one would be slightly different. And I had always been intrigued with the concept of 3-D. As a kid, one of my earliest memories is of my father taking me to see *Fort Ti*, a three-dimensional film. So it occurred to me that a *Friday Part 3* and 3-D would be a perfect combination. I also had a feeling that this might be the last one. To be honest, that is what I was hoping. I was also simply anxious to direct another film. So that is what brought me back for *Part 3*.

FRANK MANCUSO, SR.: The sameness of the content, if you will, often cried out for a hook to hang the advertising on. You'll even notice that, after *Part 2*, we suddenly started to add more to the title than just a number, whether it be "in 3-D," or "The Final Chapter." It was almost like a wink—and it was definitely intentional.

The idea for the 3-D was born out of the fact that the process is so visceral, and horror movies are so visceral. I thought of my first memories of seeing *House of Wax* in 3-D. The interesting thing about the *Friday the 13th* films is that, for me, they often play as much as a comedy as horror. Not camp—at least back then—but in terms of the dynamic of the experience: the screaming in the theater, the people jumping out of their seats, and then the laughter from the audience, not at the movie, but at the reactions of each other towards the movie. It was as an

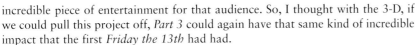

incredible piece of entertainment for that audience. So, I thought with the 3-D, if we could pull this project off, *Part 3* could again have that same kind of incredible impact that the first *Friday the 13th* had had.

And it *was* a project to pull that off, because at that time 3-D in the theaters was non-existent. We literally would have to create the projectors, install the screens and school the operators on how to project it. And it would be a massive release on over a thousand screens. It wasn't a *House of Wax* in two hundred theaters or whatever. This had to be across the board. We could not open a *Friday the 13th* on just a handful of screens. It was always about that huge opening weekend.

FRANK MANCUSO, JR.: Going with 3-D was more of a nod to the overall experience, and our belief that this probably would be the last one. Remember, at that point this wasn't a "franchise" in today's sense of the word. It really was about a carnival atmosphere of, "Let's just go out, have fun, and be done with it." The only problem was that at the time, everybody had a different 3-D system. So we hired this guy, Marty Sadoff, to come out and work on the movie and who was, at the time, probably as knowledgeable as anybody could be about the 3-D process.

MARTIN JAY SADOFF, 3-D Supervisor: I had always been fascinated by 3-D ever since I was ten or eleven years old, when my dad took me to see *The Creature From the Black Lagoon*. I had to sleep with the lights on for a week. I never forgot it.

I had grown up in Buffalo, where we were Frank Mancuso, Sr.'s neighbors. At the time he ran the Paramount branch in Buffalo. One day I invited him to come

Left: Director Steve Miner takes a break during filming *Friday the 13th Part 3* in 3-D.

Top: 3-D Supervisor Martin Jay Sadoff (seated) and crew prepare for the day's work as Steve Miner (far right) looks on. Notice the title on the slate reads "Crystal Japan"—the code name under which *Part 3* was filmed.

Middle: Jason and crew (clockwise from left): Richard Brooker (in makeup), director Steve Miner, Camera operator Eric Van Haren Noman, associate producer Peter Schindler, script supervisor Kathleen Newport, camera operator Steve Slocomb, and director of photography Gerald Feil.

Bottom: Producer Frank Mancuso, Jr., grabs a quick nap.

Friday the 13th Part 3's elaborate lodge set was built from the ground up. Seen here both in use (**overleaf**) and under construction (**opposite page, top**).

and see this 3-D test I shot. He said, "If I ever become the head of Paramount Pictures, I'll take you to L.A. and we'll make a movie." And that was the end of it, because I always thought he would become the head of distribution at Paramount. Instead, he became the head of Paramount itself.

Then around late 1981, I get a call from Tony Bishop, who would be one of the producers on *Part 3*, and he says, "I was told to call you. We were thinking of doing a *Friday the 13th* in 3-D." I went right on salary for Frank Jr. My job was to pick a 3-D system and figure out how to coordinate the glasses, and if we were going to make all those glasses, how would we get glasses to theaters? How many of the projectors had to be modified?

All this had to go into it before they actually made the decision to make the movie, because Frank Sr. really made the decision that Paramount was really going to try and revive 3-D. If they were going to put it into major theaters, they were going to do it right. We got everybody involved—projector companies, screen companies. It turned into a mammoth challenge.

STEVE MINER: We looked at all the systems when we started, and the consensus of opinion was that they were all difficult. There was no state of the art where 3-D was concerned at the time, because all the systems are from backyard inventors who were piecing them together.

We ending up using the Marks 3-D system, an "over and under single strip" process, meaning that the left eye and the right eye are printed one above the other on a single, full 35mm frame. You have two lenses on one camera, and photograph the image on one piece of film, which, of course, makes everything easier in the editing and post-production stages. That's the way we did *Part 3*, and I believe we were the first feature film to be shot with that system.

MARTIN JAY SADOFF I met this guy named Mortimer Marks in Toronto, who was playing around with 3-D. He had put together an Arri-2C camera, which was an early Arriflex camera that was hand-held, and figured out a way to shoot single-strip

35mm on it that could focus and converge in different places. It was totally different than the way 3-D had traditionally been done. With the Marks system, the distance between your eyes would always remain the same based on the focal points of the lenses. The camera saw like your eyes saw. It was the first 3-D camera I had ever seen like this.

GEORGE HIVELY, Editor: Did you ever see that movie *Short Circuit*, with the robot with the two eyes? That's kind of what the camera looked like.

GERALD FEIL, Director of Photography: At the time, Mike Nichols was considering doing *Peter Pan* in 3-D, and I had spent the previous six or seven months traveling all over the country looking at different 3-D systems. Unfortunately, the rights were not available so that project was killed. But here I was with all this exciting new research and all this confusing information and disinformation about 3-D. And I had also just finished doing a film, *Let's Spend the Night Together*. Steve Miner had seen it, and I had met him at some event in New York and told him about my research. He asked me if I'd meet him the next day and talk about *Part 3*—probably because I'd done a couple films that had some legs and some credibility. And although I had not done a 3-D picture before, I was always interested in the technology and particularly in the storytelling aspect. 3-D is always a sleight of hand, it's all about suspension of disbelief. Which is what dramatic film is all about, so I was very happy to be asked to do it.

Although their filmmaking team was falling into place, neither Steve Miner nor Frank Mancuso, Jr. were completely satisfied with the initial script for Friday the 13th Part 3. *Phil Scuderi had hired Martin Kitrosser—who served as script supervisor on the first two* Fridays—*and his wife, Carol Watson, to co-write the screenplay. The scenario they created deviated little from the established* Friday the 13th *formula: Jason was back and still stalking the community of Crystal Lake, this time setting his sights on a group of carefree vacationers who have set up camp nearby, blissfully unaware of the*

horrors to come. But Miner and Mancuso, in their hope to streamline the script to highlight the three-dimensional effects, drafted a young Romanian-born writer named Petru Popescu to perform an uncredited rewrite. The result was that Part 3 again replicated the formula of the previous two films while injecting broader humor, upping the film's body count to an even dozen, and developing a beefed-up backstory for Jason, including a thinly-developed subplot that suggested a previously unexplored sexual aspect to the character.

Yet despite the best efforts of no less than three screenwriters, the immense technical requirements of the 3-D process commanded every second of the filmmaker's attention—often to the detriment of everything—and everyone—else. It has been said that horror films are not an actor's medium and, in retrospect, many of the cast members of Part 3 recall their experiences on the film as a rueful resignation to the demands of the technology. Part 3 would also see a location change for the budding franchise, with the production moving to California. The result was a noticeable shift in tone from the previous two installments in the series.

FRANK MANCUSO, JR.: Part 3 was the first Friday to be shot on the West Coast, and I'd like to be able to say it was some sort of big aesthetic decision. But it really was because the whole 3-D thing required, in my view, being in Los Angeles. I wanted to have more control, and we needed experts in the field right there in case we got into real trouble. I just felt more comfortable there. And Phil, who was off working on the script with Marty Kitrosser, was cool with that, so that became the location for the next one.

ROBB WILSON KING, Production Designer: Some people have complained that in Part 3, it's obvious it is the West Coast, but what can you do? It allowed us to do something different from the previous Friday movies, because we had a chance to build all the locations from the ground up. There was only one scene, the convenience store with the gang members, where we were in another location that was practical. The rest of it we created.

For the rest of the film, the script called for mountain cabins or something. I said, "That is not unique enough. I think we have to create a camp lodge—that would be really interesting." And we also needed to find a canyon that looked foresty rather than like a desert. So we found this great place in Saugus, California called the Valuzet Movie Ranch. They became like partners in the film. I think we had about $140,000 for the whole deal, which wasn't a lot for what I just described. We were begging and screaming and all that stuff. But we did it with the partnership of a lot

Friday the 13th Part 3 in 3-D was the first major production to make use of a camera system known as the Louma crane (**middle**). "I was originally told that, with 3-D, you couldn't move the camera, but that turned out not to be true," says Steve Miner. "I used the Louma extensively, which gives the film some very unusual camera movements. I think that's one of its real strengths—you feel that you're really going *through* places." Martin Jay Sadoff explains the technology: "Everything was done via motion control: the focus-pulling, the convergence—all by servo motors from this big truck. That was pretty avant garde in an era when everybody still rode with the camera. Every shot was done electronically, by crane."

The technology was not without its headaches, however. "The Louma created a lot of frustration because it's an imperfect device," recalls actor Paul Kratka. "One time it fell down (**above**), which was a real crisis situation, because you don't think of people coming close to being injured making a movie." Still, the production was able to retain its sense of humor. "The crew had t-shirts made one day," laughs Kratka. "They said, 'I Hate the Louma!'"

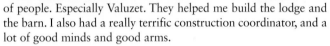

of people. Especially Valuzet. They helped me build the lodge and the barn. I also had a really terrific construction coordinator, and a lot of good minds and good arms.

GERALD FEIL: Robb is astonishingly talented. He's a terrific guy with the ability unlike any other production designer I've ever known to take whatever limitations there were and turn them into something really brilliant. The sets were designed so the corners of the floor would come out, where people could actually walk out of the screen. Even the lake itself was built forced-perspective, because we simply didn't have the room or the ability to create a real lake—that's the reason those scenes are only shot from one angle.

MARTIN JAY SADOFF There was so much thought that went into the planning of this movie that people don't realize. Nothing was an afterthought. Everything—the set design, the costumes—was done with 3-D glasses on.

ROBB WILSON KING: My favorite word for that movie was "cantilevered." It's sleight of eye—things that come at you are exaggerated to be larger than they are. I wanted the 3-D to exist constantly, which is why we built the entire lodge—three stories tall and huge—on a lake in forced-perspective. Even the whole front deck was angled. We did that with some of the rooms, too—we wanted to give the feeling that the walls could crush you, that it was suffocating. Upstairs, the bookcases all moved and turned. It was pretty interesting design-wise and construction-wise. And the coolest find of the movie was that circular staircase in the lodge—I'm really proud of that.

I also designed the lodge and the lake to be in specific proximity to each other, so that we'd always know the amount of time it would take one of our scared victims to run from here to there. We didn't want to make it too far, so in screen time you could see where they were coming from and where they were going. Then, with everything juxtaposed, it would create the kind of tension that we needed.

PETRU POPESCU, Screenwriter: I was based in L.A. and a student at the American Film Institute at the time. I had written a number of scripts and I was starting to write fiction again. I always thought of myself as writing prose, but I was struggling and needed a job. Through my agent I met Steve Miner and Frank Mancuso, Jr., who was an extremely young producer. They were doing a film in 3-D, and as is a common thing to hear as a screenwriter, they said, "We have a screenplay but it needs some work." There was a first draft and they didn't like it. They wanted somebody to pull it together and restructure it.

Before we started production, Steve Miner screened a few 3-D movies for us, and I saw Alfred Hitchcock's *Dial 'M' for Murder* for the first time. Do you remember the scene with the scissors, where the guy tries to strangle Grace Kelly with her stockings? She was lying backwards on a desk and reaching right out towards the audience. I said to myself, "This is what *Part 3* is—right here!" There was nothing to rewriting the script—the previous writers had done at least a decent job, but I ended up writing three drafts. I suggested close-ups and what people had in their hands and certain angles so things could push toward the camera. No one paid much attention to whether it was realistic.

I was never under any pressure to flesh out the characters, only to work on the circumstances of how the next kid gets slashed. There was definitely a discussion of types: "This guy has to be a good guy. This one has to be a bad girl. This one smokes. This one is sexually experienced." Those decisions were made very quickly. Nobody agonized over any of this. Because a lot of the movie is a field trip of sorts. You're out in nature, hiding behind a bush and there is the killer. So the relations between the characters are inane. There's an obligatory amount of sex, or suggestion that some of these people are couples. Because when one of them gets it, it's obligatory that the other one gets it, too. But even then, it's on the most superficial level.

If you compare the *Friday* films to say, the *Dirty Harry* movies, those have a wealth of complexity. You have a society, a bureaucracy, a system where there are problems, and this man, who happens to be a conservative right-winger in the service of society. Those kinds of premises are a lot more demanding. While a film like *Part 3* has a basic intellectual premise, in the way the killing and the victims of the killings were portrayed, it is extremely simplistic.

LARRY ZERNER, "Shelly": I was eighteen and a struggling actor. I hadn't done anything professionally. I was working for one of those research companies at the time, handing out movie tickets in Westwood to a screening of *The Road Warrior*. I was standing on a corner and these two people came up to me, Marty Kitrosser and Carol Watson. They said, "Excuse me, are you an actor? We wrote *Friday the 13th Part 3* and we think you'd be perfect!" I looked just like I did in the movie, and they took one look at me and said, "That's Shelly." Pretty amazing. I got discovered on a street corner. Me and Lana Turner.

TRACIE SAVAGE, "Debbie": By the time of *Friday the 13th Part 3* I was basically out of the business. I had worked as a child actress my whole life and knew all the pitfalls—that you could be a huge star today and no one tomorrow. So I was focusing on school and not really going out on interviews anymore. But my mother had started The Savage Agency, which to this day is one

Actress Cheri Maugans found the experience of working with the special effects makeup "a riot! We had to get to the makeup shop at six o'clock in the morning. And there I am, drinking my coffee, next to a dummy of Steve Susskind just dangling in front of me, covered in blood with a hatchet in his chest. All these macabre things—it was hilarious."

Opposite page, right: Although uncredited on the final film, legendary effects artist Stan Winston (far left) created the initial makeup designs for Jason. Here, he poses with the late actor Steve Susskind, a "dummy Jason," and director Steve Miner.

of the biggest kids' agencies in town. She called and said, "Hey, Tracie, there's an interview for a horror movie. It will film late in the spring, it won't interrupt your classes and it might be kind of a fun thing to do before you move away, and to get you some money to pay for college."

So I met with Frank Mancuso, Jr. and the casting directors. They were downplaying the *Friday the 13th* name. It was all hush-hush, but we all knew what it was. How could I not do it? What a fun movie to do as my last acting job before I was officially out of the business, and it would be something to carry with me and tell my kids about. I couldn't resist.

DAVID KATIMS, "Chuck": To be honest, I thought the script was pretty poor. It didn't make any sense. All they mentioned when I went in to audition was that they were going with a Tommy Chong look and sound for my character, so I just worked on that dialect. And I didn't have a beard and I didn't have long hair. After the audition, all Steve Miner said was, "Start growing your hair and start growing your beard."

When my agent called she was very excited. She said, "You've got a horror movie!" I thought, "Great, I've always wanted to do porn." Then she said it would pay $40,000, so I rolled up my morals, smoked them and said, "Yeah, I can play that."

PAUL KRATKA, "Rick": Tracie Savage's mother, Judy, was my agent, and David Katims' agent as well. We all studied together and all kind of got hooked up together. I went in to read for the part of Andy, and the casting directors said, "You're not right for that, but you're just right for the lead. We'd like you to come back

and meet the producer and the director. And by the way, let me tell you a little about this character, Derek"—at the time, that was his name in the script—"He lives up in the mountains. He's a carpenter. So dress accordingly."

When I came back, I wore blue jeans and work boots and a t-shirt and this parka-type thing. And I was carrying a couple of two by fours and a skillsaw. Steve Miner and Frank Mancuso, Jr. just looked at each other—it was right on the mark for them. That sealed the deal right there.

NICK SAVAGE, "Ali": I had never even heard of *Friday the 13th* before. I don't even like horror movies; they're not my cup of tea. And this was *Part 3* I was going to be in? But my agent sent me to this audition anyway, for a gang member. And I had just bought a motorcycle, so I rode it right up to the window of where they were holding the casting sessions. Steve Miner looked down to me on my bike and just said, "Okay." But hey, at the time, I was grateful for the part. Never turn down a job. There is no small part—just small actors.

PETRU POPESCU: I went to some of the casting sessions and I saw that there were boys and girls who gave good readings and those who gave bad readings, but it didn't matter. They were hired for their look, not for how they said the words.

PAUL KRATKA: I remember they were still trying to find the lead girl right up until the last minute. They kept bringing me in, week after week, for readings with all these different actresses. They really wanted Amy Steel from *Part 2*, but she was unavailable.

This page/opposite page: The young, carefree visitors to Higgins Haven, unaware of the horrors to come: heroine Chris Higgins (Dana Kimmell, background); Chris and love interest Rick (Kimmell and Paul Kratka, top); young lovers Debbie and Andy (Tracie Savage and Jeffrey Rogers, above); practical joker Shelly and his blind date, Vera (Larry Zerner and Catherine Parks, opposite page, left) and the Cheech & Chong clones Chuck and Chili (David Katims and Rachel Howard, opposite page, bottom right).

"I think the pairing of the couples was interesting," says Paul Kratka. "I think Tracie and Jeffrey were like the beefcake couple, and David and Rachel the comic relief. But Larry and Catherine—that was such an interesting dichotomy. That's not a couple you'd necessarily expect to be matched up. But I thought they went really well together. We all did." The atmosphere among the cast remained friendly throughout the often grueling, technically complex twelve-week shoot. "As a group, we were pretty tight, and all feeling lucky to be there," remembers Larry Zerner. "For most of us it was our first, and only, big movie. We had a lot of down time, and we would hang out in these trailers—hunting wagons, they called them. So we'd be just sitting around, talking a lot and having fun."

And plenty of time for extracurricular activities. "The crew gambled every day," laughs David Katims. "A match-the-pot game that could become very vicious. Frank Mancuso, Jr. lost $400 one time, and was grumbling about it as we were walking back to the set. The AD goes, 'Yeah, but you lost an hour of production time just playing the game, which is worth about $35,000.' Frank just says, 'Yeah, but I *lost.*' It was a matter of pride. He would spend several thousand dollars just to win a few hundred bucks!"

AMY STEEL, "Ginny Field," *Part 2*: You know, sometimes I look back on my career and wonder. They really wanted me for *Part 3*. They didn't have a script, but they were just going to show me some sort of outline. Then my agents got involved, and I don't know whether it was a money issue or a script issue, but I didn't do it. I think I just wanted to do different things. When you're young and cocky, you think that another great movie is going to be coming along, that Steven Spielberg is going to be banging on your door. But now I look back and I say, "I should have just gone for it. I should have done *Part 3*."

DANA KIMMELL, "Chris Higgins": Someone had seen me in another movie I'd done, *Sweet Sixteen*, with Bo Hopkins and Susan Strasburg. I met with the casting director and he immediately took me over to meet with Steve Miner. And by the time I got home they were already negotiating with my agent.

PETRU POPESCU: Almost every character in the *Friday* movies act like they don't have a head on their shoulders. They see something that says "Don't Enter" and that's exactly where they go. Only with the lead character do you have someone who is a bit more reasonable, who says, "Okay, maybe we shouldn't." The character of Chris Higgins was at least somewhat creatively satisfying to write, because she had a past. She was both easier and harder to create—I spent the most time on her. I imagined this young American girl, who, even though she isn't very grounded sociologically or whatever, at least she has a history with the monster.

The biggest discussions were around what was the exact nature of her backstory with Jason. We talked about a certain type of sensibility and drama—would a rape take the audience out of the fantasy, even though all the killings do not? We will accept mutilation of the body, but not the notion of sexual penetration—killing can be entertaining and rape cannot be. If you see a head roll in these movies, it's okay. It's like play. But if you see someone invaded or soiled—that's not amusing for anyone. So we left Chris's past encounter with Jason ambiguous.

DANA KIMMELL: I had no clue what *Friday the 13th* was. Growing up, I always loved scary movies, but I was not familiar with these. I'd heard of them, but I'd never seen any of them. Once I got the part, Steve Miner sent me home with tapes of the first two, just to see what I had gotten myself into. And they were already shooting. So I read through the script and was on set in a day or two. It was really a quick thing. So there wasn't a lot of discussion until we kind of got into the actual shooting.

It's funny, but apparently I did an interview for *Fangoria* magazine a few years ago where I talked about all these changes I requested in the movie. I honestly don't even remember giving that interview. But I do remember having a meeting with Frank Mancuso, Jr. They had a couple scenes in there about how Rick and Chris had stayed out all night, and there was a line that they had made love that night. I said to Frank and Steve Miner, "I'd be a lot more comfortable if we didn't talk

"I was amazed that the description of Shelly in the script described me perfectly—physically, emotionally, mentally. Steve Miner saw that. He said, 'Don't put on a character, just be yourself.'" Larry Zerner

about that." And they said, "Just do whatever you want," and rearranged it. I knew this series has a lot of young followers. I just thought it was good not to promote that kind of thing so much. And nobody notices, anyway.

PAUL KRATKA: I was twenty-seven at the time and I had this vision of having a torrid romance with the leading lady—and it turns out she's Mormon. Dana was just the sweetest, straightest arrow possible. A really nice girl, professional and courteous. I never got any sense that she was objecting to anything. But I can't believe Paramount would acquiesce anyway—it's not like a hundred other girls in Hollywood couldn't play her role. It wouldn't have changed the outcome of the movie, one way or the other.

DAVID KATIMS: It is understandable why Dana would set boundaries. This isn't Shakespeare. The thinking is pretty much that if you do something like this, you are not pretending that it's going to be the greatest piece of character drama. And for someone like Tracie Savage, who ended up doing some nudity in the movie, it is even a bigger decision.

TRACIE SAVAGE: Each person took care of themselves. Dana had no say over what was happening. She wouldn't have had that authority. The priority is to scare the hell out of people, and if they have an actress who was concerned about art they're going to say, "Sorry. We'll find somebody else."

I have no qualms about the nudity. It was very minimal, and there are hardly any movies on the air today where you don't see someone nude. And since then, as a joke, friends have done blooper reels for me where they've taken my nude scene and slowed it down frame-for-frame and then played it for all my friends. But I just laugh. It's not a big deal.

I did put my foot down in the scene where I'm supposed to be having sex with Andy; they wanted to have a tight shot of our faces as we were having an orgasm. The thought of that horrified

me, because that's something that's just so inappropriate. I did not want them to have a close-up shot of our faces as we're in ecstasy. That would have embarrassed me, especially as I knew I was about to pursue a more legitimate professional career as a journalist. So I just said, "Absolutely not. This is a horror movie, it's not an X-rated movie." So what they ended up doing was slowly panning down to our feet, and you saw our feet jerk as if we had just … well, you know.

DAVID KATIMS: When the material is lacking, you have to rely on yourself to make the character interesting. Chuck was definitely going to be made a comedian, so I expected to work on some of the physical comedy that we could have come up with. But, unfortunately, that was pretty much abandoned. Not that it would have made a ton of difference, but really, if we had gone with this guy as a real stoner, and using that as a comedic foil, it would have been a lot of more interesting. Have him be so wasted that he is avoiding Jason by accident, out of a drug stupor. Smoke a joint and fall on his face and have an ax fly by, things like that. Not that the movie needed it, as obviously it was very successful. But why not make it even better?

No one wanted to get into that. Steve Miner was not on top of his directing game yet. I remember him saying, "Well, try doing it different" without having a clue as to what in particular. Because my thinking is, "I'm an instrument for you, tell me how you want me to play it and I'll give it a shot." I am sure Steve's gotten much better. And he was a nice enough guy. I just didn't have the balls to say, "You know, it really would work better this way." I just did whatever they said.

LARRY ZERNER: I didn't have the temerity to stand up and ask to do anything different. I did have one big improv moment, though. Remember when I say, "Bitch" after being rejected by Vera? I said that one line right before Steve Miner was going to say "Cut!" And everybody laughed. So they kept it in.

TRACIE SAVAGE: The key priority was making sure that the 3-D effects worked. It didn't matter how the lines were delivered. It didn't matter if we stumbled or fumbled. It didn't matter if our performance was not perfect. We never did a second take because "the actor" felt it could be better. The main concern—and it was a good concern—was making sure the 3-D effects worked. And it was a very technical, very difficult thing to do. It could take two to three hours to set up lighting for certain scenes. Then we'd do one take and it was, "Okay, moving on!"

PAUL KRATKA: At times it was palpable—you could feel Steve Miner was adhering to a certain schedule and that he was aware of the budget. One time I was frustrated that I didn't get to do another take. And his comment was, "Paul, I have to be candid with you. I'm just trying to get this thing in on time. This is not the type of movie where you get endless takes to do what you think feels good in performance. It's *Friday the 13th*." It could be frustrating. Even though it's a silly horror movie, you want to do multiple takes so you can try different shadings. And there was none of that on this film.

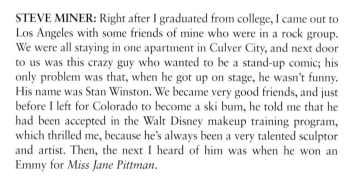

No one involved in the production of Friday the 13th Part 2 was fully satisfied with the look of Jason Voorhees that they had created. But if nothing else, it was clear that what had not so affectionately become known as "the bag" was no longer an option. The search was also on for yet another new actor to play Jason, an effort necessitated by the production's relocation to the West Coast. Coupled with another new makeup crew coming on board, radical shifts in the continuity and appearance of Jason were fast becoming a tradition of the series.

STEVE DASKAWICZ, Jason Stunt Double, *Part 2*: If you look at Freddy and *A Nightmare on Elm Street*, they used the same guy every time. But not *Friday*—because they don't want to pay more each time they use you. I was really shocked when I was told that if I wanted the job on *Part 3*, I would have to pay my own airfare out to California. And I wasn't going to do that. They said, "You don't understand, you're nobody." And I said, "No, I'm Steve Dash." Because the role wasn't that important to me. Hey, I have my morals.

RICHARD BROOKER, "Jason Voorhees": I had the weirdest audition. I actually answered an ad for the role in *Backstage West* the previous summer and never heard another word. Then totally out of the blue, in February or March, I got this phone call: "Will you come in for an interview?" I went down to the casting office and there were like fifteen of the biggest, buffest guys standing outside. I had no idea why they were there. I just walked straight in, saw two people behind the desk, and I said, "Hello, I'm Richard Brooker. I have a meeting at 2:00 p.m." It was the two casting guys. They said, "We're waiting for Steve Miner—would you mind waiting for a few moments?" So I went into this other room, sat down for a while and then Steve Miner came in and we chatted for a while. Then Steve turned around to the casting guys and said, "Book him." They said, "What about the actors outside?" Only then did I realize that the guys outside were also there for the interview. Steve just said, "Forget them. Send them home."

I didn't know it was going to haunt me for the next twenty-five years of my life.

DOUG WHITE, Special Makeup Effects: I had been involved in makeup effects since the early 1970s. I had mentored under Bert Holmes and Tom Burman, and had just started my own company before *Part 3* came along. I was actually working on this Canadian horror movie *Deadly Eyes* with Kenny Myers, who was the effects supervisor, and he was offered this job—we didn't know it was a *Friday the 13th*. But we went out to interview with the producers, and they said, "Here's the scenario. You're trapped on a farm, and think of everything there you could use to kill somebody. Come up with ten examples." So we went to lunch, came up with ideas, then came back and handed it over to them. They said, "Okay, ignore what we just said. Here's the script and this is what we're going to do." Then we found out it was *Part 3*, and in 3-D. Which actually helped us, because I had also just done this other 3-D movie called *Parasite*, with Demi Moore. So we got the job.

What was a little unusual was that when we started the show, we knew up front that they had actually already hired Stan Winston, although strictly to sculpt Jason's makeup. We would have to do a head cast of Richard Brooker, then deliver that to Stan, who would sculpt it and get approval for it. Then we'd make a mold of that and run all the appliances, bring them back to Stan, and Stan would paint them. Apparently, Stan had also done some uncredited work on *Friday the 13th Part 2*, and was a friend of Steve Miner.

STEVE MINER: Right after I graduated from college, I came out to Los Angeles with some friends of mine who were in a rock group. We were all staying in one apartment in Culver City, and next door to us was this crazy guy who wanted to be a stand-up comic; his only problem was that, when he got up on stage, he wasn't funny. His name was Stan Winston. We became very good friends, and just before I left for Colorado to become a ski bum, he told me that he had been accepted in the Walt Disney makeup training program, which thrilled me, because he's always been a very talented sculptor and artist. Then, the next I heard of him was when he won an Emmy for *Miss Jane Pittman*.

RICHARD BROOKER: I don't know the complete story, but originally Stan Winston was doing *Part 3*, and I had to go to his studio for days and days. They did a plaster cast of my head and all this other stuff, just on and on and on. Stan was also the guy

Above: The death of Debbie in *Part 3* that didn't quite come off as planned. "It was really hot on the set because we had so many lights," recalls associate producer Peter Schindler. "Poor Tracie Savage was sitting on her knees under the hammock beneath a fake body and latex neck. Well, the knife starts to come up, but instead of cutting through the fake neck, it just made a sort of tent—because the latex was melting. And there was no way to get the latex to cool down enough in the time we had to shoot the scene.. So that's why it never quite looked right."

Although the MPAA ratings board still weighed heavily on the minds of the filmmakers throughout production, *Part 3* had a relatively easy ride compared to its predecessor. "The MPAA was rough on *Part 2*, because the basic feeling was that the original film should have been rated an X," says director Steve Miner. "They were extremely unfair at times, and very subjective. But I think they eased up a little on *Part 3*."

"We submitted *Part 3* to the MPAA twice," elaborates editor George Hively. "But the cuts were actually not that severe. There were only a couple of gore scenes trimmed down, and even those cutaways were rather quick, and I feel, ultimately, actually made the scares more effective."

"I only remembered the cast by how I killed them. 'Oh, you were the poker. You were the spear gun...'" Richard Brooker

making the headpiece that I would have to wear. But by the time we started shooting, apparently somebody complained that Jason didn't look scary enough, so they brought in Doug White and his team to redesign the makeup.

DOUG WHITE: Stan wanted to do a new makeup technique on Jason because of the 3-D—I guess what you'd call a "pixilated" look, where the makeup was painted with all primary and secondary colors, and no mixing of anything else. But the producers and Steve Miner just weren't happy with it. But by then we were already shooting, and by the time it was decided that Jason's makeup needed to be resculpted Stan was no longer available. They also told me to ignore Carl Fullerton's Jason makeup from *Part 2*. They wanted a look closer to Tom Savini's work on the first one. So I was stuck with Stan's makeup and had to blend the two together. And some footage had already been shot of Jason, so the back of the Jason head had to match Stan's, yet the rest of the head had to look like an older version of Tom's. To be honest, it would have been nice to have kept better continuity with Jason between *Part 2* and *Part 3*, but at the same time the producers thought Carl's design was too far off base, largely because of the hair. As a child, Jason was completely bald, so they figured he should stay that way.

RICHARD BROOKER: Ultimately, there ended up being two different makeups for Jason. When we did the close-up stuff, there was something like eleven different appliances that they glued onto my face. That alone took six hours to apply. And for some of the scenes where you don't really see Jason, they had a "head mask" that was one big piece I could slip on and off, which was hot as hell. But the worst thing about the appliances was that we'd finish at six in the morning and everybody was tired and wanted to go home, and the makeup crew guys would rip it off my face like you wouldn't believe. My face was just raw. I'd soak my skin in some sort of orange liquid to soften it up, then I'd go home and go to sleep, and then come back and do it all over again. After two weeks my skin was like sandpaper.

DOUG WHITE: Richard was wonderful. An extraordinarily patient person when it came to the makeup. And he skulked really good. But the funny thing was, he was an ex-circus performer, and very funny, so in person, he was hardly menacing.

DAVID KATIMS: My memory of Richard was that he was the antithesis of terror. He's British and has this very refined voice, and every once in a while he would walk around with this hockey mask on, smoking a pipe and going, "Who am I going to kill now?"

RICHARD BROOKER: Steve Miner would say to me, "Jason is like the shark in *Jaws*. He doesn't have any motivation." But I don't necessarily agree with that. I studied acting for many years, and if you're playing a silent role and you can't express yourself with emotions, then what's the point? It doesn't matter whether you talk or not. If you're playing a role like that, the way you move and your body reactions can create a certain kind of character, which I think, hopefully, Jason in *Part 3* is.

DANA KIMMELL: That really was a challenge in and of itself—to make it scary because filming it wasn't a scary situation at all. That's probably the question I get asked the most by people: "My gosh,

Background: Barely glimpsed in the released film, the electrocution of Chuck (David Katims) was originally planned to be a much more elaborate effect. "They did some really interesting, pronounced makeup that you never saw," explains Katims. "The headband that I wore was scorched, my face had skin that was flailing off of it, blood was dripping out and it was very gory. It's a shame it didn't make it into the finished film."

were you frightened?" And I just look at them and say, "No, it was really fun!" It was awesome to see how the special effects were put together, and in Paul Kratka's case, what they did to make the eyeball pop out of his head. I was really fascinated by the mechanics of it all.

PAUL KRATKA: About halfway through the shoot, we switched to all nights and filmed the scene where Jason grabs me and crushes my head and my eyeball pops out. It was three o'clock in the morning, and it wasn't like we were on a soundstage. We were out in the mountains, with crickets and the cold, and you're walking from the trailer to where you're shooting, and it's some dark, unlit trail, and you've been on this film that has all this weirdness. Then they wheel out this mannequin of my upper body, head and face on a dolly. It looks exactly like me. It's very flesh-like, only collapsible so they can shoot multiple takes of the head crushing. That was spooky.

RICHARD BROOKER: The kills were probably the hardest things we had to shoot because the 3-D process necessitated so many multiple takes. It was not uncommon to do a simple stabbing sequence fifteen times. We spent hours and hours on the eyeball squeeze alone.

STEVE MINER: The toughest shot, and the one everyone remembers, was the eyeball. We needed the effect of an eyeball popping out into the audience. So, the makeup effects people put the eyeball on the end of a rod. When Jason squeezes the fake head, we just pushed the rod out to the camera lens. Then, I stood in back of the camera and told them to push it out in front of me. But, I closed one eye and didn't see the rod. We did it six or seven times until I realized that the 3-D system has two lenses, so the audience would see around the eyeball and see the rod. You don't have much fun making movies.

It is often impossible to determine at what exact moment an icon is born—and perhaps even harder to determine the originator of that icon. However, it remains without question that, as Part 3 began production, the most important step in the transformation of Jason Voorhees from slasher movie footnote into monster movie legend was about to take place. No one would ever look at a hockey mask in quite the same way again.

PETRU POPESCU: Usually in movies like this you try to justify or analyze a killer by looking at biographical explanations for why things happen. These people grew up underprivileged; they were this and that—that is sociologically interesting. But that's not *Friday the 13th.* I personally don't think Jason is a character at all. The only characters in that movie are the ones having reactions to Jason. Jason's basically a pretext for that knife attack.

I was not familiar with these films when I got the job. I had heard of them, certainly. But I hadn't seen them. But I did see *The Texas Chainsaw Massacre*—that was a brilliant inspiration. To put a mask on somebody like that, only then can you showcase them as an unnameable evil. That's what I tried to do, and that's what I thought these movies are about.

FRANK MANCUSO, JR.: I remember in *Halloween*, Michael Myers had a mask. That was certainly influential to the masking of Jason, because my experience with the folks in Boston were that they were very avid and keen moviegoers and they would pick up references to what was successful and try to spin it their own direction.

Part 2 had the bag. That was not good. But I was actually not involved with the decision to change the mask in *Part 3*. I just remember looking at tests of different masks and deciding on which one we should go with.

Despite having trained as an acrobat in his native Britain, six-foot three-inch stuntman Richard Brooker found filming *Part 3*'s murder sequences a physical challenge. "Because of the 3-D, some of the close-up stuff was an absolute nightmare," winces Brooker. "We'd have to do things again and again and again. That one scene where Rachel Howard gets stabbed with a poker (**below**)—just that one single shot took thirty-six takes to get it right. I'm standing in front of these hot lights with all of this makeup on, and wearing these heavy clothes, just dripping with sweat. And all I keep hearing is, 'Do it again!' I was there until two o'clock in the morning, just poking this girl."

"They used a stuntman when my dead body is propelled through the window," reveals actor Paul Kratka. "But because I was supposed to already be dead, the stuntman couldn't dive or really move at all. So they brought out this pneumatic ramp that propels whatever's standing on it—and they just shot him right through the window! Over and over and over, at least half a dozen times. He's hitting high, he's hitting low, and all the while they're trying to figure out the right trajectory. I just had to walk away—I couldn't watch it. I was so appalled, because if memory serves, the stuntman was paid $750 for that day's work. I was like, 'You couldn't pay me enough to do that.' Meanwhile, I had it easy. I just had to lie on the floor afterward (**top**), surrounded by breakaway glass shards and some fake blood on my face. But what that poor stunt guy had to go through!"

Above: "I always joke that I got the part because I scream really well," laughs actress Dana Kimmell, who stars in *Part 3* as heroine Chris Higgins. "That's all I did at my audition— scream!" Filming *Part 3*'s extended climax, although arduous, ultimately proved empowering for the young actress. "By then it was only emotional stuff—running and screaming. It became a survival thing. But I liked Chris because she fought back. I didn't want her to be a wimp. I wanted her to be someone who could survive—and she did."

SANDI LOVE, Costume Designer: A lot of the crew were Canadians and hockey fans, and they would have these hockey parties all the time. Those brought us all together. And I believe the concept for the idea was that, like a hockey mask protects a goalie, so too was the hockey mask a way of Jason protecting himself.

MARTIN JAY SADOFF: Now, this was the big deal of the movie—what was Jason going to look like? There were discussions and all these conceptualizations. Although it is important to remember that, at the time, no one thought these movies would endure as long as they did, so Jason's mask was really still an aside. Anyway, there is a scene in the movie where Steve Miner plays a news reporter doing a segment on TV, and which was shot very, very early on. It was actually done at the Samsung building on Wilshire and La Brea. That is the birthplace of the hockey mask. Because while Steve was off doing that, he called for a makeup test to be done, to see what the monster was going to look like and to make sure the 3-D worked and all that.

Well, no one really wanted to do the makeup. So the late Marty Becker, who was heading the effects on the film, came and said, "Well, we don't have anything, so let's put a goalie mask on him." And I used to keep my big red hockey bag with me, and I pulled a mask out. It was a Detroit Red Wings goalie mask—it was white and had a big red stripe down the middle. It didn't ultimately look much like what end up in the film—they poked holes in it and changed the markings. Then Marty Becker's team made the molds, and Robb Wilson King made various versions of it.

But the ironic thing is, it was never even meant to be a hockey mask in the first place. It was just supposed to be a way to figure out what Jason was going to look like. It was never going to be that.

PETER SCHINDLER: My recollection is that Steve Miner made the ultimate decision. I remember we shot a test with different masks, and that was the one Steve chose. It probably was everybody's idea and everybody wants the credit, but it was nobody in particular.

DOUG WHITE: Steve Miner saw the hockey mask and just loved it. And originally, we were just going to go with the old-fashioned hockey mask, but then I had built a fake Jason head and after we put the mask on it, we just said, "The mask looks awful small. We need to make it bigger." What you do to make something larger is put some VacuForm, which is a silicon ceramic fiber, over the original, which makes it bigger, then put another VacuForm over that, and so on. By the time we got to the third enlargement, I made a new mold of the mask so we could polish it up and expand it a little. And Terry Ballard, the technical advisor on the film, had already put the little red pieces on the face of the mask, which gave it that unique look. We ultimately made the masks not only for *Part 3*, but also *The Final Chapter*, because they wanted to get the old molds back.

ROBB WILSON KING: There wasn't just one hockey mask. We made different sizes to accommodate the 3-D—we created some that were oversized, for different angles, and they were fitted to Richard Brooker's face. So it really was a group creation. I certainly can't claim the hockey mask. I don't think any one person can.

LARRY ZERNER: It started as something my character would wear for a second. It just said in the script, "Jason wears a mask." Who knew it was going to be a trademark? There was no reference to go, "Oh, this mask is going to become the iconic horror symbol, along with Freddy's glove," or whatever. Although I was smart enough to ask, "Can I have the mask?" But they wouldn't give it to me.

RICHARD BROOKER: I went up to Steve Miner halfway through the production and said, "Can we just have a little scene in here where my face shows, so my mother actually believes I'm in the movie?" He goes, "No, no, no. You can't do that." So the next day he comes onto the set and he's carrying this little bag, and he says, "Here's a present for you." And I open the bag and it's a t-shirt, and on the back it says, "I Played the Monster in *Friday the 13th*." He says, "Wear this when you go back to see your mom."

As with the previous two films in the series, Friday the 13th Part 3 *would begin with a "prologue kill," a sequence before the main story begins, and usually not involving its lead characters, setting up that horror is about to return to the belea- guered community of Crystal Lake. This time, two owners of a local grocery store,*

"In the screenplay, my character had a different name, 'Derek.' But they changed it to 'Rick,' because it's one less syllable. And therefore more scream-able." Paul Kratka

fall prey to the wrath of Jason Voorhees. These sequences were the first to be shot on location in Newhall, California—only to have to be re-shot due to technical difficulties, the first sign that Part 3 would be no ordinary Friday the 13th.

As the production challenges on Part 3 mounted, exacerbated in large part by the complexities of shooting in 3-D, the atmosphere on the set grew more intense. Many of those who were there soon came to view the three-month shoot as an experience not to be enjoyed but endured. Some crew members required chemical stimulation merely to maintain the production's physically demanding and mentally exhausting schedule as the weeks of night shooting took their toll. Matters were not helped by the non-union status of the production, which offered the producers no organized support if job performance suffered. Personalities often clashed, and levity was a luxury that was rarely indulged. Part 3 remains, by many accounts, one of the more challenging shoots in the history of the franchise.

STEVE SUSSKIND, "Harold": I actually first met Steve Miner in the late 1960s. At that time he was a film editor and working part-time at a place called Pottery Barn. We weren't great buds or anything, but when I came to L.A. to pursue acting, a friend knew that Steve was doing this film, and called him to say, "Hey, why don't you use Steve Susskind?" That's how I got the role.

I'm the first kill in the movie—I get whacked in the chest with a cleaver. They had me rigged with a blood line across my chest over a piece of balsa wood that would greet the blade. Everybody behind the camera was wearing garbage bags because the blood was supposed to go everywhere. Then they call "Action!" I open the door, out comes the cleaver, it hits me square where it's supposed to and … only a little trickle. The tube that carried the blood ended up buried under the balsa wood. So all the blood went inside and all over my body. It was a mess. And not a really great omen, I guess.

CHERI MAUGANS, "Edna": At the time, I wanted to be Meryl Streep. I was interested in challenges—when you're a female at the age I was, there's the leading parts and the character parts. And the character parts are the ones that are interesting. So for me I had this whole idea of who Edna was. She was probably a cheerleader in high school but things just didn't work out for her the way she thought they were going to, and she ended up being a really frustrated mess. And there obviously was that sense of frustration in the written repartee between her and Harold.

So when I went into the audition I did not read the character as the stereotype that was written. And if you don't go in and be the character, you're not going to get anything in this business. So I came in with curlers in my hair, bad shoes, no makeup and a bathrobe. Steve Miner and I just laughed through the whole thing.

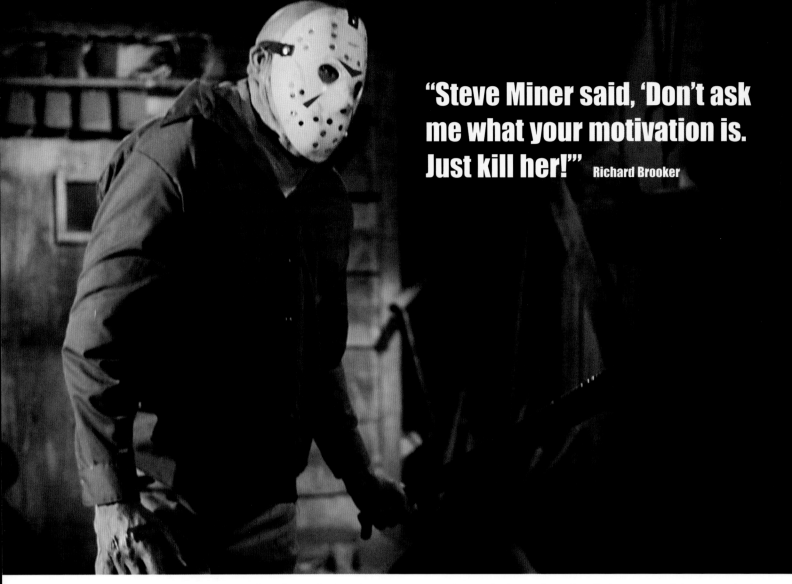

"Steve Miner said, 'Don't ask me what your motivation is. Just kill her!'" Richard Brooker

Then I walked on the set the first day, and when the writers got a look at me they made a beeline right for Steve. I knew what they were saying—I didn't fit the stereotype the way it was written, which was a fat girl who couldn't stop eating and had pimples in high school. That would have been who they would have cast. And I was not overweight, I was a pretty attractive girl. But Steve wasn't afraid of what anybody was going to say. And he wasn't afraid of his writers, obviously.

MARTIN JAY SADOFF Frank Sr. had come out to the set early on, when we were shooting the sequence where the kid goes into the grocery store. We're all set and ready to go, and Gerald Feil turns to his assistant Steve Slocomb and says, "Load camera one." And Steve replies, "You've got the film." Gerald says, "No, I told you to pick up the film." And Steve goes, "No, I told *you* to pick up the film." We've got all of the Paramount brass here and they forgot to bring the film. We had to have it brought in by helicopter. And this was like the second or third day of shooting!

STEVE SUSSKIND: The 3-D added hours to everything. One day, the only thing I did was sit down on the can, take a swig of booze and walk out of frame.

In the opening shot of the film the first time we did it, they explained to me that the camera would do a long tracking shot and a pan and so forth, and the camera would be right behind me. And it was timed so as I walked out of the store and into the yard, I'd knock over a pole that was holding up the clothesline. Then I would pick up the pole and aim its back end right into the camera. Well, the first time we did it, we did a run-through and got it on the first take. It was great.

Then we had to reshoot the whole opening of the movie. And not just the whole sequence with the pole, but the stuff in the grocery store, too. They said there was a problem with convergence on the 3-D lenses. And for whatever reason, I don't know if the marks were changed or what, but I could not nail the pole this time. Every time, it was just off left or off right or too high or too low. Finally, out of frustration—and you see it in the film—when I pick up the pole, I cheat and look behind me, to make sure I'm aiming it at the lens. And, of course, that's the one they used in the film.

LARRY ZERNER: It quickly became clear that most of the time the performances didn't matter. When we were shooting that scene at the convenience store with the gang members and I had to throw a wallet at the camera, it was, "Hit the camera!" Then after ten takes it was, "Hit the camera, asshole!"

And in the original script, the whole sequence with the gang members at the store was supposed to be much longer. After I knock over the motorcycles, there's this whole chase scene. Catherine Parks was supposed to be driving, and I was supposed to take a champagne bottle and pop it like a gun. Then it hits the gang members and they fly off their bikes. But it got cut for budgetary reasons. And then we had to reshoot all that stuff at the store anyway, because of technical problems.

ROBB WILSON KING: Making this thing was as scary as being in it. Every minute we had something that was weird, that wasn't quite right. We were plagued. For a while we had something terrorizing the set but we didn't know what it was. The lake was man-made—you'd see footprints in the sand of you just can't imagine what. And lots of snakes. Then things went missing. We

felt like the set was haunted. Although the ironic thing was that the hockey mask never went missing; I would have imagined that would have been the first thing any ghosts would have wanted.

PETER SCHINDLER, Associate Producer: I was pretty young at the time, I was thirty three years old. *Part 3* was not something I would have pursued, but I really liked Steve Miner, and it was a chance to work in 3-D. Although, it's funny, I honestly think that when you work on things like this—I mean, *Friday the 13th* is a pretty evil story—I sort of believe in karma and all this kind of stuff. It was just a very strange show to do. There was a lot of bad luck. Not a day went by that we didn't have a major production problem of some sort.

One Monday, Steve Miner and I returned to the set and walked into the lodge, and there was this hum. I thought, "Jeez, was there a light left on in here over the weekend?" Then a bee goes by. We don't think about it. More humming. We get closer to the wall and discovered that, over the weekend, what seemed like a million bees had made hives in the house. And that was the day where Dana and Tracie are supposed to walk in the lodge and have this conversation. But now we couldn't use the lodge because we had to bring in an exterminator, nor could we afford another day of shooting. So in the finished film, they are walking outside, in a field. That was a completely spur of the moment decision.

ROBB WILSON KING: We hired a mason to build this fireplace as part of the lodge set—it was huge. As a celebration for finishing the set, we lit our first fire in there, and we started getting smoked out. We couldn't breathe. Well, apparently, the mason hadn't gotten his last check, so he put a piece of glass in the funnel. If we hadn't lit the fireplace until actual shooting, it would have been devastating. Eventually, we threw a rock down the chimney and broke the glass. I learned from that experience that you have to pay your bills on time.

PAUL KRATKA: There were some real redneck crew members. They're blue collar and they have their own life and language and attitude. And on a movie set, everyone has

Above: Despite being on the losing end of Jason's machete, actor Nick Savage has fond memories of his character's duel to the death with Jason. "I had to go into the makeup shop a week earlier so they could make a cast of my arm and stuff it with bloody meat," says Savage. "It really did look real—I had to check my own arm after I saw it! Even now, children stop me in the supermarket, touch my arm, and go, 'Are you okay?'"

Opposite page: Outfitting Jason in 3-D proved a challenge for production designer Robb Wilson King. "We created a whole arsenal for Jason to pick from, and played a lot of tricks with angles and oversized killing instruments. And to seamlessly edit those things was difficult, because you don't want to give the illusion away. We often shot Jason holding a weapon four different ways, with three different sizes of instruments."

"Oh, my goodness!" laughs Dana Kimmell of filming *Part 3*'s climactic dream sequence. "Being dumped in the lake—it was supposed to be a quick one-take kind of a thing. Of course, we ended up having to do it several times." Mrs. Voorhees (**above**) was played by the wife of associate producer Peter Schindler. "That poor gal!" exclaims Kimmell. "All she had on was that makeup suit and the water was just freezing!"

Part 3 remains unique among the *Friday* films in that it is the only sequel whose characters never mention the name "Jason," leading many fans to wonder just who Kimmell's character thought she saw coming out of that lake. Quips Steve Miner: "Every story is left open just because of the greed factor. It doesn't matter if it makes sense or not!"

their specific jobs. One time I reached out to help this guy with his ladder. I was just trying to be helpful. And they really frowned upon that. It was a real no-no. When one of "those people"—the actors—offer to help, they can interpret that like, "Oh, you think I'm not doing what I'm supposed to be doing?" They thought I was a real dick for offering this really innocent, helpful thing.

One of the crew guys in particular—he played one of the cops at the end of the movie—took a dislike to me from day one, for whatever reason. And he was into guns. That was a big part of his life—he carried them and wore them. Then there was talk going around about the guns and whether or not they were really loaded. It could just be very uncomfortable.

DAVID KATIMS: The crew could have their fun with the actors. In the scene where my character goes into the outhouse, when I sat down I noticed it was really warm. I looked underneath and sure enough there is a flame coming up—they had put a blow torch under my ass. They just got it close enough to where I was like, "Oh shit!" It would have been mean if they actually burned me, but no, they just tried to scare me. That, they accomplished.

RICHARD BROOKER: There is a scene were Dana is standing on the porch of the lodge, and I come through the door and she is supposed to hit me over the head with a log. We set everything up and the camera's rolling, and I open up the door and come through smoking my pipe. Nobody laughed. All they said was, "You're wasting time! Come on!"

DANA KIMMELL: There wasn't a whole lot of time for levity; it became a survival thing. After we got through the beginning of the film, it was all night shooting. We'd get there at four or five in the afternoon. Then it was long nights, and then we'd leave at six in the morning and go home and try to sleep in the middle of the day and then come back. Foil in the windows so you could sleep all day and all that. And by the last couple of weeks, when it was just me and Richard, it was only emotional stuff—running and screaming. It got a little stressful toward the end—just doing things over and over and over, partly because of the 3-D. And we were over budget at the time.

GERALD FEIL: We went over schedule—an optimistic schedule. One always had to help the 3-D because, in the end, it's an illusion. I looked at good old black and white movies from the 1930s and '40s and saw how carefully they separated the actors from the backgrounds, because otherwise there's no 3-D—everyone will just look like cardboard cutouts. And because *Part 3* was built from scratch on a film ranch, a good square mile of background was visible from almost every place on that set. Then, when you decide at the end of the second reel that Jason is going to cut the power and everything after that is going to play in the dark, what do you do with a couple of square miles of background on the exteriors? Everything had to be lit.

FRANK MANCUSO, JR.: *Part 3* was very difficult to shoot because we needed an extraordinary amount of light, just a stupid amount of light everywhere we went. It seemed unreasonable that we had to light the set to the level Gerald said we needed. It was like working at Yankee stadium the whole time. If people were antsy or unsupportive towards Gerald, it was because we were all saying, "I hope this works, because this is looking nutty."
You had to take this giant leap of faith. It was a big jump because while we were shooting it, it never looked anything like it finally did on film.

PETER SCHINDLER: The cast were all troopers, tromping in that man-made lake at three o'clock in the morning. But the crew, they were much harder to control than the actors. They were very difficult. It was a very tough time. We had pretty much an outlaw crew. There was a lot of stuff on that set—every problem associated with the 1980's. By the second week of shooting, we had some margaritas in the makeup trailer, then certain '80s substances floating around. It started reaching a low point. We were out in the middle of nowhere, working for cash. I was just trying to keep us from shooting each other.

Being non-union was a total negative. With the quality of the work we were getting and the problems that we had, the union wouldn't have stood for it—I could've fired people and gone to the union and hired new people, which in several cases I would've done. I still could have anyway, but it's harder to replace people. If it's a union job, you know a lot of union people. You fire someone non-union, you're not sure you can replace them and find somebody who wants to work non-union. But this is what I was handed.

FRANK MANCUSO, JR.: *Friday the 13th* was always like a renegade experience. These movies were about people operating outside their job category. I started out as a production assistant and ended up being a line producer. On one movie! The guy who was the script supervisor on the first one ended up being the writer on *Part 3*. These kinds of movies could only exist with people working outside their particular job category because the fact is, quite frankly, if they were doing their job, and doing it well, they'd be working on a real Paramount movie. They wouldn't be working on this for $275 a week

MARTIN JAY SADOFF "Rough" is the wrong word. Peter Schindler was the assistant director, the associate producer and the production manager all in one—Peter controlled the set. He actually called the shots. Steve Miner got more involved as the story went on. Everything that was going into this was so far beyond Steve. Steve worked with the actors. I don't want to say anything too negative about Steve—it wasn't like he was a bad person. He just didn't know what the fuck he was doing. He wasn't on the set directing. It wasn't his movie. There were so many people and everybody kind of kept to their own thing. Steve would set up a shot

and say, "This is what I want to do. I want to have these guys run to the camera with the camera stationary." We'd say, "Steve, you can't do that in 3-D." And he'd say, "That's why I didn't want to shoot this movie in 3-D!" Then they'd call him over and say, "Mellow out—we're doing it in 3-D. It's too late. Just get on with it. Become part of the program." Then we'd try to meet and say, "This is kind of what Steve wanted. With that in mind, how to we get this shot?"

It's a shame about Steve, because Steve ended up doing one good film in his life—*Forever Young*.

PETER SCHINDLER: I really don't agree with that. I think Steve Miner knew very well what he was doing. Steve had the film pretty well storyboarded, too. He was really very meticulous.

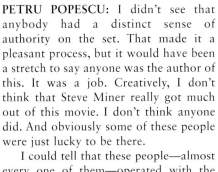

PETRU POPESCU: I didn't see that anybody had a distinct sense of authority on the set. That made it a pleasant process, but it would have been a stretch to say anyone was the author of this. It was a job. Creatively, I don't think that Steve Miner really got much out of this movie. I don't think anyone did. And obviously some of these people were just lucky to be there.

I could tell that these people—almost every one of them—operated with the audience in mind to such an extent that it was completely different than the artistic world I had been raised in, in which there was an elitist feeling that an artist does what an artist wants to do, and either the audience discovers that, or to hell with the audience. Here, there were people who were unashamedly preoccupied about how these youngsters would respond. That was very interesting, of course, if only in an engineering sense.

GEORGE HIVELY: Steve, I credit him, he did a good job working within the structure he had to. He knew when there were places where he absolutely had to have coverage and he made sure we got it and then places where he thought he could just get away without it. But the way Steve shot it, it all went together. Steve is one of those directors who has a window in his mind and he can see the screen, if you will. Too many directors, especially new directors, see everything and they keep forgetting about that it is all going to be in a little window. He had that cinematic sense.

STEVE MINER: We had a lot of problems because we were the first production to use that generation of the Marks 3-D system and we were perpetually in research and development. Then I realized it's really very simple. You just shoot with two different eyes. And if you want to bring something off that screen, it's just going to take a lot of time to rig the gag and shoot it a certain way. In that sense, 3-D is the simplest thing in the world. But it is very confusing and difficult until you work with it. I didn't know that going into *Part 3* and it took months to figure it out.

PETER SCHINDLER: One night we were lighting the lake and the lodge all the way up until one o'clock in the morning so we hadn't gotten a shot off. We start to rehearse the camera blocking, and I'm looking at my monitor as we pull back, the shot starts to expand, and all of a sudden you're seeing the lights in the frame. So I got back in the truck and I said to the crew, "Hey, we haven't shot anything yet and now we're seeing lights!

Above: Two separate endings were filmed for *Part 3*. "After we did the first cut, Steve Miner and I spent a few weeks trimming, tightening and trying alternate takes," says editor George Hively. "We also played with the way the film ended. There was one version where Chris dreams that she gets her head cut off by Jason, and then there was one with Jason's mother grabbing her out of the lake, which is what we ended up with. Because I think we all felt that you had to leave somebody behind—and that the first ending might depress people."

Not all in the cast agree with the decision. "The ending actually changed a few times, in terms of both what was shot and what was originally conceived," reveals actor Larry Zerner. "The very first ending in the original script is that, the morning after her ordeal, Chris wakes up in the canoe, then goes into the barn and finds everyone's bodies. She then decapitates Jason with a sickle. But that was never filmed. Instead, they first shot what became the alternate ending. I was there—I saw it. Chris wakes up in the canoe and hears Rick calling to her from the lodge. She paddles over to the shore, jumps out and runs to the porch. We see Rick running inside, and Chris running in tandem, and then she gets to the door, opens it, and Jason is there with

the machete. He chops her head clear off. Dana even had this wig and fake head. I remember watching that and thinking, 'What a great ending!' And they didn't use it. I'd love to see it."

Fans would, too. This alternate ending, now thought lost, has never been released. However, it can be read in Michael Avallone's 1982 novelization (**left**), now out of print. The item remains a highly sought-after collectible on the online auction market.

What are you guys doing!?" Steve Miner was in the back; he came out and yelled at me, "What do you think we're doing, just fucking around?" And I'd just about had it by that time. I was totally pissed at Steve and everything that had been happening. I'd had it with working on this thing and trying to keep everyone up. I said, "You know what? I don't need this." I put down my radio. Steve said, "You fucking amateurs couldn't film this thing with a phone book!" Then he ran over and bashed a chair to pieces.

Eventually I came back and I cooled down, and so did Steve. Steve's a great guy. It's just very hard to shoot nights. And it's particularly hard making a horror movie.

GERALD FEIL: We did our best. Peter Schindler was very good—he kept it all going on the organizational side. It was right that he went on to be a noteworthy producer. And Steve had the patience of a saint. I think it is both to Steve's credit and Peter Schindler's credit to running a set that was plagued with great difficulty and great pressure and things that took a tremendous amount of time, yet still had a good spirit.

Everybody worked very hard. Things would be demanded of the actors that wouldn't normally be demanded of actors—particularly semi-stunts that were complicated. I thought the actors, as a group, were very generous to each other, which was unusual. There were more than a few frustrations that had nothing to do with the actors or the director—they just had to do with the enormity of the undertaking.

SANDI LOVE: Grace under pressure, sure. Fun, no. What was interesting was how we would surmount problems as they arose. I think the most trying part for me was having to soak the clothes in blood every evening. After sixteen hour days, every day, it does get to you. Your mind plays tricks when you're tired.

I wouldn't say I didn't enjoy myself, but it was an emotional rollercoaster. People being pleasant one minute and intensely driven the next, all to make it work properly. Like being brought into Stan Winston's workshop by Steve Miner and told to build a body suit for Richard Brooker, to build Jason up, all while they stood and watched and talked to each other. I said, "You brought me here just to watch me?" But at least hearing that the actors had nothing but positive recollections does make me smile.

TRACIE SAVAGE: It's funny, because I don't have any bad memories about anybody. I worked for seventeen years before *Friday*. I worked with award-winning directors. I worked with Joseph Sargeant, who directed *Patton*. I've worked with big names. Then to be on this movie, it was kind of hard to take the whole thing seriously, because the impression I got was that is was just a bunch of kids having a good time. Frank Mancuso, Jr. would drive up in his little sports car every day—this was a 24-year-old kid! Steve Miner, pretty much the same thing. Sure, he took it seriously, but he was a kid with a kid's energy—and that's what made it the most fascinating. We were doing something that had barely been done before. Watching them set up shots and trying to figure out how to make it work.

MARTIN JAY SADOFF It was fucking unbelievable. The shoot was just so hard. I remember I couldn't wait to get on that plane at the end and get the hell out of there. I look back, and I don't know how I ever survived that. It was not a happy time in my life. If I had to live it over, I would love it, but I didn't love it at the time I was doing it. Here we were shooting this giant movie, and it was really like 3-D film school. "How do we do this?" Nobody would get that opportunity again. Ever.

The "3-D film school" would not end at the completion of principal photography, however. The first 3-D feature film to receive a wide theatrical release, Part 3 *was an enormous undertaking, a massive logistical effort encompassing all aspects of motion picture production, distribution and exhibition.*

The effort paid off at the box office. Friday the 13 Part 3 *opened on August 13, 1982, on 1,079 screens across the United States. By the end of its first three days, the film had grossed $9.4 million, a new record for the franchise. It also exhibited a stronger holdover than* Part 2*, assisted no doubt by the attraction of the 3-D gimmick. By the end of its run,* Friday the 13th Part 3 *had grossed $36.7 million domestically, selling over 12.4 million tickets and, until the release of* Freddy vs. Jason *twenty-one years later, remained second only to the original* Friday the 13th *as the most successful installment in the series. Whether or not the film was an artistic success, even by the standards of a franchise horror film, was arguable. Critics certainly offered scant praise aside from a begrudging acknowledgement of the effectiveness of the film's three-dimensional effects. But there was no doubt that* Part 3 *had succeeded as a commercial entertainment and once again positioned* Friday the 13th *as the cinema's reigning horror series.*

The prognosis was not quite so optimistic for 3-D itself, however. Part 3 *would prove to be the pinnacle of its '80s revival. A flurry of other 3-D films followed, including Universal's big-budget* Jaws 3-D*, and Paramount's own quickie follow-up, the Frank Mancuso, Jr.-produced* The Man Who Wasn't There*. But dwindling box office quickly killed any hope for a major comeback for the 3-D format, and Paramount's ambitious plans for the process were dashed by a contentious lawsuit with the Marks Corporation. It all ended with a whimper, not a bang: by the close of 1983, any 3-D equipment still remaining in theaters was quietly dismantled and sold for scrap.*

FRANK MANCUSO, JR.: In retrospect, I'd have to say that had Paramount known what it was they were going to have to go through in order to make this thing work, I doubt they would have done it. It was kind of a crazy idea to broad release a 3-D movie, because there wasn't any precedent. Initially, everybody thought it was going to just be a glasses issue, but the glasses were the least of it. We had to have each theater equip themselves with a silver screen and a viewing box that went in front of the lens and then they'd have to sync it all up. And we had to spend the

money to create a 24-hour hotline, for calls like, "Why isn't my 3-D working?" It was a huge deal.

MARTIN JAY SADOFF The shooting of the movie was probably the easiest part of the whole thing. The movie cost $2 million to make, but I would guess that the cost of actually getting the film into theaters at that time was about $10 million.

People have always said Paramount was embarrassed by the *Friday* movies. But if anything, it was exactly the opposite. Paramount took *Part 3* as a very serious project. And I give all the credit to Frank Mancuso, Sr. He stood by the movie. Because up until that time, 3-D movies had been released on a very limited basis. They'd make fifty prints and go to one city, and then they'd pull the fifty prints and go to another city. Frank Sr. said, "Screw it. We're going to put it in two thousand screens across the country!"

Everybody at Paramount was saying that the first two *Fridays* were big, but not really big. I remember they gave me an initial gross estimate: "If we do a *Part 3*, we think it might make $6 million." And Paramount had what was called an "A" track and a "B" track as to how a film was released—multiplexes didn't really exist then the way they do now. So you always kind of knew where you were going to play. And we were going to be the "B" run. So we went about configuring and creating all the lenses. And then a month or two before the release, Frank goes, "No, we're going to open on the 'A' track," which meant now we were going to play in all these 70mm houses—which meant another set of lens designs for the projection.

Frank really believed the moviegoing experience should be unique. He really believed that you needed something special. He said, "How hard would it be to re-equip 2,000 theaters into 3-D?" It was really a major chore because we had to get silver screens installed in all of them. We actually ended up physically making the lenses for each specific theater—the idea would be that you'd have a flat lens, a scope lens and a 3-D lens in every theater. That way once it was set-up, you wouldn't have to re-equip every time you showed something in 3-D.

GEORGE HIVELY: We were pushing like mad. It had a "hard" release date—meaning it had to open on an actual Friday the 13th. It's not like you could say, "Well, we'll go out a week later." You would lose the whole magic. There was so much to do from

Below: "When we shot the last scene, where the cops take me out to the police car and I go crazy, they weren't happy with the first take," recalls Dana Kimmell. "Steve Miner was so funny. I asked, 'Okay, Steve—what do you want me to do?' He just said, 'Uh, just do something...different.' So I just went nuts."

The first official *Friday the 13th* soundtrack release (**above**), this 1982 Gramavision compilation LP combined selected highlights from the first three films. "While they were making *Part 3*, I was working on a Broadway musical at the time, one that ultimately took up most of my life for a couple of years," says composer Harry Manfredini. "Steve Miner just said, 'Don't worry about it—we'll just use the music from *Part 1* and *Part 2*.' So believe it or not, I have never seen all of *Part 3*. I did see the first reel, and the last, but nothing in the middle. The remainder of the picture was constructed by a music editor named Jack Tillar.

"Now, as there was no score to *Part 3*, how does one make an album? Well, I just strung together some pieces from the first and second into reasonably long suites, and put them into more listenable sequences. I also re-recorded them, because in the films, the music had to fight other sound effects—rain and wind, and dialogue and crickets, and lions and tigers…"

The soundtrack LP also spun off one of the rarest of *Friday* collectibles, a promotional-only twelve-inch single of *Part 3*'s disco-infused title theme. "Harry Manfredini's publisher was a mutual friend of mine," recalls the theme's co-composer Michael Zager. "And the producers of *Part 3* wanted to get a real contemporary sounding opening and close to the movie. That's how I got involved. I had been co-leader of a band called Ten Wheel Drive, then I got into music production and I had a lot of very commercial hit records, producing for artists like Whitney Houston, Luther Vandross and Peabo Bryson. That's the reason they hired me. So Harry came over, and then I adapted the original theme and put my own thing to it. It was entirely written and recorded in an apartment over the course of a few days. And it was always going to be disco, because that kind of music was so popular at the time. We even did a single-release of it, a dance mix for the clubs. It even did pretty well. Then we made up some name for our 'group,' which was called 'Hot Ice.' I have no idea what that was supposed to mean!"

"I'm not sure if I would call the disco song fabulous," laughs Manfredini, "but it was an attempt to have a hit single utilizing some of the sounds from the score. As for that fictitious band name, well, I guess if the song was a hit, we could have gone on to do a series of disco film themes. Dancing to things like *Psycho*, *Death of a Salesman*—hey, wait a minute, that's a great idea!"

a post-production standpoint. There were a lot of opticals, all these dissolves and blow ups, the kinds of things you have to do to every film, but being 3-D it overly complicated everything. I remember one shot, we had had gotten the eyes reversed, and when you looked at it on the screen, it was all converged backwards. You wanted to throw up. All those things had to be fixed.

MARTIN JAY SADOFF They decided to have the world premiere at the Esquire Theatre in Boston, this old vaudeville house downtown. The movie was due to be screened for the press at 9 a.m. the next morning. There was a guy who was VP of Paramount Distribution at that time. He said, "Whatever you do, it's got to be on that screen at nine in the morning!" Well, it turns out the lenses at this theater could only handle about twenty minutes of light before they burned out. So here was this gorgeous theater, and we were up in the projection booth in the middle of the night, sledgehammering holes in the booth so the light could get down to the screen. They ended up billing Paramount like $100,000 to rebuild the wall in the theater.

LARRY ZERNER: The film actually opened the same day as *Fast Times at Ridgemont High*. And *Fast Times* was #7 at the box office and we were #1. For a week, Sean Penn was worried. And for two months, I was famous.

MARTIN JAY SADOFF I got a call from Frank Sr. at 11:30 a.m. on a Friday. He goes, "Two screens." I said, "Two screens what? Only two screens are up and running?" And he said, "No, we only lost two screens on the East Coast to technical problems." Then he told me the movie made its money back—"It's already in the black!" It had sold out every single showing on the East Coast from the minute it opened. The movie was a hit before the first matinee ever unspooled on the West Coast. And we ran out of glasses all over the place on the first weekend. It was incredible.

DAVID KATIMS: I remember after the screening going back and talking to Steve Miner and Frank Mancuso, Jr. I don't know how I had the balls to say it, but I said, "This is crap." And they said, "You know what, this is *Friday the 13th Part 3* and it's in 3-D. Those two things are going to make this a hit." And they were right. They knew the game much better than I did. The writing and the acting didn't matter at all.

I don't imagine any of us really feel like this was the crowning glory of our talent. I hope not. And I would include in there Steve Miner, absolutely. He has gone on to do some better work, but I would not have called him a great director at that time. And I think even he would tell you that a good film is 90 percent casting. It really is.

TRACIE SAVAGE: We all probably feel the same way. I had pretty much retired from acting after eighteen years. I wasn't really serious when I did this movie. I was a student and my focuses were elsewhere. So when I watch the movie now, I kind of laugh at my own performance. I just think, "Oh, god!" And I appreciate that.

LARRY ZERNER: There are parts that I cringe at and there are parts I think are pretty good. As the film went on, I got better. The first scene where I come out of the van—I really hate myself there. I'm really bad. I didn't know what I was doing. I wish I could do that again. But my last scene where I have it out with Vera, I like that.

PETRU POPESCU: I saw the screening with my agent. After it was over, he leaned over to me and said, "You don't want your name on the credits of something like this." So I took my name off it. I did not stay with the genre myself anyway, probably because at the time my main agenda was to be able to get back to my career as an author. These things were just somehow secondary.

RICHARD BROOKER: Horror movies are much more hi-tech now. So to look at this today, it's funny. In 1982, it didn't look funny.

GEORGE HIVELY: It was a different time. If you go back and look at some of the films that were done in the '30s and '40s and look at the editorial styles, they are much more lethargic. Then along came television, and because the original television commercials were a minute long the advertisers kept saying "We've got to be able to cram this into less space because I want to buy less time." Then thirty-second and twenty-second spots were born. Chop, chop, chop to get the message across in less time. Then that led to the MTV thing, which is just taking that style and carrying it some more.

I think that the simplicity of a movie like *Part 3*—what audiences today might perceive as a slowness—that was by design all along. There is nothing really particularly unusual or spectacular about the film. I think Steve got a script, looked at it, read it, made whatever changes he wanted to make and he had it pretty well lined up how he wanted to shoot it. I also think we were kind of holding on shots longer than you would otherwise to get the 3-D effect. And, yes, maybe we could have cut it faster. But that would not have gone over with the audience anyway, because the audience didn't have that MTV mindset then.

STEVE MINER: I do jump around a lot and have always tried very hard to do different things. Which is why I haven't talked about my *Friday the 13th* stuff in a long time. The hardcore fans remember, but I don't think I'm as well known in the genre as people like Wes Craven and Sean Cunningham. And maybe I've made some that don't work. The script wasn't very good and the acting wasn't up to par. But I think the 3-D effects worked out well, although my feeling is that at the time, a really good 3-D system hadn't yet been invented. My hope is just that I brought something different to them as a director, but at the same time I stayed within the formula and made a commercial movie.

I also think that with any hard "R" horror film you have a certain limited audience, and you're not going to have much of a crossover. Yet the core audience is very sophisticated in their own way, and you're not going to get them all in unless you have something different. It turned out that I was right, and *Part 3* recaptured the vast audience that the first film had. A big ingredient in that success was that Paramount was willing to go out on a limb with a big-time release of a 3-D film, which no one had done since the '50s.

PAUL KRATKA: I thought it was pretty scary the first time I watched it back in '82. Now, it's so corny. There was a screening at the Nuart Theater in Los Angeles a few years back, and I brought my wife and daughter and her friend. We just thought it was hilarious. And most people around us were laughing as much as we were. It's turned into this very camp experience. Yet underneath that is an extremely creative and complicated technical achievement. This was a landmark production in that respect. But then 3-D just never caught on. It just kind of lived and died that one year.

PETER SCHINDLER: You can't out-guess technology. I finished a very successful 3-D show in *Part 3* to take another successful show, *Jaws 3-D*, with the idea of great dreams. I thought it was really becoming an art form, and if I could jump in on this I would become the "Dean of 3-D" and I would have worked forever. But it never happened. I still don't regret it, though, because I learned a lot.

MARTIN JAY SADOFF Even though Paramount had never really wanted to get into the manufacturing of 3-D lenses, it got them into trouble in the end because they were sued for anti-trust. And they lost, because you can't make a movie using your own process to show it. But it was a no-win situation. If you had gone out without making your own lenses, the quality of your film would have altered from theater to theater.

I really believed that *Part 3* was going to lead to something great, that there would be a Spielberg film in 3-D. But after the anti-trust lawsuit, Paramount decided to recall all the lenses from the theaters. That was the end of 3-D. It was never going to happen.

GERALD FEIL: 3-D has a peculiar history of cycles. It goes back to the turn of the century. Interest in it peaks and then subsides and then disappears for a period of time. After *Jaws 3-D* and a few more studio movies, the process once again fell into marginal extinction. Now there's a renaissance with special-venue 3-D. IMAX 3-D is the best-looking stuff ever, but it's so incredibly expensive to produce and exhibit that it can only be in the kind of cinemas it's in now.

Part 3 does stand up. *Part 3* was the test bed for a new way of doing 3-D. What eventually evolved was a system that became known as ArriVision, a fully qualified production system. It was much better than what had proceeded it, and *Friday the 13th Part 3* was the pivot.

TRACIE SAVAGE: I joke that *Part 3* is the highest-grossing 3-D film ever produced for its time—but then there were only two other 3-D movies produced in its time. Still, it's something to brag about, isn't it?

Above: *Friday the 13th Part 3*'s opening credit sequence was a crowd-pleasing moment for the audience as well as cast and crew. "I loved the credits," says production designer Robb Wilson King. "It's my favorite thing in the movie! It was a beautiful moment, especially since I have three names, so it was this big mouthful coming at you."

"It was so exciting, because of the way the credits came off the screen," adds actor Paul Kratka. "First they came out part way, followed by a beat, and then they'd come all the way out into the audience."

Unfortunately, not all of the cast were able to share in the joy of seeing their name in three-dimensions. "I came in, got my glasses, sat down, and the credits start to roll," lamented the late Steve Susskind. "All the names are popping out, and I'm thinking, 'Any second now, I'm going to see…Steve Susskind!' Well, that didn't happen—all I got was a listing in the end credits as 'Harold.' I was so bummed!"

"There were people in the theater, ducking!"
Dana Kimmell on *Part 3*'s opening credit sequence

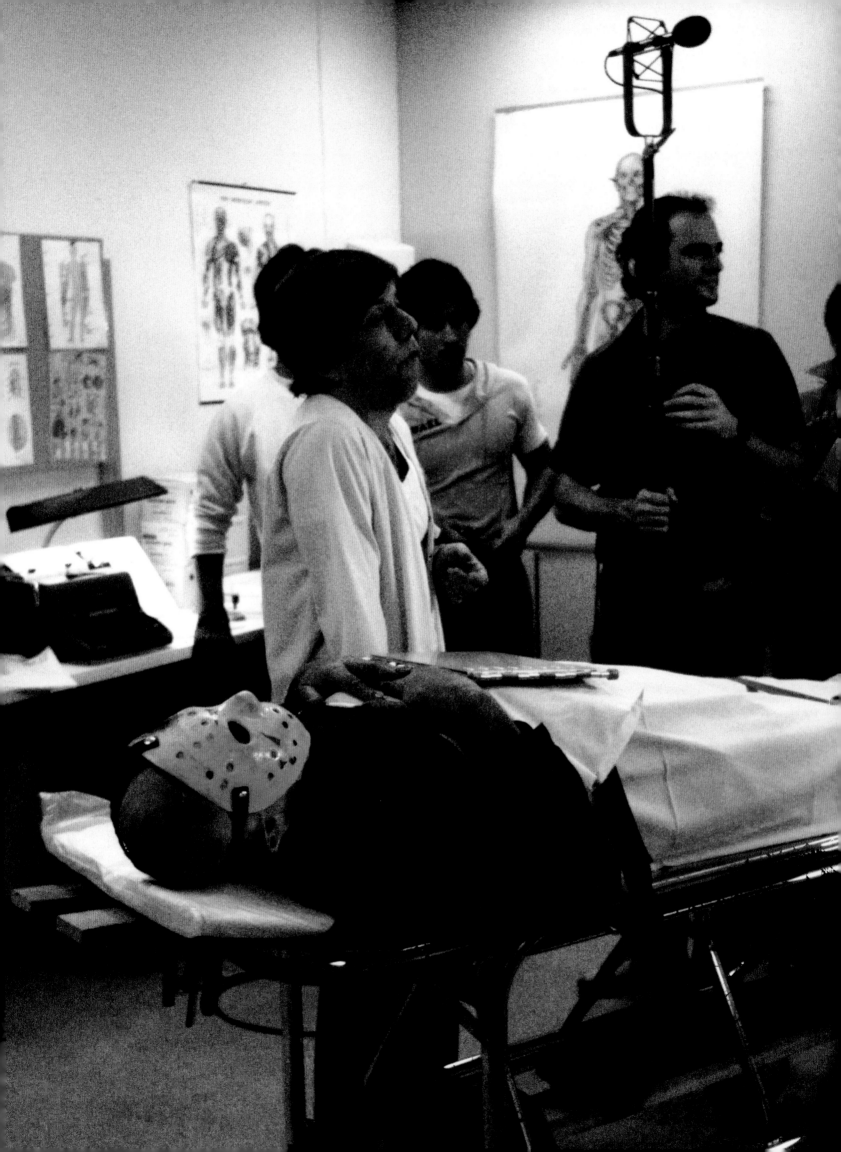

4.

Jason's Unlucky Day

By the beginning of 1984, the heyday of the slasher film was already in sharp decline. The years 1980 through 1983 have come to be regarded as the sanguine years of the genre, when all of Hollywood, from the sleaziest "independent producer" whose office was located in the trunk of his parked car on Sunset Boulevard to the highest paid studio executive, was greenlighting any film that featured a masked killer, scores of dead teenagers, an ample array of knives, cleavers or machetes and, in the best of all worlds, all three. To critics, it was an inexplicable phenomenon. But to the horror-hungry teenagers of the early 1980s it was like being let loose in a candy store with a week's worth of lunch money. Nary a week went by that a new film wasn't released that featured some imitation, variation, or regurgitation of even the hoariest slasher movie cliché. And these were not merely little-seen curios of the drive-in circuit. Following the smash success of *Halloween* and *Friday the 13th*, the major studios quickly mimicked (with varying degrees of success) the strategy Frank Mancuso, Sr. so successfully employed when he acquired Sean S. Cunningham's low-rent shocker for Paramount. Any even remotely-marketable slasher quickie was now gobbled up and treated to a wide theatrical release backed by an aggressive multimedia advertising campaign.

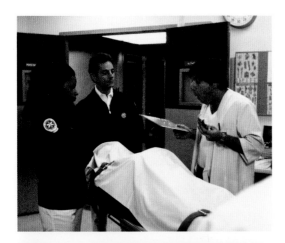

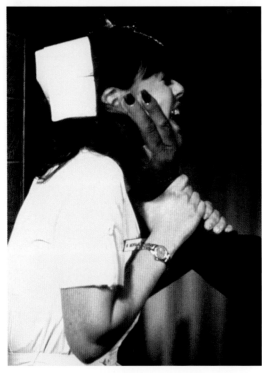

Top: As *The Final Chapter* opens, Jason is presumed dead and taken to the local county morgue, only to stalk anew. "We knew that anyone who was seeing *The Final Chapter* had, in great likelihood, seen *Part 3*," reasons director Joseph Zito. "So we felt that there was no reason to go ahead and thrust our film years into the future. Instead, we wanted it to feel as if this was all one big, continuous movie."

Above: The filming of the death of Nurse R. Morgan (Lisa Freeman)—perhaps a nod to actress Robbi Morgan of the original *Friday the 13th*?—turned into one of the most humorous moments for the crew of *The Final Chapter*. "We attached some tubing to the actress' thigh for blood to trickle down one leg," explains makeup effects designer Tom Savini. "Well, the tubing must have come loose and it became like a penis! And when it came time for the blood, a stream shot out between her legs. It got the biggest laugh on the set. Everybody just cracked up."

Previous page: Jason on the slab. "Ted White, the actor who played Jason, was a little bit freaked about being in the morgue," laughs Joseph Zito. "It wasn't that it was tough to do, but he didn't like it very much!"

The trend arguably reached the pinnacle of absurdity when the studios attempted to take the next logical step—elevating the merely exploitative to the level of respectable with an influx of imitative "adult thrillers." Slasher movies in all but budget only, these glossier, in-house studio productions boasted big-name stars and A-list directors. Yet despite the fancy logos and occasional top caliber talent, the sight of Lauren Bacall fending off a crazed stalker (*The Fan*, Paramount, 1982), Clint Eastwood hunting a serial rapist (*Tightrope*, Warner, 1984), or Oscar-winner Lee Grant catfighting with a transsexual killer (*Visiting Hours*, Fox, 1982) would not have been out of place on double bills with such unapologetic slasher fare as *Hell Night* (1983, Compass International), *Terror Train* (Fox, 1982), *My Bloody Valentine* (Paramount, 1981) or *The Funhouse* (1981, Universal). In fact, in the year 1983, nearly sixty percent of all motion pictures—not just horror films—produced in the United States bore lineage to the slasher genre.

By the time the fourth *Friday the 13th* film—ceremoniously proclaiming itself to be *The Final Chapter*—went into pre-production at the end of 1983, the series was already in danger of becoming a dated anachronism. Even its now-trusted shepherd, Frank Mancuso, Jr., had grown tired of the formula despite its enormous profit margin and the hands-on filmmaking experience it offered him. The critical and moral backlash against the slasher film was beginning to take its toll, not just on the younger Mancuso's professional reputation but Paramount's public image. Bad reviews were one thing—even the intermittent letter-writing campaigns organized by conservative parent and religious groups could be brushed off—but the contempt directed at Mancuso by the industry's artistic elite represented a potential glass ceiling that couldn't be shattered. When, in his 1981 thriller *Blow Out*, Brian DePalma used a sleazy, cynical mock-slasher film as a bookend—complete with shaky camerawork, naked, nubile females and a maniacal, heavy-breathing killer—it was impossible not to see it as a barely-concealed swipe at *Friday the 13th*, the film which had single-handedly taken down DePalma's 1980 Hitchcock homage *Dressed to Kill* at the box office. By the time Paramount announced that the final *Friday the 13th* was ready to go into production, there seemed to be little question that it was time to go out while the series was still on top. It was time to kill Jason. Once and for all.

FRANK MANCUSO, SR., Chairman & CEO, Paramount Pictures: Let it be said that, while I suppose it is possible there were concerns about *Friday the 13th* at the upper level of Paramount, there certainly wasn't at the senior level. At the time, Michael Eisner was President of Paramount and Barry Diller was Chairman. I reported directly to Barry. And I never heard anything negative about *Friday the 13th* from him. Quite simply, these films were big moneymakers and they helped our year-end bottom line.

Oh, sure, we'd get letters. But we received letters about a lot of things. Did we get the level of complaints about *Friday the 13th* compared to, say, a *Last Temptation of Christ*? Absolutely not. Nothing near that. And God bless America, because this is a free society. It is your choice to write a letter to a studio to complain about their product. But it is also your choice to leave your home and enter the theater. It is your choice to put your money down. And if you don't want to do that, you shouldn't. And that's okay.

Studios are public companies. They have stockholders. And the responsibility of the chairman, or of any senior executive, is to make the most money for the company. I don't believe, and never did, that there is a bad piece of film if people want to see it. It's not up to me, or anyone, to make that decision. It is up to the moviegoer. Yes, we had to make decisions about what to produce and what to acquire. But the public is still, ultimately, the determiner of whether your instincts are right and the product you've created is accepted.

FRANK MANCUSO, JR., Producer: I certainly would not be surprised to hear that, if you said to Barry Diller, "Name me the top fifty movies you've been involved with," he wouldn't say *Friday the 13th*. But when Paramount was greenlighting *Reds* and whatever else, there was significant exposure. But on these movies, there was none. If there was any resentment toward the movies, it was simply the fact that they were exercises in commerce. These movies introduced the idea of negative pick-ups. It said there were people involved with the company that had nothing to do with production that could generate real revenue. At that time, you have to understand that at a studio like Paramount, the distribution and marketing departments probably outweighed the production entity by a significant measure. In some ways, *Friday the*

13th gave them their own sense of pride because this was a series that had nothing to do with the people in Hollywood.

There was a moment in time where I sort of hated the *Friday the 13th* movies because everywhere I went, that's all everybody ever affixed me to. With the fourth one—which I entitled *The Final Chapter* for a reason—I really wanted it to be done and walk away. In some ways, I felt I had grown beyond it, but it was really more me coming to terms with the fact that these movies should be made by people who are pushing themselves and learning and growing. The fact of the matter was that I wasn't in a place where I could get excited about doing one of these things again. It became a chore. I was also now living out in Los Angeles, so the people in the filmmaking community weren't exactly looking at me as any particular talent. They were saying, "Oh, the *Friday the 13th* guy." I was never given the chance to even read anything that wasn't in that ilk. That became limiting and disappointing. That's why I just wanted to put an end to it.

Phil Scuderi, I'm sure, was of a different mind. But he also would have been comfortable—as he ultimately was—with me just saying, "Look, Phil—I can't do this anymore." I'm not necessarily sure he, his partners or even Paramount wanted it to be the end—they might have wanted to use it as a marketing ploy. But it wasn't a ploy for me.

STEVE MINER, Filmmaker: They stopped offering me the *Friday the 13th* movies after the fourth one. I've always wished them well—I just couldn't do them anymore. The success of that series is based on remaking the same film, over and over again. As a filmmaker, I wanted to go on to something different. And with notable exceptions, a horror film will have a limited audience. I was fortunate to get a chance to go on and make movies that had a broader appeal than any of my earlier work. You have to do what's best for you.

But I still feel I made the right choice. Without sequels, we wouldn't have a movie business. And I was able to use *Friday the 13th* as a vehicle, a training ground for the career I have today. I've had practically every job there is in film production, from being a gofer to being one of the most influential people, as an editor, producer and director. Doing so many jobs in film is really a broadening experience. You learn so much—about yourself and the moviemaking process as a whole. What more could I ask for?

JOSEPH ZITO, Director: Around 1980, I had done a remake job on a small, sort of scary movie, and I had made a short, ten-minute product reel and taken it out to Cannes. Because in order to produce these doctor jobs, I would take certain rights on the film, and I'd have to figure out how to sell those. So there I am in Cannes with this little reel, and I'm showing it to a buyer from India or something like that, and there's another guy there in the room. His name is Carl Kaminsky. He's got this seer-sucker jacket on, and apparently he had cut himself shaving, because he was bleeding in two or three places through toilet paper stuck on his face. He looks at this reel and says, "You're great! You're a terrific director! When we get back to the United States, I want you to meet some of my clients. They're great and you're great, and we'll make films!" And let me tell you, that reel did not demonstrate anything of the sort. If I could look at it now, I'd be appalled.

Of course I never thought any of this would happen anyway. But when I came back to the United States, Carl and I had dinner. Afterward, he says, "Come back to my office, I'm going to call two of my clients. These guys are going to love you." And he calls them on the phone, and says, "I met this guy Joe Zito—he's a terrific director!" Based on this crappy reel. And of those two phone calls—this is true—I end up getting two movies. I thought, "Wow. This is easy! Go to Cannes, meet a guy with toilet paper

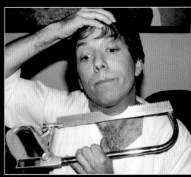

Goremeister Tom Savini returned to create the many makeup illusions in *The Final Chapter*, beginning with the gruesome death of morgue attendant Axel (Bruce Mahler). Savini explains the effect: "We started the sequence with a shot of the twist of the head, with the live actor facing forward. Then we cut to a foam, twistable torso and head for the actual turn, all the way around. Then back to the live actor, again facing backwards, with his costume also backwards, and an appliance on his front that looked like it was his back. We also had a crew member lying on the floor in back of him, portraying the actor's hands, raised up. So it went from real, to fake, and back to real. That's how we sold the effect."

"The character of Tommy Jarvis is definitely an homage to Tom Savini," says director Joseph Zito. "Tommy's obsessions are Tom's obsessions." The similarity was not lost on eleven year-old actor Corey Feldman. "Tom was great—a nice, down to earth guy, and obviously a master at his craft," recalls Feldman today. "I specifically remember the hand puppet (**this page**) I used in the scene where I'm showing off my character's makeup skills to Rob (Erich Anderson, **opposite bottom**). And I was impressed with myself because I did all the animatronics stuff myself. I just loved that whole experience—it was the first time I learned about special effects and prosthetics."

on his face, he makes a phone call and the next thing you have a movie? This is great! What a business!"

The first phone call resulted in a film called *The Prowler*, which was like a no-risk thing, the kind of movie that sort of happens before you know it and that you didn't think anybody is going to see. Then when *The Prowler* was completed, it's seen by the guy from the second phone call. A guy in Boston. He calls me and says, "This movie is great. But if I could call this movie *Friday the 13th*, we could make a fortune with it." He was Phil Scuderi. Then he says, "When I make another *Friday the 13th* film, I'll make a beeline for you and you're going to be the guy." And I never, ever thought that phone call would come. But, in fact, it did. A few months later I get another call: "I'm making another *Friday the 13th*—and it's going to be the last one we make."

FRANK MANCUSO, JR.: I sat down with Joe and I liked him, just personally. Joe eventually did ask to do a lot of different things than had been done in past *Friday*s, but we always wanted to flavor each movie differently anyway, whether it was in 3-D or *The Final Chapter*. So I went with Joe because I thought he understood what we were trying to do. He had a feel for the genre and we had a compatible personality—you could see him making the movie.

JOSEPH ZITO: The entire process of *The Final Chapter* was one of preconceptions that turned out to be different from what the reality was to be. I will admit at first blush that I had been waiting for years to get to direct a motion picture that a lot of people were going to see, and this is the last thing in the world I thought it would be. But I said to myself, "I had better not take pretense into this project. If I'm going to do this, I'd better figure out what people want to see in a film like this, and respect how it works for them."

So I studied all of the *Friday* films made up until that point very carefully. Because you had to understand you were going

into something that had an audience with certain expectations, and this had to be as good as, or hopefully better than, what they had expected. I know how pretentious that sounds, but that's the job. That's what I reached for.

When I got the call on *The Final Chapter*, there was no story, there was nothing. I had some pretty aggressive ideas about it. I thought, "Okay, maybe we can do this a little differently than the other ones. How about if we set the whole film at night?" Which is a giant production problem. "And in the rain?" Which is the most disastrous thing to suggest, production-wise. "Oh, and what if we have a kid in this one—a ten or eleven-year-old?" Which is another giant production problem, because child actors not allowed to work long hours. "And twins would really be cool! Oh, and one more thing. How about the kid has a dog?" And all of those things they agreed to! Now, when I think back on it, the arrogance to even ask for that stuff seems impossible.

To the delight of its fans—and the ire of its detractors—the Friday the 13th *series has always been about, and created for, teenagers. While the films are not dramatic enough, or comedic enough, to be considered "teen films" such as those popularized in the 1980s by filmmakers like John Hughes, the series depicted what was arguably the widest cross-section of teen characters of any of that era. Perhaps that is why, in large part, the franchise has been able to simultaneously retain a nostalgic appeal for those who first saw the films upon their initial release, while remaining vital for today's generation. The series certainly has avoided the trendy and provincial: despite their occasional sartorial mistakes or utterances of dated slang to give them away, part of the enduring appeal of the teens and twenty-somethings depicted in the* Friday *films is that they could be found anytime, anywhere, in just about any town across America. It was the filmmakers' goal that these kids be more than just the boy or girl next door. They were us.*

BARNEY COHEN, Screenwriter: I was actually in the ad business, a copywriter and concept guy. I had written a couple of screenplays, and ended up being offered a couple of *Afterschool Special*-type programs for CBS. And this was more exciting than advertising, so I quit. And one of those specials I wrote was called—goodness gracious, stay with me here—*The Inside-Out Clown*, about a fat kid who went to clown school and learned that life isn't about clowning, clowning is about life. And I don't know why he read the script, but Joe Zito—who is also, shall we say, an overweight person—called me up and said, "I love the kids you draw. I want you to write a horror film for me."

JOSEPH ZITO: When I got the job, the deal offered was, "We want you to write it and direct it." I said, "I don't really write. I know other people I can recommend." And they said, "No, no, no, we want you." So I get a contract to write and direct the film, but I ended up hiring Barney and paying him out of my salary. Later, it all got folded into the Writer's Guild of America and became a giant disaster. Because while it was in fact a negative pickup, it was released by Paramount and deemed to be a Paramount Picture by the Writers Guild of America. I never even thought to take a writing credit on the film.

Anyway, right before *The Final Chapter*, I had already been working with a writer named Bruce Hidemi Sakow, who had written a script called *Quarantine*, based on an original idea I had. And he did a really very good job of it, but we never made the movie. So Bruce and I hashed out a story together for *The Final Chapter* that became the outline. Then Barney was brought in and I worked with him on finishing the screenplay.

The method of writing the movie was absolutely unique—I can say, twenty years later, that I have never heard of anything quite like it. I would call Phil Scuderi every night at 8:00 p.m., like clockwork. I don't know if he had a television show he liked to watch at 9:00 p.m., or if he had a whole schedule of people calling him about different movies, or what, but I'd call him at exactly eight-zero-zero and somehow he would wrap it up like a television show by nine-zero-zero. And this is not a guy who was a writer, he was a theater owner, yet he had the whole thing memorized—it was absolutely mind-boggling. He would recite the script from page one to wherever we were at, and talk about the scene. I would then meet with Barney the next day, and tell him roughly what was done, implement that, and then turn that into pages. I would send those pages out to Boston, and then, all over again, the next day at 8:00 p.m., we would talk about the whole script again, including that scene. Barney and I built the script from the beginning, but it was completely visualized by this guy sitting in Boston.

BARNEY COHEN: The whole process was a lot of fun—just me and Zito in this apartment on the East Side of New York. And Zito likes to eat, so we had a fridge stocked with champagne and kishka. We would just eat and write, write and eat. I think Zito's role during the development was almost like a facilitator, explaining the producers to me, and me to the producers. That

was not normal. I can't think of another film subsequently where that happened. And I think Joe, genius that he is, is a controlling personality, and was afraid that if I talked to anybody but him, ideas might creep in that he didn't want.

The original outline was written by Bruce, who I never met, and we did use most of it. It had the basic story, the basic killing of the kids. I remember adding the family. And we changed all of the kids' characters.

JOSEPH ZITO: I just thought the films were getting stale. All these teenagers going out of the house, and on page one, Jason gets up and chases them and they're having sex and he kills them. I was looking for people we could care about. And I think Barney accomplished that with the screenplay. I don't want to build it up as more than what it is, but I'm saying at least with ours, there was some differentiation of character.

BARNEY COHEN: Joe was right on the money there. When I started writing, he said to me, "Don't try to think of any new ways to kill kids, 'cause people have seen everything. Just make them real, like your *Afterschool Special* kids, and whatever we do to them will be horrific." I had liked the first two *Friday* films, because they created characters that, for the most part, you understood and you cared about. *Part 3* was a trick movie—they killed all these kids that were better off dead anyway. So we strove to make loveable, real-world teens—even if Jason never showed up, it was still *American Graffiti*, you know? Because when you kill kids like that, people really get freaked out.

The development of the screenplay for The Final Chapter *was often collaborative, occasionally contentious, and sometimes even wacky, yet through it all the filmmakers remained focused on what they believed counted most: the characters. Enter a pair of young casting directors who, fresh to the series, were able to bring a cooler, more colorful sensibility by casting semi-known actors who were sexy, appealing and funny while still remaining relatable to the audiences of 1984. Among the cast was an Australian pop star; the eccentric artist; an ex-teen heartthrob; the passionate thespian; a budding child star; even a set of former "Doublemint Twins."*

FERN CHAMPION, Casting Director: As a casting director, it's so much more fun to find fresh, real people, as opposed to talking to their lawyers. That's what made doing the *Friday the 13th* films fun—finding new kids. There was no reason to have a star in it because it was an ensemble piece. Nobody cared about so-and-so who was in it. Who cared about anybody but Jason? He was the star. So you weren't really going after the A-list. You just wanted to make it believable, and you wanted good actors.

What was difficult was that everybody at that point was, obviously, already familiar with the series. Everyone was also very familiar with the gads of money that it made. And for the actors, these were not big-paying jobs. Their agents are saying, "How come my actors can't get more money?" while

"At that age, in our early 20's, it was just so exciting to be wanted, to be employed, to be doing anything. And this was a film! It was *Friday the 13th*! And it was fun!" Carey More

here you are having to say, "Well, the studio is puffing on big cigars, and the producers have moved to Holmby Hills." So that was not necessarily the easiest job in the world. But we didn't do too shabbily, did we?

BARBARA HOWARD, "Sara": I grew up in Chicago, and I moved to L.A. in March of 1983. My agent called me about the audition for *The Final Chapter* and I did not want to do it—am I allowed to say that? I wanted to do *The Hours*. My background was in classical theatre. I just wanted a certain kind of career that was really quality films, and not *Friday the 13th*. But my agent's like, "Go to the audition—it's Paramount! It's Frank Mancuso, Jr.!"

Of course, when you're not interested, you're completely relaxed and you audition really well. I ultimately had two callbacks. And my character didn't have a whole lot to say, did she? It was a lot of inner work—I just tried to make her a real, three-dimensional person, one who you know is going to go bad and get killed. I think I was very right for the part in that way. That really was me, those feelings. And I think Joe saw that in the auditions.

LAWRENCE MONOSON, "Ted": A couple of years before *The Final Chapter*, I got the lead in *The Last American Virgin*. That was huge, a really big event in my life. I went from complete obscurity to being kind of a teen star. And it was overwhelming for me, being this kid from Yonkers. It was difficult to deal with. I wasn't all that aware of *Friday the 13th*; certainly I knew of them, but they were not and aren't the kind of films that I like. But I think the only thing

I was getting ready to take some exams, and I think I had to miss finals for the film. And I felt a certain pressure after *Virgin*, because I hadn't worked in about a year or something.

PETER BARTON, "Doug": I started acting in 1979. By the end of '80, I was under contract with NBC. Then the teen magazines were so hungry for the next heartthrob that they pummeled me. I was on the cover of *Tiger Beat*, *16 Magazine*, all of them. And here I was, twenty-two years old and NBC was saying I'm only nineteen. Then, just as my contract was running out, under obligation, they cast me in a series called *The Powers of Matthew Starr*. Amy Steel was in it. Then I did some guest spots on *The Fall Guy* and *The Love Boat*.

By the end of '83, it had all dried up. That whole experience—I was going up and down, like on a rollercoaster. I was on such an incredible high—no drugs, just high—that when I came out the other side I crashed. That's when I wanted to give up acting, and that's when *The Final Chapter* came along. I had just been talked into doing this movie called *Hell Night*, with Linda Blair. I didn't even want to do it—they had to get me drunk to convince me. So it was a miserable time, and it was a great time. I wouldn't exchange the experience of making *Hell Night*, even though I was petrified all the way through it. So when *The Final Chapter* was offered to me, I was like, "I don't really want to do *Friday the 13th*." Eventually, I only did it because of Amy Steel—she talked to me about it. And I thought it was really cool because it was *The Final Chapter*. In my mind, I thought, "Oh, I'll be in the last one. That's kind of cool.

CRISPIN GLOVER, "Jimmy": I'm definitely a cinephile. I'll see a lot of old movies, all different kinds. And while there are some horror films that I think are good films, it's not a genre that I've ever sought out. *Friday the 13th*, that would be the only one I've done, before *Willard*, that you would call that genre. Although *River's Edge* has probably a lot more creepy feelings to it than *Friday the 13th*. So it was funny when I did *The Final Chapter*—I knew even at that time that it would be something to look back upon with a sense of humor, on some level.

JOSEPH ZITO: Crispin may get mad at me for saying this, but even during casting, I knew that he would be terrific in the movie and very, very entertaining. I also knew it would be hard because even he never knew what he would invent. We had to shoot reasonably quickly, and Crispin would be full of discovery and I'd want to mine those discoveries. So I talked to Frank and I said I would really, really like to go with this guy, but don't count on it being exactly as it is on the page. Frank weighed that and went with him anyway. I think it is very, very good that he did. It really helped the film a lot. Crispin energized the movie.

FERN CHAMPION: In all fairness, just because someone's odd doesn't mean they're bad. "Unique" is better than "weird." Crispin is just one of those, um, E.T. kind of kids. He was into his house being lit with black lights before it was fashionable. He just plays these wonderfully creepy characters.

JUDIE ARONSON, "Samantha": Right before *The Final Chapter* came along, I had actually gotten leading roles in two other movies, both in production at the same time. I ended up turning one down and accepting the other because it was a huge Universal film, a potentially Academy Award-winning thing. Then after a week of rehearsals, they asked me if I would change my name—they were having some problems with the society for Hispanic actors, because I was a non-Hispanic playing what was supposed to be a Hispanic role. And I wouldn't do it, so they ended up letting me go.

I went back to the other film and said, "Okay, I'll take it," but by that point it was gone. One minute I had two big films, and the next I had none. So when *The Final Chapter* happened I was very excited. And everyone was aware of *Friday the 13th*. Even back then, it had a cult following. Of course I had concerns, like, "Is this going to be bad for the rest of my career?" It's a B-movie, a slasher film, and there's nudity in it, so it was very scary. But it was really exciting because it was my first movie. I was nineteen.

CAMILLA MORE, "Tina": I actually went in to audition for the same role that Judie Aronson ended up getting. It was a fun reading because I thought I was doing rather a good job at it. I was a bit nervous about the nudity, and I wasn't sure I really wanted to do *Friday the 13th*, but there I was. And all of a sudden, they stopped me in the middle of the reading, and the casting agents said, "Hang on a minute. We're looking at your resume. Do you have a twin sister?"

CAREY MORE, "Terri": Camilla and I were, in fact, Doublemint twins—if you're in the acting profession and you're a twin, one day you'll be in a Doublemint commercial. And it just ridiculous how that excites people—their mouths drop! They always go, "I've seen that one!" Anyway, Camilla came home from her audition going, "Oh, God, they loved the idea that I was a twin, and so I think they're going to be writing a part in it for you!" This has happened to me a lot, in regards to acting. Being a twin, it was almost like I would get roles just by looking like Camilla. Although I had taken some acting classes, so it wasn't as if I had no experience.

The funny thing about the audition was that I didn't have to do anything. They gave me literally one line to read. I said something like, "I don't know." And they said, "Oh, fantastic! Fantastic!"

BONNIE HELLMAN, "Hitchhiker": I had known Fern Champion from New York—she had given me my first job after I got my SAG card. And she requested me for *The Final Chapter*. Then my agents came back to me and said, "You won't want to do this. There are no lines." I went, "It's a week of work! It's a major feature film!"

I went in and I met with Joseph Zito. Now, Joe is very energetic, and he talks very fast, almost stream of consciousness. And this is how he explains the scenario

Top: Doug (Peter Barton, left) and Sara (Barbara Howard) share a tender moment, one of many additional scenes shot but deleted from the theatrical version of *The Final Chapter*. "You always end up shooting a longer movie, and a lot of the things get eliminated that only seem important on paper," says editor Joel Goodman. Much of this excised material, however, can be found on the film's DVD release, as well as its frequent broadcast television airings—much to the chagrin of director Joseph Zito: "We, as filmmakers, are supposed to be involved with the TV versions of our films, but *The Final Chapter* is out there playing with scenes in it that were absolutely not ever supposed to be there. I can't even watch the TV version!"

Above: "Working with Crispin Glover was like an amusement park ride," laughs Joseph Zito. "You never knew what Crispin was gonna do." Co-star Carey More agrees: "Crispin made up that crazy dance on the spot! But while he really was eccentric, he was also very, very gentlemanly." Glover also found a fan in the young Corey Feldman. "I loved him as a kid," says Feldman, "because he had this James Dean appeal to me. He walked around with this big trench coat, blond hair pushed over to the side, and a menacing stare. I always thought he was so cool."

to me: "You're standing by the side of the road and people are going by and you're trying to hitchhike and nobody's picking you up and you get disgusted and you start to eat and suddenly you realize that there's someone behind you and you look around and then you're stabbed and you die!"

So I just went for it. I'm hitchhiking, writhing on the ground, acting all crazy. Just totally going all out. I don't know what other people do in their auditions, but I think with this kind of film you just have to be willing to go all-out.

ERICH ANDERSON, "Rob": The only other movie I had done was this really cheap little flick in Idaho, but it was a disaster—I can't even remember what it was called, and it was never released anyway. And then I played the over-the-hill, right-handed pitcher on *Bay City Blues*, the Steven Bochco show. I came in to audition for *The Final Chapter* on a total whim.

It was a Friday afternoon, in the summer of 1983, August or sometime. The audition was over at the Mutual of Omaha Building on Wilshire and La Brea, in a big conference room. And at that point the casting directors had gotten to calling Joseph Zito "Francis," as in Coppola, because he had seen like, I don't know the exact figure, but like three hundred guys for the part of Rob. I think Fern and Pamela were exhausted, but they loved Joe. Anyway, I knew it was *Friday the 13th* but I didn't really know that much about it. I had never seen any of the other movies. I had no knowledge of it at all. But whatever it was, it came down to the job being offered to me. And whatever snobbery I had disappeared in about a millisecond when somebody said, "You got the part."

JOSEPH ZITO: The casting of the lead, Trish, probably took the longest, because I wasn't looking for a certain type. It may sound strange, but I've had this conversation with casting directors and it has confused them. Despite the way the parts are written, I'll ignore that and try to find someone who just has that special something, that makes you respond to them and want to care about them. It's something that is very, very difficult to get your hands on, but when you see it, you know it. And I felt Kimberly had it.

KIMBERLY BECK, "Trish": I had a very unusual upbringing. My mother remarried and moved us to Australia when I was twelve. I wrote and recorded a song there called "Let's Take a Walk," and it was a huge hit. It was number one for 26 weeks. My stepdad, Tommy Leonetti, and I sang it and he became such a huge celebrity that they offered him his own TV show. He was like the Johnny Carson of Australia. He won awards. They even had an ice cream named after him.

I came back to America when I was fifteen and I started acting again and was under contract with Universal. By the time of *The Final Chapter*, I had also just left a soap opera called *Capitol* that I had been on for two years. I had never seen any of the *Friday* films. And I didn't want to see any of them. I still have never seen any of them. I just don't like that kind of genre at all. And this was not even a B-movie, it was really just a C-movie.

I had friends who were famous actors saying to me at the time, "Why are you doing this movie?" But they were not humbled enough to know that you do what you can. You don't do porn or

anything like that, but you do what you have to do to sustain the lifestyle that you've created. For me, I owned a home, and I had just divorced a really wealthy man and took nothing. I was struggling just to support myself and retain my dignity. It wasn't like I could be picky. And I had to fight to get that part. I had to go in and read a million times. And that, to me, is respectable.

JOSEPH ZITO: There wasn't any prior *Friday the 13th* film—or any slasher movie that I can think of, actually—that also made a kid the protagonist. It was a fresh idea. I thought that by having a family, by putting a child in there, and having a relationship between the child and his sister, and turning the mother into a victim, that we would really be making it more about people. I was trying to make something that at least had a bit more human drama outside of just the kids in a cabin in trouble. And this young boy would, of course, end up being the hero.

I had read a lot of kids. Corey Feldman was wonderful. You could look at him and your eye stayed with him, you cared about him. As a kid, Corey was a star. Of course he was already an experienced actor, so he was professional. And there was a chemistry that I thought was very good between him and Kimberly Beck. But his agents were trying to negotiate. Corey kept saying, "I'm gonna do this! I want this! I'll do whatever I have to do!" He was a great fan of *Friday the 13th*. He loved the idea—we couldn't contain him. So that sort of hurt their position. And we got him.

COREY FELDMAN, "Tommy Jarvis": I was always an avid fan of *Halloween*—Michael Myers was a hero to me. So when they asked me to be in this movie I was flabbergasted. Then I was told it was actually *Friday the 13th*. I said, "Is that the one with the guy with the baseball thing?" So I went and watched *Part 3*, which I wanted to see anyways because I was a tremendous fan of 3-D. And I loved it.

I went in and auditioned, and got a call a week or two later, saying, "We loved Corey, he's great, but Joseph Zito is a little bit concerned cause Corey is a small guy, and he doesn't look like he'd be able to lift the machete to whack the guy." I said, "Listen, I am an actor. I will act like I'm big enough to pick up the machete." They listened to me.

Like all of the previous Fridays*, the making of* The Final Chapter *would be a literal movie boot camp: a group of young kids out in the woods, working long hours under harsh conditions for very little money, despite the cache of starring in a film that they knew would be distributed by a major studio. Together, they set out to create something impossible to manufacture: authenticity.*

ERICH ANDERSON: The first day of shooting was Halloween—October 31st, 1983. All of the cast went up to Anderson's Pea House in Buellton, a town that you turn off to on your way to Solvang, California. We were shooting on this private resort lake, which really might have just been a watering hole for cattle.

We all just start hanging out, as kids do. And then there's Corey, wearing some mask or whatever, and he's got his grandfather there as his guardian—this sour dude. I said to Kimberly, "I wonder if that guy would let us take Corey trick-or-treating?" So we took Corey out to this little subdivision, about a mile from the hotel. And it was the weirdest thing. It was a carnival-like atmosphere, with all these families, and the kids were dressed up as Michael Myers and Jason, walking through the streets, scaring each other. It was a really surreal way to start shooting this movie.

JUDIE ARONSON: Corey was having problems with his family during that time. I think it started out where his mom was his guardian, and then when he made a name for himself, she got a

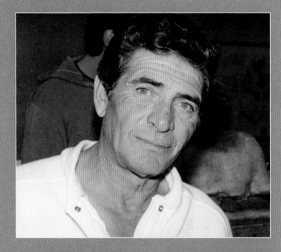

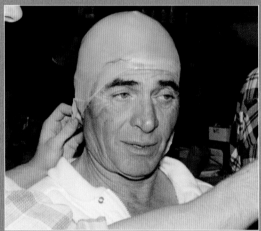

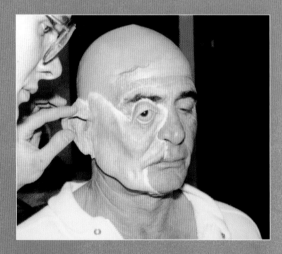

little crazy—drugs and stuff like that. It just wasn't good. So then his grandfather became his guardian. It was really hard on Corey, because here he was a little boy, and he had his old fogey grandpa on the set, trying to set limits with a bunch of teenagers around. Poor Corey just wanted to have some fun and experience life. So we took care of him as much as we could.

PETER BARTON: Corey was a sweet kid. I enjoyed his down-to-earthness then—just hanging out and friendly, and not full of himself. I think Kimberly took care of him. She had done *Peyton Place*, and Mia Farrow had taken Kimberly under her wing, so I think Kimberly had the sense to do that with Corey. She was good that way.

KIMBERLY BECK: I started acting when I was two, so I had many discussions with Corey about being a child actor. I remember I went to pick him up at his home to meet him, and I took him to some sort of Chuck E. Cheese place. It was way out in the Valley. I went to his grandparents' place and I could just tell right away that he had this sort of awful, dysfunctional childhood.

FERN CHAMPION: Corey was never a kid, you know? He was old before he should've been. His parents were going through a terrible time and he was caught. He had to fend for himself—the typical situation of coming from a split family. Great kid, but lost. So he was very vulnerable, which made it that much more interesting, because he got the character, especially the fear. He wasn't one of those happy kids. The bad news is, I think we relied on that reality. Maybe too much.

COREY FELDMAN: Kimberly and Erich were great. Everybody was great. I was probably around eleven or twelve years old, and it was so much fun being the kid on the set, because everybody wanted to take me under their wing. Yet at the same, they were a bunch of attractive young adults and they probably didn't want me around too much. But as far as I'm concerned, I loved the whole experience.

They handled the idea of a kid being around that environment very well—they were protective. I remember, originally, in the scene when Kimberly and I are coming down to the lake and we see all the kids skinny-dipping, I was supposed to chase my dog Gordon down to the water. Then Judie Aronson was supposed to walk out of lake naked, and say something like, "Oh, hi, what are you looking at?" But Frank Mancuso, Jr. thought that was too racy. "Keep the kid out!" And I had been waiting for that scene, to see a naked woman, the whole time!

JUDIE ARONSON: I was brand-spanking new in the business and I had not read the script. I guess my agent hadn't, either. It all happened so quickly. I went on the audition, had a call back and got the part right away. That was like on a weekend, and then at the beginning of the next week we were leaving for the location. I didn't realize there was nudity until it was too late—I had already accepted the part.

I come from a pretty conservative family, and I hated the idea of being nude. Hated it. So I called my agent and I'm freaking out. I had them talk to the casting people and the producers all weekend long, going back and forth and trying to make me okay with it. We ended up negotiating certain things having to do with no full frontal nudity—that it would only be from the waist up. That made me feel better. But it was still very, very scary.

LAWRENCE MONOSON: I remember the skinny dip scene—I was quite young at the time, so there was something provocative about the whole thing. But I don't have any weird morality. I think nudity, when it's relevant, is absolutely fine. I think it's the point of view of the filmmaker that either makes it gratuitous or justified. When you watch European films, people are nude all the time, and it feels wonderful, it feels natural, it feels authentic. It just feels like a human being living a life. We don't tend to be able to do that here in America. We have some sort of body disorder, and deep-seated shame. It is this sort of pseudo-puritanical society that we're all raised in.

Let me put it this way. Would I be nude in a quality film? Yes, I'd do anything. Would I ever show my butt in a movie like *Friday the 13th* again? Absolutely, positively not.

CAREY MORE: Actually, what I found most embarrassing about the whole film was that we're supposed to be these sexy twins. Everyone's looking at us going, "Oooh!" Even the boyfriends, who've got their girls, are looking at us. And we weren't really anything to look at—the outfits were so square and boring and

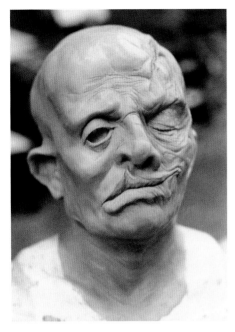
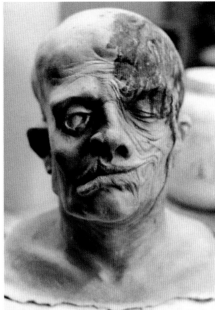

unsexy. That horrible pink shirt! And those pants! And our hair, tied in that horrible little knot! I think the whole look of the twins is dreadful. It was like we were dressed in matron's outfits.

COREY FELDMAN: I was hitting puberty at the time, so there are a lot of memorable experiences for me. It was the first time I saw a woman's bare breasts—Judie Aronson—and I was very excited about that. But what was funny was that it wasn't during the scene in the actual movie, where I was supposed to be looking at her undressing through the window. It actually was when we were shooting the scene when the campers first arrive at the house. My dog is freaking out, and Judie bends over to play with him, and she was wearing a low cut dress, and she didn't have a bra on. It was the first time, outside of my mom, that I'd seen a woman's breasts. So you'll notice in that scene I'm like, "Wow! Oh, look! At…the…dog!"

BARBARA HOWARD: I remember during Judie's nude scene, everybody was standing around—they didn't even make it a closed set. It was not done in a protective, sensitive way. You get so easily swayed. None of these people who tell you it will be fine are going to be there later, when you're feeling bad about it. They just want you to do it.

I think it's all very moralistic. You knew my character was going to die after she lost her virginity. When they offered me the part, I said I wouldn't do any nudity. And they said, "You have to, because all the other girls are." I still said no. I didn't want to be "one of those naked girls in a horror film." I've always been kind of shy—it's just my personality. So I thought I wasn't going to get the film. Then they called back and told my agent, "Okay, she can have a body double, but she can't tell any of the rest of the cast, and we're not going to shoot her death scene until the end." That was really weird. At that point I still didn't want to do it, so my agent was like, "Barb, then you shouldn't have gone in to the audition in the first place." So I ended up doing the film anyway—and I still got my body double.

The bottom line is that I was willing to not do the movie. That's why they came back to me. It was a real lesson to me about power, and I think maybe some of the other actors learned from that. If you won't feel good about yourself, if it's a part that isn't true to yourself, I don't think that anything, certainly any movie, is worth that.

PETER BARTON: I never thought I was a picky, choosy guy, but I was wondering if I wanted to get in the shower and be naked. I was actually very attracted to Barbara, so doing the shower

Opposite page: Ted White transformed. The actor did surprisingly little research to play the character of Jason. "After I decided that I was definitely going to go ahead and do the film," says White, "a friend of mine said, 'My son has got all the tapes of the other movies.' So I went over and watched one—maybe six or seven minutes of it—because I just decided I would do the same old walk that I normally do and not change anything. And that's all I did, really!"

Above: The many faces of Jason Voorhees. "I wanted him to be a thirty-five year-old version of the kid we saw in the first film," says Tom Savini, who created the makeup effects for both *The Final Chapter* and the original *Friday the 13th*. "That's why I came back—I wanted to kill Jason personally. I gave him birth and it was up to me to get rid of him. And they paid me a fortune to do it!"

scene—the close-ups—that was great. What was really kind of sad is that because Barbara wouldn't do the nude scene—which was fine—they got a body double. And I felt so bad, because here this girl is, thinking this will be her big break. But you're only a body double. And she was completely naked. It was so humiliating and mechanical: "Turn her! Put her up against the glass!"

The unfortunate part is that if it had happened to me ten years later, I would have been laughing hysterically. I would have been making jokes. Who cares? Back then I was this scared little actor who was taking it all so seriously. Not that it shouldn't be taken seriously, but it's so Hollywood.

CAMILLA MORE: To be really honest, when you're that young and ambitious, you'll do almost anything. I didn't want to do pornographic movies or whatever, but even a horror movie…I went through the script and was shocked that every single page had another, more brutal murder. It did offend me.

I think what really was important was the quality of creativity that we had with this team. Because it raises the bar if you've got people like Lawrence Monoson and Crispin Glover, and a cast that was coming up with different ways of doing things every time. I believe that because many of our cast had been successful beforehand, there was a certain spirit of, "Let's elevate this. We don't really want it to be a horror movie, we want it to be an excellent movie." Rather than just walk away having taken the money. That's a very arrogant attitude, and I don't think people in their early twenties have developed that cynicism yet.

CAREY MORE: Looking at the film now, I'm trying to think why I even needed to be in the movie. I'm not proud of the character I played in it. I'm this meek, spineless person who

Actor Crispin Glover ranks the filming of his death scene as a highpoint of making *The Final Chapter*. "I'll never forget standing next to Tom Savini with that blade stuck in my head," laughs Glover. "I had a blast, and it was an honor to be killed by someone as great as Tom."

doesn't have very much backbone. Camilla's role was slightly more fleshed out. At least she had the love scene with Crispin, and the fact that she's flirtatious with other girls' boyfriends. I don't have any of that. I was just the twin who was the goody-goody two-shoes, who's the sitting duck.

At times I was nervous. Here were all these professional actors who took it very seriously, like Lawrence Monoson—he was working on his craft in every moment he did. And here I was going, "If you want me, I'll do it." If I were given that role again, I wouldn't be quite so silent. I'd be a little bit more assertive, or give it a bit more humor. Why was I so drippy? But I suppose it's acceptable, because it could be a person. It's not like it was bad acting, it's like I wasn't acting at all. Just being.

LAWRENCE MONOSON: We were all so young and had such an incredible innocence about everything—what was exciting was just making a movie. That it was a *Friday the 13th* was not particularly significant one way or the other. And it was still a big Paramount movie.

One of the most rewarding aspects of the experience was that Crispin and I had a little subplot—I call it a little relationship. I can't believe it, but I can remember that whole sequence in the back of the station wagon, that "dead fuck" scene, where I'm typing on the fake computer. Crispin and I wrote all that. Obviously Barney wrote the movie, but they really gave us a lot of freedom to kind of expand upon the relationship of those two characters.

BARNEY COHEN: OK, here's the deal. I did not want to do that "dead fuck" thing. That was forced upon me—when Joe told me I had to write that, my mouth was open and my jaw was on my chest. Either Scuderi, or Minasian, or Mancuso came up with it. Sometimes things just get mandated, and you have to make them work as best you can. This happens all the time—everybody thinks they can write. I thought it was out of tone for the movie and dragged the movie down a little bit. Cheapened it—that's what I think I argued about a hundred times. So I consider it a feather in my cap that I made it work at all.

KIMBERLY BECK: It didn't matter that it was a stupid horror film. I remember taking it very seriously. I approached it as if I was doing an amazing movie that was going to be seen the world over. I didn't think of this as going to be a piece of shit horror movie. I don't think any of us did. I think we all thought to ourselves, "I'm just going to do the best I can." And we did.

In the three years between the release of Friday the 13th *and pre-production on* The Final Chapter, *special makeup effects wizard Tom Savini became something of a star in his own right. Dubbed the "guru of gore" by the press, few makeup effects artists in history remain as closely associated with the art of gruesome, bloody effects as Savini; in fact, his illusions have been so influential that, arguably, his is one of the most recognizable names of any personality from the 1980's slasher era outside of, perhaps, Jamie Lee Curtis. Savini even became a key component in the marketing campaigns of the films to which he contributed: when a fledgling new studio called Miramax rolled out the press junket for their 1981* Friday the 13th *clone,* The Burning, *they didn't bother to send any of the actors, including a then-unknown Holly Hunter. The only star worth mentioning was Tom Savini.*

JOSEPH ZITO: It'll offend one or two, but I'll tell this story anyway. When I came aboard, I thought it was really important to get Tom Savini. At this point, we had done *The Prowler* together and I knew how terrific Tom was. But even more important, he had conceived of the look of Jason, and as we were going for a real revelation in *The Final Chapter*, to really show Jason behind the mask, I felt it was imperative for Tom to build upon what he had created.

Tom was not an easy sell. The studio had somebody else, a very, very terrific guy, Greg Cannom, who's gone on to win Academy Awards. He's an absolutely first-rate, class-A guy. But he wanted to redefine Jason in a completely different way that wasn't related to the first film. He didn't want his work to be derived from anybody else. So I thought Tom was the only way to go.

TOM SAVINI, Special Makeup Effects: I was doing this haunted house in North Carolina and got a phone call from Joe Zito. He had the last *Friday the 13th* movie, and he wanted me to work with him on it. It wasn't until I got out there that I learned that Greg Cannom had the job first.

"Oh, it was very demented. We could have easily been arrested just for the conversations we had about how to kill these people." **Joseph Zito**

For Lawrence Monoson, performing his death scene (**background**) was the purest form of method acting. "At that time, I was very, very serious," recalls the actor. "My character was smoking pot, so I was really interested in, 'What would it be like to actually be stoned?' I thought, in a way, that this is the highest form of acting, because I won't *be* acting. So I smoked a little pot in my trailer. And it was the worst thing that I could have possibly done. I was so paranoid. Just freaking out on the set. I barely functioned. It was absolutely horrible. Once it faded away, I was like, 'OK. Experiment. Failure. Never doing that again.' Who says drugs help creativity? They're wrong."

The murder of Doug (Peter Barton, **top**) is perhaps the most physically violent moment in *The Final Chapter*. "I wanted to go against the cliché of the girl in the shower that we all know from *Psycho*," says director Joseph Zito. "So, in our version, it's the prettiest guy with the most chiseled face, the most perfect face. And what does Jason do to him? He just goes right through the glass and crushes his head against the tile. Just smashes his face. It was sort of fun in a way—I mean, not that smashing someone's head in the shower in real life should be fun—but in a movie way. I also think it interested Peter Barton, the actor, not only because it went against the cliché but because, at the time, he was still going through that teen star adulation thing."

Filming the scene was not quite so much fun for Barton, however. "Yeah, I was scared," admits the actor. "I already had been hurt on set once before, while shooting a series I had done called *The Powers of Matthew Starr*. I fell on a magnesium flare and ended up with third-degree burns and four operations at the hospital. So I was afraid during that whole scene." Manhandling the actor was also disquieting to stuntman Ted White. "Of course, it was all fake," says Jason number four, "but I still had to tell the poor kid, 'I have to make this look like real. I can't tap you. I've really got to put your head into that wall. Are you ready for that?' And Peter said, 'Well, I don't know, you're an awfully big guy!' So I talked to the assistant director and we were able to put a pad behind his head. But I still hated what I had to do to him!"

I went and met the crew and they were terrific: Kevin Yagher, Alec Gillis, John Vulich—they've all gone on to form their own very successful effects companies since *The Final Chapter*. But it must have been a very frustrating experience for them. They should have started working on the effects three weeks before I got there, but they were only allowed to work on some props and cast the head of Ted White, who played Jason. I think we worked miracles, considering the limited time that we had.

ERICH ANDERSON: Every time someone would ask what film I was working on and I'd say *Friday the 13th*, they'd ask, "Do you know Tom Savini!?" He was the star.

TOM SAVINI: When I showed up on the set, there had been a few *Friday the 13th* movies in the interim, and I had done *Dawn of the Dead*, which was like the ultimate effects movie going at the time. As soon as I got there the actors were coming up to me, asking, "How am I going to die?" And the juicier the death, the better. They just wanted to die in the most glorious ways, because, to them, that was like their claim to fame, you know? And no of them were a problem. If we had to cast their naked body, it was like, "Great, if it means I'm going to have this big, bloody death!"

BARBARA HOWARD: I think the most fun I had making the movie was the day I "died." I had come from a theatre background—where you're so used to that team feeling—and by the time we shot my death scene I had become pretty good friends with much of the crew. It was also my last day of filming. So, as if in mourning, the crew all wore black armbands. I was so touched—I've never forgotten that. It was just very sweet.

BONNIE HELLMAN: When it came time to shoot my death scene, there I was sitting out in the forest with like fifty people around me, all very serious about what they're doing. Just to get shots of my hand squeezing a banana. And they say, "Okay, we need quivering. We need vocal quivering. Now some small screams. Now, some big screams. Now, a little more quivering. And don't forget, look natural!" If you get stabbed in the throat, that's one thing. But if you're stabbed in the throat while eating a banana, that just takes it to a whole new level of absurdity.

BARNEY COHEN: Joe Zito is a really smart guy. He said a lot of things during the making of this movie that I've used throughout my career. One thing he said was, "If you scare someone in a theater, that takes about three seconds. But if you creep someone out, that lasts all night." So the goal was to create kids that were real, that it would really be a shame to see die, and truly kill 'em.

I didn't go to Vietnam. I had been drafted, but I got lucky, and I wound up going to Germany. But I did all the training, and I hung out with guys that had those hollow eyes, that sense that they weren't going to make it through the year. And I remember in writing each kill that I wanted to play with that brief moment, that look, so that nobody got killed without knowing that it was going to happen to them first, and that they had to make some kind of peace with it. And when I thought of that, it just gave me goosebumps. This ability to, essentially, announce your own death and not be able to do anything about it. Although this was something that, in all honesty, might have been the least-well-translated thing from the page to the stage.

JOSEPH ZITO: Anticipation is what makes a scary movie, certainly more than any gore we can demonstrate. When I watch films, I find it less interesting when a film dwells on the aftermath. What scares me are the things that precede the horrific moment. I'm scared when Martin Balsam is walking up the stairs in *Psycho*. Everybody thinks all we did in *Friday the 13th* was show every graphic thing that occurs in a mutilation. We didn't—we showed enough. Once that moment occurs, and once the audience has psychologically accepted it, it is not a kick to continue to stay on that. It's more interesting to get to the next moment.

JOEL GOODMAN, Editor: Early on, we made a conscious effort to establish Jason as an object of fear. We wanted to show the really awful things that this creature does so we could give the audience a reason to be afraid of him. And it was a very conscious decision to keep Jason in the shadows more. Because let's face it, a bogeyman in a hockey mask is ridiculous. That's why the less of the guy you show, the better off you are. If you imagine him, he's going to be scarier. It's the context that makes it scary. Less is more.

JOSEPH ZITO: One thing I really struggled with, and had a number of conversations about with key people, was that I thought it would be a really good thing if I could keep Jason dead long enough at the beginning. Of course, Jason's gotta be alive, but he's not just lying there and suddenly turns around and starts chasing everybody. So that is why there is that opening sequence to the movie, that starts with the tracking shot of the helicopter. Then we go through the mud with the emergency workers, finding bodies. And there is Jason, lying there with a mask on, and they throw the tarp over him. Which is ridiculous, but nonetheless, he's Jason. Then we take him to the morgue and we hold off on the moment of him coming to life. I wanted people in the theater to start shouting, trying to bring him to life, telling him to get up. In essence, making the audience co-conspirators with the filmmakers. Because if he just gets up, the audience would groan and say, "Oh, no, you already killed him last time, what's the deal?" This way, they would want for him to get up.

It became clear to the young cast and crew of The Final Chapter *that Zito's perfectionism would come into play well beyond the casting sessions. Those who soldiered under him came away from the experience with a range of emotions: many positive, some mixed, and a few bordering on hostile—particularly Ted White, a professional stuntman who became the fourth actor to win the role of Jason Voorhees. White's relationship with Zito was, by all accounts, initially positive; soon, however, Zito's battlefield mentality and, in particular, his "tough love" approach to his actors clashed with White, who was already reluctant in accepting the role. The situation eventually boiled over during one particularly long, cold, bitter night out in the hills of Hollywood while shooting the film's most harrowing murder sequence. It would not be pretty.*

JOSEPH ZITO: I wanted to change Jason. In a way, he was a little more humanized—he got some more IQ points, ya know? He would hide his bodies, he would move them around, he nails a kid to a wall, and during the climax with Tommy, he listens to reason—sort of. So Jason had to move in different ways. And since we were making a departure with the character anyway, I thought it was important to hire a stuntman who could do that and take direction.

I had made a ridiculous decision during the making of *The Prowler*. I thought, "The guy under the mask, what does that matter?" But I was wrong. It is very, very important who's under that mask. So on *The Final Chapter*, I auditioned a number of actors for the role, but we ultimately went with a guy who had tremendous experience as a stuntman and a double in many big Hollywood movies. And he was way older than any of the other Jasons. He'll probably kill me if I got this wrong, but I think he was in his sixties at the time.

TED WHITE, "Jason Voorhees": Before I did Jason I was a full-time stuntman. I doubled John Wayne for forty years. I doubled Clark Gable. Those were the two guys kept me busy most of my career, and then I doubled Victor Mature, and Rock Hudson. I did the *Daniel Boone* series for six years. I was very busy.

Before *The Final Chapter*, I had done a film called *Romancing the Stone* that Bob Zemeckis directed. I did the opening of the show—I'm the cowboy that walks in the hut to get the girl. I enter through the door, silhouetted in the frame. And I can't remember, but I think Mancini, or Mancuso—what the hell was his name?—he saw that and said, "Find out who he is. That's the guy we want for Jason."

It really was not a role. All I'm doing is killing and mangling these young kids. I hate to put it this way, but it's the God's honest truth: if it wasn't for the money, I never would have done the show. I even turned it down originally. It was on hold six weeks. But during that six weeks, greed just took over and I said, "I'll do it."

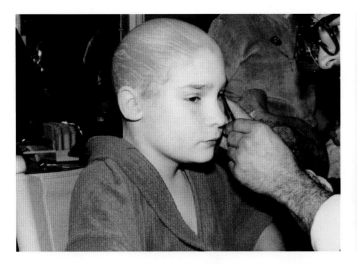

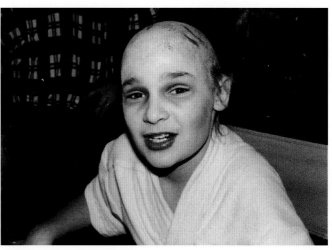

TOM SAVINI: He's a cowboy, Ted White. He would be in the parking lot, lassoing the rearview mirrors of cars as they went by.

COREY FELDMAN: Ted White was a Jerry Lee Lewis type dude, and that was hard for me to relate to, 'cause I'm not a cowboy type. He was nice and kind, but distant. You'd see him playing poker and chewing tobacco with the crew guys, but he didn't have a lot of interaction with the cast. He stayed off in his own "Jason world." But out of all the *Friday* films that I've seen, I think he did the best job: menacing, brooding, with that stance and that walk. Silent, but deadly.

TED WHITE: I did things that none of the other Jasons did. I never, ever, took off my makeup while I was on the set. And I kept away from the cast and crew completely. And by doing so, I created a little bit of a mystique. When visitors would come onto the set, oddly enough they would not come up and talk to me. They would walk around quite a ways away and just look. It was kind of a funny thing.

ERICH ANDERSON: Ted hated every single aspect of it. We were all neophytes, and Ted was a seasoned stunt professional. We made mistake after mistake, and I think that was frustrating to Ted. Also, Joe was very demanding about what he wanted. Then, the last forty scenes in the movie take place at night, and in the rain. And I don't know how many hours of makeup Ted had to go through just for the scene where Jason takes off his mask.

TED WHITE: Joe Zito and I, we started off pretty good for about the first six or seven days, but after that he became kind of a bully. And I'm not the kind of guy you can bully around. I'm not a "tough guy" or nothing like that, I just don't like to see people get hurt, or abused. I told Joe several times, "Kiss my ass," because he treated those kids like dirt. He really and truly did. I hate to tell it to you this way. They hired them for minimum. They got no money at all. I think at that time it was something like $455 a day, that's what they paid them. I'm sure not all of them had a bad experience, but it was just terrible what I had to do to them. A lot of them I had to physically handle—it wasn't where you could just make a motion, I really had to grab 'em and do it. It just wasn't pleasant for me.

FRANK MANCUSO, JR.: Personality conflicts that exist in the making of a film are like anything else in life. So many factors can affect someone's personality, and when you're together that many hours, that many days in a row, and then it's late, and everyone's tired…you can't take it seriously. Plus, I never

felt that anyone was ever trying to undermine the well-being of the movie. I certainly didn't feel that with Ted.

JOSEPH ZITO: The truth of the matter is that Ted's main problem was that he was embarrassed because of the Jason makeup. It actually made him drool—and he didn't want to be seen drooling. It wasn't an effect. It literally was choking him up, to have this thing on his teeth and all that. I know because Savini told me the story, too. But the toughest thing on this guy, and the way we really actually could have lost him, was the scene at the lake. Oh, boy.

JUDIE ARONSON: We shot my death scene in a reservoir in Coldwater Canyon—in December. They put me in a wetsuit which went from my waist down, and then the raft had a hole in the bottom of it. My body went up through the hole vertically, like I was standing up—kind of floating—with my chest and my arms hanging over the edge of the raft. Then they connected a fake back from my shoulders down. This took hours and hours and hours to set up and film, from sundown until sunup—and at night in L.A. it can get down to like 40 degrees. Even the crew were in parkas. And I'm a California girl and I'm used to it always being 70 degrees. So I get colder than the normal person anyway. But under those circumstances anybody would have. It was horrible.

TED WHITE: It was extremely cold. We'd gone through four or five takes, and they weren't exactly right. Judie said, "Please, can I get out of the water?" And Joe said, "No, we'll be with you in just a few minutes." And she said, "Please, I'm freezing to death!" And they still said, "No." Finally, I said, "That does it. Get the girl outta the damn water right now, or I walk. I'm not gonna put up with this bullshit any longer. She's an eighteen-year-old kid and she's dying in that water, and you're telling her no?" Well, they got her out. But from that minute on, Joe and I never saw eye-to-eye.

JOSEPH ZITO: The toughest thing for Ted to do was stay in the water; he wanted to come out. He didn't want to finish the scene. Judie was cold, but she was fine. That girl was absolutely, one hundred percent naked in that raft and a real trooper. Ted was the one who was cold.

Here's the real story. Ted said, "Joe, I'm getting to feel cold; I'm feeling it in my bones, I don't want to stay in here." It wasn't really a fight. The fight was this. I said, "You're not getting out of that lake." Yes, I bullied him into staying in the lake, when naked Judie was willing to stay there, and tough guy Ted wanted to get out. That's a pisser. Ask Judie about that.

JUDIE ARONSON: No, that's not true. When half of your body is in the water for that many hours it becomes really unbearable. I cried. I tried not to. I was a little bit delirious. I was out of my mind. I remember saying, "I can't do it anymore, I just can't go on," and they would be like, "A little bit more, just a little bit more." They would not let me stop, that I remember. At one point they did take me out and heated me up, but then I had to go back in. And it was just as miserable. It was just way too long to be outside in the water. Wetsuits don't matter when you're in it that long and it's cold out, and the wetsuit was only actually from the waist down, so my top part was still freezing.

JOSEPH ZITO: I'm not trying to protect the story or deny it. I just know that I was never aware of his concerns about anything but himself being too cold. He never said anything to me. He might have had a conversation with the assistant director. I would think as an experienced guy, it's very, very likely that he was an advocate for Judie. But she was okay. I don't want you to think we were completely crazy. We had professionals there—we had medical personnel and we had divers. It wasn't just like we thought, "Hey, lets go to a freezing cold lake and put a naked girl in it." Ted was right to be concerned, but we were concerned, too.

The truth is, I had no social relationship with Ted. I don't remember once talking to him outside of him being in character: "Do this" and "Stand there." I don't remember having a single conversation with the guy.

JUDIE ARONSON: I don't remember a lot about that night because I was really sick. In the true sense of hypothermia, I lost my mind. All I remember is when it ended. I couldn't even deal with taking my clothes off when I got home. I couldn't deal with getting in my bed. All I could think about is, "I need to get warm really fast." I was in college at the time and I had a roommate, so I crawled into bed with her. We laugh about it now—I just needed somebody. I was so out of it.

I should have gone to the hospital, but I didn't. I was sick like a dog after that. I was in really bad shape. In retrospect, they absolutely should have just shot it in a tank, because during the actual shot where I die, you don't see anything around the raft anyway. And I would not accept that now. I would walk off. But at the time I just tried to grin and bear it.

PETER BARTON: I'll go along with backing up the Jason guy—Zito wasn't a caring kind of guy. I'm not trying to badmouth Joe, but he was all about being hard on Judie, because it was like, "Let's get it done." I could see Ted getting upset. No doubt about it. To be fair to Joe, probably he just didn't know. But the water was really cold, and unless you're in it, you don't know how painful it is when your body starts shutting down. He should have gotten in.

We were just making a movie. I always cared about it, but I also know that like when you do television, it's more a machine kind of thing—actors don't get a lot of takes. In my experience on *The Final Chapter*, Joe never worked with me. Never. And if you start caring so much about your performance, and then they just move on, you've got to be able to let it go, because otherwise you get really angry. They couldn't care less about what the scene was about, or the acting. Their focus was on the effects, which I don't blame them for. Whatever came out of your mouth, it was like, "Fine, print. OK, next shot. Let's get to the killing." And I was a guy who liked to be coddled. But in both *Friday* and *Hell Night*, there wasn't a lot of coddling. There usually isn't, in horror pictures.

KIMBERLY BECK: There wasn't a lot of respect for the process. People were like, "Oh, just get the fucking thing done and shut up!" I don't want to say anything bad about anyone because I really was grateful for the experience. I talked to Joe a little bit about it, but then you feel kind of stupid because of the way they're approaching it. But Joe was so sweet. He was just really, really serious. But then, we all were.

BARBARA HOWARD: Joe and I—we certainly weren't close. It was not like how I've felt with some other directors that I've worked with. I didn't leave with any sort of relationship with him whatsoever. I don't think I ever saw or talked to him again. We had a better rapport in the audition process—I remember him being warmer and seeming to be interested in the character. But once we were shooting...maybe he just felt he cast well. Sometimes, after that, the director will then just get out of your way.

Actress Joan Freeman made her professional curtain call with the role of Mrs. Jarvis in *The Final Chapter*. "I had a wonderful career," says Freeman, "but as you get older there are fewer and fewer parts. I had never seen any of the other *Friday the 13th* movies, but the character—and Kimberly and Corey as my children—meant that there was enough to work with."

The fate of Mrs. Jarvis is never revealed in *The Final Chapter*, which has led many fans of the series to speculate about the exact nature of her demise. "There was one scene shot that didn't end up in the movie," says Freeman. "I'm discovered in a bathtub by Kimberly, fully clothed, just lying dead face-up underneath the water. We also shot another version which was supposed to be the original ending of the movie. My eyes are all nightmarish, and I rise up out of the bathtub at Kimberly, as if I'm not really dead. Then it turns out to be a dream. I even had a 'death mask' (**above**) made by Tom Savini."

Director Joseph Zito explains the reason these scenes failed to make the final cut. "When Trish finds her mother, I felt we already knew Mrs. Jarvis was dead, so why show it?" says Zito. "And the dream sequence of Mrs. Jarvis rising out of the bathtub—that came from Phil Scuderi and Frank Mancuso, Jr. The ending of the original *Friday the 13th*, with Jason lunging out of the lake, had been very effective. So Phil wanted another scene like it. And what we shot with Mrs. Jarvis was quite scary—she had on white contact lenses on and almost exploded out of the tub like a monster. But I just didn't feel like it added to the film."

Opposite page: "I wanted Corey to really shave his head," says director Joseph Zito of filming *The Final Chapter*'s climax, a psychological duel between Tommy and Jason. "But his guardians were worried because the television pilot season was coming up, and he wouldn't be able to get any roles in television if he was bald. I even said to Corey, 'I'll shave my head if you shave your head, how's that?' He thought that was cool, but they still wouldn't let him do it. So we ended up going with a bald cap."

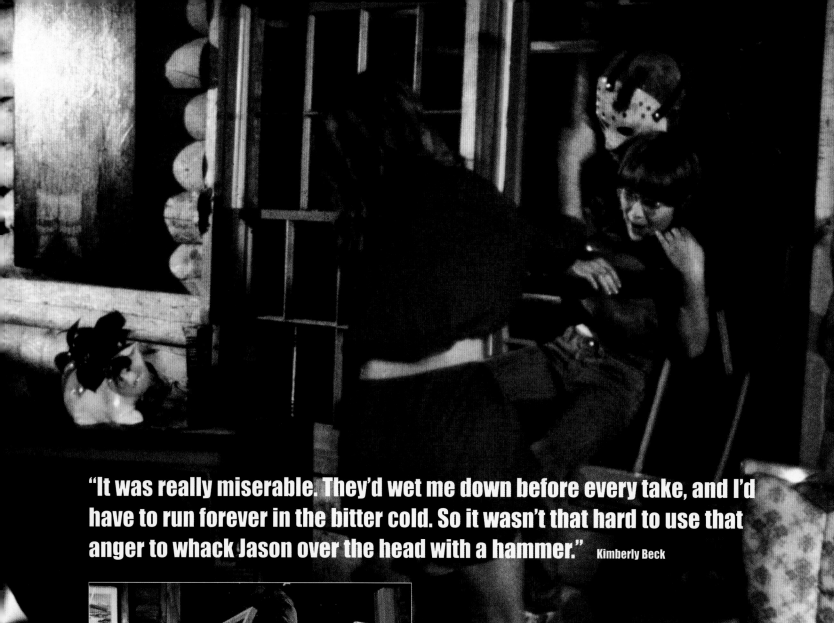

"It was really miserable. They'd wet me down before every take, and I'd have to run forever in the bitter cold. So it wasn't that hard to use that anger to whack Jason over the head with a hammer." Kimberly Beck

Above: "The most intense moment of the entire shoot was when Jason grabs me through the window," remembers actor Corey Feldman. "It was shot in one complete take—a two or three page scene. Joe Zito said to me, 'This dead body is going to crash through first, and then you'll freak out, scream, move from one mark to another, then back towards the window. And wait. Then, at some point, Jason is going to come through the window and pick you up.' So we go through the timing of the scene. Then Joseph yells, 'Action!' So Kimberly Beck and I run around, I back up to the window…beat, beat, beat…and…beat, beat, beat…no Jason. I'm thinking, 'Oh, okay, the stunt didn't work right.' And then, *boom!* Jason smashes through. This huge man comes from behind me with such force and impact that he takes me straight up seven feet in the air. And I'm only two feet tall at this time. I was losing it. It scared the shit out of me. That expression you see on my face was not acting, folks!"

Left: Makeup effects artist John Vulich (left) applies a touch-up to actor Erich Anderson during the filming of his character Rob's death scene. The grisly results provided an unexpectedly humorous antecedent for Anderson. "It was so cold and wet the night we filmed that scene, and I just wanted to get home at the end of the shoot," recalls the actor. "I had this old Air Force parka that my father gave me to wear, and I just put it on over my wet clothes because I was so tired. So here it is, six o'clock in the morning, and my car starts behaving inconsistently. And I get pulled over with blood all over me. The look on that cop's face was priceless!"

ERICH ANDERSON: Joe's thing was that he truly didn't want this to come off as a cheap horror movie. A lot of care was taken in a lot of areas. Joe wanted what he wanted, and we did it until he was happy with it. We were supposed to shoot for six weeks and we shot for twelve. We went way over. It was because Joe was a perfectionist. He wasn't concerned so much with fulfilling the needs of those paying the bills as he was determined to make a good movie. I always admired that. And in the end—at least at that time—it was considered the ace of that series, from a critical standpoint.

JOEL GOODMAN: Joe is very magnetic. He's got a certain intensity, and he kind of sucks you into his world. In an alternate universe, Joe could be a general leading people up into some kind of bizarre battle, "We're gonna take that hill!"

BARNEY COHEN: I learned a butt-load of "Zito-isms" on *The Final Chapter*. Like, never audition for a job you already have. And that no matter what you're doing, you have to work at the top of your craft. I eventually took the movie very seriously, but I didn't start out taking it seriously. I started out kidding and joking—being "better" than the material. And Zito kept calling me on it. He finally said, "You're not better than this, or you would be writing stuff that's better than this, so let's do the best we can." He was right, I was disrespecting the material. He sort of gave me enough rope, and then he said, "OK, let's get serious with this. How would you write this if it were a 'real movie?'" I think what I learned most from *The Final Chapter* is that no

matter what it is you're doing, it's what you're doing, so you've got to do it as good as you can. And that is in part thanks to Joe. I still keep that close to my heart.

After three films and nearly three dozen murders, the makers of The Final Chapter *knew that audiences would be out for blood—Jason's blood. They also knew that, if nothing else, they had to sustain a level of intensity during the film's climax that would top the three previous* Fridays *combined. But despite having three past successes—and their attendant mistakes—to learn from, the filmmakers' greatest asset was also potentially their greatest liability: audience familiarity. Now that the* Friday the 13th *"formula" had been all but perfected, there was little option but to both honor the shopworn clichés of the genre while making at least some attempt to subvert them—and all without the crutch of self-referential irony, postmodern pastiche or, most dangerous of all, campy humor.*

But the biggest challenge lay in the moment the filmmakers knew the audience had ultimately paid their money to see: Jason's demise. It had to be grand. It had to be gory. It had to be shocking. And it had to bring the audience to their feet.

JOEL GOODMAN: In a way, these movies play peek-a-boo—they're going back to these very primal experiences. There's either drawn-out anticipation, or the out of left field scare. We were very much aware of that when we constructed the movie. The classic *Friday the 13th* dynamic is the interaction, where you want the audience to say, "Don't go in the room!" Like when the main character, Trish, steps over Jason's supposedly lifeless body—you know he's going to get back up to grab her. It's a horror movie staple. What we were trying to do was not to talk down to the audience, but still do the best job possible within the conventions of the genre. Because, really, we'd be cheating you if we didn't give you that moment, wouldn't we?

JOSEPH ZITO: The audience has a very, very rare opportunity to be smarter than the characters in these films. They know that the people they are watching are deliberately doing dumb things. But it empowers the audience. It involves them in it.

A friend of mine, who is a film director, said, "Yeah, the movie was alright, but in that scene where Jason busts through the door, and the characters used those little nails—that was really stupid. Why did you do that?" We made that dumb on purpose. It's a pathetic thing for these characters to try and do, hammering with these tiny little nails, trying to hold down this door. That was exactly the point. We wanted the audience to think that those little nails aren't going to keep Jason out of this house. We did that specifically so you would feel that moment.

KIMBERLY BECK: I tried to make it as real as I could. I had to say dumb things and I had to do dumb things, but I tried to find a reason why I was doing it, so it made some sense. I tried to approach it realistically. I wanted to really be scared. I remember working with my acting coach, finding ways that were emotionally very true for me. I figured that this was great exercise and a great way for me to grow as an actor.

ERICH ANDERSON: When I got the part, I didn't know anything about the mythology of the series. I just wasn't aware of them. Culturally, I wasn't in tune with what was going on. Casting director Pamela Basker said to me, "This is what happens. You won't know this until you see the movie with an audience, but it's all these dumb kids who are obsessed with sex, getting killed one by one. And when they die, the audience cheers. So you know what would be a good task for you, Erich? If when you die, nobody cheers. That would make me feel really good if that happened." So that was how I approached the role from the beginning.

Consequently, in my death scene, I thought it was the stupidest thing you could ever say in that situation: "He's killing me!" Come on! But it just seemed natural in the moment, and it also seemed horrible. Suddenly, it didn't make Jason such an iconic figure. If he's just slaughtering dumb kids that's one thing, but killing a guy who's trying to avenge the death of his sister and two other completely innocent people? I think Joe knew that. My killing wasn't about flesh getting ripped from my body. I think it set this entire new level of terror, because all that's left is Kimberly and the little kid.

JOSEPH ZITO: Erich was an actor I didn't know before. I discovered him in casting. His was a very important character for me, mostly because of that one scene. I've read fan reviews that have attacked the moment where Rob is in the basement, and he's saying, "He's killing me! He's killing me!" They say it's silly. But it actually came out of something I read in the newspaper. A horrible story about a guy being stabbed repeatedly in a street in New York City. The guy was screaming, "Please stop hurting me, please stop killing me." And people could hear the attack, yet no one called the police.

The story was about how tragic that was, and it is. But I focused on a different aspect, that he was speaking to the assailant as he was being murdered. That there they were in conversation—this horrible, shrill conversation. Where he has the chance to realize what's happening. Instead of just being stabbed, he falls down in an opera.

BARNEY COHEN: Kids having fun with these movies—that was a phenomenon that I hadn't seen before. Joe said to me, "I'd like to ratchet up the intelligence of this talking to the screen business. People usually talk to the screen because someone is doing something stupid, but here, let's give the audience two reasonable choices on the screen." That was typified by that scene after Rob is killed, where Trish can either run outside or back down into the basement. Both choices make sense, and both of them don't make sense, so what you have is a situation where some kids in the audience are yelling for one choice, and some kids are yelling for the other choice, and you have sort of a debate going. Scenes like that were a lot of fun to construct. I've always remembered that elsewhere in my career—to try to give the audience choices.

JOEL GOODMAN: In a way, it's funny how—even back then—there was a conscious, self-referential thing going on. Which of course, with *Scream*, has become increasingly overt. But with the early *Friday the 13th* movies, there is just a little bit of it—they played out a formula and referenced other horror pictures of the time, and it is a little tongue-in-cheek, because at a certain point and on an intellectual level, it's silly. Yet on a visceral level, somehow there's a reason why it works.

BARNEY COHEN: Fans have always asked me about the ending when Tommy wears the bald cap and is telling Jason, "Remember, Jason, remember!" Well, what he is supposed to remember is the image of the actual Jason, in the water, from the first movie. I don't know why, it just seemed like the right thing to do. If you go back to the moment of death, it comes for Jason, too.

One of the things I argued with Joe about was that it's no fun to kill a monster unless the monster understands his mortality. And so, at the end, one of the things that I wanted to do, that we couldn't do, was that Jason reaches out for Trish's breast. He doesn't actually touch it, but he's at a calm moment, and you can read that Jason is getting another idea here, that finally there's something better than killing. Jason has a thought in his head that isn't murderous, it's actually amorous. And it's at that moment that he can be killed. It was a softening of Jason, like that scene in *Frankenstein* with the little girl at the well. In that moment Jason is no longer a monster—he's almost human—and where his killing almost becomes sympathetic.

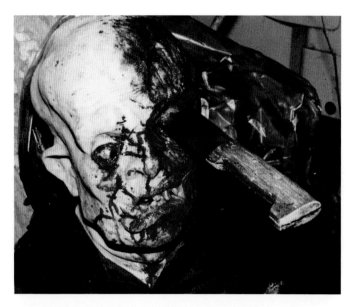

The Final Chapter's most elaborate effect was, fittingly, the demise of Jason. Makeup effects designer Tom Savini describes the effect: "It was a fully articulated, mechanical Jason, for the moment when he slides down the machete, because you could never do that with a real person. All the expressions were cable controlled—the eyebrows moving, the nose twitching and the mouth gyrating. We even had a guy inside Jason's head with a tongue on his finger, wiggling it out of Jason's mouth.

"We ended up shooting I don't know how many takes of his body sliding down that machete, different versions because of the ratings board. The machete was actually on a track inside the head. We also had the top of the head on a mechanism that would twist as if it was being sliced off. We did a number of takes of that, too. Finally, the last take was the one with all the blood (**above**), although in the finished film, we had to use a 'clean' shot with only a bit of blood in the cutaway."

Despite the grisly subject matter, working on *The Final Chapter* remains one of Savini's most enjoyable professional experiences. "We didn't work on a soundstage at all," he remembers. "Our effects workshop was in the 'war room' at Zoetrope Studios, which Francis Ford Coppola used as his headquarters while he directed a film—where he watched a zillion TV monitors. Zoetrope was exactly what you imagine Hollywood to be—all these people wandering around in period costumes, fantastic wigs and makeup. Mr. T was shooting a commercial there, Loni Anderson was doing a TV special, Kenny Rogers and Van Halen were shooting videos—it was like a dream come true. I'd be whistling 'Hooray for Hollywood!' while I worked."

TOM SAVINI: The script had Tommy Jarvis splitting Jason's head open with a machete. I didn't particularly want to do that for Jason's death, so I was trying to think of something better. I thought that Tommy, being an inventor and a special effects kid, perhaps he took a microwave oven apart. He got the shooter and put a reflector behind it, with a variable control on the voltage that goes from one to ten. Then, early in the film, when he's showing off his roomful of effects for Rob, he puts it on one and melts a toy soldier. Then, at the end, he could grab this thing and stick it at Jason's head. He turns it up to ten and cooks Jason's head from the inside, and it explodes.

I had to sell this on the phone to the money guys. They said it was logical, but they wanted to stick to the *Friday the 13th* formula, which is killing naked teenagers in the woods with household implements. And I'm thinking, "Well, a microwave is a household implement…" But I guess it was too sci-fi for them.

Then one day, one of my assistants, John Vulich, was goofing around in the shop and took a machete we had put in a zombie's head in *Dawn of the Dead*. He said, "Why don't we kill Jason with this?" So I thought, "Yeah, that's what we'll do. We'll have Tommy smack Jason in the head with a machete, do a reverse shot of the blade going in, and then go a step further—let's have Jason fall to his knees and slide

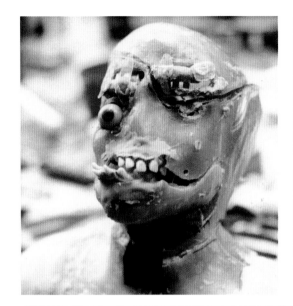

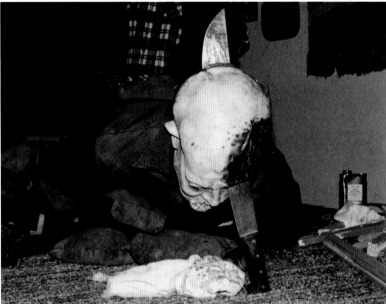
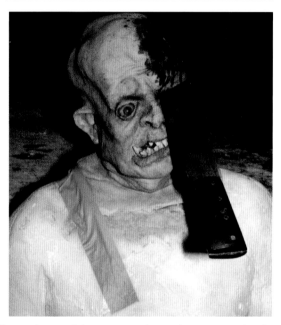

down the blade." That's what we subsequently pitched to the producers, and that's what they decided to go with. And that, really, is the ultimate death now for Jason.

COREY FELDMAN: The most horrifying experience for me on that set was when we were doing the climactic scene. I was wearing this bald cap every day for like two weeks. And because of that, I got very, very ill—your body temperature rises when you cut off the circulation to your brain. I got sicker and sicker, temperature rising to a 101 or 102 degree fever. I remember dreading having to complete that final scene because it was so much work. I was so tired. I had black circles around my eyes from the makeup, but a lot of that was real. That shot where you see me killing Jason—that is really me thinking of Joseph Zito, "Die! Die!"

Principal photography on Friday the 13th – The Final Chapter *was completed in January 1984. Paramount Pictures had originally intended to open the film in October of that year, but after early footage was screened by an enthusiastic Frank Mancuso, Sr. and a window of opportunity presented itself in the studio's spring lineup,* The Final Chapter *suddenly had a new release date—a full six months ahead of schedule. Post-production would become a madcap marathon. There was also the matter of getting the film past the MPAA ratings board. As had become the norm for the series, Hollywood's watchdogs were only too happy to make the filmmakers' jobs as difficult as they could.*

JOSEPH ZITO: I was basically going into this thing with the studio telling me in advance, "We don't quite believe in this, we're just making another one and we're going to throw it out there." It ended up being a very different experience than what the studio started out thinking. Frank Mancuso, Sr. came out and said, "Look, I believe you cannot hit this date, but we have a window of availability in April"—which is like six weeks away! "Now, you have to tell me whether you can get the film ready by that date or not. There can be no mistakes, because we're going to release this in a thousand-plus theaters and we cannot have 1,600 dark screens." I said, "I think I can hit it." Frank said, "No, you cannot *think* you can hit it—you have to tell me that you absolutely can." I said, "I had an editorial service on *The Prowler*. If you let me bring my editors, I can construct something with teams of editors and we can meet that date."

Frank agreed, but then he said, "We're going to do it in the following way: forget where you live—we're going to rent a house in Malibu for you, and you're going to move into that house. And Frank, Jr. will move into that house, and all your editors and their assistants and their apprentices will move into that house. Food will be brought in for you. You will never leave until the film is ready to be screened." So I said, "Malibu? This is really Hollywood!" Of course, being Hollywood, it was a slight lie. It wasn't Malibu, it was Zuma Beach. But it was still pretty cool.

JOEL GOODMAN: It was *Animal House*. It became like basic training. The theory was that we were going to make a maximum effort to get it done on schedule. I always got into the machismo of, "work 'til you drop," and Joe has this inexhaustible supply of energy. So then you get a couple guys together in a house and it becomes kind of a macho thing of who can work faster, and who can stay up later.

JOSEPH ZITO: We literally had apprentices sleeping in the garage. We were editing around the clock. You heard screams coming out of that house all day and all night. And there was no digital. This was all editing machines, all film. The house was just full of film.

HARRY MANFREDINI, Composer: *The Final Chapter* was the most fun I've ever had making a movie. We had a ball. It was just a riot. Craziness. There were four or five guys editing and we were trying to cut music in this house in Malibu. All the music was newly recorded. There were elements that were similar, but nothing that was just lifted and put in. It got to the point where the editors and I would be working with Frank Jr. behind us, looking over our shoulders. It was also such a panic because they were up against the MPAA, who would only screen one reel at a time. It was insane.

JOSEPH ZITO: You finish a picture and the MPAA looks at it. And they come back with some report that they're appalled. Then there's some serious negotiation process, which is such a mercurial thing, because you go to them and say, "How many frames should I cut from this?" and they're not allowed to tell you what to do. They're not allowed to be editors. They can only say "in the aggregate, we find this offensive."

The MPAA knows the practicalities of the business. They know you have a release date, and they're not going to take a major company down and not have the film ready. On the other hand, they're trying to pressure you to cut something, but they can't be specific. So it might be that you take a frame out, then you show it to them another time, and another time, and another time, and you negotiate into a position that finally everybody agrees to.

JOEL GOODMAN: We had to go back and trim things three or four times. It became a mutual wearing-down. And I think that overdoing the gore in *The Final Chapter* was always part of the plan. You certainly don't censor yourself too much in the beginning, because you know somebody else is going to be ready to do that for you.

I thought a lot of Tom Savini's stuff was amazing in this one. It's totally horrifying. When I watched the movie again recently, I found myself squirming at some of the really gory stuff. I was having the audience reaction, but I don't think that happens at all while you're working on it—when you see footage with a slate at the beginning of it, you know what you're looking at isn't real. So it does become a bit abstracted. "Is this too gory? Can we get away with this? What's the scariest thing?"

JOSEPH ZITO: I will argue with other filmmakers about this, but I absolutely believe a single frame makes a difference in how you perceive something, emotionally. It really changes how you feel about it. And you can take three frames out of an effect scene and have it work differently for you, and in fact three frames too many can have it stop working for you, too.

TOM SAVINI: The effects in *The Final Chapter* were very quick. They were almost registered subliminally. Which was great,

because Jason's death was so long and protracted, that it came as more of a shock. When that happened, you could see the whole audience shift backwards in their seats, as if they were being sprayed with blood themselves.

COREY FELDMAN: There was some serious gore involved. Not to say it isn't gory in the final version, but when we shot the scene where I slice Jason's head with the machete, I just remember thinking, "That is the most awful thing I've ever seen!" The blade going up and down inside his skull, his eyes going up and down…I was like, "Um, OK, enough. I think you got that, Joseph!"

JOSEPH ZITO: A number of the effect shots were cut back, some of them more than others. I think some even benefited, really, which is a rare thing, and some of them were hurt. But we were trying to protect the ending. The end of the movie plays very close to the way we wanted it to play. You do really see the machete enter Jason's head, you do see him slide down on the machete. That was pretty extreme for the time—you would not be likely to see that in a commercially released movie today. It was an accomplishment.

"As a guy was leaving the theater, I asked him, 'How'd you like the movie?' He said, 'It's gonna scare the shit out of you!' For a movie like this, that's better than a glowing review in *The New York Times*." Joel Goodman

With Jason's gory demise left intact, Friday the 13th – The Final Chapter *debuted on Friday, April 13, 1984, slashing its way onto 1,594 screens across North America. The advertisements promised, "This Is The One You've Been Screaming For!"—and audiences agreed. The film grossed $11.2 million in its first three days, setting an opening weekend record—not only for the franchise, but for Paramount Pictures. Not yet jaded by the concept of never-ending sequels, fans turned out in droves, propelling the film's final box office gross to $32.9 million, making it the most commercially successful sequel behind* Part 3. *Jason, it seemed, had taken his final bow and left the stage on a high note.*

Reviews were, predictably, negative. Though no attempt was made by the filmmakers to hide the fact that their movie was anything but a deliberate and deliciously manipulative thrill ride— albeit one crafted with care for its target audience—the majority of critical sentiment was pure venom, tempered only by a relief that the series had finally come to an end (or so they hoped). There were a few brief nods of praise, however backhanded, most famously from Janet Maslin in The New York Times: *"While not exactly an actors' picture,* The Final Chapter *takes pains to make its characters a little more personable than the horror-movie norm. This is unfortunate, since there is nothing to do during the second half of the film but watch them die." Maslin's views, perhaps not so coincidentally, were shared by some of the film's cast, who strove so passionately to elevate the material they had been given and were now seeing themselves on the silver screen, some for the very first time. But whatever virtues* The Final Chapter *may possess, it is still most widely remembered by fans as the first* Friday the 13th *that promised to be the last. And wasn't.*

JOSEPH ZITO: Today, the *Friday* pictures are watched alone or with a few friends on video, but a really interesting thing happens inside a movie theater with a thousand people—you can feel the collective audience identification shifting. It's almost like a horror film taking place inside the audience where they are identifying with a character, but if the character then turns them off in some way, they slide and start identifying with Jason. He becomes a hero and a villain. That really is the art of constructing one of these things. And it's not happening by accident. I think that is probably the one point that was most missed by critics of these films.

You have to have a sense of humor about reviews. It's only important that the movie work for the person prepared to buy a ticket to go see it. It's not important that it works for somebody who never in a million years would find themselves in that movie theater if they weren't paid to write about it. I remember going to the Lone State Theatre in New York, which has since been turned into a multiplex, but back then there was like a thousand seats. It's a strange, strange experience for a director. You stand in the back of a theater and you see a thousand people making a lot of noise. And at the end, they all rise to their feet, dancing around in the aisles as Corey is killing this guy. It's like a rock concert. And they're all silhouetted against a white screen. That image burns into your brain, seeing them there with their hands in the air, cheering the death of Jason. If anything, it taught me the power that a single movie image can have.

LAWRENCE MONOSON: I went to opening night on Hollywood Boulevard to see the audience reaction to the film. I did not have a good experience. I found the thirst for and love of the violence to be disturbing. The energy in the theater was frightening. I was like, "Oh, my God, what have I done?" I didn't feel physically unsafe, but I certainly wasn't going to hang around and let people know I was in the film. I'm just not a big fan of that sort of low, shocker-based, angry energy.

I imagine it's a release for some people. I don't think it's the healthiest way to release anger and fear and what have you, but it is a way. I mean, it's storytelling, and storytelling is based in ancient mythology, and certainly *Friday the 13th* is not the highest example of mythology, but it is mythic. You're dealing with simple structures and archetypes.

ERICH ANDERSON: I saw it at a cast and crew screening in Westwood. I invited my parents to see it. They were horrified. And when the experience was over, I thought it was reprehensible. I thought we were completely irresponsible to make a film like this. Then I saw it again with a paying audience. All my friends came, and I'd say that fourteen of them were back out in the lobby after the first twenty minutes of the picture. This was just not part of their culture. They were disgusted and they left—"Thanks for inviting me, Erich!" But I sat there and watched the thing with an audience, and these people were having the greatest time. They were running up and down the aisle, talking back at the screen and making fun of everybody. And it was only then that I got it.

I also learned at that screening that the camera adds ten pounds. After the movie was over, I was standing in the lobby, and this group of kids behind me goes, "That's the guy! That's the guy in the

movie!" And this girl goes, "No, the guy in the movie was fat!" Any kind of ego boost I might have gotten was completely destroyed.

BONNIE HELLMAN: I went to the theater to see it and all I could think was, "God, my head is so big!" My head was like the whole screen.

TED WHITE: We were about two days from being finished on the show, and the producers called me into the office and said, "Ted, how would you like to have your name listed on the credits?" I said, "I don't want my name on it. Just put Jason as 'Jason.'" Well, Mancuso heard that and started to give me a fit. I said, "Don't say one word to me, you little bastard. It's my name, and if I don't want it on this piece of shit, it's not going to be on it." And from that day to this, he's never spoken to me. And I've seen him several times since.

FRANK MANCUSO, JR.: I like Ted. I certainly don't have any hard feelings toward him. Because, to be honest, whoever is playing Jason—it isn't like Tom Cruise. If they take their name off a movie, it doesn't mean anything to anyone, except for maybe Ted. Maybe it was his statement about whatever he was never comfortable with about the role. But the movie turned out well and that's all that matters.

CRISPIN GLOVER: I've always been glad to be able to work. I aspire to try to do things that I like, but there are certain films that I really am proud of, and then certain films that I'm just glad I did it because I was continuing my career. But I don't regret any of the films that I've done in my career. And I certainly don't regret *The Final Chapter*.

CAMILLA MORE: I never went to see it. I was kind of selfish. I just used it for what I wanted it for—to have something else to put on my resume. I could take out the love scene and put it on my reel, and now suddenly I have a scene with Crispin Glover. That's what actors do, they build up. These little vignettes lead into bigger things. And then finally, people take them seriously. I did feel in our *Friday* that the quality of acting was above the others. Any good notices the film got I would like to think was a kind of begrudging acknowledgement that there was some sort of talent in this schlocky movie.

TOM SAVINI: The last day of filming *The Final Chapter* was the opening scene, where the police arrive and Jason's body is lying there. There was a moment after we finished the final shot, where Joe Zito said, "Jason's gone. He's dead." Then, after a long pause. Frank Mancuso said, "Yeah…it feels kinda odd to know he's really gone. Jason is dead, and Mrs. Voorhees is dead, and we've seen the last *Friday the 13th*." And I think, at the time, they really did believe it.

ERICH ANDERSON: Whenever people ask me what *Friday the 13th* I was in, and I say *The Final Chapter*, they all howl.

FRANK MANCUSO, JR.: Out of all the *Friday the 13th* films, I like *The Final Chapter* the best. I felt comfortable, creatively, with it as the end of the series. I really thought it was going to be the last. But because of the film's success, it did go on, and that was the motivation of Paramount. That's when I stepped back, as far as being involved with the series as intimately. And after that, quite frankly, for me personally it was never quite the same again.

Above: A special promotional-only poster created for the 1984 home video release of *Friday the 13th – The Final Chapter*.

5.

Repetition

It is hard to pinpoint the exact moment when a series of motion pictures becomes more than the sum of its parts. For *Friday the 13th*, that moment may have been when its popularity insisted that it outlast its own self-generated demise. For few modern movie franchises can commit suicide and live to tell the tale. No one, not even the most diehard fans of the series, expected another sequel after *The Final Chapter*. And had there never been another *Friday the 13th*, it would have been a perfectly respectable end, both creatively and commercially, to a storyline that detractors complained was already so thin that it could hardly support one movie, let alone a series of them. Jason was dead and gone, and there seemed few potential avenues left to explore that could legitimately sustain a long-term, aesthetically valid franchise. Of course, the prospect of wringing a few more bucks from one of their least expensive—and, dollar for dollar, most profitable—investments was difficult for Paramount to ignore. The surprise this time, however, was that the critics were not alone in having had their fill of all things Jason. Frank Mancuso, Jr. had surmised that the public's appetite for *Friday the 13th* had been sufficiently satiated by *The Final Chapter*, and the young producer was eager to at last graduate from the series that launched his career to bigger and better opportunities.

For the second time in the series' history, *Friday the 13th* was creatively rudderless, a ship without a captain. But once again the uncredited—yet always omnipresent—specter of Phil Scuderi would save the day. Just as Scuderi had stepped in to shape *Part 2* after the departure of Sean Cunningham, so too would he serve as the surrogate stepfather to the inevitable *Part V*—aptly (and some would argue nauseatingly) subtitled *A New Beginning*—while a reluctant Frank Mancuso, Jr. opted to take a more hands-off role as Executive Producer. Scuderi would both select a new director, one considerably removed from the sensibilities of mainstream Hollywood, and a new script that dared to do the unthinkable: it didn't bring back Jason. The most controversial chapter in the history of *Friday the 13th* was about to unfold.

FRANK MANCUSO, SR., Chairman & CEO, Paramount Pictures: It was our sincere intent for *The Final Chapter* to be the last film in the series. And then, of course, it had this huge opening success, and we had to rethink it all. This was a bottom line-based reality. Quite simply, the public still wanted to see these films. So until they really stopped coming, why not continue to make more? And sure enough, they're still coming to see them today. And how many years has it been? Twenty-five?

FRANK MANCUSO, JR., Executive Producer: I was done on *The Final Chapter*. I really was. Because I probably took the hardest hit. I can't speak for anyone connected with the first movie, but my feeling was that after *Part 2*, if somebody had issues with *Friday the 13th*, more often than not it would be my name people used. And even though you have supporters telling you, "Fuck those guys!" it ain't their name in the paper. They're not the face being associated with all of this.

However, I had this peculiar situation because my father was at Paramount, and Phil and the guys from Boston only knew me and really only wanted to deal with me. So I said, "Let me be the

point person for what I would call larger-scale decisions. I'm not going to micromanage this thing. I'm not going to be on set every day. However, I'll make sure the movie comes in when it's supposed to, and come in for the right amount." That became my approach. I would call it more of an executive producer's series of functions for *V*, *VI*, *VII* and *VIII*. I would meet with people, talk to Phil about directors, and approve the cast and the storyline and some of the more significant effects. And then I sort of gazed at it from afar. I certainly wasn't involved with any particular level of intimacy, other than when I really wanted to be.

TIM SILVER, Producer: I had been working on some *Afterschool Specials*, and one of the producers, Ken Wiederhorn, had directed something called *Meatballs 2*, which was overseen by Frank Mancuso, Sr. He invited me to meet Frank Jr. about *Part V*. I'm not even sure if I'd seen any of the movies, but I knew of the series.

I was originally hired as production manager. It was only once the film was pretty much put together—a couple weeks before we started shooting—that Frank Jr. got the opportunity to produce *The Two Jakes*, with Robert Towne directing. So he called me into his office and asked me if I wanted to produce *Part V*. I said, "Sure. How much more are you going to pay me?" And Frank says, "Nothing." But it was still a good deal so I said yes.

By the time I came on board on *Part V*, it was pretty clear, in talking to Frank and watching him work, that he needed to break free of *Friday the 13th*. I barely see myself as the producer of the picture. From a creative standpoint, Frank really controlled the film, and is largely responsible for the success of the series. The supervision of the script, the casting, the shooting … as purely a businessman who is responsible for seeing the *Friday the 13th* success continued, Frank was able to do it in the bat of an eye.

JOSEPH ZITO, Filmmaker: I had a lot of license on *The Final Chapter* because it was my impression that there was never

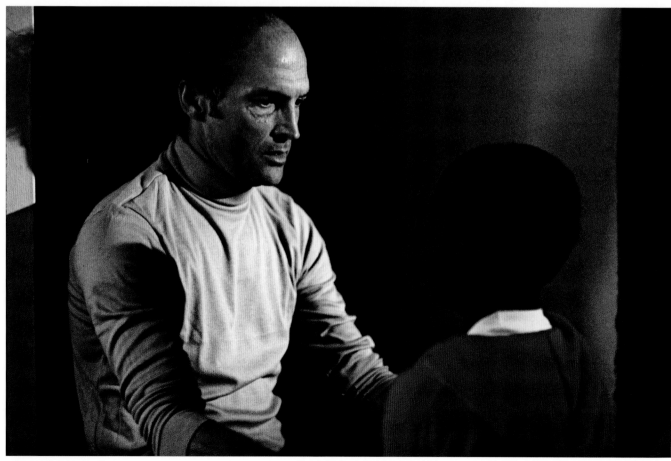

going to be another *Friday the 13th*. And that was a mixed blessing. On the one hand, it was gonna be known as the last one, and I had an obligation to the fans to not disappoint them with a cheat of an ending. But on the other hand, I thought if I could leave it open somehow, maybe Paramount would change its mind and make some more.

I didn't have this conversation with the studio, but the idea was to have Tommy Jarvis give that off-kilter look at the end, so that maybe that could help create a *Part V, VI* and *VII*. I thought—naively, I might add—"Well, if they get another sequel they're really going to win big, and maybe they'll ask me to do more films, or it will be good for my career." And what did the studio say? Basically, "Thanks." No more than that. Still, keeping it open-ended was great. It worked out, didn't it? So it's fine.

BARNEY COHEN, Screenwriter: It was obvious, once Frank Mancuso, Sr. saw the dailies of what Joe was doing, that Frank didn't want it to be *The Final Chapter*. We always assumed that the Tommy character would be the next Jason. What was strange, though, is that they didn't actually pick that up in *Part V*, or they didn't take it all the way. Joe and I weren't talking to anybody at the studio by that time anyway, but we just assumed it really would be Tommy as the killer.

STEVE MINER, Filmmaker: When we were developing *Part 3*, there was quite a bit of discussion of alternative storylines that would be a breakaway from the other films. One I pursued for a long time, with Martin Kitrosser, was taking the character of Ginny from *Part 2*. Suppose she was in a mental institution, trying to recover, and we explored a psychological approach to *Part 3*? Well, at that point, we're suddenly on new ground; we don't know if we're going to appeal to the fans that we had before, and we don't even know that we're going to create new fans. Finally, we all decided that it would have been a mistake, and we should stay reasonably within the format of the first two films. We had a certain audience that enjoyed *Friday the 13th* and we owed them the best possible film that they would enjoy within the format we'd already established.

TIM SILVER: Martin Kitrosser had written a draft of *Part V* before Danny Steinmann arrived, one that had originated back for one of the other sequels, I think it was *Part 3*. The screenplay had come to Frank from our partners on the East Coast, and it wasn't going to work for various reasons. Many things in the script would not have made it onto the screen for release. The violence tended to be of a nature that would have likely gotten an X rating. So Danny hired a writer friend of his, the late David Cohen, and they rewrote the entire thing.

DANNY STEINMANN, Director & Co-Screenwriter: I had directed and wrote a movie called *The Unseen*, with Barbara Bach. I didn't get to do a cut of the movie because they wanted to get it out right away, so I took my name off of it. What was released was a bastardized version of my film. It wasn't my vision at all. But I've always loved horror films. And then Steve Minasian and Phil Scuderi contacted me after seeing an early print of the next film I did, *Savage Streets*. They said, "Please make yourself available." They even kept me on salary for four months before *Part V* even got started.

When I got the film, they had a storyline, but Jason was dead. They'd gotten rid of their Darth Vader, which I thought was a big mistake. Fortunately, Frank Mancuso, Jr. was good. He listened. I had a lot of freedom and juxtaposed a lot of shit. What I felt was that the movie should be Tommy's story. His hallucinations, his ordeals, his trying to fight back this rage to kill. He's still plagued by the memories of Jason and Jason is still a part of him. Whether it's the real Jason or not would be the focus of the story. Who is doing the killing? And for what reason? It would be a departure from the other *Friday the 13th* films. We'd concentrate on one character, Tommy Jarvis, who we are not too sure of—we wouldn't know whether to sympathize with him, or to hate him.

FRANK MANCUSO, JR.: Part of the difficulty of any particular series of films, especially something like *Friday the 13th*, is that you cannot realistically progress the plot. You can't take it into a different realm. Otherwise, you're flying in the face of what the people want. The reason *The Final Chapter* was the end of it for me was because if I was to stay intimately involved, they would have had to radically change the formula—I was getting bored to tears.

The way Phil worked is that he'd say, "Oh, this guy's a good guy—let him do this next time." That's how I got my shot. Martin Kitrosser was the script super-

Above: Actress Melanie Kinnaman gets ready for her close-up.

Middle: Actor Shavar Ross (left) hangs out with his onscreen big brother, Demon (Miguel Nunez, Jr.).

Bottom: Actresses Juliette Cummins (left) and Tiffany Helm flank *A New Beginning* Producer Tim Silver.

Opposite page: Director Danny Steinmann (left) coaches child actor Shavar Ross. Steinmann would come to be known for his intensity on set. "Sometimes Danny could get really serious," admits Ross. "There was a scene near the end of the film, right before the big chase sequence, where I'm sleeping, and Juliette comes to put the covers over me. They had set up this high-angle shot, and originally you were supposed to see my face. But every take I was laughing, and my eyes were twitching. Danny got a little upset. But that is the only time I remember him ever raising his voice, at least around me."

"Every kill in *Part V* was cut, starting with the ax in the back," says director Danny Steinmann. "Originally, we had a wide shot of Vic coming towards the camera with the ax, then the ax bursting through Joey's back and blood spurting out all over. But the MPAA ratings board simply said, 'No good.' Now, all that's left in the final film is Vic leaving frame about to swing the ax, then a close-up of Joey screaming."

The late Mark Venturini (**background**), who portrayed the ax-wielding Vic, was already known to genre fans before *A New Beginning*, having starred in such cult classics as *Return of the Living Dead*. But the young actor was never able to realize his ambitions of fame, succumbing to cancer at the age of thirty-six. "Mark and I really bonded," remembers co-star Dominick Brascia. "We really got to like each other and we hung out for a few years afterward. And when I heard he died of cancer, I just couldn't believe it. I was really shocked. I thought, 'Here's a guy in perfect shape, and I'm the little tubby guy still kicking along.' And the ironic thing was, during the filming of *Part V*, Mark and I shared a dressing room for a couple of days. And I hated it! I thought, 'He has to kill me—we aren't supposed to be buddies!'"

visor on the first one, a good script supervisor, and he made a couple changes to the scripts that we liked, so he eventually wrote the third one with his wife, Carol Watson. So Martin was somebody who Scuderi knew and talked to and exchanged ideas with about *Part V*. And at that point, I was more of a custodian than anything else. I just wanted to make sure the films got done, that Paramount got what they wanted out of the movie. I thought, quite frankly, that it was time for other people to bring their passions to it, because I felt like I was getting totally stale on new ideas and other ways to invigorate the series. Phil was passionate about Martin's concept for *Part V*, so it would not be reasonable for me, now that I decided to take a backseat aside from a few suggestions here and there, to then start vetoing everybody's script ideas. If everybody involved really felt like this could work, then great.

While few would likely call A New Beginning *a character study, it does make a sincere attempt to explore the mind and madness of Tommy Jarvis. The* Friday the 13th *films have always centered around a single protagonist, usually a female, but* Part V *made an even bigger departure from the established formula by making its lead character a male. As the story begins, five years have passed since the events of* The Final Chapter, *with Tommy no longer a child but a young man. Due to the age and unavailability of Corey Feldman, who had quickly become one of the most in-demand child performers of the 1980s, a new actor was needed to take on the role. The script also relocated Tommy to a half-way house—in the woods, of course—populated by at-risk teens with "emotional problems" ranging from unexplained speech impediments to undiagnosed nymphomania to mental retardation and unhealthy fixations on chocolate bars. This required a new batch of young actors to portray, if no less a diverse ensemble of modern teenagers, then certainly a quirkier one. Part V also introduced a much more colorful array of adult characters than had been seen in previous* Fridays—*cops, caretakers and bona fide crazies who would populate the fictional community surrounding Pinehurst Sanitarium. In this installment, the ancillary characters would function not only as potential victims, but as suspects—with one of them ultimately being revealed as the "new Jason." Borrowing a cue from the original* Friday the 13th, *the identity of* Part V's *evildoer was—until the final reel—to remain a mystery.*

A New Beginning boasts the largest cast of any Friday *film up until that time—and certainly the most varied in terms of age, ability, temperament and attitude. Some of them came for the paycheck. Some as a lark. Some wanted to gain experience and hone their craft. While others freely admit they just came to party. It was a markedly distinct and disparate batch of personalities that often mirrored the madness that was happening on camera—and the looming tensions going on behind it.*

Principal photography on A New Beginning *began in early September, 1984, in Camarillo, California, in and around the rambling orange groves of Thousand Oaks. It would be the last* Friday the 13th *film to shoot on the West Coast. In order to maintain the secrecy of the film's storyline—and to avoid the ire of the local unions—the film was given a befitting code name: "Repetition."*

FRANK MANCUSO, JR.: We started creating fake titles. Most of the time they were old David Bowie song titles—just innocuous enough that the unions would leave you alone. Because a union was far less likely to go out and try to bust a movie called "Crystal Japan" than they were *Friday the 13th Part 3*. They knew that the train went back to Paramount and they knew the *Friday the 13th* films were successful, so they would come at you much harder. As for "Repetition," I just thought it was a funny joke.

JOHN SHEPHERD, "Tommy Jarvis": Around 1984, I had just graduated from UCLA, and had worked my way through by acting. I was taking some English classes, studying Shakespeare, meeting actors like Tim Robbins and Lance Guest. I was living down in Venice at the time, and I got this call to go on an audition for a film called "Repetition." My agent said, "It's a lead role, but it doesn't have too many lines." I read the character breakdown and I thought it was so cool. And I had also been studying with Strasberg, and I realized that because the parts I was playing were always "boy next door" and "the good son," I really needed to go against type.

When I went to the audition, I came in sweats and a heavy coat. And I ran I think ten flights of stairs. I would run up and down this fire escape until they called my name. Then when I went into the reading, I took off my jacket and just started sweating. I didn't look at them. I didn't talk to them. I was just really intense. I was very method. I could tell I struck something. Danny was really into it.

DANNY STEINMANN: The character of Tommy changed quite a bit from the original draft. Originally, they had Tommy talking a lot. I didn't want him to talk at all, so I cut back on his dialogue. And I contributed all the hallucination scenes to the script. The first scene, where Tommy sees Jason coming out of the grave, that was all added. I was allowed to throw out whole scenes or include scenes that I wrote. They were pretty generous as far as giving me a free reign to do what I wanted to do with the character.

During casting, we were panic stricken. Everything hinged around this kid being sensitive and believable. I went through fifty Tommys before we found John Shepherd. It went right up until the last day before we started filming. And if we had gone with the Tommy we were about to settle on, the picture would have been unreleasable.

"I kept asking the actor who was going to kill me to let me check his ax, because the real one and the fake one looked so alike. I was scared he might pick up the wrong one by mistake."
Dominick Brascia on filming his death scene

JOHN SHEPHERD: I remember then finding out it was a *Friday the 13th* and being really disappointed. I just thought, "Oh, gosh! I always swore I'd never do a horror film. I'm supposed to be the next Johnny Whitaker!" Plus, I was counseling kids at a church up in L.A. I had all these moms who were going to freak out if they saw my picture in the paper with a machete. And that's exactly what happened.

There were some spiritual overtones in that movie that disturbed me. *Friday the 13th* is basically a morality tale. Like in *Rocky*, where Rocky reaches down deep within himself and finds the strength to overcome. A person of faith learns that if you reach down deep enough, you'll find that you're bankrupt and you have to look outside, and that's where God is. That's the problem I had with the violence. Its worldview conflicted with mine, although I didn't have a big problem with it in concept, because it was a morality tale. Somebody takes their clothes off—you get killed. You smoke dope—you get killed. Tommy was simply a guy caught in the crossfire.

Then I talked to a good buddy of mine, a seminary student at the time. He said, "You're an actor, and in this role, I don't see that you have to do anything that compromises who you are,

Although they play onscreen lovers (however doomed), relations between actors Bob DeSimone (this page) and Rebecca Wood-Sharkey (opposite page) were anything but romantic. "Rebecca was, in real life, Ray Sharkey's wife," remembers DeSimone. "And I was a big fan of his, because of his performance in *The Idolmaker*. But I had just met him previously on another movie I had done, and he was a major junkie at that time. I was so shocked and so sad. So the night Rebecca and I were going to shoot our scenes, I was explaining this whole story to director Danny Steinmann. Then all of a sudden Danny gets this weird look on his face—Rebecca is standing right behind him. She says, 'Are you talking about Ray Sharkey? He's my husband. He just had a little problem with Valium.' I just went, 'Uhhhh…' I had no idea she was his wife! And then we had to do our big flirting scene! But ultimately we both got killed, so who cares."

Above: The filming of Bob DeSimone's death scene left one cast member queasy—Jason himself. "When I had to put an ax in that guy's head, I had to tell myself, 'It's just a movie,'" says stuntman Tom Morga. "Because even though it is fake, when you see a face and a head and you're going to put an ax into it…it's not the thrill of your day. I really did get a little sick doing that."

Opposite page: The death of Lana (Rebecca Wood-Sharkey) was another that fell prey to the "ax" of the MPAA ratings board. "They said, 'No quivering,'" says director Danny Steinmann. "So we had to completely cut out the shot of the ax going into her stomach, and all her suffering. Now, all you see is her lying on the ground."

Sure, it's a horror film, it's a *Friday the 13th*, but everybody knows what it is. It's not like you're sneaking some secret worldview in, trying to convert people to some strange thing. It's a roller coaster ride. And you're the good guy! You kill Jason at the end!"

So I think I rationalized it. The reason I found I could do the film was because evil was punished. Mercilessly and graphically. I wouldn't have a problem with that or nudity in a script that ultimately had a redemptive worldview. *Part V*, it really did speak to me. Tommy really was this isolated guy who is caught in this world with all these kids partying, and this demon is haunting him. For me, I was really doing Boo Radley.

SHAVAR ROSS, "Reggie": I was about fourteen years old. I was doing *Diff'rent Strokes*. I worked a lot around that time. And back then, *Friday the 13th* was hot. The only funny thing was that, while my parents didn't mind me doing it, they would only allow me to sign on as long as they took out all the curse words. That's why, throughout the movie, instead of "Fuckin' A!", I said, "Freakin' A!"

MELANIE KINNAMAN, "Pam": If you go back over all of the *Friday* movies, you notice that the people who make these films love to see blondes running. I knew how to run and I was blonde, so I had an edge. I also knew, from an acting stand-point, that it was real easy to be bad in these things, and I certainly did not want to be bad. So I did a quick horror film study. I went back and looked at Jamie Lee Curtis' horror films and watched other *Friday the 13th* movies. I realized that leading ladies in *Friday* films did not have a whole lot to do, but I was prepared to make the most of the opportunities I was given as an actress.

TIFFANY HELM, "Violet": My mom, Brooke Bundy, was an actress. So, while I wanted to have a career with a little more substance, life kind of took me in the direction of acting. Nothing was said about the film being a *Friday the 13th*—I thought the reason being that if the potential cast members knew they were going to be involved in such a money making venue, they would ask for a better contract. It was not until we were cast that the real name of the project was even revealed. But I was happy to be working.

I also thought that Violet was pretty bad-assed. I just hoped that I would have some input on her style, as Hollywood had no concept of what the alternative crowd was doing at the time—this was before pink hair and tattoos were in vogue. And I always had a good bond with the wardrobe department when I worked, so we went out and shopped together. A lot of the clothes were mine already, and the hair I had done before I even read for the part. Siouxsie Sioux was my female idol at the time, so I tried to use some of her makeup as suggestions.

JULIETTE CUMMINS, "Robin": I was an Olympic gymnast for fourteen years, but then the United States boycotted the games in 1980. It was difficult, because then I had to sit out another four years, and by that time I would have been sixteen years old. So I decided to get out, and that's when I began to pursue acting.

When I got the script, I loved the fact that it was a Jason movie. All I knew about my character was that I had to be difficult. Which wasn't too hard—I had my own little demons inside. And when you're casting, especially a film like this, it is about the whole group, that everybody fits together. Tiffany and I looked different—maybe that's why they cast us together.

DOMINICK BRASCIA, "Joey": My agent called, I read the script, and I liked it. But I almost didn't get the role initially because when I met with Fern Champion and Pamela Basker, who were casting it, they wanted me to play it one way and I disagreed. Their way was more stereotypical—I wanted Joey to be more real and not such a clichéd "slow" person. But when I met with Danny Steinmann and told him how I thought Joey should be, he agreed. And I got the part.

DEBISUE VOORHEES, "Tina": Voorhees is my real last name. It really is. And one of the casting folks knew that with a name like Voorhees she had to at least see me. But the part of Tina was already cast. It was one of those funny Hollywood stories where the director saw me after the producer had already picked somebody, and then he saw me and decided that he had to jump up and down and say, "I really want you to see this woman." The whole reason was because Danny Steinmann said I was the only woman that auditioned who understood that when Tina, in the script, curses at her guy, when she says "fuck you," she's actually flirting with him. She's not mad. All the other actresses who auditioned, they would get angry. But I flirted. And I got the part.

JERRY PAVLON, "Jake": I was afraid of doing it. I scare very easily and I don't like horror pictures. I had never even seen a *Friday the 13th* film in its entirety. So I didn't know how real it was going to be to me. Being an actor on the set and having to

deal with blood and being killed—I felt sensitive to it. And I continue, to this day, to be very sensitive to violence in pictures. The last thing like that I saw was *Goodfellas*, and I was looking under cars on my way out of the theater and wondering how the hell I'd get home safely. I'm just very affected by stuff like that.

But the other problematic issue for me, personally, in doing the film was that I have a sister who's a feminist scholar, who brought me up very well in thinking about patriarchy and sexism. So here is this opportunity to do a picture that is viewed rather famously as misogynist, and equating sex with death, and selling itself on bloody breasts and all that stuff. I had a long series of conversations with her, and we both decided that, "Hey, I'm an actor. It's an opportunity. Make the best of it. Bring something to the picture in a positive way." Of course, then I thought, "Yeah, right. I'll be around big bloody breasts, but that's a nice ideal."

BOB DESIMONE, "Billy": My brother, Tom DeSimone, being a director—he made *Hell Night* and *Reform School Girls*—he put me in a few of his movies. Small bit parts, nothing much. That's how I met Danny Steinmann. I played the teacher in *Savage Streets*, and then he grabbed me real quick. Danny told me, "I'd like to have my own group of actors that I can always count on."

At the time, there was a whole segment of actors and film-makers who were working in Hollywood but still kind of outside. I can only relate it to the music industry. When you're just starting out, you'll play a wedding or a wake—anything, just to play. It is not that we wanted to be in those B or even C movies. It was just a chance to get a credit. And I think we all knew that, once you're into a *Part 3, 4* or *5*, whether it was a *Friday the 13th* or anything else, it already has its own niche and that's where it was gonna stay. It is not going to take off and be another *Exorcist* or whatever. All you hoped for back then was a piece of film that you could put on your reel. I think it was the same thing with the directors. I don't think Danny wanted to be a B-movie horror director. I know my brother didn't. But he did what they gave him.

CAROL LOCATELL, "Ethel": My agent called and said, "We have an appointment for you for this thing called "Repetition," but it's really *Friday the 13th*." And I went, "Get out of here. Why?"

Because it was never my favorite genre. Truthfully, I thought, "Gee, how much social value is there in this?" Then I read the sides, and I thought it was all just kind of hilarious. And I knew I would have such a good time with the character.

There's sort of an idealism when you start out acting, and especially if you start in college and you're doing Ibsen and Shakespeare. And then you're doing *Friday the 13th*. But I loved that youthful exuberance—that was wonderful. The whole shoot, my character is kind of separate from everything, except for that one scene with all the kids and the sheriff, where I'm on a motorcycle or something. And all the kids, they were just so delighted to be working. Everybody loved everybody. Everybody was having a good time. That's how I remember it.

DICK WIEAND, "Roy": I auditioned for Danny Steinmann and Frank Mancuso, Jr. I had to read the scene where Roy discovers his son—who we will discover is his son—has been murdered, and he pulls the blanket over the body. It was all about making a transition from knowing that my son had died, discovering him, and then kind of going a little bonkers, which is what Roy does when he becomes "Jason." I even had to cry. All because of the "twists and turns" of the script. They said they couldn't just have a stuntman with a machete going around lopping off breasts. It required more than that. They needed an "actor."

It was a strange shoot for me. The kids were in their own little camp. I spent most of my time in my trailer. There was nobody to have fun with, there was nobody to joke around with. I thought, "Maybe it's the character and they don't want to be around me." I still don't know. Nobody was friendly. And because we shot most of it in Thousand Oaks, they would have us all meet in one place, and put us all in a big truck so we would ride back and forth to and from the set. Then I remember I drove out myself for the night shoots, because they didn't even bother to pick me up after that.

TIM SILVER: The fake title "Repetition" had nothing to do with residuals for the cast. It was used because *Friday the 13th* already had a reputation, and it's a non-union show, so we'd be an immediate target. We actually spent a little more money than we wanted to on *Part V*. The budget was a little over $2 million—less than *The Final Chapter*, where they had helicopters a lot more than we did. I don't even think they intended to spend that much on that picture, but Joe Zito had the capability to push for that. I even actually ended up housing the crew in a Motel 6 when we were out at that house—and I'm pleased I still remained friendly with most of the crew after putting them up in such a cheap place!

From a production standpoint, budget limitations played a very big part in how we selected the locations. We wanted to limit the company and not move around a lot, so we wanted to find a farmhouse and a barn that's production-friendly and that's fairly close. In fact, we tried to go a little further from L.A., but it became too big of an issue. Eventually, we found the farmhouse location out in Thousand Oaks, and we shot the sanitarium in a hospital that had been shut down.

STEPHEN POSEY, Director of Photography: I remember we had a little problem right at the beginning of the show. We shot in Camarillo and everybody lived in Hollywood or on the West Side.

And because of the hours we were shooting, we were going to work at four o'clock in the afternoon and driving home from work at seven o'clock in the morning. And because it's L.A., we were in rush hour traffic all the time. So it would take us like two hours just to get to and from work. So we said right away, "This is too much! We want to be put up in Camarillo." Because we knew we'd burn out—you can't do that. But of course they didn't want to pay for it. And that was one of the few times that Frank Jr. came out on the set. And he finally did agree and put us up in the hotel.

CAROL LOCATELL: You want to know how cheap it was? There was so little makeup—they just put some base on me, and that was it. I looked at myself and I thought, "No! I wouldn't look this neat and clean." So I went out to the road and picked up some dirt and just smudged it all over my face and my neck. That was my makeup! I even ended up wearing the wig that I auditioned in. I had just done *Sharky's Machine*, and Burt Reynolds had given me this wig as a gift. So I plopped that thing on my head, pulled my hair up inside it, and went in. And the make-up person, I remember really vividly, she said, "We'll have to keep the wig in case we need to do any retakes, but I'll give it back to you." And I'm still waiting.

JULIETTE CUMMINS: When I did *Psycho III* it was a studio movie with a big lot and a big crew and my own dressing room. You're treated like a queen. On *Part V*, I had to share a dressing room and it didn't seem like a big-budget movie at all, because all our shoots were on location, and it was sparse. A few trucks—ten, maybe. Most movies have twenty. Granted, I'd never done anything prior to *Friday*, so it still seemed like a "real movie" to me. And even though people were often tired and tempers flew between the crew sometimes, I don't remember ever not wanting be on set. Everyone was so helpful about what to do. We were so young. Sometimes, we didn't even know where to stand.

TIFFANY HELM: I was already a troubled teen, so I didn't need to do any prep work for my role. Well, I wasn't a teenager anymore by that point, but I had been such a good girl as a teen that when I hit my twenties I became a bit of a rebellious hellion. To be honest, at the time, partying was my priority. All of us cast did quickly form our own little "cliques." The only people I ended up really hanging out with were Juliette, Jerry and a couple of the crew people. I was really more interested in going out, so I was lucky to be working at all.

BOB DESIMONE: *Part V* was a set that was riddled with cocaine. It was funny, my scene in the car right before I get the ax in my head, that was basically improvised. The script just

Above: Simple in appearance, the makeup application designed for the murder of Tina was a complex—and often painful—process for actress DebiSue Voorhees. "It wasn't a fake head at all," she explains. "I went in to have a cast made of my face, and you know how you get brain freeze when you eat ice cream? This was like that, but you couldn't stop the pain. I had to breathe through straws. Then from that cast, they created a really thin mask for me to wear over my eye and nose area. and then filled it up with fake blood. And when that stuff started seeping into my eyes, let me tell you—it burned. I kept closing my eyes as tight as I could and the crew had to try and move me around to keep me comfortable. I was really glad when that day was over."

Top: Director Danny Steinmann (left) teaches actor Ron Sloan the fine art of motorcycle riding.

Above: With the film's body count topping nearly two dozen, the MPAA ratings board was particularly harsh on *A New Beginning*. The imposed cuts were to the detriment of the completed picture, according to director Danny Steinmann: "The thing that hurt me the most was that we had a rough cut preview of the film and we saw where all the 'pops' were. In *Part V* there were two really big ones, and both were cut. One in particular was when the guy on the motorcycle gets his head chopped off. Everybody jumped in the original version. It was much richer."

Editor Bruce Green elaborates on the deletion: "In the first cut, the machete cut off Junior's head and it went flying, and then it bounced about six times. We would take out one bounce and send it back to the MPAA, and they'd still say no. Then we sent it back again, with five bounces. And then it came back again. And again. Now, it is just one bounce."

said, "Billy pulls up and waits outside," no dialogue or anything. Danny said, "Why don't you just get high in the car and do what you want?" So there I am, at three o'clock in the morning, snorting this baby laxative called Mineta, which they use to cut cocaine. And I think I was the only person on that set not snorting the real thing.

However, on most sets at that time there was cocaine. I'm not speaking for the huge films, but from what I heard it was all the same. We didn't think much of it at the time, because there is a strange lure that says, in your mind, and in most of the kids' minds I knew at the time, that the drugs were there for a reason. There was always someone on the set who had it, because it keeps you awake. They were there to help us through the night. It became part of the whole routine.

In the '80s, it was also a signal that you had made it, or that you were on your way, even though you were making a B-movie. It was like a validation. Back then, there was still an innocence. There was a part of you that said, "This is cool. I've kind of arrived. I'm with the movie people and I'm doing this stuff and it is great." You thought it was all just temporary. You never realized that it could really be your demise.

STEPHEN POSEY: Drugs were a presence. That was part of the lifestyle in those days. It was flamboyant, decadent. It's really interesting—I remember when John Belushi died, that was when it really started to turn around. Because the industry was getting out of control. And, you know, not just in the film business but the entertainment business in general. It was common knowledge that drugs were being provided on sets like a reward, to keep people working. Some people that I was fond of during that period crashed and burned and never recovered. Luckily, for those of us who lived through all of that … for me, my major dangerous time was right before this period, because I was already getting old. I must have been thirty-five—I was a middle-aged guy! But it was amazing that we survived.

I remember going into the office one morning during pre-production on *Part V* after I had been up all night partying. That was one thing—I always would show up no matter what. I wouldn't phone in sick to the set—I was going to be there. And I think we were going on a location scout or something. But Tim Silver took one look at me and knew that I'd been up all night and that I was not in very good shape. I probably smelled, too. And he read me the riot act. I said, "I'm sorry. I apologize." It was in prep, but he just wanted to make sure that I was really reliable.

DOMINICK BRASCIA: It all runs together for me. I don't even know what decade we're in now. I know some of my friends—the two Coreys—that was their high time and they're still trying to relive that. That's kind of sad. On *Part V,* I hung out with John Robert Dixon, who played Eddie—we both had the same manager—and Mark Venturini, who would invite us out to all these cool parties. There'd be the best pot and the best coke. Although I didn't do coke; I'd only smoke a joint every once in a while. Anyway, these were very cool parties.

I babysat Danny Steinmann's two sons one time—he gave me these two kids to take care of for a couple of days. They were fifteen or sixteen. I remember sitting in my apartment and hanging out with them and being very self-conscious, because I couldn't offer them a joint—they were the director's sons!

JOHN SHEPHERD: The problem with a horror set is that it's very undisciplined, and the actors are all partying. It's hard to make it really good if people aren't into it. I was really into it. I said to myself, "If I'm going to do this, I'm going to take it seriously—I'm going to be the best Tommy Jarvis yet." And I had a buddy at the time, Michael Hitchcock, who is now a pretty successful writer, and who has been in Christopher Guest's movies. He was like, "If you're going to do this, you have to take it seriously. It's your first job." He encouraged me to take a volunteer position at the Camarillo State Mental Hospital, which I did for a couple months before we shot the movie. It was a lot of good internal work. Tommy was also supposed to be into masks, so I would visit creature shops and comic book places. And I wrote backstories for him, because that's what I was taught at Strasberg—you tried to really become the character.

The problem was, maybe there came a point where I really thought I *was* the character. When I got on set, I realized that if I were my usual, jovial self, this wasn't going to instill fear in any of my cast members, because we were all young and wild. So I decided I wouldn't talk to anybody unless I absolutely had to. And I was really faithful to my code in not speaking with anyone so they would look at me a little askance. They'd think twice before talking to me.

The hardest times, though, were traveling to and from the set. Because the teamsters were not favorable to a non-union shoot, we had to park somewhere out in Calabasas, and then they would shuttle us in. And when I got on the bus with everybody talking and laughing and bonding, I'd just have to zone out. I didn't even listen to music. I was just so isolated.

DOMINICK BRASCIA: DebiSue and I had a total argument one day. She was very protective of John Shepherd and she was pretty upset that I was complaining that he was "method." She just lashed into me, like, "That's the way he is! Stop complaining! Why are you always talking about him?" I was just like, "Don't worry about it. I just can't talk to this guy!" After that, from there on out, she was a little cooler to me. But I was pissed off—"Why does he have to be doing that? Just talk. Get over it!" I just didn't get him at all.

JOHN SHEPHERD: About halfway through the shoot, I blew my cover. Dick Warlock was our stunt coordinator, and he had this young guy working who was supposed to be my double. Well, Dick Warlock was the nicest guy I ever met, so it was just so hard not to talk to him. He would always try to have conversations with me and I would just grunt a "Yes" or "No." I finally made the mistake of saying, "How do you know Eddie?"—my stunt double. Dick says, "I met this guy in Phoenix. And I'm a Christian and Eddie's a young Christian, and I'm trying to help him in his career. So I brought him out here, and here we're doing a horror film, but it's been really good for him." And I had been counseling kids at this junior high church, and so I said to him, "I have faith. I go to church." And Dick just lights up. "Are you kidding me? Hey, Eddie! This guy's a brother in Christ!" He yells this across the set, in front of all these people who think I'm psycho anyway, because I haven't talked to anybody in weeks.

Below: "I think the most direction I ever received during *Part V* was how to squish a tomato," says actress Carol Locatell. "In my death scene, I was supposedly making stew, and then I get a cleaver in my face or something. Then they cut to my hand, and I'm squishing a tomato while I die. Those are the shots that these movies are about—honestly, that is my truthful recollection. I remember they were like, 'No, squeeze it this way! Squeeze it that way!' We did that far more takes of just that one shot than of anything else in the entire movie."

"The ratings board wanted to give the movie an X rating because of my death. They said a machete in the face wasn't just offensive, it was *obscene*."

Jerry Pavlon

That made people think I was even more weird. I remember talking on the set about it a lot after that. People went, "Are you really religious!? Do you go to church!?" Here I am having discussions about God and faith and heaven and hell, and, "Is it right for somebody who is religious to do a horror film?" It wasn't even like we were in church talking about it—we were on a horror film set!

Danny Steinmann had come to Friday the 13th *from a diverse background in exploitation cinema. He began his directing career with the 1973 X-rated romp* High Rise, *using the pseudonym Danny Stone. He also cut his teeth as a production assistant on Arthur Hiller's adaptation of* The Man in the Glass Booth *(1975), and as associate producer on the acclaimed telefilm* Spectre *(1977) for late sci-fi pioneer and* Star Trek *creator Gene Roddenberry. Steinmann's father, the late Herbert R. Steinmann, a noted East Coast art collector, had also dabbled in film production throughout the 1970s, providing funding for such notable genre efforts as George A. Romero's* Dawn of the Dead, *as well as the misbegotten* The Unseen, *on which the younger Steinmann also used a pseudonym. 1984's* Savage Streets *would be Danny Steinmann's first recognized directorial credit, and as the film gained a cult following among the East Coast exploitation and drive-in film scene it would come to the attention of Phil Scuderi and his partners Steve Minasian and Robert Barsamian.*

If it is true that the first day of any film shoot sets the tone for the entire production, then A New Beginning's *was a doozy. Steinmann's more hedonistic sensibilities clashed almost immediately with those of the producers. While the* Friday the 13th *series was hardly considered "high-brow," even by its fans,* A New Beginning *still needed to play in multiplexes across America. It could be bloody—that much was required. Sexy was fine, too. And certainly, it needed to be scary. But how far was too far? By the end of the first day's shooting, it was clear that wherever the line was to be drawn, Danny Steinmann was coming dangerously close to stepping over it.*

TIM SILVER: Danny had come to the movie through the East Coast people. And my impression was that he was thoroughly tense, that he was under a lot of pressure, he had a lot to do, and was on his guard. I remember sitting in the office for our first meeting, talking about the logistics of the shoot. I sensed immediately that he had a sort of macho, stand-off-ish attitude. Oftentimes, directors, when

they're looking at someone who is to effectively be their line producer, they see you as their adversary, as their opponent. And it fit with how Danny would eventually conduct himself.

For our first day, we shot what I guess was the "love scene," with a rather well-endowed woman, Debisue Voorhees. Then we saw the dailies the next day, and that's when Frank and I began to say, "Wait a minute"—because Danny was, how shall we say, particularly intrigued in the pornographic aspect of it. And we were all kind of shocked by it.

SHAVAR ROSS: I first came to the set when I had to come in for wardrobe. It was the first day or two of filming, and they were shooting that scene with Debisue Voorhees in the wilderness—the butt-naked scene! But I didn't know, and I wanted to meet Danny, so I saw the cameras and just ran right over. And they were like, "No! This is a closed set!" They had to stop the take, and Danny came over and met me, to shield me from what they were shooting.

DANNY STEINMANN: I've always loved any kind of film that played to my senses. I shot a fucking porno in the woods there. I mean, a porno except for insertion and all that. You wouldn't believe the nudity they cut out. And all that is left in the movie now is one close-up of them, going down.

DEBISUE VOORHEES: The lovemaking, and my death scene, that was all one thirteen hour day. My role was really difficult to do, because one, I was naked, and two, since the scene required that my eyes be gouged out, there were a lot of hours where I had to be led around by people in nothing but a robe, unable to see. And my eyes were burning because that stuff they use for the fake blood started seeping in my eyes. I kept closing my eyes as tight as I could, and people would try moving me around and to keep me comfortable. I wanted to get it over with. I think that's one of the reasons they decided to do it on the first day because they knew how difficult it was going to be. It was a relief when that day was through.

DARCY DEMOSS, "Nikki," *Part VI*: I was originally cast for that role in *Part V*. During my audition, Danny Steinmann asked me to lift up my top and show him my breasts. I said, "Excuse me, no, I cannot do that. It's incredibly unprofessional, and my agent didn't tell me about it. You can call my agent, and if he OK's it, I'm fine with that, because I'm comfortable with nudity." But to have something like that sprung on me? Then at my wardrobe fitting, Danny propositioned me. He wanted me to have dinner with him—I hadn't even read the script yet. And the next day, I didn't have a job, let's just put it that way. But I got paid for it, so it's fine.

I grew up in Hollywood, I know actresses, I know the dos and don'ts, and Danny was very unprofessional. I'm not surprised he never made another film after *Part V*. I think Danny burned a lot of bridges. He's wasn't handling people properly, and that's what gives Hollywood a bad name.

BRUCE GREEN, Editor: I was living on Venice Beach at the time, and I came home one day and there was a message on the answering machine: "This is Tim Silver from Terror, Inc. We'd like to know if you'd come in to interview to be editor for *Friday the 13th Part V*." I just listened to it and didn't pay it any mind—I wasn't interested. I had been an assistant editor on *Star Wars*, and I had already done *Raiders of the Lost Ark* and *Indiana Jones and the Temple of Doom*. I had also never seen any of the *Friday the 13th* movies—I'm not a horror film buff. Then I went over to my friend's house, who was also an editor, and he had the same message on his answering machine. Then we called up another friend of ours and *he* had the same message. Nobody wanted to do it. My attitude and their attitude, because they had all done similarly big movies, was, "We didn't go to film school and spend six, seven years as assistant editors to work on this crap."

Later that night, I phoned Michael Kahn, who was the editor who trained me, my mentor, and who is still Steven Spielberg's editor. I told him I had passed. And he started yelling at me: "You have to go in and do this movie! You have to interview for this film!" I said, "Why? I don't like horror films." He said, "That's not the point. If you're going to become an editor, you've got to be able to edit anything that's thrown at you. You can't say you'll just do high-end dramas. And more importantly, these are movies that are being distributed by Paramount Pictures. If these films are good enough for Paramount, who are you to say they're not good enough for you?" So I signed on to do *Part V* because I wanted to be associated with the studio. I wanted to be associated with Frank, who was a young, smart guy. And it was very helpful to my career.

I don't even remember meeting Danny until the first day of dailies. Now, this director came out of porn. And I was a bit nervous about doing this movie anyway. So I came into dailies, and there's this hardcore sex scene. And off-screen, Danny is yelling, "Fuck her! Fuck her!" I went white. And everybody in the room was silent. I was like, "Oh my God! What have I gotten myself into? It's bad enough I'm doing a low-budget horror film after hanging around with Steven Spielberg for the last five years. Now I'm doing a porn."

Frank Jr. looked shell-shocked because he hadn't been on set. We walked out of this screening room in Beverly Hills that was owned by Dick Zanuck, and I said to him, "What am I supposed to do with this stuff?" And he put his arm around me and said, "Kid, make it look like a Pepsi commercial."

DEBISUE VOORHEES: It was a very, very emotional day, because you can't be naked in front of people you don't know and not feel vulnerable. You're not human if you don't. Danny was actually really sweet and really understanding with me. I don't know how he was in the editing room, whether tempers flew a little bit, but I never really had any problems with him. He was very protective. On that day in particular, he really went out of his way to be overly sweet to me. And boy, I really don't remember him raising his voice to me—especially not then.

BARNEY COHEN: I was offered the Danny Steinmann one but I turned it down. I thought, "Once a philosopher, twice a pervert." I was actually a little bummed out Danny did *A New Beginning*. Because Danny's brilliant. I had the impression that he was independently wealthy. I know his parents owned an enormous brownstone on the East Side, with a lot of real art, of guys that you've heard of. I think his father was a big psychiatrist or something like that.

STEPHEN POSEY: I was one of the guys who was in that whole independent horror film stockpile of people of the time. I met Danny Steinmann through a connection with Tom DeSimone. I was the director of photography on *Savage Streets*. I liked Danny a lot, we were buddies, we played golf. But his background was sort of murky. He never talked about the adult films he did. He just never talked much about where he came from and what he had done. I had gotten the feeling maybe he was the black sheep of his family. I remember one

Above: Despite the majority of her death scene hitting the cutting room floor due to the stringent requirements of the MPAA ratings board, for actress Juliette Cummins, filming the effect remains a fond memory. "I had a great time," says Cummins. "When the blood started going down my neck, it was cold and I'd start laughing. I was thinking, 'I'm not getting killed. This is all pretend. This is magic. This is fun!'"

Opposite page: Another casualty of the MPAA ratings board was the "moment of impact" in the murder of Jake, played by Jerry Pavlon. "After the film wrapped, I had already moved back to New York," recalls Pavlon. "The filmmakers called me and said there was a problem with my death scene and the ratings board. So they had gone back and forth about what to do—should they reshoot it? In the end, they just decided to be clever with the editing and take the literal moment when the cleaver smacks my face out of the picture. I just had to fly back to Los Angeles to do a little looping—in the comic industry its a sound called a 'thwack!'"

Above: "My original death scene looked like a gruesome ad for heavy-duty feminine protection," laughs actress Tiffany Helm. "I was originally doing aerobics in my room, on my back with my legs in the air, scissoring. Jason comes in and, 'Wham!' He machetes me right up the middle. Well, I thought it was pretty funny. The producers did not. And director Danny Steinmann did not. They knew that the scene would not make it past the censors."

A meeting was hastily assembled. "We talked with Danny, and there was a lot of debate," remembers producer Tim Silver. "Personally, I felt that the scene was not what the original *Friday the 13th* was about—that film was a clear demonstration of how you can shock the audience as much as possible but not cross the line." The result was a new death scene for Helm: "Being that I was not exactly a 'hard body,' I had no problem changing the scene from exercising to what is there now, my dancing scene. And, by the way, that 'robot dance' is what we were doing at the club I went to at the time—I think it was just weird enough to intrigue Danny. So the scene was changed and everyone was happy."

Overlay: An original MPAA document submitted by the ratings board to the producers of *A New Beginning*. The film would ultimately require nine trips to the board before it would be granted an R rating.

February 8, 1985.

TO: ALL CONCERNED
RE: MPAA SCREENING

The following are scenes ruled by the MPAA to be "X" or "Hard X".

* Reel 3   295 - Boy hacked, blood splash, view of ch___
  Reel 3   710 - Boy killed with flare
* Reel 3   794 - Throat cut, blood seeping from throat
  Reel 5   Ax to skull, Ax to mid-section, view of corpse
                  (Lana & Billy)
* Reel 5   640 - Knife twist (Raymond kill)
* Reel 5   Sex scene too strong
  Reel 5   755 - Hedge clippers to eyes, view of ___
* Reel 5   853 - Head crush too strong
  Reel 5   857 - Outhouse kill too strong, spike through body, b__
* Reel 6   (Junior)
* Reel 6   220 - Head deca____
  Reel 7   267 - Cle____ to fo__
  Reel 7   678 - Cl___ ver striking face
  Reel 7   875 - Bu__ed kill, view of knife coming through body
  Reel 7   knife in ___ out ___ sto___
* Reel 7
  Reel 8   135 - ___ki__ in ___d out ___ ___ment
  Reel 9   502 - Jason's ha___ ____ ___bbing girl in stomach
  Reel 10   Dream sequence - ____ ___
* denotes strong X

above mentioned scenes must be recut in order for the board to
rescreen on Tuesday, February 12, 1985 at 1:00 in the afternoon.
The board will make a second ruling, and the film will be screened a____
Thursday, February 14, 1985 at 10:00am by Mr. Dick Hefner, MPAA Cha___

time, during *Savage Streets*, Danny and I were playing golf at the Malibu Country Club, and after, we went for a drive and he was in this rental Mustang. There was a giant boulder in the middle of the road and he just drove right over it. The car bottomed out on it. I said, "What are you doing!?" He just said, "Well, I thought we would clear it." Danny was a lot of fun to be around, but he had his share of personal demons.

The edgy elements in his films come from some place deep down inside him. The Danny I knew on set was a fun-loving kind of guy. But there was definitely a dark place in there. There was always that contrast. Certainly it's there in his *Friday*.

TIM SILVER: I liked Stephen Posey. There's no doubt that he's a nice man and he did a good job. And Danny, without that partnership with Stephen—I don't think he would have been able to pull the movie off. Danny was an isolated individual who was yelling and screaming when no one carried out what he needed. Stephen was good at interpreting what Danny wanted.

It's just funny, because Danny has a warm and humorous side to him. Danny was a character—he had an impish laugh. But he was an extremely paranoid individual. If he thought you were not on his side, he saw you as an enemy. And I remember finding that progressively as we shot he become more paranoid and antagonistic. I don't know whether or not he felt he was being reigned

in too much or controlled, or whether or not he was at odds with his mission. The folks from the East Coast may have been out to make a certain picture, and Danny felt he had to make it for them, but whatever it was, he felt he was being creatively constrained. There came to be a division between those who Danny thought were on his team, and those he thought weren't.

BOB DESIMONE: I think with me Danny was better, because we had a relationship. I think I got a little leeway. But he was doing a lot of cocaine. Someone would be talking to him and he would just be smiling away. Once, an actor was going over how they should play a scene, and Danny just snapped a pencil in his hand, right in front of the actor's face. Danny was enraged half the time. He couldn't control his anger or frustration on the set, even on this B-movie.

TIM SILVER: I don't mean any disrespect to Danny. Who knows what his assignment was from the powers that be on the East Coast? He was on a mission. Scuderi was the one who sent him, and Danny's job was probably to push the envelope as much as possible, in terms of sex, nudity and violence. And Frank's major effort was to reign that in so we could have footage we could show on screen. There was a constant struggle, in a sense, throughout the entire production. Everyone was looking out to

make sure that what Danny was doing was on target. But I thought Frank had the most consistent understanding of that and the best insight into what makes these movies work.

FRANK MANCUSO, JR.: My feeling was that Danny was going to be the guy directing the movie, and any director goes out there and tries to put their own imprint on whatever it is he or she is doing. Everybody's bringing their own sensibilities to the party. My real task at hand was to make sure that the creative needs of the movie were being met. At the same time, Danny's creative sensibilities needed to be expressed, but it had to be expressed in a context we were accustomed to living with. So for me, there was no reason to go out there and start hammering people because the first day doesn't go the way you want.

STEPHEN POSEY: Danny always just needed that little bit extra to get excited. I don't know how to say it other than he needed *more*. So that first scene we shot—it didn't surprise me at all. But it also doesn't surprise me how everyone else reacted. That makes perfect sense, from their point of view. This is not what the franchise was about, and I remember us all having a bunch of conversations. And after that first day's dailies, we did feel under the gun by the producers, that we really had to be on our toes to make sure that they were

satisfied with what we were doing. So it wasn't the most fun and relaxed show I've ever been on. There was always a certain amount of pressure on that set, from there on out.

JOHN SHEPHERD: I don't think any of the cast really knew about the tensions going on at the time. I certainly didn't. I really liked Danny. I remember he always wore a Yankees hat. And he came up to me one day early on and said, "Look, kid, this is your film. This is your shot. If you take this seriously and do a good job, I will treat you right and this film will treat you right." And after he gave me that power and confidence as an actor, I was able to do great work. I really had respect for Danny because he seemed to take it seriously.

BOB DESIMONE: There is a scene very early in the film, when I drop Tommy off at the sanitarium. I remember I improvised a moment where I pulled my ear and stuck my tongue out at Melanie, and she was freaked out a couple of times. But I was playing a sleazeball. So she stopped the scene and said to Danny, "He's making me nervous." And Steinmann said, "That's the idea! If you're an actress, go with it. If he's making you nervous, let him make you nervous." So I kept doing it. That's why I gave her the tongue and the ear. I was like, "That's for Danny."

CAROL LOCATELL: I sort of felt that Danny was pretty green. My sense was that he was a young guy who was gaining experience on the film just like everybody else. But he was sweet, and I never felt any tension in terms of our working together—sometimes, directors can be brutal to actors.

I was left to my own devices, really. I think most of us felt that way. Which may show, I don't know. I was given a lot of free license, especially to use the word "fuck" every chance I got. Remember my final words to the sheriff, when I flip him off? That was mine. All that screaming with the chicken, the "Hiiiiyyyeeeeee!" That was mine. And, "Will you shut the fuck up?" That was an ad lib. Although, I do think "fuckwad" might have already been in script.

JERRY PAVLON: In all fairness to everybody, the script was weak. But Danny knew that, too, to his great credit. We didn't chuck the dialogue completely, but Danny didn't necessarily go with it word for word. We all sensed the basic scenario, rehearsed it a couple of times, and then just went with it.

Will the real Jason please stand up? Dick Wieand plays Roy (**above**, second from left), the ambulance driver who, after witnessing the death of his son, assumes the identity of Jason to enact bloody revenge. Stuntman Tom Morga handled all of the scenes of Jason in costume (**opposite page**).

Do you remember that one scene at the table, the breakfast scene? That was hilarious. Now, that my character stuttered was an idea that I was presented with at my first audition. Danny just said, "You're a disturbed guy." And we worked for some time, probably half an hour, on the character in different scenes and trying different vocal mannerisms. And in that breakfast scene, as written, there is a line that is one of the worst and most comical ever written—"Y-y-you don't set a place for a dead person." That made me scream with laughter every time I tried to get serious about saying it. How can you, with any credibility whatsoever? And with a stutter? And with an audience on set watching? For whatever reason, that line keeps haunting me. People come up to me and say, "Are you the person who said that?" Because it is so completely idiotic.

COREY PARKER, "Pete": I was in New York and then I came out to L.A. I didn't have a car—I stayed with a friend and he would drive me to auditions. When I got *A New Beginning*, I had only done a couple of little things in New York. This was definitely bigger than anything I had done. And I was ecstatic—I was an actor and I had a job! Even if it was just for one night, and all I did was die.

Friday the 13th wasn't like an A-thing, even at that time. But that's what I liked about Danny and the way he was working. He

had a lot of intensity, especially once we started rehearsing and were on set. He didn't do it by numbers. I remember I brought my own clothes. The '50s thing, the way my character dressed, that may have been in the script, but in any case it was something that appealed to me and something I was familiar with. And it's funny, some people think that the characters in the scene are supposed to be gay. Especially because of the cap I had on my head. And maybe he is gay—I'll leave that up to each person. But that was my little input into the scene, my little association—Danny liked it that way. He wanted the actors to get into it and make it into something interesting. He was really open and excitable about ideas like that.

MIGUEL A. NUNEZ, JR., "Demon": *Part V* was one of my very first jobs. And I was absolutely terrified. Every minute of the day. I was totally green. I didn't know anything. But Danny was awesome. He let me make up my character's whole look myself. I did it all. I created all my hair, my clothes. I really took Demon seriously—I thought that if his father didn't want to see him, he had to be "out there," in order to make his father not want to hang out with him. Danny loved that. The song I sing when I'm sitting in the outhouse, "Ooh, Baby!"—I wrote that. That wasn't even in the script. And even today, people still come up to me and sing that song.

I loved Danny because he'd let me ad lib. He let you pretty much let you do your thing. He was one of those directors who was real conducive to actors—he let you go in and create. I thought it was a great learning experience for me. The best kind.

The Friday the 13th *films have always been known for their edge-of-your-seat third acts, usually involving a scantily clad blonde, lots of running and screaming, an eviscerated corpse or two thrown through a window, and a chair jumper of a surprise ending. But the success of the previous four films had upped the ante; by* Part V, *there was not just one heroine, there was also a hero and a child in peril. The stunts needed to be bigger, the thunder louder, the lightning brighter. And so much rain that even the Los Angeles Fire Department had to be called in one night to drench the set when the rain machines weren't enough.*

Adding to the excitement—or for some, the confusion—was that this time there was not just one "Jason," but two. While Dick Wieand assumed the role of Roy, the mild-mannered ambulance driver who is revealed in the film's bloody climax to be the face behind the alter ego of an "impostor Jason," actor-stuntman Tom Morga actually donned the familiar (yet semi-modified) hockey mask and also portrayed the "real Jason" as seen in Tommy Jarvis' horrific hallucinations. But even the new plot contrivances—and an essentially Jason-less Friday—*pleased few in the audience or behind the camera.*

DICK WIEAND: Even throughout shooting the film, I never had a finished script. All I knew was that the scene early in the film, when I see my son dead, was key, because that was the trigger—this one moment was all I had to make it clear that the murder of Roy's son could change him into the Jason imposter. Although that is a stupid idea, and I was expecting that there was going to be some good wrap-up stuff at the end—Danny told me that we were going to do different things with this movie. So I thought these big things were on their way.

When it came time to shoot the scene, I just let that moment happen, let the emotions come up and the change take place. I was trying to go nuts a little bit, yet still have it make sense. They even changed the position of the camera after we did the first rehearsal, because they realized what I was doing and came in closer. Of course, it was only when I finally saw the film that I realized that what I was trying to do didn't make any difference.

"Playing Jason is a little stranger than your average day job." Tom Morga

"I didn't know anything about the series at all when I got the film. All the casting directors said to me was, 'The children will love you.'"
Dick Wieand on Playing "Jason"

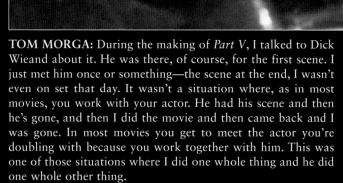

TOM MORGA, "Roy Stunt Double": When people ask if I ever really played Jason, I say, "Yes!" And when they want to know in which *Friday the 13th* specifically, I say, "It was *Part V*." Then, inevitably, they say, "Well, that Jason wasn't the real one." And I say, "Well, there *are* a couple of scenes where I play the real Jason."

The audition was funny. They brought in a bunch of guys to do the scene at the beginning of the movie, the dream sequence where kids dig up Jason's body and he stands up and goes after them. They had all of us do these mechanical Jason moves to see how well we could get up, stand up and walk like Jason. And Danny Steinmann liked what I did, and I got the job.

TIFFANY HELM: Tom was a bit slimmer than the original Jason, so I believe they had to pad him up a bit. He was a hoot. We were shooting in these creepy orange groves at night and he used to hide and jump out at Juliette and me, to give us a scare. Or sometimes he would just follow me, at a distance, really quietly, to freak me out. It worked!

JERRY PAVLON: I think to the extent that becoming a magician educates you, it also ruins a little bit of the illusion. Being on the set of *Friday the 13th* was an extremely different experience than I ever had before. There was one time when I saw Jason, with his mask in his hand, holding a cup of coffee. That's a very important image, actually, because that was more or less my experience on the set. And it allowed me to not be frightened of what would ultimately be frightening the entire nation.

DICK WIEAND: Why they made that decision to hire me and Tom as the same person also speaks of the lack of thought and concern throughout the whole movie. Tom and I look nothing alike. There was no attempt to make us look the same. Why did they not integrate us more?

I take nothing away from Tom Morga—Tom did fine stunts on the film. But he never had a kind word for me. I even asked to meet him. Near the end of the film, there's a scene where I have to lay dead on a bed of spikes. And the day we shot that, I'm standing there with my green jumpsuit on, and I asked Dick Warlock, "Is the stunt guy here. I want to meet him." So Dick took me over to Tom's trailer. And I thought he'd be glad to meet me. But he didn't come out of the trailer, he didn't invite me in the trailer. He just sort of stood there and looked at me.

I tried to improve the situation. I called the stunt coordinator and I asked him, "Some of the stuff in here is really easy, and I want to become more involved in playing the character." And I got the door slammed in my face. So I called my agent and said, "I'm trying to get more involved with this because the stuntman they hired to play Jason doesn't even look like me." He said, "The stunt coordinator's job is to keep stuntmen working. He's not interested in you. Don't worry about it. There will be better things later." And I just let it go.

TOM MORGA: During the making of *Part V*, I talked to Dick Wieand about it. He was there, of course, for the first scene. I just met him once or something—the scene at the end, I wasn't even on set that day. It wasn't a situation where, as in most movies, you work with your actor. He had his scene and then he's gone, and then I did the movie and then came back and I was gone. In most movies you get to meet the actor you're doubling with because you work together with him. This was one of those situations where I did one whole thing and he did one whole other thing.

I never got to know Dick too well but he seemed like a pretty good guy. And we did a talk show together once. I have a good feeling for him. The only thing I am not happy about is that he's signed pictures at conventions that that my image is on. I know his feeling is, well, that it's his part, and I made him look good. That's understandable. The only caveat is that fans want to have the reality. I've had fans come up to me saying, "Wasn't this really you with the mask on? Why didn't Dick say so?" I have offered to Dick that if he wants to, we could just sign the pictures together. That's what our job is—to try and get you to think that he did it all. If John Wayne was doing all the fights and the falls and stuff, you want it to be him, right? Their stuntman takes over and you're not supposed to know where.

DICK WIEAND: It was suggested that I try doing some autograph shows. I had never thought about it. I made a couple calls, and that's when I went on the Internet and realized that, while I never considered myself to really be Jason in that movie, that regardless of what I feel, the world thinks that I

am. Tony Perkins didn't do the shower scene in *Psycho*, but he's the one people think of when they think about Janet Leigh getting stabbed, and he still signed pictures of that shadow and the shower curtain.

TIM SILVER: *Friday the 13th* is an inexpensive film to produce. The hero is not a star, it's just a stuntman. He can be a scale player. He could be somebody different for each one. And the actor is not a star, either. Jason as a persona—you're not going to be looking for Humphrey Bogart or Tom Cruise in that role. And he's wearing a mask. So who cares who it is?

MELANIE KINNAMAN: It was a 90-minute film with 45 minutes of me running away from Jason. At least two weeks straight. The scene with the rain machines— I had to run into camera and stop on a certain mark. It was difficult. At one point, I hit the mark and promptly fell down. Rather than cutting, Danny said, "Keep rolling in the mud," so I spent the next five minutes rolling and screaming. When it was over, I said to myself, "I went to acting class for this?"

JERRY PAVLON: I remember watching the film after it had gone to video with a friend of mine who had never seen it, and who is not from this country. And when we came to the part when Melanie falls down in the mud, and she just keeps falling. It's hysterical how long she crawls. We could not find air to breathe in the room. We were *screaming* with laughter.

If you take an intellectual view and say, "Why isn't she getting up?", it's ridiculous. But there was a sense of wit about that even on the set. I'm an appreciative audience for Danny Steinmann because his tongue was obviously in cheek. He was sending up the genre, but without having to do what *Scream* does, which is to tell everybody in the grossest of terms that they're making fun of it. That really is for nine-year-olds. I think, in terms of that blend of horror and absurd comedy, *Part V* is still not appreciated, nor understood.

Above: "We filmed the scene where I attack Jason with a chainsaw on Halloween night," remembers Melanie Kinnaman. "I'm telling you, that was the hardest scene to do. I just could not keep a straight face. It was just so funny. I mean, here I was, standing there with this smoking chainsaw, going after a six-foot three-inch guy with a saber in his hand. I thought, 'He could kill me in a second, and they're trying to make this play like I've got the upper hand!?'"

Part V's extended chase scenes earned high marks from Kinnaman's young co-star Shavar Ross. "I always get a huge kick out of the running scene with Melanie, where she has no bra on," laughs Ross. "For one shot, they even had her purposely act scared and lean up against a wall, rain soaked— just to see her breasts. Then later, after I come out and stop Jason with the tractor (**opposite page**), she gives me this big double-dose of a hug. And she was always telling me I was cute and all that. So I had a crush on her the whole shoot. Even my stepmom kept saying, 'I think there was something hidden there.' I had a great time doing those scenes."

Left: Although the *Friday the 13th* series has been criticized for its lack of continuity between films, *Part V* saw Corey Feldman of *The Final Chapter* return for a cameo as Tommy Jarvis. "Frank Mancuso, Jr. really let me shoot from the hip quite a bit," said Danny Steinmann. "I wanted to have an opening sequence with Corey to bridge the two pictures, so Frank went out and got Corey for me and let me shoot it."

"It was supposed to be the middle of summer, but it was actually October," remembers Feldman of the shoot. "And they had no rain machine, because it was a small budget, so they just hooked a hose to a sprinkler valve of the house we were shooting at. On top of that, there is no Jason there. It's just me standing in my neighbor's backyard, freezing my ass off, going 'Aaahhhh!' And Danny Steinmann's saying, 'Oh, now you see him come out of the grave! Now he's coming after you! Now he's chasing you!' It was not the most pleasurable memory of my career. But it was short and sweet."

MELANIE KINNAMAN: Many of the things we did in that film were so hysterically over the top that I spent most of the time just trying to look at the cameramen without bursting out laughing. If I made eye contact, I would lose control. And I lost it a lot of times.

STEPHEN POSEY: I felt sort of sorry for Melanie through the shoot because she, like any actress—and like all of us working on that film—it was a step up and yet, at the same time, what did she really have to do? She's become just a couple of wet, flopping breasts. Again, this was probably, partially, the dark side of Danny, but I remember standing there and him saying, "Okay, hose her down again!" It was demeaning, but you know, as an actor, a lead in a movie—any movie—is an opportunity you can't pass up.

TIM SILVER: When Melanie was running in a wet shirt in a storm and it was clear that more was going to be seen than expected— Melanie didn't have a lot of say in the matter. I don't think it sat well with her. The nudity always posed a problem, because the actors had to agree ahead of time to what the nudity would entail. And if that envelope gets pushed during shooting, it was difficult.

JULIETTE CUMMINS: When I got the script, the big issue was how much nudity was in it. Because I was under twenty. At first, they said it was just going to be a flash of lightning and you saw me as a dead body, nude. Then they sprung that thing with the mirror—that stupid line in front of the mirror—on the set at 1:00 a.m. They had to get more T & A into the film, and I was it. And also because Tiffany wouldn't do the nudity—she was just not going to do it. So it suddenly became, "Okay, take off your robe." I had to make a decision then and there about whether I was going to do it or not. I couldn't call my agent in the middle of the night. Danny took me aside and he told me what it was going to be non-sexual: "You're just talking here—this isn't a porn thing." So he comforted me in that respect.

The funny thing is, I don't know why everyone wants me to take off my clothes. I don't have what everybody wants, giant boobs—I've got a handful and that's about it. Back then, it was a big thing to take off your clothes, and I was always asked to do it. And being young, you think it's going to affect your career and maybe you won't get hired for something else because you took it off. Nowadays, you have Oscar-winning actresses like Halle Berry doing nudity. I don't think it makes a difference now, but back then, it was a big thing. But I was and am a little bit of a rebel. I figured that nobody knew me, anyway, so was this really going to hurt me? I grew up here in the Hollywood Hills—on Ronald Reagan's old ranch land before everything started getting subdivided. I remember growing up, and I would go barefoot and topless. And my scene wasn't supposed to be sexualized anyway. But still, to this day, everyone goes, "Oooh!"

MIGUEL A. NUNEZ, JR.: It felt like I shot my death scene for like two weeks—it took me that long to die. I was outside in that outhouse, and it was freezing. And I had to do the whole death scene from top to bottom multiple times. First with the camera straight out in front with the door off. Then with the left side of the wall off. Then they put that wall back up and took the other wall off and I had to do it again. But the funny thing was, while they were killing me, they were using Jason to kill somebody else down the street. It was like a Jason factory of death.

DICK WIEAND: Even by the time we shot my death scene, they still weren't sure how they were going to explain the revelation of my identity. In the original ending, my head was supposed to go careening down some walkway or something. They even made a plaster cast of my head. But then they changed the script, and I die falling out of the barn onto a bed of spikes. And I wanted to make it an even more horrible death—I wanted to have my eyes open. But they didn't want to hear it. All they did was glue these fake spikes to my chest—which were hell getting off, by the way—and you can even see in the picture that the damned spikes are bent. It was pretty ridiculous.

SHAVAR ROSS: I remember seeing the ending of the movie and thinking it was the corniest thing. When he falls on the spikes—you can see it is a dummy! I told the production people and they were just like, "Don't worry about it. It's all in good fun." But it looks so fake.

STEPHEN POSEY: The whole ending of the movie, the surprise, is weak. I remember when it came time to shoot Roy's death, we had to do it twice because no one was happy with the final image. And I remember sitting there going, "Well, who is that!?" Even the crew were laughing, like, "Who's going to get this? What ambulance driver? No one is going to understand what is going on!" It just came out of nowhere—all of a sudden, at the very end, you had this weird connection.

FRANK MANCUSO, JR.: Was I in love with the imposter Jason? No. In retrospect, that is one of the mistakes you make when you're trying to do something different just so somebody doesn't come to you and say, "You've made the same movie six times in a row!"

JOHN SHEPHERD: They didn't have the ending written when we started, nor the coda, when I'm in the hospital after the killer is revealed. They did have something that Danny didn't like, and I actually got the opportunity to go to him and say, "I have a few ideas about the ending." Even though I didn't know the first thing about screenwriting. And Danny said, "I'd love to hear them." So my friend Mike Hitchcock and I talked about what should happen at the end, because they wanted Tommy to go on as the killer. In the original concept for the ending, he puts on the mask and becomes possessed, which I didn't like. But they wanted to have that image in there somehow. And Mike is a great writer and he had some great ideas, and we typed them up on a few sheets of that old onion fax paper. And Danny really liked it.

So what you see is what Mike and I wrote—a big crash of glass, Pam comes in, looks out the window and thinks Tommy's gone. Then Tommy's wearing the mask, standing behind her. And the next thing I know, we were shooting it. Of course, I'm thinking, "Oh, I'm going to get screen credit!" And I didn't.

TOM MORGA: I remember we shot a couple of endings. The one in the movie, and then another one where Tommy also breaks the window, but when Melanie comes in, he's just standing there, then

Above: In one of Tommy's many dream-like hallucinations, Pam (Melanie Kinnaman) finds herself at the wrong end of Jason's knife.

walks through the broken window and out into the rain. Of course, either way, it's left wide open for another sequel. Needless to say.

It had become a tradition with each new Friday the 13th *film to up the body count over previous chapters, as well as devise increasingly elaborate methods of dispatching victims, no matter how sensational or incredible. Nowhere was this more obvious than in* Part V's *final death toll, which reached an astonishing—and some would say absurd—twenty-two victims by the end of the film's 95-minutes. The question of just how much was too much weighed heavily—and uneasily—on the minds of the film-makers as* A New Beginning *neared the end of post-production.*

TIM SILVER: As far as I'm concerned, the original *Friday the 13th*—its power lied in what was only suggested. There was the fear that something was going to happen, and they really didn't linger on the graphic violence. Whereas with *Part 2* and afterward, I felt that they just pointed a camera and went right for the close-up of the gore. That wasn't necessarily appealing to me. In *Part V*, to be honest, I think that the overabundance of kills was Danny. Danny rewrote it, and because the film was weak and the story was not as strong as some of the others, that was Danny's way to try to replicate its success. There was a desperation on Danny's part. It's obvious why you set off a bomb every two pages—because you haven't got a story that's working.

BRUCE GREEN: You have to spend time setting characters up. To me, that's what it's all about. In *Part V*, we didn't set any of the characters up. Danny didn't have any interest in that. I don't want to say negative things about him, but I think the crudeness of the film came from Danny. I think that's due to his coming out of porn. In porn, it's all about the penetration shot. And *Part V* is structured like a porn film. And that's its problem.

DANNY STEINMANN: The violence in the finished film is about ten percent of what I shot. Originally, we did shoot more material with the characters. For example, the scenes with Ethel and Junior—their scenes were twice as long. And I had to take the transformation of Tommy seriously, because my focus was going to be on him. But audiences wanted to get to the kills. I did it in a way that I thought would get the biggest response. I just approached it like a cartoon. You can't take it seriously.

SEAN CUNNINGHAM, Producer/Director, *Part 1*: Read the reviews about the original *Friday the 13th*, and they will tell you it's the most bloody, disgusting, horrible movie they ever saw. But the incredible thing is, it's not there. When we did the TV version of the film, all I had to cut out was approximately twenty-two seconds. That's it! All the blood that is in *Friday the 13th* is gone. Because the anticipation is what triggers the horror, and when you see those twenty-two seconds it's a mind fuck.

After the film was a huge, completely unexpected hit, it created a whole flurry of activity and noise and spawned I don't know how many dozens of imitators. Subsequently, I think they got suspense mixed up with gore, and plot mixed up with blood. If you say, "Well, I can't fix the plot so I'll kill two other people," it's no good. It doesn't work. I think eventually the slasher moviemakers discovered that even though you can do that, it becomes your own worst enemy. Because, ultimately, gore is very numbing, and I strongly dispute the dramatic effect of it. In my opinion, you just touch it enough to make you blink, and then it's got to be gone. The impression is still there. *Psycho* is tame by today's standards, but that ambiguous figure behind the shower curtain still haunts you.

I think there's been a big change that's taken place over the last twenty years. When we first did gore back in 1980, it was a magic

trick. Now, anything you can dream of can be accomplished on film. The audience isn't surprised or particularly impressed when you do camera tricks. Remember *Terminator 2*, when we really started to see that morphing effect? And it was really amazing and cool? Well, then within weeks Gillette had a commercial where somebody was shaving and his face changed four or five times in thirty seconds. And the audience just watched it and said, "Eh." Suddenly the magic trick had lost its glamour. And now that the delight has been removed, you'd better replace that delight with something else—and that something else is the unexpected character and story twists. Which get ignored, because they're hard. But you have to tell a story that somehow achieves a resonance. If there is a lesson to be learned from any of the sequels, that may be it.

"These films are very ethnic, very blue collar. And every year it's like an event. Kids from broken homes always have *Friday the 13th* to look forward to." Danny Steinmann

HARRY MANFREDINI, Composer: I will agree with Sean and say I wish they had cut more. It's amazing how incredibly horrific the first *Friday* seemed, and now it's tame. And as a result, on the sequels, the envelope was constantly being pushed. Eventually the filmmakers knew that the MPAA would cut out a certain amount, so they went way, way over the top, so far over that the movies contained more and more kills each time. I don't know if fans what to hear this, but I've seen the versions before the MPAA cuts—I scored them—and they are just as stupid. Only gorier. To me, they are like cartoons with knives.

When it comes to these films, it's just like being a bricklayer, or a plumber. I write the appropriate music, and then I'm done. I don't have to like them to do them. And there is no question in my mind that the worst one was where the ambulance driver was impersonating Jason. I don't know how well the ideas of the plot, and the acceptability of the outcome, played to the audience. But while the series was getting stale, I do think the introduction of the Tommy Jarvis character gave it a few more breaths.

I thought my music for *Part V* was good. Over the years, I had grown considerably as a composer. Many of the differences in the scores are a result of the actual films themselves—as they evolved, they added dimensions and character elements to try to disguise that it was just really another Jason film. The score for *Part V* was a noticeable evolution. I got to write a theme for Tommy, which was also to suggest something far beyond him, that there was a total madness afoot. It was necessary to use this because it was important to "point the finger" at various characters, not just him. And to suggest that things were not as you might expect. So while the harmonic and melodic elements of the early scores are still present, the new material evolved from the old. So at least that was fun.

BRUCE GREEN: I learned something very valuable from Harry. When I first got the job on *Part V*, I went and rented a couple of the *Friday* films. And I couldn't watch them because they were too scary. Instead, I'd put it on, but I'd turn the sound off and I would high-speed until Jason would pop up and kill somebody. Then I'd watch it silent. Then I'd turn on the sound again, and that's when it hit me that it was so much about the music—especially horror, more than any other genre. Harry Manfredini is, to me, the hero of these movies. And without him, quite frankly, a film like *Part V* might have been completely unwatchable.

No matter what those involved with A New Beginning *felt about their creation, when it hit theaters on March 22, 1985 its opening weekend box office proved that there was still a sizable and hungry audience for the further exploits of Jason Voorhees. Even if it was an impostor. Cutting a swath across 1,379 screens in the United States,* Part V *became the fifth consecutive installment in the series to top the weekend box office, pulling in $8 million in its first three days. While greeted somewhat less feverishly than* The Final Chapter, *by the following Monday* A New Beginning *had already turned a sizable profit. But soon the tell-tale signs of bad word of mouth were on the horizon:* Part V *suffered a stiffer fall-off than any of the previous installments in the series. By its third weekend of wide release, the film plummeted completely out of the top ten, eventually scaring up a respectable, if far from spectacular, final take of $21.9 million. Perhaps, in the end, it was enough to justify the film's subtitle—a decent enough "new beginning" for a franchise that no one ever expected to become a franchise in the first place. Or, as some of its makers feared, was it the truly the beginning of the end for Jason?*

TIM SILVER: I think we all knew the film was not creatively satisfying. On the level of story, the film didn't work. It didn't succeed. That's probably why I've forgotten most of it. It's always more rewarding to work on films that you're glad to see out there and that you're proud of leaving behind. When you work on a film like that, it can be a horrifying experience. I don't know what I got out of it. *Friday the 13th* is not my cup of tea. For me, it was a job. I got it done and went on to the next one.

DANNY STEINMANN: I have complained a lot about other people taking over my films, but on this one I was pretty much given a true shot. I'm not displeased with the picture and I'm my own worst critic. I can't complain.

STEPHEN POSEY: When you work on a movie, and then you finally go to the cast and crew screening and everybody's there, there is always an element of embarrassment anyway. Because you're self critical. But on this movie it was magnified, because, in all honesty, it was a *Friday the 13th*. It's stupid, you know? And you know it's stupid while you're making it. But still, you think, maybe, when it's all put together? Then, there you are at the screening, the lights come up, and all you can think is, "Yeah, it's still pretty stupid."

DICK WIEAND: It wasn't until I saw *Part V* that I realized what a piece of trash it was. I mean, I knew the series' reputation, but you're always hoping that yours is going to come out better. I took a very nice girl to a screening on the Paramount lot, and I was really embarrassed for her being with me. And when it was over and we were leaving, there were cast and crew outside the theater and I just wanted to escape. I remember that some of the stuff we shot that I really liked suddenly wasn't there anymore. Then I'm hearing ad libs looped on the soundtrack that I don't remember hearing on set. These kids couldn't have been very old at the time, and here they were saying stuff like, "Blah, blah, blah…blow job!" It's just a piece of crap.

JULIETTE CUMMINS: To be honest, I didn't know how it was going to turn out even while we were shooting it. And I don't remember my first reaction when I saw it. I probably just loved the fact I was watching myself, that I couldn't believe I was on the screen. I don't know if I ever thought it was scary. I remember watching *Psycho III* with an audience and thinking it was great.

I don't remember watching *A New Beginning* and feeling that way. You have to have a sense of humor about these movies.

JOHN SHEPHERD: I saw the film at the Fox Theater in Westwood opening weekend. I had no idea what to expect. I had never seen a *Friday the 13th* movie with an audience. And I had just graduated from UCLA, so my girlfriend still went to school there and my whole fraternity—like eighty guys—came along.

Short of *The Rocky Horror Picture Show*, I had never seen anything like it. It was jam-packed, and people were standing on their chairs, screaming, "Kill 'em, Tommy!" I was so pumped that night. And I was very happy with the way they cut me, and the subtlety that Danny got out of my performance. It was a really, really fun night.

SHAVAR ROSS: I went opening night in Westwood with Corey Feldman, who was my friend at the time—we did our first commercial together—and there were fans lined up around the block. So it was a really exciting time, a great time. Kids in the crowd was standing up, yelling, "Run Dudley, run!" I couldn't believe it.

The film itself is not something I can be really proud of. There was more nudity than in the other *Friday*s. I wish it wasn't like that, because I can't show my son the whole film. I'm sure that is Danny's influence. The only proud thing for me is that after the parts I do show my son, he says, "Daddy, you survived!"

MIGUEL A. NUNEZ, JR.: I'm a big horror movie fan and I'm a big *Friday the 13th* fan. I came right out to California saying, "The first thing I want to do is a horror movie." I was just so excited to be one of the first black folks in a *Friday the 13th*. I didn't know how to contain myself. I loved it. I thought it was great.

TIFFANY HELM: Well, my best friend and I thought it would be funny to drop acid and go on opening night. And she couldn't stop giggling through the whole film—that just added to the whole evening. It was a very strange experience when the audience is applauding as Jason rises from the dead, and they whoop and holler when everyone gets killed.

FRANK MANCUSO, JR.: I would probably say *A New Beginning* is my least favorite of the series. As for the box office, in some ways, I think it didn't perform as well as the previous ones because we promised them *The Final Chapter*, so they said, "I already went last time and I thought that was the last one. I've already given you my last dollar." Yet, despite that, some of the real dedicated fans still hung on to hope. They just said, "They're doing anything, and anything's better than nothing, so I'll go see it."

TIM SILVER: It is hard to say what the ultimate effect if any *A New Beginning* had on the series. But in a very simplistic way, even if it's a disappointment on its own terms, it's already made its money before anybody figures that out. It succeeded on a business level, and that's really all that mattered for Paramount. They just wanted to keep the audience alive and keep the franchise alive. I think we pretty much knew it was unlikely that the theaters would be empty opening weekend. And we wouldn't see the long-term damage, because by the time the audience figured it out it's over in three weeks anyway.

But if I were in love with the series and I saw *Part V*, I would have been disappointed. If I have any regret, it is that it could have been a better *Friday the 13th* movie.

6.

Resurrection

The first half of the 1980's saw five *Friday the 13th* films released at the rate of almost one a year, and all had been commercially successful. But following the depressed box office that greeted 1985's *A New Beginning*, no one involved with the series could deny that a fresh direction was needed. The series could never deliver the unexpected gut-punch to the cultural zeitgeist in the way the first film did, but executives at Paramount still believed that the further exploits of Jason could remain fresh and vital. Or at least Frank Mancuso, Jr. hoped as much. Having settled, if a bit uncomfortably, into the role of the series' godfather following *The Final Chapter*, Mancuso had not grown timid, complacent or lazy. He still wanted to take risks with the series, however formulaic its requirements had become. Mancuso believed that, like Jason himself, *Friday the 13th* was never truly dead—it was only one hit movie away from reestablishing itself as the world's reigning champion of modern horror. And he would proceed just as he had on *Part V*—by finding a fresh, exuberant young director, one who could stick to the basic rules of the series while still having the freedom to put his own creative stamp on the material. There was just one marching order Mancuso would insist upon: Jason could not stay dead. It was truly time for a resurrection.

"I wanted my Jason to be a monster born out of hatred and electricity."

Tom McLoughlin

"Of all the sets we designed for the film, I'm most proud of the cemetery," says production designer Joseph T. Garrity. "It was a dream come true. We had complete control. The cemetery set was created from scratch out of an empty field **(opposite page, top)**. There was all sorts of effects—wind, rain and even a tree getting hit by lightning. We also built all the tombstones by hand, out of Styrofoam, then painted them. Although, if you notice, there are no names on the tombstones—except Jason's. That was the only one created out of actual stone. It was great fun."

FRANK MANCUSO, JR., Executive Producer: I formed my first production company, Hometown Films, around the end of 1985. I thought it was important to start separating myself from the *Friday* movies because it would have been too easy to get boxed in and never really do other things. Stylistically, Hometown tried to stay away from subject matter similar to the *Friday* movies. Even when we did *April Fool's Day*, which was one of our first movies and a sort parody of slasher movies, my biggest concern was that people were going to compare it to *Friday*.

What needs to be said is that the *Friday the 13th* films were about as close to a risk-free transaction as possible, and it was always a Paramount call to do another one. These movies were literally paying for themselves in the first weekend. And it didn't cost a lot of money to go from a *Part V* to a *Part VI*. We didn't have continuing characters. We didn't need an increasingly spectacular series of effects. We certainly didn't need anything that was extraordinary, because the central conceit of the movie was essentially simple. I remember several times where the movie would open on Friday, and on Monday, and I'd get a call from Paramount saying, "Go make another one." It was simply and purely an exercise in commerce.

TIM SILVER, Producer, *Part V*: *Beverly Hills Cop* was a tremendous success at the time for Paramount, yet the *Friday the 13th* series had netted more money for the studio. It wasn't as prestigious a project, but people forget that putting the cost— $2 or $3 million apiece—against the gross—somewhere between $20 and $40 million—allowed for a lot of profit.

I remember when we were finishing *Part V*, we sat around asking, "What are we going to call it?" It was Frank Jr. who came up with *A New Beginning*. And there was a lot of chuckling, because it's so in-your-face. It's a blatant admission that we're going to do another one. Even though *Part V* was not the creative success we hoped for, again, Paramount could afford to take a gamble because the risk was so low. And if a *Part VI* was pretty good then the series could regain its footing quickly.

TOM MCLOUGHLIN, Director & Screenwriter: I grew up in Culver City, and my dad went to USC film school in the '40s, so I had the MGM backlots to play in when I was a kid. On weekends, I'd jump over the fence and bring my friends, and we'd make these semi-horror movies or James Bond movies or *A Hard Day's Night*. Then, when I was nineteen years old I moved to Paris, where I studied fencing, acrobatics, modern dance and classical dance. I was literally right across the street from a cinema that would change movies three times a day. So all those years were just the greatest experience of soaking up everything art and film.

I came back to America wanting to make silent, visual movies, like Jacques Tati and the people I'd seen over there. Then I went on tour as a one-man performer—I did pantomimes, like Sid Caeser and Red Skelton used to do, only I tried to make it relevant to my generation, so it dealt with drugs and cars and earthquakes. But I began to see that mime was very limited and that there was only so much I could do by myself. So I got a partner and put together the L.A. Mime Company, and eventually Dick Van Dyke came and saw us and asked us to be regulars on *Van Dyke & Company*, a short-lived series in the 1970s. Then Dick started letting me write and direct for whoever was the guest star, and suddenly I'm directing Lucille Ball, Freddie Prinze, Carol Burnett. And I got an Emmy nomination, so I was in the Writer's Guild of America.

By the early 1980s I started writing comedy scripts. But nobody wanted comedy at that time, they wanted horror. So I shifted gears, but I loved horror. And I made a film called *One Dark Night*, which was released in early 1983. It didn't have a big budget—we made it for less than a million—but it also didn't have a huge marketing campaign, and there was little competition. It opened really well, even if, like most genre pictures do by the next week, it fell off like 40 percent, and by the fourth week, it was playing on the triple bill downtown. We also got mixed reviews. But it was still thrilling.

When you direct your first film, it sort of becomes your calling card and has a lot to do with what your next job is going to be. Even though I wanted to do comedy, I was now a low-budget horror movie director. So what came my way were all those sort of things, but I also got the chance to get through a lot of doors. That's ultimately how my meeting with Frank Mancuso, Jr. came about.

FRANK MANCUSO, JR.: *Part V* was a coarser movie than some of the other *Friday*s we had made, and, in retrospect, *Part VI* was an answer to that. I knew Tom McLoughlin had a different kind of mentality than Danny Steinmann, and you can't make eight movies and not have issues with people as they try to put their stamp on the films. I was also cognizant of not wanting to be stuck there every day—not because I thought *Friday* was a burden, but because I felt like it wasn't fair to tell the people I had chosen, that I had told that this was "their movie," and then sit there and hammer them every day because it isn't turning out the way I wanted it to turn out.

What was the most important thing about doing each new *Friday* was that somebody comes along who has a real passion for it, and who's fresh and hungry. You can never get somebody after they've made it. That's why you get a Tom McLoughlin—someone who wants to go out there and give it their best shot. There's a certain energy that someone who's just starting their career has, and a certain naiveté, but if you can harness that, you can't replace it. There will always be something special about somebody who comes along and says, "This is everything I've ever wanted to do."

TOM McLOUGHLIN: At that point, I didn't have a lot of control of my career choices, but I did have an agent at William Morris. And I had another deal at Paramount, a suspense thriller of some sort, although I don't know if they ever ended up making it or not. But then Paramount felt that there was still an audience for another *Friday*. My agent called and said, "They're offering you the next *Friday the 13th*." I said, "Is there a script?" He said, "No, you'd write and direct it."

I was told only this by Frank: "You have to bring Jason back from the dead—however you want to do it." I really wanted to make a comedy at that time. And Frank was really looking for any twist to keep the series going for another one. Because by the time he got to mine, he wasn't sure how much juice was left. So I sensed he was just excited by the notion that I was going to do something different with it, even if he was not a hundred percent sure if it was going to work or not.

It immediately became clear to Frank Mancuso, Jr. that Friday the 13th Part VI *would reflect an entirely different vision and sensibility from that of* Part V. *Tom McLoughlin's first draft screenplay was funnier, faster and more action-packed*

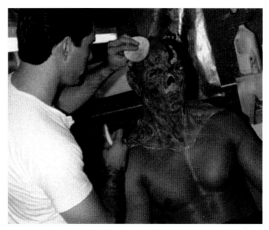

The task of conceptualizing *Part VI*'s newly zombified Jason Voorhees fell to makeup effects artist Brian Wade (**middle, left**). "We all wanted to respect what had come before in the previous films," says Wade, who worked with the effects team at Reel EFX in creating the final design. "For example, in *The Final Chapter*, Jason got a machete through the left side of his head, so we made sure he was missing his left eye. I also wanted him to look significantly rotted, because he's been in the ground for what was likely a few years, but at the same time not be a nondescript, dripping mass of goo. So I used many materials, including latex, cotton and clay, to build up stringy, deteriorated zombie-like effects over his face and hands. I'm very pleased with the final design, especially given the short time frame we had to complete it."

Above: Lead actress Jennifer Cooke (right) pals around with the mummified corpse of "Jason" and members of the Reel EFX effects team.

"The chase through the cemetery was one of the first days we filmed," recalls actor Vincent Guastaferro (**top**, right), who played Deputy Rick Cologne. "But because we were shooting at a local cemetery, which was historically preserved, we weren't allowed to leap over the graves. That's why you'll notice we're running around the perimeters of the graves. Tom McLoughlin had to block the whole scene out to look like it was *Pac-Man*. But that's another example of what a great director Tom is—he took a limitation and turned it into something interesting."

Above: Director Tom McLoughlin (kneeling) takes a break during the filming of *Friday the 13th Part VI: Jason Lives*.

than any Friday *before or since. Imbuing his screenplay with a post-modern sense of irony unique for a horror film at that time, McLoughlin seemed hell-bent on gently satirizing not only the hard-edged cynicism of* A New Beginning *and its namesake series, but the slasher genre itself.*

McLoughlin's script, although essentially ignoring the ending of Part V, brought back the character of Tommy Jarvis, completing a trilogy of sorts that had begun with The Final Chapter. *The ambitious writer-director also added a dash of mythology to Jason's backstory, a name change for Crystal Lake (redubbing it "Forest Green"), and a fresh batch of genuinely likable characters just self-aware enough that even those who literally had the words "Dead" written across their foreheads were in on the joke. And as a final clever, however self-conscious, touch, McLoughlin also pared down Part V's over the top body count to a comparatively slim—and entirely fitting—thirteen victims.*

As pre-production on Part VI began in January 1986, the young cast and crew quickly discovered McLoughlin's enthusiasm and determination to deliver a different kind of Friday the 13th. And soon any fears for a repeat of Part V's contentious production on the part of Mancuso and his producing team were quickly extinguished.

TOM MCLOUGHLIN: I was basically given carte blanche. Frank said, "Here are the films, just pick up from where they left off and see what you want to do with it." It was one of the great times of my life where they gave me a private screening room at Paramount and let me watch all the movies, back to back. And I noticed after *The Final Chapter*, it went a little sideways. So I thought, "I'm going to pick up after *The Final Chapter*, disregard *Part V*, and tie the legend together a little bit." I wanted to take the Tommy character that Corey Feldman played and do the same idea, that he was locked away, but instead of getting out and becoming Jason as *Part V* left off, he gets out and just wants to make sure that Jason is dead and in his grave. And when Tommy digs Jason up and sees him rotting, he has this horrible flashback and can't help but take out his wrath on the corpse. And of course that leads to a little divine intervention.

I thought, "If Jason's dead and we're going to bring him back, let's use the old Frankenstein device of a lightning bolt." Because if I can get the audience to buy that he's the walking dead, I can do anything, and there's no stopping him. It just gave me license to do a lot of different and neat things.

BRUCE GREEN, Editor: After *Part V*, I had edited *April Fool's Day*, and a TV movie based on *Family Ties*. Those were all Frank—he kept me busy because he wanted me to be available for *Part VI*. And despite my experience on *A New Beginning*, I was thrilled to be working, because it was immediately apparent that the script was much better, and that Tom McLoughlin seemed like a real director. Tom is great—there's a big difference in tone between Danny's *Friday* and Tom's *Friday*. Tom went into it so the audience would have fun. Danny went into it more like we were going to scare the hell out of people.

"I wanted *Jason Lives* to be about more than just teens being chased around by a guy with a machete. I wanted to have car chases and big stunts and cops with guns." Tom McLoughlin

TOM MCLOUGHLIN: Bruce Green told me *Part V* was a nightmare situation, and that Danny's sensibilities were completely different than mine. I had always been more of a gothic horror kind of person. I love Edgar Allan Poe. I love ghost stories. And *One Dark Night* dealt with death and floating corpses and claustrophobia. I wanted to get those elements into this, in an era when if you had a killer, a knife, a forest and teenagers, you had a pretty good chance of getting a film made. Maybe it's my being raised Catholic—that combination of Catholic guilt, Catholic icons, devils and demons—all my influences and beliefs sort of tied into this. You can take the boy out of the church, but you can't take the church out of the boy.

I also love surrealism. And I didn't think that it really seemed like any of the previous *Friday* filmmakers spelled out the whole thing, the mythology, other than the first movie. Of course, obviously, no one knew it was going to become a franchise. So I wanted to incorporate more of a backstory, a sense of history.

I had friends who found this terribly amusing, but I actually wrote the movie during Christmas. I was literally sitting in my living room next to the Christmas tree, writing all these horrific kills and doing my research by, going and seeing all the *Friday*s and trying to put together some assemblage of a mythology that I felt I could track how Jason got to this point. I even originally subtitled my script "Jason Has Risen," but Paramount found that a little bit distasteful, so it became *Jason Lives* instead.

VINCENT GUASTAFERRO, "Deputy Rick Cologne": Before *Jason Lives*, Tom had directed me in a play. And up until then, I'd only done two small movie roles, where I was like a gang member or something. And I looked really skinny and young and had long hair. Tom was the first one to cast me as a grown-up. I was like, "Whoa!" I didn't even know he was an up-and-

coming film director. Then my agent was called about *Jason Lives*, and frankly, it scared me. But I heard Tom McLoughlin was directing it and I got excited. Tom's an accomplished everything. He's one of the finest artists I know. I love this guy! He's capable and he has a good soul. He appears like Wes Craven and those other guys—very straight and professorial, but with a demented mind. I knew he would do something special with it.

TOM MCLOUGHLIN: The funny thing is, despite all the scary films I've done over the years, when people ask who has been my biggest inspiration, I say, "Frank Capra." It's true. Capra was my mentor. He's the only Hollywood director I actually got to have one-on-one conversations with—he even gave me notes and a quote for *Date With an Angel*, which I did after my *Friday*. Capra taught me that it's a people-to-people medium. If you care about the people, you'll care about the story. Even if you don't have as great a story as you might want, if you just like spending time with this character, that's good. That's the big thing to aspire to. I guess if you make a character annoying enough people will want to see them killed, and I felt like that was often the case with some of the past *Friday* films. So I wanted to make the characters likable so you didn't want to see them suffer. That was my huge rule in casting: get likable, accessible people, then create enough humanity so the audience is emotionally invested, because they've somehow connected with and understand the characters.

KERRY NOONAN, "Paula": It says something about Tom that all we did during my audition was sort of talk. He said, "Tell something humorous that has happened to you in the last year." I really liked Tom—he was a nice guy and really easy to connect with. The audition felt good. I think I got the job because I was free enough that I didn't really care whether I got it or not. And Paula was pretty close to me—I'm the major good girl—so I didn't feel I had to stretch it that much.

THOM MATHEWS, "Tommy Jarvis": Growing up, I just didn't know what I wanted to do. One day, a girlfriend suggested that I might try being an actor. Her remark was right out of the blue, but it triggered something in my head, and I took her advice.

Right before *Friday* came along, I was going out to readings, not getting the parts. I had already done this movie, *Return of the Living Dead*, and here I was, thinking that once it came out, that things would begin happening in a big way for me. But even after it did, and I got good notices, I wasn't getting any offers. So, I started putzing around and getting real depressed. And that film did help. But it was just that I was expecting a flood of offers and I wasn't getting any work. It was really frustrating.

I'll tell you why I did *Jason Lives*. I was in no position to turn down the lead in a film being distributed by Paramount Pictures that would be seen by a whole lot of people. No matter what some think of the *Friday* movies, they can establish that an actor can carry a picture.

TOM MCLOUGHLIN: Finding my Tommy was a question of getting someone I could believe was this kid, Corey Feldman, grown up. And we never found anybody who was exactly the right physical type, but Thom Mathews was kind of like an up-and-coming young genre actor. He already had a nice body of work—he had done those *Return of the Living Dead* movies—so I felt he brought a bit of a cult following with him. He was also a strong actor. And Frank also did not want to repeat with John

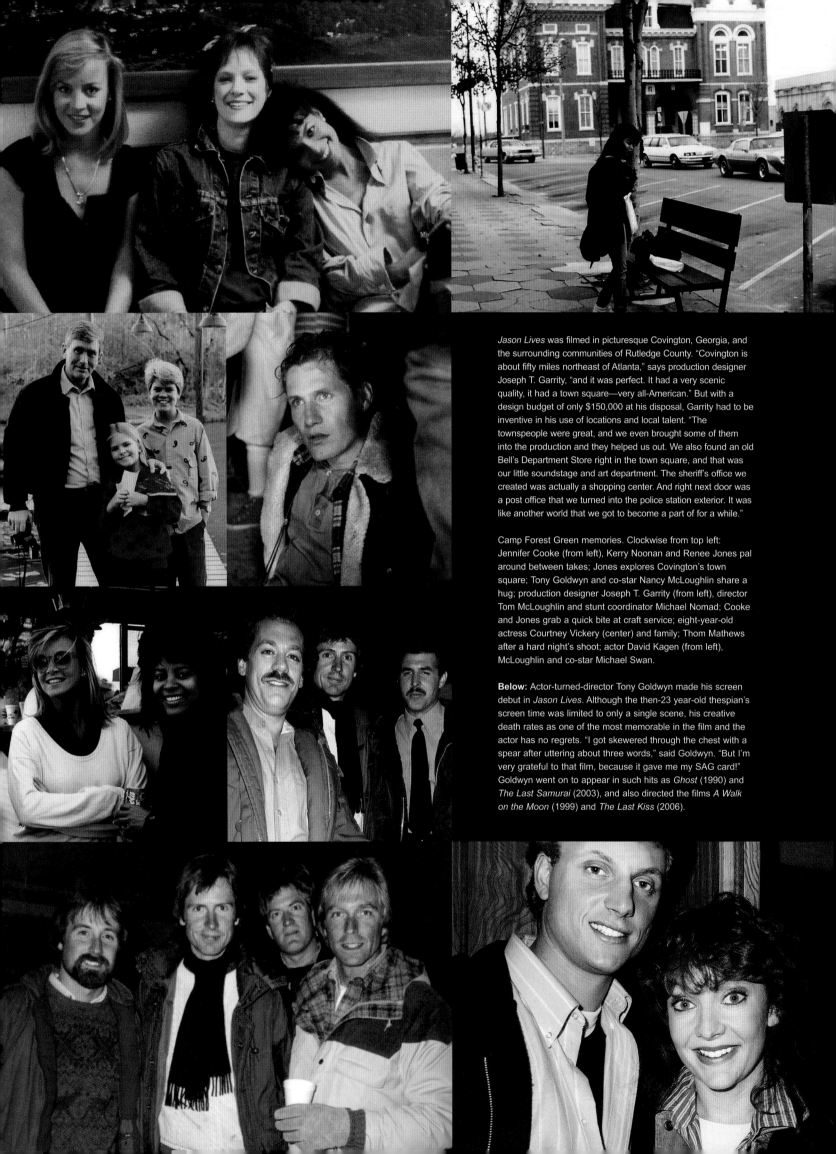

Jason Lives was filmed in picturesque Covington, Georgia, and the surrounding communities of Rutledge County. "Covington is about fifty miles northeast of Atlanta," says production designer Joseph T. Garrity, "and it was perfect. It had a very scenic quality, it had a town square—very all-American." But with a design budget of only $150,000 at his disposal, Garrity had to be inventive in his use of locations and local talent. "The townspeople were great, and we even brought some of them into the production and they helped us out. We also found an old Bell's Department Store right in the town square, and that was our little soundstage and art department. The sheriff's office we created was actually a shopping center. And right next door was a post office that we turned into the police station exterior. It was like another world that we got to become a part of for a while."

Camp Forest Green memories. Clockwise from top left: Jennifer Cooke (from left), Kerry Noonan and Renee Jones pal around between takes; Jones explores Covington's town square; Tony Goldwyn and co-star Nancy McLoughlin share a hug; production designer Joseph T. Garrity (from left), director Tom McLoughlin and stunt coordinator Michael Nomad; Cooke and Jones grab a quick bite at craft service; eight-year-old actress Courtney Vickery (center) and family; Thom Mathews after a hard night's shoot; actor David Kagen (from left), McLoughlin and co-star Michael Swan.

Below: Actor-turned-director Tony Goldwyn made his screen debut in *Jason Lives*. Although the then-23 year-old thespian's screen time was limited to only a single scene, his creative death rates as one of the most memorable in the film and the actor has no regrets. "I got skewered through the chest with a spear after uttering about three words," said Goldwyn. "But I'm very grateful to that film, because it gave me my SAG card!" Goldwyn went on to appear in such hits as *Ghost* (1990) and *The Last Samurai* (2003), and also directed the films *A Walk on the Moon* (1999) and *The Last Kiss* (2006).

Shepherd, for some reason. I can't tell you why, because I thought there was going to be some sort of obligation to keep the same actor in the role.

JOHN SHEPHERD, "Tommy Jarvis," *Part V*: It was funny. I was counseling a church youth group after *Part V* came out, and all the kids saw the film and loved it. Which, of course, gave me a lot of credibility in their eyes, that you could be somebody who had faith but who wasn't a wacko. That also made it a real dichotomy for me when *Part VI* came out, because I felt, "How can I create a character in this franchise, then tell kids you shouldn't go see R-rated films?" And here I am making not one, but two.

They sent me the script. There was even a scene in there where a little girl prays, and Jason doesn't kill her. I thought, "Maybe this is a sign from God that it's okay for me to do this." But I hadn't come out to L.A. to do horror films, and I really felt like I was better than this material. I also felt that they didn't really appreciate the work I put into the last one, because here's the sequel, and they are only offering me scale plus a bump. I said to my agent, "Set the price so high that they'll have to pay if they really want me." So I think she asked for something "exorbitant," like double scale. And it was difficult to walk away because after *Part V* came out, I ran out of money. I had to move out of Malibu to North Hollywood, and I was dating a girl who wanted to get married. So I went to work for the *L.A. Times* delivering papers and putting the inserts in them. And here I was in this blockbuster horror film! Then my girlfriend started going to seminary, and I thought, "Maybe I'm not cut out for acting. Maybe I'm supposed to be a minister." She said, "We should ask God to either open the door or close it." I said, "I think the door is closed. I'm going to seminary." So I enrolled to become a pastor.

The bottom line is that I knew in my heart of hearts that this wasn't what I was going to do. And eventually I got this other movie called *Caught*, with Jill Ireland. I played her son. It was my biggest part ever and a fantastic film and one that spoke to me personally, because it was about a kid who was on a spiritual journey which comes to faith. And I got engaged, and then married. I even went in and pitched ideas to the company that made the movie, and I've produced fourteen films for them since.

So thank goodness I didn't do *Part VI*. It totally changed my direction. I'm very thankful.

SHAVAR ROSS, "Reggie," *Part V*: I was supposed to be in *Part VI*, but that never happened. They wanted me, and Melanie, too. And it was a big deal, because they were like—"Everybody gets killed off in the beginning, so we'll knock you off, too." And my father was like, "No, he's not going to do that. My son is not going to die on film!"

MELANIE KINNAMAN, "Pam," *Part V*: I had originally signed to do *Part VI*. At that point, it was going to be a direct sequel to *Part V*. But Frank changed his mind and decided to go cheaper with it, which left me out in the cold.

TOM MCLOUGHLIN: Frank had a lot to say about casting. The only marching orders I had with the Megan character was that Frank tended to like a very attractive blond girl in the lead and pretty much all the way down the line that's what they went for in the past films—that was kind of a mandatory thing. So I was looking for what he desired, but tried to find the best actress I could. Jennifer Cooke was amazing. She had just done the "V" television series, I think. She was really sharp and funny.

JENNIFER COOKE, "Megan": Nothing else was pressing. I was available. So I did it. And it was actually a pretty fun diversion. My character, Megan, was likable and funny, and I got to drive a car fast.

DAVID KAGEN, "Sheriff Garris": I was excited because it was a terrific opportunity. No question. That's why I took it: the size of the part, the prominence of the film, and that it was produced by Paramount. I did have concerns, because I didn't know what effect these movies had on the people who watch them. I really did. And I still do—I don't know, overall, what the net effect is.

But Tom's a smart guy. He's a deep guy. I don't mean to put down *Friday the 13th*, but he's capable of other stuff. I understood this was an opportunity for him to get somewhere. I can't speak for anyone else, and I can't say I wouldn't have done the film if he hadn't been involved, but it definitely helped alleviate my fears.

"We stayed at this horrible Motel 6. You'd look out the window and the only thing on the cloverleaf was the Waffle House. So every morning, we'd risk our lives by running across the highway just to have pecan pancakes and bacon." Vincent Guastaferro on filming in Georgia

THOM MATHEWS: Before *Jason Lives*, I hadn't seen any of the *Friday the 13th* films except the original, the one with Kevin Bacon. Then after I got the part, I went out and rented the video of *Part V*. I thought I made a terrible mistake. It was awful. It was like a porn movie. Suddenly, I felt uneasy—and I had already committed myself. But I liked the script so much, and Tom so much, that I just had the confidence that he was going to make a good movie. He seemed to have a real, genuine affinity for it.

KERRY NOONAN: I had heard the guy who directed *Part V* had done porn and that it wasn't a very good movie. But I was interested to see where Tom was picking up the storyline, and where he was going to take it. We all were. So we were just pretending *Part V* didn't happen.

JOSEPH T. GARRITY, Production Designer: The older you get, the more important the choices you make become. You're torn between doing a project and not doing it. We all have to wrestle with that. Whenever I get a script that's bad, I try to find what's good in it. Because if there's not something good in it, why should I even want to be a part of it?

I think we all had heard that our film was going to take the series in a different direction, because it went bad ways prior, especially with *Part V*. We were going to pull it into a saner, tamer place. We all had many discussions together about the psychology of the films, and why it works and why it doesn't work. And what responsibility we had towards young people. Of course, what was ingrained in the series was that there was this character, Jason, and there was the death of teenagers, primarily. This needed to happen, I guess. But maybe films like this could keep violence from happening in the real world? I don't know if that's true or not. I think it has to do with who's sitting in that theater. But there's nothing wrong with putting

"One of the great things about horror movies is that their audiences are very, very verbal," says director Tom McLoughlin. "So I thought it would be fun to set up scenes and situations in *Jason Lives* that allowed the audience to literally provide the punchline. Probably the one most notable was when my wife Nancy gets killed. Her hand drops, and an American Express card floats away. And I held on that shot because I was sure that, without fail, someone in the crowd would yell out, 'Don't leave home with out it!' And sure enough, it worked. That moment always gets a great reaction."

Not everyone found the scene humorous, however. "We made *Jason Lives* in the days when product placement in movies was not commonplace like it is today," remembers production designer Joseph T. Garrity. "And American Express wouldn't give us permission. So we had to change the look of the card—if you pay real close attention, it's not quite right. But I can understand their reservations. How many credit card companies do you know who want their product associated with mass murder?"

out positive stuff. And not in the boring, Religious Right kind of way. Plus, Tom's wife was expecting their first child. I think he just wanted to lighten it all up a little bit. So I decided to do the film with him.

JON KRANHOUSE, Director of Photography: I did my first feature when I was twenty-three. I think it is what got me the gig on *Jason Lives*, actually. It was called *Brain Waves*, and there's this scene where there is an electrocution in a bathtub. We took a bunch of little tiny flashbulbs and wired them up, then triggered them to go off the same way you do a machine gun. And in the tub was this girl who was Playmate of the Year from *Hustler* or something. And she wiggles around and dies and all the lights are flashing. Frank Jr. saw that and said, "Oh, what a great death scene!" He even mentioned that to me when I interviewed for the job.

When I read the script, I thought, "This could be interesting and fun." Tom certainly wanted, visually, a more classical approach to the film. He wanted to give it a real sense of mood. But most importantly, I thought he had a very healthy sense of irony about it all—there's that line in there that the groundskeeper at the cemetery has: "Some people have a funny idea of entertainment." I think that perfectly summed up the movie Tom wanted to make.

After the on-set tensions of the three previous Friday *films, shooting another sequel in California would have been a near impossibility. The threat of a backlash from the unions was too great a risk for Frank Mancuso, Jr.'s upstart Hometown Films to take, and Tom McLoughlin's script, the first in the series to feature pre-teen protagonists in prominent roles, required that the production find a "right-to-work" state amenable to extending the hours a child performer could legally work. The locale the producers of* Jason Lives *would eventually settle upon, the picturesque town of Covington, Georgia and its surrounding communities, turned out to be a boon for the production. Quaint, accommodating and woodsy, it was not quite the authentic Camp Crystal Lake of the first two films, but it was a far more suitable stand-in than the desert hills of Southern California had been since* Part 3.

As cameras officially rolled on Jason Lives *on February 6, 1986, the crew settled in for a six-week shoot that proceeded in marked contrast to the pressure-cooker environment that dominated the last few* Friday *films. This production had a downright congenial atmosphere; if it is a cliché that the cast and crew of a film often form a makeshift "family" during production, then* Jason Lives *is the* Ozzie & Harriet *of the* Friday the 13th *series. Tom McLoughlin not only cast his new wife Nancy in a key role in the film, she became the production's unofficial den mother. Illegal substances were conspicuous by their absence, replaced by all-night* Scrabble *games, midnight bowling tournaments and, when things got raciest, the occasional round of "Truth or Dare." Finally, the makers of a* Friday the 13th *film were having fun.*

TOM MCLOUGHLIN: Even today, out of all the films that I have done in my career, when people ask me which one I had the most fun on, it literally is *Jason Lives*. To escape the prying eyes of the unions, we shot it under the title "Aladdin Sane," and we really were young and crazy. I was twenty-six. We knew we were making a *Friday the 13th*, but this was only my second film, and I was *so* into it. Everybody caught that passion.

KERRY NOONAN: The funniest thing was being picked up at the airport by a guy holding up a sign that said, "Terror, Inc."

JON KRANHOUSE: I remember being on the crew bus and coming in from the airport with some of the special effects group. As we got off the interstate and turned onto this side road going to the location, there was some huge industrial building that was very close to our motel, and it had a large sign near the entrance that said, "Two hundred days since the last industrial accident!" I leaned over to one of the effects guys and asked, "What do they do there?" And he says, "Oh, they make dynamite."

I looked at where this factory was, and the size of it, and then I looked at where our motel was, and I was sure we'd be a steaming crater by the end of the shoot.

NANCY MCLOUGHLIN, "Lizbeth": It was desolate—there was nothing there. Nothing but this stinking motel. And Tom and I had a "suite," so called because there was a lump in the middle of the room. It was such a dive. It was awful.

we shot essentially all nights. I think there was three or four days, then it was like six weeks of six day all-nighters—going to bed when everybody else in the world was waking up. Everybody would go to the bar at the Waffle House in the morning to wind down—the crew would raid you if you didn't. They'd break in, bring out the sleeping people's bodies and deposit them at the bar. It was a huge party.

VINCENT GUASTAFERRO: Nancy's extremely gracious and generous. "Motherly," and I don't mean in a bad way, like she's not hip—she's very hip and contemporary and smart and intelligent. But it's her nature to be very giving. She was like the den mother of the movie, because she and Tom didn't have children yet. When she wasn't working, she was on the set, asking "Who needs water?" She was happy and supportive of Tom. To this day, I love her.

KERRY NOONAN: The person I hung out with most was Nancy. She did her scenes and then would stay on set, so she had all this free time. She was really fun and we had a lot in common. We'd play *Scrabble*, and even hitch rides to the set back when you could still do that sort of thing.

NANCY MCLOUGHLIN: My father's a writer, his name is Bob Mott. I was Nancy Mott. He wrote for *Your Show of Shows*, a sketch show, and he was Dick Van Dyke and Red Skelton's personal pantomime writer. And, oddly enough, the only other personal writer Dick Van Dyke has ever had was Tommy—it was what got him into the Writer's Guild. My father also ended up working on *The Gong Show*, and it's funny, the one memory I have of being on the set of that show was when Tommy's brother was on it, a fire-eater. I was like thirteen or something, watching this fire-eater and watching Tom's family around him and thinking, "Oh, aren't they sweet?"

Years later, I think it was around 1979, I'm on the set of this really terrible movie called *Prophecy*, and Tommy's playing the monster. I was visiting the set with my girlfriend, whose father was in charge of security. And Tommy was climbing out of the monster outfit and I thought, "Oh, he's cute." I was twenty-one. And at the time, I didn't date, I didn't do anything. I was really shy. I thought I'd never marry, I'd never have children—when you're an actress, these are the things you give up. So Tom's looking at me and I'm looking at him and... I run and hide. For like two hours. And what did I say to my girlfriend when I saw him? "That's the man I'm going to marry." I had no idea. I didn't have a second thought about it. But I did say it. And by 1982, we were engaged.

TOM MCLOUGHLIN: That's how I met my wife, crawling out of a monster costume. I admire wives who work with their husbands. It's a whole different process than is usual between a director and an actor, but we've managed to make it work. Nancy

"It's so much fun making a horror movie. You get to act scared, get covered in blood and, hopefully, get a great death scene. And I love screaming!" Nancy McLoughlin

"I wanted to give Jason animal tendencies. Camp Crystal Lake is always going to be his territory. You can change the name but he's always going to come back."

Tom McLoughlin

and I have done a number of films together and she's a terrific actress. She's funny, she's got a great face and a great scream. I wanted to tailor a role for her in *Part VI* as one of the teenagers, although there's that old thing where when you go to horror movies, all the kids look like they're twenty-six. And I did not want to fall into that trap. So I said to Nancy, "I'm going to write a part for you as a head camp counselor and we can have a sense of humor and all that, but I won't have to deal with the whole thing of 'This person doesn't look like a teenager.' I also wanted to give her a great death scene.

VINCENT GUASTAFERRO: Tom really knows how to talk to actors, because he was one once. And that makes him get better performances. He never asked me to deal with the crap of a backstory. We just talked about what this character wanted to do. And that's great because, in terms of acting, actions define intentions. I would say to Tom, "What's this guy about?" and he'd say, "Rick Cologne is a small-town deputy, and Tommy Jarvis is the biggest criminal that he's ever had the opportunity to arrest!" Tom is completely responsible for the tone of the film and the way we as actors approached the material. Tom was very clear that he wanted much of the overt humor and jokes underplayed, almost thrown away, so the ridiculousness of saying it was more inherent than hammered home.

TOM MCLOUGHLIN: There is a lot of stylistic dialog in *Jason Lives*. I've always been a fan of the screwball comedies from the 1930s and '40s, even though that is not the way people really speak. I mean, poor David Kagen—he had a mouth full with some of the lines I wrote, my strange twists on profanity and avante garde ways of coming up with insults. But David is a very trained actor and he understood that. The same thing with Vinnie, another incredibly talented and trained actor who could go in there and be the heavy, but still be funny.

DAVID KAGEN: I look at material as a piece of music. When you play a piece of music, it does something to you. It makes you feel a certain way, it makes you dance a certain way. Certainly there were things I noticed in the script that were supposed to be fun. Tom had lines in there like "screwing the pooch" that people love. I just played it for all it was worth. I had some awareness of it potentially being over-the-top, or even campy, but I just played it for real. I think that is the case for all of us in the film—we all played it somewhere in the middle between complete seriousness and going too over-the-top. Finding that place was a very satisfying part of the work.

THOM MATHEWS: I'm not really a horror buff. I never really understood them. They never really held my attention. But after we made *Part VI*, I started to realize what filmmaking was about. It had its limits. It had the story and it had to have so many kills, but within all of that, I thought Tom made a really good movie. He tried to make the best movie he could with what he had. By the time we started shooting, any fears I initially had about making the movie were gone.

KERRY NOONAN: My favorite stage direction in the script was for the scene with the sheriff, when he is shooting at Jason: "Nothing stops this undead super-killer." I thought that was hilarious.

JOSEPH T. GARRITY: Tom wanted people to laugh and be scared at the same time, and I think he accomplished that. What is still so memorable about the film are just all those little details he threw in there, like that sign on the road during the chase scene— "Dangerous Curves Ahead." Or when those two little boys comment, "We're dead meat." That is all Tom.

DARCY DEMOSS:, "Nikki": After my bad experience on *Part V*, Pamela Basker and Fern Champion brought me back in for *Part VI*. They said, "Pretend like you never met Frank Mancuso, Jr." So I did, and I got the part. And it was so apparent the difference with Tom, the humor. When I watched the film recently—I hadn't seen it in a long time—I laughed so hard. That scene in the RV, where I'm being bounced around, that was a blast. The photos on the wall were all attached to strings that the crew were pulling—a whole bunch of little gizmos wired all over the place. And my legs flying over my head and the shoes flying off—I remember Tom showing me how to do it. It was like an *I Love Lucy* episode, not a horror film.

THOM MATHEWS: Tom could be very ambitious in ways you wouldn't expect. The toughest scene I had to do in the entire film was all dialogue, where I am in the phone booth making a call and I have to explain all this exposition to Jennifer Cooke. I remember that shot was like one continuous master with all kinds of tricky camera movements, and what seemed like tons of dialogue. It took almost ten takes just to get it right.

My role was very physical—I had to do a lot of running and jumping. Just battling Jason, and the water, and having to focus on so much. It was hard work. One night, we were shooting close-ups in the jail cell and, around 4:00 a.m., we start hearing this snoring from somewhere. It turned out one of the grips had fallen asleep. We went ahead and tried to shoot the scene, but this guy kept snoring away. I tried to keep it together but, as I was looking at Tom, I couldn't anymore. And neither could he, and we both burst out laughing.

One of *Part VI*'s centerpiece kill sequences, the massacre of a quartet of carefree survivalists (**above** and **opposite**), was cleverly conceived in the script by director Tom McLoughlin to serve multiple purposes. "I needed to somehow arm Jason with every weapon imaginable," says McLoughlin. "In the mid-1980s, the game of paintball was just starting to catch on. So I thought it would be cool that there were these big executive types out there in the woods, just having fun and playing this game, unaware that they were being stalked by a real killer. And then I could conveniently get Jason all the gear he needed."

Background: An original conceptual illustration of an idyllic sunset over Camp Forest Green. Drawn by production designer Joseph T. Garrity, the image would eventually be used as the basis for the signage seen throughout the film.

KERRY NOONAN: Thom was very nice, but he was very focused and very busy. He was in almost every scene. I really didn't hang out with him at all. He probably had a lot more homework to do than I did.

Jennifer, too … it was hard to hang out with them because they were in so many scenes that they were usually just working. And Jennifer had this age thing going, "I'm only twenty-one!" That kind of annoyed me. But she was a nice person.

VINCENT GUASTAFERRO: This is what I liked about Jennifer—her ego was so huge that she didn't need anything. I remember she was on the dock and Thom was in the water, and she had to dive in and act like she's saving him. And somebody said to her, "Are you okay?" And she goes, "Just make sure my hair looks good." But I say this because I think she had a great attitude toward the work. She didn't take it all that seriously. She knew her job in the movie was to be the hottie, and if her hair looked right that's all she needed to do. She was a very practical girl.

JENNIFER COOKE: The script said to scream on cue, and I did. I memorized my lines and showed up on time. That's about all you can do with a film like this. You can't really draw on past experiences for inspiration. I don't know about you, but I've never been chased by a monster with an ax before.

DAVID KAGEN: I started on stage, and when I came out to L.A. in 1982 or '83 I started doing television and more stage work. I did a great lead in a short movie but I hadn't done much in feature film when I auditioned for Tom. And as it turned out, Jennifer Cooke had been an acting student of mine. So we had a chance to go off and do the material before we went in, and I felt very focused and very confident and very committed. And I remember they asked her, "Which actor do you want to work with?" Jennifer said, "David." And they said, "Well, that's our choice, too." So it worked out. It was nice to know that she respected me, so there wasn't the issue that I was too young to be her dad.

Jennifer was very serious. She did care. She committed herself and she worked hard. She was not a prima donna—she was not difficult. She did have a sense of humor about it, but she tried to do well.

NANCY MCLOUGHLIN: We all got along. It wasn't intense. In many ways, on a movie set, you can be a child, and you don't really have to be emotionally invested in the games people play.

In fact, we used to play this one game by the fire, kinda like "Truth or Dare," where we would ask, "If you had to be with someone on the set, who would it be?" It's dangerous, and I think people can get very hurt by the answers, but it's so much fun.

KERRY NOONAN: We used to have this saying, "It's not love—it's location."

TOM MCLOUGHLIN: One thing I was very aware of when I did my *Friday* was the sex equals death thing. I always had a problem with that idea—that kids have sex and then they get killed. Whether it was for moralistic reasons or just coincidental. Personally, I never thought there was any moral conspiracy at work, whether by past *Friday* filmmakers or otherwise. I always thought it's just that these two elements have always been

attractive. And then it just sort of developed out of that, and someone at some point said, "Wait a minute, that's now the rule—have sex and die."

I much prefer making fun out of that whole thing. That's why I only had one sex scene in mine and it was played for laughs. Having those kids be in a motor home bouncing up and down, and then having Jason look at this thing and think, "What the hell is going on in there?" Then by the end of the sequence it all turns into a big stunt. I wanted to take it to a whole different level. The humor was that this girl was having sex to this song and trying to get the guy to last through the thing, then when the power went out, so did he. And if you listen really close, after his big moment, we put a sound effect in there—you hear him take his rubber off. It was subtle little joke we played when we were mixing the movie. It was safe sex!

KERRY NOONAN: The *Friday the 13th* movies are morality tales—the people who get killed are the ones who do bad things. Tom is very Christian and he didn't want that stuff. We're not all doing drugs, and our one sex scene is comical. There is even that scene at the end of the film, when little Nancy prays to bring Tommy back to life—that religious influence is definitely in *Part VI*. Paradoxically, that means the violence is that much more unexplainable. It's more random. We're not being punished for anything—we're just getting killed because we're there. It's an interesting twist to the normal *Friday* formula. But it's a paradox because here the movie has a Christian influence, yet people are being killed for no reason! I find that very interesting.

DARCY DEMOSS: I love Tom. And Nancy. They're great. But interestingly enough—and this is moviemaking—while we were shooting the love scene, Tom said, "I think we're going to lose your top." I went, "Excuse me?" It's not in my contract, which is why contracts make or break careers. The scene didn't need it anyway. It was what it was. So I said no. I don't remember there really being a choice. I think the producers probably said, "I think we need to lose her top, we need more sexy stuff in here." Because there wasn't any nudity in Tom's film at all. There really wasn't. And they were going to make me the girl. And I prefer not to. So much more is left to the imagination when you don't see everything.

TOM MCLOUGHLIN: I think I gave Darcy the option to take her clothes off. I can't remember at this point whether it was a definite "I won't do it" on her part. I know I had made a conscious choice not to do it, and I'm not sure if that is because it was purely the "easy" thing to do. Not that every good actress won't do nudity, but I felt like I was going to get a better caliber of talent if I did that. If it said "nudity required," there are a lot of actresses who say, "This is the beginning of my career. I'm not going to start this." And I know from working with Phoebe Cates. She told me she was upset that she made that choice in *Fast Times at Ridgemont High*. She looked gorgeous, but every

Above: "I'm just this little tiny person, and I think I have the longest fight scene with Jason out of anybody on the movie," laughs actress Darcy DeMoss. "Usually, Jason just walks up to his victim and you're dead. But I had to fight with him in this tiny little closet of an RV. And it seemed like it took forever to film—we just fought and fought and fought. I ended up with battle bruises and war wounds the next day. But it was so much fun!"

"It's like all of a sudden you get to put a baseball uniform on, and you're the pitcher in the ninth inning of the World Series. It's an incredible feeling." CJ Graham on playing Jason

time she did another picture, there was an expectation that you were going to see Phoebe strip. And as I said, I was trying to break some of the clichés and have a sense of mythology about it, so that it wasn't all about having sex.

KERRY NOONAN: All I can say is that, hopefully, one day people will start asking, "Why is it that only women are naked in these movies?"

In keeping with the tradition of the previous Friday the 13th *films, the sixth installment would again see a new actor take on the role of the indestructible Jason Voorhees. But this time, the decision to build a "new Jason" would not only come down to one of cost, or even expediency, but of genuine creative concern. The Jason that Tom McLoughlin conceived, the Jason "born of hatred and electricity," was now a member of the walking dead. McLoughlin's Jason needed to move differently, react differently, kill differently—and so, too, did the professional stuntman who played him. But as with* Friday the 13th *Part 2, a last-minute replacement needed to be brought in when the original performer that had been cast as Jason failed to live up to the expectations of the producers. Although the stuntman they ultimately chose was not a stuntman at all, but rather an ex-military "grunt" with no previous acting experience, the decision ultimately proved inspired. The Jason Voorhees of* Part VI *was more feral, methodical and single-minded than ever before.*

TOM MCLOUGHLIN: I'm gonna let out a little secret I don't think people know, well, maybe only if you're a hardcore fan. When we started *Jason Lives*, we had a different Jason. Initially, he was played by a stuntman, Dan Bradley. He did the first day or two, all the daylight stuff and the paintball stuff. Then Frank Mancuso, Jr. calls and says, "You have to replace Jason. He doesn't look right." And Dan is a terrific guy and was doing a great job. But it was a studio mandate, so I had to quickly shift gears, shoot a bunch of scenes without Jason, and cross my fingers that we could find somebody else real quick.

NANCY MCLOUGHLIN: All Dan did was eat, apparently. He gained forty pounds or something in a few weeks, enough that every day they had to take out his outfit. And the dailies were coming back and Frank was *livid*.

TOM MCLOUGHLIN: We didn't know who we could get, then the late Marty Becker, the effects coordinator, says to me, "Well, there is this guy I've met, he hasn't acted before and he just got out of the Marines. He's a real, 'You-tell-him-what-to-do-and-he-does-it' kind of guy. And a really nice guy." So I said, "Well, if you feel he is right, bring him down to Georgia." And in comes CJ Graham, this fairly attractive-looking, tall guy—nicest guy in the world. I said to Marty, "Are you sure?" And he says, "I'm telling you—this guy is great!" And he was. He was like a machine.

CJ GRAHAM, "Jason Voorhees": Mine is not so much "A Star is Born" story as "A Goofy Person is Born." I had no experience. Zero. Nada. I ran a nightclub in Glendale called Excess. We had a hypnotist there named Jack Laughlin, and he brought in the crew that had done *Friday the 13th – The Final Chapter* to do the special effects for this $10,000 production he was doing to promote his show. And in his show, when the subjects are under hypnosis, there's a horrifying scene where Jason slashes through the screen to scare them. And Martin Becker saw it and was looking for somebody physically big—

I am 6'3" and 250 pounds—to play Jason. He said, "CJ, do you want to do this?" And I said, "Why not?" I didn't know what a SAG card was.

I originally went down to interview for the part before they had hired anyone else, and I met with the stunt coordinator, Michael Nomad. Michael was comfortable with my military background and that I could, in fact, complete the mission. However, Frank Mancuso, Jr. was a little hesitant because I had no background, no experience, and I'm not a stuntman. So I didn't get cast. But I still thought it was kinda cool to get on the Paramount lot and meet Frank Mancuso, Jr. And I didn't think about it again.

TOM MCLOUGHLIN: The second I met CJ I knew he was perfect. He had this almost Terminator, machine-like quality, from being a marine. It was vital that Jason be truly scary. When I first got the job and asked Frank, "Can I add humor to *Friday?*" all he said was, "Fine. Just as long as you don't make fun *of* Jason." So that is one of the reasons why I put in that whole thing with Tommy, where he goes to the sheriff and warns him about Jason. "It's still Camp Crystal Lake to him!" It was about animals and territory. I have coyotes around my house that sometimes walk up and down the street at night. It's their turf. It has been for generations. And the fact that we're here doesn't stop them from coming and eating our cats and dogs— they even got a baby a few years ago. It's those same sort of feral tendencies that I wanted to give Jason. The moment where he's watching the RV go up and down and he kind of cocks his head like a dog—that's exactly what I wanted.

CJ GRAHAM: I got a call one Saturday to come back for another interview with Frank Mancuso, Jr. And after the meeting, I got another call to ask if I could be in Covington by Monday morning. So I'm slam-dunk, bing-bong gone.

I immediately met with Tom and Michael Nomad and they told me what they wanted. And it's not an easy task. How do you show somebody you're pissed off when you're dead? My goal was to figure out how to convey the anger, the dominating presence of this demon, without being human and without being robotic. Tom wasn't looking for Frankenstein from the 1960's. I needed to be menacing, in control, and express intent with the physical turns of my head and body. Because you can't raise your eyebrows. You can't scream and yell. Everything had to be based on the way I cranked my head or turned my neck. Remember that old thing with *Taxi Driver*—"You talkin' to me?" Well, as Jason you don't have that opportunity to practice in a mirror. You had to actually turn and be able to relay those words solely with your posture.

I remember the very first scene I shot, when I approached the RV. I walk up, I stop and you see my head turn a little bit. I remember Michael telling me, "I want you to take a deep breath. I want you to push those lats out in the back, so all you see is mass from behind." And it was like, all of a sudden, you get to put a baseball uniform on and you're the pitcher in the ninth inning of the World Series. It is an incredible feeling.

DARCY DEMOSS: When I first got to the set, it was dark because we were filming at night. And they had these fog machines going everywhere, and CJ was standing next to the trailer. And they're like, "Hey Darcy, go stand next to CJ." I was like, "Eeek! Why me?" But they just wanted to get a light reading. So I was standing next to him, and I say, "You look really scary." And CJ didn't quickly turn around—he just *slowly* tilted his body towards me. He was playing the role. It was so creepy. But that's CJ. He was a great Jason.

"Tom McLoughlin told me he wanted Paula's death to be real bloody. But I got a bit too carried away, and sprayed blood everywhere—there were brains and guts all over. It was like someone literally exploded in the room!" Jim Gill, Reel EFX

Opposite and **above**: Filming the extended cat-and-mouse murder of Paula was a highpoint for actress Kerry Noonan. "I just love my death scene," raves Noonan. "I love the fake-out at the door. Although I was a little disappointed that I didn't have the experience of working with elaborate makeup or having a body cast made. Because I just get pureed into like thirty buckets of stage blood, all offscreen. But I remember asking Tom McLoughlin after we shot it, "Hey, since you never see my dead body, can I come back as 'Bride of Jason' in the next sequel?"

NANCY MCLOUGHLIN: Everybody was in love with CJ. His heart was really good. He has such a presence. And he was above it all—in a really proper way. The role was really demanding physically and he was uncomfortable a lot, but he chose to take the high road and it made all the difference in the world. A lot of people are troublemakers—you just see it. They're people just trying to disturb things. And it's so infinitely unkind to the group—it's just unfair to the production or the director. "Why aren't we all on the same boat here?" But CJ really made sure that nobody got hurt.

TOM MCLOUGHLIN: CJ never complained. It was always simply, "Yes, sir, whatever you want." And it's a grueling job playing Jason—the long hours, the freezing cold, going into the lake, and doing fights.

It was a pleasure getting to know him off camera, too. He's just a very good person. It's interesting that playing Jason is something that people like CJ end up doing, because they can go to the dark side on cue, and then be completely normal and nice. I was very fortunate to get him.

VINCENT GUASTAFERRO: When we were in Georgia, it was very remote. Now, I'm not putting those folks down, but the kind of people who live in out the woods and are really into Jason are a little spooky. And when thirty or forty of them show up on set and say, "We want to see Jason! We want

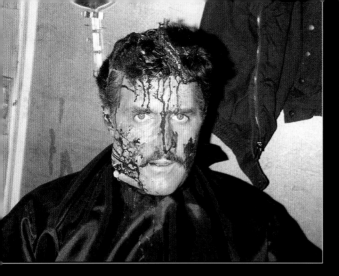
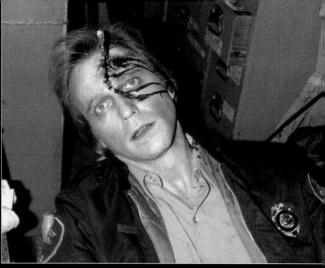

o see Jason!"—they chant it. So Tom would have to get CJ to ome out of the trailer with his mask on and wave at them. And they were ecstatic.

Even with a happy cast and crew and a gentle giant for a Jason, production on Part VI *was not without its trials and tribulations. The real villains of a* Friday the 13th *movie were still the same: the lack of budget and the dawn's breaking sun. Yet ultimately even the typical production anxieties experienced on set among the filmmakers—in particular a growing resentment by an ambitious director toward his clockwatching producer—took on a playful tone. Tensions never lingered, and by the end of the shoot, whatever residual animosities there may have been would be diffused by one big, fiery punchline.*

DON BEHRNS, Producer: My first film job was in the early 70s, as a Production Assistant on a blaxploitation movie called *Candy Tangerine Man*. It was about a guy who lived a double life—businessman during the day, and at night he was out pimping and shooting up guys. And just a couple of films later, I had worked my way up to production manager, and that's how I met the late Debra Hill, who was a script supervisor on some of those films. And I put up with her nonsense, so one day she called me saying, "I'm living with this guy named John Carpenter and he has $300,000 to make a movie called *Halloween*. You want to production manage it for me? I'm producing." I said, "What!? You've never produced before!" But she was a smart lady. I ended up working on both *Halloween* and *The Fog*.

I had a mutual acquaintance of Tom McLoughlin who recommended me for *Jason Lives*, so I met Tom, and Frank Mancuso, Jr. It was my first producing shot. It's funny—I never had a particular affinity for horror films. It just sort of happened that way. Once you start doing them and a few become successful, people look to you to do more. And I remember Tom had this marathon of the *Friday* movies right after we got to Atlanta—all five in a row. I couldn't separate one from the other! Although the ironic thing is that I guess Danny Steinmann had directed *Part V*. I did something called *The Unseen*, which Danny took his name off of. And it's a good thing he vanished off the face of the Earth after *Part V*. He was an asshole to work with and a very incompetent director.

Anyway, on *Jason Lives*, we were given a rough budget of around $3 million. More than the past *Fridays*, but Tom's script was ambitious. Going over it, there were things in there that, right away I knew were going to be particularly expensive

TOM MCLOUGHLIN: What I kept asking throughout the making of the movie was, "We've only got under $3 million dollars here, but what hasn't been done before in a *Friday*? How can I do an underwater sequence? How can I do a car chase? How can I do more than just kids in cabins and knives and running around?" We managed to do it, and stretched the boundaries every way we could. Perhaps I bit off a lot more than I should have. It sounds stupid, but car chases are cheap if you shoot them during the day, but because we did it at night you had to light the forest, you had to get stunt drivers and it wasn't even that great of a car chase. But despite the time and trouble it took to shoot stuff like that, at least it was something new for the fans, as opposed to just another one in a tent or whatever.

JOSEPH T. GARRITY: Production managers are in that precarious area of being between the creative side and the financial side. I do recall that there was a little bit of animosity between Tom and Don. Tom probably wasn't getting what he needed. I don't remember anything that we seriously felt we did not get, and in retrospect, I think Tom should be really happy with what he was able to pull off.

VINCENT GUASTAFERRO: I met Frank Mancuso, Jr. right after the casting process. He was a very hip young man at the time, with long dark hair. He emanated authority. And, quite honestly, he seemed like the son of a rich guy. But he was very enthusiastic about the movie, and Tom, and he seemed very nice. He was not an ominous, dangerous force like Don was. He was more like the gregarious, gracious presence and the big overseer. Let's face it—his name is Frank Mancuso, Jr. and we all knew that if he had said no, the movie would be over.

I remember Don being a very tense on-set presence. He didn't show up as a guy who spread the vibe of, "Hey everybody, I hope it's going well. What can I do to help out?" He showed up as a wrist-glancer. And, at the time, he was a little sinister looking—I don't know what he looks like now, but back then he had a beard and wore an Australian cowboy hat. I have to say, in sticking with my artistic brothers and sisters, and after this many years of experience, I know the line producer's job is to show up on the set and act in such a way to keep things going. But I've also worked with enough of them to know that there's a way to wield authority on a set with grace. Most of them choose to have a good relationship with the director. I look back on it and say Don was either very green, or nervous, or he just wasn't very good at it. I don't think Tom was reaching beyond budget

DON BEHRNS: We came in just barely under budget. Frank was happy about that. There's only so much money to spend on a movie like this. But everything creative I left up to Tom. I was a hired gun. I didn't get involved with that stuff except when it seriously affected being able to make the schedule.

We stuck very close to the script. A couple times, I urged Tom to move along because I wasn't sure we were going to stay on schedule. And I know a couple times he got kind of pissed off at me—particularly when he found out I was getting a bonus if I brought the picture in on time. But that was something Frank wanted.

NANCY MCLOUGHLIN: Don was usually in a corner, counting money or something. But as is often the case on most sets, people look for a bad guy. Here, I think Don was doing a good cop, bad cop thing. His job was to be stern and keep Tommy on track. That's a difficult job. And bless Don's soul— I think he and other people in that position put up with the flak they receive. And I think Tommy, or any director, who fights their battles is all the better for it.

DAVID KAGEN: It was more of a TV schedule. You did three or four takes and then you'd move on. But, hey, I did a Corman film where it's one take and then you print and move on to the next setup. This was not that bad. So I didn't feel that kind of pressure. Tom did. Tom would start shooting and really focusing on the details and there would be constant pressure to move it along. Such as getting the shot of the American Express card floating down exactly right. I knew Tom wasn't happy about that and there was a certain level of tension. But it was that kind of budget.

VINCENT GUASTAFERRO: I remember that when Nancy McLoughlin got killed, she was supposed to have a well-fit breathing apparatus so she could be underwater without being in jeopardy. But in the interest of time, they ended up doing the shot with her holding her breath instead. I remember Tom getting pretty upset that they were asking him to get it done in such a way that would jeopardize any actress. And then on top of that, I'm sure he had trouble separating himself from the fact that it was his wife they were screwing with. You have to take the side of the artist on that. Any producer who's asking you to do something unsafe in the interest of time is crazy.

DON BEHRNS: Trying to remain compatible with the director... it's difficult in a situation like that, because you want to see him get all the chances he needs to make it right,

> **"Whenever there were times when we needed to rough in an extra murder, we'd all sit around the office and ask, 'How has Jason not killed anybody?'"** Bruce Green, Editor

but you have to stay responsible. There are a lot of people expecting you to bring it in on budget. If you don't, that'll stick with you. Tom and I had a couple of big fights—mostly over him moving too slowly and reshooting stuff over and over, like the shot of the American Express card floating in the water. Directors will tend to do that. Sometimes you just have to let them take the extra time and hope they make it up on the next shot. It's a tough lesson to learn. Who are you working for—the producers? The director? And who's going to benefit you the most when the film is over? I'm not sure I ever learned that lesson.

NANCY MCLOUGHLIN: I'm sure I just said, "I'll do it! I don't care!" So stupid! My whole body was submerged and I'm literally viced into this puddle. Then the regulator stops working—they didn't test it for mud, or more accurately, Georgia clay. And the clay is going down my throat. Then it gets later and later, and they decided to get rid of the regulator. So here I am, it's like 18 degrees below zero with the wind chill factor, I'm viced in with no regulator, just trying to relax my body so I can hold my breath longer. And then I hear people talking about lunch. I'm just thinking that everybody is going to go eat and leave me down there for dead. It was a very tense moment.

Afterward, when I washed off, I had to go to the camp showers, which weren't heated or enclosed. It was ice cold with nothing to stop the wind from coming in, at three in the morning. So the costumer stayed with me, but the crew kept walking by and there was mud all over my face. That was the most unpleasant moment of the entire experience for me.

TOM MCLOUGHLIN: CJ also almost nailed Nancy in the scene when he puts the spear through the window. We didn't have money for stunt doubles. He was supposed to aim at a certain place, and Nancy was just supposed to fall and get out of the way. Oops.

NANCY MCLOUGHLIN: I usually don't question Tom as a director. I just go with it—which is probably why he likes working with me. So this time he says, "We're using a real spear, just move quick!" And I'm like, "Okay!" But the spear slid instead of breaking through the glass, and it was like *this* close to my head. I'm an idiot. I think Tom's feeling then was—and I don't think he feels this way now—that real weapons make for real fear. And they could have floated a body in the mud—but they wanted it to feel real. That's always been Tom's excuse.

But hey, Tom wrote a part just for me in the movie, and it was fun. I love screaming. Frank Capra once said, "Keep

working." I love having that actor's attitude that you take a big role or a small role. To be honest, *Jason Lives* is not a movie I take too much else from. But I did grow. I learned that it's about acting and friendships. And that you have a responsibility not to whine.

JON KRANHOUSE: Tom had a very clear vision of what he wanted, and I think that's probably where the conflict came in with Don. Relationships are very important on a film set, because if you're spending sixteen hours a day with someone and you think they're a jerk, it's not going to work. I thought it could be adversarial but in a good, friendly way. It was hard conditions, and you've got to find ways of keeping things jovial, even if Don at times maybe was the butt of the joke. I think Tom in his heart knew that helped keep everyone together in a cohesive, productive way. And I really think Don knew that as well.

It all came to a head when we shot that scene where the RV crashes. Don had dibs on the RV's much lusted-for rooftop swamp cooler. And said cooler was atop the Winnebago when it met its fiery demise. And that was quite intentional on Tom's part: "If he wants it I'll be damned." But Don thought since the motor home was to be destroyed, why waste a perfectly good cooler? Couldn't Tom agree to save it for Don's personal use, and have it removed from the vehicle before the stunt? But Tom had heard a lot of "No's" from Don, and now it was Tom's turn. He absolutely insisted the cooler stay atop the RV, and be destroyed, if only for the sake of art. The issue became such a public snickering point that many whoops and guffaws were heard during dailies as the air conditioner beautifully disintegrated upon impact and cartwheeled down the road, then out of frame. But Don was a very good sport about the whole thing.

DON BEHRNS: My side of the story on that one is that I had a motor home of my own, but I didn't have a generator or an air conditioner on it. So our transportation coordinator had found this nice motor home for the movie that had a great air conditioning unit, and I said, "Why wreck it for the movie? No one's going to know the difference." I even very carefully took it off and put it away. But the end of the film, it mysteriously was gone and back on the camper. I was so pissed!

VINCENT GUASTAFERRO: Oh, man—the blowing-up of the trailer! I wouldn't have missed it for the world. It was the very last thing we shot, and there was pressure to beat the sunrise. It took all night to get everything set up so the ramp was just right and the explosion just right. And I swear to God we were racing minutes until dawn. The sky was going to get

bright any second. It was the first time I'd ever witnessed that kind of pressure and a deadline, because if they didn't get it that night, they would have had to go another day, and there was no budget for that. But they pulled it off. Once that shot was gotten and it was a wrap, the entire set exploded. You would have thought we won the Super Bowl.

TOM MCLOUGHLIN: That was our big stunt. And it scared the hell out of me because we didn't have a Hollywood stuntman, we had a "good ol' boy" from Georgia—and he shows up in this Evel Kneviel jumpsuit. Seriously. I kept turning to the stunt coordinator and asking, "Are you sure this guy can pull this off?" We've essentially had the whole camper rigged so that if it collapsed, it still wouldn't hurt this guy, and they strapped him into this thing like he was going to the moon. But I still thought, "I hope to God we didn't just kill this guy." Then the RV goes, it hits the ramp, takes off into the air, crashes, there's fire, and it's *perfect*. We even had four or five cameras on it. Then this guy climbs out of that thing like he has just been hit over the head with a baseball bat—and gives the thumbs-up gesture that's he's okay. It was a huge relief.

 After that, everybody wanted to be back on the plane to go home, so we had a little get-together in the parking lot of the Waffle House, and that was it. Ours was a wrap breakfast. It's sad when you have to break up, but, as it turned out, we all had to get back together again to shoot additional stuff. It wasn't over yet...

Despite the best efforts of Tom McLoughlin and his cast and crew, the early cut of Jason Lives *did not fully meet the expectations of producer Frank Mancuso, Jr. That it was as funny and action-packed as any summer popcorn movie was fine. Even calling it a "nice"* Friday the 13th *movie would not be derogatory. But McLoughlin's attempt at reducing the* Friday *series' requisite double-digit body count—and its ever-more gruesome parade of creative murder sequences— was vetoed by Mancuso. The solution came in the form of one of the most dreaded words in Hollywood parlance: reshoots. By the end of post-production,* Jason Lives *would have additional scenes, a higher body count and a brand-new ending. Yet, ironically enough, what wasn't added was more blood*

Above: No matter what you call it, it's still Camp Crystal Lake to Jason. This sign, created by production designer Joseph T. Garrity, can be briefly glimpsed during *Jason Lives'* climactic battle sequence.

Opposite page: The completion of *Jason Lives'* climactic battle sequence required additional reshoots. "We shot most of that scene down at an Olympic-sized swimming pool at the USC campus in Los Angeles," recalls director Tom McLoughlin. "But the only thing they wouldn't let us film was the moment when we slice into Jason's head with the outboard motor. The school didn't want any gunk in their pool." So McLoughlin came up with an unusual solution. "I called my dad up in Culver City and said, 'Can we come out and use our family pool?'" the director laughs. "We brought the whole unit out to his backyard, and totally destroyed his pool. It was so bloody and gory. But for my dad, it was one of the greatest moments of his life—that his son was making a feature film in his backyard."

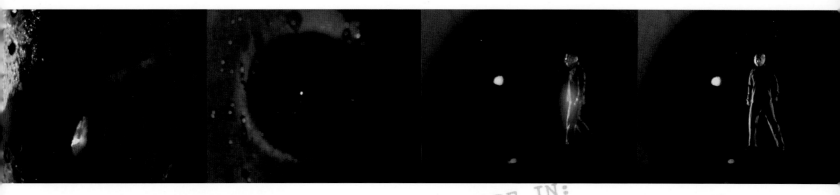

"This was the sixth *Friday* movie, and I thought Jason had become the James Bond of horror. So I wanted a title sequence to match."

Tom McLoughlin

HE'S BACK
AND YOU WON'T WANT
TO BE ALONE.

JASON LIVES

FRIDAY THE 13TH PART VI

A novel by SIMON HAWKE
based on the screenplay written by
TOM McLOUGHLIN

NOW A MAJOR MOTION PICTURE FROM PARAMOUNT PICTURES.

"At the end of *Part VI*, I wanted to introduce Jason's father, mainly because nobody had gone down that road before in the previous movies," says Tom McLoughlin of his original scripted ending. "To me, that would have made for one eerie epilogue—that there was somebody else out there that was the father of this unstoppable being. But Frank Mancuso, Jr. and the studio did not want to go to that next level. Which I can understand, because once you put that out there, does that mean you would have to focus on Jason's father in the next film instead of Jason himself? Still, I hope that someday, someone will come along and tell us what happened to Jason's dad."

Although McLoughlin's ending was never filmed, it was adapted by Simon Hawke for the 1986 novelization of the film (**above**). Now out of print, the paperback remains a sought-after collectible among fans of the series.

there was still one pivotal group of decision makers who would not be swayed by Tom McLoughlin's kindler, gentler *Friday* the 13th: *the Motion Picture Association of America's ratings board.*

TOM MCLOUGHLIN: Something I learned from the many, many directors that I studied is that if you can get the audience to laugh, then they would be much more open to experience the hard stuff. A lot of films just want to be pedal-to-the-metal horror, and unfortunately they have characters that the audiences laughs at instead of with. But if there's too much humor, you can overplay your hand and undercut the tension. It's a tough balance. I felt we got away with it because at the time we did the movie, nobody had really seen that blend of horror and comedy before.

BRUCE GREEN: I believe there is a definite relationship between comedy and horror. From the standpoint of my training as an editor, comedy is the most frame-specific genre. Just a frame or two in or out, and the joke lives or dies. I would say horror films are also very frame-specific. How far can you milk the audience? How long do you leave them on the edge of their seat until you let Jason jump out at them? It's tricky.

HARRY MANFREDINI, Composer: I think there is no question of how the director changes my work, *Friday* or otherwise. I loved what Tom McLoughlin did with *Part VI*. He was a real fan of the series and tried to add wonderful touches. He was also one of the best experiences I had with a director—I wish I could get a chance to work with him again. I was very aware of what he was trying to do, and it inspired me to become more aware of the music I was adding.

I was also aware that Alice Cooper was going to be contributing some songs to the film, but it did not change my approach. Nor, really, did the humor. As far as the comedic tone, I don't remember actually writing any intentionally "funny" music. I just tried to capture some of what Tom was trying to incorporate into the film. Music doesn't have to actually sound comical to underscore something that is humorous.

TOM MCLOUGHLIN: When I saw *Halloween*, it was amazing—I had never seen audiences jump the way they did in that theater. And that became the bar for all us filmmakers at the time—how many "jump" scares could we get? But, to be honest—did every shock have to accompanied by that John Carpenter sound, "Eeeeeeeee!" Could you do it more subtly? That's the missive I gave to Harry Manfredini, to try and score this so the audience wouldn't be so alerted to what was happening, or about to happen, but to instead allow the audience to do it for themselves.

Harry came with the package. It seemed like he had a fairly steady gig—Frank just said, "Harry's the guy!" But after I said to him, "I know you do every movie, and I know there are certain aspects we have to put in here, but I really would like a more Gothic score," I think he thought that was pretty exciting. He really brought some different things to *Jason Lives* than he had done in the past *Friday*s.

HARRY MANFREDINI: What was ultimately disappointing was that Tom's film was changed from his original conception. There was a test screening, which did not produce the results wanted, or at least that Frank Jr. wanted. Tom had all sorts of cool intellectual things in the film at one point—there were only thirteen murders, and all sorts of references to the characters and filmmakers involved with the original *Friday the 13th*. Then, after the screening, some kills were gratuitously added and characters introduced solely to get offed. I thought, after the changes, the slickness paled a bit. But some people think that is all these films are about.

TOM MCLOUGHLIN: We had our first screening of the film, which was my first cut, at a little theater and recruited an audience from a local shopping mall or something. And this audience had arrived three hours early, and the line snaked around the Paramount lot. They came to party—they were young and punked and stoned and drunk. They screamed and talked through the whole thing. I'm not exaggerating—we had that little sucker that controlled the volume all the way up and I still couldn't hear anything that was going on. It was just one big massive wall of sound from the audience. And, of course, every time there was a kill it would go up ten more decibels.

Afterward, I went up to Frank and asked, "Did it work? Did it not work? They never shut up!" He goes, "No, it's great. We just need five more kills."

BRUCE GREEN: I've never worked with Oliver Stone, but I'd be willing to bet that if you went to him and said, "If you cut this and this, the film would make an extra $15 million," he wouldn't do it. He'd say, "I don't care. I'm making my vision." With *Friday the 13th*, if marketing people go to the filmmakers and say, "If we can cut this and this, we can guarantee you'll make an extra $15 million opening weekend," the filmmakers will do it.

TOM MCLOUGHLIN: That's what I hate about the preview process. It's like a monster without a head. If one person out of five hundred makes a laughing sound, somebody goes, "It's funny? Oh, it's funny!" And they can turn the whole screening process around. I've seen that repeatedly. In previews, you can literally sabotage someone's film.

I was a little bit upset. My whole thing was that I wanted the film to have thirteen kills, to have this weird sense of logic to it. I was very proud of the fact that I was staying with these little rules that I had come up with. But Frank Jr. said, "No. We need more characters to kill off." I said, "What do you mean? We're all out of money!" And Frank goes, "No, no, no, your producer saved a ton of money. We're fine. We can go shoot two more days!"

Frank's thing was that we were going to go out to Griffith Park in Los Angeles and shoot some additional stuff. That's where we added the death of the caretaker and the two kids getting killed on the motorbike. Plus, we beefed up Sissy's death. Before, she got pulled out through the window and then you never saw what happened to her until her head rolled out of the cop car. Now, we added a shot of her head being twisted, pulled up and off. It was incredibly gory—and you saw all this skin stretch and all this stuff in her neck and then it snapped off.

Ultimately, these additions resulted in sequences that are kind of interesting. And one of the images I am glad is now in the film is when one of the kids sees Jason, after Jason has just killed the caretaker. I always found it very unsettling. Jason turns and looks at the guy who has discovered him, and then starts the chase. That is one of the great nightmare images that that we have—you're watching something that you shouldn't be watching, and suddenly the monster sees that you are watching and he comes after you. It's very small and basic, but we didn't already have that in the film, so at least that was, to me, a very nice addition.

VINCENT GUASTAFERRO: The violence in *Jason Lives* serves the plot in many ways, so it's not gratuitous. And in horror movies, it's obligatory. You have to have it to scare people. But I thought Tom was really good at setting up the possibility for a violent act, building the tension, but then not ever showing a slash. Tom was trying to show that you don't have to be gratuitous to get the effect. Did you ever see *One Dark Night*? A bloodless horror movie, but it's scary. The guy is very good at what he does.

I remember talking to Tom about this. He said there were trends in censorship. If one movie was too sexy, the censors would come out and say, "No more bare breasts." But you could still say, "Okay, let's use more horrible language." Then that would get progressively worse, and then there would be no nudity or bad language. But you could still slit people's throats. And then they'd think *that* was way too violent, and say it would be better to show more boobs. And it all cycles back again.

TOM MCLOUGHLIN: Ultimately, we had nine screenings with the MPAA. We had to keep chopping and chopping. It was difficult, because it wasn't like they were objecting to any one scene—nothing was excised completely. So much of what happens with the ratings board is based on the climate at the time and they govern accordingly. This was still when all everyone was making were *Friday the 13th* and *Halloween* clones. And just a few years before, we were all shocked when the MPAA gave *One Dark Night* a PG. I think the only reason they did was because they were so happy that, at that time, a horror movie was being made that was actually doing an Edgar Allan Poe thing with puss and maggots and corpses and stuff.

Friday was my school about the MPAA. It taught me to make sure I cover myself, because you don't want to totally sacrifice a sequence and you want to be as real as you can be in portraying a specific scene. Everything I've done after that I've done three versions of—"Here's the X version, the R version and the PG-13." Before and during *Friday*, I don't remember consciously saying, "We're going to do three different versions." I think we just went for it because Frank's whole thing is to give the fans what they want to see.

I wanted all the kills to be humanly impossible to do. I don't want to say the film was "bloodless," but they were sort of stretching reality. Pushing Darcy's face through the wall of the RV, or bending the Sheriff backwards in half, or lopping off the

Above: The task of creating *Jason Lives'* James Bond-inspired title sequence fell to title designer Dan Curry, who had also designed the opening credit sequences for *Friday the 13th Part 2*, *The Final Chapter* and *A New Beginning*. "To create the illusion that Jason is hacking his way out of his own eyeball," says Curry, "I had a large plywood box made with a round hole in one side of it. I then put a big black garbage bag inside filled with milk, which I sliced from the inside with a razor blade, and the milk would gush out in the same pattern that the slash of the machete makes across the screen. And because white milk against black plastic is very opaque, I could tint that red so that it would look like blood. Then, after the blood gushed by on the screen, it would leave a residue with the title of the film. I thought it worked really well, and people still really remember that sequence."

(THEME FROM THE MOTION PICTURE "FRIDAY THE 13TH, PART VI: JASON LIVES")

Above: With his 1986 hit single "He's Back (The Man Behind the Mask)," legendary shock rocker Alice Cooper became the first mainstream music artist to contribute to the soundtrack of a *Friday the 13th* film. "Over the years, many musical artists had expressed an interest in getting involved with the movies," says executive producer Frank Mancuso, Jr. "But when the idea of Alice Cooper came up, it just made perfect sense. Not only from a marketing perspective, but the general spirit of the movie and Alice's music—*Jason Lives* was just a more fun type of *Friday the 13th*. And, at the time, MTV had really started to become a truly substantive, youth-oriented marketing tool. How could we pass up the opportunity to put Jason in his first music video?"

There was one person, however, who was still a little disappointed in Jason's MTV debut. "I was just dying to do the music video, but the record company wouldn't let me," admits director Tom McLoughlin. "At the time, they had a core group of guys and all they would direct were music videos. Now that strict hierarchy has changed, but at the time it was very frustrating. And the funny thing is, I used to be in a band when I was really young called TNT. I was the lead singer, and we were a total Alice Cooper type of group—purely visual, with costumes and makeup and the whole thing, and we'd blow up tons of shit onstage. So I still think it would have been great if I had been allowed to do that video."

Opposite: The domestic theatrical one-sheet poster for *Friday the 13th Part VI: Jason Lives.*

heads of three survivalists at once—that was all planned to be larger than life. I felt I had to figure out unique ways of doing supernatural kills, because once we brought Jason back from the dead I had this license to do all kinds of wild murders. Ultimately, in that sense, *Jason Lives* maybe was not as hurt as it could have been by the cuts. Or, at least, compared to the other *Fridays*.

Ratings board wranglings and last-minute reshoots notwithstanding, Paramount Pictures was confident that Jason Lives *was a better, smarter, faster and funnier film than* A New Beginning. *Although* Part VI *was originally slated to premiere at the tail end of summer 1986, Paramount, optimistic that* Jason Lives *could turn out to be its most mainstream* Friday *yet—and eager to capitalize on the few remaining weeks before the target teen audience returned to school—bumped up its release date to August 1st. In a further attempt to broaden the film's appeal, the studio recruited legendary shock rocker Alice Cooper to contribute three songs to the soundtrack, including the pop-inspired single, "He's Back (The Man Behind the Mask)."*

By the time Cooper's music video was enjoying heavy rotation on MTV, Jason Lives *debuted on 1,610 screens across America. Even if the studio's ramped-up marketing campaign for the sixth entry in its longest-running film series wasn't enough for Jason to reclaim his title of "King of the Slashers," then early reviews of the film should have ensured its success—for* Jason Lives *earned the one thing that had eluded all five of its predecessors: the occasional positive notice. The prognosis was good for a commercial—and profitable—return to form for the series.*

Yet, despite Paramount's best efforts to breathe new life into the franchise, Jason Lives *was a relative disappointment at the box office.* Part VI *was the first* Friday the 13th *that failed to capture the #1 spot at the box office during its opening weekend, and although the film grossed a respectable $6.7 million in its first three days—right behind another horror sequel, James Cameron's* ALIENS—*its final tally of $19.5 million (for 6.25 million paid admissions) made* Part VI *the lowest-grossing* Friday the 13th *sequel up to that date.*

Arguably a slasher film ahead of its time, in the nearly two decades since its release Jason Lives *has come to enjoy a fondness and appreciation among a good number of* Friday *fans and genre historians alike. Considering that the film pre-dates by nearly a decade the post-modern thrills of* Scream—*filmmaker Wes Craven's self-referential ode to the slasher genre—*Jason Lives *seems positively prescient. Yet even on the heels of the unsatisfying* A New Beginning, Friday the 13th Part VI *still turned a profit, ensuring that Jason Voorhees would rise to kill again.*

KERRY NOONAN: There was some kind of wrap party, but it wasn't that exciting or cool. It was in a warehouse or something. But CJ, after the shoot, was managing this restaurant up at Universal in Hollywood at the time, and the sad thing was that they wouldn't let him off for the cast and crew screening. We were all upset, so we decided we'd all go to his restaurant afterward. And the manager became really excited that we were all coming there, and they played that MTV video with Alice Cooper and tried to get us all to dance for CJ, and made a big deal out of it. So that was nice that we were able to give "Jason" a proper premiere.

JON KRANHOUSE: With the marketing and the advertising, the Alice Cooper thing, and the summer release, Paramount was willing to roll the dice and spend a little bit more to get the profits back up. *Part VI* was a hope for a comeback for the franchise. I guess that didn't quite happen.

TIM SILVER: Starting with *Part VI*, in a way, *Friday the 13th* was not as much of a sure-fire deal anymore. *Jason Lives* didn't open as strongly as *A New Beginning*. Ours opened at number one, because it was coming off the heels of *The Final Chapter*, which had a lot of production value. Even if *Part VI* was great, its box office in the first week would not be strong because *Part V* took the wind out of the sails of the franchise.

TOM MCLOUGHLIN: Initially, *Jason Lives* was just perceived as another *Friday the 13th*. I think we all were ready for the usual horrible reviews that these movies get. But when you have a character break the fourth wall like I had in the film, and look right in the lens and say, "Why did they have to go dig up ol' Jason?"—much to my shock and everyone else's, we actually got some good notices from the bulk of the critics. Throwing away the Siskels and Eberts and people like that who, of course, immediately gave it a thumbs down. But most reviewers just said, "You can't hate a movie that's making fun of itself."

THOM MATHEWS: With the constraints that we had—the budget, the rules of the genre, the reshoots—Tom did a really good job. He had certain menu items we had to fulfill with that movie, but it was nicely shot, it had a lot of diverse elements to it, and I think all the actors did a good job. And some of the deaths were great!

NANCY MCLOUGHLIN: In all honesty, when Tommy got the movie, I had reservations. I love my husband desperately, I'm just not a fan of these types of movies. I never had any interest in doing one at all. I didn't like the darkness of it. I did wish it was something else. And what breaks my heart is that it bothers Tommy when I'm not a fan of one of his films.

But I can honestly say what he did with the material is great. But to say whether I like the movie film... these movies just don't hold my interest. That sounds mean—I thought *Jason Lives* was funny and good. There was nothing I thought was inappropriate about the way it was done. I thought it was done beautifully. And I think that made it the best of the series. And it was humorous. Tommy has such a beautiful gift.

FRANK MANCUSO, JR.: I thought Tom did a good job. It was more of a fanciful approach to the series, so in that regard I was kind of happy. I thought the movie had found a nice place to go after *Part V* and that it brought another level of humanity to the material like I thought we achieved on *The Final Chapter*, although in a different way than Joe Zito had.

I don't know whether audiences of the time were ready for more comedy in their horror. As you do something over and over like the *Friday* movies, you become more comfortable with what it is, and the rules of it. When you first start out, your notions are pretty defined. Like, if you were making a stew and you're comfortable with certain spices, then you start to say, "Well, maybe some of this and a little of that isn't going to hurt us." It all becomes a judgment call. Perhaps some of the things that were tried could have gone too far in one direction so it ruined the mood, but I think we were just trying to experiment a little more. And it was my belief to let young filmmakers like Tom explore their passions and bring their own flavor to the series.

VINCENT GUASTAFERRO: I think *Jason Lives* is unique among the genre, at least up until that point, because of three elements. It was the first one to use little kids and put them in jeopardy. It was the first one to use contemporary rock music. And it had a sense of humor. I thought this one was better than the other *Friday*s. Some of the others took themselves a little too seriously.

JOSEPH T. GARRITY: I think Tom's film, in retrospect, was part of a reaction to what the 1970s were. In some of the horror films of that period, there was a certain nihilism, a sense of futility. I think around the time we did *Jason Lives*, there was a lot of hope coming back for the world to become a better place, and a yearning for a renewed spirituality. To question why we do what we do. Is the Bible true? Did someone make it up? Is there a God? I don't want to make *Part VI* out to be more than it is, but at least Tom thought to even think about those questions at all, even if it was just in the context of this little horror movie.

TOM MCLOUGHLIN: For me, *Halloween* was the beginning of a new wave of horror movie—babysitters and a masked killer and a knife. John Carpenter made a brilliant film out of no money and a lot of talent. Then everybody tried to do spins on babysitters in jeopardy or kids out camping in the woods or some kind of a masked killer. But there were so many of them that I felt like, if I was going to make one, I wanted to try to put a different spin on it. That's always the toughest thing as a filmmaker: how do you make sure you please the fans, but also, hopefully, attract people who normally wouldn't embrace this kind of film? That was the goal I set for myself—that the comedy would work with the horror, that my *Friday the 13th* still delivered, yet it wasn't just another Jason movie.

In general, there has been negative response to *Jason Lives* from hardcore horror fans—that there wasn't enough sex leading to the decapitation or whatever. And the line that is still quoted more than any other from the film, in both positive and negative responses to it, is the one when the caretaker looks into the camera, breaking the fourth wall, and says, "Some folks have a strange ide'r of entertainment." It has been taken almost like a question. Are you making fun of the audience? Are you making fun of the genre? Are you making fun of yourself? It really sparked a lot of interest. I just tried to create a rollercoaster ride where there were laughs and screams and you had fun with it. Any time I noticed a sequel being successful, it's because you've taken another genre or another element and challenged the formula. Put Sigourney Weaver in a monster movie and have her be tougher than the alien, and you've got something.

Cut to many years later, and I was sent a script called "Scary Movie" by Kevin Williamson. Of course that ultimately became *Scream*, but I passed on it because I'd kind of made this movie already with my *Friday*. Ultimately, at least what I am seeing right now is that there's a new generation that is discovering these movies. And I'm thrilled to read the emails from kids that are seeing it for the first time and enjoying it. There are a lot of people that didn't like mine because it wasn't as violent or as sexual or whatever as the others. But on the other hand, there were a lot of people who loved it because it was the one that went a little bit off to the side—which is what I, as a filmmaker, needed to do. And definitely for the slasher genre, it was something new.

7.

Jason's Destroyer

By the end of 1987, *Friday the 13th* was a series in transition. Its first six installments had grossed nearly $200 million in the United States alone, and Jason Voorhees had grown into a highly recognizable icon whose hockey mask and bloody machete had become synonymous around the world with murder, mayhem and big profits.

Yet, the future of the franchise was anything but assured. The slasher boon of the early 1980s was not only on the wane, it was practically extinct. Audiences were now turning to mutating monsters and biomechanoids to get their cinematic chills. The biggest horror hits of 1986 were James Cameron's action-horror sequel *ALIENS*, David Cronenberg's critically-acclaimed remake of *The Fly*, and the PG-13 thrills of *Poltergeist II: The Other Side*. Then, in the spring of 1987, director Adrian Lyne's *Fatal Attraction* was released to block-buster box office and rave reviews. The film tells the tale of a suburban husband who, after a brief fling with a co-worker, becomes the unwitting target of the woman's psychotic—and eventually knife-wielding—revenge. Although blatantly mining many of the conventions of the slasher film, with its A-list cast including Michael Douglas, Anne Archer and Glenn Close, coupled with stylish direction and glossy production values, this horror film earned Academy Award nominations, not scorn.

Fatal Attraction also captured the cultural zeitgeist of the time in a way that no "slasher" film had since *Halloween* and *Friday the 13th*, spawning a host of imitative "suspense thrillers," all boasting major stars and similar plotlines: affluent suburbanites under threat from all manner of rampaging psychos—from spurned roommates (*Single White Female*, Columbia) and crooked cops (*Unlawful Entry*, Fox) to disgruntled tenants (*Pacific Heights*, Fox) and even deranged nannies (*The Hand That Rocks the Cradle*, Buena Vista). Perhaps these films' not-so-subtle lifting of slasher movie clichés was some sort of compliment, however backhanded, to the subversive influence of films like *Friday the 13th*, but one thing remained clear: Paramount's once-lucrative horror series was in trouble. The steadily declining returns for *A New Beginning* and *Jason Lives* gave critics and industry detractors even more fuel to declare that *Friday the 13th* was no longer Paramount's lucky day—or at the very least, that horror fans were demanding more intelligence behind their lust for blood. Jason may have been down for the count but he was far from out—especially if Frank Mancuso, Jr. had anything to say about it. The now 29-year-old producer's willingness to take risks with the *Friday* formula, as evinced by the tongue-in-cheek tone of *Jason Lives*, was, he still believed, exactly the creative shot in the arm the series needed in order to thrive. The road Mancuso chose next, however, come as a surprise even to the series' diehard fans. *Friday the 13th* was about to make a detour from the silver screen to the small screen—albeit in a form that no one could have ever quite expected, or anticipated.

FRANK MANCUSO, JR., President, Hometown Films: *Friday the 13th* came about as a TV series because Paramount Television wanted to get into the syndication business. They chose *Star Trek* and *Friday the 13th* as two recognizable titles because they felt there was enough of a core audience that they'd be able to get people to watch without big star power. Mel Harris, who was running Paramount Television at the time, came to me and said, "We want to do a TV series and we want it to be *Friday the 13th*—but it doesn't have to have anything to do with the movies." I said, "But that's a double-edged sword. What happens if people show up expecting Jason? They'll be pissed off. Then there are other people who won't tune in because they think they're going to see Jason." But Mel just said, "We're really comfortable that this is going to work and we really want you to do it. And you can do anything you want for an hour—twenty-six episodes a year."

LARRY B. WILLIAMS, Co-Creator, *Friday the 13th: The Series*: Steven Alavansky was a creative executive at Paramount when they opened their syndication division in the 1980s. He was their number two guy behind Mel Harris. Steve and I became friends when he was working as a producer on a film called *Blood Beach*, and I had also just written my first feature, *SpaceCamp*— I ended up with story credit on that. So when Steve got the gig at Paramount, he knew my writing, and contacted me and asked if I'd have any interest in bringing ideas to Paramount for a television series based on *Friday the 13th*, because they were looking for a way to make it work.

All they had was the title. And as I remember it, they were trying to avoid using Jason so as not to have to pay money to the rights holders if he, or any of the other characters from the films, were used. But even by itself, the title *Friday the 13th* would carry some weight. I thought it was an impossible task, that people were going to reject the show outright if they turned it on and Jason wasn't there. But I still wanted to make some connection to Jason.

So I started noodling it in my brain, and I came up with my own mythology. I said that Jason was Jason, but if you put that mask on anybody, they'd become evil. Then I took another step back and asked, "Where did he get the mask?" Then I had my

key. So I started thinking about "The Haunted Mask," and Faust. I thought, "Here's the pitch. There's a shop in New Orleans and the guy is going broke because his things aren't selling and what he needs to do is make a deal with the devil, who brings in objects and a manifest. And the devil's deal to the owner is, 'You will get wealthy selling this stuff, but if you break with me, I get your soul.'"

So I came up with the notion that if I had a shop where everything was haunted, and if at the beginning of every episode we'd show the front of the store, that among forty other junk items in there we'd have, hanging from a string, the hockey mask, which would slowly turn. I wanted the show to open like that, with the mask turning and glinting. That was my suggestion—but it didn't get incorporated due to the fear that they would have to get and pay for additional rights to use the Jason character.

FRANK MANCUSO, JR.: My initial approach was still to change the name of the series. I felt the title would work against it. Eventually, we did this focus group study where we showed them an episode. And it turns out there were people interested in it, but who wouldn't have sampled it if it was called *Friday the 13th*. So I said to Paramount, "We just got the best answer in the world. If we change the title, people will watch it. Call it 'The 13th Hour' and make it more like *The Twilight Zone*." And still, Paramount said no.

LARRY B. WILLIAMS: If we called it "Curious Goods"—it's just not going to sell. There was a thirteen-minute pilot shot. It was before the show was accepted by Paramount. I wrote this pilot episode, which had additional characters and we did in thirteen minutes a mini-version of what an hour show would be like. Frank Mancuso, Jr. directed it. Frank was really involved.

They carried it to NATPE and pre-sold the show. They went out with *Star Trek: The Next Generation*—which came out the same year as *Friday the 13th*. The sales people at Paramount were geniuses. Everyone was surprised at how successful that sale had gone that first time out. It would have been illegal for them to say that if you want *Star Trek*, you have to take *Friday the 13th*, too, but they sure made it sound that way.

FRANK MANCUSO, JR.: One of the reasons I decided *The Series* would be an interesting challenge and a great opportunity was because, on a network show, you're going to have all the freedom you want as long as it comes in on time and on budget. It's like your dream of the week. And the great thing about the show was that, because it was syndication, we never got any network notes telling us what to do. If we wanted to shoot a show in black and white, we shot a show in black and white.

It was a lot of work. I ended up doing significantly more on the show than I originally thought I would. Which is not to say I didn't intend to, just that it represented a rather large commitment of head space. I didn't have a staff of ten writers out there doing their stuff. We'd hatch a season of episodes just out of my head. Some ideas would be two pages long, others five paragraphs, but we'd outline what the basic concept of the episode was, what it was about, the setting, and who was in it. And for twenty-six episodes a year—it was very challenging to keep it going and keep it fresh. It was also when we began to utilize Canadian talent, as we shot the show up in Toronto because of costs.

It was certainly a different experience than the *Friday the 13th* movies had become for me. I enjoyed the process and the freedom of *The Series*. I always had fun doing it.

The first episode of Friday the 13th: The Series *debuted in national syndication on September 28, 1987. The premise of two cousins who inherit an antique shop in which all of the inventory carries a curse from the devil bore no connection whatsoever to the film series that shared its name, but that did not prevent the show from being an immediate hit. By the end of the 1987-88 season,* Friday the 13th: The Series *ranked as the second highest-rated syndicated television series, right behind* Star Trek: The Next Generation. *But the success of* Friday the 13th *on the small screen only exacerbated fears among diehard Jason fans that the fate of their favorite hockey-masked anti-hero might be permanently sealed. Would the popularity of the Jason-less television series spell the end of his big-screen exploits, or worse, inspire a radical—even homogenized—change to the familiar formula? But cursed antiquities were the least of Jason's problems. Since Michael Myers had*

Debuting on September 28, 1987, *Friday the 13th: The Series* ran for three successful seasons in first-run syndication. The show's original cast (**opposite**, from left) starred John LeMay and Robey as distant cousins Ryan Dallion and Micki Foster, who inherit a cursed antique shop known as "Curious Goods." Chris Wiggins (center) played Jack Marshak, an eccentric antiquities dealer who comes to the aid of Ryan and Micki, helping them solve the mysteries of the store's haunted past. LeMay would eventually exit *The Series* after its second season, replaced by Steven Monarque (**above**).

"*The Series* was a great experience," says LeMay. "I was working every day for two years, and I came out of that a much more confident actor. But it always seemed to me, especially at the beginning, that it was kind of hit or miss. There were some really great episodes, some mediocre ones and a couple of really bad ones. I also don't think I was exactly what they bargained for when they hired me. They wanted somebody who would stick out their chin a little quicker than I did, while I wanted to make Ryan more intelligent and vulnerable."

Interestingly, the director of LeMay's final two-part episode, "The Prophecies," was Tom McLoughlin, who had helmed *Friday the 13th Part VI: Jason Lives*. LeMay would eventually return to the *Friday the 13th* franchise when he starred, as an unrelated character, in 1993's *Jason Goes to Hell: The Final Friday*, making him the only actor to appear in both incarnations of the *Friday* franchise.

Playing the telekinetic Tina was emotionally exhausting for actress Lar Park Lincoln. "I wanted to make Tina and her problems real, instead of comical and stupid," says Lincoln. "Many actors will draw on very bad things to play a character like this, and to make themselves cry onscreen. But I drew on very happy things—tears of joy instead of sadness. Otherwise, those negative feelings can stay with you over a long shooting period. It also would have made Tina a depressing character, which she definitely was not."

taken a sabbatical after 1981's Halloween II, Jason Voorhees had not faced a genuine challenger until the arrival of a horribly scarred, razor-fingered dream stalker named Freddy Krueger.

In 1984, Wes Craven—who more than a decade earlier had teamed up with Sean Cunningham on the groundbreaking Last House on the Left—gave life to a new cinematic terror: A Nightmare on Elm Street. Produced by a then fledgling distribution company called New Line Cinema for just over one million dollars, A Nightmare on Elm Street tells the story of the "Springwood Slasher," a reviled child murderer named Freddy Krueger (played with sadistic glee by Robert Englund). After being freed on a legal technicality, Krueger is burned to death by the parents of his victims, only to return with the power to terrorize and murder the next generation of Springwood's children in their collective nightmares. Freddy struck an immediate and resounding chord with horror audiences, eventually spawning six sequels of his own and officially putting New Line on the map as "The House that Freddy Built." Though certainly sharing many of the tried-and-true conventions of the standard slasher film, A Nightmare on Elm Street dared to break new ground by being scary, imaginative, well-acted and surprisingly literate. Filled with surreal and often startling dream imagery coupled with fantastical special effects, the Nightmare series took the low-rent "Karo-syrup-and-latex" approach to slasher films past to a new level, employing such cutting-edge techniques as matte paintings, rotoscoping and elaborate physical effects to go along with the requisite blood and gore. What's more, Freddy, unlike the mute Michael Myers and the thoroughly un-jocular Jason, could not only kill—he could talk. Krueger's witty banter and clever one-liners became such as staple of the Nightmare series that one critic labeled Freddy "the Henny Youngman of horror." And unlike Paramount Pictures, who had never put much stock in the idea of mass marketing Jason, New Line wasted no time in exploiting (and cashing in on) their newfound golden goose. By 1988, Freddy

was everywhere: on T-shirts, posters, lunch boxes and bed sheets. He even hosted his own "Guest VJ" hour on MTV, and it wasn't long before he had his own television series—Freddy's Nightmares, a return to the weekly horror anthology format popularized by The Night Gallery and The Twilight Zone (with the irascible Mr. Krueger standing in for Rod Serling).

But one thing was now certain: if Jason was going to retain his title as King of the Slashers, he had to remain relevant to teenagers of the late '80s. No longer could he be content prowling the woods of Crystal Lake for more unsuspecting camp counselors to kill—he had to beat Freddy.

Although an idea was already stirring in the mind of Frank Mancuso, Jr. to pit horror's reigning terror icons against each other in one movie, complicated rights issues would cause those plans to be indefinitely put on hold. In the meantime, Jason would have to find another foe to battle first.

FRANK MANCUSO, JR.: Tom McLoughlin was the first director I had talked with about doing a "Jason vs. Freddy" movie. That was something that would have gotten me excited. It would have been like going back to Dracula vs. Frankenstein and updating it. But New Line would never agree to let Paramount release it domestically, which was the big stumbling block. The idea was that Paramount would distribute it here and New Line would distribute it overseas, but they just wouldn't go for it.

DARYL HANEY, Screenwriter: Freddy didn't need them because Freddy was much bigger than Jason. By that point, the Freddy movies were doing so much better at the box office, and I think they were generally better respected.

They ultimately named this thing The New Blood for a reason—that's what they were hoping. I guess because Paramount couldn't have Freddy, the idea was to recreate the series a little bit. Creatively, the series had run out of steam. Part VI made just enough money to justify making a sequel. My guess is that the feeling was, "We can still make a profit off these things and they're cheap to make and they have a built-in audience. They're kind of a sure thing." By this point, it was a franchise.

MICHAEL SHEEHY, VP Creative Affairs, Hometown Films: At the time, I remember not really wanting or asking to have my name on any of the *Friday* films, although I did get a kick out of being involved with the story meetings and the development meetings because the franchise had gone on so long. But Barbara Sachs had been there a while, and when I was first brought aboard, my title was VP, and she was a Senior VP. Anyway, she became Associate Producer on *Part VII*, as well as *Part VIII*, and really became the driving force of the movies for Frank.

DARYL HANEY: Barbara was the first person I had contact with. I pitched her a few ideas and she shot them all down. I only had one more. I said, "I notice that at the end of these movies, there's always a teenage girl who's left to battle Jason by herself. What if this girl had telekinetic powers?" Barbara immediately said, "Jason vs. Carrie. Huh. That's an interesting idea." Then we talked once or twice before I had to go back to New York. The next day I had literally just flown in and walked up the stairs of my old apartment, and the phone rang. It was Barbara saying, "You got the job."

From then on out I was constantly on the phone with Barbara back in L.A. and we were talking about the script. Her whole thing was that she wanted it to be unlike any other *Friday the 13th* movie. She wanted it to win an Academy Award. I wanted to do it very by the book and she forced me to get involved with what would become this whole stupid disaster.

FRANK MANCUSO, JR.: We were doing the *Friday* television series and I was doing a lot of other movies. It was important to be able to have some people to take over the *Friday* film franchise. Part of the reason was because we had enough productions going on that I needed help and I also really wanted somebody to sit in on these things, to be sure we, as a company, were maintaining a close watch on what was going on. I wanted people who would be up at four o'clock in the morning and have the energy to go ahead and make the right decisions. I also knew that if they ever got into difficulty, they would call me. My reference point was that these movies made me. These movies introduced me to moviemaking. These movies taught me how to do this more complicated stuff I was doing now. There is something to be said for that.

DARYL HANEY: Barbara had already done this preliminary outline, this whole concept that it was going to be like *Jaws*. There was a corporate guy who was going to build these condos at Crystal Lake. The community was saying, "You can't do that because all these murders happened here and Jason will come back." And the corporate people were like, "No, we don't care. We just want money." And it was great to take some jabs against capitalism and all that, but I never believed in it. It took a long time for Jason to appear. And the climax she came up with had this girl trapped in a boat or helicopter while Jason closes in. I was just thinking, "Why does everything have to be so overdone? Does there have to be condos and motorcycles and a helicopter and all this shit?"

I got the job in June, started working on the thing in July, but it wasn't until the fall that Barbara finally showed a copy to Frank. So Frank reads it, and he hits the roof. He said, "What the hell is this? This is horrible—this is not what I want!" So I got called into a meeting with him. Frank tells me to take *The Final Chapter*—which he considered the best of the series—and basically knock off its structure.

After that meeting with Frank, the first thing Barbara said to me was, "Ready to paint by numbers?" And I thought, "You're acting like this was such a creative process before this, but I wish Frank knew that I'd wanted to do something much closer to the original." But I couldn't really express anything to Frank because there were all these political games. I didn't want to be seen as this foil to Barbara—after all, she was the one who hired me. I was just a tool, which is what writers are to these people. So I executed a bunch of drafts of this thing, utilizing *The Final Chapter* as my template. And we were getting close to Christmas by the time they brought in the producer and hired John Carl Buechler.

JOHN CARL BUECHLER, Director: I always wanted to be a director since I first came to Hollywood, but I knew that nobody was going to give me a shot just because I made some student films. So I negotiated my way into the director's chair

Below: John Carl Buechler at work, directing stars Lar Park Lincoln (below, left) and Kevin Spirtas (bottom, left).

An accomplished effects artist before becoming a director, John Carl Buechler earns high praise from his cast and fellow filmmakers for his work on *The New Blood*. "I really liked working with John," says Heidi Kozak, who played Sandra, one of *Part VII*'s ill-fated campers. "He was so much an actor's director, and he took such good care of all his kids. He's also not a fly-by-the-seat-of-your-pants director—he really is very detail-orientated and always had a very clear vision about what he wanted and what he saw." Michael Sheehy, one of the Hometown Films executives involved in the development of *The New Blood*, recalls being impressed with the easy-going manner Buechler had with his cast. "I visited the set once, and I remember being struck by how laid-back Buechler was," says Sheehy. "For a horror film with all these young actors and scary situations, I kind of expected a very intense energy. Instead, John is sitting in his director's chair with his shoes off. He spent a lot of time sitting and overseeing, as opposed to pacing around and yelling like a lot of other directors might be when working with young actors."

by way of effects. I had a knack for sculpting and painting, and Rick Baker was kind enough to allow me the opportunity to apprentice with him and Stan Winston. I began to make a name for myself by doing effects shows, working on a lot of movies, and developing screenplays.

In late 1987, my agent at the time gave me a call and said, "John, how would you like to direct a *Friday the 13th* movie?" And my response was, "Why? Haven't they already made enough?" I didn't know that there was anything new to do with a *Part VII*. I thought it was a joke.

MARTIN JAY SADOFF, Co-Editor: There were talks, especially with *Part V* and *Part VI*, of really bringing in a major director, to really make it something special—it was actually spoken to bring Fellini in to do a *Friday the 13th* movie! He would do something really macabre. But after it was batted around for a while, it came back that this is a franchise, and people who are used to the franchise want more of the same.

"When you have a whole group of young actors at some remote location, how can you not have fun?" Heidi Kozak

MICHAEL SHEEHY: I think the formula was bigger than what we thought somebody like a name director could bring to the table to elevate it. I know when I was going after directors, I was going after people who had demonstrated some expertise in the horror genre. I wasn't going after directors who were outside of that—and major filmmakers certainly weren't approaching us about directing a *Friday* movie.

I'd seen John Buechler's movies *Troll* and *Cellar Dweller* and I thought they were pretty good. And I liked that he had this background in effects. The guy was just passionate about horror movies. John seemed to be a logical candidate. Then Frank met with him and liked him, too.

DARYL HANEY: I used to go over to Hometown and it was a really loose atmosphere. They'd have a whole group of videos lying around of movies by people they were considering to direct. Barbara put in this movie, *Troll*, and she said, "What do you think of this?" I watched the first few minutes of it and I thought it was horrible. Every frame was just off. She said, "Well, I have a feeling this is who we're going to get."

Then John came in, and we barely exchanged two words with each other. My impression of him was six feet of walking mediocrity. I really didn't like him very much. I thought he had a stick up his ass. And I couldn't understand where he got it from. Who the hell was he? I remember I was over at the office one night and I heard him on the phone: "Yeah, honey, I'm still here at Paramount." I just knew he was digging on hearing himself say that. I could hear it in his voice. He was really into it: "Oh, it's so beleaguering to be at the studio."

He would give me notes that I thought were really bizarre. Like, "Some kids are sleeping in the van and some are in the house. Why? Please explain this." And my attitude was like, "Not everybody's going to be able to sleep in the house. The van is perfectly comfortable. Why not? What's the big deal?"

JOHN CARL BUECHLER: I wasn't the screenwriter—you've got to look at the poster to tell you who it was. He actually came up with the *Carrie* premise, and wrote several drafts. But I wasn't incredibly pleased with it. It was the same stupid people doing the

same stupid things. I wanted a much bigger movie. Finally, we all took stabs at it, because it was getting close to shooting.

Over-the-top fantasy is where my roots are. I like horror films, and I like supernatural, but I'm not crazy about slashers. I got excited because I thought with *Part VII* we could bring the series to the next level, where it's more good versus evil—it's a real monster, as opposed to a guy in a closet waiting to jump out with a knife. I also got excited about doing what is essentially the last couple of reels—that's where I think the movie works its strongest. I got excited about the Tina story. It was all a little bit of a departure for the *Friday* films. I wouldn't say it's more adult, just more comic book, more—how shall I say—high-concept.

DARYL HANEY: My guess is that the structure was basically my own, but they went with end scenes that changed a lot of my lines. I don't know how much of the screenplay even is me anymore, except the names were kept the same and a lot of the methods of death were identical.

Ultimately, we got into a contract dispute. I was to be paid $30,000 for the treatment, a first draft, a revision and a polish. The standard thing. But they didn't want to pay me $30,000. I did like fifteen drafts on the script, and then I was released. They gave the final polishes to some union writer who didn't even use his own name. Manuel Fidello, the credited other writer on the movie, that's not even a real person. So here is this pseudonym getting a credit and he was paid with half my bonus, and the other half went back into the movie.

It was all sort of anticlimactic in the end. I was ripped off money. I was made the fall guy in this strange scenario with Barbara, who was whimsically changing the script from minute to minute. It was all sort of like wham-bam-thank-you-ma'am. It's like a machine, and they ran me through it and ground me up and threw me out the other side. It was a very, very bitter lesson in the ways of Hollywood, but I guess that's how we get wiser.

The film that would become Friday the 13th Part VII: The New Blood *would be prepped, cast, shot, edited and scored in the span of just over five months—a breakneck pace even by the standards of low-budget, quickly-made genre movies, much less a well-known franchise film to be distributed by a major studio. Once again, a diverse group of actors were invited to come in to read—this time for a film entitled "Birthday Bash"—but few were fooled by the false title, especially as the script's description of "Ethan, the hockey-masked killer" meant this could only be another* Friday the 13th. *But unlike the familial relationships that developed on the set of* Jason Lives, *the cast and crew of* The New Blood *found it challenging to create a harmonious working environment.*

LAR PARK LINCOLN, "Tina": I grew up mostly in Texas but my dad was Army, so we moved around a lot—seventeen schools at last count. Then I lived in L.A. for almost fifteen years. I came out there with nothing, but it was a very lucky time period where the blonde, blue-eyed girl was popular on every TV series and horror film. So I worked a lot.

When I was auditioning, it wasn't called *Friday the 13th*—it was "Birthday Bash." My late husband would read all my scripts to help me out, and he's going, "This is *Friday the 13th*!" I go, "Oh, please!" And he begged and begged and begged and begged, and finally I went in on it. So it was like a big tribute to him to do it.

KERRY NOONAN, "Paula," *Part VI*: Oddly enough, I got an audition a year or two after I did *Part VI* for some other horror movie. I went in and realized, "Oh—this is *Friday the 13th Part VII*." They had changed it to "Ethan, the hockey-masked killer."

This page: Another group of naïve campers, another group of potential victims. Clockwise from top left: Kevin Spirtas shows some skin; Heidi Kozak (left) and Susan Jennifer Sullivan grab a quick tan before the massacre begins; Sullivan (right) plays hard to get with Jeff Bennett; Diane Alameida (right) spurns the advances of Craig Thomas; post-makeover, Diana Barrows gets ready to party; Susan Blu, all smiles.

"Terry Kiser (third row, right, as Dr. Crews) played such a wonderful villain," raves director John Carl Buechler. "I think before *The New Blood* he had only been showcased as a comedy guy. But you can only do comedy if you understand tragedy. And horror, in a way, is a lot like comedy—the build up, the anticipation, and the delivery of the punchline is very similar. And Terry knew that. He can be intense and underplayed at the same time."

In addition to *Friday the 13th Part VII*, Kiser has appeared in over forty motion pictures. But he is perhaps best known for his acclaimed performance as the titular "living corpse" in the hit comedy *Weekend at Bernies* (1989) and its 1993 sequel, *Weekend at Bernie's II*.

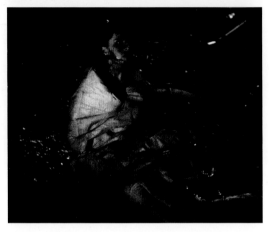

Above: "I still get people writing me and asking, 'Dude! Did you write the sleeping bag death? That's my favorite!'" laughs screenwriter Daryl Haney. "That seems to be one of the more popular deaths in the series." The audience-pleasing moment has been cited as the "Greatest Kill" on many *Friday the 13th* and horror-related websites. Its conception came to Haney from a childhood memory. "I used to shove my brother into a sleeping bag when I was a kid. Maybe that's why fans like it so much—they can relate to it!"

Opposite: The first actor ever to play the role of Jason more than once, veteran stuntman Kane Hodder would eventually don the hockey mask four times. His debut in *The New Blood* was a memorable one for the performer. "The very, very first shot I ever did as Jason was for the dream death of Michael, played by Bill Butler," says Hodder. "It was one of Tina's visions, and a really fast shot. I'm standing in the kitchen, holding up Bill, who's impaled on a tent stake. And in that moment, it felt really natural. I felt like I was born to play this character."

The death of Michael is also memorable for actor Bill Butler, although for a very different reason. "When my character dies in the movie, oddly enough, I'm going pee in the forest right after my car has broken down," laughs the actor. "And whenever someone gets killed in a *Friday the 13th* movie, one of several things has to happen: you're either having sex, or your car breaks down, or you're peeing. So at least I got two out of three."

I'm thinking, obviously, Jason. I was reading for the telekinetic girl. I was a little too old, but I was always playing teenagers. I knew the casting director really well, and the director was there. I said, "Um, I have to tell you I've done one of these." They're like, "One of what?" I said, "I was in *Friday the 13th Part VI*." And the director goes, "Oh, that's why you look familiar!" Needless to say, I didn't get the part.

KEVIN SPIRTAS, "Nick": My birth name is Kevin Blair Spirtas. I grew up in St. Louis, Missouri. As a kid, I performed a lot and sang a lot, and when I was eighteen, around 1981, I went to New York, where I got *A Chorus Line*, and then I toured with that show across the country, which brought me out to Los Angeles. Once I realized there was such a grand opportunity in TV and film, that was really it.

I remember being called in for a movie called "Birthday Bash" and I met the director, John Carl Buechler. I went in, I read and I left. I really did not think anything of it. Then when I got home that night my agent called me and said, "They want you for the lead in the new *Friday the 13th* movie." I went, "What *Friday the 13th* movie?" He goes, "Well that's the thing you just went in on." I remember seeing the very first *Friday the 13th* when I was in high school, and loving it—so when I got cast as Nick in *Part VII*, I was thrilled.

BILL BUTLER, "Michael": I moved to L.A. when I was seventeen years old. I was living in my car. I had no talent and no contacts. But I met John Carl Buechler through my friend John Vulich. I said to Buechler, "John, I'll sweep the floor, anything. I just want to learn about moviemaking." So he taught me how to paint and make molds, and one day he asked me if I had ever thought about being an actor. I said, "Truth be told, that is what I want to do." So he hooked me up with Charlie Band and I ended up doing a lot of films for Empire Pictures, traveling back and forth between Italy and the U.S.

One day I was in Buechler's shop when I heard he was doing *Part VII*, and I flipped out. I was a huge fan of the franchise. I begged John to let me audition. And when you go up for a *Friday the 13th* movie, they don't give you many lines. It's you in an office with eight people eating ham sandwiches, and they're like, "He's coming after you! He's stalking you! He's killing you!" And you do it over and over again. Or maybe I just look good with an axe in my face. Because I ended up getting the part.

JEFF BENNETT, "Eddie": This was my first film. Before that it was all guest spots on TV and some commercials for Sprite and KFC. I was living in Los Angeles at the time with a house full of actors, all starving. All we had was a big avocado tree in the backyard, so I'd harvest the avocados and fix that with rice. We lived on that for months and months. So I was so excited to get this job. I knew this was a *Friday the 13th*, but I just thought, "It's a major film—this is it!" And the funny thing is I ad-libbed a line in the audition that wasn't in the script. I said, "I've got a date with a soap on a rope." And I swear that's why, the next day, I got a call that I'd been cast. They even kept that line in the movie!

DARYL HANEY: I didn't write most of those fucking lines, like that horrible thing where the kid goes, "personal penis enlarger" and, "I've got a date with a soap on a rope." I died a million deaths when I heard that, because people are going to think I wrote something so stupid. It was horrifying.

DIANA BARROWS, "Maddy": When I went in the first few times to read for Maddy, as written she was kind of geeky, a nerd who wasn't so attractive. And she stayed that way throughout the whole film. Then I get this call from my agent that they've changed the script so that halfway through the film she would be transformed and become pretty. And they tell my agent that while I was this incredible, terrific actress, they had a doubt about my being sexy.

I was in New York so the deal was that I'd have to fly back really quick. And even with my jet lag, I got dolled up for the audition. It wasn't that hard because the first few times I went out of my way to look really gross with potato sack clothing and greasy hair. So I put on this super micro-miniskirt and these ultra high-high heels. It was just like the movie—"Touch up, my ass!" I went in, did my audition and the feedback was, "Amazing legs." And the rest is history.

SUSAN BLU, "Amanda Shepherd": I was doing a lot of voice-overs, a lot of cartoons, and then I bumped into Anthony Barnao, the casting director, and he said, "Come on, I want you to read for this. We're having a terrible time finding the right person to play

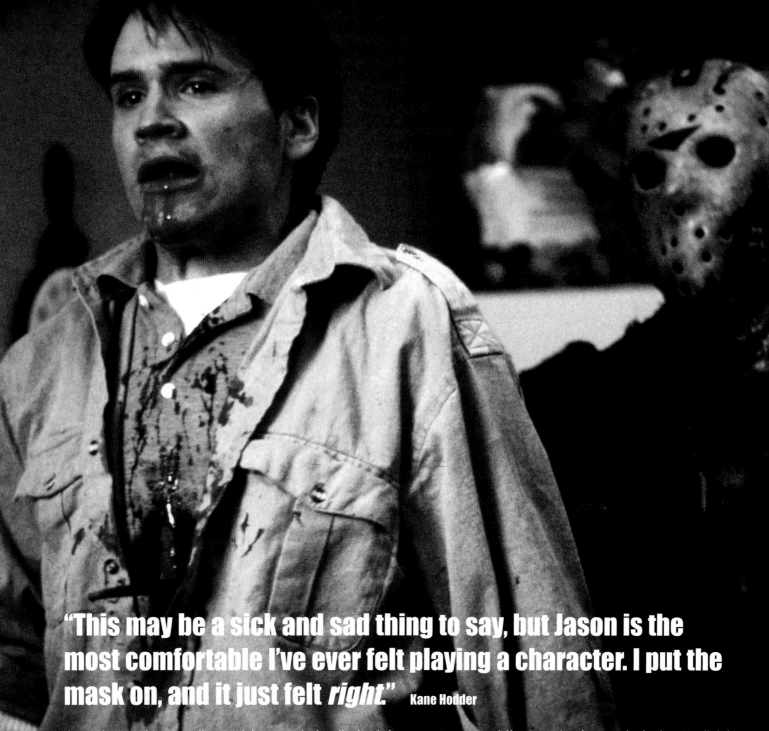

> ## "This may be a sick and sad thing to say, but Jason is the most comfortable I've ever felt playing a character. I put the mask on, and it just felt *right*." Kane Hodder

the mother." And I was really scared, because I had really decided that I wasn't going to do on-camera anymore. I was going to stick to voice-overs and animation, and then all of a sudden, out of the woodwork came this.

But I always loved horror movies. I grew up on *Frankenstein* and all the classics. And I thought that you're not an actor until you've done a *Friday the 13th*.

HEIDI KOZAK, "Sandra": When I went to audition for *Friday* they were looking for actresses who could bring these characters to life. But I was a little disappointed in who my character eventually became in the final script. I was supposed to be a swimmer on the swim team, and originally she was more developed. And the last script we got, it just didn't seem as developed as it was before. Even with some of the other horror movies I did, like *Slumber Party Massacre II*, I was able to dig into something, but I felt that with *Part VII*, that was all written out. It was really hard to get a handle on who this

person was or to differentiate her from anybody else. We all did the best we could.

DARYL HANEY: I'm embarrassed about how the characters were all such stereotypes. One would be kind of nerdy, one would be bitchy, one would be the jock—whatever. That's as good as you can make a film like that under the circumstances. You've only got a minute to establish who they are and then they get killed.

MICHAEL SHEEHY: I have always thought the *Friday* movies worked because you establish Jason, you establish the victim, and then really milk the moment for maximum tension before the kill. So I was somewhat disappointed in the way John handled the victims in *Part VII*, because Jason would just appear and kill them almost on the spot. I felt the movie might have suffered a bit because of that immediacy. But I guess when you have that many people dying, you can't spend ten minutes with each one of them.

DIANA BARROWS: We shot lots of scenes that didn't make it into the final cut, although that is par for the course in Hollywood. But I was disappointed, because there was a whole sequence developing the relationship between Maddy and David. Maddy even smoked grass for her very first time with him before her death scene. That was so much fun. There were also all these other sequences and little subplots with the characters that never made it.

SUSAN BLU: John was so good at what he did. He really cared about the actors. He really took his time with you to try and develop real characters within this horror movie. It wasn't just about Jason looking as horrific as he could. It wasn't just about the death scenes. It was about a lot of fragile acting between the doctor and myself, and between my daughter and myself. There was meat and substance to it.

BILL BUTLER: When you're an actor, there's a certain pecking order. The leads who have the meat and potatoes kind of hang together, and then everyone in the smaller roles tends to form their own cliques. I was really intimidated at first, especially with Kevin and Lar. But then I got to know them—they were so nice to me. We all became friends for the two months or so we were there together.

But Lar was not the most popular person on the set—I don't remember her being very nice to a lot of the crew. I remember she was especially hard on the costume person, something about the way her character looked, and her hair.

JEFF BENNETT: I remember everybody thought Lar Park Lincoln was a bitch. I don't think I ever even spoke to her. Although her character had to scream and cry a lot, so I suppose she had to concentrate. But she didn't pal around with anybody. I also think the situation was difficult for some of us actors because John Carl

Buechler was only talkative with Lar and Kevin. John obviously adored Lar. Everybody else were basically just pieces in a puzzle.

JOHN CARL BUECHLER: I think Lar Park Lincoln is one of the most beautiful and talented actors in the world. She blew everyone away with her reading. There was no question in my mind that this was the girl that had to play Tina. So I recorded all of the readings and played them back for Frank Mancuso, Jr. He rejected her four times. I kept having her come back in with different hairstyles and tops, and had her read it slightly different. Finally, when the hairstyle was right and the top was right, Frank said, "That's the girl! Why didn't you show me her in the first place?" So I got the girl that I wanted.

LAR PARK LINCOLN: Directors tend to fall in love with their leading ladies. And directors tend to search for an actress that they have been seeing in their mind, that has that quality they are looking for. So I think sometimes they forget that we're acting, and they fall in love with what you're reading. And as an actress, that is what you have trained to do, but that's not who you are. I think John wanted Tina's to be a story that stood alone. That you could come in and watch *Part VII* even having not seen the others, nor have to see anything after. And I was certainly very attracted to my character having her own separate storyline.

I didn't really realize it a lot at the time, but there was a real separation between not only my character and the rest of the cast, but me as a person as well. I thought it was because they were all getting killed and I wasn't. But I stayed within the character the entire shoot. I did not get involved personally with anyone else. Because the character was supposed to be sixteen or seventeen and, of course, I was lying and saying that I was eighteen or nineteen, when I was really twenty-three or twenty-four. And I had been married five years. I had to be very careful, because neither I, nor my husband, wanted anyone to know that we were married. I knew that if someone had seen me as a married woman who was running businesses they would have never seen me as Tina—mentally tormented, young and left alone. It would have never happened.

HEIDI KOZAK: Lar had more experience than anybody else other than Kevin. She had been on a TV series, and she took it very seriously and she really knew what she was doing. She even gave me advice about auditioning. She really had that way about her: "I know what I'm doing. You guys are all beginners." But she was always so nice to me. And John just loved her. That was part of the problem, too, with Kevin, because John was so into Lar as a director that Kevin kind of became this outside, difficult thing to deal with. It created a lot of tension on set. I think it came more from Lar, because she kind of decided she didn't like Kevin.

LAR PARK LINCOLN: My times with Kevin weren't my favorite memories. They weren't good. We did not get along. Our personalities just really clashed. We didn't really have any fights or anything like that—we just were not connecting. I think it had a lot to do with him not knowing who he was at the time. So we had our little jokes at Kevin's expense, none to be repeated. It was a difficult situation.

Once again, in order to avoid the watchful eye of the local unions, the Friday the 13th *machine would journey south, this time setting up camp in Mobile, Alabama and its surrounding environs. Production of* The New Blood *would become a thoroughly riotous affair, enlivened by all-night partying, run-in's with local racists, a gun-toting crocodile wrangler, copious quantities of controlled substances—and plenty of covert "male bonding."*

JOHN CARL BUECHLER: *Part VII* was probably the quickest studio movie ever made. I got the gig in November and it was in theaters in May. That is a heck of an undertaking in that amount of time. I was in a blind panic to get the movie out. There were six weeks of principal photography, and we did all the live action and special effects simultaneously, shooting with one unit and an additional camera. The plan was to shoot all the interiors first, because we could do those quicker. And everything needed to be built because of the telekinetic scenes. None of that was practical. So that was all done in a warehouse in downtown L.A. Then the production moved to Alabama for logistical reasons—we were hiding, because it was a non-union film being made by Paramount.

For me, *Friday VII* was three separate movies. The first act was *Firestarter*. The second act was the standard stalk-and-slash Jason movie. The third act was "Terminator vs. Carrie." I think, stylistically and visually, that shows. We opted for more of a soft, white look rather than the harsh look that most of the movies had. That made the women prettier and the effects more forgiving—the whole thing just had kind of a mystical quality. I wanted *Swamp Thing*. Less gritty reality, because it's a fantasy film. It's a monster movie more than a slasher movie.

Many of the most spectacular moments that John Carl Buechler conceived and executed for *The New Blood* were excised to appease the MPAA ratings board. "With the 'ax through the face" gag (**opposite**), we had a geyser of blood that shot out," explains Buechler. "And the guy's head that gets squeezed (**right**), well, Jason eventually smooshes it down to the size of a walnut, and there's blood all over the place. It was really ridiculous, but I wanted the effects in *Part VII* to be really over-the-top. Because *Friday the 13th* is not necessarily about the body count, it's about the event. You have to create something that makes the audience go, 'Wow!'"

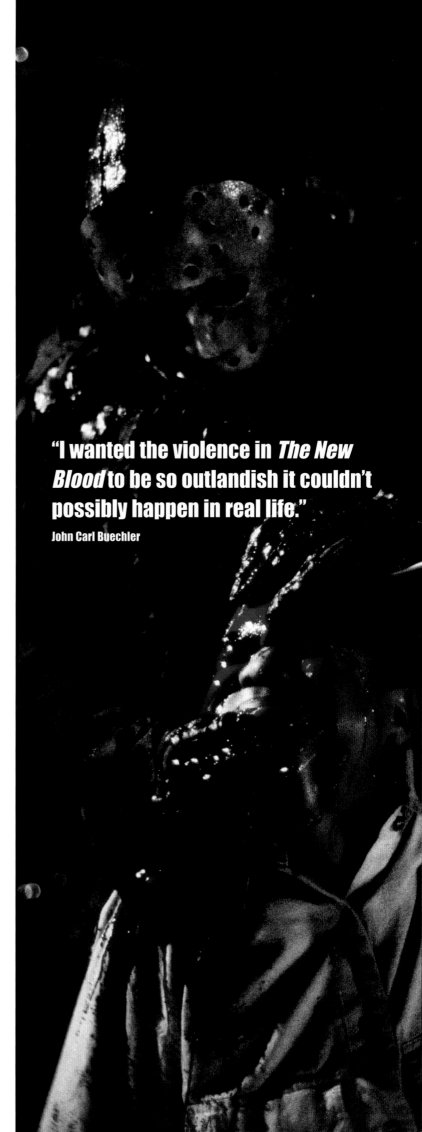

"I wanted the violence in *The New Blood* to be so outlandish it couldn't possibly happen in real life."
John Carl Buechler

"The night we shot my death scene, I had one of the worst colds I'd ever had," laughs actress Susan Blu of her character's bloody demise at the hands of Jason Voorhees. "It was also my last day of filming, so I was already hoarse and raspy from running around and screaming through the whole movie. But *The New Blood* was my last hurrah to on-camera acting before I switched over to doing voice work full time. So what better way to go could you ask for than being killed by Jason?"

DARYL HANEY: John had this idea about going and shooting someplace in the south, so he went away and did this big location hunt. I saw the tapes he brought back, and I remember the one from Alabama, where he was showing the Spanish moss and everything hanging from the trees. And I thought that was really dopey, because it's a dead giveaway we're not in Connecticut or wherever the movies are supposed to be set. But, of course, when did consistency ever matter with these things?

BILL BUTLER: The area was pretty wild, untamed. We shot on the outskirts of this town where there literally were alligators roaming around and a guy on set every day with a shotgun. We called him the "gator man." His job was to stand by camera, and if he saw an alligator or crocodile attack, to shoot them.

HEIDI KOZAK: It was the South so there were some weird vibes. I was with Craig Thomas and Diane Alameida at the local bowling alley, and the people there—it wasn't that they had a problem with them bowling, but they made some kind of comment about them being black. All of a sudden I remember thinking, "We're not in L.A. anymore."

DARYL HANEY: One of the things I really wanted to add to the cast was at least a little bit of diversity. I wanted to have some "black" faces on screen. Because in the past *Fridays* it was so fucking lily-white up there.

BILL BUTLER: I was just so happy I didn't have Heidi Kozak's death scene, where she goes swimming in the water and Jason pulls her down. 'Cause not only were there crocodiles in that

water, but it was freezing, I heard she caught hypothermia, or an actress form of hypothermia.

HEIDI KOZAK: It was ridiculous. But I was fine. When I set my mind to do something, I just do it. And I remember when I came out of the water, John grabbed me and threw towels around me and held me. He was so sweet. They got me in this warm trailer with heaters running inside and hot chocolate. They really took care of me.

LAR PARK LINCOLN: It was fourteen degrees, and for some reason the crew felt they needed to hang the thermometer off the camera, as if to remind us. It is miserable in those conditions. I don't know how Heidi got into that water—and she did get sick that night. She is just so tiny and beautiful. You could have given me all the money in the world, and I ain't walking into that dark water. It was so cold we had to put ice cubes in our mouths just to make sure you wouldn't see us breathing. And I sucked on a lot of ice—although that's the only thing I sucked on. Apparently other people did more than that.

JEFF BENNETT: Almost everybody in that movie was gay—it was like "Fri-Gay the 13th." Really. And looking back, I could have had a lot more fun on that set. I wasn't willing to look at my sexuality at that time. Back then, it was not something you discussed. In the '80s, there was like only one gay person on TV, and that was Mr. Furley on *Three's Company*, and he wasn't even really gay. It took me another two years to finally come out. And I remember one of the reasons was because I was like, "If Kevin Spirtas is gay, then I am, too!"

I did eventually have a thing with Bill Butler. We saw each other a couple of years after the movie, at a party, and it was right after we had both just come out of the closet. And I remember he was roommates with Viggo Mortensen at the time. I could tell from the way he described him that he was in love with him.

BILL BUTLER: That set was on fire. Jeff Bennett, Craig Thomas—they're like a gay pride parade. There was a lot of hanky-panky. I slept with half the cast. Just kidding.

LAR PARK LINCOLN: It sounds like more fun was happening when I was asleep than when I wasn't. I only really worked with the other cast during the party scenes, and I was married and trying to hide it, so I spent most of my time in my room, alone. I remember we all got these great crew jackets, and I love doing arts and crafts and things like that. And I had one of those little engraving pens that write. So I would spend many an hour in my room, in the middle of the night, engraving the backs of big *Friday the 13th* buttons I made that had Jason faces on them, and embroidering them onto these jackets. That was probably the most exciting thing I did the entire shoot.

HEIDI KOZAK: When you have a whole group of nineteen to twenty-year-olds at some remote location, you can't help but have fun. I think we ended up in Alabama a whole extra week because of the rain, but that was fine with us because we were staying at this great little Marriott hotel. We had dinner together, went bowling and had parties in everybody's rooms. Eventually, people started kind of bonding and going off in their little cliques. And there was this game going on at the hotel, where you fill up these cards to win stuff, and we were all into that—collecting our tickets. It was a blast.

BILL BUTLER: You have to understand, this was the '80s. I can't speak for any of the cast other than myself, but most of the crew were all having fun on a variety of party favors. I was right in the middle of it. I partied my ass off. It was just so fun. Of course I can't party like that anymore, because back then it didn't take me three weeks to recover.

That's what I learned most from my *Friday the 13th* experience. Not to drink six Bloody Marys and do a half a gram of coke in one night. It's true, actually—never mix, never worry.

With six previous films and one television show to its credit, Friday the 13th was already—and undeniably—a full-fledged franchise. But unlike the Nightmare on Elm Street series, one ingredient the Friday films lacked was a recognizable face behind their hockey-masked wearing villain—someone who, like the great movie monsters of yesteryear, could claim the role of Jason Voorhees as his own—not just for genre fans, but for the press and the public at large. If Jason never quite needed a genre actor as distinguished as a Christopher Lee, Peter Cushing or Donald Pleasence to wield his machete, then certainly, as Robert Englund proved in his career-making role of Freddy Krueger, a little old-fashioned PR never hurt a movie maniac. Enter Kane Hodder.

KANE HODDER, "Jason Voorhees": When I was in high school, I visited L.A. once and went to Universal Studios. I saw a stunt show there and was just so intrigued by it. And I had always done crazy stuff as a kid. I thought, "Oh, man, that's a great way to make a living." So I went back to high school, but decided to come back between semesters during the summer and see about going to stunt school. And once I got in, I never looked back.

I didn't know anybody in the stunt business at all, which makes it a hundred times harder—I didn't realize how ridicu-lously hard it would be to break into it. I knocked around for eight years doing other stuff and the odd stunt job here or there. Gradually I started working more and more. I eventually got my SAG card and my first professional gig was in 1977, on an old TV show called *Emergency*. Then came *House*, which was the first movie I ever got a stunt coordinator credit on—I did that for Sean Cunningham. So it's ironic that I would start working for him in 1985, and by 1988, I would become Jason.

CJ GRAHAM, "Jason Voorhees," *Part VI*: To be quite honest, I always speculated it would be cheaper to just hire a new guy every time to play Jason, because otherwise you end up in a Freddy Krueger situation, where the actor would be able to demand $250,000. So it is cheaper. But is it beneficial? I don't know.

When I originally did *Part VI*, it was not my intent to be an actor or a stuntman. Then once I got into it, I thought, "Wow, wouldn't it be cool to be the Boris Karloff of the '80s?" Because I am a big boy—I'm bigger than Schwarzenegger—I'm too big to be a leading man. So the best thing I could do would be to capitalize off that bad boy thing and be the big monster character. That could have been a stepping stone to get my name within the market—every time you need that menacing character that wears prosthetics and has to be bad guy, who would you call? CJ.

If I had a shot to do *Part VII* and *VIII*, I would have probably stayed in L.A. and pursued things. But I understood that there was some type of relationship between Kane and the director of *Part VII*. And I've met Kane. He's a great guy, and he's done a great job. He's gone on to make Jason his own.

KANE HODDER: I don't think there was anything that CJ did wrong. If they went with me it was because John Buechler was pushing for me. I had done a movie called *Prison* that was directed by Renny Harlin, and John was the makeup effects supervisor on it. I was the stunt coordinator. And if you know the

The death of Dr. Crews by way of Weed Whacker (**below**) was conceived to be one of the most crowd-pleasing kills in *The New Blood*. But the MPAA ratings board had other ideas. "Dr. Crews was so vile that the audience wanted to see him dead," says director John Carl Buechler, "and they knew that eventually there was going to be a confrontation between his character and Jason. To pay that off was a thrilling moment in the movie for me. Unfortunately, the impact of his death was greatly minimized due to the ratings board. We even had an intestine and a stomach that was pulled out and wrapped around the blade—you didn't get to see it. There is so little onscreen now that it all falls a little flat."

movie at all, I'm also the guy who comes up out of the ground strapped into the electric chair. And this character is supposed to have been dead for twenty-five years, which meant three full hours of prosthetics. When we were about to shoot, Renny Harlin says, "You know what would be good? Let's put live worms all over you." I said, "Sure. But hey, Renny, when I'm supposed to come up out of the ground and scream, let's have those worms coming out of my mouth." So I put a bunch of nightcrawlers in there, which was no big deal to me. And Buechler was like, "Wow, that's who I want to play Jason. Someone who has a real passion. Who will just go for it, and who understands and enjoys the process."

JOHN CARL BUECHLER: When I first mentioned Kane to Frank Mancuso, Frank said, "He's not big enough." And I said, "He's a great stuntman and he moves well and he's a good actor." Frank always took convincing. And my feeling was that I intended to do a pretty intensive makeup effect all over his body, and if I had too much bulk to work with, it wouldn't work. I didn't want 250 pounds of hamburger. So we did, for the first time ever in any *Friday the 13th* movie, a screen test for Jason. I put a skull cap on Kane, and a bulked-out thing with some skeletal elements coming through. And Frank saw it and said, "I see what you mean. Go for it."

KANE HODDER: During the screen test I had to stalk around, walk, and look. I also brought a good friend of mine with me, Alan Marcus, who is another stunt guy. I beat the shit out of him—I literally dragged him across the floor by his hair. Then at the end, I walked over to where the producers were sitting, glared at them, threw the table up against the wall with one hand and just tossed it away. That probably helped to convince them.

JOHN CARL BUECHLER: Kane gave Jason a personality at last. The previous Jasons, to me, just seemed to be there, with no real agenda. They were almost like Michael Myers, in that he's sort of disinterested in what he's doing. He just does it, mindlessly. There was more rage to Kane's portrayal. There was intention. He's like a Harryhausen figure—he's got that internal drama going on. And that isn't automatic. Kane deliberates and figures that out and makes it a moment. Even under all the makeup, Kane could emote. Which I think gave *Part VII* an edge that the other movies didn't have.

KANE HODDER: I just always thought Jason was a great character but they didn't really do enough with it. I don't think of Jason too much in terms of character or deep motivations. I assume that he's pretty instinctive and that there aren't too many thought processes going on before a kill. Some of the previous guys, their problem was thinking about it too much. I usually just did whatever felt natural to me. Because the few times I did really think it through beforehand, I'd watch it on film and think, "Shit, that wasn't as good as it should have been." It shouldn't look like acting.

As far as my Jason walk is concerned, it is not that different from how I really walk anyway. I think it's just mainly the way I would hold my body and the way I'd turn my head. And, personally, I never thought Jason looked as scary if he was running.

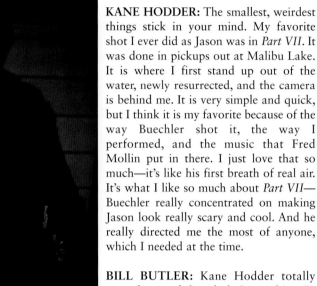

It made him look too human. That is one of the things I've never allowed my Jason to do—I don't care how ludicrous it is that his victims run but he doesn't. He always catches them anyway.

LAR PARK LINCOLN: I love Kane, but who couldn't? He's an absolute doll. And he's a very fine actor. I think the reason his Jason is so good is because you could see his eyes working, him thinking. Some people would just play it like a monster. But Kane acts within, and with, the suit.

KANE HODDER: The smallest, weirdest things stick in your mind. My favorite shot I ever did as Jason was in *Part VII*. It was done in pickups out at Malibu Lake. It is where I first stand up out of the water, newly resurrected, and the camera is behind me. It is very simple and quick, but I think it is my favorite because of the way Buechler shot it, the way I performed, and the music that Fred Mollin put in there. I just love that so much—it's like his first breath of real air. It's what I like so much about *Part VII*—Buechler really concentrated on making Jason look really scary and cool. And he really directed me the most of anyone, which I needed at the time.

BILL BUTLER: Kane Hodder totally turned around the whole Jason thing. In *Part V*, they were getting some skinny guy from the valley to play him. The reason Kane is such a good Jason is that he is completely fearless. He lived, loved, ate and breathed this character. He's also the funniest person you'll ever meet. He would literally put his head through a cinderblock if you asked him to. And another thing about Kane is he can vomit on command. He'd do it right there. He's the king of vomiting and farting. Right before they'd call action, he'd fart. And the suit he had to wear—it was a scuba-diving outfit and it reeked of swamp water. So everywhere he went it stunk to hell. It was hilarious.

KANE HODDER: Bill Butler called me Stinky Voorhees. He thought the costume that I wore, with all the latex, smelled pretty bad. So that was my nickname. And yes, I can vomit at will, as a matter of fact, thank you.

JOHN CARL BUECHLER: My intention from the beginning was to redesign the look of Jason, specifically to reflect all the damage that had been done to him during the previous movies. When you do a sequel, you must keep in mind all that has come before but also build something new. Jason is a roadmap. I got tired of seeing a guy in a gray costume with gloves and a hockey mask and there was nothing wrong with him. So I made a *lot* wrong with him: you see his rib cage hanging out, and when we

Above: The aftermath of the murder of David (Jon Renfield) was almost completely excised from the theatrical release of *The New Blood*. In both the theatrical and original versions, Jason kills the character with a knife to the stomach. The subsequent decapitation was never shot, although in early cuts of the film, Jason is seen carrying David's head around like a trophy. This deleted scene was not included on Paramount's 2003 DVD box set release of the film, and remains unseen to this day.

Above: "I think we must have shot that fifty times," laughs director John Carl Buechler of the death of Melissa (Susan Jennifer Sullivan). "It was all about trying to get the most effective hit. We did it every which way—we smacked her in the head with a rubber ax, then we cut off a rubber ax and stuck it on her head, and did several reverse shots of that. We even hit a rubber head with a real ax a few times." Unfortunately, most of the hard work of Buechler and his effects crew wound up on the cutting room floor. "What ultimately got in the final film was only a brief part of the impact," explains Buechler. "The rest was cut out by the censors. The final result was a composite of three separate angles—one of the real actress at the door, another of a young stunt lady getting hit with an ax, and then finally a shot of the stuntwoman being thrown across the room and landing behind a television set."

TINA

JASON BACKHANDS NICK

C/U TINA

NICK'S POV JASON COMING

BANDS ON MASK - SQUEEZE INTO
JASON'S HEAD - TIGHTENING

MASK SPLITS

Top: To prepare for the role of the psychically gifted Tina Shepherd, actress Lar Park Lincoln did extensive research. "I met with some psychics," Lincoln explains, "and they were mostly concerned that I not play a 'fake psychic,' where you go into some silly trance or body-shaking thing. I was told that when you have a vision, it just comes over you. So I really tried to make Tina a real person who wasn't crazy— she's just this normal girl who had something strange happening to her, and within her."

Right: John Carl Buechler's original storyboards for the unmasking of Jason.

pop off his mask you see a hole in the side of his face, full of scars—eye whacked out, motorblade to the face—all those things are reflected in the makeup. *Part VII* is a natural progression of what he should have looked like at that time.

I was also absolutely aware and appreciative of the *Friday the 13th* timeline, something that may not have been the case in the other films. Jason was dead for ten years before our movie began. And that was when Tina was supposed to be a little girl. So how many years have advanced since? Let's say she was ten years old and now she's sixteen. That's the way I balanced it.

"Tina just never stops running, screaming and crying. That girl is a major migraine!" Lar Park Lincoln

DARYL HANEY: I had forgotten Tina had the gift of prescience as well as the gift of telekinesis. And she can raise the dead. This was a very gifted girl, obviously—one serious psychic babe! Realistically, it probably shouldn't have had precognitive sequences in the first place. John added that later on—that sort of *Eyes of Laura Mars* touch. It may have also been put in to ensure that there was always something happening on screen, that it wasn't just a lot of kill scenes.

JOHN CARL BUECHLER: Barbara Sachs was a pain in the ass. She was a little Hitler. She made comments like, "Isn't this couch too yellow?" But the thing she hated the most was my Jason makeup. She hated his look. She said, "It looks like a frog. It doesn't even look like a human being." I really got in trouble for showing Jason's face when his mask cracked off. They didn't want me to do that. He stayed without his mask until the end of the movie. He didn't just put it back on again. It's *Part VII*, for God's sake, it's about time. I said, "You're going to take his mask off anyway, so let's make it a dramatic moment! Make the mask pop off because she's using her telekinesis!" But Barbara wanted me to wait until the very end, when he was on the dock, and you saw his face for only a moment. But I thought that then you don't have a real, solid confrontation, unless you can see the eyes glaring back at you. So I did it anyway.

DARYL HANEY: It's ironic that John, like me, would end up fighting with Barbara, because she was the one who got him the job.

MICHAEL SHEEHY: I have to admit, I also lobbied with Barbara for the delay in the revealing of Jason's makeup. Because once you do that, the cat is out of the bag. If he remains enigmatic in the mind of the viewer, he's scarier than whatever maggot-infested makeup you can conjure up. People project all their own fears and insecurities onto whatever is behind the mask. Sometimes less is more, and I think that character proved it.

Although it would take another fifteen years for Jason to have his day in the ring with Freddy Krueger, the makers of The New Blood *were determined to make the climactic showdown between Jason and Tina just as satisfying. The final twenty minutes of* Part VII *still rank as some of the most visually dynamic of any* Friday the 13th *film, with Jason being put through the kinds of tortures usually reserved for his victims. Whether being clobbered by a decapitated head, electrocuted in*

a puddle of muddy water or flattened by an entire porch, it seemed that, in the character of telekinetic Tina, Jason may have finally met his match.

JOHN CARL BUECHLER: Even during production I knew the MPAA was going to be hard on this film. So the only thing I really had to fall back on, to ensure the film was still dynamic, was the over-the-top mechanical effects—the big moments in the film that were not makeup-oriented. And one of the main reasons I wanted to do the film was because Tina's telekinetic abilities allowed us to stage big events that hadn't been seen in previous *Fridays*. That's also why I really needed Kane for the role, because he could give me that amazingly powerful, dynamic motion, and he understood stunts.

KANE HODDER: During filming of the scene where Tina drops the porch on my head, we didn't really know what that roof was going to do. The idea the effects crew had was to make the middle six or eight feet—the portion that was going to clobber me—out of balsa wood, but the rest of it would be all real structure. But if you really think about it and you know anything about balsa wood, depending on how it is positioned, it's almost as strong as regular wood. So when it came down, it fucking drilled me into the stairs. I think it weighed seven hundred pounds.

The funny thing is, if you look at the scene again, watch what appears to be Tina—it's not her. It's a stunt double named Paula Moody. It's an over her shoulder shot looking at me. Then the roof falls in and she goes, "Ooh! That was harder than I thought!" You can totally see her jump. No one expected that, least of all me.

LAR PARK LINCOLN: I'm so breakable, so at first I only did one stunt, when I fall through the floor into the basement boiler room. And I land on a mat, so that didn't hurt. But after that they gave me a T-shirt that said "Stuntwoman," so of course I'm like, "Oh, I can do that fall on the pier, too!" Well, after sliding on the pier about eight times later, I was like, "What was I thinking?" I was so bruised and beaten up. That scene was hell. I thought I was going to die shooting that. It was shot in one long, continuous dolly, like two minutes long, and then in the end Kevin and I run and jump on the pier—chest down. And there was no mat. I had boobs, yes, but after hitting that pier twenty times in a row, I think I lost a whole cup size.

JOHN CARL BUECHLER: I'm not extraordinarily happy about the ending—it was changed. For the last scene where Tina's dad comes out of the lake and grabs Jason, we created a whole mechanical head that's eyeless but has teeth and flesh clinging to it—it was brilliant. But it was decided that it was too monstrous for this picture, too fantasy-oriented, so what we ultimately ended up with was the actor who played Dad coming up from out of nowhere. I wanted this ghastly vision to come up, grab Jason and pull him under the water. It would have been great, it would have been dynamic, and that's exactly what the movie needed—a visual effect. But once again Barbara Sachs vetoed it. She would only let me put straight makeup on that guy. He'd been under the water now for ten years and somehow he looks exactly the same. And that is why I think fans still laugh at that today.

SUSAN BLU: I had to do the last scene that was going to be shot in the house, the one that blows up. Well, the crew had already wired it, and I walk in to prepare, and I see all these little fuses sticking out. I asked, "What are those things?" And of course, people are smoking close to the set, too. And they're like, "Oh, those are just the explosives for the house to blow up tomorrow night." And I went, "Are you nuts!?"

"People have said that Jason is little more than a moron who doesn't realize that he's dead. And maybe that's true. He's so stupid, he doesn't know he can't die." John Carl Buechler

Opposite: The fiery climax of *The New Blood* was a highly memorable scene for stuntman Kane Hodder. It also set a record for the longest onscreen "burn" in cinema history. "Back in 1988, fire stunts like this were done pretty routinely," says Hodder, who also served as the film's stunt coordinator. "But you almost never saw the ignition of the flame on camera—it was done through editing. But because the character of Tina had the power to cause objects to burst instantly into flame, we wanted to see it all happen live, on camera. So our mechanical effects coordinator, Lou Carlucci, rigged an actual cannon to blast fire out of the furnace right at me. I ended up being on fire for a full forty seconds. It was the most difficult fire stunt I have ever done."

JOHN CARL BUECHLER: We built both those houses specifically to blow them up. There were cameras all over just for that one shot—at least five or six. I was actually out on a boat in the lake, getting the master. I was peering over the edge when the explosion hit, and I felt warm and wet at the same time—at first I thought it was my blood. Then I realized it was just the heat over the water, and the impact throwing it on me. It was astounding.

KANE HODDER: It was such a tremendous explosion—the only explosion I've ever seen in all my years in the business that was actually so fast, so powerful and so immediate that your eye couldn't actually follow it. It was gone before it registered in your brain. It was an amazing sight.

If production of The New Blood *ended with a bang, its rushed post-production schedule would end with a collective cry for help. Few films—even* Friday the 13th *films—have come under such harsh and unrelenting scrutiny from the Motion Picture Association of America's ratings board, who demanded that Paramount resubmit* Part VII *no less than nine times before granting the film an R rating—prompting director John Carl Buechler to publicly fume that his film had not just been edited, but eviscerated. Scoring of* The New Blood *also proved troublesome. Despite the presence of not one but two composers, the new music for* Part VII, *while integrating many of the familiar* Friday the 13th *motifs, pleased few.*

BARRY ZETLIN, Editor: I suppose everyone who works on a *Friday* has a different experience, but for me, having never done a studio picture, it was fun. I have no Mancuso horror stories—I think his involvement was, "We have to get this done." He didn't think it was trash, he just thought it was business. And the business is that it has to be an R-rated film and you have to meet the deadline and you have to have so many prints. There was never a judgment as to, "Why do I have to sit through all this crap?"

The real horror? That was the MPAA.

JOHN CARL BUECHLER: I don't like to show a blueprint for murder. I try not to get into the mind of the killer. Jason is a dark, evil, unstoppable force of nature. So I was really torn. I thought that if you're going to do a kill, it has to be an event. It's not necessarily the body count. It has to be a moment in the film that makes people go, "Wow." And because, at the time, and probably still today, the ratings board doesn't allow you to do anything extraordinary, I felt we would need to rely on other things to create a visceral impact.

My first sense of the picture was to go more surrealistic as opposed to all-out blood-and-guts, which I feared would be removed anyway. It was, however, decided through various meetings to go more for the traditional stalk-and-slash. And I endeavored to do everything I could to make that work. Because if I was going to do one of these things, I was going to do it *Re-Animator* style and go for broke, hopefully to the point where it's so gratuitous that it would become funny, as opposed to down-right serious, stark reality.

Unfortunately, some of the stuff I wanted in the script was kind of excised early on. Tina had these dream-like states where she had flashes of clairvoyance. I thought this would be a terrific opportunity to do some surreal moments, just like the Freddy movies. For example, when Tina flashes that her mom is going to die, she should see something symbolically representative of that. In the movie, it's just Jason stabbing her mom. I thought it'd be cool to see Jason as a little boy holding Betsy Palmer's head, and the severed head saying, "Help me, mommy!" But the response was: "It's too over the top, people won't get it." As far as I'm concerned, that's what these movies are—they are over the top, and that's why you do them. And I know I could have gotten that past the censors.

What ultimately happened is that I didn't get to fully go with the more surrealistic approach I wanted, but what we did strive for—extremely heavy and grisly on the effects, and huge on mechanical stunts—didn't work, because the ratings board would not allow anything like that to be onscreen. Subsequently, this is the most bloodless *Friday the 13th* ever seen. Horror is pretty much like telling a good joke—it's a build-up and a punchline. My punchlines were all removed by the MPAA.

BARRY ZETLIN: I remember it was the morality that bothered the ratings board the most. Have sex—get killed. Do drugs—get killed. They were specific that you couldn't cut directly from a sex scene to a murder—you had to cut to something else and then come back. We could show a couple skinny dipping, but then had to go back to the house party, and then cut back as Jason comes and kills them. Or, you could see a couple in bed, but then you had to interrupt it with other people talking before you could cut back as Jason comes in for the kill. There were all sorts of strange things like that.

The whole situation became comical after a while. We'd try all sorts of ideas to make it work for them, then go back, and still it wouldn't pass. It just seemed to keep going and going. And it always perplexed me, because you're making this film for a specific audience that wants to see this—they want to see what Jason is going to come up with next. A part of me agrees with trying to keep the world more civilized, but part of me says, "Come on!" I get annoyed at the whole concept of censoring and editing a slasher film—even saying the words "editing a slasher film" sounds like an oxymoron.

JOHN CARL BUECHLER: I will say it. I will call them censors—not the ratings board. Because that's exactly what they do: censor. The MPAA is a group of housewives in Encino that basically decide what you can and cannot see, and ultimately we as artists are bent to their whim. I had a feeling they'd want to go after the film, and particularly me, who's known specifically for doing makeup effects. They had their eye on me. The movie got seven X ratings! I felt my film was castrated. If you go to make a horror film and it's about people dying, the event is the death. You can spend a lot of time setting it up, fixing anticipation, filling in the red herring and being tense, but without the punchline it falls flat.

And it's not an issue of fairness. We were in a rush to get it out, so we didn't fight—we just acquiesced. *Indiana Jones and the Temple of Doom* had someone ripping hearts out of people, but that was a big union Paramount movie. I don't think that anyone will recognize it as a serious depiction of reality. It's a big fantasy, it's a romp, it's a rollercoaster ride. *Indiana Jones* made no special contribution to society by virtue of its great story. They just spent a hell of a lot more money. And they got a PG! And I have nothing against it. I don't necessarily say that all movies have to be graphic and intense, but in some situations, they do. Spielberg's been getting away with this shit for years. He doesn't call them horror films, he calls them war movies. *Saving Private Ryan*—give me a break, man—that's one of the most horrifying movies I've ever seen. Of if you've seen *Gladiator*, you've seen more makeup effects in that movie than ten *Friday the 13th* movies combined. There is a double standard.

FRANK MANCUSO, SR., President of Production, Paramount Pictures: You can't make seven films in a series that are all basically the same in terms of content and not expect the MPAA to quickly and acutely become aware of what the films were attempting to do. But did I, personally, ever think the MPAA were unfair? Probably not. I am sure the filmmakers feel otherwise. And I am sure if you ask my son if he felt they made him cut too much out of these films, he would feel otherwise as well.

But, heavens, no—we never thought about releasing the films unrated. Paramount was and still is a signatory member of the MPAA. So we couldn't. It was never a question of not supporting the filmmakers or being embarrassed of the films. We simply did not have that option. It just was never a possibility.

BARRY ZETLIN: My fondest memory of the battle with the ratings board was the sleeping bag. In the first cut, we'd crack up at how many times we had Jason banging this poor girl against a tree. And by the end of the process, it was down to one whack. It always came back with, "Just cut one more bang on the tree!"

KANE HODDER: The sleeping bag, that is the one rare case I'm glad they did cut, because I think it was better with one simple hit. It was bang, boom! Even though it was more gruesome with the rest of the impacts.

I had no problem with the violence of *Friday the 13th*, and I never have. It is a certain type of movie that appeals to a certain audience. I've always just wanted to make those people happy. That is just my opinion. Because if you cheer someone getting slammed against a tree in a sleeping bag, you're just enjoying the craziness of it. They are cheering Jason and not taking it seriously, which is perfect.

JOHN CARL BUECHLER: I ended up shooting all these big makeup effects, and hardly anything got in. Eventually, I went back and added some reveals of some of the kills, because so much had been cut out. When Tina finds all the bodies in the forest, I added that because it gave a more visceral punch. I also added more scares, like the cat jumping out of the closet, and a little more of Jason stalking in front of the house. And that 3-D shot, where you see Jason throw this tent spike into the camera. Anything I could to make up for what we were losing.

LAR PARK LINCOLN: We had to go back several months later and shoot all those inserts in L.A. I had to drive from the Valley all the way out to this horrible place in Compton, in this area they tried to make look like the swamps of Alabama. And a lot of us looked a lot different by then, with different hair color. It was pretty silly but a lot of fun. I can remember having to stand and scream at dead bodies that weren't there, all to the tune of traffic driving by a few blocks away.

JOHN CARL BUECHLER: We also shot a different coda to the movie that never made it. After the ambulance goes away, we had a shot pushing into the lake. A fisherman pulls a fish out and suddenly the boat starts rocking, and Jason comes out in a big splash of water. The end. They didn't want it. It was excised for reasons I still don't understand.

Opposite, center: Director John Carl Buechler's original design for the character of Tina's father (John Otrin). According to the director, the makeup was eventually vetoed by the film's associate producer, Barbara Sachs. "That original design was very profound," explains Buechler. "I wanted this ghastly vision to come up, grab Jason and pull him under the water. Barbara thought it was too monstrous and too fantasy-oriented. But it would have made a heck of a lot more sense than what we ended up with, which was just the actor wearing a straight makeup."

DARYL HANEY: Frank originally wanted that. It was kind of a motif with these movies where, once everything seemed to be fine, something would come flying out of the water.

What's also funny is that while we were working on *Part VII*, *Fatal Attraction* had opened and it was huge. And at the end of the movie, Glenn Close comes flying out of a bathtub. I remember Frank came in one day and said, in a very loud voice, that he had seen a screening of it with a bunch of other executives, and at the end of the movie somebody leaned over to him and said, "Who produced this movie—Frank Mancuso, Jr.?!"

FRED MOLLIN, Composer: By the time *Part VII* was happening, I think I had already been doing the music for the *Friday the 13th*: *The Series* for about a year. And I think on some level, I deserved some kind of good merit medal. I think what happened was that Barbara Sachs, who was also involved with the TV series, then got involved in the movies. And I also think they paid Harry Manfredini either no money or very little money, and were just going to use his existing scores from the previous movies. But they ran out of music after about half the movie. That's when [producer] Iain Paterson called me and said, "Listen—how about scoring the other half?"

HARRY MANFREDINI, Composer: I was working on another film at the time for Sean Cunningham called *DeepStar Six*. As I do not "farm out" music, I am only able to do one movie at a time. And I think the post-production schedule on *Part VII* was not flexible enough for me to come in. And what is strange is that at the same time I was also being offered a *Nightmare on Elm Street* sequel. Anyway, I chose to work with Sean, and did not contribute anything new to the score for *Part VII* at all. I have never even seen the film.

JOHN CARL BUECHLER: It was all an issue of money, honestly. I said to the producers, "Fred's stuff sounds too synthy. It's okay for TV, but this is a movie. Let's make it bigger and more dramatic." And I think they eventually saw the logic of my reasoning. I wasn't crazy about Harry's music, either. Although, in the end, actually Manfredini's stuff was great, but Fred's stuff was kind of weak. It just wasn't rich enough for me. It seemed too sentient.

One thing I didn't like at all was the score for the opening credits at all—it doesn't sound like music. It's not a good introduction. You want something driving, dramatic, and that just wasn't it. But Fred did do some nice things. He created a theme for Tina, which was good, and that John Carpenter-ish, *Halloween* type of music later on. But that had to be mixed with Harry's stuff, which was obviously more dramatic and bigger and orchestral and fun. So maybe it all sort of clashed.

FRED MOLLIN: I don't remember getting too much direction from John. In fact, I don't think I ever met John Carl Buechler—I don't ever remember hearing John's name. By the time I came on board, Iain was so involved himself in doing the final post that he and Barbara just felt comfortable knowing that I would deliver and liked what I did. And it was a ridiculously crazy deadline, although I'm used to that. I think it was about three weeks, which is really not that bad. And it was only half the movie—the other half of the score was Harry.

I didn't have any trepidation. I had never seen the other movies, so I didn't have any baggage, and I didn't really have a working knowledge of what Harry had done. I feel like I didn't step on his toes because he was still half the composer on it. I kind of liked that. I like that it wasn't just me. But I'm being bone-honest here. I'm not going to blow smoke up your ass and say I was wonderful. I don't think I did that great. I think I did the best job I possibly could have in trying to marry Harry's live sound with my electronic sound. And I think I did a pretty good job—I don't think you spend too much time in the movie listening for which are Fred's cues and which are Harry's cues.

There are still many parts of my score that work quite well for me. I do like the opening credits—I went with a non-melody motif. I thought if it was very percussive, it would add a lot of tension. And the score for the end credits I thought worked well, too. So to hear that John liked things like Tina's theme makes me feel good. Obviously, my job was to please.

A scant six months after the start of pre-production, Friday the 13th Part VII: The New Blood *debuted on May 13, 1988, on 1,796 screens across the United States. The film's opening weekend suggested the "New Blood" of the title was apt, for the film returned the franchise to the number one spot at the box office, earning $8.2 million in its first three days. The subsequent fall-off, however, did little to reverse the financial slide that had begun with* A New Beginning. *With a final gross of $19.2 million, for 4.7 million paid admissions, the run-of-the-mill performance of* The New Blood *seemed to indicate that while the franchise continued to bring in its dedicated fan base, it wasn't winning over any new audiences—or enticing those who had abandoned the series after* The Final Chapter. *As if to twist the knife in Jason's side even further, 1988 would prove to be a banner year for Freddy Krueger.* A Nightmare on Elm Street 4: The Dream Master *debuted on August 19, 1988, earning a franchise-best three-day opening weekend of $12.8 million. With a final tally of $49.1 million,* Nightmare 4 *not only exceeded the commercial success of the original* Friday the 13th, *but Freddy had done it on his third sequel. It seemed that, finally, Jason had been unseated by the competition. But that didn't matter much to Jason devotees who turned out in droves for the latest exploits of their favorite masked maniac. Jason may have been buried by the competition… but he was still a long way from being dead.*

JOHN CARL BUECHLER: The day that it opened, we had a premiere at the Grauman's Chinese Theater in Hollywood. The audience was going nuts, absolutely reacting to all the things you anticipated they would react to. It's always a rush. That's the moment where it all becomes worth it.

KANE HODDER: Even to this day, that movie got the best reaction out of the audience of any of the *Friday*s I've seen. That

Above: John Carl Buechler and friend pose for a promotional photograph.

Opposite: Paramount Pictures' domestic theatrical one-sheet poster for *Friday the 13th Part VII: The New Blood.*

Background: Dated September 9, 1987, screenwriter Daryl Haney's first draft script of *Friday the 13th Part VII* was titled "Jason's Destroyer." The film would eventually be resubtitled *The New Blood* for theatrical release.

was such a great feeling. Just knowing that people were enjoying my work so much—I had never had that kind of feeling before, as an actor or a stuntman, ever.

LAR PARK LINCOLN: I remember seeing the poster, it was the first time I ever saw myself on a big billboard. It was so exciting. And the premiere—I loved it. Then I saw it in Westwood with a bunch of friends and I wore big glasses and tried to disguise myself. It was really stupid, and I got chased out to my car. It was one of those memories that, as an actress, you never forget.

KEVIN SPIRTAS: We put our feet in the footprints in front of the Chinese and kind of did the tourist thing. Then we walked in there, and it's a huge screen and a completely sold-out crowd. And as one death would happen, and another, and another, the crowd would be counting. "One, two…!"

DIANA BARROWS: The premiere was fantastic. There is no better venue than the Mann's Chinese in Hollywood. It was unforgettable. The whole audience was so interactive, and personally, it was loads of fun to receive vicariously, through Maddy on the screen, all this advice, and live reactions from people in the audience.

BILL BUTLER: I first got invited to see a rough cut and I thought I was going to have a heart attack, because there was no music. You can never watch a horror film without music. I thought it was the worst thing I saw in my life. I left there crying, thinking I would never work again. I thought Buechler had failed miserably. I even told my agent not to tell anyone I was in it.

Then I saw the finished film at the premiere. My parents went and I invited all my friends—I even warned them that it sucked—but with that music, I could not believe how good it was. I was thrilled. They also let the public in that night, and when I got killed, these black girls behind me were like, "Fuck him! He's a nerd anyway!" And my mom stands up and says, "That's my son you're talking about!" It was nearly a brawl. It was awesome.

JEFF BENNETT: I had loved the first *Friday the 13th*, and I also thought the acting was good in the first couple of them. But this one is really bad. I thought it stunk. The writing was awful. And I know I was bad in it, too. I went with my agent to a screening before opening night at Paramount. She was quiet throughout the whole movie. And after it was over, she said, "You did okay. I thought you tried too hard in that one scene." So she obviously didn't like me in it. At the time I thought my acting was pretty good. But I look at it now, and it's like, "Wow. I should have been a CPA or something."

DARYL HANEY: I was walking down Times Square one day, back when it was all crack addicts and stuff, and I saw that *Friday the 13th Part VII* was playing on a triple bill with like a Kung Fu movie and something else. I thought, "What the fuck?" So I paid my money and I walked in and it was already showing. And everyone was talking to the screen—which is the ideal scenario under which to see these movies.

I was immediately struck by how horrible the movie looked. It had this ugly white and blue light on everything. It just looked like a really bad slide show, which is exactly how that Buechler movie *Dolls* had looked to me. And once the movie finished, I would have had to sit through two other movies to see the beginning of it, and it was already so depressing. Why depress myself even more? So I never saw the whole thing. I think fucking *Part V* is better directed than *Part VII*. It's horrible.

It's really quite tragic because I do think I'm a really good writer. Looking back, I should have written under a pseudonym, but everybody has to do sub-par stuff at the beginning of their career. I didn't realize the Internet was going to come along and it would never be forgotten. In addition to the low standing of the films critically, I was treated so shoddily on the project and was ripped off money and just had such a horrible experience. In a way, though, it was the perfect introduction to Hollywood, because nothing has really been any different since. What I went through on that project was pretty much par for the course. But then you think, "It was a *Friday the 13th* movie. What did you expect?"

MICHAEL SHEEHY: *Friday the 13th*—it's a double-edged sword. Yes, there is an established formula, and there is a lot more security in that than in making a movie from the ground up. At the same time, when you've got that much success, you can really end up with egg on your face if one particular movie doesn't perform. You've got a history of six movies that have worked fairly well. If this one doesn't work, then you feel responsible.

Certainly we wanted our box office to continue to do well, but I think each time we just set out to make the best, scariest movie we could make. *Part VII* still made millions and millions of dollars and allowed us to do all sorts of other movies because of its success. I only remember a sense of fun with it at that point.

FRANK MANCUSO, JR.: You rarely know the real reason why you're doing something, especially early in your life, when you're doing it. At this point I had this very peculiar love/hate relationship with the *Friday the 13th* movies because on the one hand, they gave me very significant wealth very early in my life and on the other hand, they defined me in a way I wasn't prepared to accept. Because *Friday* was the first stuff I had done, people always identified me with it. So you spend half your time convincing people that their perspective of you is not *you*. For me, the reputation of the *Friday* movies didn't allow me to totally enjoy their success because with it came all of this negative stuff.

I don't think anybody looked at those movies and said, "Wow—what a filmmaker." It was more of a successful execution of a marketing scheme that people related to more than the virtues of any particular movie. More often than not, my contemporaries in the industry would never see them. All they'd say was, "Look at this fucking *Friday the 13th*. It knocked out our movie that was really good and it's a piece of shit."

Permanent Record and, to a lesser extent, *April Fool's Day*, are interesting by-products of the *Friday the 13th* films. *Permanent Record*, especially, was, to me, a personal statement to the people who didn't like the *Friday* films, or more precisely, thought they were out there to do ill to the world. *Permanent Record* was my way of saying, "This is me. This movie, from a content point of view, is more about what I think is relevant." And ultimately, it introduced me to an experience I hadn't had before with *Friday the 13th*—suddenly people were appreciating the filmmaking and its courage.

To be honest, the lack of box office for *Permanent Record* had far more of an impact on me than whatever happened to any of the *Friday*s. I was very intimately involved with *Permanent Record*, and I was surprised by the fact that it didn't do business. I must say that while it felt rather empty, at the end of the day I was still proud of what I accomplished. Whereas the *Friday* movies were such exercises in commerce that, clearly, if one of those movies didn't perform, I don't know that I would walk away saying I was still glad I made the movie.

JOHN CARL BUECHLER: Really, the only reason why *Part VII* kind of fell down at the box office in its second weekend was because Paramount took it out of a lot of theaters to make room for *Crocodile Dundee*, and even then it held its own. I also think there is still an argument to be made that had the film been preserved in its original, uncensored form that it would have been more enjoyable to the audience. Plus the title—that was all marketing. I just wanted to call it *Part VII*, because seven is sort of a magical number. *The New Blood*? I still don't know what that means.

Looking back, *Part VII* allowed me to explore different worlds of filmmaking. Yet I don't know if I learned anything from it. It was profoundly satisfying in many ways and profoundly upsetting in many ways. It was an independent movie made on a studio lot, but then Paramount wouldn't stand behind it. They took a totally different approach than, say, New Line did. They had Freddy appear on MTV. They'd bring press out to the set. They didn't hide it. They screamed it from the rooftops. Paramount hid their stuff. They were terrified of people knowing they were doing these films. Prior to that I had been in magazines all the time, but Frank Jr. gave me a gag order, saying, "Don't tell anyone about this movie. Don't let anybody know you're doing it." I had people call all the time and I wasn't allowed to talk to them. That was frustrating as hell.

It is also a real challenge doing a Part VII to anything. On one hand you've got the whole background of all of those other movies behind you, and the understanding and the legend is set. On the other hand, how do you bring something new to it? So we chose to go more visual, more profound, to get bigger with the effects and deliver a story that got people more involved. I don't think my movie was the same as all the others. It had different levels to it. Sure, it had the elements that drew the core slasher crowd. But if I did give anything to the *Friday* franchise, I think I brought a more classic gothic horror element—I took the most popular slasher in the world and moved it into the arena of the metaphysical. That's a big step. I'm satisfied creatively. There's a lot of things in it that I'm very proud of. I love the performances of Dr. Crews and Tina. I think Kane Hodder became the definitive Jason and is a force to be reckoned with. And I love the final battle between Jason and Tina. And now, it actually has a new life on video and DVD. Groups get together and watch these things.

In the end, all you can do is take the resources that you have available to you, and make the best picture you can.

8.

Terror in Times Square

1988 had been a year of mixed blessings for Jason Voorhees. His seventh cinematic adventure, *The New Blood*, narrowly survived a highly compressed production schedule and the cutting blades of the MPAA ratings board before landing atop the box office charts in its opening weekend. But the film was still unable to reach the profit levels of some of the earlier installments of the franchise. Even more disconcerting for the producers and Paramount Pictures, *Part VII* came in a distant second to *A Nightmare on Elm Street 4*, the latest bloody offering from Jason's biggest rival, Freddy Krueger. Yet even if the box office edge of Jason's slashing machete had dulled slightly, the outlook was still good for the future of *Friday the 13th*. All seven films in the series remained highly-profitable motion pictures whose core audience showed little intention of abandoning their favorite franchise. Its durable (if not already shopworn) formula also proved that it could withstand the injection of fresh creative ideas, including supernatural elements, bigger action sequences and even ironic satire. Moreover, the syndicated television drama *Friday the 13th: The Series* continued to fly high in the ratings, a success that, with or without Jason, only helped to increase the awareness of the *Friday the 13th* brand.

Yet no one in "Camp Jason" could deny that the film series, however enduring, needed to take even greater risks if it was to remain relevant as a new decade approached and anything resembling the 1980's already began to look passe. Many of the young fans that had grown up on the early *Friday the 13th* films were now well into adulthood—dealing with real-world issues and concerns, perhaps even starting families of their own. For many, the terrors experienced by the flighty and flirtatious teens in *Friday the 13th* were now but mere footnotes to their past adolescent angst. The once Jason-hungry teens of the early 1980s had, both literally and figuratively, graduated to the horrors of a much larger world. How Jason could continue to terrify "Generation Y" was a question left for the creators of *Friday the 13th Part VIII* to solve.

ROB HEDDEN, Director and Screenwriter: Around 1987, I was writing for a show called *MacGyver* when the producers of the *Friday the 13th* television series offered me an opportunity to write an episode for them. And I said, "I'd love to, but I want to direct it, too." They said, "No, we already have directors. We just need you to write." I insisted, and didn't hear anything for about two months. Then I got a call from Barbara Sachs, one of the show's producers, and she said, "We start shooting in four weeks, and we don't have any scripts. We need you to come in and help us." I said, "I really, really want to. But I want to direct." She said, "Fine, fine. We'll give you one."

I loved working on *The Series*. Frank was fabulous. Frank let every director make his own little movie. He turned all of us loose, saying, "Go for it!" And one day, while I was shooting an episode called "Thirteen O'Clock," Frank Jr. brought his dad to the set. And I shook his hand and I was all enthusiastic. "We're doing this subway shot, and time's going to stop, and everything's going to go into black and white, then she's going to step out and everything is going to go back to color!" Then I went off and didn't think too much about it. Then a few weeks later, Frank Jr. literally just called me and said, "How would you like to write and direct the next *Friday the 13th* feature?"

In retrospect, there must have been half a dozen other guys up for the job. So maybe bringing his father down was a kind of audition, I don't know. But on the *The Series* I was doing stuff differently, and I think they were ready to do a different kind of *Friday the 13th* movie.

JOHN CARL BUECHLER, Director, *Part VII*: I was omitted from the eighth one. Phil Scuderi was at the first screening of *Part VII* at Paramount, and he said, "Oh, you've got to do all of them. You're great!" And then I was not allowed to see him again. Barbara Sachs kind of blackballed me after that, because I did what I did in *Part VII*—I gave fans a look at Jason they wouldn't have gotten otherwise.

I would have stayed with the franchise, I would have done more. And I would have gone creepier with a *Part VIII*. My idea was that Tina has been committed to a mental hospital, because everyone thinks she was the one who killed everybody in *Part VII*. But her boyfriend Nick is back too, saying, "No, it wasn't her!" And then, of course, Jason returns and he's killing everybody, and finally there's a big showdown. That would have been a hell of a movie. But what do you call it? "Friday the 13th Part VII—Vol. 2?" So maybe I would have even tried to involve aspects of the other sequels in it. But I would have loved to have done that.

KANE HODDER, "Jason Voorhees": The two characters I wished they would bring back were, of course, Betsy Palmer, and Lar. Those two, out of all of 'em, would be the ones most fans wanted to see, even in cameos. The character of Tina was just so well received—nobody ever battled Jason like that.

LAR PARK LINCOLN, "Tina," *Part VII*: Fans always want to know why I didn't do *Part VIII*. I was asked, but we never got past the negotiations. They offered so little money that my manager at the time was like, "You are going to have such a problem being typed, so let's try to get a little more." And we weren't asking for the moon. But Paramount, of course, wouldn't pay for anything.

I actually wrote a script for *Part VIII* and pitched it to Frank. It had Tina growing into a psychologist, and she's now helping young people who have gone through similar mental problems, but survived. And, of course, Jason comes back. It was quite cool, and my husband and I had a ball writing it together. But then the offer came in and it was so pathetic. And a woman named Barbara something was one of the producers, and she said, "That's not what we are planning on doing with a *Part VIII*." So they went in a different direction. But we had big hopes with a *Part VIII* of really continuing Tina's story.

KEVIN SPIRTAS, "Nick," *Part VII*: I actually wrote a really great spec script for a *Part VIII*. It was a vehicle for me. My take was that *Part VII* was all a dream, and I killed off Lar Park Lincoln. I don't know if it would have been a Jason movie in the traditional sense, but it definitely would be great to have tried it. I still want to sell it at some point.

ROB HEDDEN: When I got the call to do the movie, I wasn't the equivalent of a *Friday the 13th* Trekkie. So the first thing I did was watch all seven of the previous movies. I especially liked the first one, and though all of the sequels have their moments, I really loved *Part VI*. Yet even if I hadn't seen all the movies, by the time of *Part VIII*, everybody knew what it was about. It was in the public vernacular. So I wanted to deliver what was expected by the fans, but also something fresh. I thought, "There's a responsibility that comes with this, but at the same time, what can I do differently than the other directors had before me?"

I pitched to Frank and Barbara in his office. I said, "Can I take Jason out of Crystal Lake? Can we take him and put him in a big city?" And Frank says, "Oh, *Jason Takes Manhattan*." I said, "God, that's brilliant! I can see the ad campaign. It's going to be great!" Because I wasn't even thinking New York. I was just thinking in a broader scope. Then they asked, "How are we going to get him to New York?" So I said, "The kids of Crystal Lake are going to take a cruise for their graduation. And no one knows exactly where Crystal Lake is anyway—it's close enough to New York that they'll buy a cruise." They all loved that. Frank said, "Cruise ship, great!"

The way I envisioned it, for the first third of the movie we'd be on the boat, then we'd get to New York at the end of Act I. Everything about New York was going to be completely exploited and milked. There was going to be a tremendous scene on the Brooklyn Bridge. A boxing match in Madison Square Garden. Jason would go through department stores. He'd go through Times Square. He'd go into a Broadway play. He'd even crawl onto the top of the Statue of Liberty and dive off. Of course, just about none of that made it into the movie.

RANDOLPH CHEVELDAVE, Producer: *Jason Takes Manhattan* was my first producing credit. I had met Frank Mancuso, Jr. kind of out of the blue, when he phoned me about locations for a project he had called *April Fool's Day*. He and the director, Fred Walton, were not able to find anything suitable in Vancouver, so I took them around Victoria, and indeed there was one place that was perfect—it looked like it had been designed for the script. I ended up the production manager on that show.

Frank and I had gotten along quite well, so years later when he was contemplating producing *Friday Part VIII* up in Canada, he called me and said, "Do you think this movie could be done in Vancouver?" But at that point there was no script, just a ten or twelve page outline that Rob Hedden had written. And Rob was signed to take it from outline to script, and if everybody was happy, then he would be assigned to direct it. And at that point, at least the outline I saw, it was only at Jason on a cruise ship, and the Manhattan part came in later. Then as I remember it, when Rob came back with the final script, all that was left was Manhattan. So it was decided, because of budgetary reasons, to only include Manhattan a little bit.

ROB HEDDEN: That is the one thing everybody says, that it is not "Jason Takes Manhattan," it's "Jason Takes a Cruise Ship." And I agree. But in my first outline it was flopped the other way. It had all this great New York stuff in it. Then the preliminary budget people took a look at it and said, "We're only going to give you $4 million to make this movie. You can't do all this. You're going to get one week in New York, if you're lucky, and the rest is going to be shot in the cheapest place we can find." And that was Vancouver. So I said, "Okay, we'll make Vancouver look like New York and we'll do it that way." But they came back again with, "You can't do the Brooklyn Bridge in Vancouver. You can't do Madison Square Garden in Vancouver. You can't do the Statue of Liberty in Vancouver." Pretty soon it was half New York, half on the boat. Then it was the last third in New York. It just kept getting whittled down and down.

Opposite/Below: Director Rob Hedden on the Vancouver set of *Jason Takes Manhattan*. Hedden had directed several episodes of *Friday the 13th: The Series* when producer Frank Mancuso, Jr., selected him to helm *Part VIII* of the theatrical film series.

FRANK MANCUSO, JR., President, Hometown Films: We were not in the position to shoot the whole movie in New York because, quite simply, we didn't have the money to do it. And no one ever thought about asking for more, because the reason the movies were making profits was because we were able to control the costs. The budgets for the *Friday the 13th* movies were always determined by the box office of the previous film, and what we thought we'd get on the new one.

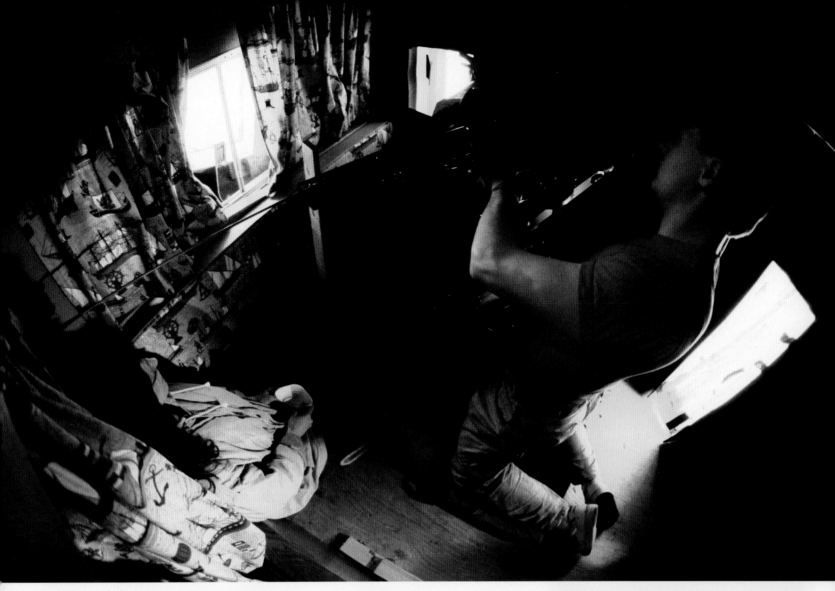

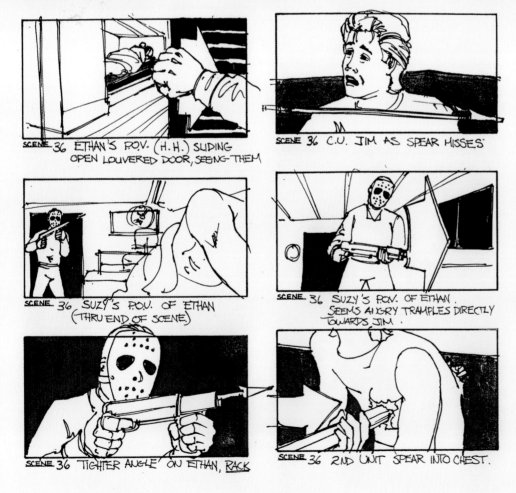

SCENE 36 ETHAN'S P.O.V. (H.H.) SLIDING OPEN LOUVERED DOOR, SEEING THEM

SCENE 36 C.U. JIM AS SPEAR MISSES

SCENE 36 SUZY'S P.O.V. OF ETHAN (THRU END OF SCENE)

SCENE 36 SUZY'S P.O.V. OF ETHAN. SEEMS ANGRY TRAMPLES DIRECTLY TOWARDS JIM.

SCENE 36 TIGHTER ANGLE ON ETHAN, RACK

SCENE 36 2ND UNIT SPEAR INTO CHEST.

Left: Rob Hedden's original storyboards for the opening sequence of *Jason Takes Manhattan*. Like many of the murder sequences in *Part VIII*, the MPAA ratings board would require extensive cuts before it would award the film an R rating.

But the opportunity was there to use the idea of New York—a monster in an urban center. That became the whole reason to make a *Part VIII*. It was a concept piece that we could let Rob run with. And we really liked Rob. He had directed a couple of episodes of *The Series*, and we all thought he did some really good work on it. And I felt he deserved a chance to break through on the feature side and this could be his shot.

MICHAEL SHEEHY, VP Creative Affairs, Hometown Films: To be honest, I don't remember how or why we ended up in New York. To me, it would have been more interesting to have the whole movie take place on a cruise ship, because it's such a confined area. Look at *Dead Calm*—that was a phenomenal film.

ROB HEDDEN: If I had already been in the ring a few times, I may have had the balls to say, "I'm not going to make a movie called *Jason Takes Manhattan* when only a half hour of the movie takes place in New York." But I was a first-time director who was thrilled to be doing a movie. And I was, and still am, a very can-do kind of person. When somebody says to me, "You've got this amount of money and this is what you can do," my answer is, "I'm going to do it. I can do it. I will do it. I'll make it the best movie I can make." And that's what I said. But I also said, "For the record, I think it should be more New York." And Frank replied, "You're right—it should be more New York. But we can't." I was not even about to walk away from it. It was too good of an opportunity. And I was excited. And I had all these great ideas. "Fine, we'll make this boat the centerpiece. We'll do a disco on the boat. We'll do all this great stuff."

I think any person out there making films considers every choice they make and wonders, "Is this going to hurt me or help me?" But at the same time, I couldn't have been more excited and thrilled to be given the opportunity. I've done a lot of stuff before and since where you mention the title and the reaction is, "I didn't see that." But there's instant recognition with *Friday the 13th*. I knew that having this franchise behind you would be a wonderful thing. These are classic movies and they'll be scaring people for generations. So I only had to doubt it for half a second: "Hmmm, am I making a mistake? No. I'm the luckiest guy on Earth!"

Production on Jason Takes Manhattan *officially set sail on February 8, 1989, in one of the most picturesque provinces of Canada—Vancouver, British Columbia. One of the challenges of casting any* Friday the 13th *has always been finding a group of talented young hopefuls on the verge of their first break who could play genuine, believable teenagers within the constrains of the formulaic plot requirements. But* Jason Takes Manhattan *would prove a particularly unique journey, combining both American and Canadian talent and setting cast and crew adrift on a luxury cruise liner for what became an exhausting, nearly three-month, shoot.*

Writer/director Rob Hedden also chose to cast his lead actress—the resilient, beautiful, yet troubled "final girl" who ultimately reveals a past connection to Jason—somewhat against the established "blonde and plucky" Friday the 13th *stereotype. But among the sea of fresh new faces, at least one familiar passenger was back on board. Kane Hodder would become the first actor ever to don the world-famous hockey mask more than once. Kane's enthusiastic and always menacing portrayal of Jason ensured that the graduating class of Crystal Lake High would have the voyage of their lives.*

ROB HEDDEN: Every character in this movie is not just some random choice. They are all people who are reflective of what I thought was going on in teenage America at that time. And that is something that is not, of course, my brilliant new idea—it has been around in all seven *Fridays* prior to mine.

In casting, I was looking for actors that I felt the audience could relate to—the trick being, of course, to find new talent who don't look too old and aren't too polished. And, too, are they going to be fun to work with? Because you don't want to be stuck on a ship for a couple of months with people that are going to make your life miserable.

JENSEN DAGGETT, "Rennie": I always just assumed that I would be an actor, because I worshiped my grandmother growing up, and she had been an actor before she got married. Her first film was *Gone With the Wind*—a little more impressive than my first film role. So I pursued theatre in high school and loved it. And when I turned eighteen, I moved to L.A. and studied with Stella Adler at her conservatory in Hollywood. I was also lucky enough to have crashed an audition with a casting director that liked me enough to get me an interview with a wonderful agent. After I signed with her, she sent me to a meeting with one of the top managers in Hollywood. I had an incredible team right off the bat—I was feeling that the whole world was open to me, and the sky was the limit. I felt like I was exactly where I was meant to be.

I remember the audition for *Part VIII* well. I met Rob Hedden and spoke for a moment about what they were looking for, and then read the audition scenes. After that, I literally had a "scream test." They asked me to scream several different ways on camera. I went all out and they seemed impressed with my vocal cords and my reading. I left there feeling pretty confident. And I had grown up watching the series, so when they called me to let me know that I had gotten the role, I was excited, even though honestly, it was not really the kind of film I had imagined doing when I moved to Hollywood. But I thought, "Okay, not everybody gets to say that they killed Jason."

ROB HEDDEN: You'd be surprised who auditioned. Renee Estevez came in. Michelle Pfieffer's younger sister, Dee Dee. Pamela Anderson, too. And Elizabeth Berkley. Elizabeth had the look, the body, the sex appeal, but there was something that was…I don't know. She was great. I can't say anything negative about anybody who didn't get the part.

But Rennie is this sympathetic innocent girl who's got this troubled past and you want to feel for her right from the get-go. How do you find innocence in Hollywood? But Jensen came in and, you know, it's so subjective, but she had that innocence and those eyes. Even her skin glowed. She had the tears, this kind of sensuous look, and the camera loved her. She was vulnerable. Plus, at the end of the day, you have to ask yourself, "Am I attracted to her?" You've got to be able to answer, "Yes."

MARTIN CUMMINS, "Wayne": In Canada in the 1980s, any movies you were getting down in the United States we'd be getting up here, too. The big American promotion machine rolls right on up. So everyone knew *Friday the 13th*—it wasn't just a American thing. But in Vancouver, at that point, they didn't do a lot of movies here yet. It was predominately a television town. Now, of course, we get plenty of big pictures up here. But back then, this was a very big deal. And I was nineteen and this was my first movie, so it was very exciting.

I went in and read for the role and it was kind of funny that I got it. Because I have never done anything like this character, before or since. I usually play the harder-edge kind of guy. Even his name—Wayne—was comical. And it was no secret that he was the character who was probably the closest to Rob Hedden himself. Rob even told me that. It was funny to be on the set, with Rob behind the camera directing me, and I'm standing there with this massive video camera that was the equivalent of one of those old brick-sized cell phones. It was a totally hilarious case of art imitating life imitating art.

Top: Although many of the graphic effects in *Jason Takes Manhattan* were heavily trimmed to earn an R rating, one sequence was completely reshot. "In the original cut, the boxer is killed by Jason shoving darts in his eyes," reveals producer Randolph Cheveldave. "But after we saw the finished film, we just thought the kill was too disappointing for the diehard *Friday the 13th* audience." Following the completion of principal photography, director Rob Hedden went back and filmed a gorier demise for the character. "I wrote a new scene," says Hedden. "Now, the boxer goes into a sauna, and Jason comes and takes a hot rock and burns it through his chest. The funny thing is, though, Kane Hodder was no longer available to play Jason, so we had to get a different stuntman. We even took Polaroids of Kane to better match his replacement. I think that's the only scene in the whole film that Kane's not in."

Opposite: *Jason Takes Manhattan* was the first *Friday the 13th* film to make extensive use of such special effects techniques as blue screen, minatures and rotoscoping. Many of the film's complex shipwreck sequences were filmed in a specially-built tank that could pump over 3,000 gallons of water per hour. Actor Gordon Currie's death scene was completed by placing a blue screen rig behind a re-creation of a portion of the ship's upper deck.

ROB HEDDEN: It's funny sometimes where the inspiration for characters, and character names, come from. In Studio City, there used to be this place called the Queen Mary, a drag club. My wife thought it was the funniest place. And there was this guy there who did Tina Turner and all these women. And his name was Julius. We just loved him because he was so funny. So the image of this big black guy named Julius just stuck in my head. I thought, "Julius—I'm going to use that name someday!"

V.C. DUPREE, "Julius": *Part VIII* was my first starring role. From what I heard, they had been looking around at a lot of other big cities for this particular character, because they wanted someone with boxing experience and a street edge kind of thing. And I'm not a big guy—5'10" and like 160 pounds. So there I am in the audition with all these local boxers who were way bigger than I was. I had like four layers of sweatshirts on and was really trying to fake it. And after the reading, Rob was like, "Awesome! I felt the character. You nailed it. But you're not fooling anybody. How long would it take you to get some meat on you?" From there on out, all I did was eat until the movie started.

The funny thing, prior to *Part VIII*, is that I didn't have any knowledge of the horror genre. I didn't even know that I was going to shoot a *Friday the 13th* until I was at the airport. At first the movie was called "Burial at Sea," and then "Ashes to Ashes." So I was in the little first-class area waiting to board, and Kelly Hu comes up to me and says, "Hey, are you going up to shoot *Friday the 13th*?" I said, "Am I what!?" That's when I put two and two together—all I knew was that they were going to pay me to go beat up some killer.

KELLY HU, "Eva": I was born and raised in Hawaii. I pretty much told my mother that I was moving to Hollywood to be a superstar when I was four years old—I didn't know there was another word for "actor." But I would have done it for free. I loved performing. I took ballet when I was a kid and jazz and acrobatics—anything that gave me an audience. Acting was just sort of in my blood.

Part VIII was my very first film ever. I auditioned for it while I was in L.A. and they flew me up to Vancouver. The only apprehension I had was that right after I got it, I was at dinner with Martin Sheen—I'm a friend of his son, Ramon—and we'd just gotten back from church. Ramon said, "Oh, Dad, Kelly's doing a movie! She's going to do a *Friday the 13th*!" Then I got lectured for like three hours, because Martin thought it was very evil. But I was so excited to be doing my first movie that even listening to Martin Sheen wasn't going to change my mind.

PETER MARK RICHMAN, "Charles McCullough": I was a New York actor—you know, an "Actor's Studio" person. And I was very sincere and hard working in developing my craft, much different than what kids do today. Rob Hedden really wanted me. And reluctantly, I did an on-camera thing for him, because for a long period of time—thirty years or so—I never auditioned. I never had to. I could just read the script and say yes or no. Then about fifteen or twenty years ago the business changed tremendously. The corporations got involved, the networks got involved, and then they started to audition people for five lines. Twenty-five actors up for one stupid part. I resisted because I thought it was below my dignity. So for a long period of time I just did not work like I used to work. But with *Friday*, my agent said that there was keen interest, so I met Rob, who is very persuasive and personable, and the next thing I know I'm auditioning.

I had never seen any of the films—they weren't high on my pecking order. It was not something where I was going to say, "Oh boy, *Friday the 13th*!" To me, this was secondary stuff. But it was a paycheck. And I was very well paid.

ROB HEDDEN: Casting Kane Hodder was one of those no-brainer kind of things. Frank and Barbara said to me, "You're the director, and if you want to cast somebody different as Jason, you should." But I'm not some guy that has to be king and say, "I have to change this just because I can, because I'm God." It's ridiculous. A good director relies on the talent of the people he or she has chosen to work on their movie. Frank and Barbara did have another guy in mind, a Canadian stuntman. They said, "Kane's great. But maybe if we get a guy up in Canada instead, we can save a few bucks." I said, "Well, yeah, but Kane knows the lore. And I'm the new kid coming in here, right? I didn't direct the last seven movies. I'm getting up to speed like everybody else." So I went with Kane.

KANE HODDER: Barbara Sachs was the one who told me they might go with a Canadian stuntman for *Part VIII*. I said, "No, I want to do it!" And she said, "Oh, really? I didn't realize that." If I had not made that call, I never would have done another Jason. I would have been like all the other guys who just did one movie. I had to push for it, but at the same time, Rob Hedden had seen *Part VII* and liked what I did.

Really, at that point, I didn't even care what the story was. I just wanted to play the character again. And it wasn't a money thing, because they certainly didn't pay me any more the second time. In fact, the only time I ever got anything decent was on *Jason X*. But I never really cared because I enjoyed playing the character so much.

ROB HEDDEN: The irony of shooting *Part VIII* was that the first half takes place on this huge cruise ship, and three days before filming we ended up losing the boat we were supposed to shoot on due to a scheduling mix-up. We had to find another boat at the last minute, and that one was half the size. I basically lived on this new boat for the weekend before filming and walked it and planned all my shots. And since it was now half the size of what was originally planned, the trick was to make it look twice as big. So that is why you never see the ship all in one shot—you see the front half, the back half, the deck. Then we used a different ship for the interiors, including the disco, kitchen, and some sets built on a stage. Ultimately, I think we succeeded, but it was an incredibly stressful situation.

RANDOLPH CHEVELDAVE: After the first boat fell through, we had an old cruise ship that used to fly the inside passage between Vancouver and Alaska called the *Prince George*. At the time it was owned by an eminent British Columbia entrepreneur named Nelson Scalbania, and had been sitting idle for a number of years, tied up to a wharf. And it could not move, the engines weren't functioning, and it needed a lot of work done to it before it could even be tugged by tugboat. But it gave us engine rooms and some terrific corridors, so we talked to Mr. Scalbania, and he agreed we could use it, and not only that, he didn't really want a lot of money for it. He said, "A dollar, to make it legal." Hey, alright! But what we didn't know was that he owed this enormous debt for

wharfing fees. I mean this is a four-hundred foot ship that had been tied up in the same spot for over two years. So when we started talking with the people who owned the wharfs, they were falling all over themselves helping us. Until they discovered that the fee for the use of the ship was a dollar, and then they stopped. So suddenly, our access to that ship was limited to the most bizarre hours. It put us on a night schedule right from the very beginning which created real problems in terms of shooting.

DAVID FISCHER, Production Designer: Prior to *Jason Takes Manhattan*, I'd worked as an art director on *Roxanne*, the Steve Martin movie. Then, out of the blue, I got a call from Randy Cheveldave. I had never even seen a *Friday the 13th* film, but I went and rented a couple of them, and from a design point of view, they posed interesting challenges. Especially, "Let's come up with some clever ways to kill people!"

Jason Takes Manhattan was also exciting creatively because it was more unique. Certainly, the ship was one of our major tasks. We had one practical ship that was in the water, a second ship that was sitting in a dry dock, and a third ship we'd use for certain interior scenes. We even built part of a boat on stage for some interiors, and then there were other sets built across town for other interiors. The real challenge was keeping it all together to make sure it all felt like the same ship. That is probably what I'm most proud of in the film. I hope we fooled the audience.

RANDOLPH CHEVELDAVE: The *Lazarus* was the other ship in the movie, and it's about half the size of the *Prince George*. And when we came to use it, it had been recently won in a poker game in Washington, and the new owner didn't know what the heck to do with it. Getting it into Canada was a huge headache, because there were all these Canadian boats that were available, so the only way to use it legally was to import a load of potatoes with the ship. Here we are supposed to be shooting a movie, and now we're a potato delivery service!

ROB HEDDEN: The *Prince George* just had to be haunted. It was an old abandoned ship with all these art deco interiors. The inside was like the maze in *The Shining*—it was spooky. And it

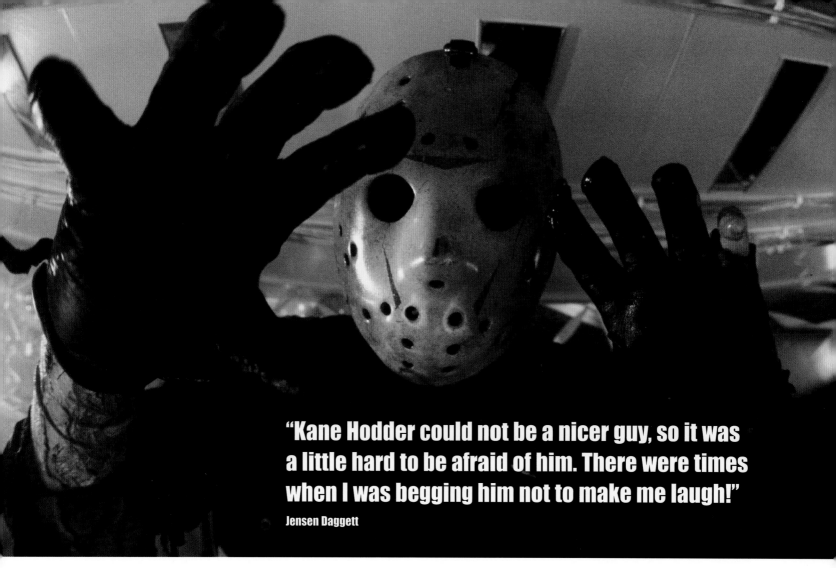

"Kane Hodder could not be a nicer guy, so it was a little hard to be afraid of him. There were times when I was begging him not to make me laugh!"
Jensen Daggett

was listing to one side. One time when the tide changed, the ramp came apart and we had to literally jump across to get off the boat. It was almost like the ship didn't want us to leave.

MARTIN CUMMINS: We filmed in Britannia, a bit north of Vancouver. The main ship we shot on was moored off of this old, abandoned mining town. On one side of the highway was this eerie ghost town, with this big old boat hanging off the other side. I think one of the reasons so many science fiction and horror movies and TV shows are shot in Vancouver is because there's constant rain, and this really desolate feeling. Even though we were on the ship most of the time, it was like we were out on the road to nowhere. It was always kind of creepy. Especially since no one is driving by at two o'clock in the morning when you're shooting. You're alone, and always aware of it.

PETER MARK RICHMAN: We shot it in Vancouver for seven weeks and it rained for six. We worked our bloody asses off. It was murder. It was freezing cold. I had to wear a wet suit underneath my clothes and I must have looked twenty pounds heavier in the film than I really am. It really was one of the toughest shoots I have ever had.

But the nice thing was that the one week my wife came up, the sun came out, and shone every day she was there. And as soon as she left, it rained.

KANE HODDER: One unique thing about playing Jason in *Part VIII* was that for every single shot they had to lay on more slime. I was supposed to look like I had just emerged from Crystal Lake after being waterlogged for however long. And the goop would soak through my costume and I was like a giant slimy sponge. There's this one scene where I'm walking down a steep flight of stairs toward the girl who's playing the guitar. These are tiny steps, and

I've got these big-ass boots on—I have big feet. And I have to walk without looking down. So I'm walking down these steps, and I'm holding my hand back to grab the rail but hiding it from the camera. That was very hard. But I turned to walk away and slipped right off the ground. And because they put the slime on me to make it look glistening, I hit the deck right on my ass.

KELLY HU: Mine was such a small role that, to be honest, I don't think they gave it much attention. There was not a lot of guidance there. But they did teach me how to snort cocaine for the "coke scene." I had never seen it before, and I certainly had never seen anyone do it. So they had to have one of the set guys build this special straw with this netting through it, and then I'd snort baking soda or something. The idea was that I'd snort it up through this metal straw and the baking soda would be caught in the net. But I could never get enough vacuumage. So then they built this other contraption—it looked like I was holding the straw, but it was actually attached to this rubber tube on the side. As I was snorting this baking soda, some guy at the other end of this tube would be inhaling it. That was a thoroughly bizarre experience.

RANDOLPH CHEVELDAVE: I've been on an awful lot of movie sets throughout the drug craze of the late 1970s and early '80s, but this was a clean set. The only drugs happening were on the screen. People had to work too hard. The entire cast was excellent. We all had a really great time. We truly did.

JENSEN DAGGETT: We were like one big shipwrecked family. We were all just so happy to be up in Vancouver working on such a nutty film. Really, we were like kids in a candy store, beginning our careers and thinking it would always be this easy and this much fun. And this may be unusual for a film with a bunch of aspiring young actors, but we really were all very supportive and

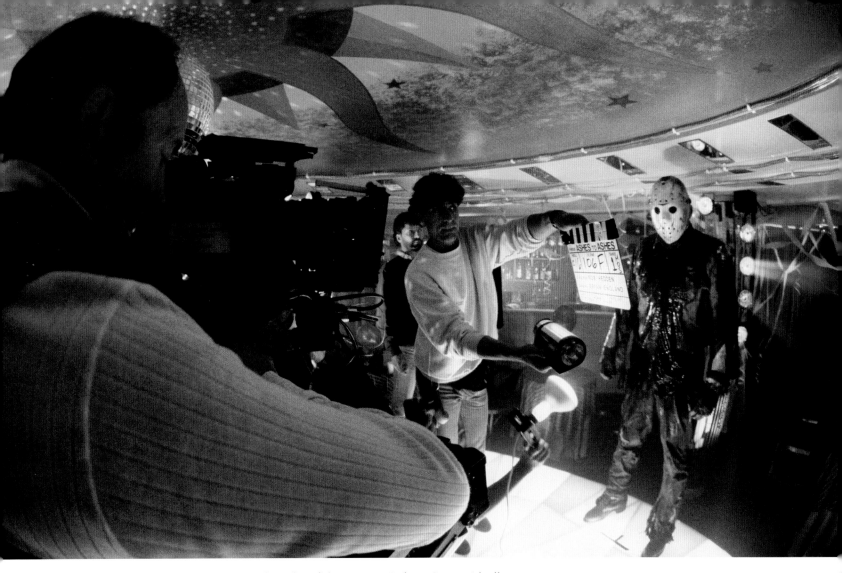

encouraging of each other. I remember a lot of shopping on Robson Street with all of the girls. Then Scott Reeves got engaged to his girlfriend and everyone was pitching in with ideas about how to do it, and where.

ROB HEDDEN: The tough thing with Jensen was that she was extremely reluctant—even adamant—about not taking her clothes off. I worked on her and worked on her, because the studio wanted her to get naked. I was like, "I totally see your side of it, Jensen. I know you want to have a serious acting career." Then I brought up all these examples of big actresses who took their clothes off. It didn't work, of course. Then I was like, "You've at least got to take your blouse off, okay? If you don't, they're going to riot in the theater. This is called *Friday the 13th*—it's not called *Driving Miss Daisy*!" But that didn't work, either.

It's really tough. You want to do the right thing by everybody. There's an obligation as a director to not exploit your cast, and at the same time make your producers and the studio happy. They were like, "Bigger boobs! More nudity! More naked violence!" Often it comes down to you standing there on a set at 2:00 a.m. with a beautiful young girl who's thrilled to have the job, but if you're a good person you're not going to use that.

I have the fondest memories of Sharlene Martin, who played Tamara. There was a shower scene written for her character right before Jason shows up. Well, Sharlene was a sweetheart but very, very nervous about getting naked. I said, "Sharlene, I'm not going to shoot this in a way that is a tight close-up with bright lights on your breasts, okay? I want this to be scary and I want it to be sexy and I want it to be titillating, but I don't want it to be sleazy. So I'm going to show you how it's going to look." She climbs out of the shower and goes and stands by the camera, and suddenly I take off all my clothes and I get in, and I do the scene. I start singing in the shower, moving my arms around and steam is coming up, and of course the whole crew is laughing. Then I come out of the shower and put my clothes back on and go, "See?" And she says, "Sold!"

RANDOLPH CHEVELDAVE: I can vividly remember how quickly Sharlene became fine with nudity. It was kind of like, within ten seconds of taking off her clothes, everything was normal again. And Rob has a hairy butt.

Above: "I really made a conscious effort to do something different with my death scene," remembers actress Kelly Hu. "I did not want to scream, because I didn't want to be the girl in the *Friday the 13th* movie who screams the whole way through. So instead, I made a lot of grunting noises and panicked sounds. But, of course, after the film wrapped, they brought in another girl during the looping sessions to dub me. I don't think they ever noticed that I wasn't screaming until they were putting the movie together. So none of the screams in the movie are really me."

"I liked Rennie because she begins the film a little repressed and unsure of herself, and is forced to become strong overnight. Or, to be more exact, over a weekend." Jensen Daggett

ROB HEDDEN: What I didn't know is that our director of photography Bryan England had decided to roll film. And the whole thing gets printed as dailies and sent back to Paramount. And the next day all the executives are watching to see if the director is doing his job and there he is, naked on the set. And they're like, "What the fuck is going on up there?" Believe me, they never let me forget it.

The specter of Freddy Krueger weighed heavily on the mind of Rob Hedden as he conceptualized Jason Takes Manhattan. *If Part VIII was going to compete—and beat—the more audacious* Nightmare on Elm Street *films, it needed more fantastical special effects and imaginative visuals. Transplanting Jason and his unique brand of carnage to a new locale would not be enough. Part of Hedden's solution was to give his heroine a series of flashbacks and hallucinations that would allow the film to not only further explore the mythology of Jason Voorhees, but deliver the audience the kinds of unexpected shocks and creative scares they had never seen before in a* Friday the 13th *film. Unfortunately, the cost of such ambitions often stretched the film's limited budget to its breaking point, eventually causing* Jason Takes Manhattan *to go overbudget and overschedule. But even with the sudden replacement of the film's lead actor and enough subplots left on the cutting room floor to fill three other* Friday the 13ths, *frayed nerves and bruised egos still wouldn't sink this voyage of the damned.*

RANDOLPH CHEVELDAVE: I think that Rob is a strange choice to direct a *Friday the 13th* movie. He does not have a dark side. Rob is a very happy guy. I would think horror would be the last genre he would be chosen for. Witness his last success, the family film *Clockstoppers*. That strikes me as exactly the kind of thing Rob wants to do.

Part VIII is definitely lighter than the other *Friday* movies. Rob and I agreed that we did not want to get really graphic with any of the violence, that we would rather creep people out with what they thought they might see rather than revolt with the amount of blood. We wanted them to be scared of the movie, not be scared of their reaction to the movie. I think that whole attitude is largely Rob.

ROB HEDDEN: We made this movie at the time when *A Nightmare on Elm Street* was really taking off. There was pressure from Frank and the studio: "Hey, freshen your movie up." That's what they did with *Nightmare*—they took an old genre and they added a new spin on it. And I thought those movies were very clever, very creative. So there are shades of supernatural and sci-fi in *Friday VIII*. There's the whole thing with Rennie seeing the ghost of young Jason, where she's hearing voices, all her delusions, and the way he dies at the end—which may or may not be in her mind. I wanted the audience to wonder of the things they were seeing, "Is this real, or is it Rennie's imagination?"

RANDOLPH CHEVELDAVE: There was one flashback scene where they were contemplating flushing Jason down a giant toilet. I actually had to argue very hard with Rob and Bryan England not to do it. And from my point of view, this was footage that would be very expensive to obtain, and all we're going to do it leave it on the cutting room floor. I thought that was pretty stupid.

ROB HEDDEN: What we did for the amount of money that we had! The thing about this movie, regardless of the story or the

direction, is that we really tried to up the production value and make it look like a real movie, as opposed to an inexpensive slasher flick.

Bryan England wasn't a famous DP but he was phenomenally enthusiastic. He hand-carried his reels to the meeting so he could show us his stuff. He was passionate. Then we looked at this film he shot, *I, Madman*. I was like, "I don't know where this guy came from, I don't know anything about him, but this is what I want my film to look like!" The color saturation, the lighting quality—there was no grain in it, it was lush, it looked gorgeous. And after he came onboard, I wasn't disappointed. Usually in these movies, it's like, "Let's shoot it quick and move on to the next setup." But Bryan would paint with light, and took his time with every shot. That included the effects—he never rushed any of it.

BRYAN ENGLAND, Director of Photography: One day, Rob came to me and said, "Bryan, I want a point of view shot of a dismembered head!" It was for the death scene of the boxer, who gets his head knocked off by Jason on top of the roof. Well, how are we going to do that? So we found this company in Canada that makes Nerf balls. We had them create a giant four foot by four foot Nerf ball we could put the camera in, and we just threw it right off the roof. Every time it bounced down into a giant trash bin, the whole crew just went, "Score!" We called it the "Nerf-cam." We were always coming up with crazy things like that.

MARTIN CUMMINS: The great thing about Rob is that there's no mystery with him. Oftentimes, directors can be afraid of actors and their crew, or they can feel like they have to talk to you in some kind of very deep and philosophical, fucked-up language. I don't need that, and most actors don't, especially when you're young. You just need you to tell me what you want and I'll do that. Rob was very passionate, but he was never pretentious about it. He knew what he was shooting and that we all should be having fun. And he kept any of the above-board tensions away from the actors; he protected us.

STEVE MIRKOVICH, Editor: I was just getting my career going. I had done a few pictures, starting with a thing called *River Rat* and a co-editing credit on *Flight of the Intruder*. Then I did *Big Trouble In Little China* and *Prince of Darkness* for John Carpenter. Then came *Jason Takes Manhattan*. Rob Hedden had called John and said, "How is this guy?" And John gave me a really good recommendation. Rob and I got along very well, and although I cannot say I was a huge *Friday the 13th* fan at that point, I thought it would be fun.

I ended up working on the film in Vancouver probably six or seven months, and the shoot was just seven or eight weeks. After wrap, Rob said, "We're gonna live with this picture, and we're gonna use every day that we have, contractually, to do it."

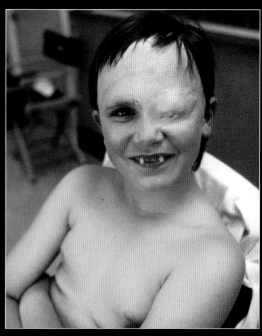

The casting of "Young Jason" in *Part VIII* proved far more calamitous than expected. The production originally hired a young Canadian actor, but the boy was unable to adequately handle the physical hardships of the film's underwater sequences. He was eventually replaced by Timothy Burr Mirkovich, the son of the film's editor, Steve Mirkovich. "No one knew how we were going to find a new actor on such short notice," recalls the elder Mirkovich. "Well, my family had come up to visit one day, and it turned out to be when the original actor playing young Jason was having trouble with one of the swimming scenes. So producer Randy Cheveldave took one look at my son and said to me, 'How would Tim feel about being the young Jason?' I said to my son, 'Timmy, it's not gonna be easy. You'll have to do some things that are hard, but you'll also be able to stay up here with me for five weeks. And you can even go on a little shopping spree at Toys 'R' Us when we're done. So, do you want to go home and go back to school, or stay up here and be a little actor?' And he just said, 'No, I wanna try it!'"

Ultimately, it was a bonding experience for father and son, although not one without its painful moments. "That scene where Jason is crying, 'Help me! Help me!' was quite a tearful day," says Mirkovich. "I know it wasn't real, but that's my son, drowning! I also watched—in agony—as they were making the whole head mask for him. All this goop over this little head, with two tiny pencil holes through the nose so he could breathe. Once, I saw his little plaster head just kind of clunk over to the side because he'd fallen asleep. But I was very proud of him."

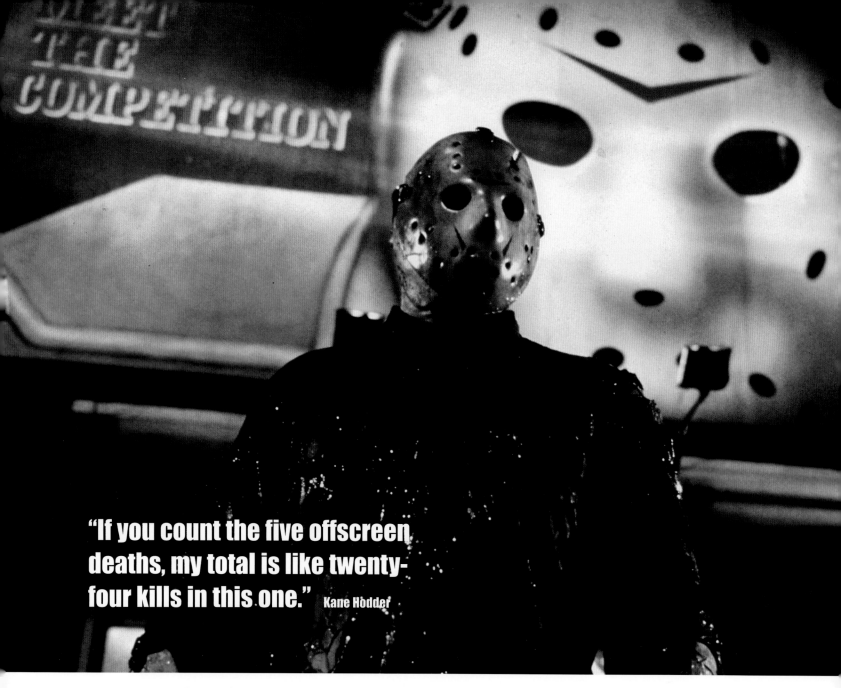

"If you count the five offscreen deaths, my total is like twenty-four kills in this one." Kane Hodder

ROB HEDDEN: The very first cut of the movie was over two hours long. Then we all looked at it, tried to be objective and decided what this movie was and was not about. And ultimately you are trying to satisfy the audience. So we decided it had to be less talk, more action. The big suspense sequences were gold, but it turned out we didn't need a lot of the character stuff I had written.

STEVE MIRKOVICH: Many times a director will be overwhelmed by the amount of film he or she has shot. I do not think I have ever worked with a director who said, "I want you to cut from here to here to here to here to here." I also do not think most directors, during the production process, can think that way, because they are shooting twelve hours a day, then spending two or three hours in their hotel room going over the shot list for the next day, trying to figure out how to solve all their problems.

Eventually, the film went overbudget. But Rob was always very communicative and very reasonable, and he was not a screamer. Which speaks greatly of him, because he had very big fish to fry during production. And, like every other filmmaker, especially a first-time director, he was under constant pressure.

BRYAN ENGLAND: There were a lot of politics on that movie, mostly for poor Randy Cheveldave. Randy got blamed for a lot of

overages, which weren't all his fault. Frank Jr. was just too busy with *Internal Affairs*, with Richard Gere and Andy Garcia, which was going to be Frank's breakthrough movie. I also felt that the original script concept, with Jason on a cruise ship, was great. Then they had the one in New York. So they just blended the two, but what happened was, instead of really going through the script and fine-tuning, it was just, "We'll figure it out on the day."

RANDOLPH CHEVELDAVE: Because there was such a hurry to get the film done, the budgeting and pre-production were done based on Rob's original outline. I only started getting involved once it was decided that Canada was the place to do it. Ordinarily, *Friday the 13th* movies were being made for about $3 million. And this one was going to get $4 million because it was an atypical entry. And by the time all was said and done, it cost about $5 million. But hey, what other *Friday the 13th* movie has a storm at sea, a sinking boat, and New York?

DAVID FISCHER: There were pressures directed at Rob from the producers, in terms of shooting only what's going to be needed on the screen. But this was his first film, and I think it's understandable that he was kind of like a kid in a candy store. It is also important to say about Rob that he wasn't just a guy doing this for the money—he was very passionate. And his energy and enthusiasm were quite high, so we were kept quite busy running

Randy's fault. It's nobody's fault. Hey, it's my fault. I'm the director. I have to take the blame to some degree. But Randy really had it the toughest because he got his ass chewed from above. There were some disagreements. But we were doing the best we could do, trying to make the best movie that we could.

RANDOLPH CHEVELDAVE: The film world, like much of the manufacturing world, is divided into blue collar and white collar. Below the line are the blue-collar guys, and above the line are the white-collar guys, and they have very, very different agendas. And when I took on *Part VIII* I had never been above the line before, and I was very nervous and very hesitant about it. And what I wasn't prepared for was that, below the line, there is a lot of camaraderie. Everybody's working toward one purpose, to make the best movie they can. Above the line, it's kind of more like some kind of club or group, where there's a bunch of people sitting around saying, "Yeah, if we did that we could make more money." It's a different environment, and certainly not an "all-for-one, one-for-all" kind of thing. Someone will knife you in the back for your job. They won't do that below the line.

I'd be surprised if I'm the first person to tell you, but Frank Mancuso, Jr. is a weird guy. I can't profess to know or ever have known the man well. I mean, he's very private, even to the point of being secretive. And Paramount was not directly involved. If they did have anything to say, they said it through Frank. And I have to be perfectly honest and say that on *Part VIII*, my contact with Frank was absolutely minimal. I don't believe he and I saw each other during the entire course of making it. He only called on the phone on occasion to ask, "Hey, how's it going?" which was probably four times during the entire production. He had a very, very hands-off approach to this one, which was quite surprising to me, because when we did *April Fool's Day* he was on the set every day. During *Part VIII*, he wasn't even in the country. But I also think that he had his hands full at the time with *Internal Affairs*. I would say that it is a fair assessment that he had his eyes on a much larger prize.

ROB HEDDEN: The times that got me were the disagreements about decisions some people wanted us to make that were morally wrong. They were either illegal or against the rules. I refused to do them. This was not long after the fatal accident on the set of the *Twilight Zone* movie, and I even brought that up in one argument I had, because a law was about to be broken—an overtime rule. The argument was, "Well, we don't have any helicopters on this movie." I said, "You're missing the point. There are going to be no accidents on this movie." I don't care if I was being paranoid about someone getting hurt. No movie is worth that. I don't care if I lose my job over it—at least I'll still be able to sleep at night.

RANDOLPH CHEVELDAVE: Many of the problems were unforeseen—just the kind of challenges that can happen when you make movies. We had to fire our original leading man one day into shooting. It wasn't originally Scott Reeves. I hadn't been involved in the original casting session, so I didn't get my first

all over the place. I'm sure, from Randy's point of view, he felt like he had his hands full, as far as keeping Rob on track and the production on schedule and on budget.

We were also trying to recreate New York City in Vancouver. That simply cost money, and it was time-intensive to go about breaking down the bits and pieces of what we needed in order to make it real and believable. Many staples of New York had to be created from scratch. The whole subway sequence—that was a big challenge. There are no subways to destroy in Vancouver, so we took an abandoned tunnel that was 1,000 feet long and ran under the city, and shipped in tons of gravel. Then we built fake subway tracks for hundreds of yards down this tunnel and built a fake subway car. And Vancouver is a pretty clean city, so here we were, going around to all these alleys and picking up garbage. We even added the graffiti. We were trying to make it all work. It was a great learning experience.

ROB HEDDEN: We were naïve and ambitious. We probably did things we shouldn't have. The problem was that the producer side of me was like, "I'd rather get more shots in the can. I can sacrifice the look a little bit to get more coverage." While the artistic side was arguing, "Oh, my God, this film is going to look gorgeous. So if it takes a little longer—if I lose a set-up or two a day—it's worth it." And that side ultimately won out.

The budget ended up being $5 million. The original expectation was about $4.2 million. It wasn't Bryan's fault. It wasn't

look at this young man onscreen until the first day of dailies came back. And he was a very nice guy, a very handsome guy. But in the dailies he just came across so gay. *So gay.* Yet in person you didn't feel that at all. It never even occurred to us

BRYAN ENGLAND: After he got fired, the boy called me that night, crying. I could see he had just gotten into the business, and he was young and scared to death. He thought he had done something wrong. He said to me, "Do you think it was because I'm gay? How am I going to explain this to my mother? My life's over." He was just wrecked by it. But it was clear after that first day that the sexual tension between him and Jensen just wasn't there. Both of these kids were as cute as buttons, but they just did not seem like boyfriend and girl-friend. He was just too sweet. So I sat with him all night, and told him he didn't do anything wrong. I felt so sorry for him. And I haven't heard from him since.

ROB HEDDEN: I was upset that I had to let anybody go. I don't even remember it being my choice. Part of me was like, "I can't bear to do this." And I don't even remember the kid. Steve Mirkovich came to me and said, "This guy is not working out." Everybody did. And they were right. For various reasons. Part of it was his look, part of it was his acting chops, part of it was his chemistry with Jensen.

"By the time *Part VIII* came along, Jason at a camp in the woods was no longer enough. It was either move him to New York or someplace else, or lose him altogether." Randolph Cheveldave

By the time of his eighth screen incarnation, Jason Voorhees was the horror film equivalent of a crash test dummy. He had been sliced, diced, hacked, slashed, pureed, burned, smashed and bashed so many times that the character had come to resemble nothing less than a lumbering, zombified human hamburger. Jason had "died" no fewer than seven times, with each successive cinematic demise designed to be more spectacular than the last. Jason's behind-the-mask visage, too, had also gone through so many metamorphoses that the challenge of creating a new look for Jason—one that could shock and surprise audiences who'd already grown accustomed to Jason's monstrous appearance—was considerable. But Rob Hedden wanted more than just another radical makeup concept and an outlandish, gory demise. He wanted to take Jason home.

ROB HEDDEN: *Part VIII* was conceivably going to be the last in the series. So I felt a real responsibility to make it a bookend to the original *Friday the 13th*. It was a daunting assignment. And the way I decided to do it was to have Jason finally die. I said to Frank very clearly: "Look, I want to kill Jason. And I want to kill him in a way that makes it feel like he's really dead and he's not coming back." And he said, "Go for it."

RANDOLPH CHEVELDAVE: Originally, Rob thought it would be a really good idea if Jason got completely melted in the toxic waste and we never saw him again. But—and as I remember it, this was Frank's idea—Jason wouldn't be completely gone; there would be something left of him. Because, of course, just in case there was another sequel, a door had to be left open a crack. Hence, the little

boy on the sewer floor at the end is supposed to be Jason, restored to who he once was before the events in the original film. I think it was a little bit of a compromise.

ROB HEDDEN: Of course, in the first film a young boy drowns and we find out it is his mother who is the one that has been killing everybody. It's not Jason. That was a great twist, but young Jason still propelled the whole thing. So in our movie, he drowns in toxic waste and turns back to that young boy. I wanted to have it come full circle. His soul has finally been released.

My intention was to set up the ending throughout the movie. That was the inspiration for Rennie's visions of the young Jason—tapping back into the first *Friday the 13th*, and the myth that Jason had drowned as a young boy and has come back to haunt and kill everybody. Rather than have a movie where people just die and there's no plot, it would all be explained in the flashback scene where Rennie is receiving a swimming lesson from her uncle. He's a mean guy and shoves her overboard to teach her to swim. And they are both aware of this whole myth of Jason still being down there. And Rennie has this total fear of the water. She literally was dragged down by Jason—it's freaked her out ever since, and now he's come back. She's having visions of him again on the ship. And it trails her all the way to the end of the movie.

Ultimately, the ending remains a controversial one. I don't know if I succeeded or failed. I'm not going to sit here and defend it and say, "My ending was total brilliance." It wasn't a simple ending. It had a little bit of thought put into it, for better or worse. But I was trying to do something different, something that would make people stop and think for a second. Yes, I took liberties with the backstory, obviously, but then so did everybody else who made these movies.

KANE HODDER: There was even a scripted line for Jason, right before all that water comes down the sewer: "Mommy, please don't let me die." The whole thing, I didn't care for it. Going back to a little kid—I just never liked it

ROB HEDDEN: Kane is a sweetheart. Then I read an interview he had done for a website a few years back, and I thought, "That doesn't sound like Kane." Because he was criticizing the ending, which he had never told me he was dissatisfied with. And he read the script. He read the ending. I discussed it with him. And he never said a word. That's what threw me. Why didn't he tell me he didn't like it? Kane is a very, very cooperative actor. Perhaps cooperative to the point that he doesn't like the ending and doesn't bother to tell me. Which now I'm mad at him for. He should have voiced his opinion, because then maybe something better may have come out of it. And there was no mystery. It was right there on the page. The studio signed off on it, Frank signed off on it, Barbara signed off on it. Everybody. Maybe that's why he never said anything?

KANE HODDER: It's probably unfair to Rob that I protested after-the-fact. I wasn't happy with it at the time, but I didn't feel secure enough in the role to say anything. I wanted to keep doing it, and I didn't want to piss anybody off. And what probably happened was that once I saw it, I disliked it more. I wasn't as unhappy with it as much while we were shooting it. It is often only after years pass that you think, "I really hated that."

ROB HEDDEN: I think another reason why the ending may not have been as well received as it could have been was because, when you do a set-up like that, you better have a pretty good payoff. The reveal of Jason's face was the scariest thing I had to do, because I'm thinking, "It took eight movies to get to this point, and we've seen his face in other movies." I had a lot to live up to. That's when I thought,

"Toxic waste! Let's melt his face and it will be great!" Because you wouldn't have time to get a good solid look at him. The idea was to camouflage the fact that he is wearing rubber and prosthetics with all this slime on it. We thought it would work.

WILLIAM TEREZAKIS, Effects Assistant: *Part VIII* was the very first movie I worked on. When I got the opportunity to work on the film, I was just so excited because I was a huge fan of *Friday the 13th* and *Nightmare on Elm Street* and *Halloween*—all the big ones. After I found out I landed the gig, I'm driving home like crazy—just shaking and screaming and honking the horn. And I so couldn't contain myself that I went right off the road, down a hill and into a ditch. But I didn't care, because I was working on a Jason movie!

I think the whole experience was what's called "paying your dues." My two bosses, Jamie Brown and the late Tibor Farkas, ran the show. I was pretty much kept in the dark during that whole movie. I wasn't allowed to go to the set. It was pretty fucked up. I didn't get an opportunity to really express myself through my art on *Part VIII*. It was just basically told, "We'll bring you the sculptures and you mold them." But at least I was working.

So I stayed in this room the whole time like a fucking hunchback. Then I see the sculpture of Jason's face. I was like, "Aw, fuck. No. No!" Because I was such a fan of the series. I knew all the previous films and all the looks of Jason. I supplied those sons of bitches with so much information on the character, and then they didn't follow it. I really liked John Buechler's design in *Part VII*, especially that he respected what had gone before. But here comes Jamie Brown, "Mr. No-Continuity," and totally takes it off track. I refer to Jason's mug in that movie as "the jack-o'-lantern"—he kind of looks like Goofy. I was definitely not happy. Especially when I wasn't allowed to sculpt it. So the whole time I was molding it, I was playing a funeral song.

ROB HEDDEN: I didn't want people to laugh when the mask came off. I didn't want it to be a big letdown. But at the same time, CGI hadn't been invented. We weren't going to have animated worms coming out of his face. We had to figure out how to do it. I had this idea of his face being melted by chemistry, where I could actually have something else going on other than just a look. So we basically put an acetone material on it, so it would bubble and melt to make it scarier than it was. And do it in a way where the lighting was kind of scary, and have him shake around a lot so you never got too good of a look at it.

BRYAN ENGLAND: No one was happy with it. I remember trying really hard to light it dark, to keep it in the shadows as much as possible. That's the main reason why, during that scene, the overhead lights in the sewer tunnel are swaying back and forth. It kind of created a strobe effect. We did that on purpose just to help cover up the makeup.

ROB HEDDEN: In retrospect, if they would have let me, I never would have shown his face at all. I think imagination is stronger than the visual anyway. I would just have gone with the *Blair Witch* philosophy: don't let them see anything. But we did everything we could, and the best we could. And we actually cut it in ways to try and accentuate the positive. At one point, we didn't show it. Then, we showed it for half as much. Then, I got a note from the studio: "No, they're going to want to see it for longer. This is what they've waited to see." So I added back another thirty-six frames. But none of these were cavalier decisions.

RANDOLPH CHEVELDAVE: I don't know if we ever got it right. But, really, what can you put under that mask so that when it finally does come off it will truly satisfy the audience? To this day, I can't think of anything that should have been there.

Whatever trials, tribulations, disasters and disappointments the makers of Jason Takes Manhattan *may have endured during the film's arduous shoot, there was one moment that would make it all worthwhile: a day that, for all those involved, ranks not only as the highlight of the whole experience of making the film, but the most memorable of their entire careers.*

Welcome to Times Square.

ROB HEDDEN: We ended up shooting one week in New York City, including the harbor scene. And even that I had to fight for. I knew that at the end of the day we had to bring this movie in for a price. But I put my foot down and said, "I'm not

"We did a lot of stuff in *Part VIII* that wasn't done in the other *Friday* movies—they never had subways or boats!" says director Rob Hedden. "David Fischer, our production designer, did a great job of making Vancouver look like New York City. It was challenging. We had to take a spotless Vancouver tunnel system that had not a speck of litter on the ground, and make it look dirty, grungy and covered in graffiti. But the funny part was, we could only get the tunnels on off hours, so we would come in, dirty the whole place up, shoot it, and then we'd have to get out of there and leave poor David to clean it all up."

Above: Cast and crew clown around after a hard day's work. From left: Visual consultant Pamela O'Har, Rob Hedden, Jensen Daggett, Scott Reeves and Kane Hodder (seated).

going to do this movie if we can't go to New York and at least get an authentic Times Square and New York Harbor." Of everything, that was the one make-or-break moment for me on the entire film.

RANDOLPH CHEVELDAVE: We didn't get a lot of money to shoot in New York. Originally, when we finally said, "OK we're adding Times Square," Frank generously allowed the budget to increase by $25,000. Well, excuse me, you want Times Square on a Friday night? I think it was forty PA's. We had police, which had to be reinforced. And by about 9:30 p.m., there was a crowd of close to 15,000 people. Time seemed to stand still.

The best reaction I saw was this woman in her mid-thirties, dressed in a business suit and briefcase—a real executive type. And there she is, on her knees, running her stockings on the sidewalk, tears streaming down her face, holding her hands forward, going, "Jason! Jason! I love you!" It was one of those moments I'll never forget.

KANE HODDER: In *Part VII*, we were either in the woods or a studio, so I didn't have any interaction with fans when I had the costume on. Now, here we are in the middle of Times Square at midnight. I had to come out and do the moment where I'm standing on the traffic island. And they had to have barriers on either side to hold people back, because this is Jason standing out there, and they're going to stop and watch. My dressing room

was actually where the MTV TRL studio is now. And I came down, got in the van, and put the mask on. Then, in the middle of Times Square, I stepped out. Cheering! Hundreds of people. I felt like one of The Beatles. I just stood there, watching. I'd look over and they just went nuts. It was so much fun. It was maybe the most exciting moment I ever had playing Jason.

BRYAN ENGLAND: I'll never forget that night. We were shooting in May, and the schools were having their proms. It was 3 a.m. and Jason would be out there and we'd be waiting to shoot and there would be these kids sticking their heads out of limousines screaming, "Jason, we love you!"

JENSEN DAGGETT: I really felt like I was dreaming. To be eighteen years old and starring in a film, and we're shooting basically on Broadway—that was something I knew I should cherish regardless of what my future held. I have done a lot of jobs since then, a lot of great locations with a lot of wonderful actors, and that is still one of the most incredible memories of my life. It was a real "King of the World!" moment.

ROB HEDDEN: Closing off Times Square and shooting a forty-foot crane shot, coming up out of the subway, then having the camera do a complete 360-degree spin—that was priceless. This low-budget *Friday the 13th* movie shooting in Times Square! I was like, "Pinch me!" It was unbelievable. It's still unbelievable. I've done movies since then—mostly TV movies—but also *Clockstoppers*, which was a $35 million movie with big CGI and *Matrix*-like effects, and nothing compares to that moment. I'm still trying to recapture it.

Rob Hedden's dream of a fresher, more audience-friendly Friday *continued throughout post-production. Already anticipating a harsh reaction from the Motion Picture Association of America, Hedden had designed most of* Part VIII's *graphic kill sequences to be shot and edited in a multitude of ways—a pre-emptive plan to avoid the long, drawn-out battles with the ratings board that had plagued the previous installments. Working with editor Steve Mirkovich, Hedden continued to take creative risks with the film's style and pacing, often employing radical jump cuts in time and space along with inventive new sound effects trickery.*

STEVE MIRKOVICH: We received an X rating on our first try, and had to go back probably two or three times. It was not crazy. I don't think it was nearly as intense a situation as it had been on past *Friday*s, at least from what I had heard. But the MPAA hates the franchise. They just do.

ROB HEDDEN: When Frank saw my first cut of the movie, he said, "Can you beef up the blood a little more?" I said, "Yeah, I've got more." I had already anticipated the MPAA, so I first turned in a cut to Frank that I thought could get past the ratings board. But Frank said, "Screw the ratings. Give me a movie that the fans want to see."

The joke was that the MPAA made me cut everything back out anyway. It was a very different political and cultural atmosphere back then. You look at *Jason Takes Manhattan* and it's tame compared to any R-rated movie today. And they were really, really strict on these movies in particular. I just watched *Total Recall* with my kids the other night, and that movie is like three times more violent than any *Friday the 13th*.

We had to lose a great deal. The very first kill in the movie, when Jim and Suzy are on the ship and Jim pulls the prank on her and pretends he's Jason—in my first cut, the spear gun goes all the way into his body, and Jason yanks it back out and there is blood and guts all over it. That had to go. Or when Tamara gets killed in the theatrical release, she just screams and we cut to the horn on the ship going, *Burrrmmmm!* Which is a trick I learned from Hitchcock—cut right from the moment of impact to some blaring noise. But originally, I had an additional shot of the aftermath, where you see Tamara lying naked on the floor with about two dozen glass shards stabbed all over her and blood everywhere. Even with Kelly Hu we had to trim. There is no blood when she gets strangled, but when she lands on the dance room floor, we had inserted a much louder hit, a ball-crush hit. And the MPAA just said, "Take out that sound effect if you want to keep that scene."

STEVE MIRKOVICH: I remember specifically one of the cuts, where there was a shadow of a wrench coming down and smacking somebody in the head. On set, somebody was standing offstage and throwing blood on the wall. Well, in the original cut, it was like a *bucket* of blood. But we had to tone it down to like a cup. Only then would the MPAA forgive us.

ROB HEDDEN: I had no illusions. It's like if you marry a woman who is really overweight and you go into the marriage saying, "In two months, I'm going to have her skinny," you're kidding yourself. You marry somebody for who they are, love them for

who they are. When I went into *Jason Takes Manhattan*, it was like, "This is the genre. I'm not going to reinvent what people love. I'm going to try to enhance what people love. And what these fans want is to see people get murdered in creative ways."

I think that may have been one of the factors why I put a little more humor into my *Friday*. Because I am not a fan of slashers, per se. And this is not a documentary. Nobody's really going to get their head knocked off their shoulders, and it's not going to roll into a dumpster. That doesn't happen in real life. So if I'm going to glorify it a little bit, I still want there to be a little bit of a wink, too.

Some people like the humor and some people don't. The hardcore fans found fault with the fact that it maybe was a little over the top. But I think good horror movies use humor to release the tension. For example, when Jason arrives at the pier in New York, I just thought, "Let's put a joke here. Let's put a billboard of a hockey player that Jason sees right when he lands. Then he looks at it and kind of cocks his head." We also did the same thing with the gangbanger guys in Times Square where Jason kicks the boom box. I wanted subtle things like that to get a laugh in the theater.

KANE HODDER: Those things seemed funny at the time, but I thought they were just too much. Jason shouldn't be played for laughs.

ROB HEDDEN: We did some other bizarre things. Right before Rennie smashes the car into the wall, when she's trying to kill her delusion or whatever, the thing goes—*dunk-dunk-dunk*. The whole theater goes silent and we just put in these little stings— *boom-boom-boom*! And when my kids first watched it, years later, they laughed. And I asked them, "Did you laugh because it was stupid?" And they said, "No, no, no. We liked it." But they

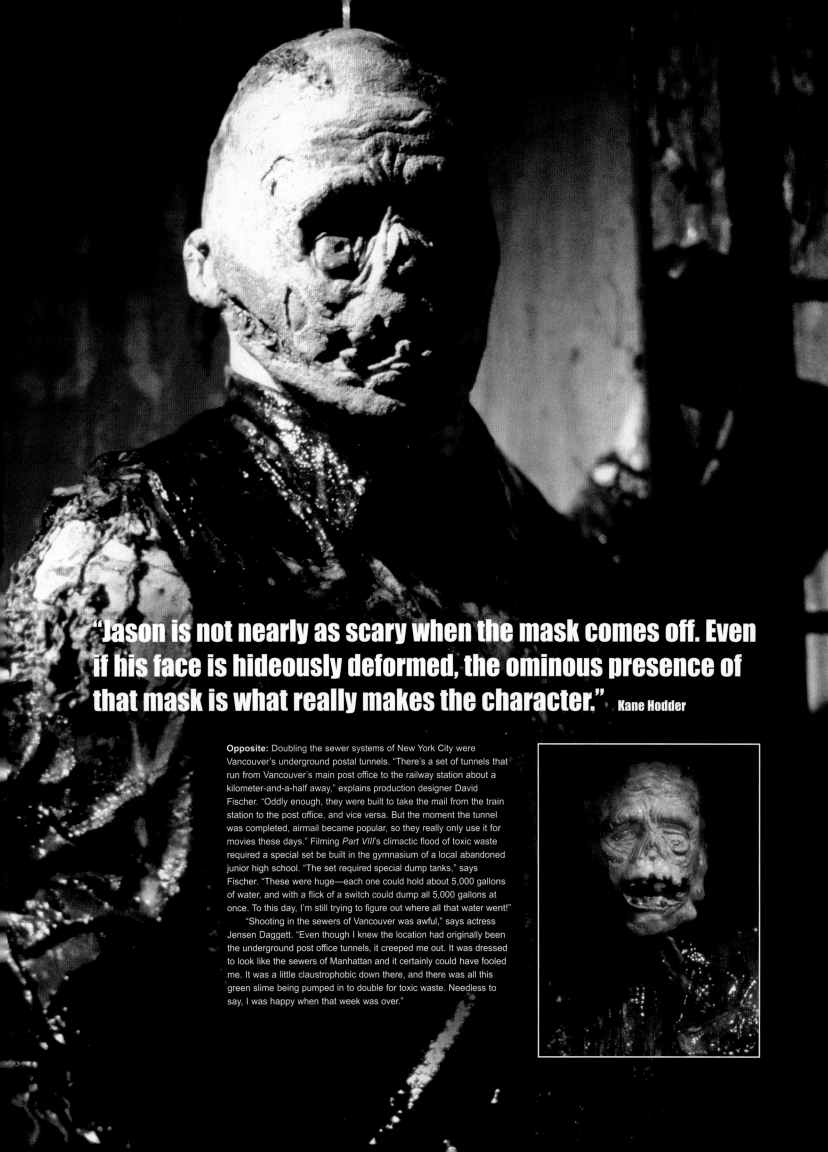

"Jason is not nearly as scary when the mask comes off. Even if his face is hideously deformed, the ominous presence of that mask is what really makes the character." Kane Hodder

Opposite: Doubling the sewer systems of New York City were Vancouver's underground postal tunnels. "There's a set of tunnels that run from Vancouver's main post office to the railway station about a kilometer-and-a-half away," explains production designer David Fischer. "Oddly enough, they were built to take the mail from the train station to the post office, and vice versa. But the moment the tunnel was completed, airmail became popular, so they really only use it for movies these days." Filming *Part VIII*'s climactic flood of toxic waste required a special set be built in the gymnasium of a local abandoned junior high school. "The set required special dump tanks," says Fischer. "These were huge—each one could hold about 5,000 gallons of water, and with a flick of a switch could dump all 5,000 gallons at once. To this day, I'm still trying to figure out where all that water went!"

"Shooting in the sewers of Vancouver was awful," says actress Jensen Daggett. "Even though I knew the location had originally been the underground post office tunnels, it creeped me out. It was dressed to look like the sewers of Manhattan and it certainly could have fooled me. It was a little claustrophobic down there, and there was all this green slime being pumped in to double for toxic waste. Needless to say, I was happy when that week was over."

couldn't even tell me exactly why. It was just outrageous and odd to them. We just tried to make it different.

RANDOLPH CHEVELDAVE: I think one of the decisions that we all agreed upon was that Jason is now, to some extent, a supernatural character. Whether he is just extremely fast, or can actually cease to exist in one place then exist in another, it really didn't matter. So long as the movie consistently obeyed that rule and didn't deviate from it, we'd be OK. And I, for one, thought it was effective.

STEVE MIRKOVICH: You just had to take yourself out of what is real. I mean, the whole idea of Jason drowning and coming back to life in the first place is preposterous. So, yes, he should be able to have some bigger-than-life strengths. He can just be there. Because the forgiving part of the audience is, "Alright, this might not be logical, but you scared me, so it's okay." If the payoff works, sometimes we don't care how we get there.

When I was editing *Jason Takes Manhattan*, I was not aware at the time that we were trying to do anything to bend logic. We simply said, "What will work? What is going to keep people on the edge of their seat? What is going to make this fun?" Fun for us, as filmmakers, was to scare the shit out of people and give them what they asked for, which was more blood, more guts, and just do not stall. I don't think anyone crucified us for that.

Jason Takes Manhattan would also be the first Friday the 13th *to make it to screens entirely without the contributions of composer Harry Manfredini. The conspicuous lack of Manfredini's trademark score, along with a unique opening credit sequence and the use of moody, rock-inspired songs on the soundtrack, ensured that at the very least,* Jason Takes Manhattan *would sound like no other* Friday the 13th *that had come before.*

ROB HEDDEN: Fred Mollin was chosen as composer because he had scored the entire *Friday the 13th* television series. He was completely dialed in. Frank loved him, and I loved him. We knew he could deliver anything we wanted. And he was highly enthusiastic.

It was not that Harry Manfredini was old news—he is still the best. Fred just had a really fresh sound, different from what had been done in the other movies. It was like, "We're making a new *Friday* here. We're making one that's not going to be at Crystal Lake. We're making one that's going to have supernatural overtones. We're making one that has some humor. So if it is going to be different, let's tweak the music, too."

FRED MOLLIN, Composer: It was a thrill and a challenge. At the time I hadn't toiled that much in features, whether it was *Friday the 13th* or not. So I was excited. And unlike with *Part VII*, I talked at length conceptually with Rob. I wanted to please him. We had long discussions about what should be done—not musically, but emotionally. Partially because we were on a very tight schedule, so I had to deliver some score and just keep going. And I am really more of an instinctual composer, anyway. I definitely wanted it to be percussive, aggressive and dynamic. I think it was. It was different than the previous *Friday*s. I'm not saying it was better—I love Harry. But I remember being extremely proud that *Part VIII* came together as well as it did. I certainly am far happier with it than *Part VII*, which was a different experience. I think Rob happens to be such a gifted guy. I love his sensibilities. Yeah, *Part VIII* has got a campy flair—obviously even more campy now. But that is what gives it its charm. It brings you back to that era. That's the nice part about it.

Although, to be honest, I can't really listen too much to my *Friday the 13th* stuff today because the technology is so much more advanced. The sounds are so much better now. You don't hear loops today—I hear certain things in my scores back then and they sound obvious. Again, it's all a matter of era. Compared to the 1970s, what I was doing in the '80s was wildly inventive and technologically brilliant. But compared to today—I could slaughter it now.

ROB HEDDEN: One thing I really wanted to do was open the movie in a very unusual way for a *Friday the 13th* film. I wanted fans to know immediately, from the first frame, that this was going to be surprising and fresh. It wasn't going to be just more of the same.

I wrote a whole opening credit sequence that was totally different from any *Friday* film. The kids on the boat that we will soon meet are supposed to be listening to a late night radio station out of New York, and we're seeing a montage of the city. And it's a dark, mysterious New York, which, of course, is also foreshadowing what is to come. And then one of those bizarre-o late night DJs comes on, doing a riff. That was the intention—what we're hearing isn't narration, but instead a disc jockey's voiceover. A "3:00 a.m. in New York" kind of thing.

I also wanted to put some kind of a song at the beginning of the movie, too, as opposed to just score. Something that had vocals in it. My original request was to use this song off of Robert Plant's *Now and Zen* CD. It was great. And when Frank heard it, even he said, "This is so perfect." It was dark and mysterious and sexy, and had an unmistakable Led Zeppelin feel. Just a really great piece of music. And we weren't even thinking MTV. I just figured it would be cross-promotion by default—it would help him and it would help us. Unfortunately, we never got to Robert Plant. Instead we got his publishing company and they wanted a trillion dollars for it.

Fortunately, Fred has a great pop sensibility. Frank said, "Come up with something that has the same feel, and we'll use that." And Fred came up with this great song called "Darkest Side of the Night." Everybody listened to it and we said, "It's not Robert Plant. We all know that. But it's really good. And no one will know that Robert Plant was originally supposed to be singing the opening of the movie, anyway." Although now they will.

FRED MOLLIN: The Robert Plant song had a very cool vibe to it but they couldn't spend the money on it. So they called me and said, "Write one! Make it in the same groove and tempo—make something in a similar mood." And of course I couldn't go too close to the original in any way, shape or form, so I came up with a whole different vibe. And even though the vocal had nothing to do with the other song, they liked it. It just set the mood.

By the way, I had never even heard the Alice Cooper song from *Part VI*, which had a sort of campy quality. And Rob didn't want to go campy. They wanted to evoke a little more mood. It's always a challenge to write lyrics for something like this, because you never want to write things that are on the money, on the nose—you're not going to write a song in what I call the *Gilligan's Island* school of songwriting. "Here comes Jason down the street/He's the guy you want to meet." We couldn't do that.

Anyway, I ended up writing the song with Stan Mizer, and we recorded it at his place. All I had was some footage from the movie. I knew what the footage was for the opening titles—it was a montage of New York. And I just said, "Fuck—let's talk about the dark side, the seamy side of the city," and the lyrics just came from that. I just made sure there was nothing that was very literal and that it just set up the mystery, but within a pop vibe as opposed to a score. I remember being very proud of that cut. I think it added to the uniqueness of the movie.

Jason Takes Manhattan effects artists William Terezakis (from left), Jamie Brown and the late Tibor Farkas, with friend.

If anyone thought that the battle between Jason and Freddy was only in the minds of the series' makers, the summer of 1989 disproved all such theories. Friday the 13th Part VIII: Jason Takes Manhattan was due to open on July 28, a mere two weeks before the arrival of the latest Freddy installment, A Nightmare on Elm Street 5: The Dream Child. It was an event heralded by the genre press months in advance. "It's the box office battle of the summer!" declared Fangoria magazine in one of its many over-the-top cover stories. Yet because the Nightmare series' profits had been on the rise just as Friday the 13th's had begun to decline, the odds-on favorite was Freddy. But the eventual outcome would surprise everyone—they both lost.

Opening on 1,683 screens in the U.S., Jason Takes Manhattan pulled in $6.2 million in its first three days, a new low for the series. Its final box office take of $14.3 million, for 3.6 million paid admissions, was hardly encouraging, and Jason Takes Manhattan became the lowest-grossing installment in the franchise to date. Although the film still proved profitable given its relatively modest budget—especially when profits from home video and ancillary markets were factored into the equation—one would be hard pressed to call Jason Takes Manhattan a hit by any standard.

Freddy, too, faced a sudden and surprising level of audience apathy. The Dream Child opened to a slightly better $8.1 million weekend gross, but it, too, wilted in the box office sun, eventually grossing a disappointing $22.2 million—an embarrassing come-down from the nearly $50 million earned by Nightmare 4. Perhaps Freddy's relentless overexposure had worn thin even among the series' fans. Or had audiences finally grown tired of Jason, Freddy and the "pop slasher" phenomenon? Whatever the case, the lackluster result inspired Frank Mancuso, Jr. and Paramount to take a step back, reflect on nearly a decade of success, and look toward a possible future that, for the first time, did not include Friday the 13th.

JENSEN DAGGETT: I thought the finished product was an interesting twist to the Friday the 13ths that I had seen before. It tried to incorporate a big city, a ship and even toxic waste—it was so very '80s. It was a lot to undertake. And I thought the performances were good. But it was not quite as scary as I remembered other Fridays from my past. That may be because I was there to witness the shooting of it, or it could be because I was very young when we used to sit home on a Friday night and rent those movies. So I would be curious to know how the fans would rank the suspense factor of ours.

V.C. DUPREE: I went to the premiere at Mann's Chinese, and then after that, Kane Hodder hired a limo, and we went out and did the rounds down in Orange County. And the surreal part was that every drive-in we passed, there's your face—fifty feet tall! And as this was my first starring role, it all was just so larger than life.

After we got to Orange County, we pulled up and I saw tons of kids and people outside this one theater. And they just swarmed the car. They had already seen the movie and somehow they knew we were coming. That was my most memorable moment of the whole experience.

PETER MARK RICHMAN: I saw it at the premiere. I don't know what I thought of it. But I do remember some guy, who had interviewed me in the past and who writes stuff about a lot of films, was sitting in front of me. And I remember him saying, rather loudly, "For Christ sake! Why would he ever want to do a picture like this?" Well, that did not feel particularly good.

KELLY HU: I was happy with the movie in general, although I'm never happy with my own work. Ever. But it was just exciting to be a part of something like that, something with such a great following.

I remember that my parents didn't see it with me—they saw it after I went, just to see it in a real theater. And they actually timed the movie from start to finish, and decided that I died exactly halfway through the movie. And my mother was hiding her eyes—she couldn't look when I died. My father just came to me and said, "Good death scene!"

MARTIN CUMMINS: I was down in Los Angeles for pilot season, and Rob called me and invited me and my dad to see it at the Mann's Chinese. And I had never seen one of those movies. To be honest, they are not my cup of tea. I'm the guy always turning away from the screen during horror movies. But I thought it was just hilarious. But the funniest thing is that my little British grandmother went to see *Jason Takes Manhattan* at the local movie theater by herself, just because I was in it. And I remember her coming to me afterward, telling me, "Darling, you know I went to see your movie. And I hope you don't mind, but I left after the gentleman with the hockey mask killed you."

ROB HEDDEN: Frank and Barbara warned me before I even shot a frame of film that this movie would get trashed, review-wise. So I was prepared for the worst. But this was my first movie. And when you put your heart into something and try to do the best job you can do, and then somebody tells you in a few paragraphs that you're a piece of crap and you shouldn't have even been born, well, it still hurts.

It's funny, there were a handful of good reviews. Leonard Maltin liked it, which shocked me. But also the guy who was the regular reviewer for *Daily Variety*. He said the direction was stylish and a bunch of things like where I was like, "Oh my God, I can't believe it!" However, when all the reviewers came out and said, "What is this crap about Jason taking Manhattan?" I sat there and I nodded. They're right. I cannot defend that. That was the only thing that hurt for me, because I'm the writer and director. Maybe if they would have only been able to read my outline, they would have gone easier on me.

You have to ask, however, that even if I had made a different *Friday the 13th* movie, if it would have been Jason in Manhattan and ninety-nine percent of it would have taken place in New York, and it would have had a $10 million budget, and I would have been able to do all the things I wanted to do, would it have made any more money? Maybe. I don't think the critics would have given it any more praise. And I really believe that if I had

had that extra money and made a real Jason in New York movie, it still wouldn't have made more profit. Because let's say it made another $5 million at the box office. So what? It would have cost more, too. It would have been a wash.

I'm sure Paramount was always hoping for it to make more money than the last one. It didn't make as much money as *Part VII*. Maybe they thought they'd done as much as they could do, and that it's never going to get better than *VII*. The difference is that *VII* cost less money to make than *VIII*. So they made less profit even if the box office was the same. Maybe if they hadn't released *Nightmare on Elm Street Part 5* two weeks later, and my movie had made an extra $10 million, it would have been different. But the fans would still have felt the way they felt about the film.

RANDOLPH CHEVELDAVE: I kind of regret not being of an age and sufficient experience to have done one of the earlier *Friday the 13th* movies. Because I think by the time *Part VIII* came around, it was like *The Mummy Meets Abbott and Costello*. I don't think Jason would have survived another Camp Crystal Lake movie. It was either move him someplace else, or lose him altogether. So I think from that perspective, absolutely the right thing was done.

Of course, nobody's happy when you have the lowest grossing entry of the series. At least it was up until that time. The box office for any of the *Friday the 13th* movies was always based on body count and gallons of blood. That is what the audience had come to expect. So to not deliver on their expectations was perhaps a mistake. We felt it was time for Jason to go away from the camp. But perhaps it was not time for him to become gentler. If I had to do it over again, it would be a slightly more violent, bloodier movie. I don't know if it would be possible to make it that and still have it retain some of its slyness, but I think that tightrope could have been walked more successfully.

MICHAEL SHEEHY: Frank Jr. was always looking towards the future. He had finally become more established after *Internal Affairs* went into production, along with some of the other movies we had in development, and he wanted to go beyond *Friday the 13th*. I remember Frank Jr. commenting, not long after *Part VIII* came out, that he wasn't planning on doing any more. I think everybody wants to go out and see if they can make it on their own.

Another movie, another look for Jason Voorhees. "We weren't going to have animated worms coming out of his face," says Rob Hedden. "Instead, I had this idea of his face being melted by chemistry." The director's original concept art for Jason's post-toxic waste demise (**background**) was realized by *Part VIII*'s effects team (**below**), although the final result is barely glimpsed in the finished film.

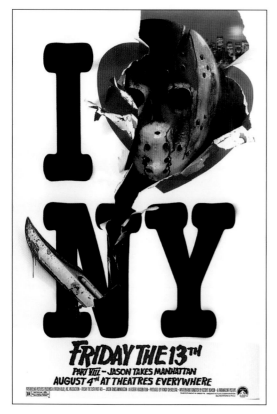

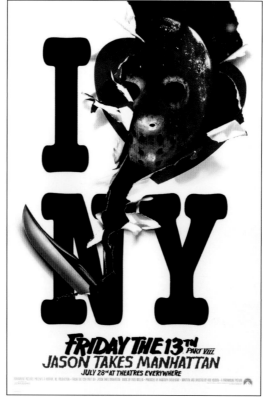

The never-ending battle between *Friday the 13th* and the Motion Picture Association of America continued to make headlines in the weeks leading up to the release of *Jason Takes Manhattan*. This time, however, the filmmakers and the MPAA were not at odds over the movie itself, but rather its poster. The film's original one-sheet (**above**, left) was initially rejected by the organization's Advertising Administration due to its depiction of Jason tearing through the famous "I Love New York" logo with a bloody knife and hockey mask. Paramount Pictures would be forced to resubmit a new, "bloodless" version of the poster, which was approved by the MPAA, and the poster began to circulate across the country as the film's July 28th release date loomed. But the controversy would not end there. The New York City Council and its Board of Tourism were no fans of the attention the poster was attracting on the city's subways and airports and threatened a lawsuit, claiming that Paramount Pictures had failed to secure permission to use the trademarked "I Love New York" logo. Although Paramount would eventually withdraw the poster from circulation (it remains a hot commodity on the collectible market), the public fracas guaranteed the film plenty of free advertising. The studio would eventually replace the offending poster with the subsequent "Style B" design (**opposite page**).

I don't know if this is what the fans want to hear, but I don't really remember any of us being affected one way or the other, because maybe we felt the film series was going to be resurrected in some form eventually anyway. We knew they weren't really going to end because they had been pretty successful. In retrospect, perhaps the only thing I do remember feeling bad about was thinking a "Jason vs. Freddy" movie could still be a smash hit. I wish I had done more to try and make that happen.

FRANK MANCUSO, JR.: It was the law of diminishing returns. There was no bigger reason than that. They were doing progressively less and less box office, and I just felt that everybody had had their fill of Jason.

FRANK MANCUSO, SR., President of Production, Paramount Pictures: I remember the decision as being something of that moment, that we would simply not do another *Friday the 13th* next year, or maybe even the year after that. Then I left Paramount in 1991, and eventually they sold off the rights to somebody else.

At the time it had probably become stale, in our minds. When you've stretched it as long as we did, I don't know if there was anything else different you could do with it. Although we did use the title for the television series, that never crossed over to the movies. So it was no different than *The Godfather*, or *Indiana Jones*. How many can you make? What new ideas can you reasonably come up with?

Look at *Star Trek*. The most successful one we had was the one with the whales, where they came back to Earth, right? And that created a new audience altogether—it brought in mainstream audiences that normally would not see a *Star Trek* film. That never did quite happen with *Friday the 13th*. It went from this level way up high, to down a little bit, then back up again, before it kind of took a while to quietly slip back down. And then it just tapered off.

ROB HEDDEN: Life's too short for regrets. I don't know why Paramount didn't make another one. They probably figured it was the end of the franchise—for them, anyway. *Jason Takes Manhattan* made them a profit, trust me—if I'm still collecting money from it, so are they. I think Frank just figured that the only place they could go after *Part VIII* was a Freddy and Jason thing, and that wasn't happening because of New Line.

Did I kill the franchise? No. They made a *Jason Goes to Hell* and *Jason X*, and of course *Freddy vs. Jason*. Honestly, I did the best job I could do, for better or for worse, and that's all I can do. Personally, it's something I'll always have. *Friday the 13th* will be around long after I'm gone. Sean Cunningham created an amazing legacy that has continued to endure. I just feel incredibly honored that I got to be a part of it and put my little stamp on it. I hope I was able to tie up all of those movies in a nice little package. I am just thrilled that I got to be involved. And nobody will ever be able to take that away from me.

There was one more farewell to come. At the conclusion of its third season in May 1991, Paramount Television would unceremoniously pull the plug on Friday the 13th: The Series. *Although it was still one of the highest-rated dramatic series in national syndication, protests, not profits, would ultimately result in the show's premature demise. Amid the vocal opposition of the Moral Majority, many of* The Series' *major advertisers became skittish at a potential backlash and began to pull their support from the show. It was a curtain call that deeply affected many of those most intimately involved with the television series, and the anger at its cancellation persists to this day.*

FRED MOLLIN: To be honest, the end of the television series was the real heartbreak. I loved the people involved. Frank happened to be incredibly supportive and a great cheerleader. He trusted me. I have nothing but great, great memories and appreciation for Frank. And the folks who ran the show, the producers, the editors, the actors, everyone involved, I just loved working with them.

I have very strong memories of being extremely angry and depressed and pissed because the family was breaking up. On top of that, I was really proud of the show. I felt that we had done three years of good supernatural TV. I really thought it was going to be a big cult show forever and that this was being pulled way too early. It really was the end of an era.

MICHAEL SHEEHY: *The Series* ended because Donald Wildmon and the Moral Majority approached a number of stations, and Paramount, and complained—having never even seen the show. He assumed it had something to do with the movies. And so some sponsors started having problems with it, too, and slowly but surely support just sort of evaporated. I remember being upset, because my perception at the time was that this group wasn't even familiar with the show. They weren't familiar with the content of it. They were creating this uproar just based on the title.

FRANK MANCUSO, JR.: I was always interested in *The Series* being on late at night, like the last thing you see before you go to sleep on a Friday night—it could be my own late-night monster series. But what happened was, because the show was very well reviewed and received, Paramount started upgrading it to primetime in numerous markets. And I was always concerned that we may be venturing into areas that were no longer appropriate for the content of the show. But Paramount was a big company, and *Star Trek: The Next Generation* always moved around the schedule, too. They'd use that *Star Trek* and *Friday the 13th* block of programming as a way to control aspects of the market. Plus, advertisers will pay significantly more for spots in primetime than they will in late-night.

In any event, as the show started to get more popular and got better time slots, that's when this Wildmon guy started to get agitated. I thought it was a joke at first, because he kept talking about Jason—I was never convinced he ever even saw a single episode of *The Series*. Except suddenly, his group started threatening the advertisers on our show, telling them, "We'll tell your constituents that they should boycott your products because you're supporting this evil show." *The Series* was going along great, but the fiscal viability of the show was always related to advertiser support. Then I started to get calls from these advertisers saying, "We love the show, we love the demographics, we love everything—but what we don't love is being on this guy's hit list. We don't need these headaches." And we started losing sponsorships.

If it was *Cheers*, and generating hundreds of millions of dollars for Paramount, it would have been different. Maybe. The studio might have had a more energized appetite to fight it. But it's the same thing that happened with Warner Bros. and rap music. Warner Bros. is making a lot of money off of that and then somebody comes out with a song called "Cop Killer" and all of a sudden Warner starts to get picketed and you're answering questions at stockholders' meetings like, "How can you take money from this when they advocate killing cops?" That's why Warner sold off Death Row Records. It wasn't about money—it was about being able to live without that headache. That's why Paramount just said, "We had a good run. We made a bunch of money. Let's not fight this."

LARRY B. WILLIAMS, Co-Creator, *Friday the 13th: The Series*: The title was both the thing that sold the show and the thing that killed the show. I was so offended when I'd read the stuff they were saying about it, because it was apparent that the people on the religious right did not watch a single episode. The truth is that this show dealt with people who were reversing evil. And what is more in the vein of the religious right than that? And what you got was someone who built his own career as an evangelist upon this tirade.

So my apologies to the people in power at that time, but you had complete cowards at Paramount. It was the only time I had any anger towards Frank Jr., because I was long gone from the show by then. But I would have been out there confronting these people, saying, "Point to it! Take any script in there and point to where it condones evil." These were morality tales. And that was the major difference between the *Friday the 13th* films and *The Series*, which was an argument I made when I first presented my ideas to Paramount.

Here again, I'm being honest. This is what bothers me. This was, in my humble estimation, the beginning of the religious right moving into the public eye with their righteous censorship. They had no business here. Paramount only decided not to continue the show because they anticipated more flak. And when they made that decision, *Friday the 13th* was the number two syndicated show in the nation. There was no refusal from any affiliate to air the show because the ratings were still good. Paramount folded. That was my judgment. And I'm not angry about it because it was "my show" at that point—only my name was still on it—it was Frank's show. But it was the beginning of the end for the creative community in many ways, because from that point on, the religious right, encouraged by that success, has stomped all over this industry.

9.

From May 1980 to August 1989, a period of only nine years, Paramount Pictures released eight *Friday the 13th* films, all of which met with varying degrees of box office success. Nevertheless, the series helped alter the language and business of the independent film industry and introduced to the world a new kind of

The Nine Lives of Jason Voorhees

movie monster—and a new kind of horror film—one that pushed boundaries and stirred controversy, particularly through innovations in the art of special effects make-up. Going to see a *Friday the 13th* film had also become a rite of passage for many adolescents, who would sneak off with their friends to the films—despite their R ratings—whispering the oft-heard teenage words of caution, "We better not let our parents find out." Surviving a *Friday the 13th* film without hiding behind their eyes or cowering beneath their seats was a sign of maturity, a ritual among peers that involved laughter, a sense of camaraderie and, perhaps, a show of bravery in the face of death—all within the safety zone of the local multiplex. The horror landscape, though, was changing. A glut of slasher films had been released in the early 1980s, brought on in no small measure by the success of *Friday the 13th*.

The genre's popularity had significantly waned by 1984, the year that saw the release of what was intended to be the last *Friday the 13th* film, the deceptively titled *The Final Chapter*. Horror movies, and not just *Friday the 13th*, were in need of a serious change in direction. As Hollywood producers scrambled around in search of the next big thing to capture the imaginations of the ever-changing youth culture of America, Jason and his teenage-slashing brethren seemed, at long last, destined for retirement.

By the beginning of the 1990s, Paramount Pictures had grown tired of *Friday the 13th*, as had Frank Mancuso, Jr., the ambitious young producer who had largely guided the series to success throughout its decade-long heyday at the studio. Although Paramount never officially announced a definitive end of their association with the franchise, after the lackluster box office of *Jason Takes Manhattan*—and the subsequent cancellation of the syndicated television series—it was probably a safe bet to assume that, at least as far as Paramount was concerned, there would be no return for *Friday the 13th*. But if the past had taught audiences anything, it was "never say never" when it comes to Jason.

A notion was stirring in the imagination of Sean S. Cunningham. Although it had been nearly ten years since Cunningham had taken a hands-on role in the franchise—and the monster—he had helped create, he decided that now was the time for Jason, like Frankenstein before him, to return to his maker.

With the job of producer now officially vacated by Frank Mancuso, Jr., Cunningham saw for himself an opportunity to discover and shepherd fresh new talent while using the profits generated by *Friday the 13th* to pursue more diverse and meaningful projects for himself. It would be a decision that would not only set into motion the rebirth of Jason Voorhees and the *Friday* franchise, it would also bring about a union between Cunningham's master creation and a new studio partner. At the time, it seemed to be a match made in heaven—finally the foundation could be laid for the long-rumored, much anticipated battle between Freddy and Jason. But first, there was one more bit of business to attend to: it was time to send Jason to Hell.

SEAN CUNNINGHAM, Producer: I look back on the movies I made and I wish I liked them more. All I see are mistakes and what I could have done better. I tried to make the right decisions but it was very difficult. It used to be, after *Friday the 13th*, that if Hollywood wanted to get kids mutilated and killed, they said, "Call Cunningham." Then after *Spring Break*, they said, "If you want to get kids mutilated and killed, or drunk and laid, call Cunningham." In 1985, I wound up directing a movie called *The New Kids*, but I was very unhappy while doing that. I just really, really didn't have a good time. It was ugly material. It was just watching two nice kids getting fucked over. So I said, "I'm not going to do this anymore. I don't want to direct dark stuff. But I don't want to retire, so I'll produce."

So I did *House* with Steve Miner, and we had a hit. I was then able to get through some difficult financial times with the *House* sequels and "Johnny Zombie," which became *My Boyfriend's Back*. By the time we did *DeepStar Six* in 1989, I had actually already hired a director, Robert Harmon, but at the last second, he bowed out and I had to come in and direct

the film. I didn't regret doing it, but that experience only underlined the fact that I had to learn more about scripts, and I had to find ways to get better material to direct. And while I was doing that, if I had to produce horror films, well, that would be okay.

The Freddy franchise was dead and, as far as I could tell, so was the *Friday* thing. It was only then that I reapproached Phil Scuderi and the original backers from Boston about getting the rights back to *Friday the 13th* so I could control the property, and I could control the money, and I could go to New Line and try to make *Freddy vs. Jason*. I could make that deal. And in that, I controlled all the rights and the cash flow, but subject to paying New Line, rather than them controlling the rights and paying me.

ROBERT SHAYE, Co-Chairman, New Line Cinema: At one time I was actually jealous of Sean and *Friday the 13th* because they had sold their film to Paramount. We had, with lots of aggravation, just made our first little film, *A Nightmare on Elm Street*. And we had shown our film to Frank Mancuso, Sr., at Paramount—and they passed on it. Sean had made it, and we were still stumbling around.

Paramount did, at one point back in the late 1980s, approach us with the idea of doing a Freddy and Jason movie. But they basically wanted what we wanted—to license them the rights to Freddy Krueger and go off and make their own movie, which we were not anxious to do. Eventually, Paramount lost whatever rights they had, and that's when Sean, who has since become a friend of mine for a long time, approached me and asked if a *Freddy vs. Jason* was still something we wanted to do.

FRANK MANCUSO, JR., President, Hometown Films: Phil Scuderi mentioned to me that they were going to make an arrangement with New Line, and I said I had this exclusive arrangement with Paramount at the time so I couldn't do it—I couldn't work for another studio. I didn't really want to go back to *Friday the 13th* anyway. I didn't have an awkward moment about it at all. And I never saw any of those other movies. But I was happy for the fans if they turned out to be good. The only thing I felt bad about was when I saw *Freddy vs. Jason*—I wish we could have done that. That was something that could have been great.

To be honest, I really don't know anything about Sean's experience with Phil and Bob and Steve. Look, these guys were not savvy movie guys. They were business guys, and they were stretching themselves into an area they weren't familiar with. And I'm sure that comes with a certain price. But Phil, God bless him, as I was moving up, if I had a movie opening up—because he was a theater owner—he would call me and tell me I was their shining star. Were it not for him, I don't know where I would have been, but I know I wouldn't have gotten there as quickly. To give a kid as young as I was the break he did, that took a lot of guts. He may have had seventy-five different reasons for doing it, I don't really know. What I do know is that he gave me that opportunity and he was always very kind and generous to me. So I am thankful for that opportunity.

FRANK MANCUSO, SR., President of Production, Paramount Pictures: Every *Friday* movie after the first one, we had the rights to distribute the product. So if the boys from Boston wanted to make one, they had to offer it to us. We could say no, and only then could they take it somewhere else. But I must say this for them: they were extraordinarily loyal people. They were very grateful that we turned this little horror film into this incredibly lucrative franchise. And until we decided to not make any more of the films, they never, ever tried to go around us, or take the series anywhere else.

GEORGE MANSOUR, Distributor, Esquire Theatres: When Phil and Steve Minasian and Bob Barsamian sold the rights to New Line they got a big chunk of money. Well, it seemed like it at the time—it's not too much now, but they maybe got $400,000 or $500,000. I don't think they ever had that ambition to really get into the moviemaking business in a big way. They didn't have the resources to go out and open a production company. These were real middle-class guys, they weren't really movie guys. Phil was a lawyer who certainly didn't go to Harvard, let's put it that way. And the other guys had accounting backgrounds. But remember, the *Friday the 13th* franchise was sold to Paramount. So in a way, they did do it.

Phil is dead, but Bobby and Steve—they're still around. They're brothers-in-law and they're still involved with a group of movie houses in New England. Lisa Barsamian, Bob's daughter, was given a producing credit on *Part 3*, but the kids never really got involved with anything. The last time I knew, they were very reluctant to have any kind of publicity or really talk to anyone. Maybe someday they'll mellow out a bit.

While it seemed the stage had finally been set for the ultimate clash between Freddy and Jason, securing the rights would be only the first hurdle in what would become a nearly decade-long odyssey of script delays and production set-backs. Initially, however, there appeared to be few obstacles. Both the Friday *and* Nightmare *franchises were in mothballs following the dismal box office that greeted their latest installments, 1989's* Jason Takes Manhattan *and 1991's* Freddy's Dead: The Final Nightmare. *But old monsters—especially lucrative ones—have a funny way of returning to haunt the present, often in the most unexpected of ways. Wes Craven, the creator of Freddy Krueger—and an old friend and collaborator of Sean*

Cunningham's—would surprise everyone when, in 1994, he announced his intention to resurrect Freddy one last time. Enticed by the potential profits that the return of Freddy's "father" might bring, New Line gave the green light to Wes Craven's New Nightmare—*an ambitious, post-modern take on the Freddy Krueger phenomenon. Again, for the first of many times to come, plans for* Freddy vs. Jason *were put indefinitely on hold. But Sean Cunningham had no desire to cool his heels or sit on a property that he had fought so hard to reclaim. Cunningham decided that if Freddy could come back for one last scare, so could Jason.*

SEAN CUNNINGHAM: I didn't come back to do *Jason Goes to Hell*, I came back to do *Freddy vs. Jason*. At the same time Wes had decided to do *New Nightmare*—or, more to the point, New Line decided they wanted Wes to do it—so everything got put on hold until after that got done. In the meantime, I said, "If we're just treading water, let's do another *Friday the 13th*, and try to get the franchise back out there."

NOEL CUNNINGHAM, Assistant Editor: Moviemaking was the family business so I always knew I'd at least give it a go. After high school, my dad was directing *DeepStar Six*, and he said, "I'll give you a PA job." And it was great—I was making more money than I ever had in my life, like $300 a week. Then I bought a motorcycle and crashed it and broke my leg, so Sean sent me to the cutting room and I ended up an apprentice editor on *Jason Goes to Hell*.

ADAM MARCUS, Director: Noel Cunningham and I went to grammar school together. I think Noel beat the crap out of me a couple of times, but by the first or second grade we became best friends. We discovered we totally shared a love of movies, and even wrote our first screenplay when we were eleven or twelve years old.

Below: The creative nucleus of *Jason Goes to Hell: The Final Friday* at work—director Adam Marcus (from left), producer Sean Cunningham and screenwriter Dean Lorey. And Marcus alone (**opposite**), with head.

"When Kane is hacking at me, he's using a *real* machete. I just thought, 'I'd better hit my mark, or he's gonna take my head clear off!'" Julie Michaels on battling Jason

Sean became a sort of surrogate dad to me. My real father lived in New York, and my mother in Connecticut, so I ended up spending a lot more time in Westport. Sean was very outspoken, but always truthful. A very direct kind of guy. He taught me a great deal—I'm incredibly lucky to have had Sean in my life.

SEAN CUNNINGHAM: Adam is an absolute bundle of self-possessed energy. And he always wanted to be the director of the play and he put on the shows—he was always like, "Do it! Do it! Do it!" He's such a type-A personality.

ADAM MARCUS: I went to NYU Film School, and as I was finishing I got two job offers. One was to write for TV, and the other was to come out and be Sean's slave for a year and he'd give me my break. So I started working for Sean, and had brought out with me a script my friend Dean Lorey had written called "Johnny Zombie" which later became *My Boyfriend's Back*. Dean wanted me to direct, but the film got set up at Disney, and when it became a bigger movie they wanted a different director on it. So I turned to Sean and said, "Come on. Give me a movie!" And he said, "Well, New Line wants another Jason movie." Now, I'll be honest. I was like, "Oh, no! C'mon, Sean. I want a career!" But what an opportunity. I was twenty-three years old, being offered the chance to direct a movie!

SEAN CUNNINGHAM: I knew I wasn't the director for this. I didn't have that passion. And I don't remember how I got to talking with Adam, but he was, or so he seemed to be, a horror aficionado. He knew this stuff inside and out. And I didn't know anything—I just did not follow these trains of thought. Boy, did I not care about *Halloween III* or whatever. I could help with this, but, talking to Adam, he really just had such a passion for it. And without that passion, the picture wouldn't be any good.

ADAM MARCUS: I remember that New Line, Sean, and all of us filmmakers involved felt like we needed to go in a new direction. I think everybody was tired of every Freddy Krueger movie getting raves, and every *Friday the 13th* movie getting torn to pieces. So we just said, "Why are we limiting ourselves? Why be confined to the same old formula?" I think that was the initial attitude we wanted to go into a *Friday Part IX* with.

Also, one of the instructions I initially received was to ignore *Jason Takes Manhattan* completely. My original treatment started after *Part VII*. Jason has been dumped back into Crystal Lake, and they dredge his body back up. This one character, an insanely strong yet kind of frail looking guy, drags Jason's body back to the camp and into a cabin where he has a science lab set up. He straps the body down and starts an autopsy, and opens up this black heart. And when he goes to pull it out of his chest, that's when Jason wakes up. But what we don't realize is that this guy is actually Jason's brother, Elias. And then Elias consumes his brother's black heart, and thereby takes Jason's power. Eventually, we dropped the whole Elias character completely from the script. But that's where the basic concept of the movie, and the idea that Jason's essence could move from one body to another, evolved from.

DEAN LOREY, Screenwriter: I worked with Sean before, and he was always saying that he wasn't going to do another *Friday the 13th* unless he could do something different with it. There had been eight movies and most of them had been pretty bad. Usually they were just carbon copies of the previous one. And there was no reason to remake the earlier movies because anybody could just go out and rent them.

We went for a new direction, keeping Jason and some of the basic elements. I also thought the other movies worked best when they had a protagonist who was a bit of a match for Jason, like the telekinetic girl in *Part VII*. I like somebody who can put up a fight, rather than a bunch of teenagers who get slaughtered one by one. We also tried to go back to the first one and get into some Voorhees family history and tie up some loose ends. Throughout these films Jason always gets killed in different ways and he keeps coming back, but the reasons are never explained. So we decided that we'd create a mythology that explains the history of Jason and explains how this could be happening.

ADAM MARCUS: Dean came up with the idea for this character Creighton Duke, a bounty hunter who had been trailing Jason for years. We thought that was a great idea, because anything that could complicate the formula in a positive way should be in the movie. We were also trying to play a bit more in the *Terminator* realm. Another choice we made was to create a group of more believable adult characters who func-

The opening sequence of *Jason Goes to Hell* went through numerous incarnations. "I read the opening of the very first script, and it was really hardcore," remembers effects supervisor Howard Berger. "It started off with a flashback of Jason as a little kid, and he and his mother are having sex! It was intense, and certainly different, but then of course things changed along the way."

"I think we all came to our senses," laughs director Adam Marcus. "I can't believe I'm saying this, but we were actually trying to go a bit more 'family-esque' with *Jason Goes to Hell*. Then we said to ourselves, 'We need to be true to the roots of *Friday the 13th*.'" The film's eventual opening sequence featured the uncredited writing contributions of Lewis Abernathy, who worked previously for Sean Cunningham on such films as *House IV* and *DeepStar Six*. "We wanted to come up with the most conventional *Friday the 13th* opening we could," continues Marcus. "Then, at the very end of the sequence, we just blew the shit out of Jason. After that, the audience had no idea what to expect next!"

"There's nothing more fun than making a horror movie," says director Adam Marcus. The cast and crew seemed to agree. Clockwise from left: co-stars John LeMay (left) and Kari Keegan lean on each other between takes; Keegan and producer Sean Cunningham; Marcus plays a little bit of air guitar; Keegan and Marcus relax between setups.

tioned as a logical part of the community. Though we eliminated Elias, we still wanted to tie in the idea of the Voorhees family tree into the mythology of the series—that it took a Voorhees to kill a Voorhees, all that stuff.

However, at the end of the day, we knew this was still the equivalent of a wrestling picture. We had to be true to the roots of the franchise. I was just not that concerned with having Jason in every frame of the film. I didn't care. I felt like the previous eight movies gave you plenty of that. But everyone who made this movie was a fan of the series, contrary to what some diehard fanatics of the franchise have said. No one was trying to hurt the series. Ultimately, we just wanted to honor the fans by giving them something different.

Armed with a script that was, by design, radically different from any other Friday the 13th, *Sean Cunningham decided that the casting of the as-yet-untitled* Jason Goes to Hell *also required a unique approach. Once again, Cunningham called upon veteran casting director Barry Moss—who, like Cunningham, had not been associated with the series since the original* Friday. *But unlike the casting sessions of the summer of 1979, Moss was being asked to look beyond the fresh young faces that Hollywood had to offer up for*

*Jason's annual summer smorgasbord, and to bring together a more experienced cast to help create a more believable—and hopefully more appealing—ensemble. For the first time in the franchise's history, not a single teenage character was featured in the script. Instead, Moss would assemble a cast of recognizable faces culled largely from series television, including Erin Gray (*Buck Rogers, Silver Spoons*), Steven Williams (*21 Jump Street*) and Allison Smith (*Kate & Allie*), as well as* Friday the 13th: The Series *alum John D. LeMay, the only actor to appear in both incarnations of* Friday the 13th *as separate characters. Even if some of the casting choices were not always unanimous,* Jason Goes to Hell *would be the first* Friday *to make a sincere attempt to cast without regard to age, ethnicity or even gender.*

ADAM MARCUS: I wanted characters that were as interesting as Jason. Tommy Jarvis was a very interesting guy too, so I think that's why he showed up a few times in the earlier movies. But otherwise, you rarely had characters in the previous movies that you wanted to root for as much as you wanted to root for Jason. So at the end of this movie, when our hero is pummeling Jason with a shovel, I really wanted people cheering him on instead, you know?

DEAN LOREY: We wanted to take a lot of the dopiness out of the character's decisions. In the other *Friday* films, people tended to do things for stupid reasons. We decided that by making the main characters a bit older and giving them real lives, outside of just being lunch for Jason, we could give them more depth and subtext.

BARRY MOSS, Casting Director: The reason *Jason Goes to Hell* happened for me was because Sean was being very generous. My mother was dying of cancer and she lived in Los Angeles. And he said, "Why don't you come cast this movie? Then you can stay at home with your mom." Which was very nice.

I certainly didn't have the same reaction to this script as I did to the first one, which I absolutely loved. I did *Jason Goes to Hell* because I love Sean, and I did it to be home. And I did believe in it enough that I could tell an actor that I thought it was a good thing for them to do. Because by 1992, it was not such a prestigious thing to do *Friday the 13th*. There had been eight of them, so it was more difficult to get good people, certainly compared to the first film.

JOHN D. LEMAY, "Steve Freeman": Before I came to L.A., I went to Illinois State University in Chicago for awhile. I was doing an

internship at the Geffen Theatre and working part time at MCI Telecommunications. There I was, looking down through the window high above, at my agent's office on Michigan Avenue, just hoping and praying that something would happen to take me away from the miserable cold and winter on the streets below. Then it happened real quickly. I did all the agent rounds and stuff, and got a couple of commercials right off the bat. And next thing you know, I was reading for a movie called *Once Bitten* that Jim Carrey ended up doing. I was being touted as the next John Cusack, who was very big at the time and also from Chicago. And all of a sudden my agent sent me to L.A. to get more high-profile representation. So I kind of got the red carpet treatment very early in my career.

I was slowly building up a resume when I got the lead on *Friday the 13th: The Series*. I was on it for two years but left before the third. It was a great experience. I was working every day for two years, and I came out of that a much more confident actor. But every interview I did during the TV series spent a lot of time comparing the show to the movies, even though the only thing they had in common was the title. So I tried to disassociate myself from it, and to do a *Friday the 13th* film right after that—I wasn't sure it was the right move.

For me, it was a job. I read the script, and I got to be the hero, and I got to live, and kick Jason's butt, and it all seemed like fun to me. And they'd created a myth around Jason and given him a curse to deal with which, in a sense, goes along the lines of the way the *Friday the 13th* series played. And Adam's enthusiasm was infectious. He really wanted to make an old-fashioned horror film, and make characters that hadn't always necessarily been three-dimensional in the past *Friday*s. That's what Adam and I initially talked about when we met, and that's what made me excited to do the movie.

ADAM MARCUS: John had done *The Series*, which actually worked against him. There were some reservations in the air about casting him because of that reason. But I liked John. I thought he had a very interesting quality. And when I described the role to John, I said, "You gotta think sort of a young Bruce Willis." I wanted a lot of comedy, and John is a very serious actor, so I think he was sort of intrigued by that. So we went for it.

KARI KEEGAN, "Jessica Kimble": I moved out to L.A. with a guy I was dating at the time and my best girlfriend, and we all had the same agent. And they both happened to be really attractive people and got auditions for the movie. But the girl who was supposed to go from our agency cancelled at the last minute. So they called me and said, "You can go—even though you're not *Friday the 13th* material." I guess, apparently, *Friday the 13th* girls are what I call "POW" girls: POW hair, POW boobs, POW butt. I was kind of a like a normal-looking girl next door girl. And I actually went in to read for the best friend—the part that Allison Smith played. I got called back, and it was like, "Kari got called back and nobody else did!" It was a big scandal.

Then I went in and read with all of the girls who were reading for Jessica, and I was in the room when they left and heard them talk about what they liked and what they didn't like. And then Sean Cunningham, toward the end of the afternoon—I think I had read with maybe eight or nine young ladies—said, "Let's see you do Jessica." This is going to sound terrible, but because I had been in the room all day and I knew what they were looking for, I just stole from all the girls what was really good. "I'll do that and that and that." Then Adam asked the girl who was the last girl to read Jessica to read a lot. I think we did every scene in the entire movie.

Finally, my competitors and I were all in this huge warehouse, and Adam Marcus said, "Can you guys go play Frisbee for a couple minutes?" I was like, "This is bizarre." I guess you can tell

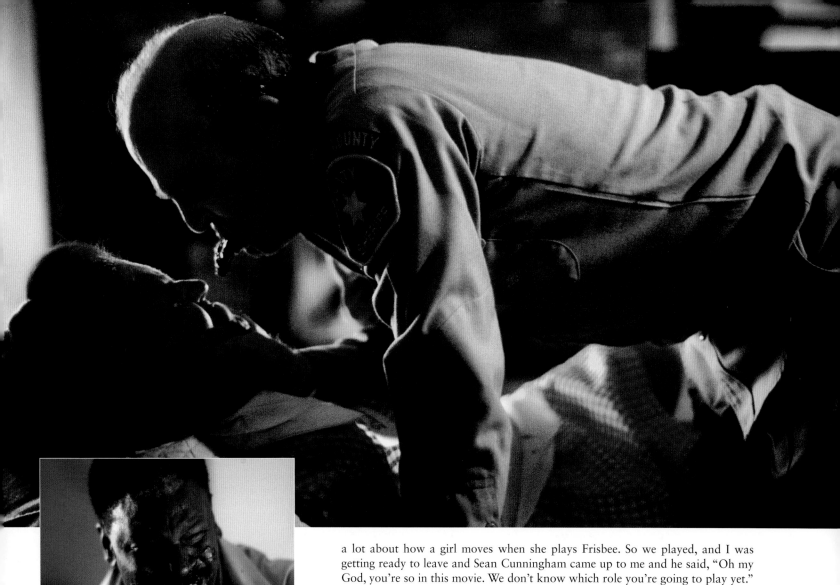

Unlike any *Friday the 13th* film before or since, the "body switching" plot device that drives *Jason Goes to Hell* owes more to such science fiction-tinged thrillers as *Invasion of the Body Snatchers* and *The Hidden* than traditional slasher films. One of *The Final Friday*'s pivotal scenes (**above**) features actor Richard Gant "ingesting" the black heart of Jason Voorhees and inheriting its essence of evil. "Quite frankly, I wish I could have done that opening scene again," admits Gant. "You look at actors like Vincent Price, who are masters at pulling something like that off, and I really wish I could have sold the moment better. But, then, what in the hell *was* my motivation?"

The "heart eating" did, however, prove to be a memorable moment for the special effects team. "There was some absolutely disgusting stuff in that movie!" laughs makeup effects supervisor Howard Berger. "But the thing that got me really sick was when Richard ate that heart. It was only gelatin, and we filled it with grape jelly, but *still*. I was ready to hurl after every take we did!"

a lot about how a girl moves when she plays Frisbee. So we played, and I was getting ready to leave and Sean Cunningham came up to me and he said, "Oh my God, you're so in this movie. We don't know which role you're going to play yet." I thought, "Oh, maybe they'll give me a smaller role like a consolation prize." And on Monday, my agent called and said, "You got the lead." I was like, "Shut up!"

ADAM MARCUS: What Kari had was a very accessible look, and she is a very attractive girl. I thought that she would have been a young mom. She and John kind of fit together, too. Sort of like salt and pepper shakers, you know? And Kari had a good sense of humor—that's something I am very strict about, that my actors have to be able to laugh and have a good time.

There was another thing Sean taught me as a kid. He said that any time you're casting somebody, no matter what for, throw a tennis ball or a Frisbee with them. Because if they can't throw or catch, then there's a whole world of things they can't do. Of course, you have to laugh at that. But seriously, if they can't, then they're going to become a pain in the ass, especially if there's any physicality involved.

ERIN GRAY, "Diana Kimble": I didn't want to do a horror film. Sean ended up calling me and said, "Well it's not really horror, it's really black comedy. I guarantee that when you go to the screening, they're gonna be talking back to the screen and laughing and nobody will be scared." Sean just sort of talked me into it. And he really was flattering and said things like, "I'm really a fan of yours and I'd really like you to do this." And there's nothing like having a producer beg—it makes the actor kind of go, "Okay, well if he really wants me *that* bad…"

STEVEN CULP, "Robert Campbell": I was a "theatre actor" at the time, but this was a lead in a movie, and I really needed to do that, even though it was a *Friday the 13th*. And the people involved were fantastic. Just the fact that Barry was casting, it made me go, "Okay, I'll read the script. I will think seriously about it."

LESLIE JORDAN, "Shelby": I love when actors say, "I won't do this because I don't want to get typecast." My commercial agency gave me a list once and said, "Check the products you won't do, like Tampax. Or, if you're vegetarian, that you don't want to do meat." And I'd do whatever. Diarrhea medicine? Sign me up. I take whatever comes my way. I've got to earn a living. Was I a fan of the horror genre? Not really. But I'm the biggest whore in Hollywood. You pay me a nickel and I'll do it.

Jason Goes to Hell was a grueling audition process. They kept having me in over and over. I kept thinking, "Good God, just make a decision!" Finally, they just switched my part with Rusty Schwimmer's. I remember Adam saying, "This is going to have a little bit more comedy than the others."

RUSTY SCHWIMMER, "Joey B.": I always say I got into acting because I had no choice. That was the only thing I thought I could do. And it was the only thing I ever wanted to do. And when I moved out to L.A., I said to my agent, "There are two things that I really need to do: a horror film and a soap opera. Because they're so bad, they're good."

The funny thing is, my agent was like, "There's this *Friday the 13th*, and even though the character's a man, I think you'd be really good for it." So when I walked in for my audition, I kind of did a fake-out on Adam Marcus and the casting directors, where I said, in this beach bunny voice, "Hi! So nice to meet you!" And they were like, "What the hell is this?" Then all of a sudden, I switched into my Chicago gangster voice: "What the fuck are you doin'!? What the fuck da you want!?" And they were dying. They asked me to do it again because they were laughing so hard. Then they brought in Leslie Jordan and put us together, and Leslie is like a little elf, and an incredible actor. And he started calling me "Pookie." Which was great, because he was supposed to be the "man," but he's so femme. And they were all laughing even harder. And right there, on the spot, Adam just said, "Why doesn't he play your husband? It'll be hilarious!" And that's a really good testament to Adam, because he was up for anything. So we ended up making up a lot of stuff just as we were doing it.

ADAM MARCUS: Casting Rusty and Leslie together was so inspired. The minute we saw the two of them together, the whole room just burst out laughing. But there's also this sort of bond that happened between the two of them in the movie—they are so loving to each other that it became more than just a sight gag, but something almost endearing. When they died in the movie, you were actually sad to see them go. That's what we were going for—we tried to get as much of a familial, loving connection between the characters in the movie as we possibly could. And genuine humanity.

RICHARD GANT, "Coroner": I had known Barry Moss and Julie Hughes when they cast me in *The Cosby Show*. They called and said, "Richard, you don't have to audition. Just come by and do us a favor and do this role." And it was wonderful, because I was fresh to it. I had never seen Jason or Freddy or any of these guys. Although at first they weren't sure what role they wanted me for—originally they had me read for the part Steven Williams eventually played.

STEVEN WILLIAMS, "Creighton Duke": The thing is, I'm incredibly talented. I'm blessed. I've never taken an acting lesson in my life. I'm the most opened-up free spirit I know! I also believe that you can't teach anyone to act. You either have it or you don't.

I was just in between shows and hanging out when *Jason Goes to Hell* came along. My agent called and said, "I've got an audition for you and it's for *Friday the 13th*." I read the script, and it was a bounty hunter, and to me, this guy was a stone-cold cowboy. I said, "If I can dress like a cowboy, I will do this role." So I had cowboy boots, a hat, and I borrowed one of those long outback coats from a buddy of mine. I just went in and said, "If I'm your guy, this is the way I want to do him." Then, when I went back, they had this strange costume for the guy, and I said, "No—I want to do him as a cowboy." And I still got the role.

ADAM MARCUS: I think what happened is, after the casting of Rusty and Leslie, that really shook things all up. Casting the two of them completely changed our perception of our own movie. And we started asking, why aren't we casting against type more? That really opened up our thinking, and gave us the courage to cast Steven Williams. And for one very important reason. We started looking back at George A. Romero's movies, and Romero's statement of constantly placing African American actors in hero roles, which to me has always been an inspiration.

Steve just made us laugh. Too many guys came in and read that material totally straight. Even the *Candyman* came in to read—Tony Todd. He was wonderful, but again, it was like he was still doing that role. We wanted someone who was as perverse as Quint in *Jaws*. Dean and I had always talked about Creighton Duke as being the one guy people would really talk about when the movie's over.

Despite his inexperience as a director, Adam Marcus strove earnestly to create an open, sociable, actor-friendly atmosphere, both on-set and off—although not one without a few quirks. Off screen there

"There is something about shooting a horror movie that brings out the kid in all of us. I loved going to lunch with a knife in my back." Erin Gray

was a conflicted lead actor, a "bounty hunter" with a fondness for dropping his pants, and an action-heroine who ended up with a broken toe, compliments of a dropped flashlight. Not to mention heated arguments over hockey masks and a budget-conscious producer still somewhat uncertain about his choice in hiring a neophyte to helm his $3 million production. But no matter how crazed the on-set antics became, both cast and crew came together in an attempt to create the most audacious Friday the 13th yet.

ADAM MARCUS: I was twenty-three. I was a dumb-ass. But I was just egomaniacal enough to think I could pull this off. There was fear. Definitely. That first day of production I was ready to blow my brains out. I was like, "What the hell am I doing!?" But the nice thing was that after the first two days of dailies came back, I remember Michael De Luca at New Line just going, "We're set. This is going to be great." And that was it. We never, ever had New Line bothering us again. I was very lucky.

I also have never liked the auteur theory of filmmaking. I think movies are made by communities of people and I think those communities have to enjoy their work. Otherwise, you know, do electrical work on someone's house, not on movies. You'll make better money, too.

STEVEN CULP: Adam Marcus was into creating this little commune during *Jason Goes to Hell*. He had us come in a week before to rehearse. We would all play basketball and games together. So I was able to come in with ideas and get feedback from Adam and everybody on the set. I felt like I was at home. There was this feeling that we're all creating something together, even if it was this silly little horror film.

RUSTY SCHWIMMER: Adam's such a good soul. What I loved most about him was that this was truly a collaboration. He had a lot of guts to listen to other people. His ego never got in the way. One time, I thought it would be really funny if I used my pinky nail to make the eyes of a Jason hamburger. Adam went, "Okay, do it!" Adam almost never negated anything I wanted to do. We were basically at summer camp and they just happened to film it.

KARI KEEGAN: Adam was very open about coming up with new ideas. I think sometimes it was out of desperation. I dropped a flashlight on the first day of shooting and it broke my toe. And this is the scene in the garage, where Steven Culp attacks me. That is the first thing I shot. And now I thought my career was ruined by a flashlight and a broken toe, because they're like, "You still have to get out of the car and run." So John LeMay was just like, "I'll carry her! It will be funny." So if you watch the movie, there's a scene where John's character is pulling me out of the house, and he throws me over his shoulders kicking and screaming and carries me to the car. And John is honestly not much bigger than me!

JOHN D. LEMAY: Adam was very generous to the actors. He wasn't tied to the script. He loved to let people discover things. And this was a daily occurrence, which made it an incredibly rewarding experience for most of the people involved.

HOWARD BERGER, Makeup Effects Supervisor: We were all like best friends. We worked eighteen hours a day and then we would spend the weekends together just having barbeques at my house, or partying at Adam's place. It was very family oriented. Adam stayed strong to what he wanted to do. He didn't back down. And Adam was young. For me, it was fine. We've worked with a lot of directors that had never shot a film but this was extremely pleasant. He was so enthusiastic and had good ideas. I think he believed in what he was doing so strongly. And he had a good support group, too.

ADAM MARCUS: I made mistakes at the time that were stupid first-timer mistakes. But I had Sean. And I gotta tell you that even though he and I had many a row, he's a great teacher. And the one thing about Sean is that with him, there is no bullshit. Even when he would be nasty, he was straight with you. Sean is also one of those guys who likes to work with everybody in a room together, all yelling and disagreeing with each other. And there were times when Sean, myself, Dean and Noel would all be arguing on the set, but some of the most brilliant stuff came out of those moments. I think that communal element was really positive and really good for creativity. Honestly, despite any fights, I don't think any of us wanted to leave that set.

SEAN CUNNINGHAM: I bought into the fact that Adam was a self-appointed expert of the genre, and that he was the representative of the audience for whom it was being made. It wasn't being made for me, it was being made for him. So we had to do those things that pleased him. When you've made a commitment as a producer to let a director direct, you have to let him do it. But I was involved much more than I wanted to be. In structural and financial ways, I would guide him. And Adam was very gracious. On some level, I was kind of his hero. Plus, he had all these shots that he thought were going to be really cool, so you want to support that.

GREG NICOTERO, Makeup Effects Supervisor: Adam had to fight. He really did. He went up against everybody. I remember him and Sean having disagreements about what the vision for the film should be. And I admired Adam for standing up for what he wanted. I'll tell you, for a guy who had never directed a film, it's very easy to be swayed by numerous voices. This person will have an opinion, this person will have an opinion. And after a while when you get inundated like that it sometimes can weaken your resolve. But he stayed true to what he believed in the entire time. And that's really hard to do.

ADAM MARCUS: I remember one of the big disagreements we had was over the hockey mask. Before I was even hired to do the movie, Sean said, "You can do whatever you want, but just get that damn hockey mask off of him!"

SEAN CUNNINGHAM: That is not true. How could you do it without a hockey mask? What was Adam thinking? I didn't have any feeling about the hockey mask whatsoever. I thought the hockey mask in *Part 3*, when it first appeared, was just a way to try and keep Jason generic. He's the bogeyman. He's not supposed to be a person. On that level, it was good. Although I did think, "Don't they have any imagination?" Because it was never explained, it was just there. It was just a device. But I never had any antipathy toward it.

"That camper being split up the middle is, without a doubt, the most disgusting moment in the history of *Friday the 13th*!" Adam Marcus

Arguably the signature kills of *Jason Goes to Hell* were the murders of two amorous campers, Luke (Michael Silver) and Deborah (*Queer as Folk*'s Michelle Clunie). The scene was actually a reshoot completed months after the end of principal photography. Test audiences had demanded more traditional stalk and slash elements in the film, and that is what they got—one of the most graphic ever seen in a mainstream film, *Friday the 13th* or otherwise. "That gag was pretty violent," agrees makeup effects supervisor Greg Nicotero. "We had a whole fire extinguisher filled with blood. Right after the moment of impact, when the weapon is thrust through the fake chest of the girl, we did a quick count of

"I've had many physical altercations in my life, so when I put that mask on, anger is not a very hard emotion for me to bring up." Kane Hodder

ADAM MARCUS: Sean's a liar and you can print that! He literally said to me to get the damn hockey mask out. Because the hockey mask was not Sean's idea. Sean had a disdain for it. He might have changed his feelings for it since, but he sure didn't like the hockey mask then. So we got it out of most of the movie. And Sean did love the idea of the body hopping and all that stuff.

RICHARD GANT: Adam was funny to me. I remember one time he walked onto the set and, for whatever reason, they had started the scene without him. The AD, for want of anything better to do, had already called "Action!" But Adam handled it with grace. He just walked on the set, looked around, and the look on his face was priceless.

KARI KEEGAN: Adam Marcus wore lifts in his shoes, I'll tell you that. Because he's short. And I only know that because I was in the wardrobe room and I was like, "Whose high heels are these that don't look like high heels?" And they were like, "*Shhhh*!" He thinks he's tall, though. He would be like, "I'm 5'10"." And I'm like, "Honey, you're 5'8"!"

RUSTY SCHWIMMER: At first I thought Sean was one of those cheesy Hollywood producer guys. But then I saw how fun he was and that he understood what he was producing here. I left with tons of respect for him. He has a great sense of humor about all this. And he's very smart, and very savvy.

If anything, making *Jason Goes to Hell* solidified my idea of having a good time while I work. You need to. This should never be a grueling job. You should be happy to wake up and go to work in the morning.

JOHN D. LEMAY: I wanted to be doing *Angels in America*. I think we all want to be doing roles that reaffirm our love of acting, and this whole idea of being able to grow and discover more about yourself through performance. But you just don't always get a chance to do that. And certainly *Jason Goes to Hell* didn't lend itself too much to that kind of enlightenment.

ADAM MARCUS: John and I had originally talked about bringing a comedic quality to his role, but once we started the shoot John suddenly wanted to get very deep into it and be very emotional about it. He almost went for a darker view of the character than we initially explored. We even ended up rewriting several scenes for that reason. For example, there's one scene that's not in the film, but I think it ended up on the DVD. It was the diner scene where they're pulling all those pranks. Those jokes were originally very big, funny and dirty. And John was sort of against that. He really didn't want to do that. That wasn't where his head was at with the character. So it was rewritten.

But John's a very good actor, and very, very serious. I'm thrilled that we cast him. He brought a certain gravity to that role. The only thing I would say for John was that, ultimately, I still wanted to get a little more sense of humor out of that character.

STEVEN CULP: It is a very violent movie. I have an ambivalent response. Because it is a lot more violent when you see it on the screen than it feels when you're actually doing this stuff on the set. I would've been happier, and we all probably would've been, if it was a lot more of a humorous, outrageous adventure, and a thrill ride. But at least from what I understood, that was simply the requirement of the franchise, as well as the studio putting their hand in and going, "This is what we want. This is what it has to be."

KARI KEEGAN: I was sure I was going to get fired every day. I was twenty-five years old. This was really my first movie, and for

everybody else, it wasn't. I was the rookie in the group and felt a lot of times like, "I'm not doing this right." I understand why actors and actresses fall in love on set because it's like instant family—it's like instant brothers and sisters and instant friends, because you depend on these people in really intimate ways. To make sure that you don't get hurt, that you're acting with somebody, that somebody's directing you. It is almost impossible not to get extremely sad when it ends.

ADAM MARCUS: Steven Williams is probably going to kill me for telling this story. There was a scene we were going to shoot that involved an effect, which required an appliance be put on Steven's leg. And he had to pull his pants down to attach the appliance. Well, the costume girls came in with one of the K.N.B. effects guys, and while they're working on the appliance, the costume girls had to fit the hole in Steven's jeans. So Steven drops his pants and isn't wearing any underwear. And all we saw were two screaming costume girls running right out of this room. Steven was definitely sort of a ladies man. He was partying so much at night that he would fall asleep on set between takes. He would just like put his head down and be asleep while we're moving equipment around him.

But I gotta tell you, I have never met an actor who came in with a better knowledge of his character, or who was more prepared. This guy was ready every second of the day, any time we needed him. He's incredible.

STEVEN WILLIAMS: I'm a very loose individual on a set. I'm going to do my thing, I'm going to have a good time, and I'm going to be gregarious. But I've been reprimanded on sets for flirting too much with the women. And I absolutely played up the sexual angle of my scenes with Erin Gray. I don't know what she had going, but that was my whole intention in terms of our scenes together. Plus, I found her to be a very good-looking woman in person. For real!

LESLIE JORDAN: I look back, and I think it was perfect I was in this movie called *Jason Goes to Hell*, because my life was in the toilet at the time. Leslie was going to hell, too. I was just an absolute mess in 1993. I was in an abusive relationship with this drug addict. He was this 6'3" cowboy from Weatherford, Texas who had a belt buckle with a turkey on it. And he had this horrendous drug problem, but of course I was going to get him sober, so I ended up in the vortex of his drug addiction. And I can remember being on the set of *Jason Goes to Hell* in a panic because I hadn't heard from him. I was afraid to go to work because I thought if I left my car keys he might take it. Then he got drunk one night and ended up shooting me with a crossbow. He eventually went to jail for attempted murder.

Anyway, all this was going on in the middle of *Friday the 13th*, and the apex of it was my death scene. Adam Marcus was so friggin' energetic, and I would come in every day exhausted from having sat up all night long worrying what this cowboy was up to and where my car was. And here was Adam, right out of NYU film school, just bubbling. And now I have to go into the french fry fryer. It was filled with bubbling root beer. So I went in, came up, and out. After the first take, Adam goes, "Oooh! Oooh! Oooh! Dude, I've got a great idea! When you go in, can you balance yourself and kind of kick your legs?" And I said, "Okay, that sounds

"One of the reasons we were really attracted to *Jason Goes to Hell* was because of the supernatural creature element," says K.N.B. makeup effects supervisor Greg Nicotero. "It allowed us to come up with some pretty cool effects, like the melting gag (**above**) where the creature comes out of the sheriff." Many of the film's fantastical effects came out of improvisations between the K.N.B. effects team and director Adam Marcus. "That really speaks to Adam's passion and enthusiasm for the film," says Howard Berger, who, along with Robert Kurtzman, shared supervisory duties with Nicotero. "Remember that little creature (**middle**) that bursts out of Kipp Marcus' neck? It was originally just going to be this little thing running around. Then, it just became this big monster. That's an example of how we were really allowed to go for it, and I think that shows onscreen."

"It was a childhood dream come true. I got to jump over handcuffs, shoot a gun, and kill Jason. What could be cooler than that?" John LeMay

good." We do another take. Then Adam again: "Hey, dude, I've got a great idea. Can you flail your arms?" I sigh and go, "Okay." Seven takes later, Adam's like, "Dude, I've got another idea..." And I just turned to him and said, "Dude, I've got a really great idea. Get the fucking shot!"

Everybody was like, "What is wrong with sweet little Leslie?"

STEVEN WILLIAMS: I wanted to give Creighton Duke some dimensions, because the man was a little bit wacky. But to this day, I don't quite understand some of those lines. What was that one about the pink hot dog thing and the doughnut? I just figured this Creighton Duke guy was crazy. So you give it ambiguity. You say something, get a crazed look in your eyes, and just let the audience try to figure out what the hell is going on.

JOHN D. LEMAY: We had our moments on the set where we'd fight about whether we were doing something that was sacrificing logic for the sake of the storyline. And for the most part, Adam really had an eye on what translated as being real. A big part of my job was trusting him to save me from all the moments where the audience ends up saying, "Why is he going into that house again when he already knows Jason is there?"

What was also interesting about doing a horror movie back then is that it was pre-*Scream*. Everybody had a great sense of humor about it, but as crazy as the circumstances in the movie are, I don't think we ever thought about pointing it out explicitly, or indicating directly that this is ridiculous. We still had to try and make it plausible. It wasn't acceptable at that point in time to call attention to the conventions of the genre the way you can today.

I also think Adam was just kind of into weird for weird's sake. And why not, in a franchise that's already over-the-top weird anyway?

ADAM MARCUS: The scene where Andy Block, who played the cop who attacks Erin Gray, is chained up by Jason and shaved—people lost their lunch at that scene moreso than any of the gore effects. It was so creepy and so not what they had seen in the other Jason movies, that the reaction was like, "What the hell did we just see?" I loved that. I was so turned on by just scaring the audience in ways other than just cutting people up.

RICHARD GANT: I found it refreshing. I liked Dean's writing, I liked his approach. In our business, you tend to know that these younger people will probably end up running the industry one day, so hopefully you make a good impression on them. Although, I have to say, that scene where I tie that cop up, I don't know...did Jason need a clean face before he killed someone?

DEAN LOREY: One of the things we decided upon was to come up with the most archetypal opening we possible could, so that the audience would believe that this was no different than any other *Friday the 13th* movie. So the girl is alone in the cabin in the woods, then we have these jump scares, and she goes running naked out through the woods. It was just about every *Friday* cliché we could pack into the opening sequence. Then, when you least expect it, pow! We blow Jason into a million pieces. That was our way of making the audience think, "Gee, maybe I'd better pay a little closer attention to this film than I normally would with a *Friday* movie."

ADAM MARCUS: Another great thing about the opening of the movie is that it is not unlike what *Scream* did a couple of years later. In the first ten minutes of that movie, they killed off the best known actress in the film. That was total genius. In *Jason Goes to Hell*, we blew up the best-known character in our film seven minutes into it—Jason himself. Like *Scream*, we started the movie off leaving people going, "I have no idea what the fuck is going to happen next!"

DEAN LOREY: But perhaps our biggest decision was to take Jason from being this unknown killer in Crystal Lake to being Serial Killer #1, to make him very well-known and establish that everybody wants to kill him. We also addressed the question of why he keeps coming back every time he's been killed. That allowed us to get a bit more tongue-in-cheek and have more fun with the movie.

ADAM MARCUS: What was terrific about Dean is that he didn't feel like his toes were being stepped on because I added a line, or an actor added a line. Both Dean and I had been actors back in New York, and we knew that we were just gonna play on set and come up with stuff as we went along.

Of course, that can be a double-edge sword. There was always that concern that you'd go too far astray. Some of the criticisms of the movie have said that. But I think one of the mistakes of horror movies is that they are so rigid to the script that they don't allow anything to develop naturally out of situations. Roy Scheider wrote that classic line from *Jaws*—"We're gonna need a bigger boat"— right on the set, okay? If you're not attuned to listen to what your actors have to say, then you're cutting yourself off at the knees.

Steven Williams was a perfect example of that. He was just so smart and funny. All that Creighton Duke stuff— Steven and I talked about it on the set, and then he just said, "What if I played him as if he is of ambiguous sexuality?" And I was like, "Dude, that's great!" And because of that, the whole jail cell exchange between Steve and John LeMay actually became my favorite scene in the movie. Because it's eight pages of gobbledygook—just so much exposition it's insane. But the audience doesn't even realize it because of the way Steven and John played it. It's just the actors doing the work. John, when he looks down at Steven touching his hair like that, it's hilarious. We were able to get laughs, but there was also this nervous thing happening to the audience because they are so unsure of where it is going. I loved that.

Adam Marcus and Dean Lorey's attempts to defy all expectations of what a Friday the 13th *film could be were not limited to the film's situations, characters and dialogue. They felt it was time to change Jason, too. Although* Jason Goes to Hell *would mark the third time actor/stuntman Kane Hodder inhabited the titular role, Hodder's reservations about the lack of screen time devoted to the series' iconic main character would later be echoed by legions of fans who wanted to know why a movie called* Jason Goes to Hell *was, for all intents and purposes, Jason-less. Glimpsed only occasionally as a ghostly specter throughout the majority of the film, only to return in the final reel for a fisticuffs battle-to-the-finish, the Jason Voorhees of* The Final Friday *made his presence known in an entirely new way. Taking a cue from* Invasion of the Body Snatchers *and* The Hidden, *the "body swapping" concept of* Jason Goes to Hell *required a host of attendant special effects far more fantastical than had ever been seen in the* Friday *series. If slug-like worms jumping from one character's mouth to another, melting heads and swirling dust devils from hell left many diehard fans scratching their heads, Adam Marcus and his special effects collaborators at K.N.B. were loving it. This was definitely not the* Friday the 13th *your big brother grew up with.*

HOWARD BERGER: Greg Nicotero, Bob Kurtzman and I had formed K.N.B. Effects in the mid-'80s, and had worked with Sean Cunningham before on *DeepStar Six* and *The Horror Show*. Then Sean called us and said, "We're doing *Jason Goes to Hell*." And we signed on just like that.

The very first script we got I really liked a lot, but it was really hardcore. I remember it started off with Jason as a little kid with his mother and they were having sex. And I kept reading it and going, "This is really intense, but I like it because it's different." Then of course things changed and many of those elements went

away. But it was chock full of stuff. That's why it was a pleasure to work with Adam, because he had such great ideas. Between Adam and Bob Kurtzman, who was really heavily involved, many new elements were added. Remember that little creature that shows up at the end, that turned into a big monster? I don't recall that ever being in the script. We just kept throwing a lot of stuff in and Adam was really open to it.

GREG NICOTERO: All the creature stuff was above and beyond the stereotypical *Friday the 13th* movie. It wasn't just about the gore gags. I really liked the supernatural element of *Jason Goes to Hell*, which was never really touched upon in any of the other films—certainly, the evil that drove Jason was never personified as a creature that could jump from person to person. And I thought that it was a good device to keep the series going, because we'd seen Jason doing the same thing over and over again for so long.

After the slasher wave hit in the early 1980s, there was a backlash. You still had your *Nightmare on Elm Street* and *Halloween* sequels, but by the end of the decade it was slowing down. That was actually a hard storm for our company to weather, but we were able to do high-profile films like *Dances with Wolves* and *Misery* to prove that we could do more than gore stuff. But one of the things that our company has always prided ourselves on is that we're the only one that's worked on every single '80s slasher character. We did a couple Leatherface movies, an *Evil Dead*, a couple of *Halloween*s, and a bunch of *Nightmare on Elm Street*s. And even at that young age we were at the time, it was fun to think that we had a hand in the sagas that people would be watching for years to come. People flip out over that stuff, because those movies influenced so many people. So now we could go, "Okay, we've done a Jason, too." I don't think there was ever an attitude of, "Oh, this is just a *Friday the 13th* movie, and *Part IX* at that."

HOWARD BERGER: Carl Fullerton's Jason is one of my favorites, as well as John Carl Buechler's in *Part VII*. Having the spine exposed and all that was terrific. So we wanted to incorporate that into our design as well, and kind of make it look like Jason's skin had grown over the mask, almost as if it had been fused into one piece. It was as if you could no longer take his mask off.

Below: Famous Los Angeles radio personalities Mark Thompson and Brian Phelps made their screen debut in *Jason Goes to Hell*. "*Friday the 13th* was one of Brian's favorite things," remembers director Adam Marcus. "One day, he went on the air to ask for a part in the next movie for his birthday. I actually heard this live in my car. I called up and said, "If you're really committed, I will write a part for you today. I'll even give you a hideously gory death." So Brian got his birthday wish—they had one great scene, they got slaughtered, and they even held a live radio show from the K.N.B. effects shop when they were getting their life casts made."

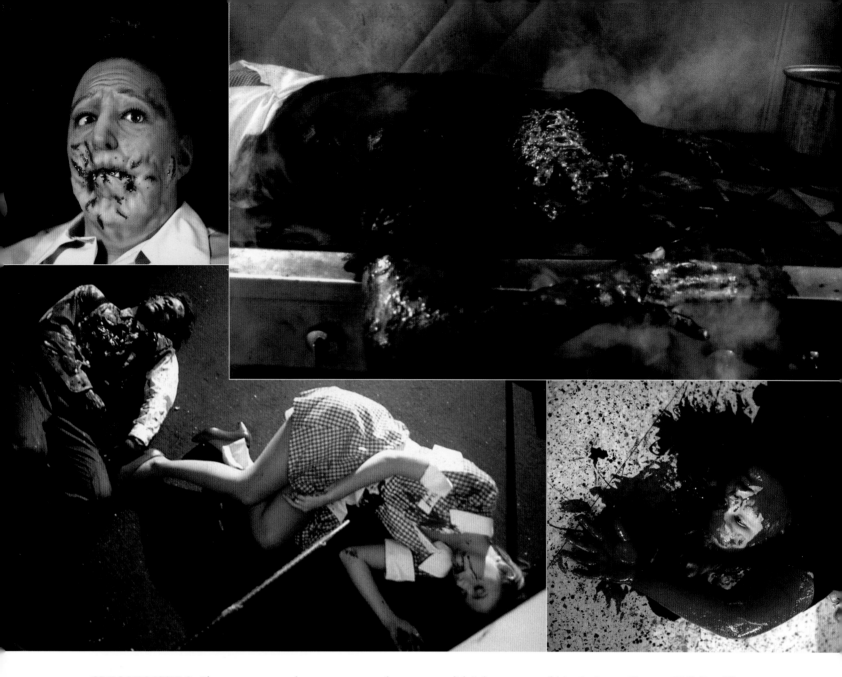

GREG NICOTERO: I know many people seem to respond very positively to the Carl Fullerton makeup from the second movie. So did we. It's really a cool look, and I always felt Carl made Jason look sympathetic but scary at the same time. He was truly frightening—you would believe that that guy would live in the forest.

We wanted to recognize what had come before but also make this Jason our own, so that's why we went with that misshapen head and a kind of bubbly texture to him. Plus, we sculpted the makeup as a full-body foam latex suit underneath the costume. Because we also really wanted the flexibility of being able to expose as much skin on Jason as we could, given the fact that we weren't going to see him through the entire movie. You really only see him at the beginning and then you see him at the end, and that's it.

KANE HODDER, "Jason Voorhees": Landing *Jason Goes to Hell* was fairly easy. I had been stunt coordinator with Sean since around 1985, so I had a relationship with him. I also played Jason in two prior movies and had coordinated all the stunts for a number of years. I think they thought, "Why change?" And Adam Marcus was someone that was a fan of what I had done with the character.

ADAM MARCUS: Kane was always our guy. I love Kane. And he loves that character. I know that he was a little disappointed that

we didn't have more of him in *Jason Goes to Hell*. But I'll say this—when Jason shows up at the end of the film and bursts through the floor boards, the audience cheered. I think I gave Jason his best send-out right at the beginning, then his best entrance, and his best send-out yet again. There's not a lot of *Friday the 13th* movies you can say that about.

KANE HODDER: From the beginning I was like, "Goddamn, there's not nearly as much Jason as I would like to see." Just as a fan. Although, when he does finally comes back at the end, it was a great, welcoming moment for the audience. But in all honesty, I still don't think it was worth not having Jason in the film as much.

I tried with several of the cast to create some sort of continuity between what I would do in my performance and what they would do when Jason was inside of them. And I didn't get really any positive response about that at all, particularly from Steven Culp, who said, "My Jason wouldn't do that." I said, "You know, you're not really playing a character—you're playing yourself with Jason inside you." My opinion is that you should do something that Jason does, not something you come up with in your fucking mind because of "your character." When you have Jason inside you, make it seem real—do something that's recognizable. I did talk to Adam Marcus, but I don't think he really cared about it, either. I really couldn't get through to anybody. I was just looking at it from a fan's point of view.

STEVEN CULP: I know Kane was really concerned that I carry on the character, that I be "Jason-like." Kane's a character. No. He's a stuntman. He's a "teamster." They're kind of rough rolling guys. I just thought he was quite funny.

RICHARD GANT: I never looked at playing Jason in me as if it was camp, although, to me, there was always a tongue-in-cheek quality to these types of films. But I think Kane liked the approach I took and that I wanted to respect the continuity. And I think I was the only one there trying to do that.

HOWARD BERGER: People think that these monsters are just guys in suits, and that anybody could do it. But Robert Englund as Freddy, or Kane as Jason—they bring a definite style to the character that no one else ever could.

JULIE MICHAELS, "Agent Marcus": Can I tell you how much of a method actor Kane is? There was one scene where he was supposed to be chasing me out of the house, and even though he wasn't in the shot, he was still working it. He decided to motivate me a little bit and stand behind the door and not tell me he was there. And I'm already freaked out. I had to be talked into this part by Adam Marcus to begin with, so they roll action and Kane jumps out from behind the door. I literally jumped out of my skin out of pure fear. And I wanted to kill him afterward!

HOWARD BERGER: I noticed that Kane didn't really fraternize with the other actors. He wasn't yucking it up. But to his credit, sometimes that can affect everyone else, because I've been on sets where the guy in the suit is being all goofy with everyone, and then when it comes time to shoot nobody buys into it—it becomes just a big rubber monster. But Kane always kept that essence. And Kane's a big guy. Even when he's not in the suit and he's staring you down, you get a little freaked out. He's very passionate and emotional. As well he should be.

JOHN D. LEMAY: Kane was a method actor, and just as scary off the set as on. But, deep down inside, he's just a sweetheart of a guy.

JULIE MICHAELS: I also love that Kane came out from behind the mask and did a cameo in the movie. And he called himself "Pussy." I loved that.

KANE HODDER: I am a pussycat—until the cameras roll. And when there's a violent scene, everybody shits their pants because I look like I'm out of control. The character isn't too far away from my real personality, so it doesn't take long to slip right in there and start tearing people up. I just always loved doing it. And I do have somewhat of a temper. It's nice to go to work and get all that aggression out, and then go home feeling very calm.

GREG NICOTERO: The funniest thing was the mood music Kane had when he was getting made up as Jason. He would have this little boom box, and he would just be like, "Hey, man, this is the music I need when I go onstage and do appearances and stuff." And it was Metallica's "Enter Sandman." I think *Jason Goes to Hell* was Kane right at the height of the whole Jason thing.

Cuts, bruises and scrapes are common on films as physically demanding as Friday the 13th, *but one particularly nasty fall near the end of principal photography would cause already-simmering tensions to reach a boiling point—and an irreparable rift to form between Kari Keegan and Adam Marcus that even the film's premiere couldn't fix.*

KARI KEEGAN: There was a scene where I had to land against a tree log, and I really hurt my neck. I severely injured myself and should have gone to the hospital, and Adam was like, "No, you're fine, you're fine." I said, "No, I am not fine, and I am not being a baby about this." So I went to my dressing room, and I called my boyfriend and he came and got me, and I went to the doctor and they said, "She has a sprained neck. She can't turn her head." It was literally two days before the end of shooting.

I happened to complain about it to my agent at the wrong time. When I called him, he was all, "What the fuck?!" I hate to say this about agents, but most of them are wannabes. They wanted to be actors, they didn't make it, and they became agents. If they can throw their power around, that's what they'll do. And mine was a real rabble-rouser who liked to flex a lot of testosterone, so this was fun for him. And he was like, "My actress is being taken advantage of and put in

The action centerpiece of *Jason Goes to Hell*, the "diner massacre," is a favorite of director Adam Marcus. "*The Final Friday* is not really a slasher movie," says Marcus. "Those movies are all, 'Set 'em up, knock 'em down.' We wanted to go more for a *Terminator* kind of thing, especially when Steven Culp (**above**) comes charging into the diner. That scene is like something out of a Sam Peckinpah film. We got to do a lot of great shots, with stylized lighting, and even slow-motion. I think it is probably the most effective scene in the film."

Top: Girls with Guns. "They armed me with some kind of crazy .44 Magnum!" laughs actress Rusty Schwimmer. "Which is so funny, because in real life, I'm so anti-gun. But once the guns came out, suddenly all of us girls in the cast got all this testosterone. Those were probably my favorite moments making *Jason Goes to Hell*. We'd all be in the back of the diner set, just shooting shit for fun, and cracking ourselves up."

a compromising position and all I have to do is call SAG!" And it sort of got blown out of proportion, and I kind of got swept into letting it be blown out of proportion.

ADAM MARCUS: It wasn't really a stunt. It was the kind of thing that, as a director, you would ask any actor to do. I wasn't putting anybody in peril. But Kari hurt herself. We sent her immediately to the hospital. Immediately. She complained of her neck and her leg. We didn't make her stay one more second to work.

Kari was a young actress. I was a young director. I think everybody sort of overreacted to that moment. That's all that happened at first. But every set, especially near the end, becomes this sort of gossipy kind of place. So there was a lot of talking going on and I was definitely sucked into that. Everybody started to kind of weigh in with their opinions. And I believe it was John LeMay who was sort of upset and insulted the most by what was happening with Kari, because he was a fellow actor. I respect that about John, and he and I spoke about what was going on. I said, "You're right. I get you, I hear you." So it was squashed at that point, but that's when Kari's representation got into it. That's when it got a little contentious.

GREG NICOTERO: Adam came to me and told me that Sean was going to direct the last couple of things on the movie. There were only two days left. I thought it was more like the studio wanted Sean to step in and finish, but there was something else on top of it as well. Kari felt pressured to do nudity, and she refused.

ADAM MARCUS: It had been a very long road with Kari. There was this whole situation with the nudity that was, in my opinion, very underhanded. I didn't feel she had been straight with me upfront that she wasn't going to do any, that she didn't want to. Even after we started shooting it, if she had gotten cold feet and just had talked to me about it, it would have been a very different situation.

The big scene was when she was in the shower, and has to cry over the death of her mother. I remember we did offer Kari a body double but she didn't want it, which I was very surprised at. I understand she's an actress, she didn't want to be exposed that way. But the job itself required that somebody was exposed. And honestly, the reason behind it was that the character was a mother—so we didn't want the fact that she had a child to desexualize her. Moms on film rarely get to be sexy. Really, what we were going for was that scene in *The Big Chill*, where Glenn Close is sitting in the shower naked and crying. She was nude, but it's so dramatic and raw. That's the way I wanted to shoot it.

KARI KEEGAN: The whole nudity thing got really funny, in an uncomfortable way, because Adam assured Sean Cunningham that he was going to get me to do a nude scene. I had spoken to my agent about it beforehand when he first sent me in. I said, "I don't do nudity."

When all is said and done, my parents have to see this. And you're going to be on film for the rest of your life. And I was young. This was not the only job in town. I had only lived in L.A. a few months when I got that one, so I had this mentality of, "It must not be that hard." So it got to the point where, when it came time to shoot the shower scene, I had a flesh-colored bathing suit bottom on and Dixie cup boobs. It was like the Madonna bra, because then there was no way they were going to be able to shoot anything. And Adam was just like, "O-kay." And no one was allowed on set except for me, Adam, the cameraman and my Dixie cups. Then there was a little snafu with the water—it was so hot. So the scene ended up being easy—I started crying because I was in real pain.

SEAN CUNNINGHAM: I started to realize that we had problems and I had to smooth it over. I did end up directing two scenes. Kari just refused to be around Adam at that point. Then he called her names, and she called him an ass. Now, it's neither here nor there. But I grew to like Kari a lot. I got her through it somehow.

KARI KEEGAN: Adam started doing some crappy things about scheduling me. He would tell me to come in at seven o'clock at night and not use me until two o'clock in the morning for a scene where I'm walking down the hallway. Sean Cunningham called and said, "What can I do?" I said, "Can we just work together—you and me?" Sean ended up directing the last couple days of the movie because I walked off the set. Adam was very, very angry because it was like, "Who is this girl? This is my movie!" And I felt sort of helpless, because I got caught up in something. I didn't mean for that to happen. And Adam got so out of control and irate on the phone with me that I was like, "You're threatening me now, so now I really don't want you to do it." If he had been cool, I would have gone into work. I would have said, "Sean, you can go. Adam, this is fine. My agent just got a little out of control."

ADAM MARCUS: Looking back, of course I would have handled it differently. I would have tried to maintain as much good will between Kari and myself as possible. I would have been stronger in some ways and more compassionate in others. I think it was mostly her representation. They were really just rude and insulting. We were all trying to work as a family and do something together, creatively. But the truth is that Kari's a very talented girl. I was happy to cast her, and I was happy to work with her. It's too bad things got a little bit screwed up.

KARI KEEGAN: I wish I had a couple more years behind me and a little more confidence, because Adam had every right to bring me in whenever he wanted to bring me in. But he wasn't doing that to other people. Even the makeup people were like, "Why are you here? We've got fifteen scenes to do!" But being young and a first-time actress, and this was my first job, I was incredibly insecure. I either thought he hated me or he was out to get me. I don't want to represent him in a bad way, either. He was twenty three years old! I was twenty five or twenty six. Overall, I really liked Adam. It all started off really well. Adam and I were buddy-buddy. It was just a couple of really bad last days.

Eventually, at the premiere of the movie, Adam and I walked in together, and it all seemed okay. I've always felt bad about what happened. But the opportunity to patch things up never really presented itself. I have a great respect for Adam and he did a great job.

Above: You can't fool a true Jason fan, even with a prop mailbox. Note the missing "o" in "Voorhees."

"Our biggest disappointment with the film was the big finale," says makeup effects supervisor Greg Nicotero. "We were so proud of what we had originally created. There was supposed to be all this stuff happening with these vines wrapping around Jason, and then we see these demons made out of earth start to come up. Then Jason is struggling, and he gets pulled into the ground. So we built a whole tabletop miniature of Jason being pulled into the ground by these swirling dirt demons. And this was before CGI had really taken hold, so how we achieved the effect was really unique—a live-action combination of full-size creatures and animated miniatures. Then I remember going to dailies and sitting there with everyone and there was some concern that maybe the visual effects of Jason being pulled into hell were just a bit too much for the studio to stomach. Or maybe they ran out of money and didn't want to spend more to complete it in post-production. I don't know—I just remember being very disappointed that all that stuff never made the final cut."

"Honestly, we were just too low-budget of a movie," contends director Adam Marcus, "and there was no CGI back then. So we cut more of it than we wanted to. But then it did sort of help give it the *Jaws* feeling. Like, show less, and let the audience imagine more. Still, I like what we ended up with. It's fun."

It has been said that a movie is really made in the editing room, a theory repeatedly put to the test by the makers of Jason Goes to Hell *during its chaotic post-production schedule. Opinions differ as to the extent of what usable footage existed at the completion of principal photography, but there is no argument that* Jason Goes to Hell *underwent extensive recutting and reshooting on its road to theatrical release. Complicating matters even further, Sean Cunningham's unorthodox technical experiments on* Jason Goes to Hell *ultimately wreaked havoc with the film's running time—and an early test screening left some audience members wanting for more traditional* Friday the 13th *stalk and slash thrills, prompting the studio to order even more changes. And all of this was before the always-contentious showdown with the Motion Picture Association of America's ratings board. The results were, predictably, bloody.*

SEAN CUNNINGHAM: There is something I think I invented, and that I originally wanted to do in the early 1980s. When you go to make a movie and you get into the cutting room, and you have a shot of somebody going out the door or whatever, actors never take cues fast enough. So it struck me that everything would benefit by going faster. I thought that if you shot a film at twenty-two frames per second instead of the standard twenty-four frames per second, you couldn't see the difference. The problem, though, was that your audio would be off if you then played back what you shot. But what happened at the time of *DeepStar Six*, which is the first film I shot at twenty-two frames per second, is that it was the advent of the harmonizer—a device that could alter the pitch of a soundtrack. So I was now able to speed up the physical action but the movie would still sound normal. And I was able to live my dream.

ADAM MARCUS: This idea is a freaking nightmare, okay? You have to change how you light everything, and all of the sound has to be dropped an octave, otherwise everyone would sound like chipmunks.

Sean's concept behind acting is that no actor can do anything fast enough. You tell them to walk through a door and they have to emote on their way to the door, okay? It is also supposed to make the action a little crisper. However, there is something about this idea that to me is just very cynical.

That's one of the reasons we had to go out and shoot more footage. Because think about it—the movie is now ten minutes shorter than it would have been. We had a 90-minute movie that became an 80-minute one.

SEAN CUNNINGHAM: It was a disaster. I didn't think about replacing Adam until we were in the cutting room, at which point he had done everything he could do, and it became up to me and the editors, and Dean Lorey to try and turn this "thing" into a movie. We cut the film down and we were able to salvage 45 or 50 minutes out of this 105-minute cut. And it was still the longest cut I'd ever seen. It felt like it ran for four days. And we went back and we shot footage and inserted it. We took it from something that was unreleasable to something that was okay.

NOEL CUNNINGHAM: There are three movies you make. There's the movie you write, the movie you shoot and the movie you cut. The movie you cut is the important one. It was Adam's first day at the rodeo, it was Dean's first day at the rodeo. A lot of beginner mistakes were made—that you have to make, and that even the really big filmmakers make. Even Robert Rodriquez puts ten minutes of deleted scenes on his DVDs. Of course, we had an hour of deleted scenes—our assembly was over two hours. There was a lot of stuff that just didn't work out, for whatever reason, whether the effects were shitty or the actor didn't get this or that. So you just start lopping off stuff, or even an entire extraneous scene.

The original cut had storylines you wouldn't believe. The sheriff and Erin Gray's character—they were engaged and about to go on their honeymoon. Now that's gone. And Kari Keegan's character and Steven Culp—they were never a couple in the first cut. That was all creative editing on David Handman's part.

DAVID HANDMAN, Editor: Both the good and the bad in *Jason Goes to Hell* came down to whether we had a decent script or not. We went ahead with production on a script that just really wasn't ready. It feels like it's been Frankenstein'd together, and it was. We just gutted the thing. We kept all the action, got rid of all the scenes that were poorly written and dreadfully acted, and wound up with a movie that was basically about people with things in their throats. It was just one vignette to another, depending on who was carrying Jason.

ADAM MARCUS: After the first test screening, the audience wanted more of the traditional *Friday the 13th* campground sex and slash stuff. And so did New Line. I was very against that, and so was Dean. Because the only problem I have had with the mythology of the *Friday the 13th* films is this constant thing that anyone who does drugs or has sex should die. That's a very Puritanical vision. In the first movie it made sense because Mom is punishing these kids for having had sex while her son dies. But Jason doesn't know that. So I just thought, "When did the Christian Right suddenly get a say in my production?"

But we were given our marching orders. And what we shot is something I'm willing to live with, because we tried to twist the conventions back around in a more positive way. I wanted to get as many guys naked as women. I think women go to see these movies just as much as men. And maybe it is easier to be afraid for a woman in jeopardy than a man in jeopardy. But if you do put a man in jeopardy, then everybody's scared. So we shot a lot of graphic nudity of both sexes in that scene. You gotta share the wealth, so to speak. Of course, most of it got cut out of the film, but rightly so. Because it was gratuitous, but at least we tried to make it more balanced.

Personally, I think the girl split up the middle is the best death in any *Friday the 13th*. And it wasn't even originally in the movie.

DEAN LOREY: Initially, we had gone back just to shoot some expositional scenes, but then when we also received those comments from test audiences we said, "OK, if you really miss that stalker stuff, we'll do something about it." So we shot a new intro for John LeMay where he picks up the campers who go to Crystal Lake and get slaughtered.

JOHN D. LEMAY: The funny thing was the reshoots at the camp. Because I actually only interact with the campers in that car before I drop them off. So, unfortunately, I didn't get to see what they shot later, with all the naked people. As is usually the case with me, I miss all the good stuff.

GREG NICOTERO: I remember when they were shooting that whole lead-up to the murder of the two campers in the tent, the two actors were both completely naked and grinding and rubbing on each other. And afterward, I said to Howard, "I feel like I need a cigarette."

DAVID HANDMAN: Frankly, I don't think I succeeded all that well in editing that sequence. It still looks like a porno movie to me.

GREG NICOTERO: Well, the nice thing about Adam, and Sean as well, was that they didn't shy away from going for it. Sean knew what the roots of the series were, and it had gotten to the point with the later *Friday the 13th* movies where you felt they were losing a lot of steam because of the MPAA. But *Jason Goes to Hell* came at the point where everyone started to figure out that, wait a minute, we can shoot the film as we want it, and release the cut version theatrically. And then on laserdisc go full out. So I was happy with the fact that there weren't any punches pulled here. It was pretty violent.

HOWARD BERGER: We had seen the movie in a rough cut that had everything in it, and we were ecstatic. Then we saw the theatrical version. I was so mad when I saw what the studio had done. They butchered the movie. I smelled trouble when I saw that poster. That was the first red flag. I hated that poster because I thought it

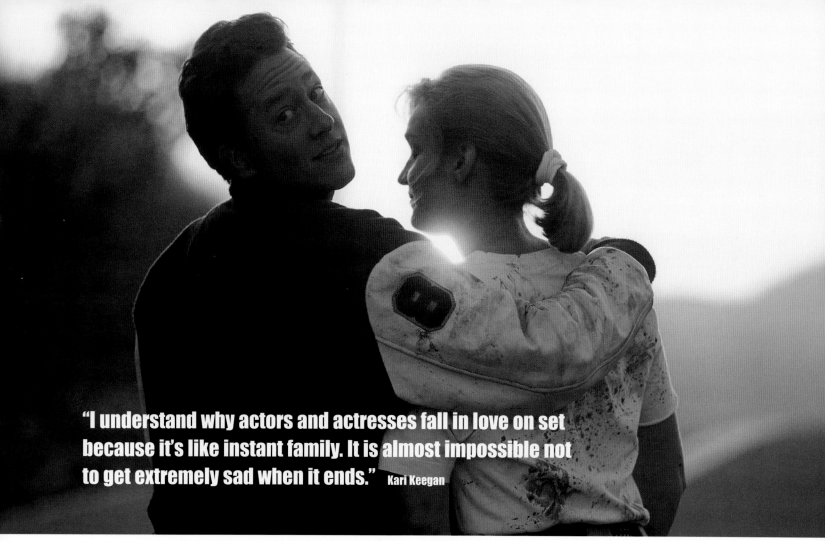

"I understand why actors and actresses fall in love on set because it's like instant family. It is almost impossible not to get extremely sad when it ends." Kari Keegan

was a complete misrepresentation of the film we had made. We all worked so hard on it, so I was really displeased with the theatrical release. At least, finally, it came out on laserdisc, and now DVD.

The box office fate that awaited the first Friday the 13th *film of the 1990s was most uncertain. Not only had it been three years since the disappointing turnout for* Jason Takes Manhattan—*an eternity in the fickle world of horror sequels—but there were few in the genre press who weren't loudly questioning what relevance Jason Voorhees could still have to the teenage demographic of 1993. Further exacerbating the studio's concerns, the entirely new approach to the franchise's established conventions left many questioning whether even the most diehard fans would embrace—or be alienated by—such radical changes to the familiar formula.*

When Jason Goes to Hell *opened on 1,355 screens on Friday, August 13, 1993, the response was tepid. The film pulled in a solid if unspectacular $7.6 million in its first three days, nabbing the second place spot right behind Warner Bros. high profile Harrison Ford thriller,* The Fugitive. *But by its second weekend,* Jason Goes to Hell *lost seventy percent of its audience, and by the end of its run would earn a less-than-stellar $15.9 million. Perhaps indicative of the depressed state of the horror genre in 1993,* Jason Goes to Hell, *despite being far from a blockbuster, was still the highest grossing horror film of the year.*

New Line Cinema, however, appeared happy with the results. Jason Goes to Hell *was never intended to reignite the languishing franchise, but rather to serve as a launching pad for* Freddy vs. Jason. *The film turned a healthy profit, and also benefited from strong sales on home video, buoyed no doubt by the first-ever unrated release of a* Friday the 13th *film on VHS and Laserdisc. Whether* Jason Goes to Hell *helped, hindered or simply had no effect on the long-term viability of the franchise, neither its fans nor its detractors deny that the film certainly remains one of the most unique entries in the series.*

STEVEN CULP: The first time I saw it I did quite enjoy myself. There was a premiere at the Mann's Chinese Theater, and we all came by limo. We were even introduced to the crowd after the film ended. It was so much fun. And the audience was so into it. I was also happy that my monster stuff came off as well as it did.

RUSTY SCHWIMMER: I saw it once, laughed my ass off, and then I was done. And I have to be happy with the film, because someone paid me to play, and I didn't have to wait tables.

JOHN D. LEMAY: I couldn't make the proper premiere, so my friends and family had one for me in Minnesota, at the Maplewood Theater in St. Paul. They arranged it so that if I signed autographs for the opening night of the show, we could have the theater early in the afternoon for all my friends and family to come—like a hundred and fifty people! And they were all so proud of me that they overlooked the fact that it was a total gross-out movie. Here I am, sitting next to my aunt and uncle and somebody's getting sliced up the middle. But they just loved it. So that was a nice memory.

KARI KEEGAN: We have become a society of pay-per-view and instant this and instant that, and there's something to be said for going to the movies and getting your popcorn and your soda and sitting down with an audience. I have seen movies that were terrible become good, because the audience made it good. You've just got to go see *Friday the 13th* with a black audience. It was the most fun I ever had in my life. After the premiere, I went to the Mann's in Hollywood for the midnight show on a Saturday night. It was awesome. My character was called "Bitch!" a bunch of times. And,

Opposite: Key art for the domestic theatrical poster of *Jason Goes to Hell: The Final Friday.* The film would undergo many title changes throughout its development and during the test screening process. Some of the alternate titles included "The Black Heart of Jason Voorhees" and "The Nine Lives of Jason Voorhees."

"Dawg, don't turn around!" It was hilarious. Then some guy behind me went, "She is phat!" I turned to my friend next to me and said, "I don't think I look that fat!" And she said, "No, that's good!"

ADAM MARCUS: I think horror movies have always suffered from the problem that they do gangbusters on opening weekend and then they drop off. That happened with *Jason Goes to Hell*, but we still did good domestic business. We came in right behind *The Fugitive*. And we were actually the number one domestic horror movie of that year—well, if you don't put *Jurassic Park* in there. I think New Line was surprised we did as well as we did. I remember my favorite thing was the front page of *Variety* after our opening weekend. It said, "Number One Goes to *Fugitive*, Rest of Box Office Goes to *Hell*."

ERIN GRAY: The only negative to the entire experience for me was when I went to the the premiere, and I'm there with this crazy, wonderful audience who are yelling and screaming and having a great time. So I'm watching this film, and I'm really getting into it—and then there's that scene at the end of the film where that blob—whatever it is—crawls up between my legs.

I don't know how to describe my reaction other than to say there was a sense of violation. And a sense of anger because you feel that you sign on to do a project and you read the script and you think that's what you're doing. And then you find out that, through special effects and other things, they add scenes and make it look like you but it's not you—so there's a sense of, "I wouldn't have done that! I didn't agree to that!"

ADAM MARCUS: That was kind of a corporate decision to make everything kind of link up easier. And I admit it's a little distasteful. It just is. And I kind of regret that shot, even though, trust me, audiences love it. It's terrifying. But I remember when we were at the screening and I saw that shot I kind of was like, "*Ewww.*"

I don't disagree with Erin. It's a little cringe-inducing. Especially for the actress who plays the role. But I gotta tell you, I had so much love for the people who were in that film. They were really brave to let me be at the helm of what they were doing. On her last day of shooting, Erin gave me from the set of *Buck Rogers* the flight wings that a new pilot would get. I was so knocked out by that. I still have it in my office.

SEAN CUNNINGHAM: New Line left me completely alone, and they were completely happy with *Jason Goes to Hell*. They made a bunch of money, so they had no complaints. And what did anyone expect? It's *Friday the 13th Part IX*! Did you see *Part VI*? *Part VII*? *Part VIII*?

For me, it was way past an embarrassment. I didn't know it when we started, but the body-morphing plot—it was a dismal idea. It's a complete fool's errand. I suspected that early on, but the finished film completely proved that. I made many, many mistakes there. If you were familiar with the series, you'd say, "How can you fuck it up? You can't." Adam came to me and said, "The last thing the fans want is to see Jason going through Camp Crystal Lake chopping up teenagers again." Of course, it was the only thing they wanted to see, and Adam delivered this movie that was *so* not good.

DAVID HANDMAN: I had fun doing it, but I don't know what it's about. I still couldn't tell you.

GREG NICOTERO: *Texas Chainsaw Massacre* and *Halloween* and *Friday the 13th*—I think it was about the kills. Then when *A Nightmare on Elm Street* came along, it created a whole new set of rules. Which is why Freddy became perhaps more popular than Jason, because those movies could have visuals—not just gore gags, but fantastical elements. I think that's again where *Jason Goes to Hell* sort of strayed from the path. Adam wanted to explore the supernatural element, and that evil is something tangible and can move from person to person, and place to place. But I think once the ground rules were set for the *Friday the 13th* films, the fans kept coming because that's what they expected to see—and they

wanted more of the same. Which is understandable, because people invest so much into the movies they love. It's the same with zombies or anything else. People don't want you to fuck with what they've come to revere.

ADAM MARCUS: I'm very proud of my Jason. I really am. We did something different. I know we really got hammered by many of the critics, but we actually got some nice notices, too. And we did stuff in our movie that was self-referential, that was cheeky. We did it years before *Scream*. But we never got any credit for that.

Some fans complain that we tried to explain too much in *Jason Goes to Hell*, that there shouldn't have been so much of the mythology. I think that's a mistake. Look at that great moment in *Jaws* when Quint gives his big speech about the U.S.S. *Indianapolis*, and that this is either a really stupid fish or a really smart fish. That's backstory for a shark! For me, it is the same with Jason. Honestly, I don't think anyone's given him enough backstory. I'm not saying that our concept was the best or whatever, but you know, I think Norman Bates isn't frightening if Norman Bates doesn't have a mommy problem. And Michael Myers was a kid when he murdered his sister. That's important to know, you know?

There are a lot of fans who should examine themselves a little bit and wonder why they keep wanting to watch the same damn movie over and over again. I don't get that. The advent of the video age allowed us to do that anyway. So there's a movie that you love? Then buy it, that's great. But don't hamper the filmmaking community because they don't want to make the same thing again and again. Because that's the attitude and the way in which these types of movies are usually made. Which I think is a shame.

Look, nothing even approaches the first *Friday the 13th*. That had a rawness and immediacy to it that I don't think anyone will match again. I think *Friday the 13th*, along with *Halloween*, really opened up a Pandora's Box—no other horror movie of this type will ever capture the zeitgeist in that way again. I also think *Friday Part 2* is terrific. I loved that. Then, I'd put *Jason Goes to Hell* kind of in third position with *Jason Lives*. They both have a really healthy sense of humor. Both wanted to take the series in a new direction. Both included a real community, a town, and more interesting characters than just Jason. I think that's fair.

10.

Evil Gets an Upgrade

With the final, crowd-pleasing coda of *Jason Goes to Hell*—featuring Jason's trademark hockey mask being dragged into the bowels of hell by the razor-sharp claw of a cackling Freddy Krueger—it appeared that the promise of horror's most anticipated screen showdown was finally about to become a reality. While *The Final Friday* was by no means a blockbuster, it successfully brought to a close a period of nearly thirteen years that saw the *Friday* franchise become the most financially successful horror film series in history. Freddy Krueger, too, had just come full circle with *Wes Craven's New Nightmare*, a wry and inventive postmodern wink at the franchise slasher craze. It seemed hard to imagine a more opportune time to stage a match-up of two of horror's reigning slasher icons—especially now that the popularity of both characters was undeniably on the downswing. Fate, however, had other plans. By the end of the 1990s, after more than a dozen writers and nearly as many screenplay drafts, the producers of *Freddy vs. Jason* were still no closer to solving the project's conceptual challenges. As the "development hell" of *Freddy vs. Jason* lingered on during the next six years, New Line was growing tired of spending millions of dollars on new writers and new screenplays.

> ## "We wanted to take a $13 million dollar budget and make it look like a $30 million dollar movie."
> Jim Isaac

Despite the best efforts of nearly a dozen talented scribes, none had successfully cracked the most basic of questions: how do you bring Freddy and Jason together in a logical and satisfying way? The *Friday the 13th* brand name was also precariously close to losing whatever box office potency it may have had. But most importantly, Sean Cunningham was running out of patience. Shortly after *Jason Goes to Hell*, Cunningham created a new production company, Crystal Lake Entertainment, to co-develop *Freddy vs. Jason* with New Line. His Cunningham Productions was also continuing to cultivate projects within and outside of the horror genre. The stagnation of *Freddy vs. Jason* was a growing financial and creative black hole for both companies. So as the new millennium approached, Cunningham felt it was time to seriously think about another Jason adventure. But if Jason was to survive into the twenty-first century, he would have to undergo his most radical re-invention yet.

NOEL CUNNINGHAM, Producer: I had been working for Sean for a while doing development. We had done the whole *Freddy vs. Jason* rigamarole for a while. We worked with the studio for a long time and the scripts were always good, just not good enough. Also, while we were trying to develop *Freddy vs. Jason*, Cunningham Productions was trying to expand without spending the money that comes along with that. That's tough. If you're an independent producer like Sean and you have three people working for you and you don't have a deal with a studio, you can easily be racking up—on the low end—$250,000 a year just to keep the lights on. Then if you want to buy property—a script— pretty much everybody else has seen it by the time it comes down to you. So most of what you get on that level is pretty much useless. So you try to develop your own stuff with new writers. So in that time we also ended up shooting this experimental short, as well as a movie called *Terminal Invasion*. But everyone still wanted to see *Freddy vs. Jason* happen, and Sean was just sitting on the Jason rights the whole time. Finally, he said, "Fuck it. We've got to do something with this. I can't just let it lay here."

SEAN CUNNINGHAM, Executive Producer: I got so frustrated with the *Freddy vs. Jason* process that I finally said to New Line, "I'm taking this away. If we're not making it, let's make something else. The franchise has to be out there in some way. And I'm not making any money on *Freddy vs. Jason*, either. So do one or the other." That's why it took so long.

But also, having made nine Jason movies, I was completely baffled as to how we could make another *Friday* that had anything new or fresh to say, or that was worthy of the fan base. An awful lot of people out there are attached to the *Friday the 13th* series and they want something new, something better. I think there'll always be a market for horror films, but not for the same one, over and over again. And to be honest, I don't know that the first *Friday the 13th* would have been successful if it were released today. By that point it was twenty years old. A *Friday Part X* had to be totally new, only with Jason still at the center of it.

TODD FARMER, Screenwriter: I didn't know if I was going to write movies, but my high school class picture is of me sitting at a typewriter. I wrote stories more than anything else. And I was always the guy at parties and camp-outs telling ghost stories, most of the time that I was making up on the fly. I moved out to Los Angeles in 1996. I dove into the trenches. There are two ways to do it. Go to school, learn what you're doing and while you're at school, you're going to make great contacts. I didn't do it that way. I just made mistakes along the way.

I met Dean Lorey through my best friend in college. I sent him a script I wrote that I liked, and he read the first forty pages and decided I had absolutely no idea what I was doing. So, to some degree, he took me under his wing, even though he's just a year older. He taught me how to write.

Dean introduced me to Sean Cunningham. I wrote a spec script for Sean that Dean had actually come up with the idea for. The plan was that Dean would direct, Sean would produce and I would write. That didn't happen, but by the end of '96 I was working for Sean as a writer and creative executive. I did rewrites, I did originals, whatever Sean wanted. And *Freddy vs. Jason* had been going on for several years. Early on, Mark Haslett , who was a vice president at Sean's company, had mentioned several times about doing a straight Jason movie. Sean basically said, "Look, I've got *Freddy vs. Jason*. I don't want to do anything to mess up that deal." Then every six months or so, we'd go back to Sean but he still wouldn't want to do anything. It wasn't until Sean got totally fed up that a tenth *Friday* could happen.

NOEL CUNNINGHAM: Jim Isaac was the one who came in at the right time and said, "Let's do a Jason movie." I'd known Jim since 1988 or '89, and he was a good friend from many of Sean's shows. He also came in and took over the directing chores on *The Horror Show*, which turned out to be a very difficult production. But Jim did a great job in trying to come in and save that. So Sean said, "Okay, we're doing another Jason. Come and develop it if you want." There wasn't a paycheck in it for any of us, but Sean gave us the shot with another *Friday* that we'd all been talking about for the last four years or so.

Jim, Todd and I sat around a table and literally came up with every scenario we could put Jason in. Nothing was too extreme or too bizarre. We kicked around different scenarios. Jason in the hood, Jason in the snow, Jason underwater. We had him fighting gangs in L.A., in the arctic, on safari, in space, the NASCAR circuit—everything. We didn't want to shut anything down.

JIM ISAAC, Director: I was thinking very broad strokes. I originally wanted to make *Friday* scary again. We are back in Crystal Lake, but it's winter and in the middle of a big storm. It would be either kids on a cross-country skiing trip that get lost, or they are already there but get snowed in. I thought that might be an interesting look for a *Friday* film. You have blood on white. I could see Jason on a frozen pond. But that wasn't a favorite idea with Todd and Noel and Sean.

Todd had picked up on this idea about space. He kind of described the trailer and what he thought was cool about it, and it did excite the room. We left there going, "Yeah, all right, this could be cool." But, in retrospect, that might have been the first of many moments when I should have fought harder for the original idea I felt the strongest about.

TODD FARMER: I thought of Jason in the distant future—like a *Blade Runner* type of deal. I like action stuff, I like science fiction stuff, and I like the idea of taking Jason and dropping him into a situation that would be foreign to him and possibly create some conflict for the character. And, personally, I always loved the idea of Jason taking Manhattan. I just thought it was funny. But in *Jason Takes Manhattan*, he really never got there. So I thought, "Well, let's stick Jason somewhere else. Let's put him in space."

NOEL CUNNINGHAM: Jason in space was kind of a throwaway. You immediately flash to the *Hellraiser* and *Leprechaun* sequels and the disasters that those were. But once we started going through every other option, there was so much stuff we could do with the concept that we actually thought it could work. Get bad-ass space marines and guns and future shit that we've never seen before. So we said, "Fuck it, this is going to be fun!"

Background and **above**: *Jason X* begins in the year 2008, fifteen years after the events in *Jason Goes to Hell*. Jason Voorhees has at last been captured and imprisoned at the Crystal Lake Research Facility for further study. With a newly redesigned appearance, including a new hockey mask, it was up to makeup effects supervisor Stephan Dupuis to reimagine the character for the new millennium. "To be honest, I was not really a fan of the *Friday the 13th* movies," admits Dupuis. "Of course, I know what the character is all about. I just really wanted to design something that the fans would like. The idea was that Jason has regenerative powers, and it has been several years since the last *Friday* movie. So we gave him a bit of hair, as well as a more clearly fleshy appearance, as if he is almost in a constant state of repair. I also wanted to go with more of a gothic version of the old Jason, hence all the shackles and chains, and we made his hockey mask a little more angular. That was also a great contrast for later in the film, when Jason is transformed into UberJason, which is an entirely new, wonderful creation."

Opposite, bottom: "I play a stupid doctor who deserves to die!" laughs veteran filmmaker David Cronenberg of his cameo role in *Jason X*. "David is the dean of Canadian horror films," says executive producer Sean Cunningham. "And he is a very dear friend of director Jim Isaac. So when David found out Jim was making a *Friday* film, he was an enormous help and came in for two days work. And we were very grateful to him, and he's very good in the movie." Directing his longtime mentor was a dream come true for Isaac. "Those were a great couple of days," remembers Isaac. "He was wonderful, and he tweaked his scenes a little bit. David would say, 'What can we do?' And he'd say, 'Well, last night I went ahead and rewrote a couple of things...'"

Jason X represented a unique challenge for costume designer Maxyne Baker. "The idea was that Earth was no longer inhabitable," says Baker of the film's unique "TerraFormer" suits. "You can breathe oxygen but only from environmental storages. But I didn't want to do the typical spacesuit you normally see in science fiction movies, with a big helmet and air flowing through tubes. So we came up with a design based on leather Flying Duster jackets from World War II. We made the collar bigger, changed the front pockets, and went with orange because that's the color of survival. And because the sun's brightness had become too much, everyone needed to wear a screen on their faces to protect from the ultraviolet rays."

SEAN CUNNINGHAM: When Noel and Todd came in and pitched me the idea of Jason in space, I just said, "What are you, nuts?" But they kept batting for it. They went off and came up with a treatment. Only then did I say, "Jesus, this is a terrific idea." Because everything that the horror audience would like to have is in there. It had new locations, new characters, new technology, and twists and turns that you would never expect. It was a way of rejuvenating the series, one that I sincerely thought could make the fans very, very happy.

NOEL CUNNINGHAM: After we convinced Sean, we still had to pitch the concept to Michael De Luca at New Line. But we did our homework. Jim Isaac has been a special effects coordinator forever and worked on some really big shows and knows a lot of good people, so he called in a bunch of favors. We already had lined up Stephan Dupuis, who won an Oscar for *The Fly*, to be our head of makeup effects. We also hired a couple of guys from ILM to do some pretty matte paintings. So we brought De Luca this huge dog and pony show. We showed him so much cool visual shit that he was like, "This could really rock!" And Todd is remarkable in how fast he can bang something out, and he wrote a first rough draft in only a couple of days. So when De Luca was so impressed he said, "Great! When can you have a script?" we just went, "Well, we've got a rough draft right here," and just slid it across the table. It was pretty slick and cool!

TODD FARMER: De Luca's attitude was that we weren't going to make another Jason movie. And if you put yourself in New Line's shoes, why would you? Real money was being spent for *Freddy vs. Jason*, so why go backwards? It doesn't make any sense. But we pitched it to De Luca and by the end of the meeting, he was really excited.

Ultimately, I have come to have many regrets on *Jason X*. But the first one is probably that, after we sold that pitch, I don't ever remember a celebration. I don't remember any of us ever going, "Wow! We got a greenlight!" Because from there on out, there was always a struggle, always a battle, always a fight. And it never ended, even after the movie was finished.

Whether taking Jason Voorhees out of the sanctity of his woods and into the outer reaches of space was an inspired feat of creative audacity or a foolish flight of fancy, it represented a considerable financial risk for Crystal Lake Entertainment. Jason X commanded the highest budget yet for a Friday the 13th *film—projected initially at $13 million, its negative cost was more than the previous four installments of the franchise combined. Both the producers and the director agreed on one thing: every*

FRIDAY THE 13TH CONCEPT ART | ESTABLISHING SHOT - DESERT | 5·30·99 J. GOODSON

dollar had to get up on screen. But pressures began to mount even during the earliest stages of pre-production. Creative differences and bruised egos became commonplace as the original shooting script was extensively rewritten, both with the input of original screenwriter Todd Farmer and without. Sean Cunningham had always championed an open atmosphere that encouraged collaboration, an attitude that had paid handsome dividends for him in the past. But this time, too many cooks in the kitchen quickly spoiled the recipe for success, rather than distilling and refining its essence into a single, cohesive vision.

NOEL CUNNINGHAM: "Vision" is a word that gets thrown around a lot, and I really do think, initially, all three of us, Jim, Todd and I, had the same vision for *Jason X*. We all liked the same movies. We just wanted a good shoot 'em up, scary, fun, funny, sexy action horror movie in space. We weren't trying to change the world. We weren't trying to impart any great moral lesson here. So we developed the script together, the three of us, very tightly, just going through and writing scenes and then reading them aloud to each other and saying, "Well, that didn't work," or, "That was great." And we made a whole list of other movies that inspired us.

After that, we sent Todd off to write it. But then there were some writers brought in at the last minute to fix certain problems which, in hindsight, created much bigger problems.

JIM ISAAC: Here is what's great about Sean Cunningham as a producer. He is one of the few guys I know of who, without a full green light, will start writing checks to get you moving. And here is the other side to that. Because this was a negative pickup, at the time we started Sean was using his own money. No bank loan, nothing. We hadn't gotten anything from New Line yet. So, ironically perhaps, this is what created problems for us—Noel, Todd and I—on *Jason X*.

Sean was actually with us during pre-production for quite a long time, maybe two months. Todd was writing and things were going fine. Then, I think what happened was that suddenly Sean had gotten the money situation worked out. His job was kind of done. And it was tough for him to do all that because he put a lot on the table—certainly, the movie wouldn't have been made without that risk. But then he looked around and saw all of us making a movie. Now, I think his heart was totally in the right place. And I don't feel at all that Sean was trying to undermine me or anything. Not on any level. But he started to play around with the script a bit more.

The first draft Todd turned in was really raw, but Todd could probably have done two polishes and we would have been there. Even De Luca said it was great. He just told us, "You nailed it." It was weird, sexy. There were some great funny moments, but scary moments, too. It just had a very raw edge to it that I thought worked. And I know Sean will totally disagree with me, but I think the movie would have been much better if we had stuck to that original approach.

TODD FARMER: The second draft was the one that was greenlit. And after that there were about one hundred rewrites. A couple of them were budget-related, but most were just opinions. I remember Dean Lorey called me a ways into pre-production. He had been videotaping a friend of ours who wanted to be cast in the movie. And this guy had been sent a couple of scenes from the script, and he was laughing at them because he didn't think they were funny. And Dean read the pages, and was like, "Todd didn't write this!" Because Dean knows how I write. That's when Dean said, "I think you've been rewritten."

I called Noel, who denied it. Then finally Jimmy admitted to it. I don't mind being rewritten. In a lot of situations, it's a good thing. I'm a firm believer that rewrites can make a script better.

But you can also rewrite the magic right out of a script if you're not careful. And that's exactly what we did on *Jason X*. We rewrote it so many times that it lost everything that made it even a little bit special. And when you take that away, all you have left is Jason in space. And that's a dumb idea in the first place.

JIM ISAAC: Todd worked his ass off. He wrote a first draft in three weeks and it was smoking. And his attitude was, "Tell me what to do and I'll do it." The guy would work twenty-four hours a day if he had to. Todd was also good at sticking up for what he believed in. But ultimately, he knew that if he fought too much he'd just be replaced. So eventually he'd kind of moan and groan and then just go off and do it.

For me, I was in the middle of the firestorm that happens when you're just weeks away from shooting. As a director, you're just all over the map. And now you're being told, almost like a little random side comment, "Oh, we're going to bring in somebody to do a quick polish." Today I'd say, "Stop. You're not." But, you learn, you know?

"By taking Jason into the realm of science fiction, the only limitations were our imaginations and our budget." John Dondertman

I also think we were all so excited that we even got to make a movie that when Sean would say certain things that we didn't agree with, even if we would argue it a little, in the back of all of our heads we thought, "Well, if we don't do it, he'll just take his camera and go home." To be honest, now, I feel that was my fault. I should not have been worried about that. There was no way Sean would have pulled the plug. I want to make it very clear that Sean and I never really had any negative personal words. And there is no way Sean would have done anything negative. But that is how we all felt, or at least I felt.

A perfect example is a moment I wrote for the original opening sequence of the film. We had initially conceived the discovery of Jason to be on a much larger, grand scale. The kids end up falling through this floor into the space where Jason is in cryo-freeze and all this stuff. During this search one of them finds an old condom. It's a *Friday the 13th* movie, right? And the condom has a shelf life printed on it. So the smartass kid should say, "Cool, let's test it out." To me that's like a no-brainer—they should start having sex right there. Then that's what would make the whole floor fall out, and bring them to Jason and put them in jeopardy. I thought that was a fun way to start the movie. And a sexy way. You get a beautiful actress to take off her shirt—it gives what everyone wants.

But Sean, when he read it, only had one comment. He said, "Well, finding a condom is not going to make them want to have sex. It doesn't make any sense." So he made us cut the whole scene. Now, I could have just followed him around and said, "What the fuck are you talking about? You're a high school kid and you're with this beautiful chick and you find a condom? Hell, yeah, you'd think of sex. At that age, everything makes you think of sex." It was one of those moments where I should have stopped the presses right there and said, "Sean, you're high. You don't get it." And then bring in Noel and Todd and talk about it. Maybe even get a real teenager in on the discussion. Because that is who we were making this movie for. And that, I think, became the ultimate problem with *Jason X*. I wanted to make it for teenagers. I ended up making it for Sean.

TODD FARMER: By the time we were about two weeks away from the start of principal photography, another writer had already come in and done a rewrite—John Vorhaus. I had already finished rewrite after rewrite, but my script was still a little cluttered. So John streamlined what I had done, and he was very good. But whether this was him, or the notes he was getting, I felt like we lost our edgy tone. It just no longer existed. I saw this as *ALIENS* with Jason. The kind of movie that has to come at you from the beginning and just stay right in your face. We couldn't be afraid to offend, we couldn't be afraid of going over the top. By this draft, all of the over-the-top stuff was removed. So Jim called me back and said, "I want you to come down and take another pass and put the tone back in." So I came back and did my best. And then that stuff got cut out after I left, anyway.

JIM ISAAC: There was so much stuff that was lost. I still wanted to keep what audiences had come to expect from these movies. That these kids are out there having fun and screwing up, and then Jason comes and all this shit happens. But this is four hundred years in the future, so let's really have some fun with it and utilize the possibilities. We originally had this party scene where all the kids are getting high and drunk and having sex. Only imagine they're doing it in a zero gravity sex bubble. You could really imagine coming up with some pretty wild, cool ideas with that. I liked the whole idea of what audiences expected and really bringing it into a weird and different place.

"When an actor that you've become friends with walks onto the set with a spike sticking out of their stomach and blood coming out of their mouth, it's a bit discombobulating." Lexa Doig

NOEL CUNNINGHAM: I ultimately disagreed with a lot of Jim's choices, but he's the director and it was my job to make sure, as best I could, that he had as clear a road in front of him to do what he wanted to do. And I'm sure he disagreed with a lot of the roads I laid out for him. But a lot of what Jim wanted had to be cut for budgetary reasons. Because if you have only $13 million, you can't have kids having sex and flying all over a cargo bay. And if you only have ten weeks of principal photography, you can't take a week and a half or two weeks just to shoot one sequence.

JIM ISAAC: For me, I felt that the integrity and the soul of the movie started being changed right from the beginning. And it was happening in a very slow way. It wasn't like Sean just came in and said, "Let's turn this into a musical." What happened is we started to kind of chip away at things—a little detail here, a little texture there. I started to give into some of these things, and if you don't have anybody looking after your back, at the reality of the big picture and pulling you aside and saying, "Wait a minute, Jim. Remember, you really wanted to have that," it's really going to screw you up. As the script started to go a different direction and get developed in a way I wasn't totally comfortable with, I was focusing on things like getting the crew to start working on the look of Jason, or rehearsing with the cast and that kind of stuff.

During the process of making a movie, you often get so wrapped up in the day to day issues that you have to solve. And the person who holds the purse strings, if they disagree with

something or don't like the way things are going, has the power to pull the plug. So I felt I needed to take those ideas that were presented to me and somehow try to make them work. The last thing I want to do is start to whine and complain about the script. You don't want to be the guy who is a part of the problem, you want to be the guy who is a part of the solution. And you can do that a couple of times. But if you start to do that over and over and over again, that's when things start to fall apart.

The casting of the Friday the 13th *films had grown more progressive throughout the early 1980s and '90s, as the cultural attitudes and expectations of teenage audiences began to change. White bread, wholesome ensembles were no longer the mandate of the studios and filmmakers, for fear that the exclusion of key demographics, such as urban audiences and female viewers, would mean potential lost profits. In fact, by the end of the 1990s, most of the major studios began to realize that a lack of ethnic diversity in the cast of a mainstream horror film was tantamount to commercial suicide. Inspired by the success of Wes Craven's* Scream *and its two sequels, even the most non-horror savvy moviegoer had become wise to the clichés and conventions of slasher movies. Now that the bar had been raised, the characters on screen had to be just as smart. The late 1990s also saw an explosion in the popularity of a spate of high-gloss, youth-oriented American television series populated mostly by unusually photogenic, wise-beyond-their-years teens. Shows such as* Beverly Hills 90210, Party of Five *and* Dawson's Creek, *radically changed the expectations for young actors in Hollywood. If* Jason X *was going to appeal to the kids of the new "postmodern age," the futuristic teens of* Jason X *had to be just as hip, modern, witty and proactive. And, of course, good looking.*

ROBIN COOK, **Casting Director:** When I read the script, I thought it was funny. And usually, what you do as a casting director is send out a synopsis to agents along with comments, usually something like, "Shoots in Toronto." And for *Jason X*, in my comments, I wrote in caps: "Yeah, I know, I know. What can I say?." See, for me, that was the beauty of the film—we all knew that what we were doing was camp, and that we were going to have fun with it. Kudos to Noel and Jim and Todd for taking it seriously. But for me—and I certainly take my job seriously—I loved the idea that we all knew that this wasn't *Citizen Kane*.

LEXA DOIG, **"Rowan":** I actually laughed when I received the script. When I saw *"Friday the 13th Part X."* I kind of looked at my agent and said, "I didn't know there was a *VI, VII, VIII* and *IX*."

But I thought the character of Rowan was great. She changed the whole stereotype of the scantily-clad, not-very-bright female that seems to appear in a lot of horror films, especially ones from way back when. And in the script, I also thought that all the women were integral to the action. Those who did survive wouldn't have if it wasn't for the input of everybody, including the ladies.

JIM ISAAC: One of the things I liked about the concept of space was that it would enable us to create new toys—cool weapons these kids could have at their disposal. One of the things I was tired of seeing in the other Jason movies is that the kids were always just so defenseless. They're just victims from day one. I didn't want that for *Jason X*.

ROBIN COOK: Personally, I didn't want it to be so much "Jason Meets Beverly Hills 90210." That sort of took away, for Jim and I, the camp of it. You look at the actors who are on any *Teen Beat*

or on the WB and they're all gorgeous. And nothing against Aaron Spelling. But all Jim and I really cared about was that they were fit.

Lexa just had that right kind of toughness, beauty and vulnerability. You just wanted to watch her. Yet even then I still remember having conversations about, "We really need to go even better looking." I was like, "How can you get better looking!?" Just look at Lexa. She's just so stunning.

NOEL CUNNINGHAM: I, especially, wanted good-looking people. That's a sign of the times. Film is a fantasy, an escape. Especially *Friday the 13th*. As much crap as reviewers and critics will sling on you for gathering a whole bunch of pretty, attractive people, you know what? If you gathered a huge bunch of really unattractive people, I bet your box office scores would be lower. People want the fantasy, and hopefully they can identify on some level with the characters, too. And also, with *Jason X*, it's in the future, so there's natural selection and all that. All the hot people were nailing each other. Ugly people ain't gettin' none.

TODD FARMER: I like strong female characters, like the kind in James Cameron's movies. I think they're sexier. I think they're more fun to be around. You know, a girl who'll slug you is the kind of guy I want to go into battle with, if that makes any sense. And that probably comes from my scarred childhood on the playground when the girls would beat me up during games of "kiss and chase."

That really came out with the character of Kay-EM. The idea was she was supposed to be a smart, sexy, femme-bot android, a synthetic—whatever you want to call her—and then to give her the opportunity to rage-battle with Jason.

The women of Crystal Lake, circa the twenty-fifth century. Clockwise from left: Lexa Doig as Rowan; Melyssa Ade as Janessa; and Melody Johnson as Kinsa.

"Janessa was described in the script as 'the sex kitten, with claws to match,' and I definitely think that's appropriate," says Ade. "She knows what she wants. I also think she is definitely the smartest one on the ship. But she is a bit of a control freak. So when all havoc breaks loose, we see her kind of come undone. I thought it was fun to play this very strong, very gutsy and pretty wacky woman whose vulnerabilities only come out after she loses her grip."

"You have to throw any concept of reality out the window with a film like this and just have fun," says Doig. "Because of the special effects, you are only getting snippets here or there of the overall scene you are doing. Just to create a really high, intense energy level is difficult, because you'll have hours of downtime, and then in that three minutes in front of the camera, you have to look scared, run from Jason and scream. And it's pretty difficult to associate that with anything in your real life. Because I haven't been chased by a dead guy in a hockey mask. At least not yet."

"In some of the other *Friday* movies, the concepts for resurrecting Jason could get pretty hokey," says screenwriter Todd Farmer. "So my idea was that the sex act itself is what brings him back to life. Just the idea that somebody's having sex on that ship is, for Jason, like that bolt of lightning that shoots through Frankenstein. And I remember when I pitched the concept, everyone loved it. It was like, 'Perfect!'"

LISA RYDER, "Kay-EM 14": Robin Cook had used me a couple of times before, and they were having a tough time casting the part of Kay-EM. The first time I auditioned, I walked into a room full of models—all stunningly beautiful women. And originally, the sides were really wacky, like Jim Carrey wacky. And they were trying to get the models to be "out there," and I don't think any of them could go there. Then they were trying comedienne-ish women for a while. They were vacillating. It is kind of a tricky part, because they wanted someone for Kay-EM who was babe-ish, but also funny, and strong, too.

I do think Jim Isaac did a really interesting thing with the casting. He didn't go the typical way that the 1980s slasher films went. He didn't cast victim girly-girls. He didn't cast buxom blond chicks. And in casting me he went a little bit older, because Kay-EM is supposed to be nineteen-year-old android. And by doing that, he made the character more of a mother to the kids. So that helped make the movie kind of special, or at least the casting of it.

MELYSSA ADE, "Janessa": I think there has consistently been strong female characters throughout cinema. What is exciting about this is that our age doesn't seem to diminish our potential strength. The women onboard are all young women. Janessa's a teenager. So regardless of that, we still have a full range of human emotions, we still have a full range of capabilities. And that was definitely an appeal with this project—that these young people are very capable. We're not just running and screaming from one cabin to the next. We have a problem to solve and we get down, we get dirty, and try and solve it. These kids just want to go home. That's all. And that's where you grab yourself. That's real. Whether it was set in outer space or in Tahiti or on the top of a mountain.

CHUCK CAMPBELL, "Tsunaron": *Jason X* just happened by accident. They just happened to be shooting in Toronto. And when I got the call for the audition and saw it was "*Friday the 13th Part X*." I wasn't that interested, to be honest with you. I think I only saw the first two, so by this one, I had no idea what the hell was going on! But it was cool because Robin Cook was very nice and she said, "They're not taking it so seriously this time. There's going to be a fun feel to it. Just go in and have fun and audition." I felt Jim Isaac wanted people to enjoy it. He wanted to give credit to the series, but do something different with it. So I went in and just got lucky.

JONATHAN POTTS, "Professor Lowe": There's no star system in Canada. There are certain things that I won't do anymore, that I don't want to do, but here, there's not enough money to be that choosy. People just kind of do the work. There's also not a lot of A-movies available. Occasionally you get an *X-Men*, but most of it is TV movies and low-budget stuff. And that means that the stars of these pictures are either people who are on their way up, or on their way down. So there's nobody in Canada who goes into acting thinking that they're going to be famous. It just isn't in the cards. And I think we all knew that the star of this film was Jason, anyway.

YANI GELLMAN, "Stoney": Just being a part of the whole *Friday the 13th* series is really cool. I grew up watching them, so to actually get killed by Jason is kind of exciting. Jim Isaac was also trying to really represent a sort of diversity that will occur in the future. We're sort of this ragtag band of humans that have escaped from Earth, so we're not all gonna look clean-cut and nice. We wanted to present a real human crew from all different walks of life.

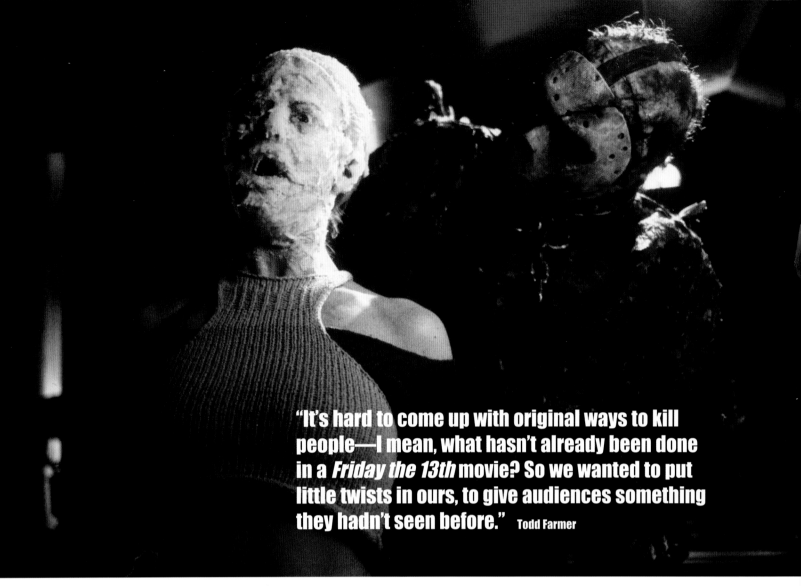

"It's hard to come up with original ways to kill people—I mean, what hasn't already been done in a *Friday the 13th* movie? So we wanted to put little twists in ours, to give audiences something they hadn't seen before." Todd Farmer

ROBIN COOK: Diversity was never explicitly discussed, but that's the way I cast it. If race is not specific in the script, that's where my creativity comes into play. For example, Peter Mensah was totally out of my head for Sgt. Brodski. Jim just wanted somebody imposing, and I said, "I've got the perfect person for you…"

PETER MENSAH "Sgt. Brodski": I grew up in England, and I was eight years old when I did my first school play. I pretty much lived on the stage until I came to Canada. I'd spent my summers in the south of France and Italy, and gotten to know that part of Europe so well that the next frontier was either Canada or Australia or something like that. I went to Canada and fell in love with it.

I think the *Friday the 13th* movies and Freddy Krueger—you could find them in England, although usually a year or two after their release in the U.S. Still, it wasn't a genre that I had paid enormous attention to, admittedly. But I was just happy to have gotten a role that I don't think was meant for a black actor. And Brodski is not a name you would usually expect to have a British accent.

TODD FARMER: Jim made a point to not exactly typecast. And I like that. I think it makes for a better movie. The beautiful thing is some of the smallest characters have the most wonderful performances, because Jim stayed in the casting room for days looking for the right people.

JIM ISAAC: Sean and I can argue about this until we die, but it was his idea to have the kids up there in space, driving spaceships and doing things as if they are these teenage geniuses. I think that is, overall, the biggest disagreement Sean and I had about the characters. I felt Sean was going more towards young sort of *Star*

Trek kids. I thought that was a little boring. Again, at first, I thought I could live with a little of that. Then it just kept going more and more in that direction.

SEAN CUNNINGHAM: Not to get too serious, but in the other *Friday the 13th* movies, as often as not, the people involved in it were victims. At least with *Jason X* these people had a hand in their future. Whether they were able to save their own lives or not, at least they were empowered. They have skills. They have a disposition. They are not saying, "Oh, what's going on?" and just waiting to get chopped on the head with a machete. They're smart, they're witty, they have power.

DERWIN JOHNSON, "Waylander": What was attractive about the script was that I thought it was very well-established throughout that these are real people with thoughts and ideas and feelings, and that we were all very specific individuals. Even Kay-EM has a very distinct personality and characteristics to her that I think feeds into the film. I think that's what makes it different from the other *Friday the 13th*s. Not only are there these explosions and special effects, but these are real people in a real situation.

LEXA DOIG: In most of these films, you know who's gonna die the minute they walk onscreen. Whereas here, because it was an ensemble cast, because each character has an integral part to play in the story, you don't always know. And when they did die, it was actually kind of emotional, like, "Oh, man, that sucks. I really liked her, or he was totally cool."

I think Rowan was a very strong person in her time, and was sort of a woman living in a man's world, to some degree. It is sort of like Ripley in the *ALIEN* films—there are definitely parallels there. Because then this whole complete chaos comes into her life.

"Kane Hodder's a big guy—huge! When he's off-camera, he's just the nicest person. But once he puts that mask on..." — **Barna Moricz**

She's got nothing left. The only thing that she does know is Jason. That kind of gives her an anchor, oddly enough, in a really sick and twisted way, to plod through the events that are happening. Because, even though she's in a complete environment with new toys and new tools and new weapons, Jason's still there and she can't really escape him. Just like Ripley and the Alien.

LISA RYDER: It was an excellent group of people and we all did a lot of bonding. We also all lived in downtown Toronto, and this is another cheap thing of Sean's, but none of us got individual transportation to the set. So it was by bus. They'd pick Lexa up first thing in the morning, then my place, then Chuck's place, so by the time we got there, there were ten people on the bus. And then we'd work all day together, and they'd drop us all back home. It was like "Camp Jason."

DERWIN JOHNSON: I remember when Jim called about a month before shooting to come and do rehearsals—I was surprised and incredibly impressed by that. He would sincerely ask, "What are your opinions?" And if you would tell him, "You know, this doesn't completely work for me," he would say, "I'm going to work on that." And he really did. You hear that so often in this business and nothing happens. But I would come back the next day, and there are new pages with the writer going, "We took your input seriously, and here it is. Does this work for you now?" It was totally fantastic.

JONATHAN POTTS: Isn't that ironic—for a Jason movie we get a month of rehearsals! And I mean real rehearsals. We literally played out each scene, and Geoff Garrett, the associate producer, videotaped them on a little camcorder so Jim could look at them afterward, seeing us walking and talking and getting ideas.

NOEL CUNNINGHAM: We were still making major script changes even while we were casting. There was one character who was supposed to be a love interest for Rowan. He was even going to survive throughout the entire film. But the romance angle just never gelled. We were looking at the script one day and it was like, "Why do we have this character?" And one of the most heartbreaking things I had to do was talk to the actor we already hired and say, "You're a really good guy—it's not about your work, it's our bad, but you're fired." Telling somebody four days into rehearsal who was the second lead in the film—he was floored! I felt so bad. But it was a good thing to do conceptually, because we had enough things clogging up the movie already.

JIM ISAAC: That was typical of the script changes that were happening, even throughout rehearsals. And it was really starting to affect me because it was happening as we were getting so close to shooting. But I think the lowest point was one day when I was rehearsing with the actors, and Sean had brought in Lewis Abernathy to do some uncredited rewrites. Now, Lewis had written for Sean before on *DeepStar Six* and contributed to the opening of *Jason Goes to Hell*. And he is a character. We all love Lewis. We were all like a family. So that is why I think I can say what I'm about to say.

Here's Lewis sitting in the corner of this big old room that all the actors are rehearsing in. And Lewis is spreading script pages out all over the floor. He's this big guy acting like, "I'm gonna be the script doctor. I'm gonna fix all the shit that's wrong with you assholes. You don't know what to do." Maybe he was half joking, half not, who knows? But it had been a very long day and I was tired and getting very frustrated—especially because Todd Farmer was already into rehearsing his role as Dallas. This script had been Todd's baby, yet he's trying to help by not getting involved in this situation with all these script changes. He's not coming up and saying, "Fuck it, I'll walk."

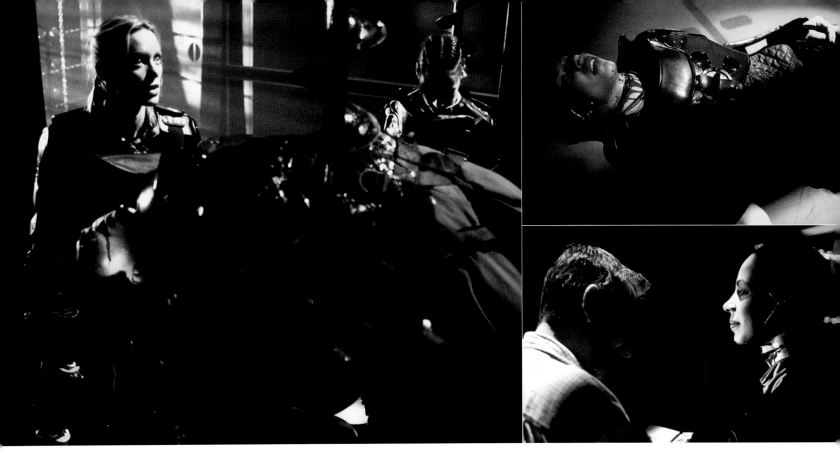

So I'm in my office at the end of the day and I'm pretty pissed. I've been rehearsing actors all day and I'm not sure if the pages we are doing are even going to be in the movie I'm supposed to start shooting next week. And here comes Lewis. I'm totally dead tired, I haven't slept in days, and here's this big guy just looking down at me. And he says, "Okay, Jim. Here's what I want you to think about: space pirates! Just think about that. All these kids are on this ship out to rob and plunder, and then Jason comes on board and wreaks havoc." I just sit there. Then I go, "Lewis, I shoot on Monday. This is literally the week before principal photography. You see those kids over there, the ones that I've been rehearsing with? They're not fucking space pirates!" That was it. That was the moment when I really felt like I was fucked. I'm supposed to shoot a movie next week, and I don't even know what script to pick up.

Unfortunately, the situation on the set of Jason X *would only grow more contentious during principal photography. Moviemaking is often about making spur of the moment decisions as much as it is the result of careful planning and coordination. But both cast and crew acknowledge that much of the energy and rawness of the original script continued to be diluted—if not completely eviscerated—as production went on. A source of even more consternation and concern was the film's limited budget—although ample by* Friday the 13th *standards—but ridiculously low in comparison to the big-budget action extravaganzas with which the film needed to compete. Stuck somewhere in the middle of the age-old battle between art and commerce was the cast. Largely unaware of the escalating conflicts between the film's core creative personnel, the actors naturally sided with their director. Few enjoyed the experience. Most simply endured it.*

TODD FARMER: Pre-production was one thing. But production, that was madness. Making the film was a nightmare.

NOEL CUNNINGHAM: It was a circus. Tons of people, tons of effects shots. Pyrotechnics. Stunts. Lots of action. Big, huge sets. We only had one exterior shot in the whole movie, and that was just an element—*Jason X* was shot entirely on a set. We had a $22 million film that we were trying to do for $13 million.

JIM ISAAC: The budgets for the *Friday* films had been getting smaller and smaller, and I felt that eventually the franchise would die out and end up going straight to video. So much time and money have been spent on movies that turned out to be bad. So with *Jason X*, I said, "Let's put every dime on the screen. Let's not do a Jason movie for $3 or $4 million. Let's raise the stakes. Let's prove we can do a movie for under $20 million that still looks A-list." Because if we approached this movie like just another low-budget slasher, then that's what we would end up with.

JOHN DONDERTMAN, Production Designer: Jim Isaac called me and said, "We want to make a film unlike any other Jason movie that's ever been made. We want it to look better than any Jason movie that's ever been made and we want it to look better than any science fiction movie that's ever been made." So it seemed like I couldn't lose.

The big draw was that we got to create everything. We could create this whole space station down to the last doorknob—all the monitors, consoles, the typography, everything. The sheer amount of detail was a quantum leap from my past experiences. Normally, you don't get to do that.

JAMES OSWALD, Art Director: Making *Jason X* was almost like being in an old Hollywood studio, where you had craftsmen of different disciplines all working under one roof. I'd never had an opportunity to work on a show where I could just walk down the stairs into this workshop where these guys are sculpting this crazy stuff. And I never worked on a show that was so effects-intensive. On *Jason X*, every single day, there was something new happening. That was very satisfying.

CHUCK CAMPBELL: I thought the whole futuristic aspect of the movie was a blast. It felt massive, like shooting in a huge air base. You could take a baseball and throw it from one end to the other, and it'd never hit the back wall.

JOHN DONDERTMAN: We had, at our busiest time, about eight people in the art department, about eighty carpenters and painters, plus the props team and the set dressing team of up to a dozen people. We were working two shifts a day to get everything complete. But everyone has their own little universe, and what could

"Kane used to really crack me up," says director Jim Isaac. "I did, sometimes, want Jason to do things that weren't completely consistent with his character. Kane would just look down at me and say, in that very deep voice, 'Jason doesn't *do* that.' And I'd be like, 'Oh, OK!' There was always this feeling that, at any point, he might reach down and grab the top of my head and squeeze if he didn't like the direction I was giving him."

happen was that everyone's universe seemed to be the most important. So there was this constant kind of jockeying for position, but at the same time we still really had to work with each other. It was an interesting dynamic.

STEPHAN DUPUIS, Makeup Effects Supervisor: Film is such a strange medium. It's like having a whole bunch of strangers suddenly thrown together who have to collaborate. It depends on the director and it depends on a lot of things. You get so many elements. So many things can go wrong and so many things can go right.

Jason X was like a family affair. Much of the crew had known each other for so long, and Jim had always wanted to direct. So it was fun to see him finally get to do it. Plus, he was very easy to communicate with. Sure, we could all argue about something, but if you don't agree with somebody, well, you just make it look like an accident.

TODD FARMER: *Jason X* was a unique experience for me because I was the novice on the crew. Here are these people, some of whom have won an Oscar, and they're making a Jason movie—which makes me think it should have been a lot better than it was.

JIM ISAAC: It was really difficult on the crew. I really couldn't deal with the script issues going on, because I had all these people asking me what color I wanted this or that and all these other details. I mean, I begged and begged and begged to have a locked script—like two months before we shot at least—because it was a very technical movie. And the last thing as a director that you want to do is give your crew new pages every day. They're working their asses off trying to get something done that they've been working on for days, and now they have a whole new friggin' script and they have to break the whole thing down again. Or they finish something and all of a sudden it isn't even in the script.

I felt like the crew liked me. But I could also tell they were really frustrated. The morale just gets down. They get tired of it all. There were times I should have regrouped, where I should have just gotten everyone together and told them that I see this going a bad direction, or at least in a direction I'm not comfortable with. They deserved that. Every little detail in a movie helps create the tone of the picture. It is just like rewriting a script—if you chip away here and you chip way there, for whatever reason, whether it is because of budget or because of time, it starts to become a different movie. The art department matters. The costume department matters. You take away their ability to do their job to the best of their ability, and you end up with a shell of a movie. But I have to say, again, it's my fault. I'm the director, and it is my job to have a vision, and the balls to fight for it.

DAVID HANDMAN, Editor: *Jason X* was a negative pickup and New Line wasn't involved until the movie was delivered. Perhaps it's strange or ironic, but maybe some of the creative problems on *Jason X* were because no one was getting notes. And without a studio to fight with, in many ways that just made it harder for everyone to be on the same page. Because you're fighting each other instead.

NOEL CUNNINGHAM: There are some producers who nickel and dime everything, and there are some producers who just oversee and manage everything and just try to stay out of everyone's way. That is what I was trying to do, and I don't know how successful I was. I just wanted to lift any kind of roadblocks out of the way so that Jim could just go and shoot. Jim was very competent and he had been through the ringer a number of times before, and together we were pretty much helming the thing. I had also been friends with Jim for about twelve years before *Jason X*. It just seemed like he knew the material, he knew the

movie we were trying to make. Jim is really smart, but I always had problems with certain parts of the script. Ultimately, I wasn't always sure about a lot of Jim's choices.

Finally, I just backed off because Jim was directing. I said, "Okay. If you understand this then go for it. Prove me wrong." I wouldn't call it a clash at all, but there was always that sort of underlying dynamic there.

JIM ISAAC: Sean, certainly at the beginning, respected Noel's creative sensibilities. Noel knew the fans and the series. He got it. And I knew that whatever he lacked in experience in filmmaking or producing, ultimately that wasn't the problem. It was having somebody to fight for our vision.

Noel had his heart in the right place, there's no question. Certainly at the beginning. I really thought that Noel had a good sense of where I wanted to go with the movie, creatively. Noel, Todd and I, we all wanted the same tone. So it must have been horribly difficult for Noel to be in that situation, and then to be working for his dad who he doesn't want to disappoint. But my feeling was, "Noel, you go fight those battles for me, all right? If I want something different and I'm busy, you go get in a room with your dad and make it happen for me." That's what a producer does.

DAVID HANDMAN: One day, Sean came into the editing room while I was working on the cargo bay scenes. At the time, footage was only trickling in, yet I was getting all of these shots that were lasting an incredibly long time. So I mentioned to Sean that I thought we were going to be short on our running time, and he goes back to Toronto and tells Jim Isaac, "I want all these shots to be really long so we can vamp with the cargo bay." Meaning, if we're short, we can beef up the screen time with all these really pretty shots of people and guns and them being chased around. Well, that was a big backfire, because it was boring and nothing's happening. And the thing about Todd's script was that it was so tight and so funny, and you didn't want it to bore people at all. That scene was originally about Kay-EM and her fight with Jason—that's a big action scene and now we've cut all her screen time very short.

Ultimately, I made Jim spend time on shots that he really didn't need at the expense of other things. It took all of the fun out of the original feel of the movie. I felt bad about that.

JIM ISAAC: Well into principal photography, Todd was gone. Sean was still writing pages. Sometimes we'd get them the night before, or even during shooting the next day. To be honest, I didn't like the pages. I didn't agree with the pages. The actors were flipping out. My assistant directors wanted to smash their heads against the wall. But I loved my cast and my crew. I just feel bad for the cast because I really worked hard to find young, energetic actors who were willing to try and make this something good. And now pages are being thrown at them at the last minute, and there I am not truly endorsing them. But what could I say? I feel bad that we didn't allow the actors to do their best work, and that's my job. They certainly didn't have enough time to work with what they were given.

I really wanted the acting in *Jason X* to just blow every other *Friday* movie out of the water. But what was happening with all the rewrites is why, sometimes, when you see a movie, an actor is brilliant in one moment and not so brilliant the next. You think, as a moviegoer, "How did that happen?" Well, a million things could happen. These actors all worked their asses off. They were sometimes given pages and pages of things that didn't make sense. They really did the best they possibly could. I think they really came through for me. It was tough.

LISA RYDER: Sean Cunningham was on set and came in with a bunch of his own rewrites all the time. Sean had his say, definitely. Every movie is like that, though. There are tons of examples of directors and producers with differing visions, and they have to come to some sort of midway. But Jim Isaac has a total sense of humor, and I don't think he's really from the horror genre. I don't think that was a huge interest for him. He was pushing toward the comic. So perhaps that midway point between Jim and Sean was never quite found.

DAVID HANDMAN: What we wound up shooting was not what Todd's script was. It misses a lot of that humor. It was kind of a battle of staying true to the original script. Sean wanted a *Friday the 13th* movie, and that's what he sold. We couldn't just go in and make a comedy. But at the same time, the people at New Line—De Luca thought the script was hilarious. I think he would have liked a comedy. But that's not what the franchise is. Personally, I think there's some hilarious stuff there. It was a cartoon—that's what we were trying to make.

There was also an enormous amount of dialogue stuff that we took out. There would be scenes, like the girl who gets sucked out the airlock, Janessa, where she's standing at a console basically directing traffic around the ship. And she's saying stylized, futuristic dialogue that she has no idea about. So we don't believe it and we don't care about it. They're words the audience has never heard. Or during that scene where the crew is re-animating Rowan's character—these are high school kids throwing around these words—it's just boring stuff. A lot of that was, again, because of Sean's fear of being short, but in all honestly, Sean also thinks that kind of stuff is dramatic. He thinks that is what people respond to, that all that dialogue makes an audience feel like there's an emergency. But, as far as I'm concerned, it just goes in one ear and out the other. You had to get rid of all that stuff.

JONATHAN POTTS: There were a lot of script changes on the spot. My sex scene with Melyssa Ade, where she has those huge nipple clamps on me, was hilarious. That was all Jim—"I have this great idea! It's so twisted!" That scene lets us see just how warped Jim is. And shopping for my outfit for that scene was also a riot. Maxyne took me down to a "He-and-She" sex shop in Toronto. And there I was, standing in the middle of this store, trying on negligee and bra tops. We even took Polaroids of different outfits to make sure there was a big enough opening in the bra so the clamp could get on my breast. And no one batted an eye.

TODD FARMER: Dialogue is always the thing that changes the most when you make a movie, and it changes drastically, right up to the day of shooting and even through editing and looping. As a screenwriter, you never know where it's gonna end up. On one hand, that's the beauty of it. You start seeing scenes acted out and the actors can bring to it things that you never imagined, and it's just wonderful. When it's working, there's a freedom of creativity that makes it all worthwhile. It makes all the headaches okay. On the other side of it, like it happened on *Jason X*, the script went through a lot of rewrites long after I left. Which is weird, because as the credited writer on the movie, you get blamed for them.

LISA RYDER: When I found out I got the film, I did waffle. I just assumed that it was going straight to video. I was like, "I don't want anyone to see this." And then I walked on set, and I met Jim, and because of his enthusiasm, and the talent that was on board, I started thinking, "Maybe this will be really cool and really funny. Maybe it will actually work." But as things went along, we started to worry that it was getting too campy—that it was never going to work.

Chuck Campbell and I had a really tough time with our love scenes—especially the kissing scene and the "nipple" scene. They were weirdly written. So Chuck and Jim and I got together and did a bit of rewriting. It was not exactly improv, on-the-spot stuff, but every once in a while, someone would add a line. It went through a kind of evolution. I guess something was lost in the translation. Because we certainly wanted to keep their relationship sweet and light—romantic, actually. Like that one scene where they kiss and then she goes, "We have a better chance of survival now."

I really wasn't willing to go to the graphic, "let's get a close-up of her getting uploaded" kind of stuff that was written. I wasn't into that, and I don't think Jim was into it, either. The dialogue needed a little bit of work. Most of the dialogue in *Friday the 13th* movies is sexual-cheesy, and we just didn't want that. And there has to be that, I guess, because of the tradition of the series. But we all saw an opportunity to do something that was a little bit of an actual relationship.

JIM ISAAC: What happened with those scenes is a perfect example of us trying to get some of the wild elements in the original script back into the movie. Even as watered down as some of those moments are, I was sincerely trying to recapture that initial tone. I mean, having him twist an android's nipples around and then they drop off—that's weird sex. Of course, you have to have a sex scene in a Jason movie, but can we just get kinky with it? Those are the kinds of things that I thought, ultimately, would be fun for the fans. Again, that was just me trying to put back in what I wanted originally, even if they are just bits and pieces.

TODD FARMER: I'm sure my first script had some one-liners in it. But it was a completely different tone. I would say the story of *Jason X* is the same, but it's of a different character and attitude. The jokes came out of the action, not out of the characters' mouths. A lot of that stuff happens on set. I think the jokes in the film are kind of corny. It is not the kind of humor I prefer. But what do I know?

I know one scene I always loved that never quite made it was where Weylander and Crutch are in the cockpit of the main ship and they're readying the escape shuttle. Then something happens and Weylander has to leave. Originally, after Weylander walked out, there was Jason, and it became this big action chase sequence. And in that scene was all this humor that was coming out of the situation—the kind of humor people often resort to when they are in a scary situation. It is not like a lot of the humor that is in the film now, where somebody says, "He's screwed," and we cut to a guy dead on a giant screw.

Although the character of Kay-EM 14 is integral to the action of *Jason X*, one of the character's biggest sequences was ultimately cut from the finished film. "We shot this great setpiece in a house of mirrors," recalls actress Lisa Ryder. "I'm walking around with my big gun, and Jason keeps appearing, and I'm blasting away at all the mirrors. There was a whole bunch of terrific action stuff, but that all got cut. I was really disappointed!"

JONATHAN POTTS: On the set, it was always that fine line. We would have a scene and we were like, "What do you guys think? Should we play that joke a little bit, or should we ignore it and just go kind of straight?" We'd look at each other and say, "Fuck it—let's make it funny. That's what I want to see." Jim was definitely on the same page as everyone else. We all knew we couldn't turn this into a truly scary movie again, nor go totally for the campy, making-fun-of-ourselves thing. Yet, you couldn't ignore the obvious, either. Because what were we making? We were making a tenth movie in the *Friday the 13th* series.

CHUCK CAMPBELL: For the cast, it was a big fun-fest. Whether it was exploding a head or spinning on a drill bit. And I welcomed the experience of working with all the blue screen. It is very technical work, but challenging. And it was so funny—any time we'd look at a screen or have some kind of monitor, there was nothing there. It was all *Star Trek*-pretend.

LEXA DOIG: Acting against the special effects was like being a kid when you play house. It's a bunch of cushions in your living room, but if you can get back to that frame of mind it

is really fun and challenging. It is really difficult to try and create a reality when you can't associate that with anything in your real life. I haven't been chased by a dead guy in a hockey mask in my personal life, at least not yet. So I don't really know how it feels. And the way the movie was shot, because of the special effects, it's only snippets here and there. You just try and pump yourself up and just keep that really high, intense energy level going throughout the entire process. It is really very hard to articulate.

But the special effects guys were fantastic, because they're very descriptive, and they would show all of us actors the conceptual drawings and what the intentions were for any individual scene. Plus, Jim used to do effects himself, so he was great about reminding us every now and again where we were supposed to be at, emotionally, during a scene.

DAVID HANDMAN: I was cutting the film in L.A. while they were shooting in Toronto. I didn't get to experience the shooting of *Jason X*, and there's a certain vibe that happens during production. The ability to sit down with a director and watch dailies, and go to the set and get the feel of it—I think that was really

"When those red, cat-like eyes are staring directly at you, peering out from behind that devilish chrome mask, you can't help but be frightened."

Lexa Doig on UberJason

missed on *Jason X*. I couldn't really tell Jim what he should be doing tomorrow because I still needed to see the film he had already shot. There are a lot of visual jokes that Jim wanted to tell, but he couldn't shoot them because they ended up shooting all this other stuff that we eventually got rid of anyway.

I remember specifically there was a shot planned for Janessa's death scene where she gets sucked out of the airlock. That was a shot Jim wanted to get and he had it all scripted and he couldn't get it. To me, that was the money shot. You get that at all costs. You don't make the director spend time doing other things if it means he's not going to get that shot. Because otherwise the scene isn't about anything.

NOEL CUNNINGHAM: I wish we could have gone back and done a couple weeks' worth of reshoots, just go and spend the money. But we flat-out didn't have it. Sean simply wouldn't give it to us.

TODD FARMER: Sean's opinion at the time was that if we had just done what he said, we would have had a better movie. My opinion was that if Sean had stayed out of the way, and if Jimmy would have listened to me, we would have had a better movie. But I'm sure Jimmy will say, "If everybody would have listened to me, we would have had the best movie of all." This is all why real moviemakers get paid a lot of money, because they can work through those kinds of situations. We couldn't.

Of all the risks the makers of Jason X *would take with the* Friday the 13th *formula, none was riskier than their reinvention of Jason himself. The sight of a hockey-masked mongoloid stalking nubile young teens in the woods was as archaic to today's teenagers as the black-caped, plastic-fanged Bela Lugosi as* Count Dracula *had been to the kids of the 1980s. If Jason was going to be blasted into outer space, a beaten-up hockey mask and a K-Mart machete would not be enough to bring him into the twenty-first century. Evil needed an upgrade.*

TODD FARMER: We knew that *Freddy vs. Jason* was coming out eventually. We also knew that, time-wise, *Jason X* would take place after the last Freddy film and after the last Jason film. So we wanted to let Freddy and Jason have their time and not interfere with that. So we moved *Jason X* ten years into the future, so it takes place around the year 2010. Which is a good thing, because then we could have the freedom to create our own Jason, and do it in a way that wasn't tied to the last Jason movie.

JIM ISAAC: I think that we all agreed, at some point, that these kids had to rebuild Jason. There had to be a moment when they totally creamed him. I mean, just rip him to pieces. Then, through some weird new technology, he comes back to life as something totally new. I just said, "Wow. Here's an opportunity for us to create a new Jason. Something really different and wild." So Todd went off and wrote something that was really fresh and cool.

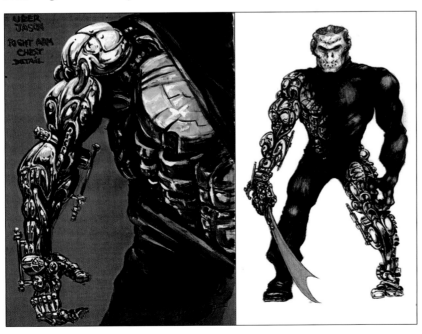

This page: Conceptual art drawings of the UberJason suit by makeup effects supervisor Stephan Dupuis. The entire design process took months of research and careful planning on the part of Dupuis and visual effects supervisor Kelly Lepkowsky. "We came up a few months early to Toronto before principal photography started," says Lepkowsky. "We built a small-scale mock-up of the UberJason character—what we called 'the cat,' because of his red eye. Stephan sculpted it, and everybody absolutely loved it. Then we began the process of creating the suit by taking castings of Kane Hodder's body to create a form that was almost like a sculpted UberJason suit, which created a whole new set of challenges." Creating the suit tested the imagination of Dupuis. "The production of the UberJason suit was really challenging because it was made out of so many different materials. You've got the metal parts, which are VacuForm, and they're attached to foam pieces with Velcro. And the black part of the suit is leather. And the tendrils that grow into the metal are silicone. So all of that had to be blended together. It took months of experimenting to get right."

TODD FARMER: I wanted to take Jason somewhere different. He's somebody the audience still roots for, even though he hacks up young virgins. So I wanted to give the fans an opportunity to really cheer when he comes back. And I honestly can't remember who actually first pitched the idea for "UberJason," but I remember everybody loved it. There was a moment of silence in the office when we talked about it.

NOEL CUNNINGHAM: UberJason was one of the big things that turned the tide for setting the film in space. The initial thinking of it was much more raw and cobbled together. It was also kind of a holdover from one the *Freddy vs. Jason* script attempts, because in one of those scripts there was a scene where Jason breaks into a sporting goods store and there's a big goalie display and one of the mannequins is wearing a big chrome hockey mask. Jason kind of looks at it and switches masks. That was probably the genesis of the whole UberJason concept, to ramp up his look a little. It was just, "Fuck—let's put him in something high-tech and futuristic. If you thought he was bad-ass before, now he's a cyborg bad-ass! Bigger, stronger, sleeker, meaner and better!" At least that was the intent.

MELYSSA ADE: I thought UberJason was just an extraordinary feat of imagination. It's absolutely incredible that, collectively, minds came up with the concept, the design, and built it and lit it. It's like a piece of art. It really is like a beautiful, beautiful painting. And that's what I keep telling myself on the set when I was scared—it's a painting!

STEPHAN DUPUIS, Makeup Effects Supervisor: By the end of 1999, months before pre-production started, I was already designing UberJason. Because it was like, "How are we gonna pull this off? The guy with the hockey mask with a machete winds up in outer space!" To be honest, I was not thinking whether fans of *Friday the 13th* were going to be thrown for a loop or not. I had no idea because I'm not a fan of the *Friday* movies. I saw the first one a long time ago and I knew what the character, Jason, was all about, but that's it.

So UberJason is a completely new creation. It doesn't have a lot to do with the old Jason apart from the mask and a wonderful new machete. And you gotta laugh at the camp element, too. It's like "Sinbad Goes to Mars" or something.

NOEL CUNNINGHAM: It came out of the word "biomechanoid." He had been blown to bits and had just kind of been rebuilt. In the earlier versions, he would have had a lot more flesh on him and things poking through. Then, of course, we realized that wouldn't work—we couldn't make that happen in the suit. It would have been impossible to execute. That's when UberJason became more polished and shit. But I loved what Stephan did. It looked really cool.

STEPHAN DUPUIS: I have always bought a lot of art books, from different artists and illustrators and painters, and that's usually where

I get my inspiration—comic books, cartoons, you name it. Because you get these fantastic, evocative illustrations. Then the challenge is, can we translate it or try to adapt that into three dimensions? With UberJason, I just began by doodling and just having fun. I was trying to think of the actual mechanical lines of the robot itself. I was also thinking about Maria, the robot from *Metropolis*. That sort of design. I just made all the lines more art deco-ish. Another influence was Burt Ogard. His dynamic anatomy has these really cool, very beautiful anatomy lines. So it was a mixture of those two things that informed the look of UberJason.

I got a lot of leeway. I just made several drawings of what I thought it should look like. Then Jim Isaac looked at about maybe four or five and took the best parts of each and put them together.

KANE HODDER, "Jason Voorhees": The first time I read *Jason X*, I knew it was the best *Friday* script we ever had, and it was only a rough draft. I was excited. And I thought UberJason was great. It was a chance for a whole different look for the character.

Working in the UberJason suit was difficult, however, because all that metallic-looking stuff was made of separate plastic pieces attached to the suit. And some were so big, like my entire arm, which was encased in silicone, that I couldn't bend it. Same with one of my legs. I really had to exaggerate my movements, even my head turning. The suit kind of minimizes what you are doing, so you think you are doing everything really broad, but it doesn't come across like that. I really wanted to make my movements a little smoother and more deliberate, not quite as haphazard as my other Jason. It was a real challenge, and I'm not sure how well it came across.

TODD FARMER: The funny thing is, I always knew Kane would play it. No one ever doubted that he wouldn't.

LISA RYDER: Kane's a very strange dude. He's very sweet and polite and nice, but then he has this strange side of him. He's kind of method. He has "K-I-L-L" tattooed on his inner lip. And he growls at you before a take. I think it's because he's such a nice guy, he needs to distance himself from his co-actors when he's trying to kill them. He feels a responsibility to fans to perpetuate that image of himself. It's his thing. He was actually fighting for Jason's motivation!

KANE HODDER: Although I was happy when I first read the script, I was even happier when Jim Isaac got the job. Because he is a fan of what I did before, which always helps me because then the director allows me to have input. I have been playing this character so long that I have opinions on how things should be

Above: "The great thing about UberJason is that it gave us free reign," says makeup effects supervisor Stephan Dupuis. "Not only to redesign his appearance, but to outfit him with new weapons. Of course, Jason without a machete is like Freddy without his razor fingers. So we created some great new machetes for Jason, too."

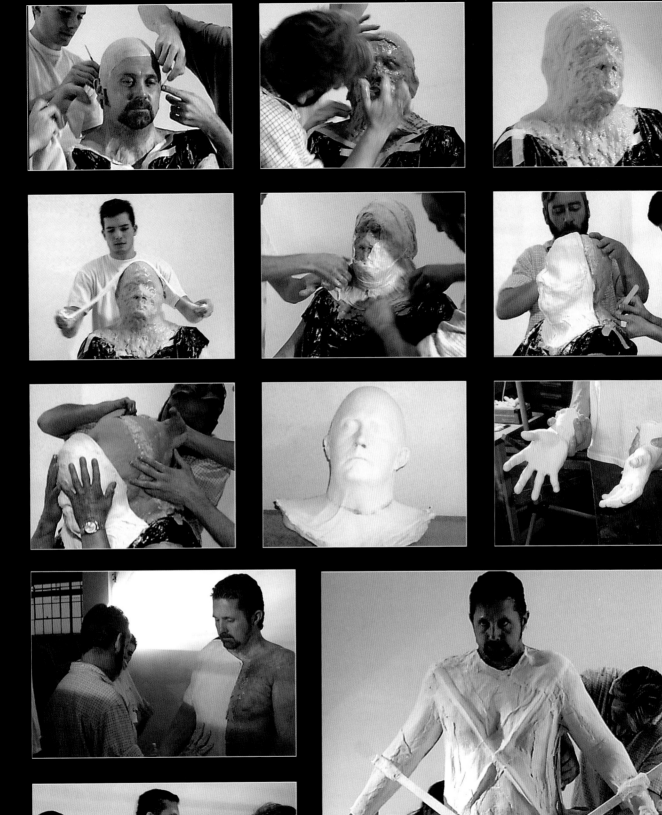

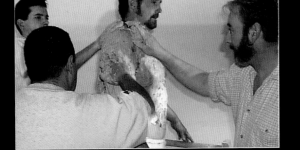

This page: The many stages of UberJason. "We actually created an 'UberJason suit,'" says makeup effects supervisor Stephan Dupuis. "We made a head and full body cast of Kane Hodder. Then, it was like he was just sort of sliding inside a banana peel—the suit had two long zippers along the sides. He was in and out of it in only fifteen minutes. Compared to some of the elaborate makeups he had to wear on previous *Friday*s, he was pretty happy about that."

done regarding Jason. And Jim was all for my opinions. Not necessarily that he agreed with everything I said, but he certainly listened.

CHUCK CAMPBELL: I was in the production office one day, and Kane comes walking around the corner, in full UberJason makeup. Red eyes and everything. I turned around and I must have looked absolutely terrified, because Jim Isaac said, "If you can react like that on the set, it will be perfect!"

MAXYNE BAKER, Costume Designer: Kane's a real character. At our first costume fitting, we set him up in the strait-jacket costume he wears at the top of the movie. And he's bound up in it, with chains and all kinds of things wrapped around him. And he's being very good about it. Then I was trying to take a Polaroid, and I said, "Kane, do you mind moving back a little bit so I can get all of you in the picture?" And he took two steps back and fell right through the fitting room wall!

NOEL CUNNINGHAM: Jim Isaac's family would come up to the set, and one time it was his son's birthday, so there was another dozen or so eleven-year-olds on the set. And of course they all wanted to meet Jason. So we introduced them to Kane. He was in his makeup chair, and he took off his mask and was just all friendly, like, "Hey kids, how's it going?" So they now had all let down their guard. Then we led the kids around for a tour. And over at one part of the studio, off to the side, were all these fake Jasons. Well, Kane went the opposite direction and went into the prop closet and laid down on the ground as if he was another Jason dummy. So the kids come into the room and we're like, "Oh, here's another Jason dummy. Look how life-like it is!" Then they lean over, and Kane just lunges up at them and hollers. And they all just screamed. I've never seen kids run away so fast!

If production on Jason X *had been a painful—if not occasionally excruciating— experience, then at least post-production allowed for a little respite from the madness that had preceded it. While neither Jim Isaac nor Noel Cunningham were completely happy with the raw footage,* Jason X *was still a pioneer of a new wave of digital filmmaking. Shot on film, then converted entirely to high-definition video to aid in the creation of its extensive and elaborate visual effects shots,* Jason X *has the distinction of being the first feature-length film ever to be completed entirely in the digital realm. It was also brighter, glossier and slicker than most of the dark, noir-ish science fiction fare that followed in the wake of such trailblazing genre films as* Blade Runner *and* ALIEN. *The film's unique visual style also earned some unexpected leniency from the Motion Picture Association of America's ratings board. Perhaps the* Friday the 13th *film that suffered the least due to cuts imposed by the MPAA, the final cut of* Jason X *would remain largely intact on its journey to an R rating—much to the surprise of its producers.*

NOEL CUNNINGHAM: To be honest, after we finished principal photography I wasn't jumping up and down. I was happy with some of the stuff we got. But we really did attempt something very ambitious, not only for a *Friday the 13th* movie, but for a smaller-budgeted sci-fi action film. We prepped the thing for like eight months, and we had our computer guys working for over a year on the CGI effects. Before we really even had a script they were already working on spaceships.

With *Jason Takes Manhattan* they tried to widen the franchise. But unless you really make the commitment to it, it just doesn't work. We made that commitment, and it became a very big project, whatever one thinks of the final outcome.

JIM ISAAC: There was a lot of misconception when *Jason X* came out that it was shot on high-definition video. It wasn't. *Jason X* was shot on 35mm film, and then transferred to high-definition. The reason I did that was that I had so many visual effects in the movie that it would have been impossible to do all that I wanted in film resolution. We first did a test, and then decided that was indeed the way to go. And once we started going down that road, my feeling was, well, what if we did that to the entire film? What if we were to shoot it, take the entire film to digital, do all the work, plus the timing and the effects, and then scan the entire movie back onto film? What would happen? No one had done it at that point. And I think the movie looks beautiful. It's got depth, and I was able to do some very cool things with the color timing. I do love that about the movie.

One of *Jason X*'s standout scenes was the "Virtual Crystal Lake" sequence. Through the use of virtual reality technology, the film's protagonists attempt to trick Jason by making it appear as if he has been transported back to his original stomping grounds. The scene was like a homecoming for Kane Hodder (**opposite page, top**, with director Jim Isaac). "It was a lot of fun to be on the spaceship as Jason," says Hodder. "But it still felt so much better to be back in the woods. It always feels more natural. And the sequence is, I think, one of the best in the film."

The filmmakers also saw it as a wry commentary on the *Friday the 13th* series' well-known clichés and conventions. "I think the early *Friday* films were much more like morality plays than *Jason X*," says producer Noel Cunningham. "Back then it was 'sex and drugs will get you killed.' Today, people don't really give a shit about sex and drugs so much, and that was why we came up with those lines in the Virtual Crystal Lake sequence, where the two girls say to Jason, 'You want to smoke some pot and have premarital sex?' (**Opposite page, bottom**) That was a definite nod to the old school slasher movies, and the fans really seemed to get that humor."

However, not all of the crew were as enthused as the younger Cunningham, particularly the film's casting director Robin Cook. "I didn't end up casting those parts," says Cook. "I just wouldn't. My casting assistant ended up doing them. I just felt that scene was gratuitous. Jim Isaac didn't want to do it, either. But the producers felt it was important. Because, quite frankly, it helps foreign sales if you have a few seconds of nudity. I didn't want any part of that." Jim Isaac, for his part, continues to have mixed feelings about the use of nudity in the sequence. "It wasn't like I was against seeing breasts," laughs Isaac. "I like breasts. There's no problem there. I just didn't want to have nudity in the film for the sake of it. But if we were going to do it, I wanted to have fun with it, and make it really silly. And, after all, we are doing a *Friday the 13th* movie. I didn't want to pretend otherwise. Ultimately, I think the scene works really well and always gets a great response from the audience."

KELLY LEPKOWSKY, Visual Effects Supervisor: For the non-technical movie viewer, it probably doesn't mean anything, which is good, because it should look just like any other picture that they've ever seen. But what it is going to mean for audiences in the future is that it will allow films that have a lower budget to be able to do the kinds of spectacular effects that we're used to seeing in big Hollywood productions. I do truly think *Jason X* may have helped open a lot of possibilities for filmmakers, because one of the challenges we had set for ourselves was that we wanted the film to look big and exciting on a budget that's much more modest than a big Hollywood spectacular. If anything, it showed people that you could have a whole new level of control in post-production.

JOHN DONDERTMAN: One of the things we wanted to stay away from with *Jason X* was the type of science fiction movie where it's very dark and menacing. We wanted to do the opposite, so that the world of *Jason X* was actually a place where you would believe people live—a place you could spend years in. And when Jason arrives, there's a contrast. So we looked at old movies and new movies, comics, NASA images, even science fiction-style architecture. *Jason X* also had to be designed for a certain age group. Ultimately, I wanted the audience to be inspired by the visuals.

DAVID HANDMAN: I think the visuals and the humor are what helped us on *Jason X* with the ratings board. The movie has got a storybook quality to it that I think got us through a lot of the potential problems with the content. And it's set in the future. It wasn't like the more typical in-your-face slasher type of stuff.

The changes we had to make for the MPAA were very minor. Certainly far, far less than *Jason Goes to Hell*. But little has changed about how the ratings board works. They still don't give any guide-

"When I first read the script to *Jason X*, I was very happy. And then when I heard Jim Isaac was going to be directing it, I was even happier because I knew he would do it right." **Kane Hodder**

lines. They just say, "This is unacceptable. Show us a different version." You have no idea how far and you don't want to go back any further than you have to. Where's the line? Personally, on *Jason X*, I think we took out more than we probably needed to in the first place. Because we had no idea how they would respond.

GEOFF GARRETT, Associate Producer: Originally, the MPAA were only supposed to deal with Sean and Jim Isaac, but it ended up being me who had to keep the relationship with the ratings board. After we first submitted it to them, they called and said, "We have a couple of things before we can rate it R that we need to talk about." And even before that phone call I was nervous. Because the *Friday* movies have always been problematic for the MPAA, and Sean has had a sort of tumultuous relationship with them that dates all the way back to *Last House on the Left*. So here I was on the phone, trying to keep the most business-professional attitude I could. And then the guy on the phone from the MPAA goes, "You know what? We really had a good time. You have a fun little movie here." And I didn't know how to respond! I was so not expecting them to comment on the quality of the film at all. I was expecting them to tell me, "This is an NC-17." And they ended up being really great to the film.

I remember the blood on David Cronenberg when he gets speared—that was all done digitally. Even the blood was enhanced. The MPAA did say that was way too much, so we just removed the blood we added. We also had to lose one revolution of the "screw kill." But that was about it. We almost felt like we were getting away with something. And I was sitting there going, "Did you not see the guy crawling along the ground with his guts hanging on the ground, or the dead body of the pilot spread across the console?"

NOEL CUNNINGHAM: If you go for exploitation, the MPAA will be a little harder on you, but if you're trying to do a good job and the violence is just part of the movie, they're much more lenient about it because they understand. *Saving Private Ryan*, for

example. There is so much gore in that. But it's there for a reason—to show the horror of war. It's "legitimate." It's only if you get too crazy with it that they object. It's the same thing with video games now—the same claptrap that's going on.

Although Jason had finally won a battle with the MPAA, there was still one more obstacle to overcome. Jim Isaac and Noel Cunningham had always envisioned Jason X *as a sequel that looked more to the future than the past—and that included its soundtrack. Harry Manfredini, despite having composed the scores for eight of the previous nine installments of the series, was far from the filmmakers' ideal choice. Ultimately, it was the elder Cunningham's insistence on using his trusted veteran composer that ensured Manfredini would get the job at all.*

DAVID HANDMAN: If you ask Jim what he regrets most about the movie, I think it's the music. Harry Manfredini was the wrong composer. Everybody wanted a fresh take and Harry didn't really deliver anything fresh. Unfortunately, Harry kind of took us back into old *Friday the 13th* territory. To me, his score sounds like he had the movie playing and he was just writing along to it. It isn't really a conceptual score. There were no themes at all—each character should have a theme. I found that to be the weakest aspect of the whole movie.

JIM ISAAC: Sean was just over *Friday the 13th*. He was tired of it, he'd done it, it's not his scene. Horror films aren't his thing, and he's the first guy to admit it. I'm not saying he's not a filmmaker— he loves the process—but he really wants to do serious dramas and work with actors and all those things. But a hip, sexy, weird, edgy, scary horror film? That's not Sean. So he just said it directly, "I'm not gonna be involved creatively with *Jason X*."

So it was very frustrating to then not be given the freedom we wanted with the score. I really wanted the music to be intense. And that, to me, had to a lot to do with getting something new. I also wanted to go with some actual songs—I wanted to make *Jason X* really hip. This is nothing against the score we did get, or Harry's music. I think the music that he did on the other movies is great. I just wanted a different signature for *Jason X*.

NOEL CUNNINGHAM: My father showed up about a month before principal photography started. He had been dealing with another film he was working on. He'd always said he was going to be totally hands-off. But there were certain times where we disagreed enormously, and other times he really helped out. There is no one better than Sean when it comes to the money. But, at the same time, the fact is that we had two different goals, both in how we thought the movie should be made and what movies we liked to go see. We're two different generations, of different schools of thought. Harry's always been involved with the *Friday* films and Sean wanted to bring back the regulars. That was a decision Sean made unilaterally that really pissed off Jim and I. We wanted a much more techno score.

Still, part of the situation was my fault. Even under the best of circumstances, I still think Harry's score would have been lacking, but he was not aware of the post-production schedule. It was unfortunate. It was insanely rushed. We kept asking him and telling him and saying, "We need to hear some stuff." And he had just rebuilt his studio and was having problems with it. Finally, it was like, "Harry, when are we going to hear some stuff?" And he was like, "How about the weekend of the 12th?" We'd be like, "Harry, that's opening weekend!" And he's like, "What!?" It was one of those 'i's I never dotted or 't's I never crossed. As a producer, the responsibility for any deficiencies in the score ultimately fell on me.

HARRY MANFREDINI, Composer: Over the years, I've learned there are good things about the movie business and bad things about the movie business. One of the bad things is that there are few people who are truly loyal. But Sean's always been loyal. Even as far back as *A Stranger is Watching*, he really pushed to try and hire me. He hasn't always succeeded, but one of the things I value most about my *Friday* experience is the friendships I've made. That is something I cherish.

With *Jason X*, I liked having the chance to write different types of music, to make the film about more than just Jason. I also liked that the characters were so sure they had superiority over Jason, and tried to be proactive. And I loved Jim Issac.

As for the themes, I did come up with softer ones. I just made them up. I get the feeling, and the dramatic sense of the piece, and then I start to listen in my head. There were also certainly musical considerations I made for the Lexa Doig character, as well as the pomposity of the teacher, and the coolness of the robot.

Even if Jason X *had been an ordeal for its makers, there was only more insult and injury to come. During the film's yearlong production, massive changes had taken place in the upper executive ranks of New Line Cinema. In a much-publicized, highly acrimonious split, Michael De Luca would exit his position as President of Production in early 2000, and with him went* Jason X's *biggest champion at the studio. With no one within the company immediately stepping up to support the film,* Jason X *would suffer the humiliation of being left on the shelf for over two years. By the time New Line released the film on April 26, 2002, much had changed both in the world of digital filmmaking and in the sensibilities and expectations of the moviegoing public. The art of computer-generated effects was growing by leaps and bounds, and younger audiences, weaned on such visually stunning action spectaculars as* The Matrix *and* Spider-Man, *cared little about budgetary battles and behind-the-scenes feuding. There was also a question as to whether or not there was still an audience for the further adventures of Jason—much less "Jason in space." It had been almost a decade since* Jason Goes to Hell, *and even if the PlayStation generation was still discovering the* Friday the 13th *films on home video and cable, to many,* Jason Voorhees *represented a face of cinema's past, not its present. Moreover, the gore quotient in motion pictures had also lost its ability to shock, with the average video game filled with far more graphic and violent imagery than anything that could pass muster with the MPAA. Regrettably,* Jason X *was in danger of seeming like a dated anachronism even before it hit cinemas.*

Opening on 1,878 screens across the United States, Jason X *failed to ignite the box office. It pulled in a mere $6.6 million in its first three days, landing a distant third behind Paramount's thriller* Changing Lanes *and the first-place finisher, Universal's* The Scorpion King, *which took in over $18 million in its second weekend. But* Jason X *would fare even worse in the long term. By its second weekend, faced with the onslaught of Sony's* Spider-Man, *the film lost sixty-five percent of its audience. With a*

Above: British-born actor Peter Mensah plays Sgt. Brodski, the commander of a team of "grunts" who must face off against the unstoppable Jason Voorhees in *Jason X*. "I saw Brodski as a very straightforward character, and not a very modern one, really," says Mensah. "He definitely belonged to a time when soldiers were soldiers and fighting is all they knew. I thought my job in the film was to act as a foil to Jason. Obviously, Brodski can't match him in strength, but he has that same kind of resilience. Even if Brodski knew he'd never win the war, he still had the courage and the willingness to stand up to Jason and fight to the death. Which he did."

The most visually complex and effects-intensive of the *Friday the 13th* films, *Jason X* utilized cutting-edge CGI technology, combined with such traditional processes as green screen and wire work (**opposite page**) to achieve its futuristic illusions. "We actually had an entire 'Green Room' for all of the green screen work," says visual effects supervisor Kelly Lepkowsky. "That allowed us to take any model or any actor and place them in front of any environment we wanted. Of course, it is a technique that has been around for quite a while now in film, but through the use of CGI, we could take it one step further. We also used green screen for many pieces of the background of our sets, which we could then replace in the digital realm with all sorts of fantastic things."

The film's cast also enjoyed working with the process, although it was sometimes a physical challenge. "Any time an actor can be placed in a really uncomfortable position with a green suit on them, it's still cheaper than CGI," laughs Lisa Ryder. "In fact, it's like $1,000 per second cheaper. It's so funny—any time in the film you see just my head talking (**background**), that's me with a green dog collar on!"

The identical key art was used on both the soundtrack CD (**above**) and theatrical one-sheet for *Jason X*. Not everyone was pleased with the finished product, however. "I thought that UberJason should be kept a secret," says screenwriter Todd Farmer. "Then he turns up on the movie poster. It was like putting a penis on the poster of *The Crying Game*. UberJason is kind of a goofy idea, but if you're watching the movie for the first time I thought it would be a hoot. People would leave the theater saying, 'You've got to see *Jason X* because you're not going to believe what happens!' But no one listened to me."

The lack of a signature theme song was also a disappointment for the film's producers. "I really wish I could have convinced New Line to give us the budget to get a great rock song," says associate producer Geoff Garrett. "But that's the good and bad part about being a negative pickup. If *Jason X* had been a studio movie, we could have budgeted the money from the get-go. Jim Isaac was even friends with the guitarist from the group Train, and Jim was going to get them to contribute a song. Instead, we ended up having Ethan Wiley and his partner put together a little something for the film."

Wiley was no stranger to Sean Cunningham, having written the screenplay for *House*, and directed its first sequel, *House II: The Second Story*. "I'm also a musician and had recently put out my own CD," says Wiley. "Jim Isaac called me and they were already in final mixing on *Jason X*, but he said that they wanted something dark and very brooding for the end credits—something upbeat and energetic for when the audience was leaving the theater. Almost, 'gothic-horror-rock-sci-fi,' as Jim put it." Wiley ultimately composed two songs for the movie with co-writer John Sholle—"X is the Loneliest Number" and "Jason's Jam." Although neither song ultimately appeared on the film's official soundtrack CD, Wiley continues to make them available on his official website, www.meanbunny.com. "We literally came up with the concepts for the tracks in a couple of hours, and recorded them over a weekend. But I think Jim was pleasantly surprised, because after he heard them he called and said, 'It's perfect—exactly what we need.' So it worked out really well."

Despite its lack of box office success, *Jason X* has amassed its own dedicated fan following and inspired a series of spin-off comic books (**opposite page**) and young adult novels.

final gross of only $13.1 million, for 2.2 million paid admissions, Jason X earned the unfortunate distinction of becoming the lowest-grossing entry in the franchise. Although the film found a second life on DVD, selling over half a million copies, Jason X was nevertheless regarded as an interstellar dud.

NOEL CUNNINGHAM: When we started *Jason X*, it was Michael De Luca's project. And when we finished it, Michael had resigned from New Line. All of a sudden, there's a whole new crew of people there, and none of them had any real vested interest in it. It was part of the old regime, so nobody wanted to get their fingers dirty. Or they didn't want their marketing budget to suddenly have $25 million chopped off to promote it. It was the red-headed stepchild that just gets dumped on a doorstep.

TODD FARMER: The truth is that New Line didn't have any money. They had put all their eggs in *The Lord of the Rings* basket and then De Luca left and he was the only guy we had ever talked to at New Line about *Jason X*. You have this movie sitting on the shelf that none of these executives have any affection for. This happened to a lot of New Line movies—we weren't the only ones. Yet there was too much money invested in it to let it go straight to video. Plus, if they were going to do that, they would have released it immediately. There would have been no sitting on it.

JIM ISAAC: It was crazy. The film had been sitting for so long that it started getting bootlegged on the Internet. I started to get these emails from fans who would tell me, "I've been invited over to a friend's house to watch a bootleg of *Jason X*." I would always email back and say, "I know it's tempting, but please don't go!" I wanted people to see it on the big screen like we intended. I was always concerned that people who were watching a lousy-quality tape would judge it based on that and be swayed, and that would create negative buzz. Of course, bootlegging is something I would prefer not to happen, but it is something that we, as filmmakers, really can't control nowadays.

TODD FARMER: Does it bother me? Yeah. Do I understand it? Sure. If I were a fan and I had waited that long, I'd probably download it, too. When people come up to me and say, "Well, *The Matrix* was bootlegged, too." Well, of course! *The Matrix* was giant. It was a huge movie. If it lost $5 million in bootlegs, it can afford that. *Jason X* couldn't afford to lose $5 million in bootlegs. That would have given us an $11 million opening weekend. It would have made all the difference in the world. We were also sandwiched in between *The Scorpion King* and *Spider-Man*. It almost didn't matter how much we grossed. We were going to be destroyed regardless.

I remember opening weekend. I got together with friends, all of whom were more than willing to go with you to see it and give you support, because most of them are writers and they've all been through this process. I went to see *Jason X* with Dean Lorey and his wife, and Kurt Wimmer, who wrote *Thomas Crown Affair*, and John Gerr who did *Romeo Must Die*. I remember we went to the theater and it was only a quarter full. And they were all just like, "Don't worry about it—it doesn't matter. You got a movie made!" It was still one of the more depressing moments of my life. Next time I have a movie open, I'm going to Disneyland. I don't want anything to do with it.

KANE HODDER: New Line Cinema said *Jason X* didn't deliver, blaming the lackluster box office on performances or whatever. Really, you took two years to release the goddamned thing. How stupid do you have to be to say, "The box office of that movie wasn't very good?" You let it fucking sit, only so people could see it on the Internet for free. You can't be that ignorant.

HARRY MANFREDINI: One of the sad things that happened with *Jason X* is that because it sat on the shelf for so long, the special effects were outdated by the time it hit theaters. When it was shot they were pretty cool, and by the release they were passé.

DAVID HANDMAN: I still believe that everything about *Jason X* was better than *Jason Goes to Hell*. You're not only talking about the difference between a $15 million picture and a $3 million picture, but Jim Isaac was also a producer, and basically brought the visual effects department with him. It wasn't the same feeling as with Adam. And Todd's script was very different—I think it's still the most unique horror script I've ever read.

PETER MENSAH: I give them credit for taking a franchise that had been kind of out of the public's consciousness for a while and making a fun movie. Because fun is needed. This isn't brain surgery here—this is entertainment. And considering the directions film is moving right now—with all the special effects, the Hong Kong action influences, just the sheer amount of explosions—I give a good amount of credit to these guys for trying to keep it fresh.

When I saw *Jason X*, I was pleasantly surprised. Because I just didn't know how it would turn out when I was making it. And some of the scenes had me howling, which is great. The fact that there's a sense of humor in there is what I was really hoping for. Because if we took it too seriously, where's the enjoyment? Without talking down to the material, though—it had to be done tongue-in-cheek. You just can't explain *Jason X*. You're not supposed to.

CHUCK CAMPBELL: I didn't really expect anything from it. It was such a fun experience to make the film that if it went straight to video it didn't really matter. I certainly didn't look at *Jason X* as a career-advancing movie for me. I just made a lot of friends and paid off my MasterCard bill.

NOEL CUNNINGHAM: I actually wanted it to be much scarier, but that was a creative decision that Jim made with the comedy. There are no scares in the movie. There were tons of scares in the script.

KANE HODDER: I hate to agree, but there wasn't much suspense in *Jason X*. But I do think it was a better-made film than the other *Friday*s. There was more money in it, certainly, and it was of higher quality. But I have to say my favorite is still *Part VII*.

JONATHAN POTTS: I didn't have any illusions—I knew what it was. I was just looking forward to being in a lead role in a film that would actually be in theaters, that people would talk about, and be in magazines. And it was on the Web all over the place. I don't think for any of us it was like, "This is it, man. People are going to see this and we're going to be on our way." But I also knew someone might watch it and say, "Hey, I like that guy." Roger Ebert reviewed the film and even mentioned my name. He tore it to shreds—he hated it—but he said, "Professor Lowe," and I was like, "Yay! He mentioned me!" I was just thrilled to be a part of it.

TODD FARMER: I wish we had a name actor in the film, although I think everyone in the cast did a fine job. I wish we'd kept UberJason a secret. I wish the script hadn't been rewritten so many times. If we had stuck to that and not gone so crazy with the rewrites, we would have had a better movie. There's a huge list of regrets.

Jason X is not a very good movie. It's not Sean's fault. It's not Jim's fault. It's not Noel's fault. It's not my fault. We all screwed up. We were four guys fighting these stupid battles and we should have been having fun and making the best movie we could make. That's not what we did. We let the fans down, we let ourselves down. And we cost ourselves a lot of money.

SEAN CUNNINGHAM: "Jason in Space" might have been really successful. I don't regret having figured out how to make the movie, but it was always a gamble. So we did it, and then all people said was, "Hmmm. Jason in Space—I'll catch that on cable." They just didn't want to go to the theater to see it. I don't think any of us really knows why, and we never will. And it wasn't that Jim did a bad job or anything. Jim is a good guy. A great guy. *Jason X* just didn't work on that kind of commercial level.

NOEL CUNNINGHAM: You know, it was actually probably easier that the film sat on the shelf as long as it did, because then you have that distance from it. Otherwise, if it is still your whole life and then it comes out and doesn't do anything you're truly devastated.

Still, I haven't seen the film since opening night. I just can't watch it. There are so many missed opportunities. In hindsight, there are things I could have and should have done differently. But all in all, we came up with a fun little movie. It's nothing to be ashamed about.

TODD FARMER: I wrote the movie I wanted to write—so what if they made a different movie? It doesn't matter. I'd like to do it again. It's only when it gets to a point where you're not passionate about it that it's going to suck. And I never had to deal with that. I always wrote what I wanted to write. Maybe that's why I got rewritten—because I wasn't writing what they wanted.

That's a rude awakening for any writer out here. We're not brilliant as far as the industry is concerned. We literally are just the guys they bring in—we don't do anything special. But the truth is that there would be no movie without us because we're the only ones creating anything original. We're taking a blank sheet of paper and creating a story out of it. Everybody else takes that and goes from there. So I know what our original intention was and we got nowhere near that.

JIM ISAAC: I would have done *Jason X* so differently now. There's no question about it. At the time, my thinking was I wanted to do something new for the franchise. And it wasn't just about the action. It was about doing something a little edgier. Scarier. A little more fun. I never wanted *Jason X* to be perceived as a parody. It was just that I had seen so many *Friday*s that were so similar to each other. I wanted to give the fans something newer, different and fresher.

The final product is not what I had originally imagined, or what we pitched originally to New Line. And that happens all the time. I learned with *Jason X* that you have to always, always fight for what you believe. And more than just doing it right, and on time, and on budget, you're fighting for your vision. Because you can't please everybody. Maybe the only thing I do know, the one thing I did learn from all of this, is that you can't always be a nice guy directing a movie. It's a collaborative effort, no question. But there is a point where the whole goal is to convey your vision to all the other artists on the project. And when you get everyone on same page, only then can they make your vision even better. Way better. But you have to guide them. And that's when you really come up with something cool.

11.

Winner Kills All

New Line Cinema has long been referred to as "The House That Freddy Built," a sobriquet that founder and CEO Robert Shaye would be among the first to acknowledge. Bolstered by the success of Wes Craven's seminal 1984 shocker, *A Nightmare on Elm Street*, followed by its seven lucrative sequels, New Line would, over the next two decades, rise from obscurity as a fledgling distribution company specializing in often-undistinguished exploitation fare, to the most successful and well-known independent studio in Hollywood. Today, New Line has amassed an impressive and diverse roster of box office hits, including the blockbuster *Rush Hour* films, the phenomenally successful *Austin Powers* franchise, and the Academy Award winning *The Lord of the Rings* trilogy. But New Line would not forget its less-than-humble roots—or its debt to the razor-clawed villain who made their success possible. So even after a nearly ten-year gestation period that was both costly and frustrating, the studio did not waver in its commitment to bringing the long-anticipated showdown of *Freddy vs. Jason* to the screen. Working in tandem with Sean Cunningham's Crystal Lake Entertainment, a reported six million dollars was spent developing some eighteen drafts written by over a dozen screenwriters—including some of the most well-paid "A-list" writers in the business.

"Teens have sex—Jason kills them. Teens have sex—Freddy kills them. It was inevitable that these two guys would duke it out." Robert Englund

Even amid all of the false starts, outlandish concepts and seemingly never-ending rewrites, the key to crafting a logical, satisfying and ultimately entertaining *Freddy vs. Jason* remained elusive. Diehard fans had been waiting for years to witness the ultimate battle between their favorite horror icons, and both New Line and Sean Cunningham were determined not to let them down. But *Freddy vs. Jason* needed to be more than just an amalgam of Jason and Freddy's "greatest hits," or a run-of-the-mill slasher sendup with Freddy and Jason at the center of a WWF-style showdown. The dramatic question of *Freddy vs. Jason*—how to get two distinctly different horror villains into the same ring in a clever, believable way—would have to be answered to Robert Shaye's satisfaction before he would consider green-lighting the project.

ROBERT SHAYE, Co-Chairman, New Line Cinema: *Freddy vs. Jason* was always in the air. There wasn't any great navigational plan in mind. Just really, truly and honestly an overweening desire to make the movie, which I think a lot of fans were waiting for, as good as possible.

NOEL CUNNINGHAM, Development Executive, Crystal Lake Entertainment: Originally, New Line was very excited: "Whoa! *Freddy vs. Jason*! That's going to be a kick-ass show!" But when you really sit down and start to think about it, you go, "Okay, what happens? You have two main characters—both of whom are villains. One of them doesn't exist in the real world, and the other one doesn't talk. How do you create a movie around those two characters?" It's damn near impossible.

SEAN CUNNINGHAM, Producer: If you're going to put them in the same movie, are you going to be able to give fans what they expect from both of these characters? What's the experience of watching a Freddy movie? What's the experience of watching a Jason movie? How are they different? And it wasn't just the rules

of each franchise we were worried about, like, "Oh, the virgin has to survive." Or, "The pothead must die in the fourth reel." None of that really applied. It just had to do with the core emotional experience. How are you going to handle Freddy and Jason in the same movie without one contradicting the other? That was a puzzle that we had to address.

ROBERT ENGLUND, "Freddy Krueger": I had always gotten a little defensive when people were whispering, "They're trying to milk the last dime out of these franchises!" Because, in fact, *Freddy vs. Jason* is fan-originated. I remember as far back as 1984 or 1985, guys were coming up to me and going, "What would happen if Freddy Krueger ran into Jason in an alley? Could you kick his ass?" It's always been a curiosity.

The concept of a "versus" movie is not a new one. It has been around for a long time. And there's a great tradition of mixing and matching in the movies. I never wanted a *Freddy vs. Jason* to be "Abbott and Costello Meet Freddy and Jason," but *Ghostbusters* was, and is, a great concept. And there were other great horror mix-ups, whether it be the Wolf Man or Frankenstein or Dracula. So the idea of *Freddy vs. Jason* is of a great, long tradition.

ADAM MARCUS, Director, *Jason Goes to Hell*: Back when we were making *Jason Goes to Hell*, Dean Lorey, Noel Cunningham and I were trying to come up with more gags to put in the movie. Then I said, "You know, doesn't New Line own Freddy outright?" And the wheels started turning. I called Mark Ordesky and Michael De Luca at New Line, and asked, "Can we have the claw?" And it was very funny 'cause they were a bit covetous of it. They asked nervously, "What are you going to do with it? And why?" But when we told them our idea, they flipped.

I remember the first test screening after we finished the film. When that moment hit, when Freddy's claw lunged out of the ground at Jason's mask, the entire test audience got up on their feet and cheered. And Mike De Luca, Bob Shaye and Mark Ordesky were standing in the back, and they all just looked at each other with such glee. Mark and Mike even high-fived each other. I think that's when *Freddy vs. Jason* was really born.

Development on Freddy vs. Jason *began in early 1994, a few months following the release of* Jason Goes to Hell. *The writing team of Cyrus Voris and Ethan Reiff, who had recently scored a modest hit with Universal's* Demon Knight, *would become the first screenwriters to pitch a* Freddy vs. Jason *concept to New Line—but far from the last. Meanwhile, Sean Cunningham turned to Lewis Abernathy, his screenwriter on* DeepStar Six *and* House IV, *to develop a different take on the project. But six years, a dozen writers, and nearly twice as many drafts later,* Freddy vs. Jason, *like the title characters themselves, seemed stuck in hell. Although the resulting scripts were often wildly disparate in concept, approach and tone, one particular element introduced in Abernathy's early draft appealed to both New Line and Cunningham: the "Fred Heads"—a cult of nihilistic teens who look to the long-dead Freddy Krueger as their "spiritual leader." The Fred Heads would remain the one constant on* Freddy vs. Jason's *long and often chaotic road to production. And they almost survived. Almost.*

LEWIS ABERNATHY, Screenwriter: *Freddy vs. Jason* was already in development at New Line when I started working for Sean Cunningham around late 1993. I felt we should make fun of ourselves, but in a way where you don't know that we're making fun of ourselves. I also felt that Jason should be a good guy. It's almost like a comic book. Go ahead and turn him into *Spider-Man*. Make it a PG-13 movie. Turn it on its head, but let's not make the same old dark, dreary stuff about a guy in a hockey mask. I also had the idea that Jason was going on this murderous rampage to get back at the guy who drowned him—and that camp counselor was Freddy Krueger.

SEAN CUNNINGHAM: Lewis came up with some really fun stuff. And that was the first time these characters had been able to co-exist in any form, so it was really kind of cool. We had a meeting between Lewis and [former New Line President of Production] Mike De Luca. Lewis was in *Titanic*—and James Cameron came in to say, "I believe in Lewis, he's going to do a great job." But as it turned out, Lewis went in a direction that De Luca didn't like, so he ended up hiring someone else.

RONALD D. MOORE, Screenwriter: Mike De Luca was definitely a fan of Brannon Braga and I because of our work on *Star Trek: The Next Generation*. We had a sit-down meeting with Mike and he gave us carte blanche to come up with a concept.

The key decision for us was that we wanted to take either Freddy or Jason's point of view. We felt like if they were both bad and they were both villains, you won't root for either one of them. And if that's the case, it doesn't really matter who wins. And there was something interesting about taking the less accessible of the two—Jason, the guy who never even speaks—and making him sort of the anti-hero of the piece. That's what intrigued us. So we put Jason on trial, and the hero of the movie was his defense attorney. We were trying to comment on sequelitis and the franchise aspect of it all. It was interesting pop culture stuff that we were examining. And this was also right in the thick of the OJ Simpson trial and the media circus surrounding it.

Wes Craven had done *New Nightmare*, which had already broken the fourth wall a little bit. But that film was not a hit. New Line didn't mention any specific problems with the self-ref-erential angle of our script at the time. They just said of *New Nightmare*, "It didn't do that well at the box office."

After we turned in our second draft, we were greeted with silence. For weeks, if not months. In fact, I don't think we ever heard from them again. It was just, "Okay, guys, great. Thanks! We'll get back to you." But that's common in Hollywood—people don't want to call and give you bad news. So we just shrugged it off. It was disappointing, but we had just got *Star Trek: First Contact* so we definitely had enough on our plate anyway.

DAVID J. SCHOW, Screenwriter: *Freddy vs. Jason* was the easiest screenwriting job I ever got. I had written *Leatherface: The Texas Chainsaw Massacre III* for New Line, and also had done a polish on *A Nightmare on Elm Street 5*. I just happened to be in New Line's offices one day, and literally I got this job with Mike De Luca looking up at me and saying, "You want to take a crack at this?"

My script roughly fell into three parts: The first part was mostly about a guy who communes with Freddy in his dreams and is, in fact, the head of a cult of Freddy fanatics called the Fred Heads who want to bring Freddy back from the dead, and do it by any means necessary. The second part was about resurrecting Jason from Camp Crystal Lake, because he has to fight Freddy. Finally, in the third act, they have to hypnotize Jason with a drug so he can fall asleep and enter a dream version of Camp Crystal Lake, where we see a glimpse of his backstory with Freddy. Then, at the right moment, the kids have to wake up Jason so he can bring Freddy back out into the real world and do battle.

In looking at the *Freddy vs. Jason* they ultimately made, you can see some of the concepts that had already been kicking around for awhile. If any of that is similar to the finished movie, it may have started with my draft.

Below: *Freddy vs. Jason*—the bastard child of a hundred rewrites—was finally released from development hell by co-screenwriters Mark Swift (with machete) and Damian Shannon. It would be a long road from script to screen for the pair. "We wrote *Freddy vs. Jason* together in a little coffee shop," says Swift. "And we had these little goals along the way. First it was just, 'I hope this movie gets made.' Then it we just hoped to get screen credit. Finally, when the movie was about to be made, it was, 'I hope we just get a picture of ourselves on the set. Wouldn't that be cool?'"

"It was really exciting to be on set," continues Shannon. "As a horror fan, just to think what it would be like to see Freddy and Jason on the same screen—and have yourself included in that experience—is the ultimate."

ETHAN REIFF, Screenwriter: We wrote from scratch, but there were big elements that everybody sort of liked. They liked the Freddy cult. They liked the idea of the drug that can put you to sleep. But I think those were the only two things we were handed, like, "Okay, do a version of this."

The one major thing we felt we were contributing was to tie the origins of these characters together and to not pull any punches. We literally had a scene where you see Freddy Krueger as a young adult camp counselor having just raped Jason by the lake. I still remember my brother reading that draft and saying, "I can't believe you guys actually did that."

CYRUS VORIS, Screenwriter: Our thing was like, "One's a child molester and the other one is, for all intents and purposes, a disturbed, molested child." And then Jason has an ax to grind against Freddy. Because he's the guy who molested him and threw him in the lake and let him drown. So that seemed like a good driving motivational thing.

The other thing was, Freddy at that time had started to become a sort of hero in the genre pop culture. There was the *Freddy's Nightmares* TV show where he was a kind of *Extreme Justice* host. Like, "If you mess up, kids, you're going to get what you deserve." And it was freaky. It was like, "What the fuck? He's a fucking child molester or child killer. Why is he a hero?" And we didn't want to shy away from what was the genuinely evil about it.

NOEL CUNNINGHAM: Was this the best script of *Freddy vs. Jason* that could have been made? Probably not. But it was good. It was certainly the best one we had by that point. And then Rob Bottin was brought on for a little while to direct it, and he brings with him a whole cache of effects knowledge. We also had David Goyer and James Dale Robinson rewrite it.

SEAN CUNNINGHAM: I never wanted to change all the things that worked well in the Freddy or Jason movies—I just wanted to add stuff that had never been there before. But in order to accommodate Mike De Luca—and I don't regret this—I was willing to work with any writer he decided on. Finally, with Cy and Ethan, they worked with me for several months and we turned in a draft that I thought was pretty successful. And it really had a lot of elements of Lewis Abernathy's original draft, who I started with in the first place. But De Luca just flat-out hated it. Then *Scream* opened and it was, "It's a brand new ball game now. We can't do the same old stuff." So De Luca basically just threw it all away.

MARK VERHEIDEN, Screenwriter: I believe most of the drafts up until that point dealt with the idea of this Freddy cult. But that was the one thing I reacted very negatively to. I came back and just said, "You've already got Freddy and Jason. You don't need these goons running around." I liked the idea of trying to connect Freddy and Jason to the history of the other movies. So I introduced some of the characters from the previous films in there, too.

I eventually wrote two drafts—the first I delivered in August 1999, and the second by the end of the year. I suppose my experience was probably like a lot of the other writers—there are no big, "You're done, buddy!" discussions. You just don't hear much until you read in the trades that they've hired writer number nine or whoever.

ROBERT ENGLUND: It was a rough time. I wasn't really privy to a lot of what was going on. I had heard a lot of people at New Line suggest that a lot of the writers were just coming in and taking the money and not taking it seriously. Or they

thought New Line wanted it to be more camp and self-referential than they did. All I knew was that every director and special effects guy who I would hear about being connected to this film was somebody I wanted to work with. But, for a variety of reasons, it was never coming to pass. And while I was waiting, it was getting to the point where I was having to turn down other jobs because it kept seeming like *Freddy vs. Jason* was going to happen at any minute. So it was getting a little frustrating.

In early 2000, New Line Cinema would undergo an extensive shake-up in its executive ranks, starting with the well-publicized split of longtime President of Production Michael De Luca. And with De Luca went Freddy vs. Jason*'s biggest—and perhaps only remaining—champion at the studio. Yet the event ultimately turned out to be a blessing in disguise. Robert Shaye, newly energized and with a fresh new team of executives in place, made* Freddy vs. Jason *an even greater imperative.*

Prior to his departure, De Luca heard one final pitch from two enthusiastic young screenwriters looking for their first big break in Hollywood. Enter Damian Shannon and Mark Swift.

MARK SWIFT, Co-Screenwriter: Damian and I met at USC in 1988, although we both eventually left—Damian went to NYU Film School, and I went to Johns Hopkins in Baltimore. Then we hooked up again and started writing after that, working on our first screenplay. So I guess we were friends first before we were screenwriters. And we're both big horror fans.

When we came in to New Line to meet about *Freddy vs. Jason*, we were pretty nervous. We took it as a challenge and a huge opportunity. I loved *A Nightmare on Elm Street* and I loved *Friday the 13th*. Just to be a part of that history—we couldn't pass it up. So we created a mission statement that we gave to New Line about how we would do the movie. We just wanted to keep the story in tune with what we'd seen before. We didn't want to change the mythologies. We just wanted to take these two histories, combine them, and then ask, "What are they going to fight over?" And we also didn't want to make either of them the butt of the joke anymore.

DAMIAN SHANNON, Co-Screenwriter: We decided that the story should start right from the last scene of *Jason Goes to Hell*—the point where Freddy grabs Jason's mask. We asked

ourselves what that meant—why was Freddy grabbing the mask? We felt we needed to understand what the friction was between these two guys. Why are they trying to kill each other, without making Freddy the one who raped him? We wanted to take Freddy and Jason back to their roots, and to see these characters restored to their former glory.

MARK SWIFT: We pitched Mike De Luca our approach and he was very excited. We were hired by the end of December 1999. Then shortly thereafter, Mike split New Line, and there was a regime change. Suddenly, there were no *Freddy vs. Jason* fans left at the studio. We had to get everyone re-excited, or this movie that had taken almost ten years to get greenlit was again going to die. So that's when we did a forty-page treatment, our list of the "rules" for *Freddy vs. Jason*, an executive summary and all this stuff, just to try and get the studio to believe in us again.

ROBERT SHAYE: *Freddy vs. Jason* kind of languished because it was difficult to find a production executive within New Line, up to and including our head of production at that time, who really cared a lot about it. Then when we changed our head of production, we renewed this imperative to Toby Emmerich that we have to find someone who is going to get behind this. And we came up with a somewhat unlikely candidate, this wonderful woman named Stokely Chaffin, who loves the genre and could really jump in.

STOKELY CHAFFIN, Production Executive, New Line Cinema: I had worked with Neal H. Moritz before, and we had produced the *I Know What you Did Last Summer* moves and *Soul Survivors.* I always loved horror movies and horror movies always find an audience. People are always going to love these movies. Seven years ago I heard the idea of *Freddy vs. Jason* and I went, "Genius! That's perfect! What a great event picture." Then seven years went by, and I get *Freddy vs. Jason* as a project. For me, it was always meant to be.

When I started, there had been a million drafts before—literally seventeen scripts by twelve different writers. Fortunately, there was a treatment done that basically had the sketched out story of what the movie should be. That was the one done by Shannon and Swift. I read the treatment and basically felt, "Well, there are some problems here, but it looks pretty good. Let's see what we get when the script comes in." And we did get a really good script.

MARK SWIFT: Ultimately, it came down to Bob Shaye. Sometimes, it's dangerous when anybody at a studio takes a personal interest in your project, but in this case it was a good thing because he's a horror fan. Although, in his mind, he'd also been burned before. Wes Craven convinced him to do *New Nightmare,* and it didn't turn out well financially, at least in terms of domestic box office. But Bob still got behind us and made *Freddy vs. Jason* happen.

Finally, Freddy vs. Jason *had a greenlit script and an energized new executive to champion it. Now all it needed was a director. The studio wanted someone who would respect the legacy of both the* Friday the 13th *and* A Nightmare on Elm Street *franchises, while at the same time bring a fresh new sensibility and visual style to this most unique—and decidedly American—horror hybrid. Ironically, they would have to go halfway around the world to find their man.*

STOKELY CHAFFIN: I had made the foolish proposition to every agency in town that I would agree to meet any director who wanted to come in for *Freddy vs. Jason.* I probably took sixty meetings with directors of all kinds, from music video to commercial directors to people who had made only one feature or a short. The problem we had was that there were people who loved the characters and knew everything about the movies and had seen all of them fifteen times, but didn't have the experience. And then there were people who had the experience, but were kind of like, "Yeah, I think I saw one back in the theater way back when." And we're like, "What are you doing here? Why would you want to take this on if you don't care about these characters?"

RONNY YU, Director: I think it's funny that a movie I made, *Bride with White Hair,* received a lot of attention in the Western world. I didn't intend to make it like a horror movie or a slasher movie, but somehow, in the West, people look at it as a horror or slasher movie, and they send me scripts assuming I'm a slasher movie director. But I'm not.

In 2002, I was living in Sydney, Australia, and I got a call from New Line saying, "Would you mind if we flew you over to talk to our boss, Bob Shaye? He has a project for you." I said, "Sure. What project?" They say, "A good project. You're going to like it, especially since you're always telling people you want to make a real American movie. And this is a real, *real* American movie." I called my agent and he said, "You might like it. Take the flight, go to Hollywood and have the meeting." So I came over, and then they told me it was *Freddy vs. Jason.*

STOKELY CHAFFIN: When we originally put together our top list of five or six directors for *Freddy vs. Jason,* Ronny Yu was on it. I just expected him to say, "Thanks so much for your interest, I really appreciate it, but it's still no." But he was open to it. We could tell. So we kept reeling him in a little bit, and said, "Well, why don't you just come here for a meeting and we can talk about it further?" We practically begged him.

Then he came into Bob's office and acted out a scene from the script. He stepped on Bob's toe and spun him around, and I was going, "Oh God, what are you doing!?" But even if you could only understand Ronny's every third word, you could feel his passion for the material.

RONNY YU: Bob asked me if I had seen any of the *Friday the 13th* or *Nightmare on Elm Street* sequels. I said no. He said, "You mean no Jason, no Freddy?" It's funny, because the same thing happened with *Bride of Chucky.* I had never seen a *Child's Play* film. But I think my lack of knowledge about Freddy and Jason worked in my favor, because the studio was looking for somebody who could come in with a fresh take and some new ideas.

Then they gave me the script and said I needed to tell them yes or no right now, because they'd waited for so long. Nine years or something like that. They also wanted to start in two months. I had to come out to America in May 2002 and they were supposed to start prep by June. So I read it, but I still said, "Thank you. I'm heading back." And they said, "Why? Why? Why?" I said, "I'm not so sure about the script. I think it still needs some massaging." But then Bob and the other New Line executives said, "Ronny, do whatever you want to make it right, to feel comfortable."

"The key to Jason's anger is very simple. Anyone, no matter what culture they come from, would be pissed off if someone tried to mess with their mother. Jason's just like, 'Don't fuck with my mom!'" Ronny Yu

Once I was given that sort of freedom, I said okay. At that moment, I was just looking at it as a fun movie. It wasn't until after I accepted it that I started to think, "Oh, God, I hope this Chinaman does not screw this up!"

With its director officially signed on and pre-production commencing in June 2002, writers Damian Shannon and Mark Swift set about writing a new draft of Freddy vs. Jason *tailored to Ronny Yu's vision. But Yu, feeling that the script still needed streamlining, called in* Blade *scripter David Goyer to do an uncredited rewrite. The result was major changes in both plot and character, with Goyer refashioning Shannon and Swift's admittedly lengthy, perhaps even unwieldy, 130-page screenplay into a tight, economical blueprint for a crisp, action-packed 90-minute movie.*

One person who would not participate in the final development process, however, was Sean Cunningham. Although neither Cunningham nor New Line ever wavered in their enthusiasm for Freddy vs. Jason, *the film's day-to-day production chores ultimately would be turned over to executive producer Doug Curtis.*

MARK SWIFT: Sean became a producer in name only. We never had a meeting with him, and we never talked even on the phone. We never saw his script notes. I guess New Line sort of shielded him from us. *Jason X* was a disaster, and it killed *Freddy vs. Jason* for a while. I think New Line lost a lot of faith in not just *Friday the 13th* but the whole question of whether there was still an audience for *Freddy vs. Jason*. The next thing we knew, the studio was testing the idea in malls, figuring out whether thirteen-year-old kids would want to see this movie. We thought we were in real trouble.

CYRUS VORIS: I think New Line would have loved just to buy Sean out and then do whatever they wanted. But, you know, give Sean credit—he was one of the creators of the property, it was his baby and he owned it, so he wanted to be involved. It was more important for Sean to actually have some involvement than

In *Freddy vs. Jason*, Canadian actress Paula Shaw was cast as Mrs. Voorhees, the role that was made infamous by Betsy Palmer in the original *Friday the 13th* and its first sequel. The recasting of the much-beloved character caused much controversy amongst fans. "Sean Cunningham asked me to do the last couple of films," says Betsy Palmer, who was approached to reprise the role in both *Jason X* and *Freddy vs. Jason*. "I said, 'How about a piece of the action? You won't even have to pay me a salary.' Because I got about thirty bucks in residuals from the first two movies, while Sean and the studio made millions and millions of dollars. But Sean said, 'Oh, no, we can't do that,' and I ended up being offered SAG minimum. And it was only a couple of dumb scenes. It was ridiculous. So I said, 'No, thanks.' Then they upped it to $10,000, then $20,000, but I still said no."

"We really tried to get Betsy," says *Freddy vs. Jason* executive producer Doug Curtis. "We even met her agent's original asking price. It wasn't outrageous, although it was really more than our budget could afford. But we thought it was so important for the fans. Then, eventually, at the last minute, her agents called back and simply said, "This is not what she wants to be remembered for."

Following in the footsteps of Palmer was initially daunting for Shaw. "At my age, I'm sure you can imagine I'm not a big fan of the *Friday* movies," laughs the actress. "But I really wanted to do a good job. So I went out and rented the first film. It was a challenge—I wanted my work to be a continuation of what Betsy did, but not be an imitation. I think ultimately she seeped into me, by way of osmosis, and I took on her essence. I have so much respect for her as an actress and her performance as the character. "

"He's the first character that you look at and say, 'Oh, yeah, he's gonna die!'"
Jesse Hutch on Trey

Perhaps the signature creative death in *Freddy vs. Jason*, the now-infamous "bed kill" (**top**) ranks as a highpoint for co-screenwriters Mark Swift and Damian Shannon. "When Damian and I went to the first test screening, during the bed kill, the crowd was so loud you couldn't hear the dialogue during the next two scenes," marvels Swift. "That, for Damian and I, was one of the great moments, because that was one of the scenes that was filmed just like we wrote it. So to have the audience love it like that just felt terrific."

Filming the scene was also memorable for actor Jesse Hutch, who plays human bookmark Trey. "I loved working with all the special effects, and just hanging around the studio to see how it was all put together," says Hutch. "But it was funny, when we shot it, I had to be totally in the moment. My spine had supposedly been broken in half, I've got blood all over me, and I'm crushing a beer can in my hand. Well, on the first take I got so into it that I spit the blood out of my mouth and hit the director of photography right in the face. He wasn't very happy about that!"

just to get a bunch of money. So that was always the thing. But probably to this day, even though *Freddy vs. Jason* became a big success, I'm sure there's still tension between Sean and New Line.

DOUG CURTIS, Executive Producer: Sean chose not to be involved. I didn't even meet Sean until three weeks before we started shooting the movie. At one point he decided he wanted to be involved, but the studio said it was too late, which dumbfounded him. Ultimately, the trade-off was that we put his daughter, Jessica, on the film as an associate producer. She was a very smart girl and a very good producer.

But I'll tell you the most important thing about Sean: he was the most gracious person I've ever known in my life. He sent me a gift basket on the first day of shooting that said, "Good luck, buddy." Then he sent me another basket at the end of shooting that said, "Congratulations." Ultimately, he should be very excited and proud.

SEAN CUNNINGHAM: I was glad *Freddy vs. Jason* was getting made, but I had strong feelings that there were deficiencies in the script. I had been wrestling with *Freddy vs. Jason* for years, and I felt I had learned to understand storytelling much better than I had earlier. I also thought the hiring of Ronny Yu spoke to the difficulties of working within the studio system. "Shooters" are often hired to be directors, and Ronny is a good example of that. Ronny is a great visualist, but he doesn't have a clue about what he's shooting in terms of telling a story. But Ronny was somebody who was going to get the movie into production, and at that point I was happy with anything just to get the fucking picture made.

Ultimately, you don't want somebody on set who's bringing negative energy. You want to keep it positive, and who will do the best you can with what you've got. So I shook everyone's hands and told them how supportive I was. I also was involved in the promotion of the movie, because I felt that was the least I could do, and that it was part of my job. And I'm certainly not going to look a gift horse in the mouth.

RONNY YU:. Throughout the shoot it was basically just me and Stokely. She really supported me on all the battles and changes in the script.

I did get a ton of notes from Mr. Cunningham saying, "These are the rules. Don't bend them!" So I did my homework and spent two weeks going through all seventeen movies. The balance I tried to work out was, how do you satisfy the hardcore fans of both franchises as well as excite people outside of that? I took myself as an example, because in the beginning I wasn't that familiar with the films at all. And it was different than *Bride of Chucky*—that was campy because how seriously can you take a two-foot-tall doll?

In the end, after looking at all of the films, I thought that every one of them had their good parts. But I particularly liked the first *Nightmare* and the first *Friday*—the Sean Cunningham one. I thought we should go back to the roots. I decided that I can't reinvent these two long-lasting American horror icons. My job is to respect what's been laid down for so many years and just turn up the entertainment level a notch.

MARK SWIFT: A couple of months before shooting, around July of 2002, we did meet with Ronny two or three times and incorporated his notes. We turned in our last draft in August. Originally when they looked at our script, New Line said that it would cost $60 million, and that's a lot of money. I give credit to Ronny and those guys—they did it for $30 million. Some stuff had to go. So they hired David Goyer to do a polish, and that turned into him writing pages while they were shooting. He's responsible for a lot of the dialogue in the finished film and most of the characters and material that was cut.

STOKELY CHAFFIN: The script was overly long and complicated and very, very dense. So we timed the script, and it came in at two hours twenty-eight minutes. We're like, "You know, this is not the *American Beauty* of horror films and it probably shouldn't be two hours long." So David Goyer came in. He made it a more cinematic movie. He was so good at streamlining the material that you never even noticed what he took out.

MARK SWIFT: When you lose scenes, in order to keep story, you have to have characters speak about what's missing. Then you run into a situation where a lot of the characters are just talking plot, which is never enjoyable. What also happens in the process of making something shorter is you combine characters. Obviously, stuff has to get lost, but there are so many little things that would have made the movie that much better. But that's part of making movies. They wanted it to be fast and they wanted a quick running time.

RONNY YU: I wanted *Freddy vs. Jason* to move lightning fast, with the whole thing taking place over two or three nights. Even now, after the fact, I look at it and I think we should have brought Freddy and Jason into it earlier. Just get them in the ring.

DOUG CURTIS: I thought the writers were afraid that the audience wasn't going to get it. But the audience gets it because they've already seen the movies. And if you don't know it, you're not even in the theater because you don't give a shit about it.

DAMIAN SHANNON: Goyer made a lot of smart cuts—great editorial changes—and did them without losing any scenes. However, some great Jason highlights at Crystal Lake were lost, as well as an epilogue that really wrapped up the characters of Lori and her father. We also tried to keep the Freddy one-liners disturbing, kind of like dark comedy. We wanted to turn him back to what he was like in the first one. That really didn't end up in the movie, either.

MARK SWIFT: My favorite line in the original *Nightmare on Elm Street* was when Freddy holds up his glove and says, "*This* is God." That's the kind of stuff we tried to go for. And Bob Shaye had a rule: "I don't want Freddy to say more than four or five words in a sentence." He really wanted to keep it short. But as we got cut down, it seemed like Freddy had to explain stuff. He'd turn to the camera and say, "I think I'll let Jason play for a while." That's the kind of stuff that irked me.

Freddy vs. Jason's crew at work. **From top**: Ronny Yu, with claw; executive producer Doug Curtis (left) and production designer John Willett; and director of photography Fred Murphy (left).

Opposite: "Recreating the Elm Street house was a real challenge," says production designer John Willett. "There were no accurate drawing records kept from any of the earlier *Nightmare* films. We had to try and find a suitable house in Vancouver, which is very difficult. Obviously, we would never find exactly the same house, but we could find the bones of a place that we could then transform. Another challenge was that, because of our budget, we had to go inside the house and shoot most of the interiors on location, too, which is unusual because normally you build that stuff on stage. Finally, at the last minute, we found this great house in a perfect neighborhood. It's not quite identical, but it was about eighty percent the same. A lot of fans get nervous when that one little detail is off here or there, but I really felt we achieved the same look and spirit of the original."

I remember the first line of the script was always: "Full moon. Dark trees. A misty lake." We always started at Camp Crystal Lake. But in the rewrites, the studio felt the audience needed a sort of refresher course, so that's how the movie came to start with that Freddy voice-over at the beginning. Now he gives this entire speech, where we never really wanted him to talk, ever. We just thought that would make him more scary.

By the time casting sessions for Freddy vs. Jason *began in late July of 2002, the trend of casting extremely photogenic, budding young stars whose faces would bring a high-gloss, "we're-hipper-than-you" attitude to slasher films of the new millennium, had begun to subside. But the influence of* Scream *and its imitative ilk continued to be felt. It was now cool, even a sign of status, for a young star on the rise to appear in a horror film. Jason and Freddy had also been staples of the genre for nearly two decades, which only added to the cache of landing a role in* Freddy vs. Jason. *Even if the project was not totally considered A-list, its casting directors had a far larger talent pool to choose from than any of the past* Friday the 13ths. *As* Freddy vs. Jason *would also be shot in Vancouver, the final ensemble was a mix of American and Canadian talent, both the usual unknowns as well as recognizable faces from film, television and even pop music.*

DAMIAN SHANNON: We wanted half the kids in *Freddy vs. Jason* to seem like they were in a *Friday the 13th* movie and half of them to seem like they were in *A Nightmare on Elm Street* movie. And, of course, all of these films are full of clichés, but we wanted to embrace that. We wanted the virginal girl. We wanted the party kids. We also wanted a unique blend of minorities, because that's what they started to do in the later *Nightmare* movies. I think we came up with a pretty good mix in our screenplay.

RONNY YU: When I look back at all the characters in both franchises, there's almost no value to them. Their only purpose is just to get chopped up or killed. Here, the writers were very smart, because they created characters who turn the tables around. In the beginning they're victims, but then they think, "Ah, why don't we use ourselves as bait to bring these two together and let them fight it out while we watch?" The characters become the actual means by which to bring the two monsters together.

MATTHEW BARRY, Casting Director: Whether it's a comedy or a horror film, you want good actors in films for their respective genres. A lot of young actors will come in for a *Freddy vs. Jason* and and act like *Starsky & Hutch* and it's wrong. That's one of the problems with Hollywood—kids come out and they're not trained. We wanted some good, trained people. We also wanted unknowns. And the studio agreed, because they already had the franchises in Freddy and Jason. What else did they need? It doesn't make any difference if Ashton Kutcher is in it. That was great for us because it meant we got to break some new kids—there's nothing more exciting than that.

CHRISTOPHER MARQUETTE, "Linderman": I actually didn't get to read the full script for *Freddy vs. Jason* before I said yes to it. I knew what it was and I just really, really wanted to do it. Instead of thinking that this was just a good part for my career, I thought, "Wow, what an amazing experience to be a part of something so big!" And I'm the type of actor who thinks it can be difficult to make a really great performance out of a horror movie, only because it's really hard to make it real. I saw it as a huge challenge.

KYLE LABINE, "Freeburg": I actually auditioned for the role of Linderman first. I guess they saw a different part for me and they brought me back for Freeburg. Which is funny, because my character is the stoner, and I've never smoked a joint in my life.

And then I waited a long time until I found out I got the part, because I had heard they were having issues about racial diversity in the film—that is, that it might be too much of an "all-white" cast.

MATTHEW BARRY: Diversity was a huge factor, absolutely. As casting directors now, we don't want to make a "white" movie. We want to add some flavors to it. And it's not just ethnicities. It's gender as well. Because do you know who goes to these movies? Women.

The character of Mark, Jason Ritter's best friend in the movie—that character was originally written for a Latin kid. And we had wanted to cast a Latino actor we had already found, but then he went and took some low-budget scale movie because he didn't want to do a horror movie. It was like, "We aren't going to find any fucking Latin actors in Vancouver!" But we had hired Brendan Fletcher for a smaller role in the movie, and he was so good that we decided to test him for the Latin role. And he was phenomenal. He kicked fucking ass. Ronny loved him: "Great acting! Great acting!" So he came back the next day and all he did was open his mouth and he got the job.

BRENDAN FLETCHER, "Mark": Although I was more of a Freddy fan growing up, I knew there was a following for both of these characters. So I leapt at the opportunity to be a part of a Freddy movie, let alone a Freddy and Jason movie. It's like *Batman vs. Superman* or *Godzilla vs. King Kong*. So I was right in there.

JESSE HUTCH, "Trey": I quickly picked up on the fact that I was playing the dickhead—which is weird because most people who know me don't think I'm a dickhead. Yes, he's a mean character, but he also doesn't realize it. For some reason, when people see Trey in the film, they find him to be funny. I didn't play him that way, but that's why I'm guessing he comes across as funny because it's like, "Who is this guy? Who says that?"

KELLY ROWLAND, "Kia": I remember being on the set with Beyonce when she did *Austin Powers* and thinking, "This looks so cool! I want to do this!" This opportunity really just landed in my lap. I remember my agent even asked me before I went out on the audition, "Will this bother you? How would you feel about doing a scary movie?" I was like, "I don't care! That sounds like fun!" Plus, Freddy and Jason—that's history.

I actually went into the audition with the idea that I wasn't going to get it. I had heard all these stories about how hard it was to act scared, and I have the most punk-ass scream anybody's ever heard. So nobody was more surprised than I was that I got the part.

MATTHEW BARRY: Of course, the studio wanted some kind of hip-hop quotient for the movie. We interviewed Eve and Pink and all these other hip-hop artists and most of them just couldn't act their way out of a paper bag. But Kelly came in and she was really determined. Her audition actually wasn't the greatest—she was missing something. But then she called and said, "I'll work with you. I really want to do this." And she had a solo album coming out at the time, so we had to work around her schedule. But she was like, "If I need to push here and push there, I'll do it because I really want to be a part of this." She wanted it bad. So we did a satellite audition where she was at the New Line office in New York and we were at the New Line office in L.A., and that was a slam-dunk. She kicked ass.

The class of Springwood High, 2003. Clockwise from above, this page: Christopher Marquette as Linderman; Jason Ritter as Will; Monica Keena as heroine Lori Campbell with director Ronny Yu; Brendan Fletcher as Mark (from left), Keena, Rowland, and Katherine Isabelle as Gibb.

New Line Cinema co-chairman Robert Shaye, who has made numerous cameo appearances in the *Nightmare on Elm Street* films, returned in *Freddy vs. Jason* (**opposite center**, with Yu) as the principal of Springwood High. "Robert used to be an actor before he founded New Line, and he likes to do cameos," chuckles executive producer Doug Curtis. "And when Bob calls and says he wants to be in the movie, you put him in!"

RONNY YU: She was just a down-to-earth, normal girl, and so serious about what she's doing. She had the perfect attitude. Kelly was our one fantastic discovery. She was just so natural, and likeable as a person.

MATTHEW BARRY: Casting the lead, Lori, was the hardest. We literally went down to the wire and saw everybody. Every bad fucking actress—probably close to three hundred from Los Angeles to New York. We also had had a lot of people turn the role down.

Monica Keena was someone Ronny and myself and my casting partner Nancy Green-Keyes really fought for. I discovered Monica on a film called *Crime and Punishment in Suburbia* and I knew what she could do.

MONICA KEENA, "Lori": Auditioning is the hardest part of this whole process. Once you have the part, the pressure's off and you have time to develop your character. But the audition process—you have to prove yourself in five minutes or less.

I'd never really done a horror movie before. And it was kind of an interesting concept to finally have the two most famous villains in horror movie history battling each other. I thought that would be kind of cool to be involved with.

I was never really a huge fan of either *A Nightmare on Elm Street* or *Friday the 13th* growing up because they scared me too much. And I always sort of swore that I would never do a horror movie, just because I can't watch them. But I thought this one would be kind of fun. And it's something very different from anything I've done. I usually do dramas and independent movies, so this was a totally different realm. It was just kind of exciting.

With the start of principal photography looming on the horizon, Freddy vs. Jason *at last had its cast in place. Or so it seemed. Twenty-two-year-old actor Brad Renfro had been hired to star opposite Monica Keena as "Will," the film's troubled young hero. Renfro had earned early acclaim for his performances in such films as* The Client *and* Apt Pupil, *but had also made tabloid headlines with his "bad boy" reputation, which included arrests for drunk and disorderly conduct and the alleged theft of a speedboat. Although Renfro's subsequent departure was officially attributed to "creative differences," the production would be forced to find a suitable replacement with only a week to spare.*

MATTHEW BARRY: Here's the truth about the casting of Brad Renfro. We all loved Brad. He's a great actor. But his agents lied like motherfuckers. Flat out fucking lied. We called about his reputation and they said, "Yeah, he was fucked up. He hasn't worked for a while. But he went back to Tennessee, checked himself into a spa and got cleaned up." We said, "Okay, we want to have a deal based on a meeting with Ronny." Everybody was okay with that.

Then New Line went and made a deal without Brad meeting Ronny first. Doug and Nancy and I were furious. Because Brad comes up to Vancouver and they hate him. He doesn't look the role. He's fucked up. He had done some things up there that I won't say.

DOUG CURTIS: Ronny originally really fought for Brad. He really wanted him. But the day Brad walked into our office, he looked like a street bum. He was drunk, he was beyond unkempt—he looked like an eighty year old in a twenty year old body. Then later he got fucked up on heroin and lied about it. And he disappeared for a week—we didn't know where he was, we just knew he was out on a binge. It was bad.

MATTHEW BARRY: Even after that we still wanted to talk to Brad, but his representation said, "Well, he's in Phoenix now. He's cleaning up and getting in shape for the film." Eventually, we didn't cast him, but on top of all that, his representation says, "We want his salary." They wanted to be paid! We said, "Go fuck yourselves. You have some fucking nerve." But it's really sad about Brad because the kid is talented.

So with a week to go before shooting, we had to scramble. We had tested this one kid, Ian Sommerholder, and we liked him a lot, but Ronny thought he was too pretty. Jason Ritter had actually come in before and he was okay. But what Nancy and I like to do—especially Nancy, God bless her—is give people a second chance. "Come in and work with us, then we'll put you on tape." Some actors won't do that and they'll blow their chance. But Jason did. And we wanted to

fight for him. So we coached Jason to get into the emotional depth of the character. Was he better than we expected? Absolutely. He was terrific in the film.

JASON RITTER, "Will": Because both of my parents were actors, I grew up around the business. I wanted to get into it when I was real young and drop out of elementary school. But my parents said I had to go to college and learn how to do it the right way. My father also wanted me to be realistic about it. Acting is a scary business to watch your children go into, and Hollywood is a difficult, scary place that's filled with rejection and heartache. He just made sure I studied, that I was trained in theatre and things like that. But he never really stopped me. He and my mom made sure my head was screwed on right about it, that I wasn't going to have any misguided notions that you just walk into this town and get handed a part. It takes a long time to get to the point where they're offering scripts to you.

RONNY YU: Luckily, the casting directors came up with Jason Ritter. We flew Jason up to Vancouver and he and Monica did a rough read-through. We all liked him, and the studio liked him. I looked at some of his work and I thought he was a really good kid. And then when Nancy said, "Guess who he is? He's John Ritter's son!" I just went, "Wow. What a coincidence—I directed his dad in *Bride of Chucky!*" Sometimes life is so weird.

Even with its two young leads in place, Freddy vs. Jason's biggest casting controversy was yet to come. Few would argue that the biggest stars of the movie were not its human characters at all, but its monsters. And it would be nothing short

of heretical to suggest that anyone but Robert Englund should have slipped back into the dirty red and green sweater he had made famous seven times before. Actor-stuntman Kane Hodder, however, was not as recognizable as the face behind Jason Voorhees' iconic hockey mask. Still, it was never a question among genre fans that Hodder, who had already played the role four times previously, would be asked to reprise the role in Freddy vs. Jason. *But as the start of principal photography approached, rumors began to circulate on the Internet that not only was Hodder out of the running, but that the film-makers were plotting a startling reinter-pretation of the character, one sure to alienate the franchise's most ardent followers. While some of the gossip bordered on the outlandish—the most popular rumor being that, at one point during the film, Jason would speak—and even cry—the recasting of Hodder ulti-mately proved true.*

The performer the producers would eventually choose to wield Jason's machete was six-foot-three, Canadian-born Ken Kirzinger, who faced the unenviable task of not only filling Hodder's venerable boots, but successfully interpreting the film-makers' new vision for the character. The Jason Voorhees in Damian Shannon and Mark Swift's screenplay, while not a complete re-invention of the character, does attempt to delve deeper into Jason's psychological mindset than any previous Friday the 13th *film, as well as more fully dramatize key moments of his backstory. Jason's look is new, too, with a slightly redesigned hockey mask, blackened skin and a more streamlined build. Even if the bold steps the filmmakers took with the character were vindicated by the subsequent success of the film, the departure of Hodder remains a hotly-debated subject among diehard fans, and a contentious sore point for the actor.*

> ## "I don't think Jason even knows the difference between right and wrong. That's why I feel sorry for him." Ronny Yu

MATTHEW BARRY: Who else could play Freddy? Robert was always in, and he loves it. Although Robert wasn't getting hired a lot at the time, which is sad because he's a really good actor. So we weren't worried. There might have been some fuss over money, but I think he ended up doing *Freddy vs. Jason* for $1 million. It never even crossed our minds to look elsewhere.

ROBERT ENGLUND: Freddy's been very, very good to me. I've had friends that are much better actors than I am, that had to quit the business because they couldn't survive the auditions or the rejections, or people who just didn't realize how good they were. So I'm certainly not going to whine now, having been in the business for thirty years and having had hit movies for the last twenty.

SEAN CUNNINGHAM: Robert had been on board since the very beginning. It was a very conscious understanding that a *Freddy vs. Jason* would not go far without him. And even over all the years when this was an on-again, off-again project, he remained on standby for us, and I think he even turned down jobs when we thought we were really close to going but then it fell apart.

Casting the role of Jason was another matter. It was New Line's decision to hire a new actor for the role. It was not a consensus. A lot of people, including me, thought they should have stayed with Kane Hodder. But the studio wanted to try something different, to make it fresh. To me, it was done for no good reason. But, at some point, the people that write the checks get the cut, if you know what I mean.

Having said that, I think Ken Kirzinger did a terrific job. I like Ken, and I like Kane. Still, and this is nothing against Ken, I feel that it was a mistake to not go with Kane. Of all the people who had anything to do with *Freddy vs. Jason*, Kane was the one that I think was not treated as well as he should have been.

KANE HODDER, Actor & Stuntman: Maybe some of the other guys who have played Jason didn't think it was that big of a deal, but to me it was always a tremendous honor. I loved playing the character, every single thing about it—I believe that was part of my success in the role. And it had always been my dream to kick Freddy's ass.

Way back in March of 2002, I got one of the first *Freddy vs. Jason* scripts once it had been given the green light. And I thought, "We're looking good here now. If they are giving me the script, obviously they want me to play the character." And this came from New Line directly. I even had a meeting with an executive there, as well as a great talk with Ronny Yu—at least, I thought it went very well. Maybe that was just a meeting to satisfy whomever. Then I was made an offer. One of the producers of the film called and said, "We want you to do it, but we don't have much money and this is what we can offer." And he gave me a number. My only question was, "Does that include residuals? Was this a buyout situation?" The answer was, "I'm not sure. Let me check on that."

After that, I started getting weird feelings whenever I would call over there. I started thinking, "Something's going on." I talked to another New Line executive, and they said, "Well, you're not out of the running, but we're thinking of going in a different direction. I said, "Different direction?" They tried to tell me that they wanted someone with more expressive eyes and all this stuff.

MATTHEW BARRY: Kane came in and basically said, "This means a lot to me. I have a lot of fans. Don't take this away from me." But in the end, you always have to do what's best for the film, and Ronny thought recasting Jason would be the right thing to do. And, to be honest, so did I. Kane was physically too big. He didn't fit the image that Ronny was going for. Ronny wanted to focus on

Jason's eyes. And he felt Kane was a little too cartoony in the last few films. It was about movement, too, at least compared to the other films, where Jason just kind of walks around like Frankenstein. There's a lot more to him in this one.

RONNY YU: Jason was born with a disability. I can relate. I had polio when I was about nine months old. Jason has this sort of rage in him—he grew up hated. This is just me talking here, but I find him sympathetic. Even though he's a mindless killing machine, I don't think he was given a choice—I don't think he even knows the difference between right and wrong. Even his mother taught him the wrong thing. But he has such a respect for her that he would do anything she tells him to. So that's why I feel sorry for him. He has this just one track mind to kill people. For me, that's pretty powerful.

I had no problem with Kane. Kane did fantastic work. But the studio thought it was a good idea to change. They were thinking that this is a whole new franchise, and another new actor to play Jason could give the movie a little different flavor, including updating his costume and look. Ultimately, it was not my call—it was really New Line's. Although I agreed it was a great idea because then we could inject new ideas into *Freddy vs. Jason*.

ROBERT ENGLUND: I believe that Ronny had a different concept of Jason's physical nature in mind. I just think he was looking for more of a tall, skinny, Anthony Perkins kind of character.

DOUG CURTIS: Ronny didn't really care. To Ronny, it was a non-issue, but Stokely, to her credit, didn't want the guy. She thought Kane wasn't scary, that he was too chunky. To me, it just needed to be somebody who could pull off the Jason swagger with some intelligence and not be a total robot, and who could convey what turned Jason into this monster.

RONNY YU: I was certainly worried. Even until the day I screened the movie for fans, I was worried. Because I would go onto the Internet and there's all these angry fans. So I called Jeff Katz, who was working for Stokely. Because

"We filmed the rave scene out in the middle of nowhere, in a cornfield that smelled like cow shit," laughs actor Christopher Marquette. "It's really a place I never want to go to again. It was really scary, desolate and dirty. On top of that, they had this flammable blue goop everywhere, for the big moment when Jason, on fire, comes slashing through the cornfield. It was really frightening, because the goop is still there even after the fire goes out, so if you get it on your shoe or elbow, you could totally go up in flames. It was pretty hard to concentrate on your acting when you are scared of being burned to death."

Below: Jason's ensuing rampage was a logistical feat for the film's makeup department, who had to create complex mechanics and appliances for an almost non-stop barrage of gore. "That rave scene became like a fucking triathalon," remembers makeup effects supervisor William Terezakis. "You'd finish stabbing someone in the chest here, then you've got to run over there and inflate Jason's lung, then go back and stab someone else, then bust some other guy's leg. It was like one gag after another, and they were just working us like fucking animals. In total, there were twelve of us on set handling different units all at the same time, because they often had three cameras going at once. I could hear the circus music playing as we ran. We even resorted to getting vitamin B injections in our necks to keep going. It was brutal, but fun."

Top: Lochlyn Munro played the part of Deputy Scott Stubbs, one of Springwood's finest who finds himself at the wrong end of Jason's machete. The actor has appeared in such genre films as *Dracula 2000* and *The Tooth Fairy*, but is perhaps most famous for his comedic role as the under-endowed Greg Phillippe in *Scary Movie* (2000). **Above,** *Freddy vs. Jason*'s makeup team applies the finishing bloody touches for Munro's death scene.

Opposite page: "That hair is not mine!" laughs actor Kyle Labine, who plays stoner Freeburg in *Freddy vs. Jason*. "The producers decided after I was cast that I would wear hair extensions. And it was horrible. Especially at first, because when they first put the extensions in, they are very long until they cut them down to size. So for the first couple of days, I had this *total* mullet. I wasn't too thrilled."

Jeff is the expert when it comes to these franchises. I asked him, "Hey Jeff—will this upset the fans?"

JEFF KATZ, Development Executive, New Line Cinema: I'm on the Internet all the time. I was literally checking this stuff twenty-five times a day because I'm obsessive-compulsive. And there were all these rumors about what we were doing. The most ridiculous? The one that was around for the longest time, one that had this whole sect of Jason fans really upset, was that we were going to have Jason talk. That would have been interesting. Frankly he's been beat to shit so many times I don't know what he'd say. How could he form a word?

Anyway, Kane has his fans, obviously. But with a new guy, we could bring something new to the table. And ultimately, Ken's Jason is more to-the-point, and more brutal.

KANE HODDER: It's hard to even put it into words. It was such a slap in the face, especially not to be given any kind of official reason for it whatsoever. It's very difficult to phrase this correctly. I've been trying to think of a way to say it so that doesn't sound like I'm a pompous asshole. But I don't think they realized the following that I have with the fans. Because if they had, I don't think it would have been so easy for them to decide to recast, which is part of the problem with *Freddy vs. Jason*. Whoever made the decision to not use me was under the impression that they just needed a big guy in a mask. "That's fine, whatever, it doesn't matter, he's just walking around stalking people." And that's not true.

To top it all off, the same week I found out I wasn't going to be playing the character in *Freddy vs. Jason*, I was asked by New Line to go to Texas promote the release of the *Jason X* DVD. For free! They wanted me to do it out of the goodness of my heart, and they're screwing me out of my character. That's a tough thing. Maybe it sounds shitty, but the timing was so terrible, I was like, "I don't think so." If there had been a little time in between, I may have reconsidered.

The fans are the only ones who are loyal. Loyalty really doesn't exist in this business, for the most part. That's the way it is. At least I know there were some people who were on my side.

GREG NICOTERO, Effects Supervisor, *Jason Goes to Hell*: In Kane's mind, Jason is so much about body language, and Kane spent a lot of time perfecting that. Kane really finessed that performance. And there are a lot of people that don't understand that. Certain performers bring a character to life. Or kill it. So that when you see another guy in Jason's outfit in *Freddy vs. Jason* you know it's not Kane. I thought it was really sad that he didn't get a chance to continue that. He really believed that his nuances brought Jason to life. And they did. He's absolutely correct in saying that, just as he's absolutely correct in saying that you could never have someone else playing Freddy Krueger—so why would you have someone else play Jason?

JOHN CARL BUECHLER, Director, *Part VII*: It was so stupid. I don't understand it. It makes no sense to me. You can't separate the physical presence of Jason from Kane. He didn't just fit the suit right—he created a character that made the suit work. Kane is an amazing actor. He's never false. That man charges into a scene—no matter what, it's passionate, it's what he is. He throws his heart and soul into it.

TODD FARMER, Screenwriter, *Jason X*: I have always wished *Freddy vs. Jason* the best, but they were morons for not hiring Kane. He deserves it. He's the only guy who kept this thing alive for ten years, talking about it in every interview and convention he did. There's the right thing to do and the wrong thing to do. But Kane will be fine.

KANE HODDER: Eventually, they had an open casting call—I know a lot of people who went in on it. And they end up hiring a Canadian stuntman. So what does that tell you? They wanted someone with more expressive eyes, or someone who was cheaper and more convenient?

KEN KIRZINGER, "Jason Voorhees": This just fell into my lap. I've done a fair bit of acting in my past. I started out as a stuntman and then they started handing me lines playing a thug. Eventually I did get an agent and started doing some acting. But then my stunt career really took off and I got into coordinating.

When I went in to interview for the job on *Freddy vs. Jason*, the producer liked my looks. I got a call a couple of weeks later, "Would you like to come in and audition for it?" I'm six-foot-five, two hundred and twenty-five pounds. It wasn't a real complicated audition. I came in, waved a knife in the air, flexed my muscles, walked around in the mask and they hired me on the spot. They also had me read a scene and react. I was wearing a mask, and they did close-ups of my eye and had me walk around the room and react to a scene they read from the script

DOUG CURTIS: We tried out a lot of guys, but you could see it in Ken's eyes that this guy was a tortured soul. The other thing was that he even doubled Kane as Jason in *Jason Takes Manhattan*. And Ronny liked him right off the bat. Ken's a very articulate guy. He has a gracefulness about him. He never fought Ronny on anything—it was always, "Is this what you want?"

KEN KIRZINGER: The experience in *Part VIII* definitely helped me land the role. But Kane's a pro and we've both been around a long time. *Freddy vs. Jason* was just an opportunity that came along that I took advantage of. New Line made the decision that they wanted to go with a different Jason—Kane realizes it has nothing to do with me getting the job. And even though Kane hates losing the part, I hope he's happy that I got it, somebody that he knows. At least it didn't go to some dancer they auditioned or something. I hope there are no hard feelings.

KANE HODDER: I want it known that Ken Kirzinger only doubled me in two shots in *Jason Takes Manhattan*, and only because we were under tremendous pressure and I just didn't have the time. That's it. It's not like he did all the stunts in it. And you can see the

difference in our performances. Watch the shot after Jason gets electrocuted and walks off the subway train—Ken looks nothing like me because he swings his arms. It's fucking terrible.

Ken doesn't make it clear that this was all he did as Jason in *Part VIII*. He's not lying, but he certainly can be misleading. I just resent the fact that people were under the impression that he did a lot more on that movie than he actually did. Two shots don't qualify you to play a character. But as shitty as it is, I can't say I blame him. He wanted to get the job. He just did it in a shitty way, in my opinion.

WILLIAM TEREZAKIS, Makeup Effects Supervisor: Ken Kirzinger wasn't signed on until a while after we started filming. And when he first came to the shop, honestly, he didn't know a heck of a lot about the character. He was nervous. He asked me, "What's this guy supposed to be like? What do we do?" But, of course, he had such a big job to fill. And he really got it right away. I even have some test footage we shot, where Ken's doing his walk for the first time, and I could tell right away he was doing the right thing when I saw it. I think Ken did a great job.

KEN KIRZINGER: Even by my first day on the set, New Line hadn't okayed me yet for the part. They wanted to see me on film. So my first day was just that moment where I first walk down Elm Street. And I was so nervous because they wanted Jason to walk a certain way and they were being very specific and nit-picky about it. Thankfully, New Line saw the footage and they were happy, and I signed a contract. That was a pretty nerve-wracking night.

RONNY YU: Ken was working on the character a lot. He'd say to me, "I'm not going to live up to Kane!" I said, "Don't worry about it. Just go in and do the best you can. Look at it as a brand-

new Jason. Let's think of it as Frankenstein." Remember the way Frankenstein would walk really slow—like a silent, giant killer? And often he just stands there. Because then when he moves in for the kill, he's like lightning.

KEN KIRZINGER: Ronny's ideas about the character were very strong, so much so that it was more up to me to match what Ronny wanted than give my own point of view. He was definitely directing me. The subtleties of the movements were very important to him. He had a very specific idea that Jason would move very slowly—painfully slowly—until he actually did something, like break a neck or swing the machete. Because it just made it look that much more violent.

Playing Jason is like putting on a Santa Claus suit. You have this iconic character, and all of a sudden you're it. There were not really any other films or actors who played Jason that I looked at specifically. Of course, having worked with Kane on *Part VIII*, and him being the archetypal Jason—we wanted the fans to see something familiar. Hopefully we walked that fine line of creating something new but that fans still identified as the character.

WILLIAM TEREZAKIS: I did try to keep a continuity in Jason's look, but, honestly, if we would have followed the other movies, Jason would have been reduced to a pile of goo. Basically, Ronny wanted a reborn Jason. Something without the scars, without the ax wound in the head. Ronny also wanted Jason's main feature to be the hockey mask, so everything surrounding it is like a black frame. That would make the mask pop out, which I thought was a good concept.

We settled for a pooled-blood look, basically leaving Jason's head very black. It still has the deformities that Jason had, following the original Tom Savini cranial shape. From there, we advanced it to see what it would be in an adult stage. The concept

was that Jason's been on his back for a while, so all the blood has pooled into the back of the head and has created this darkness which is creeping up.

RONNY YU: I love the hockey mask. You can hide anything behind there. Whether you're happy, angry, sorrowful, whatever—when it is behind the mask, it's scary. It's symbolic. So I used that visual a lot in the movie.

It's funny, but initially there was some talk about, "Maybe we should add more sound to Jason?" I said, "No, no, no! If Jason gets hit by Freddy and there's a moaning sound, that totally destroys the myth of it. He can't make a sound. He just has to take what Freddy gives him and when he gets a chance to fight back, he fights back like an unstoppable killing machine." I wanted to go back to the first *Friday the 13th* and get into Jason Voorhees as a son and a killer. He has a one-track mind—like a shark.

MARK SWIFT: Damian and I thought a lot about Jason's backstory. We tried to come up with a good visual metaphor for why he does what he's doing. So we came up with the closet at the Voorhees house—stuffing these victims into it. That was another thing we had to fight for, when they'd say, "What is the closet? I don't get it." We also thought it was a way Freddy could realize he had a fear of drowning. For us that was one of the big differences

Above: "We created the entire Camp Crystal Lake set at Bunsen Lake Forest in Vancouver," says production designer John Willett. "We wanted something that looked real and audiences could immediately identify as a camp from the 1950s. It also is depicted in two different eras in the film: when we first see it, it is sparkling clean, then at the end of the movie, it looks like a scene out of D-Day, with pits and craters and blackened earth. It was a mammoth task—we had to move the beach, create most of the forest and put in all the buildings for the cabins and construction site. That is one of the sets I'm most proud of in the film."

in our draft and the finished film. When Jason opens the closet and we see those victims, we look up and see a little kid drowning. But in the movie, it seems more like he has a fear of water. And we didn't want Jason to have a fear of water because if you look at the past movies, that has never been an issue. It's drowning he's afraid of, because that's what happened to him as a boy.

ROBERT ENGLUND: I really wanted the script to exploit the nightmares of Jason, to not only have Freddy privy to what makes Jason tick, but also for the audience to have his backstory reiterated. Not only in a sort of expository plot way, but also to kind of go into the fantasy nightmare world of little Jason Voorhees, that big Jason Voorhees would remember. To me, that would make it fair, because otherwise Jason would just sort of kick my butt up between my shoulder blades. Freddy's really got to get in Jason's head. And the screenwriters solved that with *Freddy vs. Jason.* It's a great device. They get rid of all their exposition for the new fans—you got all the backstory just in that one scene where you go down through that neuron into Jason's subconscious. That was one of the things in the script that made me really happy to get on board.

KEN KIRZINGER: The motivation of the characters is different. Freddy is just pure evil—he's the bastard child of a hundred maniacs. But Jason, if his mother hadn't been murdered and he hadn't drowned in a lake, probably would have grown up to have a more normal life. Jason's just sort of a little misguided. I like to call him a "psycho savant." He lost his mom early. He's been living out in the woods and under the lake with no guidance. He's just following a mandate, "Kill all those bad kids." Jason's mother is the only person that Jason listens to, the only person he would take orders from. I mentioned it in one article that if Jason was arrested and tried, he probably wouldn't go to jail because he's insane. He

thinks that what he's doing is right. He's doing it for his mother, not for his own personal greed or anything else.

Principal photography on Freddy vs. Jason *began on September 5, 2002. Shot in and around Vancouver, British Columbia, over a period of eight weeks, the $32 million production—minus $7 million spent on script development—was by all accounts a physically demanding and emotionally draining experience. But it was especially challenging for its young cast, many of whom lacked any prior feature film experience. Adding to the tension was Ronny Yu's intense focus on the visual aspects of the film, often to the exclusion of performance considerations. Yu's temperament also varied widely on any given day—moody and unpredictable one minute, highly enthusiastic and collaborative the next. And then there was his limited command of the English language. By the end of the shoot, Yu's oft-heard battle cry of "More energy!" became both a catchphrase—and a punchline—among the cast.*

RONNY YU: Once filming started, I tried not to get myself into the position of feeling pressure because the burden can become very heavy. I just went in and trusted my own instincts. If I felt something was right, I did it. But this one took a lot of energy out of me. It was a very complex schedule because we had a very limited amount of time, especially with the unpredictable weather in Vancouver. Piecing this puzzle together was very difficult. It almost felt impossible.

DOUG CURTIS: Ronny and I became very close during the process of making this movie. Which is not easy, because Ronny can be very, very difficult. Ronny's a very moody guy. Ronny can go into these black holes of depression out of nowhere. He won't want to talk and can't be told of anything that is going on. If what's in his head isn't happening on the monitor in front of him—even though it's physically impossible—it just depresses him to a point where he can't even speak. And Ronny, more than any director I've worked with, cannot stand incompetence. If you're being paid to do a job, I don't care how small a job it is, you'd better show up with your game face on, because he is not a guy you want to come unprepared for. A lot of people got their egos seriously damaged on this movie because he didn't hold back.

My place was to just create an environment where, to the best of my ability, whatever Ronny decided to do was going to get done. I had to be the cheerleader. Because there were a lot of moments where people were saying, "Why the fuck am I doing this? I really don't know what he wants." Yet, at the same time, I've never seen a crew work harder for a director. Because, to Ronny's great credit, he is the first one to give everybody their due in the most effusive way. In the strangest way, he's so demanding that, at any given moment, people will say, "What more can I give him?" It was one of those movies where it was a love-hate thing with the director.

ROBERT ENGLUND: It was hard work, and not just because of the schedule and the nights and the cold. Ronny just has a strange pop culture sensibility. He had the whole movie completely in his subconscious; it's just like the chef that has the spices that are his secret recipe. And he never quite shared it with me or Jason Ritter or Monica Keena or Kelly Rowland. But what kept me going after a twenty-four hour day, working in freezing temperatures with blood spattered all over me and long underwear riding up my you-know-what, was to see Ronny's visual poetry on a little tiny screen in the forest. We'd all run over to the monitor, shivering, then we'd see this amazingly cool stuff, even in the video replay. It was all in his visualization. Ronny is as young and as vibrant in that kind of way as you can be. And I don't think Ronny slept at all. He was literally up for a month. It was a brutal shoot.

MONICA KEENA: Ronny had every shot worked out in his mind, and he's so specific about what he wants. I think he just has a really great eye for all of the special effects. But Ronny was also a different kind of filmmaker than I was used to. He was so very focused on the visual aspects that, a lot of the time, I had to figure out on my own what my character was supposed to be doing and how she was supposed to act, which I never had to do before. "More energy!" That was his biggest direction on the set. That should have been the catchphrase for the movie.

RONNY YU: When Monica came in to interview, I asked her to improvise a scene. Then I said, "Can you scream for me?" And then she let out the loudest and scariest scream! And on top of that, she's a very good actress. So I just said, "Okay, you're hired!" But I think that actually worried her, because then she'd think, "Did I only get the part just because of my scream?" I would have to say, "No, no, no!" But, you know, that was a big part of it.

DOUG CURTIS: There ended up being friction with some of the actors. It was a little difficult because once Ronny forms an opinion about someone, it's hard to change his mind. He never did particularly care for Monica Keena. She was too needy, in his mind. She was just being an actress—and a good one—and she wanted to give him the best she could. But in Ronny's mind, it was actually very difficult. Ronny would say, "We've got it!" And she'd say, "Please let me do another take. I think I can do better." That would upset Ronny, because in his mind if he was right, he was right. He didn't need anything else.

It was Jason Ritter, just because of his great personality, who was able to keep Monica buoyant. He just made her feel safe and really helped her get through it.

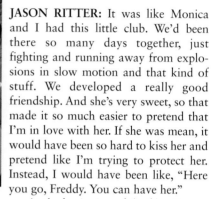

JASON RITTER: It was like Monica and I had this little club. We'd been there so many days together, just fighting and running away from explosions in slow motion and that kind of stuff. We developed a really good friendship. And she's very sweet, so that made it so much easier to pretend that I'm in love with her. If she was mean, it would have been so hard to kiss her and pretend like I'm trying to protect her. Instead, I would have been like, "Here you go, Freddy. You can have her."

At the beginning of the film, Ronny pulled me aside and said, "It's really important that the love between you guys is real." He put a little more concern into some of the acting than I would assume the other films in the franchises had. But it was still hard for the actors because when there's all this technical stuff and every shot takes a half-hour to reset, you can't be like, "I don't like the way I said that line." Too bad. You have to move on.

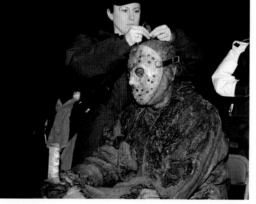

RONNY YU: When I look at the monitor, I don't look at it from a Ronny Yu point of view. I look at it from an audience point of view. I think, "If I'm the audience, would I be interested in that shot?" And when I see something I like, I jump up and down like a kid with a new toy. I try to instill that enthusiasm in everybody I'm working with.

The actors, I yell at them. Really, sometimes I do. A lot of them were first-timers—all those outstanding parts were played by very green kids. The most important thing for me is, if you cast the right person, you know that it will work. It doesn't matter how much experience the kids have as long as they understand the role. I talked to practically every single one of them, just to explain their character and tell them what I want from them. Then I'd give them

Top: Makeup effects supervisor William Terezakis applies the finishing touches to the makeup for young Jason, played by thirteen-year-old Spencer Stump. The extensive prosthetics often required marathon application sessions for the young actor. "Five hours to put it on, one hour to take it off," says Stump. "It was painful to have all that glue on my face. They even had to make a mold of my head by putting this cement stuff all over it, which was really freaky, because I'm claustrophobic." Following his appearance in *Freddy vs. Jason*, Stump has found himself a minor celebrity at the high school he currently attends. "Every once in a while, someone will still yell out, 'Hey, baby Jason!' And some people treat me like a god. Which is weird. I'm like, 'I was only in it for two minutes!'"

"It's not that Jason doesn't feel pain, he just has no fear. He's been cut up, blown up, shot, hacked and slashed, and still he keeps coming back." Ken Kirzinger

"The most fun I had on *Freddy vs. Jason* was designing the sets for Jason's world and Freddy's world," says production designer John Willett. "Both are truly nightmarish environments and, visually, are signature moments in the film. The idea was to change the color for each. We always used blues and greens and water colors for Jason, and reds, rusts and earth colors for Freddy. We felt this way you would visually guide the audience, and that they would always know exactly where the story was at any given point in time."

"The fights had to take place both in the real world and the dream world. The trick was making that happen without violating the established mythology of either character." **Mark Swift, Co-Screenwriter**

references—magazines and movies to look at. I gave them homework. But with very experienced actors, you don't need to do that much coaching, because you just watch them. I've worked with Samuel L. Jackson and Robert Carlyle—it's a totally different thing. You just switch on the camera and let them do their thing.

CHRISTOPHER MARQUETTE: Ronny was fond of saying "more energy," but that really got to become kind of a joke. I'd say to him, "Is there anything else you want me to do in this scene aside from what you saw in rehearsal?" And Ronny's just like, "No, more scared!" But I thought Ronny gave me almost complete freedom over what I wanted to do, because he trusted me. Then he got to concentrate on the cinematography and the direction and the blocking, just placing me where he wanted me and saying, "Action!" I think that's great. *Freddy vs. Jason* would have been hell to go through with a director who told you exactly what to do every time. So I was happy.

JESSE HUTCH: I'll be honest: I didn't really feel comfortable doing that bedroom scene. I had never done anything like that before. It was kept to a minimum because Katherine Isabelle was a bit uncomfortable with it as well. We just wanted to get it over with. But being a new actor, I felt like, "Oh, I guess this is what's happening," so I went along with it, but afterward I felt like, "That was a little uncomfortable for me." I thought the death could have happened without that glimpse of the two characters doing their business there. It was one of those scenes—if I never see it, I won't feel bad.

MATTHEW BARRY: Ronny was like, "Look, I want to set up the camera and go. I don't want to have to work with insecure actors. I just want them to come in, do what they do and then move on to the next shot." That made it tough, and challenging.

That's why I was especially proud of Kelly Rowland— she was determined and she wanted to work hard on it. Same thing with Britney Spears—those artists are hard workers. They're disciplined. I loved Kelly. I think she was one of the best things in the movie.

RONNY YU: Kelly didn't have the experience of a Samuel Jackson, but she did have a certain energy. It doesn't matter what kind of experience an actor has as long as you have the right attitude. I felt I had to recognize that and use that. She was very humble and really wanted to learn and was willing to try everything. She was very scared of Freddy. She would keep asking me, "Ronny, can I have my eyes shut?" I said, "No, Kelly, you cannot have your eyes shut in a confrontation with Freddy!" She was like, "Oh, man!" But eventually everything worked out great.

KELLY ROWLAND: Honey, they jump-started my engine because I was not ready. I wanted to warm up a little bit. And I'm terrified because the very first shot I did was when the Freddy claw comes out of the magazine and gets my nose. I did not want to do that scene first. I was, like, "Why did I have to start off with Freddy?"

MONICA KEENA: Kelly is one of those people that I don't know how you could ever say anything bad about. She just emits this wonderful glow and light and she brings so much more to her character than is written. Kelly was so bright. But she was definitely nervous the first couple of days. We spent a lot of time together on and off the set. We developed a rapport, so all our scenes together became very natural. It's believable we were friends in the movie because we really were becoming friends offscreen, too.

KELLY ROWLAND: The teamwork on the set reminded me of being in Destiny's Child. It's the little things that I think I'll look back on and remember. I loved how Jason Ritter was funny and always turned a dull moment into something bright and beautiful. And Monica helped me in scenes where I was really scared. There's one shot where we go into the cornfield and we're running and right behind me was complete darkness. I was like, "You've got to hold my hand. I'm gonna be scared!" And she did. I even remember the first time I met her—I was just drawn to her. Her eyes are so beautiful that they just talk to you. We didn't have to try to be friends because we were actually there for each other.

BRENDAN FLETCHER: I had this habit of going around and singing Destiny's Child songs all the time—it was one of my favorite things to do. And Kelly was actually really cool about it, even though I totally destroyed her songs. Well, I hope she thought it was funny.

JASON RITTER: I gave Kelly some singing lessons. Just kidding.

Although the creators of Freddy vs. Jason *had put forth their best effort to make the characters more than just typical slasher film fodder, no one was under any illusions as to what audiences were really coming to see. The climactic slugfest between the two titans of terror had to be nothing less than the most spectacular, knock-down, drag-out fight in horror history. The expectations of the fans weighed heavily on the mind of Ronny Yu. He knew that after nearly a decade of hope and hype, the battle between Jason and Freddy had to be so over-the-top, so outrageous, that audiences wouldn't be able to stop talking about it on their way out of the theater. And it certainly had to be bloody. But even* Freddy vs. Jason's *seen-it-all makeup effects crew was taken aback by Ronny Yu's carnival of carnage. As filming wrapped, stage blood was being ordered up not by the bucket, or even by the gallon—but by the barrel.*

RONNY YU: I didn't look at *Freddy vs. Jason* as being just another slasher movie where the audience would simply sit there, waiting for the kills and the body count. I looked at this as being an action-horror movie, kind of like *ALIENS*, something with lots of action, lots of scary moments and lots of horror. I saw *Freddy vs. Jason* as being like *King Kong vs. Godzilla*—plenty of combat and scenes of the two monsters fighting.

Somehow, I'm also a big fan of the WWF, even though I don't like it—it's just so bizarre that I keep tuning in. I also have realized what great scriptwriters those people are, because everybody in the WWF has a character, a larger than life persona. And when you see them fight, you somehow have to root for one side. So that was also one of my inspirations.

This page: Ronny Yu in action. From top: directing Ken Kirzinger (left) and Robert Englund; discussing a take with director of photography Fred Murphy (left, in background) and Englund; and coaching Christopher Marquette through a complicated dialogue scene.

MARK SWIFT: Most of the changes made to our final draft were in the third act. Our ending was not supposed to be as over-the-top. We didn't ever want to make the thing cerebral, but we wanted it to be smarter than maybe was expected. What we wrote was a lot more elaborate, with more characters and a whole subplot about a housing development being built at Camp Crystal Lake that tied into some of the other movies. We fought for that. We did our best. Then it got lost. So now, when suddenly they end up fighting at a construction site, you're like, "Why?"

DAMIAN SHANNON: We even had a reference to Tommy Jarvis in there. The developers at this Crystal Lake construction site were having problems with Tommy protesting. I think that might even have been where that Internet rumor came about—that Corey Feldman was going to be in *Freddy vs. Jason*. I also thought it would be a great idea to put more victims in between, to see people get caught between Freddy and Jason. We had a lot more people getting killed. But they just didn't want to introduce those characters.

DOUG CURTIS: The whole ending of the movie we lost because it was stupid. It involved a lot of people in a construction trailer that the audience was not invested in. It was a different movie and it was very expensive. As it turned out, I think the ending we came up with was even more expensive, but it was certainly more

exciting because it involved our two protagonists fighting it out to the death. That's what audiences were paying to see. And it is why, eventually, the movie tested so high—everybody talked about the end battle of the movie.

RONNY YU: *Freddy vs. Jason* is "more, more, more!" I told the crew to imagine that Freddy and Jason are like a T-Rex and Godzilla fighting. Are they going to hold back? No! They're going to tear each other's limbs off and go for the eyes like two animals. Let's go back to the rawness of it, the basics. I also said, "All the violence—let's go wilder so the audience will laugh at it and not get disturbed by it." These are two beasts who the audience has no emotional investment in. They smack each other in the head and it's all fake. And they never die anyway. But visually, there's a lot of excitement. I took from all those samurai movies I saw when I was little—there's blood squishing everywhere. Push it, push it, push it, so the audience has a fun time.

The movie I kept in my mind throughout shooting this was *Rocky*. The scene that really hit me is at the end, the final fight, when Apollo beats the crap out of Rocky. Yet Rocky has the spirit to fight back even though his eye is all swollen and all of that. Then he tells his trainer, "Cut it open." And they actually slice open his wound and the blood just spills out! And that for me is the rule I followed on *Freddy vs. Jason*.

MARK SWIFT: We started off writing what was probably the bloodiest film ever made, and that was because Bob Shaye at New Line told us to make it as violent as possible. Ultimately it became less bloody, but it stayed essentially the same story all the way through. Although, when we came out to visit the set, we were talking to one of the special effects guys and he was just shaking his head at some of the over-the-top stuff Ronny was doing. He was just going, "Man, this is something out of Monty Python!"

RONNY YU: One of the special effects people came up to me and asked, "Can you tell me how much blood we should order? In terms of buckets or gallons?" I said, "Gasoline barrels. Get me two dozen."

KELLY ROWLAND: Man, the fight between Freddy and Jason was really cool. Especially where I actually tail Freddy off, where we're face to face and I'm letting him have it. Those were my favorite scenes.

When I actually get into Kia mode, I just have to laugh because she just has this strength about her—that she just doesn't care what anyone thinks. If you piss her off, then that's the worst thing you've done, because she'll let you have the third degree. She's very mouthy, very sassy, and she's a worldly girl. She's very cool to be with, but don't step on her toes because she can be a real diva.

MARK SWIFT: I have a feeling that when Kelly Rowland came into the process, she thought she needed a bigger kill. She wanted to say more to Freddy—she probably wanted to talk some smack. I bet that whole speech was written just for her. So now there are a couple of lines in there that Damian and I are like, "For God's sake—tell someone, anyone, that we didn't write those!" One was when Freddy says to Kia, "How sweet, dark meat!" That was actually Englund's line. But then Kelly Rowland calls Freddy a faggot—I can't believe she did it.

"Freddy and Jason are like T-Rex and Godzilla fighting. Are they going to hold back? No! They are going to tear each other's limbs off … like two animals." Ronny Yu

Right: "Freddy and Jason have been childhood fears of mine, so doing this movie kind of freaked me out at first," says Kelly Rowland. "Then when I got to the set, everybody was so nice. Of course, they soon started to play jokes and scare me. But it was so much fun!" Ironically, the one scene that didn't scare Rowland was filming the violent death of her character, Kia. "In that scene I had all this fake blood, which is made out of corn syrup and red dye running down my head. And you're supposed to keep the blood on your face between takes so that they can take pictures for continuity reasons. But I didn't know that, and I'm a sweets fanatic. So I kept licking the blood off. Finally, my makeup artist said, 'Kelly, please stop licking the blood!'"

"Lori is the least likely action hero ever," says Monica Keena. "I'm supposed to be this very quiet, subdued, virginal character. Then all these terrible murders start happening and I have to find this strength within me and take care of everybody. I go through a huge metamorphosis during the course of the movie. I kind of turn warrior at the end." Although the *Friday the 13th* films have often been criticized for being exploitative and misogynistic, Keena feels that the role of Lori subverts many of those preconceived notions. "Women in horror movies have often been sex objects that are just there to look pretty and get murdered. But in *Freddy vs. Jason*, I didn't think Lori was victimized. She wasn't just this pretty girl running around looking hot the whole time. In a way, it's a coming-of-age story because she really finds herself, and a strength she never knew she had—she refuses to be kicked down by these monsters."

DAMIAN SHANNON: Both those lines we're not big fans of. We didn't write either of them. At least "dark meat" I can laugh at, because Freddy's a pig—he's a villain. You want to hate him. To me, I think Freddy should be able to say anything. He could be as un-PC as he wants to be. But to have Kelly Rowland say "faggot"— that doesn't make any sense.

DOUG CURTIS: I love the idea of good versus evil and of evil being so bad. We all have that dark side to us—Ronny talked about that a lot. You have to explore that. And when you get to explore it on an operatic level it becomes more fun than not. It doesn't force you to explore the dark side of mankind, it just gives you some characters who encounter it. I just think it makes for good drama.

RONNY YU: I always say that *Freddy vs. Jason* is "Four Fingers of Death vs. The Machete"—Freddy's glove is like a claw, and Jason's machete reminds me of old samurai movies. But the trick is not to be so overt that everybody says, "Oh, this is a Hong Kong movie." My goal was to make a Hollywood movie. So whatever I injected into the film had to hit the audience on a subconscious level. I had a very open-minded attitude, I listened to everybody, especially these people who've been involved with these franchises.

MONTY SIMMONS, Stunt Coordinator: Ronny is not your classic slash and gash director. He brought a whole other layer to the fight scenes on *Freddy vs. Jason* because of his Hong Kong background. Just the wirework was phenomenal. I mean, we sent these guys flying in every conceivable direction. We had them flying into objects, through walls, up stairs, down stairs—you name it, we've done it. In real life they would've been dead fifteen times, but in this world they go flying across the room through a wall and crash down two stories. They get up and they come right back at each other again. It just keeps going and going.

ROBERT ENGLUND: I was actually having trouble the second week on second unit. When they say, "You're gonna fly through the air on fire and we're gonna see it from up in the sky," they actually shoot it that way. It's amazing. And you just sort of have to surrender yourself to their incredible imagination, because it's so unrestricted.

KEN KIRZINGER: The fight sequence at the end I was particularly happy with. I did most of the stunts and I really enjoyed it. I also got my own little touches in there. There's a scene after Jason's been knocked down by the crushed air bottles

nice toys—a nice big machete, prosthetic bodies and stunt guys to play with. It was just a really fun environment.

ROBERT ENGLUND: I've never worked so hard in my life, and I'm an old dog now. Have you ever played baseball on a cold day and you caught a line drive, you know, "*Ow-ie-ka-pow-ie!*" And it was the same thing with doing the fight scenes, because even though we're padded and stuff, we're doing them over and over and over again. And, you know, in the cold you don't quite feel it. You're a little numb, so it was rough. Ken is a stuntman, so he could get in there and get a lot more down and dirty than I could. But sets are very macho and very male and you want to get in there, too. So I gave him my two cents' worth. I showed no quarter.

MONICA KEENA: It was hard to think about anything positive when you're spending fifteen hours a day covered in blood and mud. It was difficult. I had moments where I'd been doing it for weeks and weeks, and it just reached the point where I was exhausted and didn't want to see any more blood. But then I got excited all over again at the idea that I'm part of this.

When we had to jump into Crystal Lake at the end of the movie, I had the flu and it was freezing in Vancouver. It's the coldest I've ever been in my entire life. I was crying. And my clothes were too skimpy so I couldn't wear a wetsuit. Jason Ritter would have been able to, but he was so kind that he opted not to just so he wouldn't have an advantage over me.

JASON RITTER: I was trying to make Monica feel better about it because she was sick, and feeling all hot and cold. And I was going to jump in the cold water and be like, "It's fine. Jump in!" And then I jumped in and screamed, "It's freezing!"

We do lots of running, screaming, and some more running. I've never been in a movie where we're running away from fire and jumping into a lake with an explosion behind us. But it was like my little childhood dream of explosions and blood. It was the hardest part of making the film, but the most fun, too.

DOUG CURTIS: *Freddy vs. Jason* reinvigorated Ronny's career, but he was very unsure as to whether he should be making this movie or not. Ronny would always say to me, "Are you glad you're making this movie?" And what do you say to that? I'd just say, "I'm glad to be making any movie." But when I said yes to *Freddy vs. Jason*, I was genuinely happy to be making it. And the closer we got to the end of the journey, the more and more glad I got. I just became so proud of what we were

"I look at this movie like a wonderful, dramatic, violent comic book. It's like 'The Bloody Ballad of Freddy & Jason.'"

Robert Englund

This page: "We put the most amount of work into the ending," says co-screenwriter Mark Swift who, along with Damian Shannon, had the formidable task of conceiving of a suitable climax for *Freddy vs. Jason*. "Our original idea was to bring in Pinhead from the *Hellraiser* franchise, but New Line didn't own that property. So then we did a rewrite which had Freddy and Jason in hell, and a cameo by Satan." Ultimately, this ambitious finale was nixed due to budgetary constraints, says Swift. "If you go CGI, it would have looked like shit, and if you went with a real set, it would have cost far too much money."

Seen here are the original conceptual drawings by Dave Damron, who was commissioned by Swift and Shannon to help them pitch their original idea to New Line.

achieving on a daily basis. And on that last day, when it was all done and we knew that we'd pulled it off, there was just a glow about everybody.

Despite all the frustrations and aggravations and challenges and stress, we were very lucky. There were so many things that could have gone wrong, just physically. But they all went right. It was amazing. It was a movie that was just meant to be.

So, who wins? The claw or the machete? That was the question that had plagued Freddy vs. Jason *from day one. Each franchise's fans had their bets on their favorite villain, and to tip the scales in either's favor would alienate just as many as it would appease. Crafting the film's final coda would prove to be the film's greatest challenge. It would also require multiple test screenings, plenty of rewrites, and not one—but three—filmed endings. Ultimately,* Freddy vs. Jason *would end with neither a whimper nor a bang. Instead, the battle of the century would end... with a wink.*

MARK SWIFT: Originally, in our draft, we killed Will. And everyone was like, "You can't kill Will, that's insane." So then we killed Lori's father instead. At the end of the movie, Lori and her father walk into a dry lake bed, because Crystal Lake has been drained. Freddy's glove is on the ground and the father grabs it and says, "We're going to get rid of this—this time for good!" And then Freddy's arm rips through the ground and pulls him down. It was kind of an homage to the first *Nightmare*. The last image of the movie would be Lori clawing at the dirt, screaming. Freddy has essentially made her an orphan, taking her mother and father. We wanted to have this epilogue that lets you know that maybe the fight is continuing in hell.

DAMIAN SHANNON: David Goyer wrote a new epilogue which was shot involving a sex scene between Lori and Will, where Will turns into Freddy. I didn't like it. I don't think anyone did. And, thankfully, it wasn't received favorably by test audiences and was cut anyway.

DOUG CURTIS: The lowest point of making the movie was when Ronny showed the studio his cut. I felt Ronny's cut was terrific. I thought he nailed it. But the studio didn't like it. Bob Shaye didn't like it at all. He was really upset. Stokely came in, and Goyer came in, and a lot of time was spent in the editing room. There were lots of notes between Ronny's cut and the first test screening, which was about two or three weeks later.

Then, after the first screening, the audience loved the movie. The next day on Ain't It Cool News, there wasn't a bad review. Everybody raved. But then I think maybe we all got cocky. New Line said, "Well, if they love it that much, we can make it even better." And I thought the next cut was great, too. But at the second screening the test scores actually went down. They were not fantastic—in the seventy percentile positive range—but they were still above the norm. I think they overcut it. Ronny agreed.

But I think the really big problem was that now we had no ending, because the ending of the first version that we shot was so stupid. New Line just said, "Let's see what happens if there's no ending at all."

MARK VERHEIDEN: I'm not sure if any of the other *Freddy vs. Jason* drafts had this, but in mine Michael De Luca wanted me to write two endings. One where Jason "won" and one with Freddy the victor. I remember that New Line's plan at the time was to release it two ways and you wouldn't know which ending you'd get when you went to the theater. They really wanted to try to do that. It would be just another way to sort

The release of *Freddy vs. Jason* would be accompanied by not just one soundtrack CD, but two. *Freddy vs. Jason: The Original Motion Picture Soundtrack* (**left**) features twenty new and previously unreleased tracks by such contemporary rock artists as Slipknot, Type O Negative and Ill Ninon. In its first week of release, the soundtrack broke the Billboard Top 40 Album chart, and eventually sold over 500,000 copies.

Freddy vs. Jason: The Original Motion Picture Score was composed by Graeme Revell (**below**), who had previously worked with director Ronny Yu on *Bride of Chucky*. "I was really attracted by the way Ronny described the film to me," says Revell. "That it was a big WWF bout, a great ol' slug-fest." Perhaps the biggest challenge Revell faced in composing the score was paying tribute to the familiar scores for both franchises, while introducing fresh, new elements. "I did have concerns about meeting expectations. And why not? Harry Manfredini had done a great job on the past scores, and I knew that was really important to a lot of people. And Jason, of course, has his vocal effect that's so famous—"Ki, ki, ki, ma, ma, ma." So what I tried to do was create new moods that derived from those themes, and bring in my own set of ideas for the different combinations of characters."

Revell began his musical career as a founding member of the pioneering industrial group SPK, and his work as a composer has been acclaimed for its inventive use of non-traditional instruments and sonic textures. His score for *Freddy vs. Jason* is no exception, with its aggressive percussion and often startling bursts of sound. "I like to layer sounds—there's often ten things on top of each other at any given time. I also talked a lot with Ronny about the use of 'negative space,' meaning that you have to quiet things down for a few seconds before the big scare. Horror is a genre in particular that is totally dependent on peaks and valleys. It's very much about a carefully crafted set of surprises and red herrings. *Freddy vs. Jason* was a lot of fun to do."

New Line Cinema's domestic theatrical teaser poster (**left**) and theatrical one-sheet for *Freddy vs. Jason*.

of jazz up interest in it. Obviously, too, diehard fans would see it twice. That would have been an interesting way to go.

MARK SWIFT: Really, I think the ending they ended up with is the best one. Bob Shaye came up with that. It's really brilliant because there is a more definite winner, yet an argument can be made that perhaps there isn't. Although, to tell you the truth, when Jason is carrying Freddy's head out of the water I wasn't sure if Robert Englund was doing a *Looney Tunes* wink to the audience, like, "Hey, thanks for coming to the movie," or if he was really thinking about it in terms of that Freddy is still in control and he's manipulating Jason. But I like the fact that an argument can be made for both sides.

DOUG CURTIS: Ronny was the one who came up with the idea that Bob Shaye takes credit for. Fans all wanted an ending, yet they didn't want it to end. That's what's so brilliant about that ending. It leaves it open. In the minds of the people these movies are designed for, they're both winners.

SEAN CUNNINGHAM: I don't want to be too coarse a producer here, but it's possible for a wrestler to lose a match, then come back and kick ass the next time. The ending of the film reflects the overview that in any particular battle there may be a victor, but the war always continues. How do you kill two people who can't be killed? You can get yourself into a Catch-22 loop. But I think we still have a very strong, visceral ending where people can say, "That's the biggest kick-ass fight I've ever seen!" Ultimately, the biggest winner had to be the audience.

RONNY YU: Who wins? Since the moment I signed on, that is the question everybody's asking you. My mission was to satisfy the hardcore fans who grew up with these two characters. That's why I felt that no matter what we came up with for the ending, fans of both franchises have to come out feeling like they're the winner. And I'm pretty happy with what we have now. I think that did satisfy both parties.

New Line Cinema kicked the Freddy vs. Jason *publicity machine into overdrive as its U.S. release date of August 15, 2003 loomed closer. Surpassing the cost of the marketing campaigns for all ten*

previous Friday the 13th *films combined, New Line's PR assault spanned all media, including television, radio, print and the Internet, at a reported cost of $25 million—nearly equal the film's production budget. Beginning with a carefully orchestrated plan to generate early buzz, production tidbits were "leaked" to popular entertainment websites to keep eager fans alerted to every breaking development from the set. New Line also ramped up its merchandising of officially-licensed* Friday the 13th *and* A Nightmare on Elm Street *products, ranging from hats and mugs to lunchboxes and comic books. Jason and Freddy even took a trip to Las Vegas a month before the film's release, where, in an elaborately-staged event held at Bally's casino, Robert Englund and Ken Kirzinger, in full costume, participated in a mock pre-fight weigh-in and boxing match to the delight of the hundreds of fans and press in attendance. Then, on Thursday, August 14, for the first time in his long and distinguished "career," Jason Voorhees was given a proper Hollywood reception. Held at Hollywood's famed Cinerama Dome, the premiere of* Freddy vs. Jason *was a star-studded event covered by such mainstream media outlets as* Entertainment Tonight, Access Hollywood *and* MTV. *Jason may never become an A-list star, and he certainly won't win any Academy Awards, but for one bright, shining moment, he was the talk of Tinseltown.*

Still, the public reaction that awaited Freddy vs. Jason *was far from certain. While New Line Cinema and the filmmakers were —more or less—pleased with their film, the most recent box office numbers for both franchises were hardly encouraging—and the meager turnout for 2002's* Jason X *did not exactly inspire confidence. And there was still the question of just who the audience was for the film. For the kids of the 1980's who grew up on Jason and Freddy, the characters may have become beloved icons of nostalgia, but nostalgia nonetheless. And for a new generation of hip, pop-culture savvy teens, Jason and Freddy no longer represented objects of fear but rather postmodern punchlines from such films as* Scream *and* Scary Movie.

But any doubts about the commercial viability of Jason Voorhees were short-lived when Freddy vs. Jason *made its debut on 3,014 screens across the United States. Even with widespread summer blackouts threatening to close many theaters across the East Coast, nothing could stop the* Freddy vs. Jason *box office blitzkrieg. With an opening three-day gross of $36.4 million, the film not only obliterated the career-best* *debuts of both franchises, it also set a new record for the biggest opening weekend for a horror sequel. The film also showed surprising staying power during its second weekend, once again claiming the #1 spot at the box office. With a final cumulative domestic gross of $82.6 million,* Freddy vs. Jason *earned its place as the most financially successful entry in the* Friday the 13th *franchise. (Although, with 13.7 million paid admissions versus the original* Friday the 13th's *14.8 million tickets sold, it still ranks second in the series in overall attendance.)*

Of course, the cultural cache enjoyed by Freddy vs. Jason *cannot be counted only in dollars. The success of the first—though perhaps not the last—Freddy/Jason face-off brought its respective franchises full circle. Suddenly Jason Voorhees and* Friday the 13th *were no longer regarded as relics of the bygone era of exploitation slashers. But where the character and the franchise will go from here remains uncertain. Even if we have seen the last of Jason and* Friday the 13th, Freddy vs. Jason *will have served as a fitting end—and a shining testament—to a motion picture phenomenon. And the makers of this "final chapter" will one day be able to look back with a wistful smile—and perhaps even a morbid sense of pride—about bringing Jason Voorhees back to life one last time.*

CHRISTOPHER MARQUETTE: I went to the screening and the premiere. That's the first time I've been on a red carpet with more than fifteen photographers and this time it's like fifty and a ton of fans yelling out everybody's names. It was really overwhelming. That's one of the things I'll definitely never forget about the experience, just being part of that whole day. It was amazing.

DOUG CURTIS: The studio would have been happy with a $15 million opening. Still, we were all kind of holding our breath. Then Stokely called and left a message on my cell phone, but it broke up when she said, "Can you believe it made...?" She sounded drunk with excitement. I thought she'd said $8 million. But she actually said it made $18 million or some ridiculous figure, just on Friday. I was just blown away.

MATTHEW BARRY: As a casting director, I'm not proud of all the films I've done. Not at all. Sometimes you have a great cast but the films don't work out, or sometimes you have a great film but you just don't like the director's choices. On this one, I'm actually very proud. It was long and hard, but in the end it turned out exactly how I wanted it to. The kids were all great—it was more than I was expecting. It was such a great ride. And it makes me feel good to know that we're part of the big one of these franchises.

ROBERT ENGLUND: It may be a strange integrity, but I think there's a whole new point of view now on horror movies from the 1970s and 1980s. A new respect. We've become the Seattle grunge band of horror. We were lean and mean, but we somehow delivered the goods. And we were culturally significant in an accidental way, as opposed to these bloated studio horrors that are all about CGI effect after CGI effect. Everything has been co-opted since then. Mothers began piercing themselves and wearing safety pins, and everybody has contemporary hair now. But back then, both of these franchises were raw and imaginative, and were something that the kids found for themselves. So I think now, with a kind of retro hindsight, it is fun to remember back to the great times of these movies, before the age of hype and sophistication and irony.

Also, my feeling is that when the DVD box set of *A Nightmare on Elm Street* came out, we gained a new generation. I know my fan mail, personally, went through the roof. It also has a younger appeal now than it used to. Moms and dads even let their kids see them. It's become a rite of passage for twelve and thirteen-year-old boys. So I believe that generation has had their appetite whet for these movies, and were really anticipating *Freddy vs. Jason*, as well as the people who were fans originally.

I think it was a project and an idea whose time had come. And although I don't see Freddy or Jason disappearing any time soon, *Freddy vs. Jason* may, in a way, be the perfect farewell to the horror conventions of the last two decades.

DAMIAN SHANNON: Let me put it this way: after I saw the movie, I thought it would make about $60 million. I didn't expect how much it eventually made. But the thing we'll never know is, which version would have made the most money? The one we wrote or the one on the screen? Because the one thing that's most sorely lacking for me in the movie is tension. The characters being afraid and the moments of stalking. You just don't get that same feeling that you got in the early films of the franchises. Maybe that's my nostalgia. I was very young when I saw the first *Friday the 13th*, and it terrified me. I never got any sense of that here. But, at the end of the day, you have to say, "The movie made $80 million." Ronny more than pulled it off, and a lot of fans love what we did. So that's all you can really ask for.

"I suppose 'vindicated' is a good word to describe the way we all feel. We delivered a movie that the audience loved, and it's the audience that matters most." Doug Curtis

MARK SWIFT: *Freddy vs. Jason* is not perfect. I think it has a lot of problems. There's one mind that says, "If you make a piece of shit, it's just going to make the same amount of money." I don't believe that. It did have a massive drop-off. And I think the people who love it the most are fifteen or sixteen years old—guys especially. But when Damian and I were writing it, I thought it could break through to $150 million. Honestly. Look at what *Scream* did, look at what *Blair Witch* did. If *Freddy vs. Jason* had been done right, if it was dark and scary with lots of action, it would have been massive.

On the whole, I think *Freddy vs. Jason* delivered for a lot of people. I'm glad it got made. I would rather have the version that exists now than Freddy killing somebody with a Nintendo power glove. And New Line's absolutely thrilled with it. Plus, you're never going to make everybody happy. So I'm not complaining. It's pretty amazing.

TOBY EMMERICH, President of Production, New Line Cinema: In all honesty, I don't disagree with the critics. If I were being paid by the New York Times, I'd probably give *Freddy vs. Jason* a mixed review, too. But our exit polls were really strong, so the film's real fans obviously enjoyed it. I wish we could have made a movie that pleased both the fans and the critics, but that would've taken another five years and another $20 million, and that wasn't what we had to work with.

RONNY YU: Oh, the reaction, it was unbelievable. But I'm not a savior. I did not rescue anything. I just went in and tried to make something exciting. It all boils down to luck. And, really, I think it was the fans who made this happen, who really supported these characters and these franchises all these years. Otherwise, we just wouldn't have made those numbers. I'm just so happy that I delivered something that the fans really embraced.

12.

Reflections on the Water

For all of the writers, directors, actors, producers and craftspeople who have left their mark on *Friday the 13th* and its sequels, their contributions have granted them honorary lifetime memberships to a most unusual club. And while some look back on their association with the series as a mere stepping stone—or, in some cases, a roadblock—to their long-term career goals, others are proud to display their Jason-inflicted "battle scars," and boast of their struggles and ultimate survival at "Camp Blood" as well-deserved badges of honor. Presented here are the parting thoughts of many of the talented men and women whose creative contributions helped shape the cinematic legacy that is *Friday the 13th*. Their recollections shed light on the impact the series has had on their careers, their personal lives, and pop culture at large. They also reflect candidly on the series' continuing allure and speculate on what the future may hold for Jason Voorhees. Regardless of whether *Friday the 13th* survives a dozen more sequels, or we have indeed seen the last of Jason Voorhees, there is little doubt that the legend of a certain hockey-masked killer will live on long after those whose stories are documented here have passed.

But no matter when Jason Voorhees finally decides it is time to put down his machete, kiss his mother's decapitated head goodnight, and finally rest in peace (or in pieces, as the case may be), the fans of *Friday the 13th* will always have these memories—these Crystal Lake Memories—to remind us that these films did indeed matter.

TASO STAVRAKIS, Effects Assistant, *Part 1*: The first *Friday the 13th* was made on a shoestring. It was just a few people who all had the willpower to say, "We're going to do this." And we didn't know what it would be until it was done, then it suddenly became this big thing. That's what I took the most from *Friday the 13th*: that no matter what anyone thinks or says about your idea, you can make it happen—and it just might become something incredible.

ARI LEHMAN, "Jason Voorhees," *Part 1*: One thing that speaks to me about the original *Friday the 13th* is that it has to do with confronting our innermost fears, which is very spiritually liberating and can make us stronger people. I think that was the effect that being in the movie had on me—I might have been scared of horror movies prior, but afterward I gained insight. I've lived in Chicago and New York and Brooklyn and I've seen real horror situations where they, some of my brothers out there, have real respect for Jason. Maybe confronting this demon somehow helps you steel yourself to some situation—it's a fantastic thing. It has to do with imagination ... and even Albert Einstein said imagination is more important than knowledge.

VICTOR MILLER, Screenwriter, *Part 1*: Up until 1980, if I would be at a party and people would ask what I did for a living, I'd say, "I'm a writer." And of course they would say, "Well, what have you written that I know?" And I would have to say, "Nothing." But after May 1980, I can still go anywhere and answer the same question by saying, "I wrote *Friday the 13th*." And although most of the time they would be quick to say, "I never saw that, because I wouldn't go to that kind of movie," it still somehow validated me as a writer to the outside world. It did not make me a better writer, and personally, it did not solve all of my inner turmoil. But it sure made it easier to go to parties.

HARRY MANFREDINI, Composer: For me, *Friday the 13th* is a double-edged sword. It paid me a lot of money, but at the same time it's always, "Oh, you're the guy who did *that*." It just turns out that I'm good at writing horror movie music. And it is a lot of fun. But I'm sure I'll be ninety years old and I'll never escape *Friday the 13th*. There will be a *Friday Part 65* or something, and old Jason will be in a wheelchair. And on my gravestone, it'll say, "He's the guy who thought up 'Ki, ki, ki. Ma, ma, ma.'"

FRANK MANCUSO, JR., Producer, *Part 2—Part VIII*: If all anyone ever remembered me for was *Friday the 13th*, would that bother me? Probably. But my response today would be different than it would have been six or seven years ago, because I hadn't yet made films like *Species* or *Stigmata* or *Ronin*. So I have been able to show other sides of myself, creatively.

You have to have perspective. You have to know that different films you make are going to affect different people in different ways. *Friday the 13th* came at a time and a place in certain people's lives when they weren't totally ready for it, and it hit them point blank. It resonated. And as any kind of creative being, you want to engage people in a way that sticks.

Ultimately, I have no regrets. If some people still want to talk about and love the *Friday the 13th* movies, that's great. Let them have their bliss. People have just started to relate to these movies in a way that has taken them to a whole other level. And no one can control that. I just want to be gracious and say, "Thanks." And off we go.

> ## "You can't please everybody. I got a hate letter for *Jason Takes Manhattan*. It was really scary. It involved having my balls cut off. That it was the worst piece of shit ever and I should be giving blow jobs instead of making movies. Then, at the end, it says, 'But at least it was better than the last couple of *Friday the 13th*s...'" Rob Hedden

CLIFF CUDNEY, Stunt Coordinator, *Part 2*: My only concern with doing things like *Friday the 13th* was that, if I worked in B-movies too much, then I'd become known only as a B-movie stuntman. And the sad part is, ironically, those are the movies you have the most creative freedom with.

RONNY YU, Director, *Freddy vs. Jason*: The only thing different I can sense now is that since *Freddy vs. Jason*, I get to read a lot better scripts. I didn't really believe what people were telling me when I first came to Los Angeles to try and make Hollywood movies—they kept saying, "The only important thing is the box office." But I understand now that is so true. I've had bad experiences and good experiences with my past movies, and the big difference with bad box office is that people don't return your calls. At least, for now, people are returning my calls.

JIM ISAAC, Director, *Jason X*: To tell you the truth, I don't think *Jason X* helped me. In fact, it has been an obstacle in my career that I've had to get over. Since that movie, when I've gone up for other projects, I've had to convince people of a lot of things. They'd say, "We saw *Jason X* and it was fun, but it wasn't scary. It didn't kick our asses. What happened there?" So I would tell the whole story of the problems on that movie, but then reassure them that it wouldn't happen again—that I'm not going to let other people influence my vision, that the producer has to support and fight for the same things I want, and that the movie I am initially pitching is going to be the same one that ends up on the screen. The whole experience of *Jason X* was really difficult for me, for a long time. It is only now, a few years later, that I can really talk about it at all.

TODD FARMER, Screenwriter, *Jason X*: If it were ten years later and I was now your waiter, I'd probably be a little bitter about *Jason X*. But I got lucky. I knew ahead of time that *Jason X* wasn't going to help my career. I just had to get over that as quickly as possible and start writing what I wanted. Then I wrote a spec script that was very well-received and I recreated my career. But nobody called me up and said, "Wow! *Jason X* rocks!" That never happened.

BARRY ZETLIN, Editor, *Part VII*: When people want to see scenes of stuff I've done, I still always include a scene from *The New Blood*. One, I think it was very well cut, and two, I think it's very recognizable and a film that everybody's heard of. I'm proud of it.

CHUCK CAMPBELL, "Tsuarnon," *Jason X*: When you're an actor, people will always ask you what you've done. And I always include *Jason X*, because not only was it fun to make, but everyone knows *Friday the 13th*. Trust me, they don't care if you have played Hamlet, but they sure want to know all about Jason.

ROB HEDDEN, Writer/Director, *Part VIII*: I learned many, many lessons, both personally and professionally, from *Jason Takes Manhattan*. Technically, I was allowed to try all sorts of things, with equipment and style and lighting. I also learned—through mistakes—how to communicate better with people. Actors as well as crew. I'd like to think that I learned from other people who were very talented, and it rubbed off by osmosis in some way. And it inspired me to continue doing what I do. I left that movie and thought, "There are things I'm very proud of in *Part VIII*, and there are things I think I can do even better. So I'm going to keep doing this for a living. I'm going to keep writing, I'm going to keep directing, and I'm not going to ever give up, and see what happens."

I thank *Jason Takes Manhattan*, because that really was a major hurdle for me. It will always be my first movie, and I will always smile when I think about it.

STEVE MIRKOVICH, Editor, *Part VIII*: I have done a few horror movies, and I am not afraid of doing more. It is a fun genre to work in. It is not always the biggest money or the most prestigious, and you are never going to win an Oscar. But nothing is more satisfying than watching the reaction of an audience just expecting to being scared to death. You do not always get those opportunities with conventional love stories or action pictures. There is just something about the electricity that goes through a crowd when they know something is about to happen, and then you get to spring it on them. It's a terrific feeling.

KELLY HU, "Eva," *Part VIII*: You really can't go wrong with doing something like *Friday the 13th* as your first film. It's a fun franchise to be a part of. To this day, I still get people asking me for autographs on things like *Friday the 13th* posters. The fans are really the most important part of doing this—knowing that *Friday the 13th* is one of these cult films that people are going to remember for a very long time. Once you become a part of something like this, you know you'll have fans who will follow your career and always be very supportive. *Friday the 13th* fans stick with you forever.

BARNEY COHEN, Screenwriter, *The Final Chapter*: After *The Final Chapter*, my career could have gone either way. I could have become the great "undiscovered cult drive-in classic writer," or the one that everybody in Hollywood only called to do horror movies. Guess which way it went? I ended up writing nothing but horror scripts for six or seven years. Now I could boo-hoo that, but the truth is I was happy to be working and I'm still happy to be working. You know that great song, "I'm Still Here?" That's my national anthem. Because a lot of us aren't here anymore.

JOAN FREEMAN, "Mrs. Jarvis," *The Final Chapter*: You know what's funny about *Friday the 13th* for me? I've never been recognized for being in that movie, not even once. But I did get a call a few years ago from a friend of mine saying, "Did you know that you're listed on the Internet as having committed suicide?" I guess some person went onto a website with bogus information—there was another Joan Freeman who was an agent at one time, and apparently she did kill herself. So I just want to set the record straight and say that the rumors of my death are greatly exaggerated. No, *Friday the 13th* did not kill me off!

JOSEPH ZITO, Director, *The Final Chapter*: A number of my films have been sequelized and, of course, *The Final Chapter* was a sequel itself. It's a very strange thing as a director, looking at the movies that follow yours. I don't want to send the wrong signal, because it's not that you wish you had made them, it's just that you wish nobody had made them.

Still, I'm flattered by what has happened with *Friday the 13th*. I thought it was sort of cool that the character of Tommy Jarvis got continued, because it was something that I had wanted to do with the story. But I can't say I'm responsible for any of this—it's very hard to feel a proprietary stake in it. It's just that my film worked for some audiences, and that's all I was ever trying to do—make an effective movie. If a byproduct of *The Final Chapter* was that the series has since lived on far beyond my one movie, well, that's great.

COREY FELDMAN, "Tommy Jarvis," *The Final Chapter* & *Part V*: I'm not a big fan of blood and gore. I'm more peaceful than that. But the reason I like the *Friday the 13th* movies is because of the intelligence behind planning them. And none of them try to be too serious about it, but at same time end up being pretty damn good. Of course, that goes up to *Part V*, and after that I refuse to comment.

Of course, the question I get more than anything else is, "Aren't you upset that you didn't get to play you in *Part V*?" Well, I was only a kid, so I couldn't have done it. Then they say, "Well, why don't you do it now?" So I always respond that if I had my druthers, they should do a *Friday the 13th Part 20* and skip over all the middle ones. Just pick up the plotline after *Part V* and have me come back as Tommy Jarvis, and Jason and I have a final confrontation. I think that would be a lot of fun.

JOHN SHEPHERD, "Tommy Jarvis," *Part V*: I look at *Part V* now and I have a few issues with it, but when I decided to do the film I fully committed to it. I didn't look back. As a result, I'm very happy with the work that I did, and the relationships that I kept. This movie gave me an opportunity to take the training that I had, follow my heart and do the best I could. It doesn't matter that some people discount that now. Because rewards will come, even if they are not immediate. For me, *Part V* really did open up a new beginning. In many ways, *Friday the 13th* was a big turning point for me—it took me in totally new directions. And it taught me never to discount the gifts that you are given. That was something I really took away from the whole experience.

DICK WIEAND, "Roy," *Part V*: I had been running away from Jason for a long time. My marriage to my second wife lasted fifteen years, and I didn't even show her the movie until the fourteenth year. But then I realized that, like it or not, I wear the mantle for this part—I might as well embrace it. That's why I started doing the autograph shows and things. I've met some people who are huge fans of these movies, and across all age groups. I'd even say there has been a resurgence in the past few years. Some really diehard fans even come up to me and say, "*Part V* is my favorite in the series, because it's just so freaky, so quirky, so weird." It amazes me that people actually have an affection for this piece of crap.

BILL BUTLER, "Michael," *Part VII*: One thing that is really cool about being in a *Friday the 13th* movie is that, inevitably, every actor in Hollywood has been in one, too. And when you run into each other, it's like there's this weird mind-meld. You just look at each other and go, "Oh, you were one of Jason's victims, too!"

JENSEN DAGGETT, "Rennie," *Part VIII*: I learned so much about life, acting, and being a responsible adult from *Jason Takes Manhattan*. I know that it left me with a desire to work harder, and a love of taking jobs on location. I also learned a lot about teamwork and professionalism. So I am very happy that I took that job.

If nothing else, it has made me a cool aunt to my nieces, who force their friends to watch it at slumber parties. And I am sure that one day my son will be equally impressed. Who knew?

JOHN D. LEMAY, "Steven Freeman," *Jason Goes to Hell*; **"Ryan Dallion,"** *Friday the 13th: The Series*: Whatever else happens in my life, I'll always be remembered as one of the survivors. And I'll always be able to say that I helped kill Jason. Not too many people can say that.

KANE HODDER, "Jason Voorhees," *Part VII*, *Part VIII*, *Jason Goes to Hell* & *Jason X*: *Friday the 13th* has been a tremendous boost to my career, and the best part of my career. It really has. There are lots of side opportunities that have happened because of it. And the thing that will always be in my favor is that I don't believe anyone will play Jason more times than I did. Maybe I'm not the most recent, but I don't anticipate anyone else ever doing more than four movies, if they even go that far. That feels good.

CJ GRAHAM, "Jason Voorhees," *Part VI*: There is probably no horror character in this world right now that is more well-known than Jason. You can walk up to anybody, and they will go, "You played Jason? You've got to be kidding." You have more notoriety playing that part than any horror character you can think of—maybe even Michael Myers, maybe even Freddy Krueger, certainly Leatherface. Trust me—if you say you played one of those parts, they may not know you, the person, but they definitely know who you were in the movie.

JULIETTE CUMMINS, "Robin," *Part V*: My friends tell me that I should be proud I did all these horror films, including *A New Beginning*. Because someone believed in me, and I got to do a few major motion pictures. And you have to start somewhere. So you should always be proud of what you have done.

STEVEN WILLIAMS, "Creighton Duke," *Jason Goes to Hell*: It got me an interview for this book. This is the payoff for *Jason Goes To Hell*.

LARRY ZERNER, "Shelly," *Part 3*: After the movie came out, for a period of about a month, I was somewhat famous. I got my fifteen minutes. And that's something a lot of people never get. I'm grateful—at least I know I had this one thing. Plus the fact that I'm this little tiny piece of movie trivia—I'm the guy who gave Jason his hockey mask—it's an honor! I'm the only non-Jason to wear that mask. So that's cool.

Since then, it has been fun to be famous and then to fade back into obscurity. I'm an attorney now. And in the movie I say, "I'm not an asshole—I'm an actor." Now I get to say, "I'm not an actor—I'm an asshole."

PAULA SHAW, "Mrs. Voorhees," *Freddy vs. Jason*: The late Shelley Winters was a good friend of mine—we were in the Actors' Studio together and we've been close for twenty years. My generation knows her as an Academy Award winner, but kids today know her as Roseanne's grandmother on the *Roseanne* show. Yet I know that

tickles her to death. Now, I'm not trying to compare myself to Shelley, but I've done a lot of far more serious roles than *Freddy vs. Jason*. And we all want recognition, so it's exciting—I never would have thought I would have found a little piece of immortality this way, you know? It's my tiny slice of the pop culture pie. I am now part of a tradition that I had never even thought about.

KARI KEEGAN, "Jessica," *Jason Goes to Hell*: After *Jason Goes to Hell*, I said, "If I never work again, at least I can say I had one moment where I was in the company of great talent." I'll probably never win an Oscar; I'll probably never win an Emmy—and that's okay. I got to do a major movie at least once and it was seen by millions of people. There were some things about the film that weren't so great, but in general I walked away going, "I did something that so many people would kill to do."

"What's the greatest thing about being in *Friday the 13th*? I got to be a first-degree of Kevin Bacon."
Ronn Carroll, "Sgt. Tierney," *Part I*

KYLE LABINE, "Freeburg," *Freddy vs. Jason*: It's really cool knowing that no matter what happens for the rest of my life, I'll always have this. Even if I end up selling shoes, I'll always be a part of this legacy. I also think I've progressed a lot as an actor since *Freddy vs. Jason*. I'm still young, I'm still growing up, and there are changes in your life. So it's nice to have this little reminder—I can always pop in *Freddy vs. Jason* and instantly be reminded of exactly where I was at that time.

CHRISTOPHER MARQUETTE, "Linderman," *Freddy vs. Jason*: I never thought about *Freddy vs. Jason* only as a good part for my career—I thought it would be an amazing experience to be a part of something so big. And it didn't even hit me until about halfway through the movie—"Wow, I'm actually making *Freddy vs. Jason*!"

It's definitely great. It's definitely something that in thirty years, no matter how many movies or amazing things I hope I get to do, I'll look back on it and be so happy I was a part of it. Maybe I'll always be "Chris Marquette from *Freddy vs. Jason*," but that's still terrific. There are a million other films that could be judged as being better than *Freddy vs. Jason*, but these movies will always be a part of our culture. *Friday the 13th* will always be a standout on your resume.

KELLY ROWLAND, "Kia," *Freddy vs. Jason*: When you're doing music, you have to do tours. You have to go from one side of the world to another, all the time. But with movies, you film in one place for a good stretch. I never felt more settled than on the set of *Freddy vs. Jason*—it really made me feel like I had some stability. I love my music, of course, but being part of this film was really cool. I wish I could actually start over and just have the experience all over again. I was very lucky to have worked with such incredible people. I was very blessed.

KEN KIRZINGER, "Jason Voorhees," *Freddy vs. Jason*: I'm certain playing Jason will affect my life, but I don't know if it'll change it all that much. It's been fun to be Jason for a while, and already I do get to travel more. And if we do another one—great. But I'm sure they'll be making *Friday the 13th* movies long after I'm out of the business. The next guy will come along and put on the suit and my turn will be over. So I'll be happy if I can just stretch my fifteen minutes out as long as I can.

Top row, left: On January 21, 2005, actor Steve Susskind (right) suffered fatal injuries in an automobile accident in Mission Viejo, California. He was sixty-three years old. Although best known to *Friday* fans for his portrayal of Harold in *Part 3*, Susskind had appeared in over thirty motion pictures. The actor was eulogized by family and friends in a special retrospective of his work in the month following his untimely death. He also appeared at a special anniversary screening of *Part 3* at the Nuart Theater in Los Angeles on August 12, 2003 (pictured, with co-star Richard Brooker.) "Steve loved the fact that *Friday* fans were interested in his funny character Harold," said the actor's stepdaughter, Lauren Walker. "And I know he had a great time at the Nuart screening. It was a great night. Steve is and will always be missed by his family, friends and as we have discovered, his *13th* fans."

Over the course of a weekend beginning Friday, May 13, 2005, Necrocomicon held the "Friday the 13th 25th Anniversary Celebration" in Hollywood, California. The event reunited cast and crew from all eleven *Friday* films. Clockwise from top row, right: *Friday the 13th*'s Sean Cunningham (from left), Ari Lehman, Betsy Palmer and Ron Mlllkie; *Part 2*'s Amy Steel and John Furey; Kevin Spirtas and Lar Park Lincoln from *The New Blood*; Larry Zerner (left) and David Katims from *Part 3*; and *Friday the 13th*'s Palmer, composer Harry Manfredini and Adrienne King.

On January 13, 2004, New Line Cinema held a special event at the Hollywood Wax Museum in Hollywood, California, to celebrate the DVD release of *Freddy vs. Jason*. The museum unveiled wax statues of both characters, with stars Robert Englund (left) and Ken Kirzinger on hand for the induction ceremony. Among the many other festivities was a Jason and Freddy "Best Look-a-Like" contest, judged by Englund, Kirzinger and co-star Jason Ritter. The *Freddy vs. Jason* DVD would go on to sell over 2.5 million copies in the United States.

"My fear now is that New Line is going to option *Child's Play*. It's going to be Freddy vs. Chucky, and that little sucker is going to be kicking me in the shins." Robert Englund

MONICA KEENA, "Lori," *Freddy vs. Jason*: I never worried about the "Friday the 13th Curse" until this interview. Especially these days, because people are peppering their careers with all types of movies. There are actors who were in *Scream* who are doing wonderful, dramatic independent movies right now. I don't think *Friday the 13th* can really hurt you. I don't think any project can make or break your career. You will probably get typecast if you choose to only do horror movies, but most actors wouldn't do that.

JESSE HUTCH, "Trey," *Freddy vs. Jason*: In *A Nightmare on Elm Street*, Johnny Depp was killed in bed. And in *Freddy vs. Jason*, I was killed in bed. And after the movie came out, I actually saw a little write-up that said, "Jesse Hutch ends up dead in a bed—just like Johnny Depp!" It was such an honor just to see my name in print next to his. I think that's what all of us hope for when we do one of these movies. That not only is it another job, and another chance to keep on moving up and doing bigger and better things, but that we'll end up being the next Johnny Depp.

LAUREN-MARIE TAYLOR, "Vickie," *Part 2*: These types of movies are your training ground as an actor, because it's not like you get a gazillion-dollar budget. Yes, culturally they've become significant, but they really are very small movies. You really do

get to learn the ABC's of everything—of camera angles, of lighting and sound, and just how large your facial expressions can look up there on the big screen. *Friday the 13th* really does teach you about the fine workings of filmmaking.

AMY STEEL, "Ginny Field," *Part 2*: The only advice I could ever give is to just enjoy every minute, because all of a sudden it will be gone. When I started, I was living on a day-to-day basis, just going, "Oh my God! I'm making money! This is great!" And I just thought it would continue. Hollywood is really fun when you're young, and you're successful and things are happening. But as you get older, you get in the very compromising position of no longer being young and beautiful. Now I do voiceovers. I love it—you don't even have to put makeup on. I also went back to school and got my BA. So I don't regret anything—I had the best time. I'm looking back now in hindsight, and I have a great view from here.

DEBISUE VOORHEES, "Tina," *Part V*: I stopped acting in my early twenties. I was going to auditions, and I started to see all these women in their forties who were showing up for the same roles I was. They'd had breast jobs, were wearing too much makeup, and would put baby oil all over themselves and glitter in their hair. I just thought, "I don't want to be that woman. I don't want to be so afraid of not getting the next part that I'm cutting up my body." You can't stop aging. It's a reality. So I came home, went back to college and graduated with a Journalism degree in the top ten percent of my class. I'm really proud of that. And I've been working now in Texas for ten years as an entertainment journalist.

I look back on *Friday the 13th* with fondness. Even when I did *Part V*, I knew I wasn't doing a serious film. Was I entertained by it? Yes, because I knew the people and kind of laughed at it. Personally, I don't think it was a great film or anything. And I'm not sure I understand the popularity of *Friday the 13th*. But it is kind of neat that so many people do really enjoy them. What I take the most pleasure from now is talking to the fans. You don't know how sweet some of them are—they'll write me these letters and send a picture for me to sign. Some of them even say, "Oh, you're such a big movie star!" I'm like, "Well, not exactly." But to them, I am. It's just so cute.

ROBBI MORGAN, "Annie," *Part 1*: Sometimes when you're part of a project, you do it and then you're kind of done. Especially a movie—by the time it's finished and out you're already onto something else. For me, I didn't realize what was happening with *Friday the 13th* until my brother called right after it came out to say, "Robbi—this movie is huge!" It was fantastic. And still, to this day, I get recognized on the street—which is shocking, because it was so long ago and my part was so small. But I'm absolutely thrilled to have been a part of it. It was a blast.

ADRIENNE KING, "Alice," *Part 1* & *Part 2*: Unfortunately, I got a little bonus out of *Friday the 13th* that took away a little bit of the fun. Shortly after the movie came out, I had a stalker—and this was before the issue had really come into the public's consciousness. It was very difficult. It lasted for about a year and a half. Eventually it got violent. It ended with the person being incarcerated, although they have since gotten out.

It took me a very long time to cope with the whole experience, and it completely changed the course of my career. After *Friday the 13th*, I did do my little cameo in *Part 2*. Then I went to the Royal Academy in London and I studied there—kind of to redeem myself. And I was very happy because they only accept a couple dozen Americans into that program. But by 1984, I wasn't really acting anymore. I certainly didn't want to go on and become a "scream queen." I honed my craft and everything, but I wasn't secure enough to come back from the Academy and deal with a possible repeat of the whole stalker experience.

But there's nothing I can look back on and say, "I wish I didn't do that." The actual experience of making the movie was wonderful. And its success, for me, was just the most amazing thing—it was the highlight of my career. I look back at *Friday the 13th* with nothing but a smile.

JUDIE ARONSON, "Sam," *The Final Chapter*: Always read your scripts before you accept the part. Never accept any part that takes place in water for long periods of time—I'd make sure to put that in the contract now. Seriously, that is what I definitely got from *Friday the 13th*. And that it was my first movie, it was a lot of fun, and I worked with a group of really nice people.

BETSY PALMER, "Mrs. Voorhees," *Part 1* & *Part 2*: I once told my daughter, "Tell me the truth, are you ashamed that your mother did *Friday the 13th*?" And she said, "Not at all—now I don't have to tell my friends who you are anymore." The funny thing is, I did poo-poo it for a long time. I wasn't sure if I wanted anyone to know. But I've since accepted it. It's actually become fun now. It's like a badge of honor. I'm the Queen of the Slashers!

TIFFANY HELM, "Violet," *Part V*: I think one of the biggest thrills in my professional life was a couple of years after I did *Part V*. I was working for designer Stephen Sprouse and I got the opportunity to meet Iggy Pop. I was totally tongue tied. But instead of me having to embarrass myself, he just said, "Wow! You were in a *Friday the 13th*!? How cool!" I was totally shocked. So I am quite proud to have been a part of nostalgic Americana camp.

VINCENT GUASTAFERRO, "Deputy Rick Cologne," *Part VI*: I still have people who write to me and ask for autographs. It's bizarre. I mean, if you saw this movie in theaters you have to be forty years old by now. But I don't care. I'll always respond and send a signed picture.

I also have two teenage sons now, and their friends come over and want to watch retro horror movies. Then they find out I was in *Jason Lives* and they're like, "Oh my God—your dad was in a *Friday the 13th* movie?" They think I'm the coolest guy alive.

SHAVAR ROSS, "Reggie," *Part V*: This thing is still popular. I get emails from people all over the world who love it, which is amazing because *Part V* wasn't a big blockbuster. Yet I still have people recognize me on the street. They say, "Dude, man, I remember you! You're Reggie the Reckless!" Then there are people who review the films and send out questionnaires. Or send me lots of drawings they have done of me. Don't ask me why. It's just really weird!

TED WHITE, "Jason Voorhees," *The Final Chapter*: Right after I finished *The Final Chapter*, I went on to do *Starman* with Jeff Bridges. I played the hunter at the roadside diner who gets in a fight with him. And we were down in Mississippi late one night, and the local newspapers were interviewing Jeff. Then the director called him off to do a shot, so Jeff said, "Talk to Ted, he just finished a show." And they turned to me and asked, "What did you do, Ted?" I said, "Oh, I did a little nothing picture." And they went, "Well what was the name of it?" And I said, "*Friday the 13th*. I was Jason."

Well, the next night we came out to finish shooting, and they must have put that in the paper because all of a sudden there are tons of cars just jammed all around the location. Jeff said, "Jesus Christ! You're going to have a sore hand before the night's over with, buddy." Because there were all these kids, just lined up to come and get my autograph. I had no idea when I did the role how many young people loved *Friday the 13th*, and that they were even allowed to watch something like that.

RICHARD BROOKER, "Jason Voorhees," *Part 3*: I get fan mail all the time, and sometimes I even get stopped for an autograph, which is weird, since you never even saw my real face in the movie. And one time I was introduced to this girl in a bar as "the guy who played Jason," and all she asked was, "Do you sleep with a hatchet in your bed?"

DANA KIMMELL, "Chris," *Part 3*: Supposedly, when I killed Jason, that was going to be it. We never dreamed it would go on and on and on. We had no idea it would still have this following. I'm just amazed that, after all this time, people are still so involved and watching these movies.

MARK NELSON, "Ned," *Part 1*: I discovered I have a big fan base of thirteen-year-old boys. They still rent *Friday the 13th* and watch it on TV. One time, a boy of maybe twelve stopped me on the street near Times Square. He said, "Hey man, you're Ned! I'm so excited! Can you come with me and meet my mom?" It seemed to mean a lot to him, and it was fun to see how excited he was, so I said sure. We went down to this hot dog place in Times Square and behind the counter is this woman. The boy runs up to her and says, "Mom,

mom, look who I found! It's Ned! The actor from *Friday the 13th*!" Her smile faded from her face and she just said, "Oh, you should be ashamed of yourself! How could you do a movie like *that*?"

TONY TIMPONE, Editor-in-Chief, *Fangoria Magazine*: I'm always amazed by the appeal of slasher films. They're very simplistic and very basic. You don't have the deepest characters or the most intricate plotting or motivation or anything, but the fans seem to be the most loyal out of any in the horror genre. They want Freddy. They want Jason. They want Leatherface. It's amazing. They just satisfy some sort of primal bloodlust in these young people. They have a hard day at work, then go home and pop in a DVD of a *Friday the 13th* film and get out a lot of their aggressions and hostilities, all without lifting a finger.

Personally, I don't have a real fondness for slasher films, but as the editor of *Fangoria* they are my bread and butter. I have to give the fans what they want. We have been covering *Friday the 13th* from the beginning and we are always trying to find new angles to publicize and promote the movies. Because our readers really love these movies, they grew up with them, have always supported them and enjoy reading about them. So we are always having fun trying to find new angles to profile these films, and it's never wasted space.

PAUL KRATKA, "Paul," *Part 3*: What really amazes me is that not a week goes by that I don't get an email from somebody about *Friday the 13th*. And this really has only been in the last couple of years. It's like there is this intense following that goes on, like a cult-like fanaticism. I think many of them came of age during the 1980s and they've kept up with *Friday the 13th*, for whatever reason, and now with the Internet, they can track down and share their interests. And thanks to the DVD box set, there is this whole thing with teenagers discovering it—it just cracks me up.

What's really surprising to me is that most of the emails I'm getting now are from gay men. There's this following among them for these movies. I don't know what to make of it. And some of them are very blatant, like, "You were my first crush." Then some are a little more hidden in their wording. But it's the most unusual phenomenon.

JEFFREY SCHWARZ, Documentarian: When *Friday the 13th* was coming out on DVD overseas, Warner called me to do a documentary on it—I did the *Jason X* DVD and a lot of other horror titles. I thought it was an honor and I didn't want to fuck it up. I think most producers feel the same way when approached to work on something they love and that has influenced them.

I can connect it to when I was a fourteen-year-old obsessed with these movies. When I was a kid, all I wanted to do when I got home was go to my room and watch horror movies. I had pen pals who were also rejects, for lack of a better word. The fact that you can be a reject and kind of revel in it is very significant for kids. Not just *Friday the 13th*, but all horror movies.

I wouldn't have been able to say this then, but I can say it now: I think seeing these well-developed, healthy teenagers having sex and then being punished for it by an outsider who was not accepted by them—there's something very powerful about that image. Especially to someone who himself feels like they are on the fringes or feels rejected. Personally, it really enabled me to gain some strength in being an outsider. And that outsider status then prepared me for a gay outsider status as well—it was the first step in realizing that I wasn't like everyone else. Because these films' female heroines could function within the popular-girl hetero world, but they're not going to ever really be a part of it, they're always going to be outsiders. They're tomboyish. And with Jason, there was always a sense that he

was just really jealous of them, too. There was a rage there. It runs deep. That's just high-falootin' bullshit, but that's what I think now.

DANIEL FARRANDS, Screenwriter, *Halloween 6*: When I was fourteen years old I was just obsessed with *Friday the 13th* and *Halloween*. I spent an entire summer writing a *Friday the 13th* script which I was absolutely convinced I was going to sell to Paramount. Being the "professional" that I was, I sent a query letter to Frank Mancuso, Jr. pitching him my story and basically telling him why my script would make the best *Friday the 13th* ever. Astoundingly, I received a reply from him a couple of weeks later. I couldn't believe it! In his letter, Frank said that although he was currently in production with *The Final Chapter*, he was so impressed with my letter that it was the first time he'd ever taken time out to respond to anyone regarding the series. He encouraged me to keep writing and welcomed me to the motion picture industry.

For me, a kid from Santa Rosa, California who could only dream of writing movies, especially horror movies, his acknowledgment was like a blessing from the Pope. I still keep the letter framed in my office—but I always have a laugh when I read the part that says, "With it will come the end of the series and of Jason." Twenty years later, I'm still waiting for him to buy my script!

"I don't know...where's the shame in *Friday the 13th*?"
Randolph Cheveldave, Producer, *Part VIII*

DARYL HANEY, Screenwriter, *Part VII*: I had never looked up anything on the Internet about *Friday the 13th* before, but then one day I was just kind of curious so I logged on. I was really blown away by how many sites there were. I went to one of the message boards and it was all these really young teen and pre-teen kids. They were all flirting on the board. They'd be writing to each other about these personal problems in their lives: "I think I'm going to kill myself! My dad has grounded me for the next two months!" And they were naming themselves things like "Jason's Right Hand." It was kind of touching, actually.

I think Jason's appeal to all these kids has something to do with sexual awakening and hormonal hysteria. About facing up to adult responsibility for the first time, and all the fears that go with that. That is a universal part of the human experience. Movies like *Friday the 13th* will always be there for that time in your life when you need something like that to help get you through it.

KERRY NOONAN, "Paula," *Part VI*: Maniacs who come and kill teenagers in parked cars have been a staple of urban legends since the 1950s. And those are morality tales, too, because if they hadn't been making out, they wouldn't be in danger. I don't think *Friday the 13th* itself was ever an urban legend, but it certainly has created its own mythology and story that people recognize. People now say about a cliché or a convention in a movie, "Oh, that's like a *Friday the 13th*." I think the original blueprint of the movies incorporated certain motifs and themes in a powerful way, and they're still obviously speaking to people.

I think what the franchises that have been the most successful—*Halloween*, *Friday the 13th* and *A Nightmare on Elm Street*—have in common is a really scary killer that people find *just* plausible enough. They're not really believable, but people find them scary because we are of the generation who grew up knowing of faceless men who would kill you just as soon as they look at you. My mother always said, "Don't take candy from strangers!" These kinds of fears of serial killers were very much part of the collective consciousness of the time that created the *Friday the 13th* movies. I know that's what affected me as a kid. That was what I was afraid of. And that fear has not gone away, because it seems we have more people like that than ever before.

TOM McLOUGHLIN, Writer/Director, *Part VI*: I'll tell you two different sides of the coin about doing a *Friday the 13th* movie.

A number of years after I did *Jason Lives*, I was watching an HBO special about teens who kill. They had this boy on there who was about 14. They asked, "Why did you kill your friend's mom? What could have possibly been going through your head?" And he said, "Jason, man. I was thinking like Jason." It really affected me—could a movie like this truly influence somebody?

The other side of the coin was that I was once directing a play up in San Francisco, an all-out comedy. One night, after a performance, somebody was waiting for me, this very professorial guy. He says, "Are you the director?" I said, "Yeah." He says, "I noticed on your credits that you did one of the *Friday the 13th* movies." And I immediately started making excuses. "You know—it was a fun thing, blah blah blah." And he said, "I didn't see the movie, but I just wanted to thank you." I was stunned for a second, and then I asked, "Why?" He says, "Well, I'm a psychologist and we have a clinic up here in San Francisco where we work with disturbed kids. We have them put on these Jason masks and they take out their aggressions on stuffed dummies. By not being themselves and venting what they feel through this character, we've had a lot of wonderful breakthroughs. I just wanted to thank whoever is responsible for this."

Boy, was that something I didn't expect to hear. I was just so blown away that somebody of authority and experience thought *Friday the 13th* was a positive thing.

JOHN CARL BUECHLER, Director, *Part VII*: My argument has always been that what we do isn't new. You can go to any church across the world and see an effigy of a man nailed to a cross with a wound in his abdomen and a crown of thorns stuffed into his forehead. There is tremendous impact in creating visions of visceral horror, and you do it for that reason. The impact of images have sustained entire sects of religions for centuries. So to limit the artist is a false thing. Because if you legislate our ability to tell stories and take that away from us, then someone in another country, someone in the marketplace, is going to use those tools anyway.

We are artists who use this medium to tell stories, and even though they may be over-the-top, the horror film is the first true story—of the hunter who went out after the wolf. It was fraught with danger and anticipation. He struggled, he may have been wounded, but he won. Then he gathered the other hunters around the fire and told the story. It's not a bad thing to tell people a tale of horror.

When you talk about the *Friday the 13th* movies, when you talk about *A Nightmare on Elm Street* movies, or *Halloween* movies, or Frankenstein, or Dracula—they have all become icons. Think about it: after *Jason Takes Manhattan*, they stopped making *Friday the 13th* movies—they became "Jason" movies. *Friday the 13th* is not even in the title anymore. And people dismiss these movies out of hand because they are just little low-budget horror movies. But you know what? These are going to be the classics for a new generation, and they will live forever just because there are so many of them. I think that the *Friday the 13th* movies are a piece of history, and I am proud to have been a part of it.

GREG NICTOERO, Makeup Effects Supervisor, *Jason Goes to Hell*: It always intrigues me that so many people had such a backlash towards these movies, and have always stood by their guns that violence in cinema instills violence in its audience. I never believed that adage. Because if that was true, why wouldn't the converse be the same? Couldn't we show Disney movies to a bunch of convicts and rehabilitate them?

DARCY DEMOSS, "Nikki," *Part VI*: I think the people who rent those kinds of movies are responsible for themselves, and if that's what is their entertainment, so be it. Who am I to stop anybody from freedom of choice? I don't really have any concerns. I enjoy what I do, I'm very blessed, and people seem to like the films, so why not? Go with it.

BRUCE GREEN, Editor, *Part V* & *Part VI*: What's interesting about the whole backlash against *Friday the 13th* is that these movies should actually be embraced by Christian Fundamentalists. The formula is: teenage couple has sex, teenage couple dies. They should be shown in every church in the Midwest.

Above: Jason Voorhees continued to make headlines when, on December 22, 1989, one of the original hockey masks he wore in *Friday the 13th Part VI: Jason Lives* was stolen from the front porch of famous shock filmmaker John Waters. Waters, the director of such "trash classics" as *Pink Flamingos* and *Hairspray*, received the mask from *Friday* producer Frank Mancuso, Jr., and it was intended as a Christmas gift for Waters' longtime friend Dennis Dermody (left, with Waters). After a few fretful days, Waters eventually received a call from the police department that had retrieved the mask from a nearby mailbox. "I think it was a prank thing," says Waters, who listed the value of the mask as "Priceless" on the original police report. "There was a frat house next door to me, and when the story got in the papers, they must have freaked out. So they slipped it in a mailbox and anonymously called the cops. But there had been a rash of letter bombs at the time, so the police had to dismantle the whole mailbox just to get the mask out." For Dermody, an avid fan of *Friday the 13th* and a noted social commentator who has written numerous articles on the series for such magazines as *Paper* and *Interview*, Waters' gift was a dream come true. "Immediately after we got the call, John and I drove all the way down to the police station," says Dermody. "I sang, '*Ki, ki, ki, Ma, ma, ma*' the whole way. Then when we got there, the cops were all waiting for us because they were so excited. I pulled the mask out of the box, held it up high and they all cheered!"

Mr. John Waters
Your mask is at
Northern District. The
Number is 396-2455.
OFF. Plater
&
OFF. Day

Seriously, there's no violence against women in *Friday the 13th*. There is only violence against teenagers. There is not a specific misogyny. You don't watch those movies and say, "That director and that writer hate women." Frank Mancuso, Jr. told me that the purpose of these movies is this: opening weekend, teenage boys want to see them on their own. Then the second weekend, they bring their girlfriends, so they can be macho and not jump out of their seats. But the girlfriends will scream, jump into the guys' arms and then they can cop a feel. As a guy, I think that's fine. Although ask a teenage girl and see what she thinks.

"*Friday the 13th* is sort of like McDonalds now, isn't it?"

Betsy Palmer

PETRU POPESCU, Screenwriter, *Part 3*: If you like horror, you're very young at heart—even a child. People who are older never liked horror movies, anyway. It's not realistic, for one, but it's not good for the psyche. They'd say, "Why would I waste nine dollars and two hours on something I'm trying to shut out of my psyche?" Because if you start to have a lot of internalized experiences with death, like an adult will—you start losing loved ones, and you come to accept your own mortality—you are no longer curious, while a kid is always curious. That's why Jason continues to appeal to these new generations, and will probably keep on going and going.

STEVE MINER, Director, *Part 2* & *Part 3*: Younger people tend to understand that genre films are meant as a piece of entertainment, in a nightmarish sort of way, but in a fun sense. But then there are older people, including some critics, who don't understand that concept and never will. A perfect case in point is a scene I did for *Friday the 13th Part 3*, this terribly silly scene where Jason takes a guy and squeezes his head together hard enough so his eyeballs pop out. I can't imagine that anybody has been inspired to go out and squish somebody's head until their eyeballs pop out. I'd like someone to tell me this and I'll never do a violent scene again.

BONNIE HELLMAN, "Hitchhiker," *The Final Chapter*: I was teaching pre-teen kids right after I did *The Final Chapter*. And they loved to play make-believe—every single thing we did had to have Godzilla and the Grim Reaper in it. So they're already aware of death. And *Friday the 13th* is played out in an entertaining, non-realistic way. Jason's a monster. He's not a real person. Look at the old Frankenstein movies—they're meant to make you scream and throw your popcorn in the air and have a good time. It's like being on a rollercoaster.

JERRY PAVLON, "Jake," *Part V*: I am actually now a fourth grade school teacher at a private school on the upper west side in New York. And recently, one of my students had surfed the Web and hit the jackpot. He came into class one day and said, "Mr. Pavlon, I understand you were in *Friday the 13th*." And of course, upon hearing this, my entire class went berserk. Every single one of them freaked out in excitement. They asked a thousand questions. That is something of a testament to *Friday the 13th*. And tells you a lot about their success in this culture, I guess.

DAVID KAGEN, "Sheriff Garris," *Part VI*: Kids feel weak in our society. They're in an adult world and they don't know the rules and they don't have control. So maybe to some extent, by identifying with superheroes or supervillains like Jason, they're responding to the idea of power. All the unpredictableness in these movies mirrors that loss of control, but then there is that relief when it finally works out in the end. When the teen hero finally prevails through all the madness, there's a sense for the audience that, "I too can prevail."

DOMINICK BRASCIA, "Joey," *Part V*: I have friends that work at video stores, and they tell me that every year on a Friday the 13th, and on Halloween, that their *Friday the 13th* videos are all gone. The shelves are empty. People have little marathons. So I'm actually happier to have been involved with a *Friday the 13th* than if I had been in some movie that was really big for a few months and then just disappeared. It's exciting to be involved with a phenomenon that constantly rejuvenates itself.

CAREY MORE, "Terri," *The Final Chapter*: Why are people still interested in *Friday the 13th*? Is it symbolic of a certain period of life? Or just a cult phenomenon? I can't think of a thing. What is funny for a lot of us who were in these movies is that you just have a laugh about it now. It was never anything more serious than that. I haven't taken anything of *Friday the 13th* with me in my life since then. I'm certainly happy I did it, but it just means a lot more to other people than it ever meant to me. So it's really just flattering that all these kids say such nice things about me, and they're complete strangers! I really can't understand why, but it's great.

LAR PARK LINCOLN, "Tina," *Part VII*: I think *Friday the 13th* works in the same way that soap operas work—we crave a story that continues. You find a show that you love, then you follow it, it restarts the next year, and eventually it ends. Then

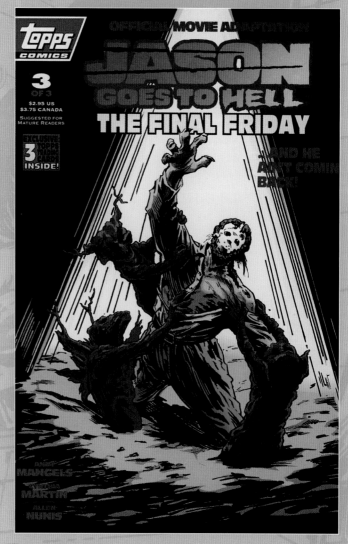

eventually it comes back for the reunion special. And wouldn't it be neat if we could see where our lives are going to go, like it was an episodic television show?

ETHAN WILEY, Song Composer, *Jason X*: I think *Friday the 13th* came along at the right time, when the horror genre needed to be brought back to its most elemental aspects. From Vincent Price and Boris Karloff onward, horror has always had a very theatrical and fantastical side to it. But *Friday the 13th* and Jason, similar to *Halloween* and Michael Myers, stripped that all away and became about cold, stark evil with no apologies. I think they pulled people back to that primal fear of the bogeyman, of that fear of that thing in the dark that is relentless, that you can't reason with. Back in the old days, maybe you could reason with Boris Karloff or Vincent Price. But you can't reason with Jason.

NOEL CUNNINGHAM, Producer, *Jason X*: I have a theory. I think one of the big allures of *Friday the 13th* was because it came at a time before HBO, before Showtime. It was the only place you could see really cool gore. The *Porky's* movies capitalized on this, too. You could see tits and sexually explicit material, and you didn't have to go to the Pussycat to see a Marilyn Chambers movie. But once you could turn on "Cinemax After Dark" and see softcore porn in the comfort of your own home, then all of a sudden the appeal is gone. Now you can click on the computer and see whatever the fuck you want. But in the early days, you didn't have that kind of access. I think that is why the kids of 1980 found *Friday the 13th* exciting and titillating, and the kids of 2005 probably find it boring.

JON KRAHOUSE, Director of Photography, *Part VI*: I think digital technology is a wonderful tool, but an awful lot of kids today don't understand the visual grammar and storytelling methodologies that have come before. I think the heyday of *Friday the 13th* was the end of the era of the practical, onscreen magic trick because, sadly, that's not what sells tickets anymore. Although I will say that I think the success of movies like *The Sixth Sense* and *The Others* is heartening. It shows people have brains and the patience to enjoy a good story, and that if you make a movie that respects the audience, they will still turn out. At least, that is my hope.

FRANK MANCUSO, SR., Former President of Production, Paramount Pictures: I believe the success of the *Friday the 13th* films was, in part, representative of a communal moviegoing experience. One that, today, is in danger of disappearing. Because kids used to be the first ones to the theater on a Friday night to see something new and different. They would be the ones to establish it, bring it home and talk about it, which then created this kind of widening of the market: "Boy, I just saw this movie, it's amazing! You have to see it!" That would then attract people who might not normally come, because even a great review isn't enough.

I believe retaining this experience is of primary importance to the future of the motion picture industry. Movies have to create something that delivers an emotional resonance, and that needs to be experienced communally. That reaction was a large part of the success of *Friday the 13th*. And we shouldn't allow that to be lost. It's Americana.

CYRUS VORIS, Screenwriter, *Freddy vs. Jason*: It's not about the initial movie anymore, or the franchise. It's about the iconographic characters. I think *Freddy vs. Jason* was such a hit with young teens because it answered that question you always had since you were a kid: who's stronger? It's like *King Kong vs. Godzilla*. And it's purely a twelve-year-old mentality that wants to see that kind of stuff.

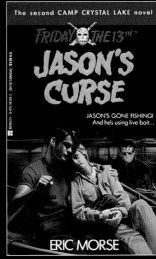

The marketing of a masked maniac. The roster of officially licensed *Friday the 13th* products now numbers in the hundreds. Comic books (**opposite**), trading cards, lunchboxes, T-shirts, model kits, even toy machetes ("Ages 6 and Up") are just a few of the items that have transformed Jason Voorhees from a symbol of pure evil into a highly marketable commodity. Jason may not be exactly family friendly, but he has certainly become as recognizable in American pop culture as Darth Vader, James Bond and Indiana Jones.

In 1993 and '94, Berkley Books published four original *Friday the 13th* young adult novels (**above**) by William Pattison (under the pseudonym Eric Morse). While copies of these long out-of-print books remain hotly sought-after collector's items among *Friday* fans, the author takes umbrage with the publisher's perceived lack of support for his Jason quadrilogy. "I thought I was going to be going to horror conventions and doing book signings," complains Pattison. "Hell, I even thought there was going to be another series of four books."

Years later, Pattison's enthusiasm for the series was rekindled after visiting a fan website which featured a section on his young adult books. "I was overwhelmed. For the next eight months I was inundated with emails from fans who were looking for my books. Eventually, these emails inspired me to start 'The Official Bring Back the *Friday the 13th* Young Adult Novels Series Campaign.' I started this campaign to convince Berkley Books and New Line Cinema to either reprint the young adult novels or start a new series of books based on *Friday the 13th*." In 2005, Pattison got his wish—sort of—when a brand-new series of young adult *Friday* books was published by Black Flame.

While the *Friday the 13th* franchise has generated millions of dollars in revenue for its investors and parent studios, the majority of the actors who worked on the films did so for Screen Actors Guild minimum scale. Subsequently, cast members share in only a small portion of the profits by way of yearly union residuals. "I call it my blood money," laughs *The Final Chapter*'s Barbara Howard. "I'm just amazed, because the *Friday* films still show up regularly on TV, especially around Halloween. Most of the checks I get now are pretty small, but it is still a nice little bonus to get every year."

"I remember being humbled by my *Friday* experience," says Howard's *Final Chapter* co-star Kimberly Beck. "Because it was a lot of hard work, and there wasn't an incredible amount of money to be made. It was union scale plus ten percent for my agent. I even tried to get more money from the producers, and they just laughed."

Yet scale wages and meager residuals seem like a bonanza to the cast of the original *Friday the 13th*. "Everyone thinks all of us actors have been making tons of money off of *Friday*, but that's not true at all," sighs actress Betsy Palmer. "My residuals over two-odd decades have been about $35 a year, and even that stopped coming a few years ago."

"Everyone who was in the first film—we don't get any video residuals at all," says actress Adrienne King (**above**, in a 1979 head shot). "Because the original film was made before the new SAG rules came into effect in 1980, which finally granted actors participation in home video profits. Now at least I get residuals from the second and the fourth film, but only because they used clips of me from the first one."

Background: Adrienne King's original SAG contract for *Friday the 13th*. Her pay rate? $785.00 a week.

DAVID J. SCHOW, Screenwriter, *Freddy vs. Jason*: I think the "Vs." movie is the last refuge of the horror franchise. After the self-referential comedy, it's the team-ups. And I think the immediate response to the success of *Freddy vs. Jason* is a rematch.

Look at what happened to the Universal monster movies in the 1940s. First thing they did after putting Frankenstein and the Wolf Man together was to say, "Well, if two were good, then five will be even better!" And here's where it will go: Freddy and Jason will team up for a rematch. Then we'll see a movie with more than the two of them—Michael Myers or somebody. Then they'll make it a "Vs." comedy. And it will be delirious. It will be Freddy and Michael and Jason and Chucky, along with Chris Rock and Jackie Chan—there's no extreme to which they won't push a property if they can get some more mileage out of it. Finally, they'll just go back and remake the first movie and start all over again

MARK VERHEIDEN, Screenwriter, *Freddy vs. Jason*: I was never quite sure why people would put down the concept of the "Vs." movie, whether it be *Freddy vs. Jason* or *Alien vs. Predator*, as being an inherently uncool idea. It all really just goes back to the comic book, and comic books are always somebody versus somebody. And that's just a really fun concept, so why have a problem with it?

It's funny, fans can treat these characters like untouchable icons that have some sort of mythic value we need to protect. And it's like, I'm sorry—these are 1980s horror movie characters, and we should just have as much fun with them as possible.

ETHAN REIFF, Screenwriter, *Freddy vs. Jason*: Going "back to basics" is fiction. You can't go back home again. You have to accept the reality with these franchises that we're now operating in a different context. James Bond can't fight Al Qaeda the way he fought Dr. No. And you can't say, "I'm gonna terrify people with this poor kid at a camp." You're just not going to be able to do that anymore if you're making a sequel to *Friday the 13th*.

So I say to just go and embrace the fantastic. Go with the fact that this is now a big professional wrestling match and try to pump it up for all that it's worth. There's probably more legitimate creative potential to that approach than to have the arrogance to put blinders on and think you can go back to the primordial soup origins of these franchises.

LARRY B. WILLIAMS, Co-Creator, *Friday the 13th: The Series*: I created *Friday the 13th: The Series* knowing that if you make evil all-powerful, then you yourself are creating a negative psychology. You are saying, "There's no reason to fight evil, guys. You might as well give up. No matter how many times you kill it, it will always come back." But I think I would have trouble selling *The Series*, or any horror script today, because now we're only concerned about how many special effects you can squeeze into a movie, and that's not my game.

Sure, *Freddy vs. Jason* was a big hit, but would it have been an even bigger one had the audience been delivered something different? I believe that, as filmmakers, we are turning up the gore and the action and eliminating the myth. But it's through myth and character that we create true fear. If you think about it, if you want to build genuine fear, you have to work with a myth that people understand. People have to feel what's at stake. If the villain involved cannot be defeated, and if the people can't be saved, there's no reason to watch because everybody's going to die anyway. But if you create a mythology and characters that you care about, you can create a film that's truly resonant.

MARK SWIFT, Co-Screenwriter, *Freddy vs. Jason*: I think my greatest satisfaction with *Freddy vs. Jason* is that Damian and I rescued it from development hell. I don't know if it ever would have been made otherwise. It was really at the point where it was on death's door. So I take the most amount of pride in the fact we at least got it out there, in some form.

It's just funny to be sitting and talking about this film today. Between then and now there were a hundred meetings, and Damian and I had to struggle. We fought every fight. In the end, it got to the point where we kind of went our separate ways from the project. But I don't want to go through the rest of my life saying, "Well, in the screenplay we did this or that!" At some point, you have to let that stuff go. The screenplay we wrote is different than the movie. I think our script is good in its own right, and so is the movie. I'm just truly and honestly happy that so many fans enjoyed the movie they had been waiting so long for.

If I learned anything from *Friday the 13th*, it is that you have to fight for what you believe in. Making a movie is not a sprint, it's a marathon. And if you are going to see it through to the end, you have to go through it all: the changes, the disappointments and the frustrations, as well as the exuberance and the glee.

DAMIAN SHANNON, Co-Screenwriter, *Freddy vs. Jason***:** I think Mark and I have done all we can with *Freddy vs. Jason*. Someone who hasn't gone through it is going to have to come up with some fresh ideas now. If they are going to make a *Freddy vs. Jason 2*, they have to bring in someone new—some sort of third character. But that can so easily become unintentionally campy. Mark and I certainly never wanted to go camp with *Freddy vs. Jason*. But, truthfully, where else can you go?

RONALD D. MOORE, Screenwriter, *Freddy vs. Jason***:** I believe a big part of what keeps people coming back to these franchises is their memory of the first one. You go and have this experience that you love, with an imaginary world, or a group of characters, and you want to explore it again. You want to see another adventure. Whether it's Jason or Freddy or *Star Trek* or *Star Wars*, it's that desire to recapture that initial feeling that propels people back into theaters again and again.

If you're a filmmaker, you're lucky if your sequel is *The Empire Strikes Back*. In my opinion, *Empire* is what makes the entire *Star Wars* phenomena what it is. If *Empire* had sucked, it would have just petered out. But *Empire* raised the stakes. And successful franchises can deliver enough new bursts of creativity and adrenaline to keep it going. *ALIENS* did that, too—it brought you back to what you loved about the first one, and expanded the world. But, at a certain point, you run out of ideas. And it is only then that the *Friday the 13th* series, and Jason, will truly die.

ERIN GRAY, "Diana Kimble," *Jason Goes to Hell***:** For as long as I've known him, Sean Cunningham's always been mentoring kids. Telling them, "Sure you can do it!" Making them believe in themselves. I did a short film for him, and the whole thing was made by college kids. Sean's like, "Let's do it in my driveway, and we'll have a thunderstorm and we'll get a hose and we'll make it work!" That's *so* Sean. He's always had this attitude of, "Let's just go do it!" And somehow, he makes it happen. And that's a wonderful gift, it truly is.

I think what I remember most about my *Friday* experience is being in Sean's presence and feeling that energy on the entire set and being part of that joy and playfulness—you don't always get that on a film set. I guess I learned, "Don't take life too seriously. We're not gonna get out alive." That kind of said it all.

SEAN CUNNINGHAM, Creator: *Friday the 13th* was originally dismissed by the critics as being exploitative and not worthy of attention. It was only after the picture started doing a whole bunch of business that people looked at it a second time and said, "There must be something good here." Then the *Friday the 13th* look-alikes showed up. And then they would be criticized, like, "Well, it didn't really have the style or panache or understanding that the original *Friday the 13th* had." From the same guy who panned my film originally! Not that *Friday the 13th* got any better, but I think that your point of view on the film changes according to box office. I only got credit for it years afterward.

The only downside of *Friday the 13th* over the years has been that, although it allowed me, theoretically, to do a whole bunch of different things, it tied me to its reputation. When people meet me, generally their reaction is, "Oh, you don't look like the kind of a guy that would make horror films. You seem like a normal person!" I hope I'm a normal person. I think that I am not obsessed with darkness. I am not obsessed with fear. As I've gotten older, my attitude toward the genre has changed. When you're dealing with horror films, I think by and large you're dealing with the phenomenon of untimely death. And when you get to be my age, you don't worry about untimely death anymore, you worry about timely death. Your concerns are very different.

But I have not once regretted being involved with *Friday the 13th*. I was blindly lucky, and it opened so many doors. It supported me and my family, and on some level it still does. It made it possible for me to sit here and talk about it. Back in 1979, I didn't know if I'd be alive twenty-five years later to talk about anything, much less *Friday the 13th*. So I'm shocked. I'm just absolutely shocked.

Will there ever be an end to Jason? I really don't think so. Even as the current audience changes and grows older, there's always a new generation to come, and they will always have to deal with this fairy tale. You just take this fairy tale and put a slightly different spin on it. I think Jason will be with us for quite a long time.

The original *Friday the 13th* culled most of its acting talent from in and around the New York theatre scene. Twenty-five years later, the film still benefits from the unfettered eagerness of its young cast who, free of cynicism and without the benefit of hindsight, saw the film less as a stepping stone to Hollywood fame and fortune than an opportunity to hone their craft in front of the camera. "I didn't even really think of this movie as a horror film," says actress Jeannine Taylor, who played Marcie. "Just a great, low-risk way to get some on-camera experience. To me, this was a small independent movie about some very carefree teenagers who are having a rip-roaring time at a summer camp where they happen to be working as counselors. Then they just happen to get killed."

Although the film's success at the box office would, today, provide a likely career boost for a young actor, the negative criticism that greeted *Friday the 13th* closed doors for many members of its cast. For Taylor, the specter of *Friday the 13th* was always hovering close by. "It was impossible for me to enjoy that it was a hit because I got disapproval from a number of people whom I respected. I went on to do a couple of New York stage productions right after the film was released, and I'd included *Friday the 13th* in my bio for the playbills. The directors of each of these productions came to me and said, 'You were in this film? *Friday the 13th*?' Then they shook their heads slowly—and disapprovingly—and walked away. And these were famous Broadway directors. But I did not take *Friday the 13th* out of my bio. I didn't want to dwell on it, yet I didn't want to pretend that I hadn't done the film, either. It was very difficult for a while. My response was to wipe it off my mental screen."

Despite any setbacks, Taylor, who was already an operatically trained singer by the time she appeared in *Friday the 13th*, went on to forge a notable career in musical theatre, winning critical acclaim in such stage productions as *A History of the American Film*, *Ladies in Waiting* and *Hijinks!* (**above**). Taylor also graduated from the noted William Esper Studio in New York, and earned a certificate from the prestigious Royal Academy of Dramatic Art (RADA) in London.

Today, with the backlash against the film having subsided, she is able to look back more fondly at her *Friday* experience. "I learned that a certain portion of one's life is completely out of one's control. My response can only be appreciative. For all the scorn and ridicule heaped upon it at the time, *Friday the 13th* became this enormous success and an iconic part of the culture. It will always be embedded in that cultural moment, and so will I. That's something a lot of people never get."

Coroner's Report

The following is a list of statistics for the *Friday the 13th* franchise. Box office numbers have been provided by their respective distributors. Figures for total paid admissions are an estimate, based upon the average ticket price of the respective year of each film's release. Ticket prices provided by NATO (National Association of Theater Owners). As the *Friday the 13th* films were R-rated and earned the majority of their grosses on weekend evenings, no adjustments have been made for child, senior citizen or matinee pricing. All video sales figures current as of August 1, 2005. Provided by VideoScan, an independent industry tracking firm.

FRIDAY THE 13TH

Production budget: $550,000
Shooting locations: Blairstown, New Jersey; Hope, New Jersey
Principal shooting dates: September 4—October 3, 1979 (28 days)
Production company: Georgetown Productions
U.S. distributor: Paramount Pictures
U.S. theatrical release date: May 9, 1980
Taglines: "A 24-Hour Nightmare of Terror"; "They Were Warned…They are Doomed…and on Friday the 13th, Nothing Will Save Them."
U.S. box office: $39,754,601
U.S. admissions: 14,778,700
U.S. opening weekend: $5,816,321
   Percentage of box office: 14.6%
   Number of screens: 1,127
   Per screen average: $5,287
   Rank: 1
International distributor: Warner Bros.
International taglines: "You'll Wish it Were Only a Nightmare!"; "Fridays Will Never be the Same Again"; "You May Only See it Once, But That Will Be Enough"
U.S. novelization: Written by Simon Hawke
   Publication date: September 1987
Date of television premiere—U.S.: July 12, 1984
Date of first DVD release—U.S.: October 19, 1999
   Unit sales: 32,497
Date of DVD release - UK: September 29, 2003
   Note: The Warner Bros. DVD release of *Friday the 13th* features what has come to be known as the "international cut" of the film. This version boasts nine seconds of additional gore footage that was excised from the U.S. theatrical release in order to obtain an R classification from the Motion Picture Association of America. Excerpts of this cut footage can be seen on Paramount Home Entertainment's *From Crystal Lake to Manhattan – The Ultimate DVD Collection* box set, released September 2004. However, as of this writing, the intact, full-length "international cut" of *Friday the 13th* remains unavailable in the U.S.

FRIDAY THE 13TH PART 2

Production budget: $1.25 million
Shooting locations: Kent, Connecticut
Production company: Georgetown Productions
Worldwide distributor: Paramount Pictures
U.S. release date: April 30, 1981
Tagline: "The Body Count Continues…"; "A Deadly Combination" (U.S. re-release with *Friday the 13th*)
U.S. box office: $21,722,776
U.S. admissions: 7,813,900
U.S. opening weekend : $6,429.784
   Percentage of box office: 29.6%
   Number of screens: 1,350
   Per screen average: $4,762
   Rank: 1
U.S. novelization: Written by Simon Hawke
   Date of publication: February 1988.
Date of first DVD release—U.S.: October 19, 1999
   Unit sales: 19,309

FRIDAY THE 13TH PART 3

Production budget: $2.25 million
Shooting locations: Valuzet Movie Ranch, Saugus, California
Production company: Jason, Inc.
Worldwide distributor: Paramount Pictures
U.S. release date: August 13, 1982
Tagline: "A New Dimension in Terror"
U.S. box office: $36,690,067
U.S. admissions: 12,431,800
U.S. opening weekend: $9,406,522
   Percentage of box office: 25.63%
   Number of screens: 1,079
   Per screen average: $8,717
   Rank: 1
U.S. re-release date: May 13, 1983
Number of screens: 520
Re-release box office: $2,108,548
   Percentage of total box office: 5.75%
   Number of screens: 520
   Rank: 10
First U.S. novelization: Written by Michael Avallone
   Date of publication: August 1982.
Second U.S. novelization: Written by Simon Hawke
   Date of publication: May 1988
Soundtrack: "Music From Friday the 13th – Parts I, II & III" (Composed by Harry Manfredini)
   Date of release: September 1982
   U.S. chart position: Did not chart
Date of first DVD release—U.S.: October 17, 2000
   Unit sales: 21,372

FRIDAY THE 13TH – THE FINAL CHAPTER

Production budget: $2.6 million
Shooting locations: Solvang, California; Topanga Canyon, California
Production company: Friday Four, Inc.
Worldwide distributor: Paramount Pictures
U.S. release date: April 13, 1984
Taglines: "Three Times Before You've Felt the Terror. Known the Madness. Lived the Horror. Now, This is the One You've Been Screaming For."; "Friday, April 13th is Jason's Unlucky Day"
U.S. box office: $32,980,880
U.S. admissions: 9,815,700
U.S. opening weekend: $11,183,148
   Percentage of box office: 33.9%
   Number of screens: 1,594
   Per screen average: $7,015
   Rank: 1
Date of first DVD release—U.S.: October 17, 2000
   Unit sales: 19,894

FRIDAY THE 13TH PART V: A NEW BEGINNING

Production budget: $2.2 million
Shooting locations: Camarillo, California
Production company: Terror, Inc.
Worldwide distributor: Paramount Pictures
U.S. release date: March 22, 1985
Tagline: "If Jason Still Haunts You, You're Not Alone"
U.S. box office: $21,930,418
U.S. admissions: 6,177,600
U.S. opening weekend: $8,032,883

   Percentage of box office: 36.6%
   Number of screens: 1,759
   Per screen average: $4,566
   Rank: 1
Date of first DVD release—U.S.: September 25, 2001
   Unit sales: 16,917

FRIDAY THE 13TH PART VI: JASON LIVES

Production budget: $3.0 million
Principal shooting dates: March 8—April 24, 1986 (40 days)
Shooting locations: Covington, Georgia; Los Angeles, California
Production company: Terror, Inc.
Worldwide distributor: Paramount Pictures
U.S. release date: August 1, 1986
Taglines: "The Nightmare Returns. This Summer"; "Kill or Be Killed"; "Nothing This Evil Ever Dies"
U.S. box office: $19,472,057
U.S. admissions: 5,248,500
U.S. opening weekend: $6,750,837
   Percentage of box office: 34.7%
   Number of screens: 1,610
   Per screen average: $4,193
   Rank: 2
U.S. novelization: Written by Simon Hawke
   Date of publication: August 1, 1986
Hit singles: "He's Back (The Man Behind the Mask)" by Alice Cooper
   U.S. release date: September 1986
   U.S. chart position: #56—Billboard Pop Chart
Soundtrack: "Constrictor" by Alice Cooper—features "He's Back (The Man Behind the Mask)," "Teenage Frankenstein" and "Hard Rock Summer"
   U.S. release date: October 1986
   U.S. chart position: #59 - Billboard Top 100
Date of first DVD release—U.S.: September 25, 2001
   Unit sales: 17,658

FRIDAY THE 13TH PART VII: THE NEW BLOOD

Production budget: $2.8 million
Shooting locations: Bayonette, Alabama; Culver City, California
Production company: Friday Four, Inc.
Worldwide distributor: Paramount Pictures
U.S. release date: May 13, 1988
Taglines: "On Friday the 13th, Jason Will Meet His Match"; "Jason is Back, But This Time Someone's Waiting!"
U.S. box office: $19,170,001
U.S. admissions: 4,664,200
U.S. opening weekend: $8,245,038
   Percentage of box office: 43.0%
   Number of screens: 1,796
   Per screen average: $4,590
   Rank: 1
Date of first DVD release—U.S.: September 3, 2002
   Unit sales: 18,370

FRIDAY THE 13TH PART VIII: JASON TAKES MANHATTAN

Production budget: $5 million
Shooting locations: Vancouver, British Columbia;

New York City, New York
Production company: Friday Four, Inc.
Worldwide distributor: Paramount Pictures
U.S. release date: July 28, 1989
Taglines: "New York Has a New Problem"; "The Big Apple is in Big Trouble!"
U.S. box office: $14,343,976
U.S. admissions: 3,613,100
U.S. opening weekend box office: $6,251,310
    Percentage of box office: 43.6%
    Number of screens: 1,683
    Per screen average: $3,714
    Rank: 5
Date of first DVD release—U.S.: September 3, 2002
    Unit sales: 15,439

JASON GOES TO HELL: THE FINAL FRIDAY
Production budget: $3.0 million
Shooting locations: Thousand Oaks, California
Production company: Crystal Lake Entertainment
Worldwide distributor: New Line Cinema
U.S. release date: August 13, 1993
Taglines: "The Creator of the First Returns to Bring You the Last"; "Evil Has Finally Found a Home"; "Horror Has Many Faces...Death Wears Many Different Masks...But Pure Evil Wears Just One...and This is Your Final Chance to See It."
U.S. box office: $15,935,068
U.S. admissions: 3,849,100
U.S. opening weekend: $7,552,190
    Percentage of box office: 47.4%
    Number of screens: 1,355
    Per screen average: $5,573
    Rank: 2
Soundtrack: "Jason Goes to Hell: The Final Friday – Music from the Motion Picture" (composed by Harry Manfredini)
    U.S. release date: September 14, 1993
    U.S. chart position: Did not chart
Date of DVD release—U.S.: October 8, 2002
    Unit sales: 38,194

JASON X
Production budget: $14 million
Shooting locations: Toronto, Canada
Production company: Crystal Lake Entertainment
Worldwide distributor:: New Line Cinema
U.S. release date: April 26, 2002
Taglines: "Evil Gets an Upgrade"; Welcome to the Future of Horror"
Worldwide box office: $16,951,798
U.S. box office: $13,121,555
U.S. admissions: 2,258,400
U.S. opening weekend: $6,649,006
    Percentage of box office: 50.7%
    Number of screens: 1,879
    Per screen average: $3,540
    Rank: 3
Overseas box office: $3,830,243
    Percentage of worldwide box office: 22.6%
U.S. novelization: Written by Pat Cadigan
    Date of publication: February 1, 2005
Soundtrack: "Jason X – Music from the Motion Picture" (Composed by Harry Manfredini)

Date of release: May 14, 2002
    Chart position: Did not chart
Date of first DVD release—U.S.: September 3, 2002
    Unit sales: 549,280

FREDDY VS. JASON
Production budget: $25 million
Development budget: $6.8 million
Principal shooting days: September 9—November 22, 2002 (53 days)
Shooting locations: Vancouver, British Columbia
Production company: New Line Cinema
Worldwide distributor: New Line Cinema
U.S. release date: August 15, 2003
Taglines: "Winner Kills All"; "Evil Will Battle Evil"; "Slicer. Dicer." (video release)
Worldwide box office: $114,326,122
U.S. box office: $82,622,655
U.S. admissions: 13,701,900
U.S. opening weekend box office: $36,428,066
    Percentage of box office: 44.1%
    Number of screens: 3,014
    Per screen average: $12,086
    Rank: 1
    Number of days at peak rank: 11
Overseas box office: $31,703,467
    Percentage of worldwide box office: 27.7%
U.S. novelization: Written by Stephen Hand
    Date of publication: July 29, 2003
Hit singles: "How Can I Live," by Ill Nino
    U.S. chart position: #32—Billboard Modern Rock Chart
Soundtrack: "Freddy vs. Jason – The Original Motion Picture Soundtrack" (various artists)
    U.S. release date: August 12, 2003
    U.S. chart position: #11—Billboard Top 200
Soundtrack: "Freddy vs. Jason – The Original Motion Picture Score" (composed by Graeme Revell)
    U.S. release date: August 19, 2003
    U.S. chart position: Did not chart
Date of first DVD release—U.S.: January 13, 2004
    Unit sales: 2,693,291
    Rank: 2

FRIDAY THE 13TH: THE SERIES
Production company: Triumph Entertainment Corp.
Distributor: Paramount Domestic Television
Number of episodes: 72
Airdates: September 1987-April 1990
Soundtrack: "Friday the 13th: The Series – Music From the Original Television Scores" (composed by Fred Mollin)
    U.S. release date: January 12, 1992 (CD)
    U.S. chart position: Did not chart

FRIDAY THE 13TH: FROM CRYSTAL LAKE TO MANHATTAN – THE ULTIMATE DVD COLLECTION
Distributor: Paramount Home Entertainment
Date of release: October 3, 2004
    Units sales: 189,361
    Rank: 18

FRANCHISE VS. FRANCHISE
The following is a comparison of the leading "slasher" film franchises. Box office totals adjusted for inflation based on 2005 average ticket prices. Installments include sequels, remakes and team-up films. All figures domestic only.

FRIDAY THE 13TH
U.S. box office: $523,022,700
U.S. box office (unadjusted): $315,635,506
U.S. admissions: 83,683,600
Installments: 11
Active years: 1980-Present

HANNIBAL LECTER
U.S. box office: $491,124,700
U.S. box office (unadjusted): $397,606,017
U.S. admissions: 78,580,000
Installments: 4
Active years: 1986-Present

A NIGHTMARE ON ELM STREET
U.S. box office: $442,659,200
U.S. box office (unadjusted): $307,420,075
U.S. admissions: 70,825,500
Installments: 8
Active years: 1984-Present

PSYCHO
U.S. box office: $388,052,200
U.S. box office (unadjusted): $102,662,736
U.S. admissions: 62,088,300
Installments: 5
Active years: 1960-1998

HALLOWEEN
U.S. box office: $386,623,100
U.S. box office (unadjusted): $216,857,643
U.S. admissions: 61,859,700
Installments: 8
Active years: 1978-Present

SCREAM
U.S. box office: $381,197,700
U.S. box office (unadjusted): $293,553,139
U.S. admissions: 60,991,600
Installments: 3
Active years: 1996-2000

THE TEXAS CHAINSAW MASSACRE
U.S. box office: $208,931,300
U.S. box office (unadjusted): $125,407,987
U.S. admissions: 33,430,100
Installments: 5
Active years: 1974-Present

CHILD'S PLAY
U.S. box office: $174,638,300
U.S. box office (unadjusted): $125,034,731
U.S. admissions: 27,805,500
Installments: 5
Active years: 1988-Present

Notes on Sources

The recollections that appear in this book have been excerpted from over two hundred exclusive interviews, conducted over a three-and-a-half-year period beginning January 2001 and ending July 2005. Additional quoted material and historical data has also been culled from various filmed productions, television programs and print articles—both published and unpublished. Photographic materials and archival documents were culled from the studio vaults of Paramount Pictures and New Line Cinema, the private archives of the many talented unit photographers who have worked on the *Friday the 13th* films, and the generous donations of cast and crew.

INTERVIEWS

Los Angeles, conducted by Peter M. Bracke:
Erich Anderson, Judie Aronson, Kevin Bacon, Diana Barrows, Matthew Barry, Peter Barton, Kimberly Beck, Don Behrns, Jeff Bennett, Susan Blu, Dominick Brascia, Joe Bob Briggs, Richard Brooker, John Carl Buechler, William Butler, Chuck Campbell, Ronn Carroll, Fern Champion, Stu Charno, Randolph Cheveldave, Barney Cohen, Robin Cook, Cliff Cudney, Steven Culp, Juliette Cummins, Martin Cummins, Noel Cunningham, Sean Cunningham, Doug Curtis, Jensen Daggett, Steve Daskawicz, Darcy DeMoss, Dennis Dermody, Bob DeSimone, Alex Diakun, V.C. Dupree, Bryan England, Robert Englund, Todd Farmer, Daniel Farrands, Corey Feldman, Richard Feury, David Fischer, Joan Freeman, Carl Fullerton, John Furey, Richard Gant, Geoff Garrett, Joseph T. Garrity, Warrington Gillette, Crispin Glover, Joel Goodman, CJ Graham, Erin Gray, Bruce Green, Tom Gruenberg, Vincent Guastaferro, David Handman, Daryl Haney, Rob Hedden, Bonnie Hellman, Tiffany Helm, George Hively, Kane Hodder, Barbara Howard, Kelly Hu, Jesse Hutch, Jim Isaac, Leslie Jordan, David Kagen, David Katims, Kari Keegan, Monica Keena, Dana Kimmell, Adrienne King, Robb Wilson King, Ken Kirzinger, Heidi Kozak, Jon Kranhouse, Paul Kratka, Ron Kurz, Kyle Labine, John D. LeMay, Lar Park Lincoln, Carol Locatell, Sandi Love, Frank Mancuso Jr., Frank Mancuso Sr., Harry Manfredini, George Mansour, Adam Marcus, Jack Marks, Christopher Marquette, Thom Mathews, Cheri Maugans, James Maxwell, Nancy McLoughlin, Tom McLoughlin, Peter Mensah, Julie Michaels, Victor Miller, Ron Millkie, Steve Mirkovich, Fred Mollin, Lawrence Monoson, Ronald D. Moore, Camilla More, Carey More, Tom Morga, Robbi Morgan, Barry Moss, Dennis Murphy, Mark Nelson, Greg Nicotero, Kerry Noonan, Miguel A. Nunez, Jr., Betsy Palmer, Corey Parker, William Pattison, Jerry Pavlon, Petru Popescu, Stephen Posey, Jonathan Potts, Bill Randolph, Ethan Reiff, Graeme Revell, Peter Mark Richman, Jason Ritter, Shavar Ross, Kelly Rowland, Lisa Ryder, Martin Jay Sadoff, Nick Savage, Tracie Savage, Peter Schindler, David J. Schow, Jeffrey Schwarz, Rusty Schwimmer, Damian Shannon, Michael Sheehy, John Shepherd, Timothy Silver, Meg Simon, Kevin Blair Spirtas, Taso Stavrakis, Amy Steel, Peter Stein, Steve Susskind, Mark Swift, Lauren-Marie Taylor, William Terezakis, Tony Timpone, Russell Todd, Mark Verheiden, DebiSue Voorhees, Cyrus Voris, Brian Wade, Blake Washer, John Waters, Douglas J. White, Ted White, Dick Wieand, Ethan Wiley, John Willet, Katherine Williams, Larry B. Williams, Steven Williams, Ronny Yu, Michael Zager, Larry Zerner, Barry Zetlin, Joseph Zito.

Los Angeles, conducted by Jeffrey Schwarz:
Sean Cunningham, Victor Miller, Harry Manfredini, Adam Marcus, Betsy Palmer.

Los Angeles, conducted by Steve Wolcott: Dan Curry, Corey Feldman, Tom Savini.

New York City, conducted by Peter M. Bracke:
Gerald Feil, Warrington Gillette, CJ Graham, Kane Hodder, Adrienne King, John D. LeMay, Ari Lehman, Lar Park Lincoln, Betsy Palmer, Amy Steel.

New York City, conducted by Jeffrey Schwarz:
Bill Freda, Jay Keuper, Betsy Palmer.

San Diego, conducted by Peter M. Bracke: Richard Brooker, John Carl Buechler, Warrington Gillette, CJ Graham, Kane Hodder, Tom McLoughlin.

Vancouver, conducted by David Pond-Smith:
Melissa Ade, Brian Anderson, Maxyne Baker, Dennis Berardi, Lexa Doig, John Dondertman, Stephen Dupuis, Yani Gellman, Derwin Johnson, Kelly Kepkowsky, Steve Lucescu, Barna Moicz, James Oswald, Dov Tiefenbach, Derick Underschultz.

IN PRINT

Balun, Chas. "Friday the 13th Part VII: The New Blood – Jason Gets Metaphysical," *The Bloody Best of Fangoria, Vol. 8.*

Bartholomew, David. "An Interview with Carl Fullerton," *Cinemafantasque,* 1981.

Buckley, Tom. "At the Movies," *The New York Times,* January 23, 1981.

Burns, James H. "Friday the 13th Part II," *Fangoria* #12, 1981.

Burns, James H. "Here's…Carl Fullerton," *Fangoria* #13, 1981.

Crisafulli, Chuck. "Friday the 13th Part IX: Jason Goes to Hell," *Cinemafantastique,* 1993.

Day, Patrick. "Injecting Life Into a Familiar Boogeyman," *Los Angeles Times,* April 24, 2002.

Dimeo, Steven. "An Interview with Tom Savini," *Cinemafantastique,* 1984.

Everitt, David. "After the Final Chapter: Friday the 13th – A New Beginning," *Fangoria* #44, 1985.

Fasolino, Greg. "Jason's Song," *Fangoria* #83, June, 1988.

Ferrante, Anthony C. "Freddy and Jason Go To Development Hell," *Fangoria* #226-#227, 2003.

Fischer, Dennis. "FX Profile: John Carl Buechler," *Horrorfan,* Fall 1989.

Flake, Linda. "Blood Money for a Rollercoaster Ride," *Premiere,* December, 1980.

Gilbert, John. "Miner Miracles," *Fear,* November, 1989.

Gilpin, Kris. "The Fine Art of Splitting Hairs and Heads on Friday the 13th Part VII," *Cinemafantastique,* January, 1989.

Gire, Dann & Mandell, Paul. "Friday the 13th: Horror's First Franchise," *Cinemafantastique,* November, 1989.

Goldstein, Patrick. "Sunny Side of Horror," *Los Angeles Times,* September 2, 2003.

Grove, David. "Crystal Lake Memories," *Fangoria* #212, 2002.

Grove, David. "When Sequels Collide," *Rue Morgue,* 2003.

Grove, Martin A. "Hollywood's Producers Focus on Pre-Filming Deals to Ensure a Payoff," *Herald Examiner,* July 1, 1980.

Gudino, Rod. "When Sequels Collide: Freddy Krueger," *Rue Morgue,* 2003.

Janisse, Kier-La. "Place Your Bets!," *Fangoria* #224, 2003.

Kit, Zorianna. "'Jason' to Blast Off," *Hollywood Reporter,* May 22, 2000.

Lawson, Carol. "Spotlight: Kevin Bacon," *New York Times,* March 25, 1983.

Mandell, Paul. "Jason Lives! The Birth of a Slasher," *Cinemafantastique,* November, 1989.

Martin, Bob. "Friday the 13th: A Day for Terror," *Fangoria,* June, 1980.

Martin, Bob. "Friday the 13th Part III in 3-D," *Fangoria* #21, 1982.

Martin, R.H. "Savini and Friday the 13th – The Final Chapter," *Fangoria* #36, 1984.

McBride, James. "Switching Channels," *Backstage,* February 15, 1991.

Mills, Bart. "Closeup: Kevin Bacon," *Movieland,* March, 1986.

Newton, Steve. "Exclusive Set Report: Friday the 13th Part VIII: Jason Takes Manhattan," *Fangoria,* August, 1989.

Pogrebin, Robin. "Touched by the Poetry of Fatherhood," *Sunday Times,* 1996.

Rowe, Michael. "Jason X: Kills in Space," *Fangoria,* #210.

Scapperotti, Dan. "Danny Steinmann on Friday the 13th Part V: A New Beginning," *Cinemafantastique,* 1985.

Scapperotti, Dan. "Friday the 13th Part II," *Cinemafantastique,* 1981.

Scapperotti, Dan. "Friday the 13th Part III," *Cinemafantastique,* 1982.

Scapperotti, Dan. "Friday the 13th Part VIII," *Cinemafantastique,* 1989

Scapperotti, Dan. "Jason Lives: Filming the New Slashfest," *Cinemafantastique,* November 1989.

Seguin, Denis. "Behind the Scenes with…Production Designer John Dondertman," *Screen International,* March 31, 2000.

Shapiro, Marc. "Freddy Vs. Jason," *Starlog Celebrity Series Presents: Freddy vs. Jason,* October, 2003.

Shapiro, Marc. "Friday the 13th Part VI: Jason Lives FX – The Critics Live!", *Fangoria,* August 1986.

Shapiro, Marc. "I Spit on Jason's Grave," *Fangoria,* September, 1986.

Shapiro, Marc. "I Wrote for a Zombie," *Fangoria,* #126, 1993.

Shapiro, Marc. "Jason's Final Foe," *Fangoria,* #126, 1993.

Shapiro, Marc. "Lake Placid: What a Croc," *Fangoria,* August, 1999.

Timpone, Anthony. "It's Not Just Another Horror-Comedy!", *Fangoria* #51, 1986.

Turnquist, Kris. "Sean Cunningham's New Look," *Box Office,* December, 1986.

Van Buskirk, Dayna. "Old Blood in New Bottles," *Fangoria* #227, 2003.

Waddell, Calum. "Return to Camp Blood," *Rue Morgue*, September/October, 2004.

Warren, Bill. "It's a Bird! It's a Plane! It's Warlock!," *Fangoria*, February, 1989.

Zeller, Steven. "A Full 'House' at the Box Office," *Drama-Logue*, March 13-19, 1986.

ONLINE

Caretaker, The. "Tom Savini Interview," *House of Horrors.com*, July, 1997.

Chau, Thomas. "One-on-One with Sean Cunningham and Ronny Yu," *UGO.com*, August 18, 2003.

Coppa, Matt. "Teacher's Pet," *Stuff Magazine.com*, February 20, 2003.

Fallon, John. "The Arrow Interviews...Daryl Haney," *Arrow In the Head.com*, 2004.

Freeman, Royce & Lucas, Petch. "Interview with Harry Manfredini," *Pit of Horror.com*, June, 1999.

Masi, Anthony. "Interview with Steve Miner," *HalloweenMovies.com*, July 28, 1998.

Murray, Rebecca. "Behind the Scenes of Freddy Vs. Jason," *About.com*, August, 2003.

Patrizio, Andy. "An Interview with Ronny Yu," *IGN.com*, January 21, 2004.

Topel, Fred. "Getting to Know Yu," *About.com*, August, 2003.

Topel, Fred. "Ready for Freddy Krueger," *About.com*, August, 2003.

Uncredited. "Fright Exclusive Interview with Diana Barrows," *Icons of Fright.com*, February, 2005.

Uncredited. "'Together' Morning Preview Attracts Record Crowd," *Box Office*, January 17, 1972.

TV, DVD & VIDEO PROGRAMS

1986 *Fangoria Weekend of Horrors* (D: Mike Hadley; Media Home Entertainment)

2002 *By Any Means Necessary: The Making of "Jason X"* (D: Jeffrey Schwarz; New Line)

—— *The Many Lives of Jason Voorhees* (D: Jeffrey Schwarz; New Line)

—— *The Making of "Friday the 13th": Return to Crystal Lake* (D: Jeffrey Schwarz; Warner Bros.)

2004 *Freddy vs. Jason: Development Hell* (D: David Prior; New Line)

—— *Meet Bob Shaye* (D: Jeffrey Schwarz; New Line)

BOOKS

Bouzereau, Laurent. *Ultraviolent Movies*. Citadel Press, 1996.

Clifford, Michelle and Landis, Bill. *Sleazoid Express*. Fireside, 2002.

Clover, Carol J. *Men, Women & Chainsaws: Gender in the Modern Horror Film*. Princeton, 1992.

Grove, David. *Making Friday the 13th: The Legend of Camp Blood*. FAB Press, 2004.

Humphries, Reynold. *The American Horror Film: An Introduction*. Edinburgh, 2002.

Lewis, Jon. *Hollywood V. Hard Core*. New York University, 2000.

McBride, Joseph. *Steven Spielberg: A Biography*. De Capo Press, 1997.

Muir, John Kenneth. *Horror Films of the 70s*.

McFarland & Company, 2002.

Peary, Danny. *Cult Movies*. Delacorte Press, 1981.

Robb, Brian J. *Screams & Nightmares: The Films of Wes Craven*. Overlook, 1998.

Schoell, William & Spencer, James. T*he Nightmare Never Ends: The Official History of Freddy Krueger and the Nightmare on Elm Street Films*. Citadel Press, 1992.

Szulkin, David. *Wes Craven's Last House on the Left: The Making of a Cult Classic*. FAB Press, 2000.

PHOTO CREDITS

1 (James Dittinger), 2-3 (James Dittinger), 6 (Los Angeles Times), 12 (Richard Feury), 14 top (courtesy Sean Cunningham), 14 middle (courtesy Frank Mancuso, Sr.), 14 bottom (courtesy George Mansour), 17 background (courtesy Sean Cunningham), 17 bottom right (*International Variety*/SSC Films), 26 top (Richard Feury, courtesy Crystal Lake Entertainment), 27 all images (Richard Feury, courtesy Crystal Lake Entertainment), 42 overlay (courtesy Crystal Lake Entertainment), 44-45 all images (Richard Feury, courtesy Crystal Lake Entertainment), 48 (John Foster), 58-59 (John Foster, courtesy Jason Collum), 60 top left (courtesy Carl Fullerton), 66 both images (John Foster, courtesy Jason Collum), 68-69 background (courtesy John Furey), 72 (Laurel Moore), 75 left (Laurel Moore), 75 right top, middle and bottom (courtesy Paul Kratka), 76-77 overleaf (courtesy Gerald Feil), 77 top right (Robb Wilson King), 77 middle right (Steve Susskind), 77 bottom right (courtesy Paul Kratka), 78 top right (courtesy Steve Susskind), 80-81 (courtesy Tracie Savage), 82 (Laurel Moore), 83 (Laurel Moore), 86 both images (Laurel Moore), 87 (Laurel Moore), 88 (courtesy Jason Collum), 89 (courtesy Jason Collum), 90-91 all images (courtesy Steve Susskind), 96 (Larry Secrist, courtesy Jason Collum), 99 bottom right (Tom Savini), 100-101 all images (Larry Secrist), 102-103 all images (Larry Secrist), 104 all images (Carey More), 106 left row, top to bottom (Tom Savini), 106 background (Larry Secrist), 107 top left and top middle (Tom Savini); 108 all images (Tom Savini); 109 (courtesy Jason Collum), 110 bottom left (Tom Savini), 112 both images (Tom Savini), 113 (courtesy Jason Collum), 114 bottom left (Tom Savini), 116-117 (Tom Savini),120 (Joe Mealey), 122 (Joe Mealey), 124-125 (Joe Mealey), 134 overlay (courtesy Bruce Green), 144 (James H. Armfield), 150 top left, top right, second row from top and left, third row from top and left (Kerry Noonan), 150 second row and right (CJ Graham, courtesy jasonvi.com), 150 third row from top and right, fourth row from top left and right (courtesy Tom & Nancy McLoughlin), 156 overlay (courtesy Joseph T. Garrity), 164-165 script overlay (courtesy Tom McLoughlin), 166 (Mark Sennett), 168 (Michael Ansell), 170-171 (photographer uncredited, courtesy Paramount Domestic Television), 175 all images (Michael Ansell), 176 (courtesy Jason Collum), 178 (courtesy Jason Collum), 188-189 (courtesy Bill Butler), 190

bottom left (Bob Villard), 190-191 script overlay (courtesy Daryl Haney), 192 (Ron Grover), 194 (courtesy Rob Hedden), 195 bottom (courtesy Rob Hedden), 197 (Ron Grover), 200 (Ron Grover), 201 top (Ron Grover), 201 bottom right (courtesy Kelly Hu), 203 top right (courtesy Bryan England), 205 bottom (courtesy William Terezakis), 208-209 background (courtesy Bryan England), 212-213 all images (courtesy William Terezakis), 214 posters and MPAA document (courtesy Daniel Farrands), 216 (Mark Fellman), 219 (courtesy Crystal Lake Entertainment), 220-221 all images (Mark Fellman), 222-223 all images (Mark Felllman), 224 all images (Mark Fellman), 225 all images (courtesy K.N.B. Effects Group), 226-227 all images (courtesy K.N.B. Effects Group), 229 all images (courtesy K.N.B. Effects Group), 230 background (Mark Fellman), 231 bottom middle and bottom right (courtesy K.N.B. Effects Group), 232 all images (courtesy K.N.B. Effects Group), 233 all images (Mark Felllman), 234-235 all images (Mark Fellman), 236-237 all images (courtesy K.N.B. Effects Group), 238 (Mark Fellman), 247 all images Ava V. Gerlitz, 250 all images Ava V. Gerlitz, 258-259 all images (Noel Cunningham, courtesy Crystal Lake Entertainment) 260-261 all images (Ava V. Gerlitz), 262-263 all images Ava V. Gerlitz), 264-265 background illustration (Stephan Dupuis, courtesy Jim Isaac), 266 (James Dittinger), 268 (Mark Fellman), 272 (James Dittinger, courtesy Doug Curtis), 276-277 (James Dittinger, courtesy Doug Curtis), 278 top left (Marcel Williams), 281 right top and middle and bottom (courtesy Doug Curtis), 282 left top and bottom (James Dittinger, courtesy Doug Curtis), 286 both images (Marcel Williams), 287 (Marcel Williams), 288 (Marcel Williams), 289 top right and middle (James Dittinger, courtesy Doug Curtis), 289 bottom right (courtesy Christopher Marquette), 290-291 (James Dittinger), 293 top right (courtesy Christopher Marquette), 293 middle right (courtesy Doug Curtis), 295 all images (Marcel Williams), 297 bottom right (courtesy Graeme Revell), 300 (Richard Feury, courtesy Crystal Lake Entertainment), 305 all images except top left (Daniel Farrands), 308 (Nels Israelson), 312 top left (courtesy Adrienne King), 312-313 background (courtesy Adrienne King), 313 (Carol Rosegg, courtesy Jeannine Taylor), 320 (Nels Israelson).

The publishers would also like to thank the unit photographers of all eleven of the *Friday the 13th* films for their tremendous contributions to this book. *Friday the 13th*—Richard Feury; *Friday the 13th Part 2*—John Foster; *Friday the 13th Part 3*—Laurel Moore; *Friday the 13th – The Final Chapter*—Larry Secrist; *Friday the 13th Part V: A New Beginning*—Joe Mealey; *Friday the 13th Part VI: Jason Lives*—James H. Armfield; *Friday the 13th Part VII: The New Blood*—Michael Ansell; *Friday the 13th Part VIII: Jason Takes Manhattan*—Ron Grover; *Jason Goes to Hell: The Final Friday*—Mark Fellman; *Jason X*—Ava V. Gerlitz; *Freddy vs. Jason*—James Dittinger, Marcel Williams and Nels Israelson.

Index

This index includes references to the films and people of the *Friday the 13th* universe. There are also references to other key films (in) and slasher villains—except Jason Voorhees himself, who appears cover to cover. Persons appearing in lowercase caps are those referenced but not quoted. Page numbers in italics refer to instances where the subject appears only in a photograph on that page.

Author's Acknowledgements

Unlike other successful long-running motion picture franchises, historical material on the *Friday the 13th* series has been comparatively scarce—I should know, I looked. Compiling the many materials contained in this book often felt like a Herculean task, one requiring months of research, countless phone calls, much begging and pleading, and just a little luck—as well as the time, generosity and support of a great many people.

Firstly, I wish to thank Sean S. Cunningham. Without his enthusiasm and encouragement, this book simply would not have been possible. His willingness to go to bat for a little-known, eager young writer gave me the courage to push ahead no matter what the odds, and never lose faith in my project. To him, I am forever indebted.

To New Line Cinema—specifically Marianne Dugan, Lourdes Arocho, Dave Sztoser, David Imhoff and all in the Licensing & Merchandising department—thank you for your patience throughout the process. And additional thanks to Helene Cornell for the many hours spent in front of the lightboard.

Although no longer the home of the *Friday the 13th* franchise, Paramount Pictures has also been wonderfully supportive of this book. Very special thanks must go to Larry McCallister in the Licensing Department, who showed such willingness to work within our limited budget and aid in our research. Shanna Wegrocki in the Paramount Archives was a tremendous asset in discovering stills—and was always there when I needed just that one more. And without the efforts of Martin Blythe in Home Entertainment, the required introductions never would have happened. I am humbled.

After having to transcribe over three hundred hours of interview material, much of it poorly recorded, I can only imagine what thoughts must have gone through the heads of my four faithful and long-suffering transcriptionists: Michael Restaino, Brian Lennox, Dana Fredsti-Thomas and Camille Kaminski. They now know more about *Friday the 13th* than they ever cared to. So to them, much praise and sincerest apologies.

The interviews conducted for this book took many months to complete. Yet there were still some participants who remained either out-of-reach or unavailable. So it is with great fortune that I was allowed to pull from other sources. Much appreciation is extended to Scott Wolcott at Toolbox Productions, Jeffrey Schwarz at Automat Pictures and Sandra Murray at New Line Cinema for granting access to interview transcripts conducted for their various projects. I would also like to thank my fellow comrades in arms—the many other journalists who have, throughout the years, delved into the demented world of *Friday the 13th*—for making my three years of research the most pleasurable of my professional career.

To Mark Matsuno and the team at Matsuno Design Group, led by John McCloy, thank you for your excellent cover design and title treatment. You have perfectly captured the moodiness and atmosphere of the *Friday the 13th* mythology. Your team also took decades-old still images and archival materials and made them look brand new. This book would have been little but a collection of mouldy old photographs without your talents. And to Scottie Gee Gerardi, your impeccable recreations of the headlines that appeared in many of the *Friday the 13th* films are even better than the real thing.

As much as this is a book about words and pictures, they mean nothing without the proper perspective and context. Quite simply, without the brilliant editing of Daniel Farrands, it would have been an incoherent mishmash. Dan took the words of so many and made them something truly special. The process took many long days and sleepless nights, and it was never glamorous and rarely "fun"—but I will never forget those times. This is his book as much as mine.

To Geoff Garrett—you are a true partner. Without your unwavering support and commitment this book simply would not have been possible. It has been an honor.

Then there is also a very special group of people who supported me throughout this three-year journey—from the highest highs down to the darkest depths, then back again. Without them I would have lost any semblance of sanity. They are, in reverse alphabetical order, Larry Zerner (you're first at last!), Joel Vendette, Adrienne King, Geoff Garrett and Daniel Farrands.

To my agent, Garrett Hicks. You have changed my life by believing in this fledgling author, and never second-guessed my choice in projects or subject matter. Words cannot express the gratitude I feel.

Finally, I would like to thank my friends and family. Few likely will ever understand this most strange obsession of mine, but all continue to love me regardless. I am truly blessed.